THE WORLD IN THE MODEL

During the last two centuries, the way economic science is done has changed radically: it has become a social science based on mathematical models in place of words. This book describes and analyses that change – both historically and philosophically – using a series of case studies to illuminate the nature and the implications of this change. In format, it offers a tourist guide to economics by focussing on specific models, explaining how economists created them and how they reason with them. This book will be of interest to economists and science studies scholars (historians, sociologists, and philosophers of science). But it is not a technical book; it is written for the intelligent person who wants to understand how economics works from the inside out and particularly the ways in which economic models have shaped our beliefs and the world we live in.

Mary S. Morgan, Fellow of the British Academy and Overseas Fellow of the Royal Dutch Academy of Arts and Sciences, is Professor of History and Philosophy of Economics at the London School of Economics and the University of Amsterdam. She has published on a range of topics in the history and philosophy of economics: from statistics to experiments to narrative, and from nineteenth-century Social Darwinism to game theory in the Cold War. Her previous books include *The History of Econometric Ideas* (Cambridge University Press, 1990) and *Models as Mediators* (Cambridge University Press, 1999, coedited with Margaret Morrison). She has also edited collections on measurement, policy making with models, and the development of probability thinking. In the broader sphere, the collection of essays *How Well Do Facts Travel?* (Cambridge University Press, 2011, coedited with Peter Howlett) marks the conclusion of a major interdisciplinary team project on evidence in the sciences and humanities. Professor Morgan is currently engaged in the project "Re-thinking Case Studies Across the Social Sciences" as a British Academy–Wolfson Research Professor, and (during 2010–11) as a Davis Center Fellow at Princeton University.

The World in the Model

How Economists Work and Think

Mary S. Morgan

London School of Economics
and
University of Amsterdam

CAMBRIDGE
UNIVERSITY PRESS

CAMBRIDGE UNIVERSITY PRESS
Cambridge, New York, Melbourne, Madrid, Cape Town,
Singapore, São Paulo, Delhi, Mexico City

Cambridge University Press
32 Avenue of the Americas, New York, NY 10013-2473, USA

www.cambridge.org
Information on this title: www.cambridge.org/9780521176194

First published 2012

Printed in the United States of America

A catalog record for this publication is available from the British Library.

Library of Congress Cataloging in Publication data
Morgan, Mary S.
The world in the model : how economists work and think / Mary S. Morgan.
p.   cm.
Includes bibliographical references and index.
ISBN 978-1-107-00297-5 (hardback)
1. Economics–Mathematical models.   2. Economists.   I. Title.
HB135.M667 2012
330.01′95195–dc23   2011018364

ISBN 978-1-107-00297-5 Hardback
ISBN 978-0-521-17619-4 Paperback

For Charles, and for Dori

Contents

Colour plate section appears between pages 100 and 101

Figures, Tables, and Boxes

Figures

Tables

Box

Preface

Science is messy. Historians write seamless accounts to make it comprehensible, and in doing so, sometimes paper over the knots and holes in scientific life. Philosophers provide sparely argued analyses of scientific method, and in doing so may avoid the many awkward rubs of detail. This book is not such a monograph: It offers neither a continuous historical narrative nor a fortified philosophy of modelling. Yet, its ambition is to offer both a history of the naturalization of modelling in economics and a naturalized philosophy of science for economics. And it does so in the spirit of those many others who eschew smoothness.

So – this book is not a conventional monograph. It is a series of historical case studies through which the philosophical commentary runs. I have long described it as a kind of travel guide: I present, as three-star tourist sites, some of the best known, and historically significant, models in economics, and use each as the basis upon which to fashion a philosophical commentary about the nature of modern economics. But readers might also find this book something like a detective's case-book: my series of investigations, as I follow the clues and fit them together, to make sense of what economic modelling is all about. Case studies are the best way that I know to figure out how science goes on. Cases not only form individual stories that capture the practices of economic science in considerable depth, but taken together they provide the materials for a broader account of how economics became, and works, as a modelling science. The messy details are important – not just because, as we know, bald narratives lack credibility, but rather because the devil is often in the detail, and thus larger, and important, matters cannot be understood and explained without them. After all, what would detective novels be if the clues were omitted as *mere* detail to the argument?

What else does this book not do – and what does it do? It does not try to give a definition of models – but it does discuss the qualities that make them useful in a science. It does not suggest that there are different kinds of models, but it does illuminate the heterogeneity of objects that count as models. It does not suggest that models are easy to characterize, but it does argue that in order to understand them, we should pay attention to what models are used for, and how they are used. It is not even-handed, but does argue that models are both very useful knowledge-makers in economics as well as being of limited use in that same domain. It is not a critique of modelling, but it does make clear how and why they may be criticised as well as how and why they may be valued.

Fifteen years of researching, thinking, and writing about models have convinced me that there are no easy answers to questions about what models are, and how modelling works. Some questions are more helpful than others. Asking: What qualities do models need to make them useful in a science? and What functions do models play in a science? are more fruitful than asking What are models? Asking: How does reasoning with models go on? and What kind of knowledge does a science gain from its investigations with models? prompt an account of modelling (in economics) as an autonomous epistemic genre: that is, as a way of doing science that has its own rationale just as do other modes of science. Answering these questions is the agenda for this book.

But those fifteen years have also persuaded me that there are lots of different kinds of things that legitimately count as models in other sciences, and that they often look and function very differently in those other sciences. Comparisons between model-based sciences are extremely useful; they operate here, only gently, as a foil. Fifteen years have also taught me that looking for how a science becomes a model-based discipline requires attention not just to the scientific modes of reasoning, but also to questions of perception and cognition as well as to qualities of imagination and creativity. The arts cannot be entirely taken out of the sciences.

I am delighted to thank all those many scholars who have helped me, argued with me, discussed issues, commented upon chapters, and generally become involved in my attempt to understand modelling. I hope that I have captured most of these by name in acknowledgement notes attached to each chapter – of course none of them are responsible for my not always taking their advice. Special thanks go to Margaret Morrison and Nancy Cartwright who were significant research partners at the beginning of my research; to Marcel Boumans, Harro Maas, and Roy Weintraub who engaged with my work throughout; and to a cohort of graduate students at LSE and in The Netherlands who responded to my enthusiasm for models in a variety of fruitful ways. Such special thanks also go to the anonymous readers for the Press, and to others who read the manuscript as a whole, for their many generous and positive pieces of advice (which, unfortunately, sometimes conflicted with each other); to Aashish Velkar who sorted out the permissions and acknowledgements; to Simona Valeriani who looked after the many figures; to Tracy Keefe and Rajashri Ravindranathan who saw the manuscript through publication; and finally to Jon Adams for his brilliant red cover design and to Scott Parris at Cambridge University Press, whose patience has been unfailing. I am grateful to the Wissenschaftskolleg in Berlin for hosting my first research work on the topic (for several months in 1995–6), to the British Academy for a Research Readership (for a second block of time in 1999–2001), and to my Department of Economic

History at the London School of Economics and my History and Philosophy of Economics group in the Faculty of Economics and Econometrics at the University of Amsterdam who have supported my work throughout. It has been a long fifteen years, but in my defence – several other things happened on the way!

Mary S. Morgan
December 2010

1

Modelling as a Method of Enquiry

PART I: CHANGING THE PRACTICE OF ECONOMIC SCIENCE

1. From Laws to Models, From Words to Objects

Two hundred years ago, political economy was overwhelmingly a verbal science, with questions, concepts, and a mode of reasoning all dependent on words. As a *science*, classical political economy of the eighteenth and early nineteenth centuries began with individuals, theorized their relations, and posited a few general laws that operated at a community level. One of the few laws that was expressed in mathematics was proposed by the Rev'd Thomas Robert Malthus, who claimed that the growth of population, driven by passions, increased in a way that would inevitably outstrip the more pedestrian growth of food supplies. So, he argued, there must also be checks at work in the world: the numbers of people were kept in

1

check either through the vices of disease, famine, and war, or by virtue of celibacy or delayed marriage. While such laws might indeed have an iron grip on economic life, it was not thought easy to perceive these laws at work amongst the complicated changing events of everyday life. This created difficulties for the *art* of political economy, namely fashioning policy in line with an understanding of those scientific principles of political economy.[1]

Economics is now a very different kind of activity. From the late nineteenth century, economics gradually became a more technocratic, tool-based, science, using mathematics and statistics embedded in various kinds of analytical techniques.[2] By the late twentieth century, economics had become heavily dependent on a set of reasoning tools that economists now call 'models': small mathematical, statistical, graphical, diagrammatic, and even physical objects that can be manipulated in various different ways. Today, in the twenty-first century, if we go to an economics seminar, or read a learned scientific paper in that field, we find that economists write down some equations or maybe draw a diagram, and use those to develop solutions to their theoretical conundrums or to answer questions about the economic world. These manipulable objects are the practical starting point in economic research work: they are used for theorizing, providing hypotheses and designing laboratory experiments, they are an essential input into simulations, and they form the basis for much statistical work. Economics teaching is similarly bounded: students learn by working through a set of models: some portraying decisions by individuals and companies, others representing the behaviour of the whole economy, and for every level in between. The use of economic models has become habitual in government policy making, in trading on financial markets, in company decisions, and indeed, anywhere that economic decisions are made in a more technocratic than casual way. In economics, as in many other modern sciences, models have become endemic at every level.

The significance and radical nature of this change in economics is easily overlooked. The introduction of this new kind of scientific object – models – involved not just the adoption of new languages of expression into economics (such as algebra or geometry), but also the introduction of a new way of reasoning to economics. And having moved from a verbal to a model-based science, economists no longer depicted their knowledge in terms of a few general, though unseen, laws,

---

1 Nineteenth-century economists often used the term "principles" in the titles of their treatises on political economy. This term denoted both their theories and analysis of law-like elements in the economic system as well as the appropriate means of good governance (which might have an ethical, even moral, quality). For example, Malthus' laws of population were almost laws of nature (they were based on individual instincts of passion and the need for food, empirical data on population growth, and hypothesized claims about likely growth of food output), while his policy arguments were designed around his understanding of these laws (for example, he was against social security schemes which, in the process of supporting the poor, would interfere with the natural checks on population growth operating within the system see Malthus, 1803).

2 For the twentieth-century development of economics into a tool-based science, see Morgan (2003a).

but expressed it in a multitude of more specific models. As models replaced more general principles and laws, so economists came to interpret the behaviour and phenomena they saw in the economic world directly in terms of those models.[3]

Despite the ubiquity of modelling in modern economics, it is not easy to say how this way of doing science works. Scientific models are not self-evident things, and it is not obvious how such research objects are made, nor how a scientist reasons with them, nor to what purpose. These difficulties of definition and understanding are exhibited in a most concrete fashion in an example that may well be the first such economic model in the history of the field.

The *Tableau Économique* is a wonderful numerical object: a cross between a table and a matrix, it presents an accounting portrait of the French economy (Figure 1.1). It shows the classes of people in the economy (farmers, manufacturers, and landowners) and has a zig-zag pattern of horizontal and diagonal lines between them with numbers on them indicating the amount of goods or money being transferred between the groups of people. It was invented in the late 1750s by François Quesnay, an economist, and physician in the court of Louis XV and thus at the centre of French political life in the mid-eighteenth century.[4] He treated the *Tableau* as a research object, using it to conduct various numerical exercises to explore the possibilities for the French economy to grow via agricultural investment and the subsequent circulation of the surplus created from Nature around the classes of people in the economy. In these exercises, various numbers for the agricultural surplus and the amounts circulated in the zig-zags were inserted, and then added downwards to determine whether such an economy would grow in a stable, balanced way, or if there was some lack of balance in the relations.

The *Tableau Économique*, as one of the earliest models in economics, makes a fine example to introduce a book on models, for it is one of the most celebrated in the history of economics. It can be regarded as the great-grandfather of models in many different economic traditions even while its own content and meaning remain somewhat mysterious. Two hundred and fifty years later, most modern economic models lack the decorative borders (and the dot-matrix qualities that make it look like a needlework sampler hanging on the wall), but are otherwise not so different. Models in economics are still mostly pen-and-paper objects depicting some aspect of the economy in a schematic, miniaturized, simplified, way. The most important point to note about this object, however, is that it was not simply a passive portrait of the economy; rather, it had the internal resources for Quesnay to

---

3 So, by the early twenty-first century, we find, for example, an account in which financial traders acting on models make markets behave like those models (demonstrating the performativity of economic models; see MacKenzie, 2006), and we find economists in newspaper columns explaining the phenomena of ordinary life by verbally reinterpreting those events as examples of these small worlds depicted in economic models (e.g., Harford, 2008, or Levitt and Dubner, 2005 and their columns in the *New York Times* and the London *Financial Times*). I return to this point in Chapter 10.

4 Examples (for there are several) of Quesnay's *Tableau* are found in Kuczynski and Meek (1972) and in Charles (2003) who discusses the development of the diagram.

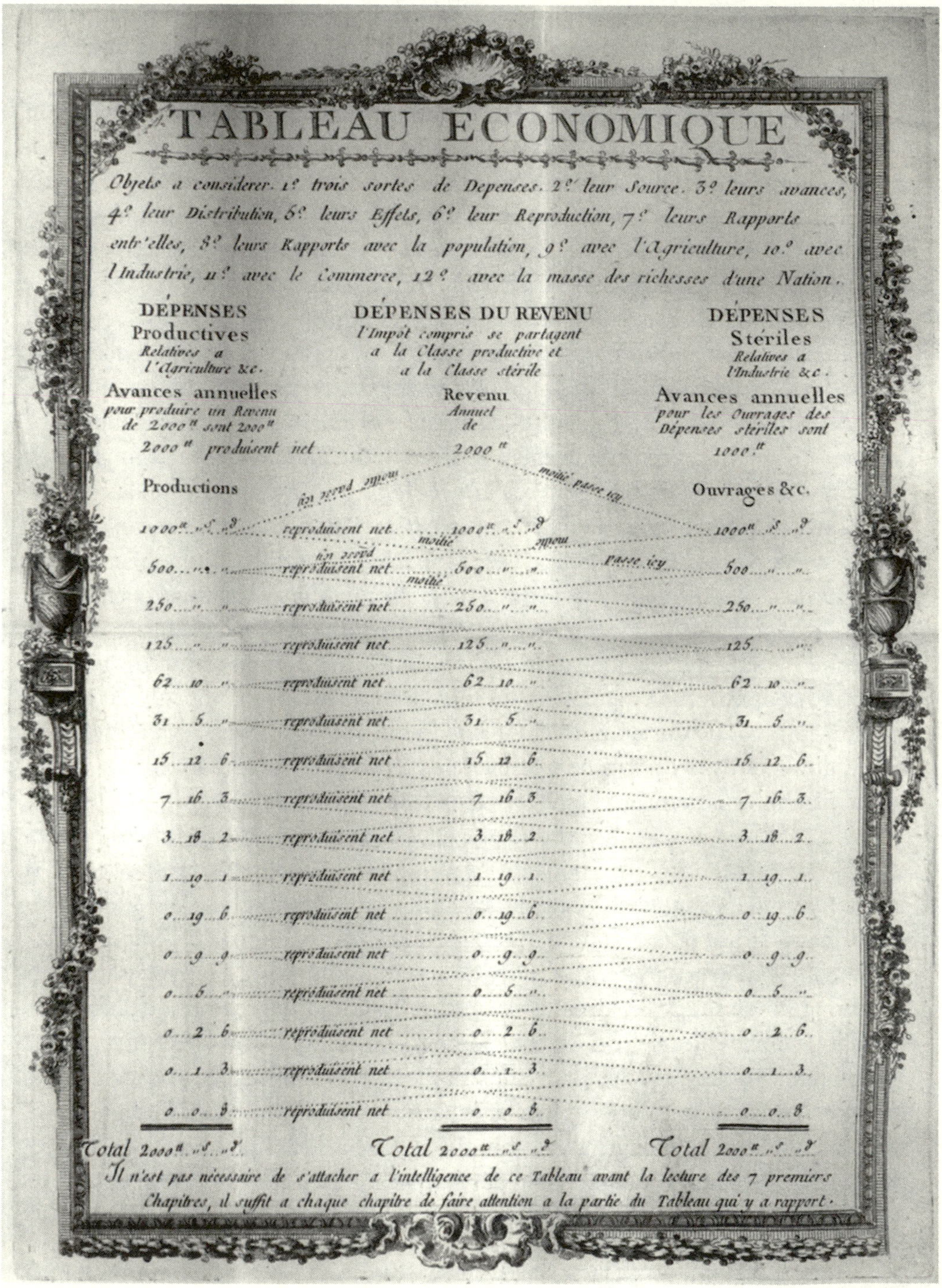

Figure 1.1. Quesnay's *Tableau Économique* (1767).

Source: Private collection. (Reproduced in Loïc Charles [2003] "The Visual History of the *Tableau Économique*". *European Journal of the History of Economic Thought*, 10:4, 527–50, 528.) Reproduced here with thanks to Loïc Charles.

investigate (by his arithmetic exercises) how such an economy as he depicted might work. It is this possibility for manipulation that turns such pictures into models for the economist.

It is also telling that Quesnay's contemporaries found the *Tableau* as difficult an object to interpret and use as do present-day economists. It is very hard for modern economists to understand how the different parts of the *Tableau* relate to each other, or to the economy he inhabited, and to reconstruct exactly how Quesnay reasoned using the object, without the evidence uncovered by historians to explain these things to us.[5] And if we think about how Quesnay might possibly have invented this research object, we can also appreciate that an imaginative and creative mind must have been at work. Such difficulties point to the cognitive and contingent aspects of models: they are objects that embed theoretical and empirical knowledge that later economists will not automatically be able to extract and articulate again, just as non-economists cannot read or use modern economic models without considerable training in the field.

Quesnay's *Tableau* is surely a special object, unique perhaps in its day, but its very specificity raises a number of questions that need answering. If such research objects are so specific to time and place, and if we need to know a great deal about their particularities to see how they work, then how can we characterize the scientific practice of modelling in a general way? This raises philosophical questions: How do economists create such research objects? What exactly is involved in scientific reasoning with such objects? How does working with such objects tell us anything about the world? That is: How should we characterize the making, using, and learning from models as a way of doing science?

The pioneer status of Quesnay's *Tableau* equally raises general historical questions. For while economists now find making and reasoning with such objects the natural way to do economics, we do not have a good account of how that happened, nor understand how it could make such a difference to economics as a science. Reasoning with models is a cognitive process by which economists acquire their knowledge and use it.[6] Sometime in the past, economists had to begin to think with such objects, and learn how to gain knowledge of economics with them, if later generations of economists were to come to reason easily with them and take it for granted as the method they should use.

That process of change: from economists reasoning with words to reasoning with models, is what this book is about. The historical and philosophical aspects of that change cannot be easily untangled. At the meta level, we can point to the considerable but gradual historical shift in the way economists reason, involving elements

5 For recent scholarship that investigates the likely sources of the *Tableau*, its various versions, and how it was used, see particularly Charles (2003) and Van den Berg (2002).

6 Nancy Nersessian (from her 1992 paper to most recent 2008 book) has been instrumental in connecting the literatures of cognitive science with that of the philosophy of scientific modelling. (See also, for examples of different approaches using this connection, papers by Gentner, by Vosniadou, and by Giere in Magnani and Nersessian, 2001.)

of both cognition and imagination that made a big difference to the epistemology of economics, that is, to how economists come to know things in economics. But to understand and appreciate fully the import of these changes, we need to look at the micro level, at the objects themselves. When we look at that level, we find we cannot understand how economists learn things from models without understanding how models are used, nor understand how they are used without understanding how they are built. But why a particular model is built, what questions it is designed to answer, and what uses it is put to, are historically contingent. History and philosophy cannot easily be pulled apart, and the cognitive and imaginative aspects of modelling prove equally sticky in figuring out how economists make and reason with models. These issues – philosophical and historical, involving elements of reasoning and imagination – are explored in the book through the investigation of a number of models of considerable significance, and long life, in the history of economics. It is by paying careful analytical attention to how these small objects are made and used in economics that we can understand the import of the big changes in economics. They provide the materials for both a naturalized philosophy of modelling in economics and a historical account of the naturalization of models in economics.[7]

2. The Naturalization of Modelling in Economics

Though the important historical and philosophical changes in economics are difficult to understand separately, a broad chronology for the historical development of modelling over the last 200 years can be outlined. There are three moments of time that are important. To begin with, we can find a few isolated examples of models in the late eighteenth and early nineteenth centuries and so call this period the prehistory. We then find, in the late nineteenth century, a first generation of modellers: a very few economists who regularly made and used such research objects. The second generation of modellers, the real developers of the method of models, emerged during the interwar period. Modelling then became widespread through economics only after the mid-twentieth century.

To make this history more concrete, and to get a real feeling for what these research objects are, I introduce a number of significant examples here. If we begin with the 'prehistory' of models, we find that not only does Quesnay's *Tableau Économique* exist as an object out of its time in the eighteenth century, but there

---

7 It is appropriate here to refer to three parallel investigations. Nersessian (2008) comes to the topic of 'model-based reasoning' from cognitive science and philosophy of science, and combines mental models, narratives, experiments, and reasoning in her account of the history of physics. Ursula Klein (2003) uses history and philosophy of science and semiotics to explore the nexus of paper tools, models, and experiments that created a shift of scientific reasoning and practice in chemistry (see also Klein, 2001). Their two accounts share many of the elements of my own project for economics, though we have put them together in somewhat different ways. Meli (2006), in another parallel, discusses how the science of seventeenth-century mechanics depended on reasoning with objects.

(a)

Now if no rent was paid for the land which yielded 180 quarters, when corn was at 4*l.* per quarter, the value of 10 quarters would be paid as rent when only 170 could be procured, which, at 4*l.* 4*s.* 8*d.* would be 42*l.* 7*s.* 6*d.*

20 qrs. when 160 were produced, which at £4   10   0 would be £90   0   0
30 qrs. .... 150 4   16   0................. 144   0   0
40 qrs. .... 140 5   2   10................. 205   13   4

$$\text{Corn rent}^1 \text{ would increase} \left.\begin{array}{c} 100 \\ 200 \\ 300 \\ 400 \end{array}\right\} \text{ and money rent in the} \left.\begin{array}{c} 100 \\ 212 \\ 340 \\ 485 \end{array}\right.$$

Corn rent[1] would increase in the proportion of {100, 200, 300, 400} and money rent in the proportion of {100, 212, 340, 485}

(b)

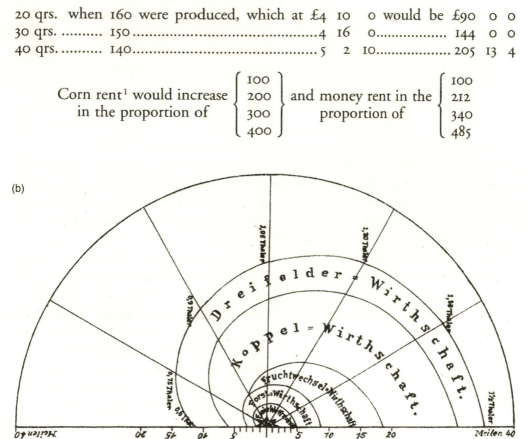

Figure 1.2. The Prehistory of Models.

(a) Ricardo's Farm Accounting (1821).

Source: Piero Sraffa: *The Works and Correspondence of David Ricardo*. Edited with the collaboration of M.H. Dobb, 1951–73. Cambridge: Cambridge University Press for The Royal Economic Society. Vol. I: *Principles of Political Economy & Taxation*, 1821, p. 84. Reproduced by permission of Liberty Fund Inc. on behalf of The Royal Economic Society.

(b) Von Thünen's Farming Diagram (1826).

Source: Johann Heinrich von Thünen, *Der isolierte Staat in Beziehung auf Landwirtschaft und Nationalökonomie*, Hamburg, 1826. Reprinted facsimile edition 1990. Berlin: Academie Verlag, p. 275.

are also very few further cases in the early nineteenth century. One is provided by a table of farm accounts developed by the English economist David Ricardo (1821) to explain how income gets distributed in the agricultural economy (one element of his table is shown in Figure 1.2a). Another is the diagram (in Figure 1.2b) of farm prices in relation to distance from towns, drawn by the German agriculturalist Johann von Thünen (1826), depicting an idealized abstract, landscape but with numbers drawn from his experience of farming at his own estate of Tellow.[8] These three objects – the *Tableau*, the accounting table, and the spatial diagram with numbers – each designed to show how the agricultural economy worked, jut out awkwardly from the sea of words that surround them in this early period of economic science.

In the late nineteenth century, we begin to see more regular occurrences of these objects we are calling models, but we may also notice that the few economists involved felt they had to justify their creation and usage of these odd research objects that they had invented to help them in their analysis. They did not yet have the concept or label of models and were indeed quite self-conscious about this activity. Three important examples epitomise this first generation of models and modellers and their understanding of the role of models. In 1879, the British economist Alfred Marshall began to draw little diagrams to explain more clearly how two countries trade with each other, in this case the curves depicting the offers of German iron for English cloth and vice versa as relative prices change (Figure 1.3a).[9] Marshall thought that such diagrams were useful if they could be illustrated with examples from economic life (and then he often presented them in his footnotes), but that if such pieces of mathematics were not useful, they should be burnt! In 1881, the Irish economist Francis Edgeworth outlined a somewhat different diagrammatic perspective on exchange relations (Figure 1.3b) to figure out the range of possible contracts that Robinson Crusoe might strike with Man Friday to gain his help in cultivating their island economy. Not being sure how to refer to this way of reasoning, he labelled his analysis with the diagram as offering a "representative particular" argument (see Chapter 3). In 1892, Irving Fisher, an American economist, designed and constructed a hydraulic mechanism to represent, explore, and so understand the workings of a mini-economy, one with only three goods and three consumers (Figure 1.3c).[10] He accompanied this work with an outright

---

8 Von Thünen's original contribution appeared in 1826; an English translation of part of the study became available in 1966, with a useful introduction. On different interpretations of his modelling project, see Judy Klein (2001, pp. 114–6), who reproduces his diagram and discusses it as a measuring device, and Mäki (2004), who analyses it as a theoretical model.

9 This was the first appearance of these curves in the history of economic theorizing about trade relations, on which Humphrey (1995, p. 41) comments: Marshall "by crystallizing, condensing and generalizing earlier insights into a powerful yet simple visual image" was able to create an object that made these relations "transparent". Marshall's 1879 diagrams and discussion were finally published in an edition of his early works edited by Whitaker in 1975, and this diagram provided the logo for the Charles Gide conference at which some parts of this paper were first presented. Marshall's views of mathematics are discussed by Weintraub (2002).

10 Fisher's thesis of 1891 was published in 1892 and republished in 1925, displaying a photograph of the mechanism in the frontispiece labelled "model of a mechanism".

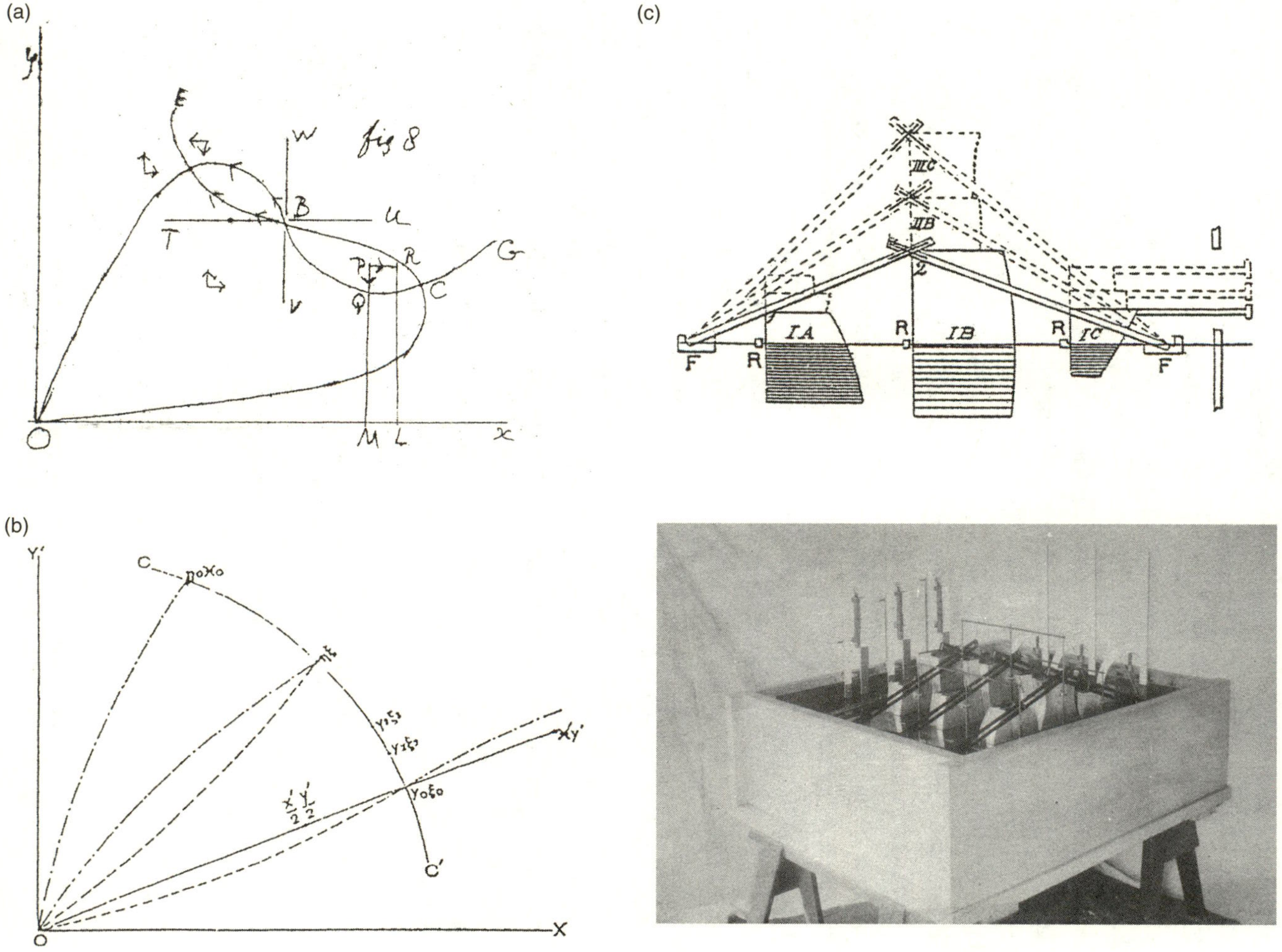

Figure 1.3. First-Generation Models.

(a) Marshall's Trade Diagram (1879).

Source: Alfred Marshall, "Pure Theory of Foreign Trade". Privately printed 1879, Figure 8, Marshall Library, Cambridge. (Reprinted, London: London School of Economics and Political Science Reprints of Scarce Tracts in Economics, No. 1, 1930). Reproduced with thanks to Marshall Library of Economics, Cambridge.

(b) Edgeworth's Exchange Diagram (1881).

Source: F. Y. Edgeworth, *Mathematical Psychics*. London: C. Kegan Paul & Co., 1881, Figure 1, p. 28.

(c) Fisher's Hydraulic Machine and Its Design (constructed 1893 from 1892 design).

Source: Irving Fisher, *Mathematical Investigation in the Theory of Value and Price*. Thesis of 1891/2. New Haven: Yale University Press, 1925. Frontispiece and Figure 9 on p. 39. Reproduced with permission from George Fisher.

defence of these research objects – mathematical, graphical, and real machines – that he designed and used for his economic analysis.

It seems reasonable to locate these three economists in the first real generation of model-makers, and their self-consciousness about their research objects as indicative of this moment of change. This late nineteenth century moment was noticed later on by Arthur Pigou in 1929, who cleverly understood the diagrams and equations we see in these examples as "tools", labelling Edgeworth as a "tool maker" and Marshall as a "tool maker and user". For Pigou, these objects were "pieces of analytic machinery", "thought-tools", or even "keystones".[11] And because economics is now dependent upon such research objects, all of these examples can today be understood as models, though, neither in the prehistory period, nor in this late nineteenth century moment, would economists have recognised them as such or used the label.

It was in the 1930s that economists really 'discovered' the idea of models. It was in that decade that these objects became conceptualized, gained the label 'model', and a fuller understanding of their usefulness developed. Two economists played an important role in this transformation, thus sparking the wider deployment of the label, notion, and usage of models in economic analysis. In 1933, in the depths of the Great Depression, the Norwegian economist Ragnar Frisch developed one of the first mathematical models of the business cycle. Because it had certain features, particularly the possibility to simulate a cyclical pattern, Frisch's "macro-dynamic system" created a new recipe for future business cycle models (see Boumans, 1999 and Chapter 6, this volume). As a recipe, it formed the basis for the first econometric model of a whole economy, built by the Dutch economist Jan Tinbergen in 1936 (1937), to see how to get The Netherlands out of the Depression. This object embedded a theory of the business cycle into the mathematical form, along with statistical information from the Dutch economy in the numbers (or parameters) of the equations. These two economists won the first Nobel Prize for Economics in 1969 for this model-based research; one of Tinbergen's model equations and a schema (from his slightly later US model of 1939) are shown in Figure 1.4a, while Frisch's model is shown later in Figure 1.6.

Tinbergen was also largely responsible for transferring the term 'model' in the early 1930s from physics, where it had usually referred to a material object, into economics to refer to the statistical and mathematical objects that he and Frisch were then developing.[12] So by the middle 1930s, the label 'model' had come into use,

---

11 See Pigou's lecture of 1929 (in his 1931), particularly pp. 2–8. Joan Robinson (1933) is more usually noted for introducing the notion of the "tool box of economics", but she was following Pigou, whose discussion, and prose, is more effective. Pigou's idea of tools was quite broad – it included not just models, but also the concurrent development of mathematical and statistical techniques. I return to the issue of "keystones" in Chapter 10.

12 Ludwig Boltzmann had defined the term 'model' in the sense of a material object model, in what has become one of the classic articles on models in the 11th edition of the *Encyclopaedia Britannica* (1911). Boltzmann there provides a good view of nineteenth-century scientists' sense of the word. Boumans argues that it was Ehrenfest who probably broadened the scope to apply to mathematical objects, and since Tinbergen was his assistant in the mid-1920s, this is a likely route for the transfer of the term into economics (see Boumans, 2005, chapter 2) though there are also scattered uses of the term by other economists in the 1920s.

Figure 1.4. Second-Generation Models.

(a) Tinbergen's US Econometric Model: Equations and Causal-Time Process.

Source: Jan Tinbergen, *Business Cycles in the United States of America, 1991–1932*. League of Nations Publications, Series II, Economic and Financial, 1939 II.A 16; Equation 6.31 on p. 137 and graph 6.31 on p. 138. Reproduced with permission from Stichting Wetenschappelijke Nalatenschap Jan Tinbergen.

(b) Hicks IS-LL "Little Apparatus".

Source: J. R. Hicks, "Mr. Keynes and the 'Classics'; A Suggested Interpretation" *Econometrica*, 5: 2 (Apr., 1937), pp. 147–159; Figure 1, p. 153. Reproduced with permission from The Econometric Society.

(c) Samuelson's Keynesian Model.

Source: Paul A. Samuelson, "Interactions between the Multiplier Analysis and the Principle of Acceleration". *The Review of Economics and Statistics*, 21:2 (May, 1939), pp. 75–78; text and equations on p. 76. Reproduced with permission from MIT Press Journals.

(a)

$$Z_t^c = e_1 Z_{t-1}^c + e_2 Z_{t-2}^c + e_3 Z_{t-3}^c + e_4 Z_{t-4}^c + (AU + IIO + F + R)_t \quad (6.31).$$

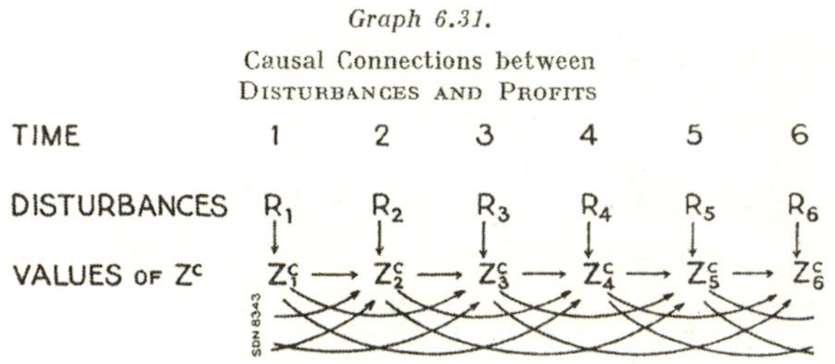

Graph 6.31.

Causal Connections between
DISTURBANCES AND PROFITS

TIME	1	2	3	4	5	6
DISTURBANCES	R_1	R_2	R_3	R_4	R_5	R_6
VALUES OF Z^c	Z_1^c	Z_2^c	Z_3^c	Z_4^c	Z_5^c	Z_6^c

SDN 8343

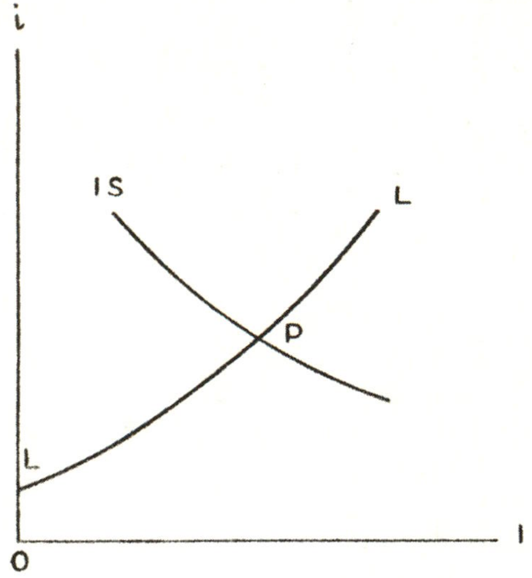

(c)

The national income at time t, Y_t, can be written as the sum of three components: (1) governmental expenditure, g_t, (2) consumption expenditure, C_t, and (3) induced private investment, I_t.

$$Y_t = g_t + C_t + I_t.$$

But according to the Hansen assumptions

$$C_t = \alpha Y_{t-1}$$
$$I_t = \beta[C_t - C_{t-1}] = \alpha\beta Y_{t-1} - \alpha\beta Y_{t-2}$$

and

$$g_t = 1.$$

Therefore, our national income can be rewritten

$$Y_t = 1 + \alpha[1 + \beta]Y_{t-1} - \alpha\beta Y_{t-2}.$$

(b)

though not everyone had noticed it.[13] For example, in 1937 John Hicks invented a "little apparatus" (p. 156), his IS-LL diagram (Figure 1.4b), to compare the workings of J. M. Keynes' new macroeconomics (of 1936) with that of the older classical system. In that same year, in another attempt to turn Keynes' theory into something more comprehensible, James Meade provided an eight-equation algebraic treatment, calling it a "A Simplified Model of Mr. Keynes' System", while soon after Paul Samuelson produced a smaller set of equations (seen in Figure 1.4c) to exemplify and explain the Keynesian relations, describing them as "a new model sequence" (1939, p. 75). All of these three 'Keynesian' models are discussed in Chapter 6.

Economists quickly broadened the scope of the label 'model' to refer to all kinds of mathematical and diagrammatic and material objects. But even then, models – as working objects and as a label – did not immediately and fully invade economics until a bit later. Only with the next new generation of economists – for whom both the label and the notion were unproblematic – did models cease to be special and became commonplace. Thus, William Baumol (1951) used the term as naturally as one might refer to a domestic weed when he referred to Harrod's (1939) small set of equations showing how an economy grows as "Mr. Harrod's Model", while Roy Harrod himself (of the same older generation as Hicks and Meade) still mused about the term as if it were some exotic imported plant:

> Many years after I had made certain formulations in the field of growth theory and after Professor Domar had made similar formulations, there began to be references to the "Harrod-Domar model". I found myself in the position of Le Bourgeois Gentilhomme who had been speaking prose all his life without knowing it. I had been fabricating "models" without knowing it. (Harrod, 1968, p. 173)

This brief history has enabled me to indicate the historical contours of when models were introduced and when modelling became the normal mode of reasoning in economists: from isolated examples in the prehistory, to a first generation of model-makers and users in the late nineteenth century, to a second generation who developed these research objects explicitly as models in the 1930s. It was this second generation who fully developed this "new practice" of modelling, as Marcel Boumans (2005) has justly labelled it. The label, the idea, and the use of models became the natural way to work for economists only in the period from the 1940s onwards.

Models are not easy objects either to define or, in general terms, describe, but those reproduced here, some of the most important models from the history

13 Nor was its meaning stable in the 1930s (for examples of its range, see Schumpeter, 1935). Although we see the term model taken up by those making models of Keynes' theoretical macroeconomic system (1936), it was not one of Keynes' terms (almost the only time he used it was in discussing Tinbergen's work, see Keynes, 1973, pp. 284–305). Keynes himself seemed to prefer the term "schema" or "schematism", which, as we will see later in Section 4.iii, has a slightly different connotation: it indicates an outline, rather than an apparatus that might be manipulated.

of economics, exemplify the sort of things that count as models in economics: either real objects, or pen-and-paper objects that are diagrammatic, algebraic, or arithmetic in form. Despite their variations in form, these objects share recognisable characteristics: each depicts, renders, denotes, or in some way provides, some kind of representation of ideas about some aspects of the economy. Yet, and this is a very important point to stress, these representations are not just pictures. Pictures of the economy go back a long way: we see shipbuilding in the eleventh century Bayeux Tapestry and building sites in the fifteenth century frescoes of the recently reopened hospital of Santa Maria della Scala in Siena. These depict the arrangements of labour and capital, show the technologies of the period, and so forth – but they are not models for the economist. As I pointed out earlier, Quesnay's *Tableau Économique* was not just a depiction of the economy but one that could be manipulated, and because it could be manipulated, it could be reasoned with. For economists it is the possibility to reason with the different kinds of representations shown in this chapter that makes them all into economic models.[14]

Hick's 1937 terminology of a 'little apparatus' nicely captures the manipulability of such research objects – they are working objects that can be played around with in various ways – even though his model is made only of paper and pen compared to the real apparatus of Fisher's earlier hydraulic model. These two examples have an obvious affinity with the material object models used centuries earlier. For example, models of the planetary system constructed out of papier maché and metal rods were used by scientists to explore the workings of the universe, while articulated wooden maquettes were made by architects to demonstrate the construction of their buildings. This comparison points to another critical point about models: they must be small enough in scale for their manipulation to be manageable in order that they can be used to enquire – indirectly – into the workings of those aspects of the economy depicted, just as those models of domes and the planetary systems were. It seems natural to take over this older sense of material models from the arts and sciences to understand the term 'model' that Tinbergen introduced into economics at that time: small-scale objects depicting aspects of the economy that can be analysed and manipulated in various ways.

But notice here how introducing this new kind of research object into economics brought along with it a new way of reasoning to that science, a method that economist-scientists now call simply 'modelling'. By the latter half of the twentieth century, mathematical modelling had become the preferred way of doing scientific and policy-making economics, and had come to inhabit a number of other domains where economists had left their mark in the scientific, public, and commercial realms. And, wherever statistical data were available, econometric modelling

---

14 The label *Tableau* is indicative that some tables of numbers may also have this manipulable quality, and so reasoning with them is also a possibility, for example, Leontief input–output tables both represent the economy and can be manipulated.

became the relevant way of working – although this book is not primarily about econometrics.[15] In other words, disciplinary arguments at all levels of economics came to hinge not just on the objects – models, but on economists' abilities to reason with them – modelling. Modelling had become *the* accepted mode of reasoning in economics in the sense that it became "the right way to reason.... what it is to reason rightly".[16]

3. Practical Reasoning Styles

This brings us to the question of reasoning method, for though we can discern some characteristics in common between those revered old models of the universe resting in our science museums and the modern mathematical models of the economy, it is perhaps not so obvious that economics shares a mode of reasoning with early astronomy.

3.i Modelling as a Style of Reasoning

Modelling is one of the six different "styles" of scientific thinking that Alistair Crombie distinguishes in his *Designed in the Mind: Western Visions of Science, Nature and Humankind*.[17] It is worth listing them all here – in the chronological order that they appeared in the history of the sciences.

---

15 The history of modelling in economics has been barely considered except in econometrics (on which see Morgan, 1990; Boumans, 1993, 2005; Qin, 1993; and Le Gall, 2007). The parallel literature on mathematical modelling – *qua* modelling – is less developed, but see Boumans (2005), who focusses on the 1920s–1930s in his discussion of it as a "new practice" in both statistical and mathematical terms. Solow (1997/2005) offers some suggestions about its takeoff in the 1950s and as a rare exception, compares the use of mathematics to the use of modelling to argue that economics is mainly a modelling discipline. Niehans (1990) recognises the "era of models" as a leitmotiv for the period since the 1930s (but does not say much about its history); and Colander (2000) portrays modelling as the "central attribute of modern economics" (p. 137). Most histories of twentieth-century economics allude to models, but the introduction of models, and their mode of argument, are largely taken for granted. Mirowski (2002) indirectly comes closest to dealing with this as an historical problem, but his questions are about ideas, theories, and techniques of economics in the context of the Cold War, rather than about modelling itself.

16 One of the peculiar signs of this acceptance (and it may be specific to economics compared to other scientific fields) is that economists rarely use the word *theory* nowadays, or if so, they use it interchangeably with *model* to such an extent that many economists find it difficult to distinguish between the two (see Goldfarb and Ratner, 2008). I return to the point in Chapter 10. The quote itself comes from Hacking (1992a, p. 10) and refers not to modelling in economics, but to a much broader claim about the nature of epistemic genres in scientific reasoning, discussed in the next section.

17 Crombie's claim – that there are basically six styles of scientific reasoning, first appeared in his paper of 1988 and the volumes of Crombie's massive three volumes: *Styles of Scientific Thinking in the European Traditions* (1994) were in draft in 1980. Thus, Hacking's review and further analysis (1992a) come after that first paper but predate Crombie's main publication of 1994.

1. Mathematical postulation and proof
2. Experiment
3. Hypothetical modelling
4. Taxonomy (the method of classification into natural kinds)
5. Statistical
6. Historical-genetic[18]

These categories label different 'styles' or 'epistemic genres' of scientific reasoning, that is, of ways of finding out about the world. They do not provide the kind of detailed descriptions in combination with a big picture analysis of how science goes on that we find in Ludwig Fleck's 'denkstil', Michel Foucault's 'epistemes', Thomas Kuhn's 'paradigms', nor Hans-Jorg Rheinberger's 'experimental systems'.[19] Rather, this set of categories provides a framework for historical epistemology in the sense that it enables the historian to track the changes in how scientists do their science. While modern economics barely makes it into Crombie's massive volumes, nor Ian Hacking's subsequent discussions, they provide the resources to understand how modelling as an epistemic style or genre came into economics and what kind of difference it made.[20]

According to Crombie (1994), modelling grew up in the field of early modern sciences and arts in the making of models of natural objects – and sprang from the desire to imitate nature, and in so doing to understand its workings. It had joint roots in natural philosophical investigations into the relationship of the Earth and the heavens (such as in astronomy) and in the craft skills found in the creation of objects such as imitation birds (singing, feathered, mechanical automata). Given these roots, Crombie labelled one of its characteristic features as involving "the construction of analogies" (1988, p. 11). Although there are good examples of analogical models in economics, analogical aspects no longer constitute a distinguishing feature of model-making in this field. It is therefore useful to broaden the canvas beyond analogies to see how the desire to understand Nature (or in the economists' case, the economy) through some form of imitation lies at the heart of modelling. And, just as there are many different genres and aims of representation in the arts, such scientific representations come in a variety of forms and disguises.

---

18 The "historical derivation of genetic development" is associated with evolutionary science. "Thinking in cases" is a seventh style added by Forrester (1996), as used for example in various branches of medicine and psychiatry. Karine Chemla (2003) has argued for an eight style – the algorithmic method. At first sight, none of these other styles seem to be connected to modelling, but as we shall see later in this book, the methods of taxonomy and classification, and the method of experiment, are both found in conjunction with the method of modelling in economics, while statistical reasoning is the basis for econometric modelling.

19 See Fleck (1935/1979), Foucault (1970), Kuhn (1962), and Rheinberger (1997).

20 As such, this account provides a parallel to Hacking's accounts for the development of the statistical style (1992b), for the experimental (laboratory) style (1992c) and for the taxonomic style (1993).

The history of modelling as a reasoning style in Crombie's account is built upon material object models, such as those in astronomy, and so we can continue to think of the planetary motion models of the Renaissance period as being exemplary for the idea of models and of how they are used for enquiry. They were built to represent the relationships – hypothesized by the early astronomers – between Earth and the heavens. They were carefully designed not just to present or illustrate known relationships but also to demonstrate those relations that scientists *supposed* to be true (their hypotheses) and thus to explain how the universe was thought to be arranged and to work. Those models that were manipulable (rather than with fixed parts) were particularly useful in enquiries into the hidden trajectories and contested relations of the heavenly bodies. It is this kind of physical activity of science in general that perhaps led Ian Hacking (1992a) to suggest that Crombie's style of "thinking" should be replaced by "reasoning".[21] Thus, we might rather think of each style as a generic kind of very practical reasoning, with different characteristics for each style.

We learn from Crombie that the adoption of any particular style of practical reasoning in any one field requires its own historical account. Take, as a parallel example to the introduction of modelling, the method of experiment. This grew up in the early modern period as a method of analysis and synthesis "to control [the method of mathematical] postulation and to explore by observation and measurement" (1994, Vol. I, p. 84). Crombie dates its main development from the thirteenth century and thereafter it took hold in various disciplines at different times and places. But typically those who would adopt a new style of practical reasoning for their science have to argue for it, as well as demonstrate its usefulness, for the acceptance of a new style generally institutes a *change* in reasoning style. This is one reason why the histories of the different sciences are so replete with arguments about how that science should be done. For example, Shapin and Schaffer (1985) analyse in detail how the method was fought over in the establishment of natural philosophy in seventeenth century England. To follow the example into economics: classroom experiments began there in the 1940s, though the activity was sufficiently limited that economists experienced their own battle for the acceptance of the experimental method within economics only in the period after 1970. Yet it is worth noting too, that in economics as in many modern sciences, the individual styles have begun to hybridize. Thus, even from the beginning of experimental work in economics in the 1940s, modelling informed those experimentalists' working hypotheses and models were found in their experimental designs (as we shall see in Chapter 7).

Finally, we can also take from both Crombie and Hacking that adopting a new reasoning style into a science does not come without significant consequences for its content. There are inevitably connections between style and content, and while

---

21 The practical aspects of this are important: for like Hacking, I find the term "reasoning" underrates the importance of the "manipulative hand and the attentive eye" (Hacking, 1992a, p. 4).

different sciences may rest on one or more of these styles of reasoning, that does not imply that any scientific system can rest on any style. For example, Quetelet's 'average man' of the mid-nineteenth century is a statistically defined concept and so unthinkable without the adoption of statistical reasoning. In economics now, it is almost impossible for economists to give an account of individual behaviour, or of the world economic crisis, which has not been defined in terms of their economic models and argued over using their model reasoning.

Any scientist's ability to reason in a chosen style is thus clearly dependent on the contingent history of that discipline, and whether that method is accepted within it. Yet, once more or less adopted within a discipline, a style, as Hacking says, becomes

> … a timeless canon of objectivity, a standard or model of what it is to be reasonable about this or that type of subject matter. We do not check to see whether mathematical proof or laboratory investigation or statistical 'studies' are the right way to reason: they have become (after fierce struggles) what it is to reason rightly, to be reasonable in this or that domain. (Hacking, 1992a, p. 10)

Once accepted by a group of scientists, a style of reasoning comes to seem natural to them, so natural that they do not question it. They neither question its historical origins, nor the objectivity of the knowledge gained from using the method, nor do they appeal to any outside or higher level for its justification. That is why, Hacking argues, once a style of reasoning is accepted in a community, reasoning rightly means to reason in that style.[22]

3.ii Modelling as a Reasoning Style in Economics

Although the broad historical contours of the appearance and spread of *models* in economics were outlined earlier (in Section 2), the processes by which *modelling* took hold as an independent style of practical reasoning are more hazy. There was, of course, no blank page in economics before modelling took over. Early economists used technical and conceptual terms (the terminology of their science), but reasoned with them in the modes of ordinary verbal argument. As modelling developed, it first partly overlayered and partly integrated with two other generic practices of scientific reasoning, namely mathematical ones in the late nineteenth century and then statistical ones in the 1920s and 1930s (in the form of econometrics). More recently it has become layered into the experimental and classificatory

---

22 Hacking even makes a stronger claim, arguing that a style becomes self-validating. For example, statistical reasoning is validated by arguments that are coherent within statistical thinking, not by ones from other styles of reasoning or some meta philosophical argument (see Hacking, 1992b, and for laboratory sciences, Hacking, 1992c). This all points to the relativity of scientific method and so the knowledge obtained by it, but it is not a radical relativity, for each of the styles is considered valid as a scientific method.

modes of reasoning (see Chapters 7 to 9). While modelling itself became deeply rooted in economics, so deeply rooted as to produce the overwhelmingly luxuriant growth that made it – in its various forms – the dominant mode of reasoning by the late twentieth century, it did so in forms that were either partly disguised or manifest in hybrids.

Treating the development of modelling as an epistemic genre – that is, as a practical mode of reasoning to gain knowledge about the economic world – does help to part the clouds that obscure the historical gaze. It reveals to us that mathematics grew up in two styles of reasoning in economics at more or less the same time in the late nineteenth century: the method of mathematical postulation and proof and the method of hypothetical modelling using mathematical models. We have already seen how the first generation of model-makers in the late nineteenth century generated a new practice of modelling, but by taking note of Crombie's categories, we can also see why it crept in unnoticed by historians who have paid more attention to the concurrent introduction of mathematical modes of arguing without distinguishing between two styles of reasoning both involving mathematics. It is fair to say, however, that recognising two distinct historical traditions in styles of scientific reasoning that both involved mathematical languages, and distinguishing between the method of hypothetical modelling versus that of postulation and proof, is not always easy. This knotty historical problem is further complicated by the fact that, as Weintraub (2002) has shown us, mathematics has its own self-image, one that changes in its relationship with the sciences. During that late nineteenth century time when these two mathematical modes of reasoning came into economics, mathematicians felt the need to have their work closely related to the sciences, though that relationship could be mediated in different ways, while for their part, economists of the time argued about the usefulness of mathematics as both a language and as a method.[23]

Nevertheless, we can contrast, as exemplars of these two reasoning styles in the late nineteenth century, Fisher's hydraulic/mechanical model of his three-commodity, three-person economy (pictured in Figure 1.3c) with the French economist, Leon Walras' 1874 mathematically described general equilibrium account for the whole economy. So, whilst Walras (amongst others) was busy introducing what might be recognised as mathematical language and the method of mathematical postulation and proof, we can also distinguish objects that we can call models, and a method of reasoning with them (including the use of mathematics), being developed by economists such as Fisher and Marshall. The fact that Fisher built his hydraulic model to represent Walras' ideas, and to figure out by exploring with that physical model the *process* by which the latter's mathematically postulated and proved general equilibrium might be arrived at, shows us the

---

23 Authorities on the history of mathematical reasoning in the history of economics are Roy Weintraub (see his 2002 and 2008); and Giorgio Israel (see particularly Ingrao and Israel, 1987/90, and Israel, 2002). For an insight into contemporary views, see Edgeworth (1889).

difference between them. The fact that both used mathematical ideas from physical systems demonstrates not only the closeness of mathematics and the sciences (but also shows how treacherous relying on analogies as indicators of reasoning styles can be). Individual economists worked with different styles of reasoning involving mathematics and the mathematical method, but as we should expect, their choices were locally determined, dependent on their own histories, times, and places and their own image of the role of mathematics in science.

Mathematics provides the languages of most modern economic model-making, and we know that economics became mathematized at the same time as it became a modelling science, but if we want the historical record to help us think about modelling, then we need to turn the terms around: in order to get at modelling in economics, we need to concentrate on the objects, on the models themselves rather than on their mathematics. Here, as we have already found, history matters whenever we are discussing any specific example of a model, for models are contingent, not timeless: we need history to understand why and how any particular model was built, how it was used, and what understanding economists gained from it. But to understand the development of modelling as an epistemic genre, we need to capture and explicate the generic qualities that we can find in the earlier models of Quesnay, and Ricardo, just as much as the twentieth century work of Frisch and Samuelson. To understand what is involved in this shift in economic science, a shift in how economists reason in economics and about the economy, we need to understand what constitutes the method of modelling in economics. Here, history begins to take second place: it provides the materials and examples for explanation, but we are instead concerned with philosophical questions about how models are made, about modelling as mode of reasoning, and about the nature of modelling as an epistemic genre.

PART II: MAKING MODELS, USING MODELS

4. Making Models to Reason With: Forms, Rules, and Resources

How do economists make models?[24] The process of model-making in economics has often been labelled one of "formalization", a term whose various meanings have so twisted and turned through the history of economics that I suggest we

---

24 The literature on the philosophy (or methodology) of modelling in economics has seen considerable attention in recent years, particularly since the formation of a specialist *Journal of Economic Methodology*. I have discussed the seminal contributions by various economists over the twentieth century alongside some philosophical reflections in Morgan, 2008/online, and surveyed the recent work in Morgan and Knuuttila (2012). Consequently, this chapter does not provide an additional survey: rather some elements are discussed in this chapter and others in the chapters that follow.

begin afresh with it.[25] I focus on two meanings of the term. First, if we think about its active form: 'to formalize', we imply to give form to, to shape, or to provide an outline of something. Second, 'formal' contrasts with 'informal', meaning lacking in exactness or in rules, whereas 'formal' implies something rule bound, following prescribed forms. Making models involves both senses: models give form to, in the sense of providing a more explicit or exact representation of our ideas about the world, and in creating those forms we make them subject to rules of conduct or manipulation. These two aspects of modelling – giving form to ideas and making them formally rule bound – are related, and if we understand how, we take a big step towards seeing how models provide the means for reasoning within economic science. I make use of some more examples of economic models to show how giving form to a model and making it subject to rules of reasoning go along together.

4.i Giving Form

All the models reproduced in this chapter – a small but representative sample from the history of the field – give representation to economists' vague ideas about the economy in various more exact forms: in diagrams, equations, pictures, and even in physical objects. How does this happen? Commentators have found a number of different ways to describe this process of 'giving form to' ideas, namely, as a process of recipe making, of visualizing, of idealizing, or of choosing analogies. It is helpful to see these four accounts as four different ways to understand how models get made rather than being either labels for different kinds of models or as terms used by the scientists/model-makers themselves. Nor are such accounts necessarily mutually exclusive in accounting for any particular model-building episode.[26]

---

25 It is indicative, for example, that at the end of the nineteenth century, the taxonomy of methods for economics given by W. E. Johnson in the Old Palgrave (the renowned dictionary of economics of 1894–6) contrasts "formal" with "narrative", although both categories fell under the term "descriptive economics"; meaning that they "describe the conceptions and facts with which the science deals". Formal methods were those which "analyse and classify" concepts and involved the "logical processes of definition and division". Both "Inductive" and "Deductive" methods fell on the other side of the taxonomy tree, under the title of "constructive" methods: those that "establish laws and uniformities" (Johnson, 1896, pp. 739–48). In contrast, most modern commentators align formal methods with mathematical methods, and thus with deduction. Some minority of economists continue to dispute the efficacy of 'formal methods' in economics, arguing that formalism is non-neutral (see Chick and Dow, 2001), or that it narrows and leaves out too much substantive content of importance compared to the verbal methods it supplanted (thus equating formal with a lack of substance), an argument that seems to hold both the language of mathematics, and the small-scale reasoning tools of modelling, equally at fault. Two recent debates about the meaning and content of 'formalism' are suggestive of the term's extraordinary range (see debate in *Methodus*, 1991, particularly contributions by McCloskey and Katzner, and in the *Economic Journal*, 1998, by Backhouse and Krugman).
26 For example, as we find in Chapter 5, both Hesse's 1966 account of analogical modelling and Boumans' 1999 account of recipe-making help us understand the process of making the analogical Phillips-Newlyn hydraulic machine (see Morgan and Boumans, 2004).

The first of these four accounts of how models are made sees the process of giving form to ideas about the economy as analogous to recipe-making. Boumans' (1999) recipe notion embeds two ideas: economists choose the model's *ingredients* – their ideas, intuitions, and bits of knowledge of how the economy works – and then combine them together and fashion them to make something new. It is critical that this model-making involves processes of *integration*: mixing and shaping and baking the elements, 'cooking' them to form something whole that is not fully recognisable from the original elements (as in chemical synthesis). It may well be that the end product is not envisaged at the beginning, for *recipe-making* is a creative process (less so for *recipe-following*, which produces more reliable and known results). For example, Ricardo can be understood to have formed his model out of a set of little accounting tables (one of which is shown in Figure 1.2a): he integrated these elements together and reasoned with them until they emerged as the accounts of a model farm representing the agricultural economy of his day (as we shall see in Chapter 2). Hicks' IS-LL model provides another good example that can be well described as recipe-making: it was fashioned to make sense of Keynes' ideas about the macroeconomy by fitting together the simplified or basic elements and relations of the macroeconomy (see Figure 1.4b, and discussion in Chapter 6). Once synthesised, the new model recipe depicted certain macroeconomic relations in a new form (the IS/LM model) that proved flexible to many different interpretations and had a remarkably long life.

A second account of model-making derives from another comparison, this time drawing on the similarities between the practices of representation in arts and sciences and inspired by Nelson Goodman's work (1978). In Morgan, 2004, I argue that the activity of model-making requires *imagination* to hypothesize how the economy might work, and then the power and skill to *make an image* of that idea. For example, Edgeworth's first drawing (1881) of the relationships between Robinson Crusoe and Man Friday (Figure 1.3b) can be understood as his imagining and imaging the set of points on his graph where they might both be willing to make a bargain to help each other. This little diagram gradually evolved into the Edgeworth Box diagram in a process that was far from self-evident but depended on the processes of imagination and image making by a sequence of different economists, each of whom used this particular way of envisioning economic relations and portraying them into these little two-dimensional diagrammatic/mathematical forms (see the example by Bowley in Figure 1.5c). In this account (described in Chapter 3), modelling, understood as a way of giving form to economic intuitions, involves a kind of envisioning power.

A third account of model formation understands it as a process of 'idealization'. Philosophers of science have used this notion to explain the practices observed in mathematical modelling in physics (e.g., McMullin, 1985). Modelling there is portrayed as a process of picking out the relations of interest, and isolating them from the frictions and disturbances which interfere with their workings in the real world to give form to simpler, and 'ideal', world models (e.g., 'in an ideal world,

Figure 1.5. Models: The Variety of Forms.

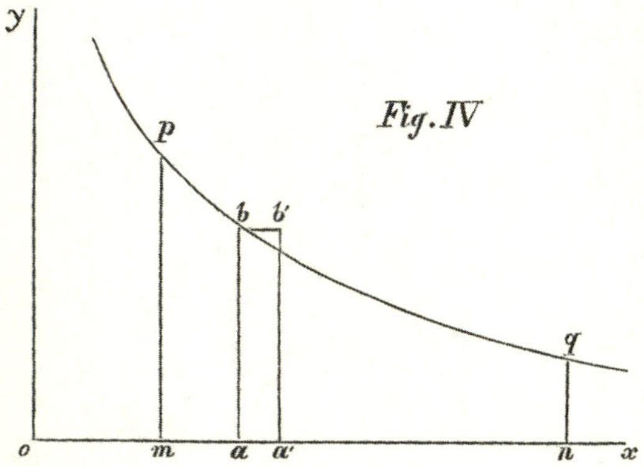

(a) Jevons' Utility Curve.

Source: William Stanley Jevons, *The Theory of Political Economy*, 1871. London: Macmillan & Co., Figure 4, p. 49.

(b) Fisher's Arithmetical and Mechanical Monetary Balance.

Source: Irving Fisher, *The Purchasing Power of Money*, New York: Macmillan, 1911; Arithmetic Balance, p. 18; Mechanical Balance, p. 21. Reproduced with permission from George Fisher.

(c) Bowley's Version of the Edgeworth Box.

Source: Arthur Lyon Bowley, *The Mathematical Groundwork of Economics, An Introductory Treatise*. Oxford: Clarendon Press, 1924; Figure 1, p. 5. Reproduced with permission from Oxford University Press.

(d) Phillips' Plumbing Diagram.

Source: Bill Phillips' undergraduate essay "Savings and Investment. Rate of Interest and Level of Income". Undated, 1948–9, p. 1, Figure 3. University of Leeds, Brotherton Library, Newlyn-Phillips Machine Archive.

(e) Luce and Raiffa's Game Matrix.

Source: Duncan R. Luce and Howard Raiffa (1957) *Games and Decisions*. New York: Wiley; matrix, p. 95. Reproduced with permission from Dover Publications.

(a) *Fig. IV*

(b)

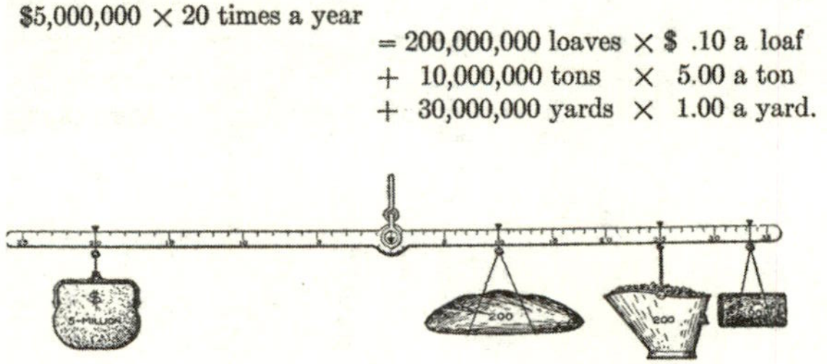

$5,000,000 × 20 times a year

= 200,000,000 loaves × $ .10 a loaf
+ 10,000,000 tons × 5.00 a ton
+ 30,000,000 yards × 1.00 a yard.

(c)

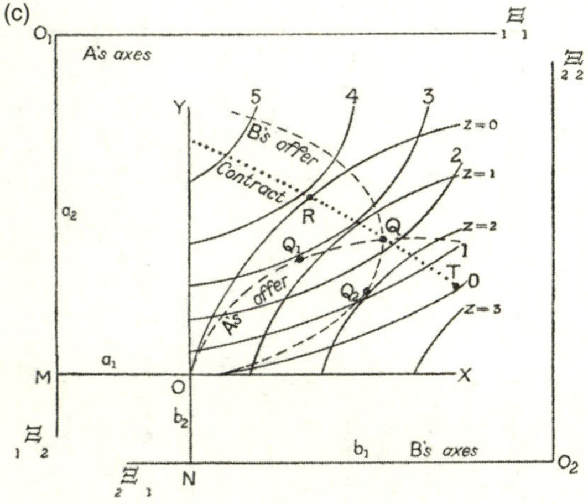

(d)

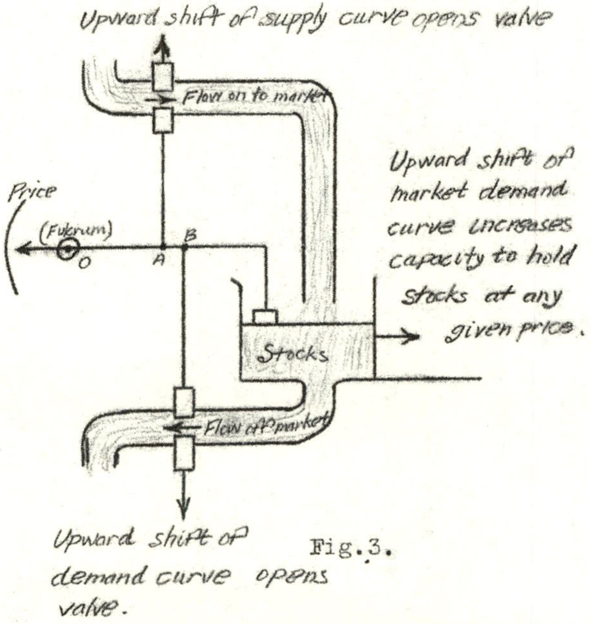

Upward shift of supply curve opens valve

Upward shift of market demand curve increases capacity to hold stocks at any given price.

Upward shift of demand curve opens valve.

Fig. 3.

(e)

$$H: \begin{array}{c} \alpha_1 \\ \alpha_2 \end{array} \begin{array}{cc} \beta_1 & \beta_2 \\ \left[\begin{array}{c} (5,\ 5) \\ (6,\ -4) \end{array}\right. & \left.\begin{array}{c} (-4,\ 6) \\ (-3,\ -3) \end{array}\right]. \end{array}$$

there is no friction'). Such accounts have also been used to understand model formation in economics. Thus, Nancy Cartwright has used the term to discuss how economists made models to get at causal capacities in the economy while Uskali Mäki has used it to describe how economists isolate particular accounts (models) for theorizing purposes.[27] As an example here, Jevons' graphed economic man's experience of utility as dependent upon only two dimensions, its intensity and duration (Figure 1.5a). He did so because, by his own account, these were the two most salient elements in motivating mans' economic behaviour. This idealization enabled him to leave aside six other dimensions of utility that Bentham had suggested in an earlier verbal account. But this simplification also made it possible for Jevons to represent man's behaviour in making consumer choices into a form where he could treat the problem mathematically.[28] Such idealization processes of giving form to economic models can be described as the formation of ideal types (using Max Weber's account, 1904 and 1913) or even as a process of drawing out a caricature (see Chapter 4, and Morgan, 2006).

A fourth strand of literature, following Mary Hesse's (1966) work, argues that model-making, or giving form to a model, depends upon our cognitive abilities to recognise similarities and our creativity in exploring those similarities.[29] Scientists choose models on the basis of similarities seen in the form, structure, content or properties between two fields and investigate these similarities in a systematic way. For example, Fisher (1911) chose a mechanical balance as a model for his economic "equation of exchange" between money and goods because he recognised the similarity between the elements and their relations (see Figure 1.5b and Morgan, 1999). This ability to recognise similarities, and so to choose a form for a model, is only the first step, for it usually requires a lot of further work to fill out that form into a full model. In another example, Phillips drew the little plumbing diagram (Figure 1.5d) to help him to understand how the stocks and flows of a good interact in a market. With the collaboration of the monetary economist Walter Newlyn, the model grew into a large physical hydraulic machine of the economic system as a whole (see Figure 1.7 and Chapter 5).[30]

---

27 For example, von Thünen's model has been described (by Mäki, 2004) as arrived at by the process of "isolating" real-world aspects away for theoretical purposes, whereas it could also be understood as a process of "causal idealization" (in Cartwright's terms) since von Thünen used numerically based observations about his own farm in his model. On the general arguments on idealization in economics, see Cartwright (1989) and Mäki (1992); a survey with further references is provided in Morgan and Knuuttila (2012); Hamminga and De Marchi (1994) provide an important collection of earlier papers on idealization reviewed in Morgan (1996).

28 Historical work suggests that Jevons' gave form to his model not just through a process of idealization, but through an inspired transcription of ideas from several other fields and drew on his own working experiences and on his creativity as a scientist (see Maas, 2005).

29 See also Gentner (2001).

30 Marcel Boumans (in Morgan and Boumans, 2004) has described the move from such a metaphor to a model as a move from a vague to a more exact form of representation: from the one-dimensional representation of a metaphor to the two-dimensional analogical model, as in the little diagram by Phillips of a market as a plumbing arrangement of Figure 1.5d, or to fully formed three-dimensional model as in Fisher's built hydraulic machine of Figure 1.3d (see Chapter 5).

More recently, economists have themselves suggested that the point of modelling is not to *recognise* analogies, but to *create* them, rather as Fisher designed his analogical model of the gold standard mechanism in the late nineteenth century (see Morgan, 1997). For example, Robert Lucas argues his modelling of the business cycle creates "a mechanical, imitation economy".[31] Robert Sugden has argued that modellers create "credible worlds", where the credibility claim rests on some observed similarities in model outcomes, for example, between those of a checkerboard puzzle with the analogous pattern of segregated housing.[32] In seeking to capture not the workings of real economies but to mimic some aspect of it via an imagined analogous world, these practices of design take us back to one of the historical roots of modelling in the arts where craftsmen built mechanical birds that would 'sing' but did not suppose that birds were mechanical automata.

The activity of giving form to a model has been characterized in four different ways here, and exploring and analysing these different ways of thinking about model-making provide the subject matter of the next several chapters of this book. But in this chapter, I am less concerned with the differences in these accounts than with the things that they have in common. When we look at the examples of models presented in this chapter, it is not obvious what these general qualities of model-making might be. But certain points can be made, which, in part, arise from this very variety in the nature of the objects that get made.

To begin with, these accounts all understand the scientist-economist as acting in this process of model formation. It is obvious, but important to remember, that models are created by a knowing economist-scientist for a particular purpose. Whether the scientist is best described as making a new recipe, using his or her imagination and imaging powers, idealizing from some other account, or choosing between different analogies, the point is that models don't make themselves.

Another shared feature is that, in making models, scientists form some kind of a representation of something in the economy. While the activity of creating a model can be described variously as representing, depicting, imagining, or imaging, more generous terms such as rendering or denoting, often seem equally pertinent and accurate as descriptions of the activity of model-making. The very different ways economist-scientists have of getting to their models, *and* the sheer variety of forms they have created, support this pluralistic language. The important point

---

31 Lucas (1980, p. 697); he most famously said of his business cycle models that "A good model, from this point of view, will not be exactly more 'real' than a poor one, but will provide better imitations". (1980, p. 697), leading to a discussion of the artefactual character of the results of such modelling – see Hoover (1995) and Boumans (1997).

32 The notion of designed analogies or similarities is consistent with Sugden's writings on how models are made and used in his discussions of the checkerboard and other examples (see his 2009 and 2002); see also Chapter 9 here. The development of 'simulation' in the 1960s as a way of using models shares a mimicking aim, but without necessarily sharing any particular view of the nature of models (see Chapter 8).

here is that whatever term is used should not unduly limit our understanding of what models are and how models work as a means of enquiry.[33]

These accounts of model-making also suggest that forming models is not driven by a logical process but rather involves the scientist's intuitive, imaginative, and creative qualities. When we look at the variety of objects displayed in this chapter, it would be difficult to see what, if any, such a logical process could possibly be that would cover all these instances. The importance of these creative qualities in the scientist's model-making activities may reflect the long-ago roots of scientific modelling in the decorative crafts. We found these evident in the *Tableau Économique*, but they remain in the delight that economists take in creating 'elegant' models.

Model-making is a skilled job. Perhaps it is not yet evident, but will become so in the chapters that follow, that learning how to portray elements in the economy, learning what will fit together, and how, in order to make the model work, are specialised talents using a tacit, craft-based, knowledge as much as an articulated, scientific, knowledge. It is not easy to pinpoint in any general way these skills of articulation and construction, or to see how economists acquire them except through apprenticeship. Perhaps, like Pigou, it suffices to note that some economists have considerable talent in model-making, and that these talents of the scientist-economist are recognised in the artefactual nature of the models that are made. Economists recognise these talents in terms of the qualities of the models themselves, where their term 'fruitfulness' indicates a model that is not just well put together and easy to use but easy to extend, generates interesting findings, new questions, and so forth. Economists' skills in articulating and crafting models, along with their imaginative and creative abilities, turn up in different ratios in different episodes of model-making, but they are all essential to the process of giving form to models.

---

33 Although philosophers of science tend towards using the terminology of 'representation', it is the subject of huge debate for the term raises a number of important and difficult problems. First, as discussed here: what is the process of representation? I am sympathetic to R. I. G. Hughes' (1997) argument (following Nelson Goodman) that 'denoting' is a better term for the activity of model-making than representing, for it makes clear that the models stands in relation to its economic system "as a symbol for it" and that while there is "no representation without denotation", denotation is "independent of resemblance" (1997, S330-1). Second, how is a representation defined? (Are models best thought of as maps, descriptions, structures, axiomatic systems, fictions, etc., or as artefacts with flexible representing relations?) The approach taken in this book, as in Morgan and Morrison (1999), is more concerned with how scientists use models than with an analysis of them as philosophical objects, so I use this awkward term representation as a descriptively useful one, without apology, and leave the philosophical problems for elsewhere (see Morgan and Knuuttila, 2012), and for others (addressed in recent volumes edited by Grüne-Yanoff, 2009 and by Suárez, 2008; see also Knuuttila, 2005). Third, what is the nature of the representing relation? The importance of this last lies in the view held by some philosophers that models have to represent the world accurately – for example, have a structural isomorphism to the world – in order for us to make truthful deductions about the world from them (for an early discussion in philosophy of social sciences, see Brodbeck, 1968). I reframe this as an inference problem later in this chapter (Section 5) and more fully later in the book.

4.ii Becoming Formal

Each of these four processes of understanding model-making: recipe-making, visualizing, idealizing and choosing an analogy, describes an act of giving form to ideas about the economy. But by representing the economy in a particular form, the economist-scientist at the same time creates an object that must obey certain rules – which brings us to our second sense of formal: meaning subject to rule and rigour in contrast to that sense of informal. Since in each particular case, these rules form the rules of reasoning with that model, they effectively determine the economist's valid manipulation or use of that model. Where do these rules come from? And, what kinds of rules are involved?

Rules for reasoning with a model come from two distinct aspects of the model. First, when an economist reasons with any model, he or she must obey certain reasoning rules according to the kind of the stuff that the model is made from, or language it is written in, or the format it has. So, these rules could be those of geometry or algebra, of mechanics or hydraulics, etc. depending on the model. Reasoning with Fisher's equation, for example, was subject to the rules of arithmetic; in contrast, reasoning with his mechanical balance model was subject to the rules of behaviour, and so manipulation, of mechanical balances (both in Figure 1.5b). Samuelson's equations model (in Figure 1.4c) can be manipulated following the formal rules for working with equations – either algebraically or arithmetically in a simulation (and he does both, as we shall see in Chapter 6). An important point about these kinds of rules are that they are given and fixed by the substance of the model, even where that model is a paper representation of a material model (as in Fisher's mechanical balance). They are 'formal' rules in the sense that they are not made them up each time the economist works with a particular model, rather, they come ready made from the form or language the modeller has chosen for that representation.

Second, and in contrast, allowable manipulations of the model are also determined and constrained by the economics subject matter represented in the model. For example, Samuelson's model of the macroeconomy must be manipulated in a certain order, not just because the economic relations have a certain time order (found in the equations' subscripts) but because of the implied causal links given by the economic content. In other cases, the characteristics and ambitions of model economic man are used to motivate how the resources of an economic model are used. For example, the reasoning in the Prisoner's Dilemma model is determined by the economists' view of how the economic model man will act in the world of the model. But – just as with the earlier *Tableau Économique* (in Figure 1.1) – the matrix of numbers depicting the Prisoner's Dilemma game in Figure 1.5e needs to be accompanied by a text account of the economic rules for the situations that the numbers represent before they can used in reasoning (see Chapter 9). These kinds of rules of manipulation don't come with the form, they come from the economic concepts and content that the model-maker uses in making the representation.

These two kinds of rules – the formal rules (those given by the form) and the economic rules (those given by the subject matter) – taken together provide the means of reasoning with a model.[34] For example, the little hydraulic diagram from Phillips is designed to work according to the hydraulics pictured, but is simultaneously subject to the rules of reasoning from the economic content enshrined in the arrangements of the parts: where demand and supply, and price and quantity, can be changed in particular ordered ways (Figure 1.5d). Usually the model form is designed so that these two different sets of reasoning rules will be complementary in the way that the model works. But sometimes, particularly with analogical models, they may turn out to be in conflict – as indeed, happened with Fisher's mechanical balance, where his economic rules of adjustment at first sight were at odds with the mechanical ones of the balance; Fisher found a way to resolve this dissonance by revising his economics (as we will see in Chapter 5). By the late twentieth century, these different sources of rules in a model might no longer be separately recognisable, for modern economics had reached the point where (just as McMullin [1985] noted in his discussion of physics) the concepts and arguments of economics are so thoroughly intertwined with, and even drenched in, the terms of their habitual mathematical expression that they can no longer be pulled apart. So modern economists looking at Jevons' graph of utility (Figure 1.5a), for example, will find it difficult to separate out the economic content from the mathematical argument he made with it.

For the purposes of our investigations of modelling, we can now appreciate how formalization here means that the economist-scientist both gives form to his or her ideas and simultaneously makes them rule bound in the model. The model is formed to represent their ideas about some aspects of the economic world, and their reasoning with the model is bound by the rules appropriate to that particular model – given by both its economic content and its language format. These two different sources of rules – from a model's format and from its subject content – determine and limit how each particular model can be used, and so, *constitute the kinds of right reasoning that are possible with that particular model.* So when we look at how an economist reasons with a model, we should expect to find some very specific reasoning rules being used. But what are these rules of reasoning to be used on?

4.iii Reasoning Resources

I argued earlier that representations become models only when they have the resources for manipulation: this unlocks the puzzle of how any particular model

---

34 We might describe these as syntactic and semantic rules – those that come from the format (or 'language' structure in which the model is formed) being syntax, and those that come from the economic meaning (the interpretation of the elements) being semantics. But this usage would not map onto traditional philosophy of science usage, where the 'syntactic versus semantic view of models' refer to different views of the relation of models to theories. A version of this explained for economists is found in Hausman (1992).

can be reasoned with.[35] Here we return to Frisch, who recall was one of the first to produce a mathematically expressed model of the economic system as a whole in an attempt to figure out how the elements of the economic system when put together could create business cycles in economic activity.[36]

Frisch's first version of his model, in his now classic paper of 1933, was a schema of economic activity (shown in Figure 1.6a here, on which capital letters indicate stocks and lowercase letters indicate flows). It depicts his account of the main elements in the economy: some are "visualized as receptacles" (the circles) and "others may be visualized as machines that receive inputs and deliver outputs" (the squares) (Frisch, 1933, p. 173). He called it a *Tableau Économique*, surely a reference back to Quesnay's famous invention, and we can see that like that earlier example (Figure 1.1), Frisch visualized quite a complicated set of circular flows (indicated by arrows) around the elements in the system. Relative to Quesnay's *Tableau Économique* however, in which both numbers and ordering are specified in his 'table', Frisch's schema lacks the resources for the kind of model manipulation that Quesnay was able to do. Quesnay could use his numbers, and their ordering, to reason about the nature of the system he had depicted, and by playing around with these numbers, explore various different kinds of systematic behaviour in his model world and learn new things from so doing. Frisch's diagram shows the elements and their links, but these can be used only for a verbal description of the relations, and verbal reasoning about them, but not for more rewarding explorations that would tell him anything much about the behaviour of his system; indeed, without those arrows, the scheme could hardly be reasoned with at all. Frisch's schema has limited resources for verbal reasoning and none for numerical manipulation. It was, however, just a starting point.

From this scheme, Frisch developed a more simplified little mathematical model connecting y, the annual production of capital goods, with x, the annual production and consumption of consumer goods (there are no stocks held), and z_t, the amount of production going on at time t (Figure 1.6b). This little mathematical model of the economic system had the resources – of both mathematical and economic content – for Frisch to present it as a kind of machine: its form and content could, with certain manipulations, produce a dynamic pattern. This version of the model had sufficient resources for him to carry out simulations (by putting some parameter values in the equations) to show that the model could generate a cyclical pattern in productive economic activity. This was an important outcome, since one of Frisch's main reasons for making the model was to demonstrate that cyclical patterns could be generated by such a system of equations (see Chapter 6).

---

35 Amongst the older tradition of philosophical writings on models, Black (1962), mentions manipulation of models, but offers little in the way of discussion or analysis.

36 The story of Frisch's model has been told several times in the history of economics: Morgan (1990) concentrates on its place in the history of econometrics; Boumans (1999) on it as a new recipe in modelling the business cycle; and Louçã (2007) on its analogical aspects.

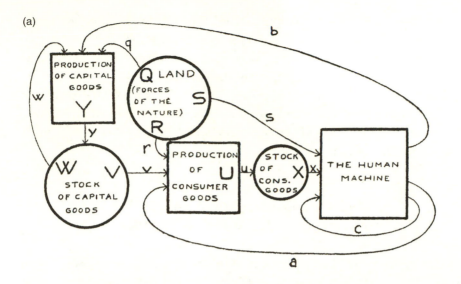

(b)

$$(1) \qquad z_t = \int_{\tau=0}^{\infty} D_\tau y_{t-\tau} d\tau$$

$$(2) \qquad \dot{x} = c - \lambda(rx + sz)$$

$$(3) \qquad y = mx + \mu\dot{x}$$

Figure 1.6. The Reasoning Resources in Models.

(a) Frisch's *Tableau Économique*.

Source: Ragner Frisch, "Propagation Problems and Impulse Problems in Dynamic Economics". *Economic Essays in Honour of Gustav Cassel*, 1933. London: George Allen & Unwin Ltd. Figure 1, p. 174. Reproduced with permission from Ragner Frisch.

(b) Frisch's Macro-Dynamic System.

Source: Ragner Frisch, "Propagation Problems and Impulse Problems in Dynamic Economics". *Economic Essays in Honour of Gustav Cassel*, 1933. London: George Allen & Unwin Ltd., pp. 177 and 182. Reproduced with permission from Ragner Frisch.

In this example, the contrast between Frisch's *Tableau Économique* and his little mathematical model shows the importance of the presence of model resources that can be manipulated in order to make the object useful as a model. In the schema, there are resources that can be reasoned with, but they can not be manipulated in such a way that you gain any understanding about the possibilities for business cycles to occur from such reasoning. Recall that the rules for reasoning or manipulation come from the model in two distinct senses – from the format (or language) it has, and from the economic content. The schema has quite a lot of economic content, content that can even be reasoned with to some extent, but the format is that of a picture and pictures do not (generally) contain rules for their manipulation. The equations have less content in the sense that there are fewer elements and causal links, but the form (or language) of that content (equations) enables the use of a deductive mode of manipulation so that Frisch can reason mathematically about the nature of the business cycle with this version of his model.

These examples from Frisch enable us to understand not only how the reasoning rules come along with the particular model that is built, but also how necessary the resources are to provide materials to reason with. But this does not explain – in a more general way – how those model resources are used, nor to what purpose, though there are certainly hints in Frisch's example. I turn now to suggest a more general account of model reasoning.

5. Modelling as a Method of Enquiry:
The World in the Model, Models of the World

It is easy enough to say that modelling constitutes an epistemic genre, but we still need to figure out how it functions as a way of doing economic science. Scott Gordon, in his history and philosophy of the social sciences, argues that "the purpose of any model is to serve as a tool or instrument of scientific investigation" (1991, p. 108).[37] This forms the starting point for my claim, in the latter half of the book, that economists use models to investigate two different domains: to enquire into the world of the model and to enquire into the world that the model represents.

Model-making – as we have already seen – is an activity of creating small worlds expressed in another medium. The economist represents his/her ideas about certain elements of the economy: the system as a whole, or people's economic behaviour, that they want to investigate or understand into other forms: into bits of mathematics, diagrams, machines, and even – sometimes – strictly defined verbal portraits. The models have certain qualities – they are smaller-scale, and it is supposed, simpler, than the real world, made of quite different materials, and their sense of representation, imitation, or similarity might be quite opaque.[38] I take up these awkward qualities of the way economists render their accounts of the world into models in Chapter 10, but for here, the point is rather that these representations – by design – contain economists' intuitions, or the things they already know, or both. That is, sometimes these small worlds in the model primarily represent speculations and theories about the economic world; the economist may be agnostic about how far they represent the workings of that world, or even deny that they do so at all (as we saw with Lucas), regarding them perhaps as parallel or imagined model worlds. At other times, models are created primarily to incorporate (in some form) features they already know, that is, to embody what the economist takes to be essential

---

37 Of course, I am not the first to see models as instruments of enquiry in the social sciences (arguably, Max Weber (1904, 1913) thought of his ideal types in this way – see Chapter 4), but few suggestions along these lines explore how such instruments work.

38 A nice parallel is found in the studies of geologists who built small boxes and filled them with different materials to see what happened when big physical shocks hit them as a simulation model for earthquakes (see Oreskes, 2007). On smallness see Chapter 10.

features of the relevant section of the world, how the parts relate, how the elements interact, and so forth, as with Frisch and Tinbergen. Most often, the 'world in the model' represents a combination of both economists' ideas and their knowledge.

These small objects, models, then have a stand-alone, autonomous, quality, that enables them to lead a potentially *double life* for, I argue, *models function both as objects to enquire into and as objects to enquire with*. That is, they are objects for investigation in their own right, and they help the economist-scientist investigate the real-world economy.[39] Model investigations offer economists the possibilities to speak both to their ideas and to their experience of the world at the same time, but characterizing such work as a method of enquiry, exploration, even discovery, still presents us with quite a puzzle. How do models provide such a method of enquiry that enables this double life to go on? My answer is that model reasoning, as a generic activity in economics, typically involves a *kind of experiment*.

Advancing the argument that appears later in the book, I suggest that we can characterize model reasoning as a kind of experiment in the following way. Models are made to address some particular purpose, and so working with a model typically begins with the economist asking a question related to that purpose. To answer the question, the economist makes an assumption that fixes something in the model, or changes something in the model, that is, in the diagrams or equations, or other material, that the model is made in. He or she then investigates the effect of that assumption, or change in the model, by manipulating the resources of the model in a model experiment to demonstrate an answer. That demonstration is deductively made, for it uses the reasoning rules given in the language format and in the carefully specified economic content of the model. The process of demonstration itself prompts a narrative about the economic content. This combination of *questions*, *experimental demonstrations*, and *narrative answers* forms the way in which the economist explores a particular model (see Morgan 2002 and Chapter 6). From experimenting on the model, economists investigate and come to understand, in the first instance, only the world of the model. How such experimental investigations into the model might also provide some understanding about the world that the model represents is a messier problem that I return to shortly.

Let me begin with the easy part of this double life of models: *models as objects to enquire into*. Economists investigate the world in the model using this mode of experiment to understand their economic ideas or theories. This seems odd: since they created that little world in the model, wouldn't they already understand it? Not

39 The ways that models function in these two domains in economics is not well accounted for by the standard views in philosophy of science that have tended to worry about the definition of models and to treat them either as mini-versions of theories or as efficient descriptions of data from the world. As we will find in the chapters that follow, the diagrammatic models of the Edgeworth Box, Ricardo's arithmetic chains, and Samuelson's mathematical model of the Keynesian system all function as independent forms: they embody ideas and knowledge about the economy, but are themselves neither theories or data descriptions. In Morrison and Morgan (1999), we argued such construction was responsible for the observed practical autonomy of models that enabled them to mediate between the mathematics of theory and the empirics of observation (see Chapter 2).

so, for if ideas about the world can be expressed very simply, economists don't need a model to think with. But as soon as they abstract two or three characteristics of economic man together, or isolate two or three hypothesized relationships from the economy at once, it becomes difficult to reason about what happens when they are combined. That is why economists create models in the first place, and why they need this kind of experimental approach in order to answer questions about this small person or world in the model.

Investigating the world in the model through such experimental means is the way that economists explore their theories and intuitions.[40] By asking questions and making such investigations, they understand the implications of their intuitions, explore the limits of economic behaviour that their models imply, codify and classify the various different outcomes that some more general theory might overlook, and are prompted to develop new hypotheses about the behaviour of the elements represented in the model. For example, Samuelson wanted to know the effect of increasing government expenditure. He found by his experiments on the little mathematical model in his 1939 paper that the model could generate cyclical behaviour, explosive growth, or gradual decline in the elements of the model, according to the numerical parameters he inserted into their relations. These model explorations provided some surprising answers about certain aspects of the Keynesian account of the world as well as generating more understanding about the various extant theories of business cycles.

The second part of this double life of models is the way that economists use *models as objects to enquire with*, for it is clear, from the way economists work, that the small person or world in the model also serves as an object to investigate the aspect of the real people or real world that it is taken to represent. This aspect of model work is much more difficult to characterize than the way economists use models to investigate their ideas and theories.

Philosophers have problems at this point, and for good reasons. Their justly sceptical argument goes as follows. If the model is an accurate representation – in some way – of the relevant parts of the economic world or of economic man's behaviour, and if those elements can be treated in isolation, then it might be that the results gained from model experiments can be applied directly and unambiguously to the world, and give truthful statements and valid explanations about those things in the world.[41] These 'ifs' are big ones – for how does the economist know if they have an accurate model of the world? Or, that it can be treated in isolation? It is this ignorance that creates philosophers' worries about modelling, and,

40 Crombie assumed some kind of a one-for-one relationship: that "a model embodies a theory" (1994, Vol. II, p1087), and on this basis, that the method of models offered "a characteristically effective scientific combination of theoretical and experimental exploration." This is certainly a useful hint about experiments (which he does not expand), but the account of how models are formed in this chapter, and various examples discussed in Chapters 2–6 suggest that the relationships between theories and models are varied and not easy to characterise.

41 See, for a recent discussion, Cartwright (2009).

most especially, their concern about the status of the representation involved. But of course, it is just such problems – and this same lack of knowledge – that lead economists, like scientists in other fields, to adopt modelling as a mode of investigation in the first place!

It may help to clarify my account of modelling as a double method of enquiry in economics if we compare it with two of the other reasoning styles mentioned earlier: the method of mathematical postulation and proof and the method of laboratory experiment.

If we portray mathematical modelling as a version of the method of mathematical postulation and proof, then we could say that economists *postulate* the economic world in the model and so could quite reasonably expect to make mathematical truths about that world in the model. This account works well for *enquiries into* the world of the model: models can indeed be truth-makers about that restricted and mathematical small world. But as economists recognise, these are not truths that they can transport unconditionally to the world that the model represents. Economists (just like their astronomer forebears) understand that a model stands in for their economic universe to enable them to explore certain properties of that world represented in the model. But whether they can come to valid conclusions about the behaviour of their actual economic universe is a much more difficult problem, as they know themselves.

If we make the alternative comparison with laboratory experiments, we get an idea of how economists use a model as an object to *enquire with*. In this way of understanding modelling as an epistemic genre, economists *hypothesize* how the world is when they represent it in the model, and then experiment with that world or person in the model to see how it behaves. Then the important question of whether the results of the experiment on the model can then be transferred to the world that the model represents can be considered an inference problem. So, by treating model enquiries as a form of experiment, the question of how this mode of reasoning connects models to the world switches from a truth-making problem to an inference problem, though no less difficult to answer.[42] This is why I suggest that we view modelling as a method of investigation and enquiry more akin to the method of experiment than to the method of postulation and proof.

Of course, model experiments in economics are usually pen-and-paper, calculator, or computer, experiments on a model world or an analogical world (such as an hydraulic machine), not laboratory experiments on the real world. This has implications for the inferences that can be made. There are two issues here: one is the form of the inference arguments, and the other is the power of the inferences that can be made.

---

42 Others have suggested that the model-world relation might be thought of in inferential terms, but without seriously considering the nature of the inference in practical terms, or whether the inferential relation lies in the original construction of the model, or rather in its subsequent relation back to the world (see for example Suárez, 2004 and Woody, 2004; and the essays in Grüne-Yanoff, 2009).

Inference arguments from model experiments are informal: when economists talk of 'testing their models' (having already assured themselves of their internal mathematical qualities and coherence) they are interested in judging the usefulness of their model experiments by comparing the behaviour of the model world to that of the real world in a kind of matching or bench-marking process. They may compare the model experimental behaviour of their thin model of economic man with the behaviour of real economic people, or surmise how a particular policy change instituted in a model compares with the equivalent actual policy in the world. A characteristic feature of these informal inference arguments from economic models is that they often involve narratives in making inferential or explanatory accounts that serve to link results *from* the experiment made into the world in the model *to* events in the world that the model represents (discussed in various ways in Chapters 6 to 9).[43]

These informal comparisons made from model experiments to the world clearly lack the formal decision rules based on probability measures found in statistical inference, and that are used to validate and make inferences from econometric models. But it is worth remembering that inferences made from laboratory experiments also lack formal decision rules. Laboratory scientists, like modellers, depend upon both tacit and articulated knowledge in making sense of their experimental findings and judging their relevance within the laboratory.[44] And, like model work, laboratory scientists face the same question of whether their experimental results can form the basis for inference beyond the laboratory, namely the problem of external validity.[45]

But in another respect, clearly, the experiments made on models are different from the experiments made in the laboratory, and the inferences that can be made differ in principle. This has nothing to do with the formality or informality of the inference argument, but rather, as I argue in Chapter 7, it is because model experiments are less powerful as an epistemic genre. It does make a difference to the power and scope of inference that the model experiment is one carried out on a pen-and-paper representation, that is, on the world in the model, not on the world itself. While model experiments may *surprise* the economist with unexpected results, laboratory experiments may *confound* the economist-scientist by producing results that are not only unexpected but potentially unexplainable given existing knowledge.[46]

Let us look briefly at a more complicated example to see how the model is both an object to enquire *into* and an object to enquire *with*, holding these notions of questions, deductive experiments using the resources of the model, and informal inferences, in mind. The Phillips-Newlyn Machine (shown in Figure 1.7 and

---

43 See Morgan (2001, 2007).

44 It is precisely this difficulty that has led Deborah Mayo to advance her framework for making inferences from experiments (see her 1996), which recognises that such inferences depend on the knowledge of the scientist in making relevant pre- and post-experimental judgements.

45 See Chapters 7 and 8, and Guala (2005, chapter 7).

46 See discussion in Morgan (2003b, 2005).

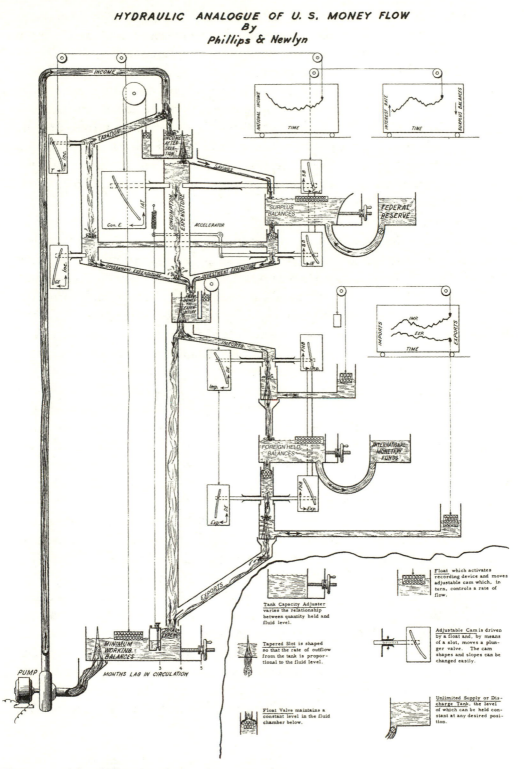

Figure 1.7. The Phillips-Newlyn Hydraulic Machine.

Source: The James Meade Archive, Box 16/3, BLPES Archives, LSE. Reproduced with permission from the estate of James Meade.

discussed fully in Chapter 5) is a big apparatus – a real hydraulic model – of which we can see here only a drawing. The physical model itself operates according to the language rules of hydraulics, with the flow of water around the machine controlled by physical valves. But the overall form and parts of the of the machine are designed to imitate the stocks and flows of money (red water) around an economy, and the behavioural functions of the economic relations are drawn into the small rectangular "slides" that can be seen on the drawing; these in their turn control the opening and closing of the valves in the hydraulic system. Despite its complexity, and even without knowing what these economic relations are, we can see how the rules of form (hydraulics) and content (monetary macroeconomics) are instantiated in the Machine.

The next point to see is how the Machine's resources are reasoned with in an experimental mode of investigations by using the rules of language and content. The economist sets up the model to answer a particular question, such as: What will happen if I increase the money in this system by increasing the liquid in the "money tank" fed by "the central bank" (at the top right)? This is the experimental intervention (or manipulation) into the world of the model. The pump circulates this increased liquid through the machine, the valves control the flows according to the economic relations ascribed in the model, and the model demonstration churns out a set of outcomes of this experiment: the effects of this change in the amount of money on the income in the economy is automatically charted in one of the top right-hand corner graphs.

The Machine model has tremendous resources: it can be set up to answer any number of questions – and thus associated model experiments. With some of these questions the economist can *enquire into* abstruse points in economic theory, for example, as to whether the interest rate is determined by the stock or flow of investment funds. Such questions and experiments about the world in the model make demonstrations that enable those theories to be compared with each other. And once economists have discovered how their world in the model works, they use this knowledge to generate further questions about those theories. Another set of questions are prompted by different historical or current situations that turn up such as financial crises or great depressions. These deliver experimental outcomes for the world in the model that economists will compare with the events that they observe in the world. That is, with these questions, economists *enquire with* the model into the world that the model represents. Economists may come to explain or reinterpret or find a new understanding about some aspects of the real-world behaviour through these experimental means.[47] That is how, by experimenting with the model, economists can gain understanding and provide explanations of *how the*

---

47 Economists also use this model-generated knowledge to teach others their insights, for example, economists used the Phillips-Newlyn Machine to demonstrate and explain the UK Government policy changes (an experiment with the Machine screened by the BBC and visible now on a video in the London Science Museum next to the Machine).

economic world in the model works and use these in an informal way to *reflect on the workings of the real economy* that the model is taken to represent (see Morgan and Boumans 2004, and Chapter 5).

So, modelling as a style of reasoning in economics works as a method of enquiry comprising probing questions, manipulations to provide demonstrations that are both deductive and experimental, and informal inference arguments involving elements of narrative that offer explanatory or interpretative services. These characteristics are explored in a nutshell format for Ricardo's model farming experiments in the next chapter. And, with a wider gaze, these characteristics of the style of practical reasoning of modelling are explored in different ways, and at much greater depth, in the second half of the book.

6. Conclusion

Reasoning with models enables economists to enquire directly into their theories or ideas about the world, and enables them to enquire indirectly into the nature of the economic world. They reason about the small world in the model and reason about the big economic world with the model; they reason about the thin economic man in the model and reason about real people with the model man. Yet, critically, these two spaces of exploration are not always clearly demarcated: in working with models economists often simultaneously investigate the world in the model and the world their model represents. In this sense, reasoning with economic models is like reasoning with astronomical models. Those models exemplified astronomers' theories about the arrangements of the heavens, and could be used to explore the full implications about those ideas at the very same time as being used to offer explanations or accounts for particular observed events or patterns in the behaviour of the heavenly bodies. Economic models, like those models of the planetary system, are objects to enquire into and argue over, but *at the same time* ones to take to the world and explore it to gain understanding, insight, or explanations from doing so.

The comparison between astronomical models and economic models that has woven its way through this chapter is not just an heuristic comparison that helps us see how economists use models, but reminds us that the modelling style of reasoning has an illustrious history. Indeed, the scientific revolution of the sixteenth and seventeenth centuries was not just one of content, but of styles of reasoning. Modelling has been portrayed as the working method of Galileo no less, and continues to be prevalent in modern natural sciences.[48] Despite this ancestry, economists are not quite sure that the method has a credible scientific respectability. Models are relatively small and simple compared to the economic world, they are made of different materials, and cannot well be applied directly to that world. Even so, like those

---

48 Hacking, for example, recognises it as the basic method of "cosmology and cognitive science – none other than the chief modern instances of the Galilean style...." (Hacking, 1992a, p. 7).

models of the universe of earlier days, economic models may capture the heart of the problems that economists seek to understand. Modelling is not an easy way to find truths about the economy, but rather a practical form of reasoning for economists, a method of exploration, of enquiry, into both their ideas and their world. That is the thesis of this book.

Acknowledgement

Elements of this chapter were written for an address "Forms and Tools in 20th Century Economics" to the Association Charles Gide September 1999 in Paris, at their meeting on the theme "Modèles formels et théorie économique: histoire, analyse, épistémologiques". I thank Annie Cot and the Scientific Organising Committee of that society for their invitation, memorable for the imposing room in the Sorbonne in which my talk took place. The argument was subsequently presented at Duke University in February 2000. More recent elements of the chapter have been developed for talks to development specialists at Bonn (ZEF), at Rotterdam (econometrics seminar), at the University of Oslo's 75th Anniversary of their Institute of Economics, at the Summer Institute for History of Economic Thought at George Mason University, at Les Treilles, France for a workshop on style in science, at the University of Toronto (HPS seminar), at Chung Cheng University, Taiwan (conference on "Models and Evolution in Economics and Biology"), and at University of São Paulo, Brazil (Symposium on the "History of Post-War Economics"). I am grateful to those who commented on all these occasions. I particularly thank: Roy Weintraub for our many conversations about the history of mathematics in relation to economics; Marcel Boumans for many discussions of modelling; Charles Baden-Fuller for commenting so carefully on various drafts of this chapter; and Sheldon Steed for research assistance.

References

Backhouse, Roger E. (1998) "If Mathematics Is Informal, Then Perhaps We Should Accept that Economics Must Be Informal Too". *Economic Journal*, 108:451, 1848–58.

Baumol, William (1951) *Economic Dynamics*. New York: Macmillan.

Black, Max (1962) *Models and Metaphors*. Ithaca, NY: Cornell University Press.

Boltzmann, Ludwig (1911) "Models". In *Encyclopaedia Britannica* (11th ed, pp. 638–40). Cambridge: Cambridge University Press.

Boumans, Marcel (1993) "Paul Ehrenfest and Jan Tinbergen: A Case of Limited Physics Transfer". In Neil De Marchi (ed), *Non-Natural Social Science: Reflecting on the Enterprise of More Heat than Light* (pp. 131–56). Annual Supplement to *History of Political Economy*, Vol. 25. Durham, NC: Duke University Press.

(1997) "Lucas and Artificial Worlds". In John B. Davis, D. Wade Hands, and Uskali Mäki (eds), *New Economics and Its History* (pp. 63–88). Annual Supplement to *History of Political Economy*, Vol. 29. Durham, NC: Duke University Press.

(1999) "Built-In Justification". In Mary S. Morgan and Margaret Morrison (eds), *Models as Mediators* (pp. 66–96). Cambridge: Cambridge University Press.

(2005) *How Economists Model the World to Numbers*. London: Routledge.

Brodbeck, May 1968 [1959] "Models, Meaning and Theories". In May Brodbeck (ed), *Readings in the Philosophy of the Social Sciences* (pp. 579–601). New York: Macmillan.

Cartwright, Nancy (1989) *Nature's Capacities and Their Measurement.* Oxford: Clarendon Press.

(2009) "If No Capacities, Then No Credible Worlds. But Can Models Reveal Capacities?" In Till Grüne-Yanoff (ed), *Economic Models as Credible Worlds or Isolating Tools?* Special Issue of *Erkenntnis* 70:45–58.

Charles, Loïc (2003) "The Visual History of the Tableau Économique". *European Journal of the History of Economic Thought*, 10:4, 527–50.

Chemla, Karine (2003) "Generality above Abstraction: The General Expressed in Terms of the Paradigmatic in Mathematics in Ancient China". *Science in Context*, 16:3, 413–58.

Chick, Victoria and Sheila Dow (2001) "Formalism, Logic and Reality: A Keynesian Analysis". *Cambridge Journal of Economics*, 25:6, 705–22.

Colander, David (2000) "The Death of Neoclassical Economics". *Journal of the History of Economic Thought*, 22:2, 127–43.

Crombie, Alistair C. (1988) "Designed in the Mind: Western Visions of Science, Nature and Humankind". *History of Science*, 26, 1–12.

(1994) *Styles of Scientific Thinking in the European Traditions*, Vols. I–III. London: Duckworth.

Edgeworth, Francis Y. (1881) *Mathematical Psychics.* London: Kegan Paul.

(1889) "Opening Presidential Address", Section F: Economic Science and Statistics, *Nature*, Sept. 19, 496–509.

Fisher, Irving (1892/1925) *Mathematical Investigations in the Theory of Value and Prices* (thesis of 1891). New Haven: Yale University Press.

(1911) *The Purchasing Power of Money.* New York: Macmillan.

Fleck, Ludwik (1935; 1979 translation) *Genesis and Development of a Scientific Fact* (translated by F. Bradley and T. J. Trenn). Chicago: University of Chicago Press.

Forrester, John (1996) "If *p*, Then What? Thinking in Cases". *History of the Human Sciences*, 9:3, 1–25.

Foucault, Michel (1970) *The Order of Things: An Archaeology of the Human Sciences.* New York: Random House.

Frisch, Ragnar (1933) "Propagation Problems and Impulse Problems in Dynamic Economics". In *Economic Essays in Honour of Gustav Cassel* (pp. 171–205). London: Allen & Unwin.

Gentner, Dedre (2001) *Analogy in Scientific Discovery: The Case of Johannes Kepler.* In Magnani and Nersessian, 2001, pp. 21–40.

Giere, Ronald (2001) "Models as Parts of Distributed Cognitive Systems". In Lorenzo Magnani and Nancy J. Nersessian (eds), *Model-Based Reasoning: Science, Technology, Values* (pp. 227–42). New York: Kluwer Academic/Plenum Press.

Goldfarb, Robert S. and Jon Ratner (2008) "'Theory' and 'Models': Terminology Through the Looking Glass". *Econ Journal Watch*, 5:1, 91–108.

Goodman, Nelson (1978) *Ways of Worldmaking.* Indianapolis: Hackett.

Gordon, Scott (1991) *The History and Philosophy of Social Science.* New York: Routledge.

Grüne-Yanoff, Till (2009) [ed] *Economic Models as Credible Worlds or Isolating Tools?* Special Issue of *Erkenntnis*, 70:1.

Guala, Francesco (2005) *The Methodology of Experimental Economics.* Cambridge: Cambridge University Press.

Hacking, Ian (1992a) "'Style' for Historians and Philosophers". *Studies in the History and Philosophy of Science*, 23:1, 1–20.

(1992b) "Statistical Language, Statistical Truth and Statistical Reason: The Self-Authentification of a Style of Scientific Reasoning". In Ernan McMullin (ed), *The Social Dimensions of Science* (pp. 130–57). Notre Dame, IN: University of Notre Dame Press.

(1992c) "The Self-Vindication of the Laboratory Sciences". In Andrew Pickering (ed), *Science as Practice and Culture* (pp. 29–64). Chicago: University of Chicago Press.

(1993) "Working in a New World: The Taxonomic Solution". In Paul Howich (ed), *World Changes: Thomas Kuhn and the Nature of Science* (pp. 275–310). Cambridge, MA: MIT Press.

Hamminga, Bert and Neil De Marchi (1994) [eds] *Idealization in Economics*. Amsterdam: Rodopi.

Harford, Tim (2008) *The Logic of Life*. London: Little, Brown.

Harrod, Roy (1939) "An Essay in Dynamic Theory". *Economic Journal*, 49:193, 14–33.

(1968) "What Is a Model?" In N. Wolfe (ed), *Value, Capital and Growth* (pp. 173–91). Edinburgh: Edinburgh University Press.

Hausman, Daniel M. (1992) *The Inexact and Separate Science of Economics*. Cambridge: Cambridge University Press.

Hesse, Mary (1966) *Models and Analogies in Science*. Notre Dame, IN: University of Notre Dame Press.

Hicks, John, R. (1937) "Mr. Keynes and the 'Classics': A Suggested Interpretation". *Econometrica*, 5, 147–59.

Hoover, Kevin D. (1995) "Facts and Artifacts: Calibration and the Empirical Assessment of Real-Business-Cycle Models". *Oxford Economic Papers*, 47:1, 24–44.

Hughes, R. I. G. (1997) "Models and Representation". *Philosophy of Science,* 64:S325–36.

Humphrey, Thomas, M. (1995) "When Geometry Emerged: Some Neglected Early Contributions to Offer-Curve Analysis". *Economic Quarterly*, 81:2, 39–73.

Ingrao, Bruna and Giorgio Israel (1987) *The Invisible Hand*, English edition (1990). Cambridge, MA: MIT Press.

Israel, Giorgio (2002) "The Two Faces of Mathematical Modelling: Objectivism vs Subjectivism, Simplicity vs Complexity". In P. Cerria, P. Fregiglio and C. Pellegrini (eds), *The Application of Mathematics to the Sciences of Nature* (pp. 233–). New York: Kluwer.

Jevons, William St. (1871) *The Theory of Political Economy*. London: Macmillan.

Johnson, W. E. (1896) "Method of Political Economy". In R. H. Inglis Palgrave (ed), *Dictionary of Political Economy*, Vol. II (pp. 739–48). London: Macmillan.

Katzner, Donald W. (1991) "In Defense of Formalization in Economics". *Methodus*, 3:1, 17–24.

Keynes, John M. (1936) *The General Theory of Employment, Interest and Money*. London: Macmillan.

(1973) *The Collected Writings of John Maynard Keynes*, Vol. XIV, ed D. Moggridge. London: Macmillan.

Klein, Judy L. (2001) "Reflections from the Age of Economic Measurement". In Judy L. Klein and Mary S. Morgan (eds), *The Age of Economic Measurement* (pp. 111–36). Annual Supplement to *History of Political Economy*, Vol. 33. Durham, NC: Duke University Press.

Klein, Ursula (2001) [ed] *Tools and Modes of Representation in the Laboratory Sciences*. Boston Studies in the Philosophy of Science. Dordrecht: Kluwer.

(2003) *Experiments, Models, Paper Tools: Cultures of Organic Chemistry in the Nineteenth Century*. Stanford, CA: Stanford University Press.

Knuuttila, Tarja (2005) "Models, Representation, and Mediation". *Philosophy of Science*, 72, 1260–71.

Krugman, Paul (1998) "Two Cheers for Formalism". *Economic Journal*, 108:451, 1829–36.

Kuczynski, M. and Ronald Meek (1972) *Quesnay's Tableau Économique*. London: Macmillan.

Kuhn, Thomas (1962) *The Structure of Scientific Revolutions*. Chicago: University of Chicago Press.

Le Gall, Philippe (2007) *A History of Econometrics in France.* London: Routledge.

Leontief, Wassily W. (1946) "The Pure Theory of the Guaranteed Annual Wage Contract". *Journal of Political Economy*, 54, 76–79.

Levitt, Steven D. and Stephen J. Dubner (2005) *Freakonomics.* New York: Harper Perennial.

Louça, Francisco (2007) *The Years of High Econometrics.* London: Routledge.

Lucas, Robert E. (1980) "Methods and Problems in Business Cycle Theory". *Journal of Money, Credit and Banking*, 12, 696–715.

Luce R. Duncan and Howard Raiffa (1957) *Games and Decisions.* New York: Wiley.

Maas, Harro (2005) *William Stanley Jevons and the Making of Modern Economics.* Cambridge: Cambridge University Press.

MacKenzie, Donald A. (2006) *An Engine, Not a Camera: How Financial Models Shape Markets* Cambridge, MA: MIT Press.

Magnani, Lorenzo and Nancy J. Nersessian (2001) [eds] *Model-Based Reasoning: Science, Technology, Values.* New York: Kluwer Academic/Plenum Press.

Mäki, Uskali (1992) "On the Method of Isolation in Economics". In Craig Dilworth (ed), *Idealization IV: Intelligibility in Science* (pp. 317–51). Amsterdam: Rodopi.

   (2004) "Realism and the Nature of Theory: A Lesson from J. H. von Thünen for Economists and Geographers". *Environment and Planning A*, 36, 1719–36.

Malthus, Thomas R. (1803) "An Essay on the Principle of Population". Everyman edition, 1914, reprinted 1982. London: Dent.

Marshall, Alfred (1879) "The Pure Theory of Foreign Trade". In John K. Whitaker [ed] (1975), *The Early Economic Writings of Alfred Marshall, 1867–1890*, Vol. 2, Part III.5. London: Macmillan for the Royal Economic Society.

Mayo, Deborah (1996) *Error and the Growth of Experimental Knowledge.* Chicago: University of Chicago Press.

McCloskey, D. N. (1991) "Economic Science: A Search Through the Hyperspace of Assumptions". *Methodus*, 3:1, 6–16.

McMullin, Ernan (1985) "Galilean Idealization." *Studies in History and Philosophy of Science*, 16:3, 247–73.

Meade, James E. (1937) "A Simplified Model of Mr. Keynes' System". *Review of Economic Studies*, 4:2, 98–107.

Meli, Domenico Bertoloni (2006) *Thinking with Objects: The Transformation of Mechanics in the Seventeenth Century.* Baltimore: Johns Hopkins University Press.

Mirowski, Philip (2002) *Machine Dreams: Economics Becomes a Cyborg Science.* Cambridge: Cambridge University Press.

Morgan, Mary S. (1990) *The History of Econometric Ideas.* Cambridge: Cambridge University Press.

   (1996) "Idealization and Modelling" (A Review Essay). *Journal of Economic Methodology*, 3:1, 131–8.

   (1997) "The Technology of Analogical Models: Irving Fisher's Monetary Worlds". *Philosophy of Science*, 64, S304–14.

   (1999) "Learning from Models". In Mary S. Morgan and Margaret Morrison (eds), *Models as Mediators: Perspectives on Natural and Social Sciences* (pp. 347–88). Cambridge: Cambridge University Press.

   (2001) "Models, Stories and the Economic World". *Journal of Economic Methodology*, 8(3), 361–84.

   (2002) "Model Experiments and Models in Experiments". In Lorenzo Magnani and Nancy Nersessian (eds), *Model-Based Reasoning: Science, Technology, Values* (pp. 41–58). Dordrecht: Kluwer Academic/Plenum Press.

(2003a) "Economics". In T. Porter and D. Ross (eds), *The Cambridge History of Science*, Vol. 7: *The Modern Social Sciences* (pp. 275–305). Cambridge: Cambridge University Press.

(2003b) "Experiments Without Material Intervention: Model Experiments, Virtual Experiments and Virtually Experiments". In H. Radder (ed), *The Philosophy of Scientific Experimentation* (pp. 216–35). Pittsburgh: University of Pittsburgh Press.

(2004) "Imagination and Imaging in Economic Model-building". *Philosophy of Science* (Proceedings of the 2002 Biennial Meeting of the Philosophy of Science Association), 71:5, 753–66.

(2005) "Experiments versus Models: New Phenomena, Inference and Surprise". *Journal of Economic Methodology*, 12:2, 317–29.

(2006) "Economic Man as Model Man: Ideal Types, Idealization and Caricatures". *Journal of the History of Economic Thought*, 28:1, 1–27.

(2007) "The Curious Case of the Prisoner's Dilemma: Model Situation? Exemplary Narrative?" In A. Creager, M. Norton Wise, and E. Lunbeck, *Science Without Laws: Model Systems, Cases, Exemplary Narratives* (pp. 157–85). Durham, NC: Duke University Press.

(2008/online) "Models". In S. N. Durlauf and L. E. Blume (eds), *The New Palgrave Dictionary of Economics*, 2nd ed. London: Palgrave Macmillan http://www.dictionaryofeconomics.com/dictionary

Morgan, Mary S. and Marcel Boumans (2004) "Secrets Hidden by Two-Dimensionality: The Economy as a Hydraulic Machine". In Soraya de Chadarevian and Nicholas Hopwood (eds), *Models: The Third Dimension of Science* (pp. 369–401). Stanford, CA: Stanford University Press.

Morgan, Mary S. and Tarja Knuuttila (2012) "Models and Modelling in Economics"; forthcoming in Uskali Mäki (ed), *Handbook of the Philosophy of Economics* (one volume of the *Handbook of the Philosophy of Science*. General Editors: Dov Gabbay, Paul Thagard, and John Woods). Amsterdam: Elsevier/North-Holland. Available at: http://papers.sspn.com/sol3/papers.cfm?abstract_id=1499975.

Morgan, Mary S. and Margaret Morrison (1999) [eds] *Models as Mediators: Perspectives on Natural and Social Science*. Cambridge: Cambridge University Press.

Morrison, Margaret and Mary S. Morgan (1999) "Models as Mediating Instruments". In Mary S. Morgan and Margaret Morrison (eds), *Models as Mediators: Perspectives on Natural and Social Science* (pp. 10–37). Cambridge: Cambridge University Press.

Nersessian, Nancy J. (1992) "In the Theoretician's Laboratory: Thought Experimenting as Mental Modelling". *PSA Proceedings of the Biennial Meeting of the Philosophy of Science Association*, 2, 291–301.

(2008) *Creating Scientific Concepts*. Cambridge, MA: MIT Press.

Niehans, Jürg (1990) *A History of Economic Theory*. Baltimore: Johns Hopkins University Press.

Oreskes, Naomi (2007) "From Scaling to Simulation: Changing Meanings and Ambitions of Models in the Earth Sciences". In Angela Creager, M. Norton Wise, and Elizabeth Lunbeck (eds), *Science Without Laws: Model Systems, Cases, Exemplary Narratives* (pp. 93–124). Durham, NC: Duke University Press.

Pigou, Arthur C. (1931) "The Function of Economic Analysis". In Arthur C. Pigou and Dennis H. Robertson, *Economic Essays and Addresses* (pp. 1–19). London: P. S. King & Son.

Qin, Duo (1993) *The Formation of Econometrics*. Oxford: Clarendon.

Rheinberger, Hans-Jörg (1997) *Towards a History of Epistemic Things*. Stanford, CA: Stanford University Press.

Ricardo, David (1821) *The Principles of Political Economy and Taxation* (3 editions: 1817, 1819 and 1821; 1821 reprinted in Piero Sraffa and Maurice H. Dobb (eds), Vol. 1:

Collected Works and Correspondence of David Ricardo (1951). Cambridge: Cambridge University Press.

Robinson, Joan (1933) *The Economics of Imperfect Competition.* London: Macmillan.

Samuelson, Paul A. (1939) "Interactions between the Multiplier Analysis and the Principle of Acceleration". *Review of Economics and Statistics,* 21, 75–78.

Schumpeter, Joseph A. (1935) "The Analysis of Economic Change". *Review of Economic Statistics,* 17:4, 2–10.

Shapin, Steven and Simon Schaffer (1985) *Leviathan and the Air-Pump.* Princeton: Princeton University Press.

Solow, Robert M. (1997) "How Did Economics Get That Way and What Way Did It Get?" *Daedalus,* 126:1, 39–58 (reprinted fall 2005, *Daedalus*).

Suárez, Mauricio (2004) "An Inferential Conception of Scientific Representation." *Philosophy of Science* (Proceedings of the 2002 Biennial Meeting of the Philosophy of Science Association), 71:5, 767–79.

    (2008) [ed] *Fictions in Science: Philosophical Essays on Modeling and Idealization.* New York and London: Routledge.

Sugden, R. (2002) "The Status of Theoretical Models in Economics". In U. Mäki (ed), *Fact and Fiction in Economics: Models, Realism and Social Construction* (pp. 107–36). Cambridge: Cambridge University Press.

    (2009) "Credible Worlds, Capacities and Mechanisms". In Till Grüne-Yanoff (ed), *Economic Models as Credible Worlds or Ioslating Tools?* Special Issue of *Erkenntnis,* 70:1, 3–27.

Tinbergen, Jan (1937) *An Econometric Approach to Business Cycle Problems.* Paris: Hermann & Cie.

Van den Berg, Richard (2002) "Contemporary Responses to the Tableau Économique". In S. Boehm, C. Gehrke, H. D. Kurz, and R. Sturn (eds), *Is There Progress in Economics?* (pp. 295–316). Cheltenham: Edward Elgar.

Von Thünen, Johann Heinrich ([1826]1966) *Von Thünen's Isolated State* (English translation of *Der isolierte Staat,* 1966, translated by Carla M. Wartenberg; ed Peter Hall). Oxford: Pergamon Press.

Vosniadou, Stella (2001) "Mental Models in Conceptual Development". In Lorenzo Magnani and Nancy J. Nersessian (eds), *Model-Based Reasoning: Science, Technology, Values* (pp. 353–68). New York: Kluwer Academic/Plenum Press.

Walras, Leon (1874/1954) *Elements of Pure Economics,* translated by William Jaffé. London: Allen and Unwin for the American Economic Association and Royal Economic Society.

Weber, Max (1904) "Objectivity in Social Science and Social Policy". In *The Methodology of the Social Sciences* translated and edited by Edward A. Shils and Henry A. Finch, 1949 (pp. 49–112). New York: Free Press.

    (1913) *The Theory of Social and Economic Organisations* (translated by A. M. Henderson and Talcott Parsons, Part I of *Wirtshaft und Gesellschaft,* 1947). New York: Free Press.

Weintraub, E. Roy (2002) *How Economics Became a Mathematical Science.* Durham, NC: Duke University Press.

    (2008) "Mathematics and Economics". In Steven Durlauf and Lawrence Blume (eds), *The New Palgrave Dictionary of Economics,* 2nd ed. London: Macmillan; Available online at http://www.dictionaryofeconomics.com/article?id=pde2008_M000372&goto=M&result_number=2269.

Woody, Andrea (2004) "More Telltale Signs: What Attention to Representation Reveals about Scientific Explanation". *Philosophy of Science* (Proceedings of the 2002 Biennial Meeting of the Philosophy of Science Association), 71:5, 780–93.

2

Model-Making: New Recipes, Ingredients, and Integration

1. Ricardo, the "Modern" Economist?

David Ricardo is revered by many economists as the first 'modern' economist – and equally blamed by others – for having introduced abstract reasoning into economics. Both sides believe him to have initiated a style of economic argument characterized by the use of small, idealized examples that seem to be hypothetical and unconnected to the world in which he lived, but Ricardo himself found them useful in arguing about practical problems and events. This description of his way of arguing suggests that Ricardo was one of the pioneers of economic modelling.[1]

Consider first an example widely known to economists: Ricardo's argument in favour of free trade based on his notion of comparative advantage. He made his case using a little numerical example of the trade in wine and cloth between Portugal and England, drawn from the experience of his day. Though Portugal could produce both goods with less labour (i.e., she had an absolute advantage in the production of both goods), his verbal argument with the numerical example showed how it was advantageous for both countries to specialise and produce only that good in which they each had a comparative advantage (England in cloth and Portugal in wine) and then to exchange those goods with each other.[2] The numerical example works so well that it has continued to feature, sometimes even with the same countries and goods, to demonstrate the theory of comparative advantage in modern textbooks (even though economists no longer believe in the labour theory of value that underlies the way the numerical example worked for Ricardo). This 200-year-old example fits the way that modern economics is often taught at an elementary level in terms of a small world, a world of two goods and two consumers: Ricardo's example seems already a modelled world.

But this little 2 × 2 world, and the ease with which modern economists can use it, makes a misleading introduction to Ricardo's work for two reasons. First, Ricardo's writings in political economy are generally not at all easy to follow for the modern economist trained in modelling, for they are characterized by long chains of verbal reasoning with numerical chains incorporated into them rather than diagrams or mathematical equations.[3] Second, these difficult numerical chains sit within a very different tradition: economists of the classical school thought, and argued, in terms of laws and principles, not models. They did not habitually make nor reason with models of the economy: especially created, small-world examples of how bits of

---

1 There are several candidates for the title of 'first modern economist', meaning one who uses the technologies of modern economics, and a variety of national heroes to choose from. For example, Cournot on the French side, and Jevons, on the British side, both score highly for the introduction of mathematical and statistical methods. The claims for Ricardo relate to his development of abstract reasoning, associated here with modelling, for whom the comparable German claimant might be von Thünen, though as Chapter 1 showed, Quesnay's *Tableau Économique* has priority claims as the 'first' model. O'Brien (1975) claims: "Ricardo's system was, if not entirely the first, certainly the first sweepingly successful example of economic model building" (p. 37). He describes Ricardo as "inventing these techniques" and "Ricardo's deductive method .... as a process of heroic abstraction" (p. 42) (a process labelled "the Ricardian Vice": see Schumpeter, 1954, pp. 472–3). As this chapter shows, my view is that Ricardo's model-building was a mixture of inductive and deductive work, and not a process of abstraction – on which see Chapter 4.

2 This example occurs in his *Principles of Political Economy and Taxation* (1817/19/21), chapter 7. I thank Robert Went (see his 2002) for the information that there had indeed been such a switch, with Portugal giving up making textiles and specialising in wine to trade with English cloth during the eighteenth century (though this change was not necessarily fully to the advantage of both countries, nor a free market decision).

3 Perhaps because Ricardo is known as the 'first modern economist', a number of economists have confessed to me that they once thought they ought to read Ricardo, but gave it up as too difficult!

the economic system might work. For them, the economy was governed by laws, general and strict, just as the natural world was, and the task of the economist was to discover, or formulate, those laws taking account of the evidence of the day and of history.

Ricardo's work does not *look* as if it contains, or relies on, such things as models and he did not consciously *work* in a scientific tradition that used models to reason with. Yet, this chapter shows that Ricardo was indeed something of a pioneer in modelling, though his models, like most economic models that reach us from the past, are not self-evident things. Consider briefly a less well-known numerical example, in which he successively adds teams of ten labourers at a time to cultivate a field. Following its first appearance in a footnote, this numerical example becomes the site on which his famous laws of distribution are demonstrated. It is also the numerical example from which Ricardo discovered just how easy it would be for an economy to end up with no growth. In other words, this case turns out to play a critical role in his principles of political economy, as we see in this chapter, though the idea of adding more and more labourers to the same plot of land may seem to us strangely unreal. Was he so remote from the agricultural realities that he did not know about ploughs and horses!? What economic problem was Ricardo attacking? How did questions about agriculture come up in the economic debates of his day? Can we make sense of Ricardo's reasoning with such numerical examples? Why did his use of these numerical accounts look like experiments? And how did he fit these numerical chains together to play such an important role in his work?

To understand Ricardo's numerical chains, and his reasoning with them, requires little mathematical skill, but very considerable knowledge of the economics and of the economy of that day, as provided in the first part of the chapter. Only when we have that knowledge can we begin to appreciate how each of these numerical chains embedded not just Ricardo's ideas about the economy but also evidence of the day (such as the prices of wheat, and agricultural experiments), as we find in the second part of this chapter.[4] When pulled together – as ingredients of a recipe are – these numerical accounts formed a model, indeed quite a sophisticated one, for, by integrating together the separate numerical accounts, he built up a 'model farm'. And he used that model for 'model farming': processes of reasoning that enabled him to figure out the laws of his economic system. I discuss, in the final part of the chapter, how these numerical chains did more than illustrate Ricardo's arguments and more than support his propositions: rather they functioned to *demonstrate* Ricardo's laws of distribution.

So Ricardo's model farm provides a wonderful example of how the process of model development creates understanding for an economist, and how, by providing

---

4 Historians of economics have not paid a great deal of attention to these numbers, with the exception of Barkai, who correctly argues that Ricardo supported his theoretical propositions "by means of a model, the core of which is, as usual for him a numerical example" (Barkai 1986, p. 596). See also Barkai (1959), Gootzeit (1975), and O'Brien (1975, pp. 121–9).

some unexpected results from the new mix of elements, economists learn from developing the ingredients and integrating them into these small-world accounts. I start by explaining why Ricardo was so knowledgeable about agriculture so that we might grasp, in what follows, the originality of his way of arguing in economics.

2. Ricardo, His Economy, and the Economy of His Day

2.i David Ricardo, Esq.

David Ricardo was born in the east end of London in 1772 into a Jewish family of successful financiers.[5] He fell in love with the Quaker girl down the street and married in 1793; their marriage was a happy one and blessed with children, but created family cuts on both sides. Yet he was already sufficiently established to make his own way in the City of London, and enjoyed a successful career there, particularly in helping to finance the British government's engagement in the Napoleonic Wars. His interest in economics dates from 1799, when he picked up a copy of Adam Smith's *Wealth of Nations* during a family stay in Bath, and he began to write pamphlets and papers on matters of finance and currency. In 1814, having made a very considerable fortune, he began to buy country estates and lent out money on mortgages, including one on a potentially wealthy coalfield and industrial area on the edge of Manchester.

In almost his first letter from his country estate, Gatcomb Park in Gloucestershire, in reply to advice from Sir John Sinclair, founder and President of the Board of Agriculture, Ricardo wrote:

> I have not quite given up the Stock Exchange; for a few months in the year, I mean to enjoy the calm repose of a country life. Though I have a few acres of land in hand, I am not yet become a farmer. I leave the management of them wholly to others, and hardly take sufficient interest in what is going on, to make it probable that I shall ever be conversant with agricultural subjects ... (October 31, 1814)[6]

---

5 Ricardo's published works, and a large proportion of his letters, and other items, have been edited for publication by Piero Sraffa with Maurice Dobb (1951–1973). They are referred to here under the title *Works*, followed by the volume number, and for these biographical details, see *Works, X*. Historians of economics have written at impressive length and depth about Ricardo and his economics. The classic studies remain Mark Blaug (1958) and Denis O'Brien (1975 and revised, 2004); Samuel Hollander (1979) provides a (not uncontested) account of Ricardo's ideas; Terry Peach (1993) handles problems of interpretation; and Murray Milgate and Shannon Stimson (1991) discuss Ricardo's radicalism. Donald Winch's (1996) intellectual history of political economy in the period provides important background. See also many papers written about Ricardo collected by John Cunningham Wood (1985–94).

6 See letters 65–66, *Works, VI*, pp. 149–50. Sinclair, one of the major Scottish landowners and agricultural activists of the day, was but a mere acquaintance of Ricardo.

As good as his words, Ricardo lived partly in London, particularly during the period when the Houses of Parliament were sitting, for he had become an MP for a 'rotten borough' in 1819. Yet, he was a radical reformer, on the side of constitutional reform and widening the suffrage until his untimely death in 1823. In addition to his political activities, he remained active in economic and financial affairs, as evident in a long and diverse correspondence with such as Jeremy Bentham, Maria Edgeworth, James Mill, and of course his good friend and fellow economist Thomas Malthus. But he always loved to return to his country life, and when writing from Gatcomb, Ricardo was lyrical in discussing its beauty, seen from his walks and rides into the surrounding countryside.

The picture we have of Ricardo as an economist is one who knew, from experience, the practicalities of finance, money, and banking, and used that understanding in his writings on political economy to great effect. Yet – but this is only at first sight – we do not get the same impression that he was knowledgeable about farming and the land, despite the fact that such country estates, as Ricardo's pictured here (Figure 2.1), were not just a pretty house and park – they typically had their own farms.[7] And while Ricardo never became a gentleman-farmer, unlike some of his friends from the City, the evidence gives us good reasons for thinking that he was no less well informed, or less able to judge, the agricultural realities of his day than Malthus, who was for many years the parson of a rural parish before becoming the first professor of political economy in England.[8] For example, Ricardo's comments on his estate's farming activities quickly turn into economic arguments, as we find in this letter, written from Gatcomb Park to James Mill:

> The country here is looking very beautiful – our haymaking is now in full vigor, and no superabundance of agricultural labour in the market. The barley and oats I am told do not look well, but the wheat is promising. The manufacturers have full employment for their men; Osman [Ricardo's son] told me yesterday that Mr. Hicks was employing his men extra hours, and of course giving them extra pay. If the labouring class, in Agriculture, and Manufactures, are doing well, we must console ourselves for the misfortunes of landlords and tenants – they form but a small proportion of the whole population, and it is no small comfort to reflect that the losses they sustain are more than made up by the prosperity of other capitalists. (July 9, 1821)[9]

7   The estate of Gatcomb Park (now known as Gatcombe Park, home of Princess Anne) included the lordship of the manor of Minchinhampton and the land amounted to more than 5,000 acres.

8   "You are not *half a country gentleman*, nor a *particle of* a farmer", wrote Ricardo's good friend, Hutches Trower – another emigre financier from London, in November 1817 (Letter 235, *Works, VII*, p. 207), who had already become fully engaged in country life, suggesting that Ricardo pay particular attention to the planting of trees, and recommended two books that he should keep by him (Letter 102, 23rd July, 1815, *Works, VI*, p. 237).

9   Ricardo's *Works, IX*, p. 13. James Mill was his great debating companion and intellectual mentor. When both in London, they regularly walked together and argued about politics, economics, philosophy, and much else, though Ricardo's letters to his friend rarely comment on his own

Figure 2.1. Gatcomb Park, Country Home of David Ricardo.

Source: Piero Sraffa: *The Works and Correspondence of David Ricardo.* Edited with the collaboration of M. H. Dobb, 1951–73, Cambridge: Cambridge University Press for The Royal Economic Society, Vol. VII: *Letters, 1816–1818,* facing p. 1. Reproduced by permission of Liberty Fund Inc. on behalf of The Royal Economic Society.

GATCOMB
The Seat of
To whom this plate is

PARK,
David Ricardo Esq.re
inscribed by S.g & H.S Storer

Emery Walker Ltd ph.sc

London Published Feb.y 1 1821 by Sherwood Jones & C.o Paternoster Row

When Ricardo became a large landowner and lord of the manor, he duly became an active member of that class in all the ways that would have been expected of him. The parish of Minchinhampton, in which Gatcomb Park was situated, was both an agricultural parish (mainly arable, with pasture for sheep) and a manufacturing one (woollen broadcloth was the local industry), with a sizeable population.[10] He helped in the local parish, supporting the rector in rebuilding almshouses, starting a school and infirmary, and so forth.[11] He was elected sheriff of the county of Gloucestershire for 1818, an evident sign of establishment success and local respect.[12]

At the same time, we also know that his interest in political economy had begun to deepen and to widen from matters of currency, bullion, and trade to those of agriculture and politics as early as 1811, three years before he became a landowner.[13] By 1814 he was actively writing and lobbying against 'the corn laws' (where 'corn' refers to wheat and small grains rather than maize), which had long restricted the import of cheap corn.[14] What is less well-known, but understood from his letters, is that in September 1814 he had been reading the House of Lords' Report into the Corn Laws (or more correctly into the ".... State of the Growth, Commerce and Consumption of Grain...") and briefly discussed the "Evidence" section of that report with Malthus. Ricardo complained that the report "discloses some important facts, but how ignorant the persons giving evidence appear to be of the subject [of political economy] as a matter of science".[15]

This "Evidence" will prove important later: it consisted of the witness reports of those who came to give evidence to the committee and verbatim accounts of their cross examination by committee members. The statements range across different

---

landscape (though see *Works, VII*, Ricardo's letter to James Mill, p. 170; p. 277, 12th August, 1818 and letter 274, p. 305).

10 The 1801 census recorded 3,419 people in 692 houses rising to 5,114 people in 1,116 houses in the 1831 census. This and other information about Ricardo's country estate and the local industry has been gleaned from Herbert's (1976) *Victoria County History of Gloucestershire*. Vol. XI: *The Stroud Valleys*.

11 For example, he started a local school in Minchinhampton in 1816 on the Lancastrian system, with 250 boys and girls as pupils in 1818 (see Herbert, 1976, p. 206).

12 However, he never became a magistrate for the county: possibly it was his Jewish birth, though he became a Unitarian after his marriage; perhaps it was because he was not a member of the land-owning Whig elite. See biographies by Weatherall (1976) and by Henderson with Davis (1997) as well as *Works, X*.

13 These interests and their dating can be seen quite clearly from the relevant *Works, III* and *IV* and in his letters, Vols. VI–IX.

14 He was consistent in opposing petitions for help from the landowners and farmers when prices of grain fell – see, for example, his remarks in *Works, VI*, p. 47. However, it was not the case that he let his sympathy with the plight of the labourers interfere with his views on the 'poor law'. He was certainly a charitable man, but decried the incentive systems inherent in the poor law.

15 Malthus found the report to be on his side: "It contains as you observe some very curious information. The evidence is a little suspicious, though it is a good deal such as I expected from [my] Theory" (Letters 58 and 59, Ricardo to Malthus 30th August, 1814 and Malthus to Ricardo, 11th September, 1814 *Works, VI*, pp. 130 and 132).

forms; there were personal descriptions, discussions about prices, and a wealth of numerical farm-accounting statements presented by individual farmers and land-lords.[16] The second witness was one Edward Wakefield, who in 1815 was to become Ricardo's land agent, and from then on regularly sent him letters informing him of his duties as a good landlord, his tenant farmers' problems, the difficulty of finding reliable new tenants, the state of the market for land, and the prices of produce.[17] And from the point at which he entered Parliament in 1819, Ricardo gained a fur-ther wealth of knowledge of the agricultural experience of Britain of his day, partic-ularly as he sat on the Select Committee investigating agricultural distress in 1821 and 1822. He used such knowledge in his speeches in Parliament, in his writings about agricultural issues, and in framing his policy positions.

All this suggests that far from being a wealthy absentee landowner uninterested in farming, as he had appeared to be in 1814, Ricardo certainly became very knowl-edgeable about the land and engaged with agricultural matters. Now, to make sense of and appreciate Ricardo's numerical reasonings in his political economy, we need a better sense of the economic issues of his day and how they were perceived by economists, such as himself, working in the classical tradition of his time.

2.ii Economics Matters, Experimental Farming Matters

The two big issues for political economists of Ricardo's day were the growth of population and the high price of basic food that contemporaries blamed on the restrictive tariffs known as the corn laws. Agriculture lay at the heart of both questions.

The problem of the apparently explosive growth of population was prevalent on the tongues of the chattering intelligentsia, for it presented the most intracta-ble question. For historians of economics, that question has been most intimately connected with the work of Ricardo's great friend and fellow economist, Thomas Malthus.[18] Recall that classical economists thought and reasoned in terms of laws or principles that, like laws of nature, were understood to govern the economy. In accordance with this stance, but with an unusually concise form, Malthus' ideas about population were proposed in two numerical 'laws': that food supply grew arithmetically while population growth (if unchecked) would grow geometrically. He argued that the effects of these two laws were shorter-run periods of misery, alternating with comparative well-being, as economic activity fluctuated around this constraint fixed by the ability of nature, and so farmers, to provide food for the rapidly growing population.

---

16 The long set of tables of data that appeared separately attached to the report are not called 'evidence' but 'accounts' (almost reversing modern economists' connotations of these terms).

17 These unpublished letters from Edward Wakefield can be found at the University Library in Cambridge. Unfortunately, Ricardo's letters in reply are not part of the collection.

18 For the ways in which the population question spread into many aspects of life and ideas in the period, see James' 1979 book about Malthus.

The issue of the corn laws, the legal tariff on grain that prevented imports of cheaper foreign grains, was equally hotly debated as the most immediate and important policy question in political economy. Ricardo first addressed this problem in his 1815 pamphlet known as his *Essay on Profits* and concluded that the tariff, by keeping the price unreasonably high, was to the benefit of the landlord but to the detriment not just of the labourer but also to the capital holder.[19] Corn (wheat) prices had been extremely high from 1795 because of poor harvests and the Napoleonic Wars. Indeed, prices had been high enough to cause food riots, changes in the 'poor law' (or legal system of localised social welfare), and the extension of arable farming into newly enclosed areas. (Ricardo commented on such riots that occurred in London in March 1815 in one of his many letters to Malthus.[20]) In that same year of 1815, Ricardo's new country parish of Minchinhampton found the cost of poor relief had risen to £2000 and 230 people were on permanent outdoor relief.[21] As prices fell from their peak, farmers complained and landlords' rents were threatened, raising demands from both groups for further tariff protection under the corn laws, while the labouring class was not in favour of such restrictions for prices of corn and so bread prices still remained high.[22] Parliament had investigated the corn laws in 1814, but the farming interests (farmers and landlords) won the day of course, for labourers had no vote, and the tariff remained.[23]

For both Ricardo and Malthus, the population problem was a given – it was the result of the iron laws of political economy. The health and growth of the farming sector were critical for the well-being of the economy as a whole, for agriculture had not only to feed the growing population but also, to a considerable extent, employ them. At that time, agriculture and its associated activities still formed the largest sector of the economy (despite the beginnings of industrialisation, the ongoing success of commerce, and the fast growth in urban centres). The farming interests themselves were well aware of their central role, and the immense importance of

19 See *Works, IV*: "An Essay on The Influence of a low Price of Corn on the Profits of Stock", 1815.
20 *Works, VI*, letter 77, p. 180. These riots were not only urban affairs. Machine burning and the burning of grain barns were a feature of the period: his good friend Trower wrote to Ricardo about a neighbour's experience in July 1816 (*Works, VII*, p. 45).
21 This was against a number of households, which probably lay between 700 and 1,000 households; see Herbert (1976, pp. 188 and 201), who also states that "from 1814, the poor in the house were farmed" (p. 201), which I take to mean were set to work on farms within the parish.
22 At their peak in 1812, prices had been around three times the late eighteenth-century level. Somewhat suddenly, there had been a fall in the price of corn due to a bumper harvest in 1813 and, after peace in 1814, prices fell further. In 1815, they were still around double the prewar level, though just below the level at which protection came in. See D. P. O'Brien (1981, p. 167) on the discussion of high prices and their effects and Dorfman (1989) for the following fall. The full series of corn (small grains) prices can be found in Mitchell and Deane (1971). Rents per acre, which had been rising steadily since the 1790s, levelled off around 1815, but at double their prewar level: see Turner et al. (1997) and Offer (1980). See Hilton (1977) on the politics of the corn laws and Snell (1985) on the poor law of the period.
23 There was some alteration, the 1815 act abolished the sliding scale of duties on imports and replaced it with import prohibition when the price was below 80sh, with free imports over that price.

farm productivity, in these two problems of political economy. But for the farmers, the provision of both food and employment were practical matters to be solved, rather than matters of scientific law.

Economic and political historians have long been aware of the importance of the tariffs on corn as indicative both of the class war between the agrarian elite and farm labourers and of the rural–urban power struggle as Britain underwent urban-isation. Historians of economics have seen how such struggles depended on the contemporary perception of how incomes were distributed between such groups – or as classical economists of the day expressed it – upon 'the laws of distribution': that is, of what determines the share of output between their three economic classes of landowners, farmers (capitalists), and labourers.[24] (Of course, the historical issues stretch further than this, for Ricardo's account of distribution laid the groundwork for Marx's analysis of class interests and so point to a later history of momentous political and economic events.) Agrarian historians have long been aware of the importance of experimental agriculture that drove the technical changes that sup-ported the massive increase in agricultural output in that period and so prevented the kind of food crises Malthus had envisaged. The connections between the argu-ments over the corn laws, food security, and distribution are manifest.

Yet one link remains unexplored by historians of economics, namely the com-mon ground and unexpected connection between the two practical domains of political economy and experimental agriculture, and in particular the fundamental importance of these links in Ricardo's work. His account of distribution depended on substantive elements from practical and experimental farming in three respects. First, the experiments undertaken in farming at that time provided subject matter for his political economy. Second, his numerical accounts paralleled, in numerical form, the reports of real experiments in farming. Third, the way he used his numer-ical accounts – his way of reasoning with them – constituted a form of experiment that might be called a 'numerical experiment'. His political arithmetic, or as I shall suggest, his model and modelling, mirror the numerical expression and content of agricultural experimental work. So to understand Ricardo's modelling in political economy, we must know something of this tradition of agricultural experiment.

The late eighteenth and early nineteenth centuries were an age of experimen-tal farming in Britain, with the purpose of improving the productivity and output of the farming sector.[25] There was a strong proselytising, even missionary, element in these activities; successful experiments were to provide information, advice, and even exemplary procedures for others to follow. Experimental reports such as the supposed 500 odd found in Arthur Young's *Farmer's Tours* of the 1770s (see Mingay, 1975) and William Marshall's *Experiments and Observations Concerning Agriculture and the Weather* (1779) went alongside agricultural handbooks

---

24 See particularly Overton (1996) on agrarian and economic history, Hilton (1977) on economic
   and political history, and Winch (1996) on the history of economics and its political dimensions.
25 A broad survey of the movement, and its literature, is given by Wilmot (1990).

outlining best practice, such as Alex. Beatson's *A New System of Cultivation* (1820/21). Experimental investigations in the first two decades of the nineteenth century, the period of Ricardo's work in political economy, ranged over animal husbandry, fertiliser testing, cultivation methods, work organisation and machine performance, and so forth just as they had earlier focussed on the virtues of animal breeding and the importance of drainage, new crops, and crop rotation. Technical change based on such experiments was an ongoing process.[26]

There was also an usually high level of political involvement in agriculture: a number of the Whig aristocracy, owners of large land holdings, were intent on improvement and were active in developing their own experimental farms. Their great agricultural shows, particularly those held at Mr. Coke's (later Earl of Leicester) estate at Holkham Hall, Norfolk, and the Duke of Bedford's estate at Woburn, were sites where the latest practices were reported, new breeds shown, and visitors escorted around the experimental plots. These events had become high points of the social, political, and agricultural season in the early years of the nineteenth century. Experimental agriculture thus occupied a secure location within a politically forceful landowning and farming elite. The personal interest shown in farming by George III had turned it into a fashionable pursuit, and the new agricultural societies provided institutional entrepreneurship.[27]

The scientific experimental tradition from chemistry was also revitalised during Ricardo's years by the Board of Agriculture's establishment of an annual course of lectures by Humphry Davy in 1803, repeated until 1812.[28] Such scientific work complemented rather than replaced the work of practical field experimenters, and it was not necessarily regarded as a different kind of endeavour. Accounts of experimental activities and findings called on the work of chemists such as Dr. Joseph Priestley alongside those of famous agricultural commentators such as Arthur Young and practical experimentalists such as William Grisenthwaite, whose *A New Theory of Agriculture* of 1819 also appeared as a series of letters in the *Farmers' Journal*.[29] Davy's own *Elements of Agricultural Chemistry* of 1814 (from his lectures) interwove the agricultural experimental farming reports from the 'great improvers'

---

26 County surveys formed the main body of agricultural information of the day from which this variation can be understood (see Marshall's 1817 county reports to the Board of Agriculture in the second decade of the century – the exact period of discussion for Ricardo's work here). For a recent review and reassessment of the agricultural revolution see Overton (1996) and Allen (1994) (and for specific chapters on innovating techniques of the period, see G. E. Mingay's [1989] edited Vol. VI in *The Agrarian History of England and Wales*). On Young's reporting of experimental farming, see Mingay (1975, chapter II:4). Good examples of specific contemporary reports of technical matters, such as crop rotation, can be found in the *Farmers' Journal* of the period, for example, September 22, 1810 (p. 176); September 14, 1812 (p. 403), and November 1, 1813 (front page).

27 See "Agricultural Literature and Societies" by Nicholas Goddard in Mingay (1989).

28 See Berman (1972) on the scientific connections of experimental farming.

29 His letters can be found, for example, in the issues of September 7 and 21 in 1818 addressed to "Mr. Coke". For an account of the early history of experimental work in farming and agricultural science, see Russell (1966, p. 67, and chapters 2 and 3).

(the Whig landowners) with the reports from Young and findings from eminent scientists.

The 'practical farmer' was an important contributor to all this, for any interested farmer could join in this practical science by experimenting on his own land and write to report his findings to the farming newspapers of the day. This was not necessarily high science, nor did it require the huge investments of the wealthy landowners. Significantly, experimental reports by practising farmers and landowners (as opposed to those by 'scientists') described not just the agricultural experiment and its outcomes, but also the associated costs and profits. Experimental reports were sometimes reported in financial terms, and if farmers reporting 'successful' experiments did not provide the monetary arithmetic that demonstrated increased profit as well as productivity, they found their claims of 'improvement' open to question.

Ricardo knew about all this. He was familiar with the experimental farming activities of his day, for no intelligent and engaged political economist moving in both the political and landed gentry circles, as he did, could have remained ignorant of them. We already know that he knew about the practical experimental work of farmers from his reading of the "Evidence" section of the House of Lords Report on the corn laws in 1814 (above). We know that he also knew of the agricultural activities of the Whig landowners as well as of the new system of agriculture, for he refers in one letter to the annual agricultural meetings (known as a "sheep-shearing") of 1821 at Holkham Hall as "Mr. Coke's annual feast".[30] His letters pointed to the importance of agricultural improvement both as a necessary requirement for growth and as an obvious part of the experience of his day, although he does not seem to have been directly a participant in experimental activities.[31]

But there is another surprising signal from which we can appreciate his familiarity with the agricultural improvements of his day and the experimental element involved. The writing in his *Principles of Political Economy and Taxation* (his main contribution to economic science, which appeared in three editions in his lifetime: 1817, 1819, and 1821) is very formal, but he very occasionally moves from neutrality to the first person singular voice – and he does so precisely at the point when he discusses the possibility of increasing agricultural output through introducing new technology and changing farming practices![32] (This is indirect evidence, but

30 See Ricardo's letter to Mill of August 28, 1821 (*Works, IX*, pp. 45–6). In fact, this was the last of these great events, which, though they had been going for more than forty years, had become large scale only in the early nineteenthth century. For information on the these meetings, see Goddard (1989, pp. 377–8).

31 I have found no evidence that Ricardo's tenants were involved in agricultural experiments, but certainly Wakefield was concerned about employing best practice farming. And, the erstwhile owner of Gatcomb Park, Edward Sheppard, father of the immediate previous owner Philip Sheppard, had experimented in sheep breeding on an estate at Avening (in the next door parish to Minchinhampton) that had previously been held under the same ownership.

32 There is another obvious case later where he is discussing investment along similar lines, and he writes as the farmer-investor in his chapter "On Machinery".

pertinent and all too easily overlooked – so easily that I will need to point it out when we reach that event in the next section.) And, in these places, he writes in the first person as both capital investor or farmer (making profits) and as landlord (collecting rents) – the two roles that he has been careful to keep separate in the rest of his chapter. These are not just roles, but classes in the economic system, classes that share between them the total products of the economy. As such classes they feature in Ricardo's model farm, as we shall see.

3. Constructing Ricardo's Numerical Model Farm and Questions of Distribution

My purpose in this section is to show exactly how Ricardo integrated his knowledge of contemporary agricultural experience and experiments with his economic ideas in his construction of the accounts for a numerical 'model farm'; and that it was through his numerical experiments using this 'model farm' – 'model farming' – that he formulated his laws of distribution. But to show all this, I need to explain how Ricardo's numerical accountings are put together and to follow their sequence through with Ricardo to the point where they demonstrate his laws of distribution. This requires working through some rather dense material.

Let us begin where Ricardo began. As Blaug argues, "Ricardo's *theoretical* system emerged directly and spontaneously out of the great corn laws debate of 1814–16".[33] But it was Ricardo's familiarity with the kind of *evidence* given in that debate that was critical both for the development of his mode of arguing and for the way in which his system 'emerged'. In his first pamphlet against the corn laws of 1815, Ricardo used a couple of large tables to argue and demonstrate his points, and was surprised to find that this mode of reasoning led him to some new findings. However, his argument was constrained by the fact that a table is essentially a two-dimensional object, and he wanted to develop a numerical argument about the interactions of several variables (see Appendix 1).[34] As his investigations into growth and distribution in the economy proceeded further in the more thorough

---

33 Blaug (1958, p. 6), italics mine. Ramana (1957, p. 198) has, like Blaug, argued that this pamphlet by Ricardo – along with contemporary ones by Malthus, Torrens, and West – were the direct outcome of the 1814 investigations into the corn laws by Parliament. By comparison, Edward West's 1815 pamphlet on rent, which appeared just before Ricardo's, used numerical arguments in a somewhat similar way to Ricardo, but in no way matched the extended table of Ricardo's pamphlet, nor the continuity and complexity of the numerical accounts he produced in his *Principles*. Malthus' 1814 pamphlet on the corn laws and 1815 pamphlet on rent contained no use of numbers, tables, or farm accounts while Robert Torrens' 1815 pamphlet used numbers to a very limited extent; both began to use Ricardo's more sophisticated numerical examples in their later writings. On Marx's use of numerical examples, and artefactual elements in them, see Reuten (1999).

34 Although many tables are constructed to show lots of things varying together, such elements are usually tabulated against one dimension, namely time. Ricardo had to juggle his three variables: rent, capital, and profit, in order to display their interrelations within a two-dimensional table.

treatment in his *Principles*, he abandoned his attempts to argue with large tables and used a sequence of smaller numerical chains. Each of these illustrated and demonstrated a different part of his argument as relevant for the particular topic in each chapter.

Here is where we shall see how the experimental farming of the real economy of Ricardo's day (discussed in the previous section) – in content and numerical expression – was mirrored in the numerical accounts that formed his model farm. Ricardo's numerical examples appear in different forms, sometimes running through the lines of text, sometimes as a set of mini accounts, and sometimes in footnotes. This is also how the farming experiments were reported in the period – sometimes running through text, and sometimes as a set of farm accounts. I shall show some of both the farming reports and Ricardo's numerical examples – his 'accountings' (as I shall call them) – in their original forms. By comparing them, we can see how Ricardo's political economy used the same kinds of reports that appeared in agricultural experimental work, and that, in content, he discussed real problems of the agriculture of his day.

But while the numerical accounts look like illustrations of the text, in fact, they are not quite that: they play a rather special role for they function as reasoning tools complementary to the verbal argument.[35] Each one enabled him (and his readers) to reason through what would happen in his model farm economy in rather concrete form (the set of accountings) if different actions were to be taken under various circumstances. We can think of these reasoning chains as offering numerical experiments, in the sense that one thing at a time is allowed to vary so that its immediate effects can be set out, its side effects traced out, and the final outcomes judged. And, as befits experiments, Ricardo usually makes it very clear which other things are being held constant: the *ceteris paribus* conditions are set out and noted each time, and each numerical experiment plays out its demonstration through a series of related changes, or a scenario, as successively more of something is added (e.g., more capital, more manure, etc.). These model farm accounting experiments effectively provide numerical 'simulations', showing the different eventualities of different scenarios. It is these numerical experiments that mirror or parallel the real agricultural experiments of his day.

Each of these accountings formed an ingredient in his model farm, and later in this section we will see how he integrated these ingredients into his model farm. We will also see how his numerical experiments with that model farm – that I call model farming – led him to some unexpected, even surprising insights into the nature of that small-world economy, insights he understood as relevant to the economy of his day. This points us to the way in which unexpected results can emerge when a new formal mode of reasoning is adopted, and in later chapters of this book, I shall explore this idea, and the notion that experimentation is a more general quality of model functioning (see Chapters 7 and 8).

---

35 This importance of this independent representational function is discussed further in Chapter 3.

3.i The Numbers in Ricardo's *Principles* and Experimental Accounts

For Ricardo, the fundamental problem of political economy was to understand the distribution of gains between the economic classes. He had set for himself the challenge of understanding the laws that determined this distribution, that is, the shares of produce that go as rent to the landlord, profits to the capital holder, and wages to the labourer. His opening remarks of the Preface to his *Principles* make this clear:

> The produce of the earth – all that is derived from its surface by the united application of labour, machinery, and capital, is divided among three classes of the community; namely, the proprietor of the land, the owner of the stock or capital necessary for its cultivation, and the labourers by whose industry it is cultivated …
>
> To determine the laws which regulate this distribution, is the principal problem in Political Economy … (Ricardo, *Principles*, 1821, *Works*, I, p. 5)

Ricardo takes the correct analysis of rent to be critical to determining what these laws are. So, though he begins his *Principles* with a standard account from classical economics about labour as the source of value, he then moves immediately to the question of rent and this drives his account through the following pages until his laws of distribution are laid out a few chapters further on.

Rent is defined by Ricardo as:

> … that portion of the produce of the earth which is paid to the landlord for the use of the original and indestructible powers of the soil. It is often, however, confounded with the interest and profit of capital, and in popular language, the term is applied to whatever is annually paid by the farmer to his landlord. (Ricardo, *Principles*, 1821, *Works*, I, p. 67)[36]

But the definition does not motivate much on its own. Ricardo wanted to make his account of rent absolutely clear: how rent arose; how the amounts were determined; how it was affected by agricultural investment; and most importantly, how it featured in the distribution of income. For these purposes, a static account would not do, for the economy was in a period of rapid change, and Ricardo needed to demonstrate how his laws of distribution applied over time and how changes in each element affected the distribution to the other classes. In this context, the problem of population growth was an important consideration. It was not just the immediate factor – the necessity of growing more food to feed the growing population (the Malthusian problem), but also the more generally perceived agricultural/rural problem of poverty due to lack of work, for as the population grew, not only was more food required, but more labour was also available. Ricardo's account of the distribution of the product therefore needed to be supple enough to take both these issues – food output and employment – on at once.

---

36 In this section, page numbers refer to the 1821 edition of the *Principles*, provided in Sraffa's edition (*Works, I*), and reproduced by the Liberty Press for the Royal Economic Society in 2004.

Ricardo's numerical accountings were motivated in his argument by the problem of increasing output of food, with solutions coming from attacking the problem in different ways. In the first substantial numerical account, Ricardo proposes that farmers will bring in additional (more marginal) land into cultivation and he uses this to show that, under such circumstances, rent will arise. Although the case example of bringing new land into cultivation as a way of increasing food output for the growing population might seem contrived, this was far from the case. Despite the island constraint and relatively high population density for the period, there was an ongoing process of enclosure of common pasture (or 'wastes') and a consequent increase in arable acreage in England during this period. These were the well-known realities of the day.[37]

I quote Ricardo here, not just because it is the first numerical accounting, but because it provides a good example of his running text form of this. As readers will see, these extracts from Ricardo require patience, not only to overcome the stylistic devices of a 200-year-old text, in which the logic of the words and numbers complement each other, but also to appreciate that Ricardo is in the process of gradually assembling the set of ingredients for his model farm through his series of accountings. It is helpful also to bear in mind that he uses quarters of grain as his unit of account.

DOCUMENT 1:
Ricardo's Accounting 1: From his Chapter II: On Rent, *Principles*, 1821, *Works*, I, pp. 70–1

Thus suppose land – No. 1, 2, 3 [of three different qualities] – to yield, with an equal employment of capital and labour, a net produce of 100, 90, and 80 quarters of corn. In a new country, where there is an abundance of fertile land compared with the population, and where therefore it is only necessary to cultivate No. 1, the whole net produce [after supporting the labourers] will belong to the cultivator, and will be the profits of the stock which he advances. As soon as population had so far increased as to make it necessary to cultivate No. 2, from which ninety quarters only can be obtained after supporting the labourers, rent would commence on No. 1; for either there must be two rates of profit on agricultural capital, or ten quarters, or the value of ten quarters must be withdrawn from the produce of No. 1 for some other purpose. Whether the proprietor of the land, or any other person, cultivated No. 1, these ten quarters would equally constitute rent; for the cultivator of No. 2 would get the same result with his capital whether he cultivated No. 1, paying ten quarters for the rent, or continued to cultivate No. 2, paying no rent. In the same manner it might be shown that when No. 3 is brought into cultivation, the rent of No. 2 must be ten quarters, or the value of ten quarters, whilst the rent of No. 1

---

37 As shown, for example, in the evidence to the *Lords Report* in 1814; see also Mingay (1997).

would rise to twenty quarters; for the cultivator of No. 3 would have the same profits whether he paid twenty quarters for the rent of No. 1, ten quarters for the rent of
No. 2, or cultivated No. 3 free of all rent.

This numerical chain forms the first part of Ricardo's accounts for his model
farm. It was designed not only to outline the process of increasing output by bringing new land into cultivation, but also to show how rent arose and explain its level
by connecting it with the fact that the same amount of labour and capital produced less output on the poorer quality of land than on the better. This argumentation, and the numerical outcomes, depended not only on Ricardo's definition of
rent, but also upon two classical economic assumptions, namely, the tendency of
profits to equalize and that the profit rate is determined on the least productive
land. Under these two formal conditions, as the accounting shows, rent is the difference in net produce (after wages are paid) between the more and less productive land – so that landlords gain, as rent, the excess profits of the farmer on the
better quality land.[38]

Ricardo's second alternative – and associated numerical accounting – to solve
the need for increased food by a growing population was to increase capital inputs
on the same land, again another well-observed feature of his day. He assumes that
successive capital investments will increase output (but at a declining rate), yet
profits on each unit of capital must remain equal.[39] His accounting numbers show
how rent arises as the difference between the levels of profits with different doses
of capital (Ricardo, *Principles*, 1821, *Works*, *I*, pp. 71–2). That is, on both the more
marginal land case (wherein the additional labour employed produces less output) and the more enhanced capital case (wherein capital is understood to embody
labour), rent will arise because "... rent invariably proceeds from the employment
of an additional quantity of labour with a proportionally less return" (*Principles*,
1821, *Works*, *I*, p. 72).

It is not only rent that rises under these circumstances, but also the relative
price of agricultural produce. This outcome follows from the classical economics
'labour theory of value', which holds that it is labour alone that creates value, and
that there is a direct relationship between labour input and value. If more labour
has to be used to produce the same amount of a commodity, the value of that commodity will rise relative to others and vice versa. The implications for agriculture
follow:

> The most fertile and most favourably situated land will be first cultivated,
> and the exchangeable value of its produce will be adjusted in the same

---

38 Later in the book, Ricardo develops this example by adding taxes and tithes.
39 Reich (1980) finds contemporary evidence to support Ricardo's belief in declining returns to agricultural investment, despite the period of improvement. Blaug argues that this classical assumption was widely believed at the time to be correct (Blaug, 1956, pp. 159–60).

manner as the exchangeable value of all other commodities, by the total quantity of labour necessary in various forms, from first to last, to produce it and bring it to market. When land of an inferior quality is taken into cultivation, the exchangeable value of raw produce will rise, because more labour is required to produce it. (Ricardo, *Principles*, 1821, *Works*, I, p. 72)

He also assumes that all improvements in agriculture are labour saving and therefore lead to a fall in the price (or relative value) of the good:

If they did not occasion a fall in the price of raw produce they would not be improvements; for it is the essential quality of an improvement to diminish the quantity of labour before required to produce a commodity; and this diminuation cannot take place without a fall of its [the commodity's] price or relative value. (Ricardo, *Principles*, 1821, *Works*, I, p. 80)

In his third numerical account, Ricardo discusses another feature of the period – namely technical change in agriculture – as a way of increasing food output to feed the growing population. This most interesting passage shows not only how Ricardo tabulated some of his numerical accounts, but also his familiarity with at least two of the main elements of the experimental farming results of the day: the importance of manure and the role of root crops. Although the introduction of root crops as part of a rotation system had been the work of "Turnip" (Lord) Townshend in the eighteenth century, the best crop rotation for any particular location was still very much a part of the experimental farming of Ricardo's day. For example, Rudge, in his 1813 account (for the Board of Agriculture) of Gloucestershire (wherein Gatcomb Park lay) provided a long accounting of crop rotations in both physical and monetary terms.

This is also the passage that shows us Ricardo thinking as a farmer – for it is at this point that he becomes a farmer in the first person, discussing the possibility of *himself* introducing a "course of turnips" (into the field rotation of crops), or of *himself* introducing a more "invigorating manure" to his fields. (This is a rare use of the informal first person singular in his book, which usually remains strictly formal.) We can see that he so far enters into the issues of agricultural improvement that he speaks to us of himself as a farmer lowering rent – a benefit to the farmer, but to himself as landowner in real life, a loss in income that he will have to bear!

DOCUMENT 2:
Ricardo's Accounting 3: From his Chapter II: On Rent, *Principles*, 1821, *Works*, I, pp. 80–1

The improvements which increase the productive powers of the land, are such as the more skilful rotation of crops, or the better choice of manure. These improvements absolutely enable us to obtain the same produce from a smaller quantity of land. If, by the introduction of a course of turnips, I can feed my sheep besides raising my corn, the land on which the sheep were before fed becomes unnecessary, and the same quantity of raw produce is raised by the employment of a less quantity of land. If I discover a manure which will enable me to make a piece of land produce 20 percent more corn, I may withdraw at least a portion of my capital from the most unproductive part of my farm. ..... If, by the introduction of turnip husbandry, or by the use of a more invigorating manure, I can obtain the same produce with less capital, and without disturbing the difference between the productive powers of the successive portions of capital, I shall lower rent; for a different and more productive portion will be that which will form the standard from which every other will be reckoned. If, for example, the successive portions of capital [invested in the same land] yielded 100, 90, 80, 70; whilst I employed these four portions, my rent would be 60, or the difference between

$$
\left.\begin{array}{l}
70 \text{ and } 100 = 30 \\
70 \text{ and }\ \ 90 = 20 \\
70 \text{ and }\ \ 80 = 10 \\
\\
\overline{} \\
60
\end{array}\right\}
\quad \begin{array}{l} \text{whilst the produce} \\ \text{would be 340} \end{array} \quad
\left\{\begin{array}{l}
100 \\
90 \\
80 \\
70 \\
\overline{} \\
340
\end{array}\right.
$$

..... If, instead of 100, 90, 80, 70, the produce should be increased [through "improvement" such as manure] to 125, 115, 105, 95, the rent would still be 60, or the difference between

$$
\left.\begin{array}{l}
95 \text{ and } 125 = 30 \\
95 \text{ and } 115 = 20 \\
95 \text{ and } 105 = 10 \\
\\
\overline{} \\
60
\end{array}\right\}
\quad \begin{array}{l} \text{whilst the produce} \\ \text{would be increased} \\ \text{to 440} \end{array} \quad
\left\{\begin{array}{l}
125 \\
115 \\
105 \\
95 \\
\overline{} \\
440
\end{array}\right.
$$

But with such an increase of produce, without an increase of demand*, there could be no motive for employing so much capital on the land; one portion would be withdrawn, and consequently the last portion of capital would yield 105 instead of 95, and rent would fall to 30, or the difference between

$$
\left.\begin{array}{l}
105 \text{ and } 125 = 20 \\
105 \text{ and } 115 = 10 \\
\overline{} \\
30
\end{array}\right\}
\quad \begin{array}{l} \text{whilst the produce will* be still} \\ \text{adequate to the wants of the} \\ \text{population, for it would be 345} \\ \text{quarters, or} \end{array} \quad
\left\{\begin{array}{l}
125 \\
115 \\
105 \\
\overline{} \\
345
\end{array}\right.
$$

the demand being only for 340 quarters.

*omitted footnote

We begin to see here how his model farm is gradually being built up, for he repeats his second accounting showing increasing investment in the top part of the 'table', but then incorporates the effect of a technical change in the bottom half. His discussion and numerical account are given in the form of a numerical experiment. And it is a complicated experiment. In the first stage there is a variation in capital input and we see the variation in output as the 'treatment' is varied. In the second stage, there is the same variations in capital inputs, but with the application of manure (or equivalent technical improvement) and this creates a further set of output data using the same variations in capital inputs at the same time – a kind of double experiment. The experiments show that with technical change increasing output at all levels of investment on his model farm, less capital investment is needed to produce the same amount of food and rent falls.[40]

This numerical experiment can be neatly compared with an actual field trial experiment on the application of manure reported in a weekly, the *Farmers' Journal*, in 1817 by a farmer, or perhaps a landowner, from Tetbury, less than 10 miles from Ricardo's country estate:[41]

DOCUMENT 3:
Extract from a letter to the *Farmers' Journal*, May 19, 1817, p. 154

METHOD OF EMPLOYING THE AGRICULTURAL POOR

SIR,   *Tetbury, April 26, 1817*

..... Several portions of land in a large field, in equal divisions, were marked out, and all planted with potatoes of the same kind, the same soil, the cultivation the same in every respect, except that in one division no manure was put on the ground before planting with potatoes. All the other divisions were manured with different quantities of manure, progressively increasing from ten cartloads per acre up to

---

40 From this, Ricardo argued that after technical change, the original output of 340 can be produced with just three units of capital, so that if the population was already fully provided for, the final unit of capital could be withdrawn bringing net produce back to 345, but also reducing rent by 30. Thus, in this account, technical change can affect both the amount of capital (that needs to be invested in agriculture) and rent. (See O'Brien [1975, pp. 126–9] for discussion of the assumptions and possible artefacts of the numbers chosen in this numerical experiment.) This tendency of the profit rate to fall with technical change has been called "Ricardo's Paradox" – see Offer (1980).

41 *Evans and Ruffy's Farmers' Journal and Agricultural Advertiser*, more generally known as the *Farmers' Journal*, was a weekly paper, the first agricultural newspaper, and lasted from 1807 until taken over in 1832 (see Goddard, 1989). I don't know if Ricardo read the journal, but its readers were certainly familiar with his views reported in the paper and felt entitled to take issue with them. On one occasion at least: January 17, 1820, a correspondent from Bedfordshire outlined a set of hypothetical farm accounts assessing the impact of the corn laws in a letter explicitly addressed as "Questions to Mr. Ricardo".

forty, which was the highest quantity put on any division; the consequence was, that the crop without any manure, cost £6. per acre, including rent, &c. and produced 24 sacks per acre, which sold, at 5s per sack, for exactly £6.; and, therefore, left no profit whatever for the grower, or interest for his capital employed. The other divisions produced from two and a half to four sacks additional for every additional cart-load of manure (which was chiefly sweepings of the streets of a town, and cost 5s the load when on the ground); and the highest, manured at 40 load of manure to the acre, yielded 160 sacks of Potatoes per acre, which at 5s per sack is £40. or £150.per cent profit.....

A. L.

This neat example shows how Ricardo's numerical farming experiments in political economy grew up alongside and mirrored the agricultural experiments of his day. The reporting of this exemplary experiment also looks like some of Ricardo's numerical experiment accounts that run through the text, while the kind of tabular appearance that we see above in some of Ricardo's work can also be found in some of the many other farming experiments reported in various accounting formats in that same journal in the period, as we will see later.

Let me move now directly to the fifth numerical account in Ricardo's series.[42] This is the one I mentioned at the beginning of the chapter, where he adds labour to the field in units of ten men at a time, and that sent me on this quest to understand the content and style of Ricardo's strange reasoning style. For the first time, prices of corn and rent in monetary form have appeared in the example. (Note that the prices quoted here are within the normal range of corn prices for 1815-23: £4 or 80 shillings being reasonable; £5 or 100 shilling being high; 1817 was an exceptionally high year, being around 120 shillings or £6.) The addition of the monetary unit of account, which runs alongside the output account, makes this fifth accounting more difficult to follow, even when the reader has worked carefully through the previous accountings (numbers 1–3), which contain the ingredients to help make sense of this one.

The rationale or motivation for this next accounting (Document 4) is not so clearly given as for the earlier examples. As a final footnote to Ricardo's chapter "On Rent", it offers itself as an explanation of an otherwise cryptic statement about the nature of rent under circumstances of increasing labour input: "First, he [the landlord] obtains a greater share, and, secondly, the commodity in which he is paid is of greater value" (Ricardo, *Principles*, 1821, *Works*, I, p. 83). The accounting experiment

---

42 The fourth numerical account (1821, p. 82) is hardly developed in Ricardo's chapter but gives figures to consider alternative improvements to agriculture – those resulting from "such as the plough and the thrashing machine, economy in the use of horses employed in husbandry, and a better knowledge of the veterinary art, are of this nature." (1821, p. 82). These involve capital inputs that save labour directly rather by altering the fertility of the land.

is designed to make sense of this, and, as we can see (below), Ricardo assumes that with successive doses of extra labour, as with extra doses of capital investment, output will increase but at a declining rate, and so rent increases in terms of quarters of grain as labourers are added. But in each round of adding labourers, the price of a quarter of grain also rises (recall from above: the labour theory of value of the classical economists argues that as more labour is required to produce an equivalent amount of corn, the value of the corn must rise). So landlords get a double benefit: they get more grain (as rent) and the value of each quarter rises, which explains the cryptic comment above. This accounting also unravels one of Ricardo's apparently paradoxical statements earlier: "Corn is not high because a rent is paid, but a rent is paid because corn is high" (1821, p. 74). This statement may seem opaque, but its causal structure is clear to anyone who has worked carefully through the numerical accountings. Once again, because of its importance, I provide the full text for this accounting:

DOCUMENT 4:

Ricardo's Accounting 5*: From his Chapter II: On Rent, *Principles*, 1821, *Works*, I, pp. 83–4 footnote

To make this obvious, and to show the degrees in which corn and money rent will vary, let us suppose that the labour of ten men will, on land of a certain quality, obtain 180 quarters of wheat, and its value to be £4 per quarter, or £720; and that the labour of ten additional men will, on the same or any other land, produce only 170 quarters in addition; wheat would rise from £4 to £4 4s. 8d. for 170: 180: : £4: £4 4s. 8d; or, as in the production of 170 quarters, the labour of 10 men is necessary in one case, and only of 9.44 in the other, the rise would be as 9.44 to 10, or as £4 to £4 4s. 8d. If 10 men be further employed, and the return be

$$160, \quad \text{the price will rise to £4 10 \quad 0}$$

$$150, \quad . \quad . \quad . \quad . \quad . \quad . \quad 4 \ 16 \quad 0$$

$$140, \quad . \quad . \quad . \quad . \quad . \quad . \quad 5 \ \ 2 \ 10$$

Now, if no rent was paid for the land which yielded 180 quarters, when corn was at £4 per quarter, the value of 10 quarters would be paid as rent when only 170 could be procured, which at £4 4s. 8d. would be £42 7s. 6d.

20 quarters when 160 were produced, which at £4 10 0 would be £ 90 0 0

30 quarters . . . . . 150 . . . . 4 16 0 . . . . 144 0 0

40 quarters . . . . . 140 . . . . 5 2 10 . . . . 205 13 4

Corn rent would increase in the proportion of	$\begin{bmatrix} 100 \\ 200 \\ 300 \\ 400 \end{bmatrix}$	and money rent in the proportion of	$\begin{bmatrix} 100 \\ 212 \\ 340 \\ 485 \end{bmatrix}$

---

*This accounting 5 might be somewhat easier to follow as reformatted here. Holding L (land) quality and K (capital) constant and increasing Lb (labour) inputs (assuming declining output with successive units of labour), the accounting is:

L Qlty	Lb	O'put Qtrs	Price per Qtr	Rent Qtrs	Money	Money Index
1	10	180	£4	0	0	0
1	+10	+170	£4.4.8	10	£42.7.6	100
1	+10	+160	£4.10.0	20	£90.0.0	212
1	+10	+150	£4.16.0	30	£144.0.0	340
1	+10	+140	£5.2.10	40	£205.13.4	485

This accounting in Document 4 starts off relegated to a footnote, and so looks as if it is a minor point. And in the context of the other accounts earlier in the chapter, the addition of more labourers to the field can be understood as another solution to the population/food problem. But the example soon comes to form the basis for two further extensions to the accounts that move Ricardo to his laws of distribution.

The first part of this move towards the laws of distribution is in the chapter "On Wages", where Ricardo extends the numerical account of adding men to the field as in Accounting 5, to explore the effect on wages of the increase in the price of corn as more labour is used on the same land in his Accounting 6. In the second development, in the chapter "On Profits", Ricardo explores the effect on farmers' profits of increasing labour input. In this numerical Accounting 7 (Figure 2.2, below), Ricardo first repeats his numbers of the effect of increasing labour input on wages and price of corn (as in his Accounting 6), and then explores the consequent effect of all these things working together on the farmer's profits and on the landlord's rent.[43] In other words, Ricardo adds in two more ingredients of the model farm accounts: the effects of increasing labour usage on wages and profits. This enables him to use this numerical accounting in a demonstration of how the whole product is shared between the three classes: farmer, landlord, and labourers. Because of its importance once again, I provide here Ricardo's full accounting statement, reproduced from the definitive Sraffa edition (as Figure 2.2).

This final numerical account is extremely important. It is the place where we can see the model farm fully built, and we can see how it constitutes the medium in which his arguments about distribution – and his laws of distribution – emerge and are demonstrated in full.[44] The accounting experiments with the model farm show that as more labour is employed and food output grows, profits decline and

---

43 Reich (1980) attempts to analyse how far the share of rent rose during Ricardo's life and to look at the empirical basis for Ricardo's arguments about rent in corn and rent in money. I merely note here that Ricardo assumes that wages consist of a corn amount and a money wage amount and uses numbers that are close to the prices of corn and money wages paid in his time.

44 See O'Brien (1975) on interpretations, and Barkai (1959) on consistency in the example.

When Wheat is at

$$\begin{matrix} £. & s. & d. \\ 4 & 4 & 8 \\ 4 & 10 & 0 \\ 4 & 16 & 0 \\ 5 & 2 & 10 \end{matrix} \right\} \text{ wages would be } \left\{ \begin{matrix} £. & s. & d.- \\ 24 & 14 & 0 \\ 25 & 10 & 0 \\ 26 & 8 & 0 \\ 27 & 8 & 6 \end{matrix}$$

Now, of the unvarying fund of 720*l.* to be distributed between labourers and farmers,

When the price of Wheat is at

$$\begin{matrix} £. & s. & d. \\ 4 & 0 & 0 \\ 4 & 4 & 8 \\ 4 & 10 & 0 \\ 4 & 16 & 0 \\ 5 & 2 & 10 \end{matrix} \right\} \begin{array}{l} \text{the labourers}^2 \\ \text{will receive} \end{array} \left\{ \begin{matrix} £. & s. \\ 240 & 0 \\ 247 & 0 \\ 255 & 0 \\ 264 & 0 \\ 274 & 5 \end{matrix} \right\} \begin{array}{l} \text{the farmer} \\ \text{will receive} \end{array} \left\{ \begin{matrix} £. & s. & d. \\ 480 & 0 & 0 \\ 473 & 0 & 0 \\ 465 & 0 & 0 \\ 456 & 0 & 0 \\ 455^3 & 15 & * \end{matrix}$$

* The 180 quarters of corn would be divided in the following proportions between landlords, farmers, and labourers, with the above-named variations in the value of corn.

Price per qr. £. s. d.	Rent. In Wheat.	Profit. In Wheat.	Wages. In Wheat.	Total.
4 0 0	None.	120 qrs.	60 qrs.	
4 4 8	10 qrs.	111.7	58.3	
4 10 0	20	103.4	56.6	180
4 16 0	30	95	55	
5 2 10	40	86.7	53.3	

and, under the same circumstances, money rent, wages, and profit, would be as follows:

Price per qr. £. s. d.	Rent. £. s. d.	Profit. £. s. d.	Wages. £. s. d.	Total. £. s. d.
4 0 0	None.	480 0 0	240 0 0	720 0 0
4 4 8	42 7 6	473 0 0	247 0 0	762 7 6
4 10 0	90 0 0	465 0 0	255 0 0	810 0 0
4 16 0	144 0 0	456 0 0	264 0 0	864 0 0
5 2 10	205 13 4	445 15 0	274 5 0	925 13 4

Figure 2.2. Ricardo's Model Farm Showing His Laws of Distribution.

Source: Piero Sraffa: *The Works and Correspondence of David Ricardo*. Edited with the collaboration of M. H. Dobb, 1951–73, Cambridge: Cambridge University Press for The Royal Economic Society, Vol. I: *The Principles of Political Economy and Taxation, 1821*, from p. 116. Reproduced by permission of Liberty Fund Inc. on behalf of The Royal Economic Society.

rents take up their share while real wages remain constant. These distributional outcomes are each consistent with Ricardo's previous findings with his separate accountings, but the effect of combining these ingredients is not easily predictable. And it is the combination that 'determines' the laws of distribution, the task he had set himself out to solve in his Preface. Using these numerical accountings integrated into a model farm, he had succeeded far more effectively than with his earlier 1815 table in deriving results about a complex system of relations.

Finally comes the unexpected 'punchline' to these laws of distribution: Ricardo continues his numerical experiment to discover that if more and more men keep being added to the field, there comes a point where the whole of the distribution, beyond the amount that goes to labourers as a subsistence wage, goes only to the landlord (£2880 in rent or 144 quarters of grain) while the farmers' profits fall to zero. And since profits must equalize at the lowest rate set in agriculture, this sets a base level of zero profits for the economy as a whole. This would mean no further capital investment in the economy and so no growth. While this state of stagnation had been envisaged and feared by classical economists, it was Ricardo's model farm that succeeded in demonstrating how it might happen.

Whereas Malthus worried about population growth because of the vice and misery that accompanied it, for Ricardo the more serious danger was that, in the absence of any technical change, as more and more of the population were employed in farming, profits would fall so far that there would be no investment, and so stagnation in the economy. For both Malthus and Ricardo, these outcomes were tied up with their numerical reasonings. For Malthus, those outcomes *came from* his proposed *numerical laws of population* (that population grew geometrically, and food supply arithmetically). For Ricardo, it was the other way around: *the laws of distribution* and their surprising effects *were discovered from his reasoning with his numerical accountings*, that is, *his laws emerged from reasoning with his model farm.*

Not all Ricardo's contemporaries appreciated the innovative way in which he argued with his model farm. Ricardo reported that the premier French economist of the day, Jean-Baptiste Say, had complained that he (Ricardo that is) "had made demands too great on the continued exercise of thought on the part of my reader, and had not sufficiently relieved him or assisted him by a few occasional examples, and illustrations, in support of my theory."[45] Perhaps the problem was that some readers of that day did not realise that they were being given helpful examples in these numerical chains, while to some current readers, it is the particular examples, such as adding many more labourers to fields, that seem a little odd.

In the broad context of the overall argument in Ricardo's *Principles*, this example of adding labourers to the same fields initially looks as if he was just covering the case for completeness of his argument – an artificial, hypothetical case. But when he continues with this accounting, and uses it as the basis for his account

---

45 Letter from Ricardo to Trower describing Say's response; *Works*, Vol. VII, p. 178.

of distribution among the three economic classes defined in classical economics – landlords, farmers/capitalists, and labourers – we become aware that it is a very important case indeed. Although the example does not seem to fit into the traditional range of agricultural experiment and agricultural improvements (of adding manure or of introducing new adding machinery), it turns out that this example, of adding more and more men to a field, is not at all a hypothetical case but rather an actual proposal of Ricardo's day. Adding labourers to fields was tried by a number of experimenting farmers during this period because of a contemporary policy debate on 'spade husbandry', a debate that spoke directly to the fundamental problems that Ricardo was dealing with in political economy. This combination of policy and scientific interest meant that this example would not only make sense to his contemporaries but also made it the relevant case for exploring those issues of distribution that interested him.

3.ii The Spade-Husbandry Debate

The 'spade husbandry' debate took place between about 1816 and the mid-1820s, just the time that Ricardo was writing his *Principles*.[46] This debate, over the productivity effects of employing large numbers of labourers in agriculture engaged both with the issues raised in the experimental farming of the day about the productivity of different forms of agriculture, and with contemporary worries about the condition of the labouring classes. On the former point about productivity: spade husbandry was a labour-intensive kind of cultivation, a generic technology rather than any one particular technique. Proponents argued that employing labour in spade husbandry would increase yields per acre so much that product prices could fall *and* labour could be paid more. It might be understood as something like the agricultural sector equivalent of Adam Smith's well accepted, but still somehow magical recipe for manufacturing epitomised in the pin factory, in which the productivity gains from the division of labour were so great that employing more labourers would lead to a more than proportional increase in output, spreading wealth through the nations.[47] Opponents argued that increased labour usage must increase labour costs and therefore prices, despite a possible rise in yield per acre. So, in an immediate sense, the efficacy of spade husbandry was an open question of the day – open to argument and to experimental test. But for Ricardo's *Principles*, the spade-husbandry solution – of adding more men

---

46 Discussions about spade husbandry pre-, and postdate this particular period of intense debate, and are associated with both radical reformers' or utopianists' and paternalists' solutions to poverty in the middle nineteenth century (see Chase, 1988). Archer (1997) argues that the provision of allotments (spade-husbandry small plots) was associated with periods of rural unrest from Ricardo's period through until the 1840s; Moselle (1995) discusses the profitability of such small-scale farming; while others consider settlements such as the Chartist land colonies as a solution to urban poverty (see Armytage, 1958).

47 West (1815, pp. 24–5), writing about rent just before the debate really got going in the weekly papers, suggested indeed something like this analogy.

to the fields – was precisely the solution that, according to Ricardo's account (in Accounting 7), had the power to reduce profits and so capital investment to zero. Stagnation – the most dreaded worry of classical political economists and the most notable prediction – would necessarily follow.

Yet the real problems had also to be taken seriously. There was a particularly high level of 'distress' caused by a lack of employment in the late 1810s, due to the sudden fall in prices of arable crops that induced farmers to lay off labourers, and this in turn added to the burdens on the parish-based poor law supporting unemployed labourers. And remember that it was the parish, via its landowners, that held the financial and moral responsibility for looking after the poor and destitute, a matter that could certainly not be ignored by a landowner such as Ricardo whose several country estates employed many farm labourers and in a period in which the new industrial opportunities for employment in factories were still in their infancy. Ricardo's own country parish saw a considerable increase in the number of poor supported by the parish in these years. These were the short-run and immediate problems for each farmer, for each labourer and for every parish, that is, for the local political economy. The spade-husbandry debate addressed both productivity and poverty issues. Proponents of spade husbandry claimed that their techniques increased yields and increased labour employment, and so reduced expenditures on the poor, thus potentially killing not two, but three, birds with one stone.

Spade husbandry appeared to offer landowners the possibility of providing profitable (to the landowner) employment to local unemployed labourers as an alternative to supporting those same people via the local poor law. For a visionary utopian scheme, there was Robert Owen's 1819 proposal, discussed in Parliament, for a model community using spade husbandry as part of a gardening utopia.[48] A capitalistic agriculture alternative was found in Sir John Sinclair's proposal in 1819 to set up a joint stock company for a big investment in spade husbandry on marginal land.[49] This widely publicized scheme was designed to put large amounts of the unemployed labouring poor to work, but also to be profit making, and so be attractive to potential investors.

Judging by the *Farmers' Journal*, spade husbandry was subject to many actual experiments as well as to these two projected schemes of Owen and Sinclair. In this connection, recall that Mr. A. L.'s manure experiment of 1817 (reported in Document 3) appeared under the title "Method of Employing the Agricultural Poor": it employed considerably more labour, as well as increasing output, and the writer added a note linking his letter to the spade husbandry debate. On April 5, 1819 (front page, and p. 106), Mr. William Falla of Gateshead reported a number of experiments, including one in which he extrapolates from his real experiments to provide calculations for an extremely labour-intensive version of spade husbandry

---

48 See for example, Ricardo's speech on the plan, *Works V*, pp. 30–5.

49 This scheme was to cultivate 10,000 acres of land close to London by spade husbandry. See *The London and Provincial Sunday Gazette and Political Inquisitor*, February 7, 1819.

For breast-ploughing and burning, first time, I pay 10s. per acre.
For breast-ploughing, second time...................... 5s. per acre.

Making total   15s. per acre.

At these prices my labourers have earned, this season, 25s. weekly; an adequate compensation, when wages are at 9s. per week, generally.

Horse Ploughing.				*Manual Labour.*			
1st time, proverbially *brushing*, man, boy, and five horses, three quarters an per acre day, at 18s. per day the team.........	£1	2	6	1st time, breast-ploughing, &c....................	£0	10	0
2d time, ploughing in the seed, ditto	1	2	6	2nd time, ditto........... One man 2s., boy 1s., two horses 6s. ...... 9s.	0	5	0
Two men to tread the ground and level the land, 1s. 6d. each, and drink 6d. per acre..............	0	5	4	Two horses to drag 6s., boy 1s. .... 7s.			
Extra seed, half a bushel..	0	4	0	16s.			
				Perform three acres per day, say one third expence per acre	0	5	4
	£2	14	4		£1	0	4
				Saving of expence..........	1	14	0
					£2	14	4

I have not included water furrowing, they are so near alike in both ways.

Impressed with these advantages, I trust it will not appear too *enlightened* to adhere to a system which gives, for a period of three months, to the labourer nearly treble wages, and affords so self-evident a saving to myself. This I trust may account for any roughness which has appeared in my remarks, which only *frets* the smooth tribe, who have, without knowledge, opposed a practice pregnant with benefits to the community at large.   I am, Sir, your obedient servant,   A. RASP.

Figure 2.3. Newspaper Report of a Farming Experiment with Spade Husbandry.

Source: *Farmers' Journal*, November 6, 1820, p. 354, extract from letter entitled: "On Cultivation, Chiefly by Manual Labour".

involving "transplanting 232,320 plants [wheat seedlings] at 4½p per 1000" by hand![50] "A. Rasp," a farmer from Gloucestershire, reported (see Figure 2.3) on the

50 *Farmers' Journal*, January 10, 1820 (front page), "C. W. P. in Gainsborough" provides calculations from hypothetical spade husbandry of the "garden" type. On June 26, 1820 in the same journal (again on the front page), an anonymous "Cultivator" of Hampshire reports his actual experiment on the use of spade labour in potato cultivation.

advantages of manual over horse ploughing in working the soil, providing exact details of his cultivation methods for beans and the reasons he uses them; he also details the cost to himself and the good return in wages to the labourer from his cultivation experiment, neatly reported in parallel columns.[51]

By contrast, Mr. J. L. James, writing on a field version of spade husbandry, reported his observations in a way that substitutes lyric qualities for the prosaic details and serious accounting usually provided in these reports:

DOCUMENT 5:

Extract from a letter to the *Farmers' Journal*, May 10, 1819 (front page)

ON SPADE HUSBANDRY

SIR,   *London, April 30, 1819*

...... having read in your Journal Mr Crowther's letter on Spade Husbandry, with his invitation to all persons to witness its method and produce, I turned my horse with the intention of merely riding through his farm .... I was so struck with the number of hands I saw bespangled over its fields, as it were like stars in the sky, that I resolved on a more minute examination. ......

I then saw a field, which this spring had been breast ploughed (what we call drenchering,) and burnt, and a number of men were then employed in breast-ploughing in the barley, at 12s per acre, and it certainly left the land lighter and more likely to produce a great crop than if it had been ploughed with horses: the men I found could earn, some 10s., some 12s., and some 15s. weekly according as they were more or less expert hands. We then inspected several fields, about fifty or sixty acres of wheat, which it appeared had not been ploughed but twice in eight years, and it certainly had a most promising appearance. ... The whole parish seemed like a large machine, impelled by the prime mover, and all its subordinate parts performing their necessary offices with the regularity of wheels and pinions. .....

J. L. James

The spade husbandry debate petered out in the early 1820s, and judging from the discussion in the *Farmers' Journal*, it remained an open question whether, or perhaps under what local conditions, and for what crops, spade husbandry would show increasing yields (at least over some range) as labour input rose, or, as in Ricardo's numerical example, decreasing yields. Ricardo remained committed to the classical economic view that technical change was always labour saving (as we

---

51 There appear to be some errors in the accounting, but the general point is made.

learnt earlier), but he remained interested in the productivity claims of spade husbandry. He expressed himself open to the evidence in his speech on "Mr. Owen's Plan" in Parliament in 1819, and he discussed the merits of the method in his notes on Malthus text in 1820, and in reporting Mill's views in 1821[52]:

> Mill does not shew the effect that would be produced by spade husbandry, but the effect that would follow from an increasing people, which should constantly require an additional proportion of the population to be employed in husbandry. He would recommend spade husbandry, if it could be shewn that the capital and labour employed in it, yielded more than an equal capital and the same quantity of labour in plough or machinery husbandry. (Ricardo, *Works, IX*, p. 56)

The point here is not the validity of the productivity claims, but rather that we have found, in these spade husbandry experimental reports, an obvious contemporary reference point – and one known to Ricardo – for his case of adding labour to fields, as well as many examples of the accounting format. And it is also particularly notable that we find in this farming literature not only the reports of real agricultural experiments on this question, but also accounting for the kind of hypothetical farming or scenario calculations that Ricardo himself used in his model farming. The most obvious difference in these agricultural accountings compared to Ricardo's numerical accounting experiments are that the categories of rent and profit are not always separated out. In the contributions to the *Farmers' Journal* there tend to be only two factors: labourers and the farmer, suggesting perhaps that the contributors were yeoman farmers. In contrast, in the earlier 1814 *Lords Report Evidence* about the corn laws, witnesses were usually either tenant farmers or landlords' agents and generally separated out capital returns from rents in their accounts quite carefully. The second difference is that contributors to the debate, farmers or landowners, provided a commercial analysis showing their own profitability, not a general analysis of political economy in order to discern the law of distribution of the classical system as Ricardo was striving to do with his model farm.

4. Ricardo's Model Farm and Model Farming

According to Alan Bennett's play *The Madness of King George* (1995), both farming and the adjective 'model' were in fashionable use in Ricardo's time. The term 'model farm' actually came into circulation only somewhat later; nevertheless, I feel no qualms in using it for the numerical accountings that Ricardo created

---

52 Ricardo confessed he did not agree on the general principles of Owen's plan but did think it would be a good idea to ascertain the facts of the method (*Works, V*, p. 31 Speech in Parliament, December 16, 1819 on "Mr. Owen's Plan"). On Malthus, see *Works, II*, pp. 38–9.

and 'model farming' for the way he used them to understand the economic system.[53]

4.i Three Model Farms in One

Ricardo developed his model farm accounts to investigate particular questions about the nature of rent and the problems caused by population growth, and to determine the laws of distribution. To answer these questions, he created a set of accounts for an imaginary farm, but not in one move. Rather, as this history has shown, these accountings were built up step by step through his successive chapters, so that the model farm and its behaviour emerged only gradually as different possibilities were posed and answered. The model farm was not a simplified version of a real farm, for the numbers and their relations did not come, number by number, from a particular set of farm accounts. Nor can we describe his set of numbers as an abstract version of such a farm – they seem all too concrete. Nor were his numerical accounts deduced directly from the laws of the classical system, though they obeyed them. Rather, the model farm he developed was an independently conceived object, using typical numbers from the agriculture of his day and with the elements constructed to behave according to his ideas about the different elements involved. To use the language of Chapter 1, he formalized his ideas and knowledge – in the sense of giving form to them and making them rule bound, in the model farm accounts. His model farm accounts were the places where both specific agricultural facts and his concepts and ideas about rents, profits, and so forth were brought together and integrated with the laws of political economy of his school.

But there is something very unusual about Ricardo's model farm. Of course it was only a pen-and-paper object, but *it represents and functions as a model in three different senses at the same time*, as:

- A model farm that worked according to the various definitions, concepts, and laws of political economy in his *Principles*,
- A model of real individual farms in terms of contemporary numbers and particular experiences, and
- A model for the whole farming sector since the effects he worked through were those that would be evidenced at the aggregate economy level, not the individual farm level.

---

53 The film version of Alan Bennett's play (1995) finishes with "model" almost as a refrain. Though this was indeed the period when model farm buildings were being built (see Martins, 1980) and the term "experimental farm" was occasionally used, the term "model farm" as a vehicle for the diffusion of best practice farming (not just buildings) became widespread only in the mid-nineteenth century (as a search of the journals reveals).

Let me justify these claims and explore the elements that enter into Ricardo's model farm so that we can understand more clearly how there is only one model farm, but it can represent and function in all three of these domains.

4.ii A Model Farm that Worked According to Ricardo's Economic Ideas

The first thing to stress is that the model farm Ricardo created through his numerical accounts is not quite what historians of economics have called "Ricardo's corn model" to refer to the general economic relationships of the system that Ricardo posited. Rather the model being discussed here is Ricardo's numerical model farm, a pen-and-paper object, whose construction and behaviour depend on the incorporation of a number of Ricardo's definitions, concepts, and assumptions of classical political economy and his views of how these were related together. Ricardo's model farm represents the elements of that system of political economy, and therefore should behave according to that system, but it is *not* itself the system of those relations. It has a separate existence that allows it to function autonomously.[54]

The main definitions, concepts, and assumptions that go into Ricardo's numerical farm model – as far as they are reported in this chapter and in the order they came into the accounts – can be listed as follows:[55]

DOCUMENT 6:
Elements of the Classical System Used in Ricardo's Model Farm

(a) Categories of the classical system: three economic classes: landowners, capital holders (farmers) and labourers.
(b) Problem addressed: population growth and the various suggested solutions for increasing food output.
(c) Definition of rent as the return to landowner of the productive powers of the soil.
(d) Law of profit rates to equalize.
(e) Assumption that the profit rate is determined on the least productive land.
(f) Determination of rent as the difference in net produce (after costs) between the most compared to the lesser, and to the least, productive land.

---

54 See Morgan and Morrison (1999, chapter 2).
55 This list includes all the ones needed for the model farm accountings, but they were not always fully listed each time in the discussion of the accounts in Section 3 above. Nor have I covered all of Ricardo's accounts, so the list above is not necessarily exhaustive, but is sufficient for the accounts discussed in this chapter.

(g) Law of declining returns to increases in capital and labour inputs in agriculture.

(h) Assumption that all technical improvements are labour saving, so productivity is defined in terms of labour required.

(i) Core assumption of classical economics: the "labour theory of value". Labour determines the value of a good; if less labour is needed to produce the good, the value of the good is lower and if more is needed, there is a higher value of the good. (With (h) above, the *ceteris paribus* consequence of technical improvements is a fall in the value of the product because less labour is needed.)

(j) Convention that wages consist of a monetary amount and a corn amount.

(k) Distribution of the product is shared three ways according to the 'classes' of the classical system, but the distribution itself is determined by the various definitions, assumptions and laws above.

(l) Tendency law of the profit rate to fall.

If we were to go back into Ricardo's numerical accountings, we would find that all these elements of the classical system (definitions, concepts, assumptions, and laws) were gradually embedded into the workings of the model farm as the sequence of accountings built up. For example, at critical points, as we have seen, the labour theory of value dictated the way prices changed in response to changes in output due to technical change or to additions of labour. And we have also seen how rent was not treated symmetrically with profit and wages: land was not a factor of production whose costs must be covered; rather, rent arose only due to a shortage of land of the best quality. This last point (item f in the list) was the most distinctive element of Ricardo's particular version of classical economics. Ricardo's final account for his model farm, Accounting 7, reproduced in Figure 2.2, is consistent with the full list of elements, and the numerical experiments worked according to the behavioural and accounting assumptions of this list. But there was no one element in that list that determined how those model farm accounts were structured, nor could the numerical farm model be deduced from them for there is no one-for-one equivalence between the elements of the model farm accounts and the set of conceptual elements in that list. The model farm is a separate object in which each of those conceptual elements has found representation. Of course, as we have seen, these were not the only things that might be found embedded in the model farm accountings.

4.iii A Model of an Individual Farm in the Period

At this point we might remember where we started the chapter – namely with the criticism by some that Ricardo is thought to be responsible for making arguments using abstract examples that seem remote from the actual economy of his time.

This is clearly not tenable in respect of his work in this area, for there are three ways in which we have seen that Ricardo's model farm accountings held strong empirical content and so can be taken as a model of actual or typical farms of his day.

First, the numbers used for the numerical cases. Ricardo liked to pretend that the numbers he dealt with in his text bore little relation to the numbers of his economy in order to claim generality for his resulting 'principles':

> In all these calculations I have been desirous only to elucidate the principle, and it is scarcely necessary to observe that my whole basis is assumed at random, and merely for the purpose of exemplification. The results, though different in degree, would have been the same in principle, however accurately I might have set out in stating the difference in the number of labourers necessary to obtain the successive quantities of corn required by an increasing population, the quantity consumed by the labourer's family etc., etc. (Ricardo, *Principles*, 1821, *Works, I*, p. 121)

However, as I have already suggested, many of his numbers were *not* randomly chosen – the price of corn, the level of wages, and so forth were all ones within the range of figures in typical farm experience of the period.

A second aspect of the model farm's attachment to his world came in the *content* and *form* of Ricardo's numerical accountings compared to the experimental farming reports of the time. We have already discussed the characteristics of the experimental farming of this period, when big landowners ran experimental farms and practical farmers undertook experiments on their own fields to determine the best crop rotations, the best forms of manure, and the best methods of cultivation. We can see how these were paralleled in Ricardo's sequence of accountings, which suggested taking more land into cultivation (via enclosure and extending arable cultivation); by increased capital investment; and by innovations in agriculture such as crop rotation, manuring – even by spade husbandry. His model farming experiments were all closely related to the actual farming experiments of his period. We have also seen how Ricardo's numerical accountings looked very much like the reports of these farm experiments. Sometimes, as in the manure experiment reported by Mr. A. L. from Tetbury, these reports were in running text; other times, as in Mr. Rasp's accounts for his spade husbandry experiment, they were tabulated into a set of accounts detailing physical outcomes and the profit to be expected, or that had been made, from their experimental interventions. Similar accounts were typically offered as evidence in official reports or in agricultural surveys where the experiments were not controlled field trials but reports of the normal variations from crop rotations – a kind of continuing natural experimental activity of many farmers of the day.[56] These ways of reporting agricultural activities – by laying out

---

56 As we know, Ricardo was certainly familiar with these reports that figure in the "Evidence" attached to the House of Lords' 1814 report into the corn laws. Such kinds of reports are littered through the county studies for the Board of Agriculture of Ricardo's day.

numerical accounts – suggest another way in which Ricardo's numerical examples can be seen as being well attached to his world. In this parallel, Ricardo's farming accounts can be understood as experimental farming reports for a 'model' farm with some very special economic features and using hypothetical economic science experiments, not physical agricultural experiments.

Third, Ricardo's numerical examples chosen for his model farming, and the motivation for each, could all be related to lively discussions in political economy of the day. As we have seen, population growth not only formed one of the primary problems for political economists, but was also one of the main items of contention in broader intellectual circles. The newly established census of population, begun in 1801 (and continuing at 10-year intervals) had seemed to confirm Malthus' worries, and the various aspects of increased population were widely understood to provide serious policy problems in the provision of adequate food supply, and employment and poverty relief for the growing numbers of labourers. For Ricardo in his arguments with Malthus, the important contemporary economic issues had been the effects of population growth on wages and economic growth, and the dynamic relationship between wages and the well-being of labourers. In this context, Ricardo's model farm experiments showed him that whereas technical change in agriculture might, in the short run, increase food output in line with population growth, the increased workforce effect of population growth remained the longer-run problem. This was the fundamental reason why Ricardo used the example of adding more men to fields throughout his discussion of distribution issues, for it was this numerical experiment that most effectively captured the whole set of economic concerns of the day. That it was also the case in his model farming which crystallized the dismal predictions of classical political economists – because it demonstrated a process that drove profits to zero – was an unexpected and surprising outcome.

4.iv A Model Farm for the Whole Agricultural Sector

The third way in which the model farm functioned for Ricardo was as a version of the agricultural economy as a whole. How do we know this? An individual farmer who sets about experimenting with manure will gain a return in additional output, but an individual farmer adding labourers to a field will hardly alter the price of corn, for that is determined by all the farms together in the aggregate. But in Ricardo's example, the price of corn does alter, so that clearly Ricardo's farm accounts functioned not only as a model of the individual farm, but as a model of the agricultural sector as a whole. This has not gone unnoticed. Blaug argues that in Ricardo political economy, "the whole economy is a giant farm, distributing its product among landlord, tenant farmer, and hired laborer" (Blaug, 1968, p. 508). O'Brien refers to this as "Ricardo's 'collectivization' – the treatment of the agricultural sector as one giant farm" (O'Brien, 1975, p. 130). An alternative view, suggested by Patten (1893), is to think of Ricardo taking an individual farm, farmer, labourer, and landlord to represent the agricultural experience of typical landlords, labourers, and so forth, and thus representative of the general whole. Either as the typical farm that stands in for the whole, or as the giant aggregate farm, Ricardo's model farm accounts thus do double duty as representing both the individual case and the aggregate.

However, this double duty does create certain problems of interpretation, and O'Brien even refers to this aggregation as a kind of 'trick' (O'Brien, 1975, p. 123). For example, in the reproduced Accounting 7 (Figure 2.2), the numbers in the top part of the table relate back to the variation in Accounting 5 (Document 4), in which we are thinking about individual farms with outputs varying along with increasing doses of labour inputs, while the bottom half of the table is for just one of those lines: a farm using one set of labourers harvesting 180 quarters of grain. Yet, as Barkai noted, Ricardo moved from this latter "pattern of the distributional shares of the product for a single dose only" to attribute it "to the *economic system as a whole*" (Barkai, 1966, pp. 287–88).[57] This raises a question as to whether the revealed laws of distribution for that specified individual farm carry over to those farms with other doses of labourer, and so raises doubts about the system as a whole. While the pattern may transfer across, the levels or proportions may be different. These are the kinds of interpretation difficulties that have worried the few scholars who have wrestled with these numerical pieces in order to produce a consistent version of Ricardo's system.

5. Model-Making: Creating New Recipes

5.i Ingredients

Ricardo's model farm was created out of conceptual elements and out of empirical elements. These ranged from conventional items (such as definitions and laws, along with numbers from farming), but also less obvious empirical elements (such as the experimental farming tradition). Marcel Boumans (1999) gives an account of this mode of model-making as a process akin to developing a new recipe. He suggested that we think of all these conceptual and empirical elements as ingredients that have to be integrated together to form a model, much like the ingredients of a new kind of cake have to be chosen and then mixed together. But though the form of Ricardo's numerical accounts mimicked those of experimental farming reports, the model farm that Ricardo created did not follow the existing recipe of real farming accounts; instead, his farm was conceived as a new recipe – a new model in economic science, where the ingredients of his accountings operated according to the laws, concepts, and definitions of that science.

57 See also Barkai (1959).

By virtue of its clever construction involving elements of both, Ricardo's model farm mediated between his ideas about how the economy worked and the practical economic realities.[58] Morgan and Morrison (1999, chapter 2) suggest that the possibilities for models to function autonomously in science in this way, and so enable scientists to investigate both their theories and the world, depend on a certain independence of the elements used in their construction. Boumans' recipe analogy shows us in what sense these elements are independent – namely as a list of separate ingredients: the small world in Ricardo's model was made up from some ingredients that relied on empirical information and others that came from the fundamental laws of classical political economy.

Boumans' recipe analogy also nicely indicates how model-making involves a degree of flexibility. A model, like a recipe, needs to be open in the sense that it can incorporate some variations in the set of ingredients. We see how this fits Ricardo's work – not only did the numerical accountings define a model farm in which a combination of conceptual elements were fitted together, but they were also fitted together in such a way that would be flexible to the different ideas about how an increased population might be supported according to contemporary experience of agricultural change. That flexibility to different elements, to suggested questions and so solutions, was a feature of his accounting that allowed them to be extended to answer a number of questions about the world depicted in the model – both as individual farm and as aggregate farm.

But there are limits here. A recipe in which all the ingredients change, or are put together in a very different way, is no longer recognisable as the same recipe and there is no reason why such a new recipe should give us anything edible or a new model be useful or fruitful. A model that is completely flexible and open to all questions and uses might prove doubtful in providing definitive outcomes, as might one in which the elements are not sufficiently integrated together. A degree of constraint in model design would seem to be a necessity. Ricardo's model farm was supple enough to be used to discuss a range of eventualities – both theoretical and empirical – as we have seen in the series of accountings. But it was also constrained by its elements in ways that meant that the spade-husbandry case – in its strongest claims – was problematic for his model farm.

The strong case for spade husbandry envisaged that the introduction of more labourers would increase yields per acre and per labourer, for example, through different kinds of ploughing (substituting labour and light ploughs for heavier horse-plough teams), more hoeing, and hand transplanting of seedlings, to such a degree that more labourers could be profitably employed, and that their wages could be kept high. Such a claim for labour working in agriculture was incompatible with other ingredients of Ricardo's model farm, for he assumed declining yields per labourer as labour input was increased and that all technical changes were labour saving.

58 See Wise (1993) for a discussion of mediating technologies in other contemporary sciences.

Such assumptions were compatible only with the weaker claims of spade husbandry, namely of increasing yields per acre, but not per labourer (as in his accountings 5–7), and so prices of corn rose as this happened because of the labour theory of value. Thus the strong productivity claims of spade husbandry could not be incorporated into the behaviour of Ricardo's model farm – unless of course the model farm were to be reconstructed in some of its fundamental ingredients. He did not do so. Even though spade husbandry might have provided the real economy solution to the economic problem that worried him, such a solution could not be easily incorporated into his model for some of the less flexible elements of the recipe forbade it.

5.ii Fitting Things Together: Integration and Reasoning Possibilities

An important insight that comes from Boumans' analysis is that integration of the elements in the model does not just happen; it has to be effected by some kind of moulding process or device that creates something whole out of the bits. In Boumans' cases, this moulding is done by the choice of mathematical formalism. In Ricardo's case, the integrating device for his model farm is an accounting convention: it is neither the accounting conventions of double entry books, nor even the simple conventional expenses and profit/loss accounts preferred by his contemporary farmers. Rather, Ricardo uses a set of more general accounting conventions to provide the integrating element in his numerical accountings, namely, that the total output must all be allocated to the economic factors, that all the items must add to the total, and that inputs and outputs must balance in both real and monetary terms. It was these principles that both moulded and held Ricardo's model farm accounts together. Such an integration is critical to the use of a model and to how productively it functions.

Words are certainly adequate to state the labour theory of value, or the definition of rent, or the role of adding manure, or even the tendency of the profit rate to fall. But what happens when you put these elements and events – and more – together? Many times, Malthus and Ricardo argued their way over the same ground as we have just covered in model farming: the ground being the likely progress in the economy towards growth or stagnation; the impact of population growth, of extending cultivation, of technical change in agriculture and their effects on wages, on rent, on profits, on investment; on the progress of the agricultural sector versus manufacturing; and on the differences between nominal and real wages. We can see, in the many written interchanges of correspondence between Ricardo and Malthus, that they found it very difficult to argue these complex cases with just words. They used the verbal methods of classical economics to reason about the problem, to sort out the *ceteris paribus* conditions, and to get their arguments to work according to their instincts. But they found themselves falling into convoluted reasoning chains, and often failed to convince each other.

Both Mathus and Ricardo sometimes used small numerical examples in their arguments with each other.[59] But such examples were developed more persuasively by Ricardo into his model farming accounts, and these then provided him a way around this problem of making convincing cases about any system involving so many elements and so many variable aspects – as any political economy that had pretensions to be about the world must do. We can recall, from earlier in this chapter. The difficulties Ricardo had in using the two-dimensional table of his *Essay* in order to see what happened when he put several variables together, where each was behaving according to its own specified economic laws. Creating the model farm in his *Principles* enabled him to overcome the dimensionality constraints of reasoning with a table for it enabled him to integrate the different conceptual elements, definitions, laws, and so forth (listed in the last section) together along with the empirical elements of agriculture that he believed important. This was not something that could be done verbally, and as he already knew, was difficult to do in a table with only two dimensions.

Ricardo used the series of pen-and-paper experiments with his model farm – model farming – not just to answer particular questions with particular outcomes and stories, nor just to show how the various individual elements of his economics fitted together but also – most importantly – to show how they worked together in all their possible variations. In the process, Ricardo's model farming moved from simple experiments with only one element of variation (ones that almost constituted thought experiments) to a multidimensional experiment in which the variation in many inputs and outputs could be shown together. Turning the elements (his ingredients) into a model farm, a farm that also acted as representative of the agricultural economy as a whole, enabled him to solve – in an interesting and innovative way, two major problems. One was the problem of how to show lots of things happening at once and the other was to show how his various ideas and assumptions work together at the same time to create a particular set of outcomes. These are things he could not have achieved just with the written text. They depended on his forming a model and reasoning with it, that is, on his model farm and in his model farming.

This reasoning relied on his model farm not just because that model formalized these ideas – gave form to his ideas, nor because it also made them behave formally – it made them rule bound (see Chapter 1). The reasoning also depended on the way the elements of that object were held together by the *integrating device of accounting*, so that the bits were forced into behaving consistently with each other. This meant that when one bit of the puzzle was changed, it had immediate

---

59 Their numerical arguments are particularly a feature of the period 1815–16, when Ricardo was working from his *Essay* to his *Principles*. These numerical examples occur again in 1820 when Ricardo is writing notes on Malthus' new *Principles* (1820). At this later stage, they both used such numerical calculations not as illustrations, but as ways of thinking and to demonstrate the results of their theorizing to each other. Malthus tended to drop these thinking tools in his published work, whereas Ricardo incorporated them.

implications that other bits must also change – the set of ingredients that went into the model were independent, but they were not all independently available for manipulation at the same time; it was only as an integrated whole that the model could be properly experimented with.

We see all this most obviously in Ricardo's final accounting (reported in Figure 2.2 in Section 3), where all the elements worked out in previous accountings are brought together to determine, and to demonstrate, how the general distribution works. Each bit of the puzzle – development of rent, increased labour input, increased prices, effect on money rent, and so forth – had been discussed in previous accountings. The final farm accounts integrated all the parts so that they worked together and enabled him to show the overall outcome in a scenario of changes in inputs, outputs, prices, rent, profits, and wages.

It is this final accounting that *reveals* Ricardo's laws of distribution – these laws of distribution dictate what happens to the share of wages, profits, and rent as changes occur in the economy. These laws of distribution are not the set of assumptions (listed in Document 6 earlier) that were built into the model farm accounts, nor are they self-evident from studying individual elements, their behaviour, or the structure of the model farm. Rather, they fall out of his model farming, out of his way of melding the evidence, relationships, and conceptual elements, together using the accounting conventions, and using the model in an experimental way. Ricardo used his model farm, and model farming as *the means to* discover how the distributional outcomes are determined. So, the laws of distribution and their determination are not illustrated by the numerical accounts, nor are they merely shown by working alongside Ricardo through his experiments with the model farm, rather they are *demonstrated* in the sense that they *deductively emerge* from the creation and use of the model farm as an integrated set of farm accounts.

Appendix 1: Numerical Argument in Ricardo's 1815 Essay

Ricardo's 1815 pamphlet known as his *Essay on Profits*, was fully titled "An Essay on The Influence of a low Price of Corn on the Profits of Stock".[60] This essay contained the first statement of Ricardo's system of political economy and his laws of distribution, but was only an important half-way stage in *the way that he argued for these laws* – a way that marked something of a departure in economic argumentation. In this 1815 essay against the corn laws, Ricardo was primarily concerned with the relation between the price of corn and profits. He discussed

---

60 See Ricardo, 1821, *Works, IV*, pp. 1–41. As with all works by Ricardo, there is a debate about this 1815 table and what it does and does not show about Ricardo's 'corn model'. See O'Brien (1975, pp. 132–5) for an analysis of the table and the extent to which other arithmetical examples could be constructed consistent with Ricardo's assumptions. Hollander (1979) discusses the table as a numerical showcase for what is known as the 'Ricardian model', referring to the more generalizable theoretical claims of the Ricardian system.

the relative distribution of returns to the landlord and the farmer (capital holder) from capital investment in agriculture and from extending agriculture onto unused or more marginal lands as a way of increasing produce to feed the rising population. His analysis, shown through numerical argument, suggested that it would be better to import cheap corn than use capital in agriculture with a declining profit rate.

The first part of his argument in the 1815 *Essay* used a running arithmetic example that was then reported using a table (reproduced here), actually an elaborate double table of hypothetical farm accounts, in which he needs to show how both rent and profits change as investment takes place. In the top half, he shows the effect of increased inputs of capital (measured in quarters of wheat) on less fertile land, or equivalently land that was further from market, so that there is a declining net product in wheat (after paying costs) on each capital input. Because of the principle that "the general profits of stock being regulated by the profits made on the least profitable employment of capital on agriculture" (1815, p. 13), the profit rate must be the same on each capital input. The excess profit over costs on the more fertile land compared to the less fertile land goes as rent. The top part of the table shows, with great elaboration, what happens to profits and rent for each section of capital input, as successive units of capital are applied and the profit rate is equalized. It needs this degree of elaboration because each time another portion of land with attendant capital input is drawn into cultivation, the numbers for profit on capital and rent change on all previous portions of land, so they all have to be shown again for each change in capital investment. This is done by showing the changing inputs of capital on the left hand side, the changing rate of profit and net output in the next two columns and then in successive columns the effect on profits and rents for all the sections of land for that capital input. This device of reporting each column separately allows him to show the process going on (in Figure 2.4).

There are three points of *economic content in the table* that we should note here that are relevant for the chapter. First, as yet, the table did not show the position of the labouring class in the distribution analysis, although his essay and letters of the period show that he was fast working out the full explanatory account of distribution that appeared intact from the first edition of his *Principles* in 1817. Second, although he argued about, and used his table to demonstrate, the effects of increased capital investment and increased cultivation of marginal land, his argument with the table purposely assumed that there was no technical change in agriculture (though again, such changes were discussed in the essay). This assumption was precisely made to point out the dangers of falling profit levels in the absence of technical changes, such changes being the main means by which capital would otherwise continue to find profitable investments. Third, his table demonstrated why he argued against the tariffs on corn: if cheaper foreign corn could be imported, there would be no need to expend cultivation and capital onto more marginal land where the profit rate would fall.

TABLE, shewing the Progress of Rent and Profit under an assumed Augmentation of Capital.

Capital estimated in quarters of wheat.	Profit per cent.	Neat produce in quarters of wheat after paying the cost of production on each capital.	Profit of 1st portion of land in quarters of wheat.	Rent of 1st portion of land in quarters of wheat.	Profit of 2d portion of land in quarters of wheat.	Rent of 2d portion of land in quarters of wheat.	Profit of 3d portion of land in quarters of wheat.	Rent of 3d portion of land in quarters of wheat.	Profit of 4th portion of land in quarters of wheat.	Rent of 4th portion of land in quarters of wheat.	Profit of 5th portion of land in quarters of wheat.	Rent of 5th portion of land in quarters of wheat.	Profit of 6th portion of land in quarters of wheat.	Rent of 6th portion of land in quarters of wheat.	Profit of 7th portion of land in quarters of wheat.	Rent of 7th portion of land in quarters of wheat.	Profit of 8th portion of land in quarters of wheat.
200	50	100	100	none.													
210	43	90	86	14	90	none.											
220	36	80	72	28	76	14	80	none.									
230	30	70	60	40	63	27	66	14	70	none.							
240	25	60	50	50	$52\frac{1}{2}$	$37\frac{1}{2}$	55	25	$57\frac{1}{2}$	$12\frac{1}{2}$	60	none.					
250	20	50	40	60	42	48	44	36	46	24	48	12	50	none.			
260	15	40	30	70	$31\frac{1}{2}$	$58\frac{1}{2}$	33	47	$34\frac{1}{2}$	$35\frac{1}{2}$	36	24	$37\frac{1}{2}$	$12\frac{1}{2}$	40	none.	
270	11	30	22	78	23	67	24	56	25.3	44.7	26.4	33.6	27.6	$22\frac{1}{2}$	27.6	12.4	29.7

	When the whole capital employed is	Whole amount of rent received by landlords in quarters of wheat.	Whole amount of profits in quarters received by owners of stock.	Profit per cent. on the whole capital.	Rent per cent. on the whole capital.	Total produce in quarters of wheat, after paying the cost of production.
1st Period	200	none.	100	50		100
2d Ditto	410	14	176	43	$3\frac{1}{2}$	190
3d Ditto	630	42	228	36	$6\frac{3}{4}$	270
4th Ditto	860	81	259	30	$9\frac{1}{2}$	340
5th Ditto	1100	125	275	25	$11\frac{1}{2}$	400
6th Ditto	1350	180	270	20	$13\frac{1}{4}$	450
7th Ditto	1610	$248\frac{1}{2}$	$241\frac{1}{2}$	15	$15\frac{1}{2}$	490
8th Ditto	1880	$314\frac{1}{2}$	$205\frac{1}{2}$	11	$16\frac{1}{2}$	520

Figure 2.4. Ricardo's Table from His 1815 Essay.

Source: David Ricardo: "The Influence of a low Price of Corn on the Profits of Stock" [1815] from Piero Sraffa: *The Works and Correspondence of David Ricardo*. Edited with the collaboration of M. H. Dobb, 1951–73, Cambridge: Cambridge University Press for The Royal Economic Society, Vol. IV: *Pamphlets and Papers, 1815–1823*, p. 17. Reproduced by permission of Liberty Fund Inc. on behalf of The Royal Economic Society.

There are three points about Ricardo's *mode of arguing* that are worth making. First, although in principle the top table events could be happening simultaneously, the bottom schedule assumes that these are sequential events, and cumulates the totals as if for successive periods. In the England–Portugal trade example mentioned at the beginning of the chapter, we can view the two situations with or without trade can either as alternative scenarios or as a change between times. In the 1815 table, it is essential that this is a time process, for Ricardo's thesis is based on the assumptions

> that no improvements take place in agriculture, and that capital and population advance in the proper proportion, so that the real wages of labour, continue uniformly the same; – so that we may know what peculiar effects are to be ascribed to the growth of capital, the increase of population, and the extension of cultivation, to the more remote, and less fertile land. (Ricardo, 1815, p. 12)

So, Ricardo is interested in the growth process and the use of increased capital inputs in solving the problem of feeding the increased population. Time would not be necessary, if each addition could be thought of as an alternative scenario, but it is necessary here in that the table reflects the classical economists' concern with feeding a growing population while at the same time worrying about the "tendency of the profit rate to fall" over time. In an economy as whole, Ricardo proposed that this profit rate is determined by agricultural profits and if profits fall to zero there, they fall everywhere, so investment ceases and stagnation follows.

Second, Ricardo shows his delight in the way the table demonstrated something strange and new in showing that increased capital input would first raise profits in quarters of wheat and then reduce it while rent and net produce both continued to rise: "This is a view of accumulation which is exceedingly curious, and has, I believe, never before been noticed" (Ricardo, 1815, p. 16). Ricardo took this finding to be an essential element of his set up, rather than an artefact of the numbers chosen in the table (on which, compare Reuten's [1999] account of Marx's numerical arguments). The point for us is that it gives a first inkling of how economists can learn things by using a set of accounts or a numerical 'model'. It is the results that seem counterintuitive or surprising that alert the economist to the fact that something new has come out of the model-making and model-using process.

Third, in the context of this chapter's discussions, we might want to note his disclaimer, footnoted before the table, that "It is scarcely necessary to observe, that the data on which this table is constructed are assumed, and are probably very far from the truth. They were fixed on as tending to illustrate the principle....." (1815, p. 15). Given his familiarity with the political economy of his day (even before he became a landowner), and the evidence of his letters, there is reason to be quite suspicious of such statements.

Acknowledgement

This chapter grew out of a paper first given to my departmental colleagues in May 2003; at the History of Economics Meeting at Duke in July 2003; at the Economic History Seminar, Oxford (November 2003); Seminar: "Knowledge and Society", Institute of Historical Research, London (December 2003); the "Histoire et Philosophie de la Mesure" Université Paris 7 (December 2003); the University of California, San Diego, Science Studies Group (January, 2004); and finally a LSE workshop on the "Facts" project (see working paper Morgan 2005) in May 2005. I am grateful for comments on all these occasions. My thanks also to Lesley Stringer, Márcia Balisciano, and especially Xavier López del Rincón Troussel for splendid research assistance; and to librarians at the University Library in Cambridge and Goldsmiths Library (Senate House) in London for help with Ricardo papers and pamphlets. Parts of this chapter were drawn from *Experimental Farming and Ricardo's Political Economy of Distribution* (LSE Working Papers on "The Nature of Evidence: How well Do 'Facts' Travel?", No. 03/05, Department of Economic History, 2005).

References

Allen, Robert (1994) "Agriculture during the Industrial Revolution". In R. Floud and D. McCloskey (eds), *The Economic History of Britain since 1700*, Vol. I: *1700–1860* (pp. 96–122). Cambridge: Cambridge University Press.

Archer, John E. (1997) "The Nineteenth-Century Allotment: Half an Acre and a Row". *Economic History Review*, 50:1, 21–36.

Armytage, W. H. G. (1958) "The Chartist Land Colonies 1846–1848". *Agricultural History*, 32:2, 87–96.

Barkai, H. (1959) "Ricardo on Factor Prices and Income Distribution in a Growing Economy". *Economica*, 26, 240–50.

(1986) "Ricardo's Volte-Face on Machinery". *Journal of Political Economy*, 94:3, 595–613.

Beatson, Alexander (1820/1) *A New System of Cultivation*. London: Bulmer and Nicol.

Bennett, Alan (1995) *The Madness of King George*. London: Faber and Faber.

Berman, Morris (1972) "The Early Years of the Royal Institution 1799–1810: A Re-Evaluation". *Science Studies*, 2:3, 205–40.

Blaug, Mark (1956) "The Empirical Content of Ricardian Economics". *Journal of Political Economy*, 64, 41–58.

(1958) *Ricardian Economics*. New Haven, CT: Yale University Press.

(1968) "David Ricardo". In David L. Sills (ed), *International Encyclopaedia of the Social Sciences*, Vol. 13 (pp. 507–12). New York: Macmillan.

Boumans, Marcel (1999) "Built-In Justification". In Mary S. Morgan and Margaret Morrison (eds), *Models as Mediators: Perspectives on Natural and Social Science* (pp. 66–96). Cambridge: Cambridge University Press.

Chase, Malcolm (1988) *'The People's Farm'*. Oxford: Clarendon Press.

Cunningham Wood, John (1985–1994) *David Ricardo: Critical Assessments*, 7 volumes. London: Croom Helm/Routledge.

Davy, Humphry (1814) *Elements of Agricultural Chemistry*. London: Longman, Orme, Brown, Green, and Longmans.

Dorfman, Robert (1989) "Thomas Robert Malthus and David Ricardo". *Journal of Economic Perspectives*, 3:3, 153–64.

Farmers' Journal (1807–1832) Originally *Evans and Ruffy's Farmers' Journal and Agricultural Advertizer*. Various issues.

Goddard, Nicholas (1989) "Agricultural Literature and Societies". In Gordon E. Mingay (ed), *The Agrarian History of England and Wales*, Vol. VI: *1750–1850* (pp. 361–83). Cambridge: Cambridge University Press.

Gootzeit, Michael J. (1975) *David Ricardo*. New York: Columbia University Press.

Grisenthwaite, William (1819) *A New Theory of Agriculture*. London: Neville.

Henderson, John P. with John B. Davis (1997) *The Life and Economics of David Ricardo*. Boston: Kluwer.

Herbert, N. M. (1976) [ed] *Victoria County History of Gloucestershire*. Vol. XI: *The Stroud Valleys*. Oxford: Oxford University Press/University of London.

Hilton, Boyd (1977) *Corn, Cash, and Commerce: The Economic Policies of the Tory Governments, 1815–1830*. Oxford: Oxford University Press.

Hollander, Samuel (1979) *The Economics of David Ricardo*. University of Toronto Press; London: Heinemann.

House of Lords (1814) "First and Second Reports from the Lords Committee appointed to enquire into the state of the Growth, Commerce and Consumption of Grain, and all laws relating thereto". July 25, 1814, *Parliamentary Papers, 1814–5*, Vol. V.

James, Patricia (1979) *Population Malthus: His Life and Times*. London: Routledge and Kegan Paul.

Malthus, Thomas R. (1814) "Observations on the Effects of the Corn Laws". Reprinted in *The Pamphlets of Thomas Robert Malthus* (1970) (pp. 95–131). New York: Augustus Kelley.

(1815) "An Inquiry into the Nature and Progress of Rent". Reprinted in *The Pamphlets of Thomas Robert Malthus* (1970) (pp. 171–225). New York: Augustus Kelley.

(1820) *Principles of Political Economy Considered with a View to Their Practical Applications*. London: John Murray.

Marshall, William (1779) *Experiments and Observations Concerning Agriculture and the Weather*. London: J. Dodsley.

(1817/1968) *The Review and Abstract of the Country Reports to the Board of Agriculture*, Vol. 5. New York: Augustus Kelley.

Martins, S. W. (1980) *A Great Estate at Work*. Cambridge: Cambridge University Press.

Milgate Murray and Shannon C. Stimson (1991) *Ricardian Politics*. Princeton, NJ: Princeton University Press.

Mingay, Gordon E. (1975) *Arthur Young and His Times*. London: Macmillan.

(1989) [ed] *The Agrarian History of England and Wales*, Vol. VI: *1750–1850* Cambridge: Cambridge University Press.

(1997) *Parliamentary Enclosure in England*. London: Longman.

Mitchell, B. R. and Phyllis Deane (1971) *Abstract of British Historical Statistics*. Cambridge: Cambridge University Press.

Morgan, Mary S. (2005) "Experimental Farming and Ricardo's Political Economy of Distribution". LSE Working Papers on "The Nature of Evidence: How Well Do 'Facts' Travel?", No. 03/05, Department of Economic History.

Morgan, Mary S. and Margaret Morrison (1999) *Models as Mediators: Perspectives on Natural and Social Science.* Cambridge: Cambridge University Press.

Moselle, Boaz (1995) "Allotments, Enclosure, and Proletarianization in Early Nineteenth-Century Southern England". *Economic History Review*, 48:3, 482–500.

O'Brien, Dennis P. (1975) *The Classical Economists.* Revised 2004. Oxford: Clarendon Press.
    (1981) "Ricardian Economics and the Economics of David Ricardo". *Oxford Economic Papers*, 33, 352–86.

Offer, Avner (1980) "Ricardo's Paradox and the Movement of Rents in England, c. 1870–1910". *Economic History Review*, 33:2, 236–52.

Overton, Mark (1996) *Agricultural Revolution in England: The Transformation of the Agrarian Economy, 1500–1850.* Cambridge: Cambridge University Press.

Patten, Simon N. (1893) "The Interpretation of Ricardo". *Quarterly Journal of Economics*, 7, 22–52.

Peach, Terry (1993) *Interpreting Ricardo.* Cambridge: Cambridge University Press.

Ramana, D.V. (1957) "Ricardo's Environment". *Indian Journal of Economics*, 38, 151–64.

Reich, M (1980) "Empirical and Ideological Elements in the Decline of Ricardian Economics". *Review of Radical Political Economics*, 12:3, 1–14.

Reuten, Geert (1999) "Knife-edge Caricature Modelling: The Case of Marx's Reproduction Schema". In Mary S. Morgan and Margaret Morrism (eds), *Models as Mediators: Perspectives on Natural and Social Science* (pp. 196–240). Cambridge: Cambridge University Press.

Ricardo, David (1815) "The Influence of a Low Price of Corn on the Profits of Stock". In Sraffa, Vol. IV.
    (1821) *The Principles of Political Economy and Taxation* (3 editions:1817, 1819 and 1821; 1821 edition reprinted as Sraffa, 1951, Vol. 1).
    Collected Works. See Sraffa (1951–1973).

Rudge, Thomas (1813) *General View of the Agriculture of the County of Gloucester, Drawn up for the Consideration of the Board of Agriculture and Internal Improvement.* London: Sherwood, Neely and Jones.

Russell, John E. (1966) *A History of Agricultural Science in Great Britain, 1620–1954.* London: Allen and Unwin.

Schumpeter, Joseph A. (1954) *History of Economic Analysis* (ed: Elizabeth B. Schumpeter). New York: Oxford University Press.

Snell, K. D. M. (1985) *Annals of the Labouring Poor.* Cambridge: Cambridge University Press.

Sraffa, Piero (1951–1973) *The Works and Correspondence of David Ricardo.* Edited with the collaboration of M. H. Dobb. Cambridge: Cambridge University Press for The Royal Economic Society; reproduced by The Liberty Press, 2004.

Torrens, Robert (1815) *Essay on the External Corn Trade.* London: Longman, Rees, Orme, Brown and Green.

Turner, Michael E., J. V. Beckett and A. Afton (1997) *Agricultural Rents in England, 1690–1914.* Cambridge: Cambridge University Press.

Weatherall, David (1976) *David Ricardo: A Biography.* The Hague: Martinus Nijhoff.

Went, Robert (2002) *The Enigma of Globalization: A Journey to a New Stage of Capitalism.* London: Routledge.

West, Edward (1815/1903) *Essay on the Application of Capital to Land* (Reprint of Economic Tracts, Series 1, No. 3. Baltimore: Johns Hopkins University Press.

Wilmot, Sarah (1990) 'The Business of Improvement': Agriculture and Scientific Culture in Britain, c.1700–c.1870. Historical Geography Research Series, No. 24.

Winch, Donald (1996) *Riches and Poverty: An Intellectual History of Political Economy in Britain, 1750–1834*. Ideas in Context, 39. Cambridge: Cambridge University Press.

Wise, M. Norton (1993) "Mediations: Enlightening Balancing Acts, or the Technologies of Rationalism". In Paul Horwich (ed), *World Changes: Thomas Kuhn and the Nature of Science* (pp. 207–57). Cambridge, MA: MIT Press.

3

Imagining and Imaging: Creating
a New Model World

1. Introduction

The Edgeworth Box is an economic model with which all economists are familiar. It began life in 1881, underwent substantial development over the next decades, and continues in use today: a modern version is shown in Figure 3.1. It is a small-scale, manipulable, diagrammatic object – undoubtedly a model – made to represent the exchange relations between two individuals. It introduced important new conceptual materials into economics and has functioned primarily as a device for theorizing with. The form, the content, and the history of this model can all be taken as exemplary both for the development of modelling in economics and for the movement to make economics a mathematical science. These late-nineteenth-century developments of modelling and mathematization are intimately linked in the discipline, though it is not clear exactly how, nor why it matters.

The pioneers who introduced mathematics into economics in the late nineteenth century argued that it would make economics more scientific, because economic ideas expressed in mathematics are expressed more exactly, and reasoned about

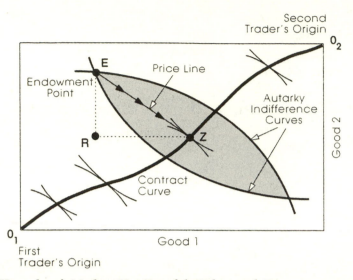

Figure 3.1. Humphrey's Modern Version of the Edgeworth Box.
Source: Tom Humphrey "The Early History of the Box Diagram" (1996). *Economic Quarterly*, 82:1, 37–75, figure 1. Reproduced with permission from the author, Tom Humphrey, and The Federal Reserve Bank of Richmond.

more rigorously, than when expressed in words. These claims are also constitutive of what is involved in the activity of modelling, for, as I argued in Chapter 1, model-making gives *form* to ideas about the world and in the process gives *formal* rules to reason with. Yet, mathematization and model-making are not the same move: all models require a language of representation, but these need not be mathematical ones.[1] The model of economic man was developed (as we shall see in Chapter 4) primarily in verbal terms, and each new version formed a specific portrait of a model man to argue with. Analogical models are sometimes found produced in the original language of the analogy rather than in mathematical descriptions of them, such as Fisher's mechanical balance or the Newlyn-Phillips hydraulic machine (both found in Chapter 5), and these necessarily obey the language rules of those analogical objects and fields.[2] And while it is fair to say that, historically

1 As argued in Chapter 1, mathematics came into economics in the late nineteenth century, both in modelling and as the method of postulation and proof. This 'mathematization' was controversial within the economics discipline, though historians of economics have largely taken for granted the terms of those historical contests, from the pioneers and detractors, as ones of methodology and modernism. A notable exception is Weintraub (2002), whose wonderfully idiosyncratic study successfully challenges the received view in many different respects. His chapter 5 (with Ted Gayer) addresses the issue of mathematics as a neutral language, and is particularly relevant here.

2 Historians of economics have also paid considerable attention to the importance of analogies and metaphors in the content expressed in mathematical economics (Mirowski, 1989) and to the evolution of such ideas (e.g., Ingrao and Israel, 1990). These are valuable metaphor-lead histories. Yet not all analogical thinking provides for a ready-made mathematical economics (see Boumans, 1993, and more broadly, my Chapter 5), and if mathematics came into economics not from subject-analogies but via formal analogies, that is between the form of economic ideas and mathematical forms, this takes us back to mathematizing as a change of language (see my Chapter 4 discussion of mathematical idealization).

considered, the mathematical languages became preeminent in model-making, to treat this development merely as a matter of language choice not only misses how and why modelling relates to mathematization in economics. It also risks seriously underestimating what was involved in modelling as a significant development in the practical reasoning modes of economics. So there are cognitive issues about these historical changes in the way economics is expressed that need to be seriously considered and clarified.

But there are deeper issues that stem from the synchronous development of mathematics and modelling. New forms of expression within a discipline involve not just a change of method and the ways that scientists do their work, but also changes in the things that they express. As scientists imagine their world, and make images of that world in new forms, they also form new concepts to work and argue with. Modelling as a new way of visualizing the economy, and mathematics as a new language of expression, both prompt conceptual change. New ways of expressing economic ideas – models and mathematics – lead to new things being expressed. So the cognitive struggles these new processes of visualization entail are rewarded by the new conceptual developments that come from them.

In this chapter, the focus is on the joint processes of visualization – imagining the economic world and making an image of it – in creating small model worlds. I start with the cognitive aspects of these changes in ways of expressing economics and move into the conceptual aspects of these new modes of visualization before turning to the historical development of the Edgeworth Box to show how – in practice – cognition and visualization are interconnected.

2. Acts of Translation or a New Way of World-Making?

If we start out by thinking of mathematics primarily as a language, then we might portray mathematical model-making as a process of translating economics from words to mathematics. But in general there is no reason why translating between two such different kinds of language, from the older verbally expressed economics into mathematical forms, should be easy. The problem of translating words into mathematics might be compared with translating from words to drawings. The difficulty of this latter action is succinctly expressed by Ivins (1953) in discussing how an artist could depict a botanical specimen, that he had not himself seen, from a verbal description by someone who had:

> It is doubtful if any much more intricate intellectual process can be imagined than the translation of a linear series of verbal symbols, arranged in an analytical, syntactical time order, into an organization of concrete materials, and shapes, and colours, all existing simultaneously in a three-dimensional space. (Ivins, 1953, p. 160)

Any account of the transition to modelling using mathematical modes of expression in economics needs to recognise a similar kind of cognitive depth in the problem.

Understanding model-making in economics as a process of translating verbal economics into mathematics not only understates the cognitive tasks involved, but also mistakes the nature of the problem in two ways. First, there is the question of deciding on the appropriate mathematical language, for there is not one mathematical language but many. Second, there is the problem of knowing what it is that is to be transcribed.

First then, even where there is a simple translation from words into mathematics, the choice of mathematical language – and so form – is not necessarily obvious. Economists can translate a straightforward verbal discussion of supply-and-demand behaviour into mathematics, but they still have a choice of ways to represent the behaviour. They might translate these hypothetical schedules of how people behave into two intersecting lines on a diagram (as Alfred Marshall did, as we see in Chapter 7) or translate it into two equations – but the semantics and syntax of these representations differ. Many economists assume that they are exactly equivalent (and even say that they are 'formally' equivalent) but they are no more equivalent than, for example, a couple of sentences written in Dutch and translated into English. In that case, the words themselves will have different connotations of meaning (the semantics), the sentence structure may well be different (the syntactics), the symbols will be different (the words representing things will be different), and some languages will require more symbols to express the ideas than others. And, as I pointed out in Chapter 1 – these different formal languages have implications for the rules of manipulation of those models. So, rather than characterizing model-making as a process of mathematical translation, we might better say that it means choosing a kind of mathematics that enables economists to represent the aspects of the economy that interest them into an appropriate form.

The second problem might be labelled as one of transcription. Even if the laws of economics are written in mathematics, as some nineteenth-century economists certainly believed, they are not there waiting to be transcribed.[3] Economists don't know for sure what those laws are; as Irving Fisher suggests, they perceive them only dimly:

> The effort of the economist is to *see*, to picture the interplay of economic elements. The more clearly cut these elements appear in his vision, the more elements he can grasp and hold in mind at once, the better. The economic world is a misty region. The first explorers used unaided vision. Mathematics is the lantern by which what before was dimly visible now looms up in firm, bold outlines. The old phantasmagoria disappear. We see better. We also see further. (Fisher, 1892, p. 119)

The intuitions that economists have about the economic world, and wish to express in mathematics, may be very opaque and they use their imaginations to create model

---

3 See Le Gall (2007), who refers to such economists as 'natural econometricians', ones who believed that careful use of statistics will reveal these mathematical laws.

versions of the world as a way to explore those ideas. Here mathematics can be helpful for, as Fisher (1892) argued, the mathematical method is the manipulation of symbols as "aids to the human memory and imagination", where "a symbol may be a letter, a diagram or a model" (pp. 107, 106). So this activity of modelling helps economists to express their intuitions, and indeed, they may come to understand their ideas about how the world works only by making such small-world images.

Thus, both terms, 'translating' and 'transcribing', underestimate the task of making an economic world in a model through mathematization. Translating is not a rote activity but one in which material choices with consequences have to be made. Transcribing makes a strong ontological commitment: it suggests that the laws of economics are written in mathematics and economists merely had to figure out how to decipher their own Book of Nature. Recognition of the presence and importance of model-making in the mathematization of economics suggests not acts of translation, or of perception and transcription, but rather ones of cognition and of portrayal as economists sought to understand their world.

These terms – of finding appropriate formulations, or of turning intuitions into representations – suggest that we might gain from thinking about mathematical model-making as acts of creation. Nelson Goodman's *Ways of Worldmaking* (1978) stresses how scientists and artists are involved in making sense of the world in similar kinds of ways. Both groups make versions of the world as a way of understanding it and giving us insight into how it works.[4] Understanding mathematical modelling as a process of world-making focusses on economists' ability to create new accounts of the economic world, ones that would enable them to see further or see more clearly. Portraying scientific modelling as acts of representation akin to those of artists enables us to appreciate the role of both imagining and imaging in world-making, and so the relevance of a term that has connotations of both these, namely, visualization. This term is more naturally fitted to artists' work, and certainly needs to be broadly interpreted if, as I intend, it is to apply to the ways scientists make their accounts of the world. For economists, as for any scientists, the process of making accounts of the world involves conceptual as much as perceptual work. It takes both intuition and imagination to develop the abstract concepts required to portray the economic world into a model. If we view modelling in economics as the struggle to envision how the economic world works and express that conceptual understanding in new forms, including mathematical ones, we get to the broad and deep sense of visualization that I mean. In model-making, visualization and understanding are inseparable.[5]

4 I interpret Goodman's idea that both scientists and artists make versions of the world as that both groups make representations of the world. Goodman is careful not to use the term representation so broadly; R. I. G. Hughes (1997) interprets Goodman's ideas in the context of model-making as 'denotation'.

5 De Marchi (2003) is one of the few to have discussed this cognitive aspect of visualization in the history of economics (see also the other papers in the 'mini-symposium' on visualization edited by Leonard, 2003). Two books of essays that interpret visualization broadly within the history, sociology,

3. Making the Mathematical Economic World in Models

How does this analysis of what it takes to create new forms of expression in economics relate to the historical process of such a change? The arguments above suggest that to make economics in the more exact forms provided by mathematics, economists needed not only those more exact languages, but they also had to imagine mathematical representations of the world – that is, models – within which their economic ideas could be expressed, just as to verbalise a particular idea about economics requires a verbal description of the economic world in which those ideas make sense. We all take our verbally described economic world as a matter of habit. That verbally expressed economy – the nouns, verbs, descriptive phrases and relations between them that economists still use – grew up over the past centuries in such a way that their theories and descriptions of the economic world could be expressed within that domain, within that version of the world. The habits and the conventions of any symbolic system necessarily constrain what can be expressed for, as Goodman wrote: "Though we make worlds by making versions, we no more make a world by putting symbols together at random than a carpenter makes a chair by putting pieces of wood together at random" (1978, p. 94). But those habits and conventions do not prevent innovation, for economists continue to revise and remake versions of the economic world in whatever their adopted language.

Creating a mathematically expressed economics was, historically, a process similar to that of creating a verbal economics. Economists made their mathematical versions of the economic world, just as their forebears had made their verbal ones, from many different sources of inspiration. It was no simple linear process. Weintraub (2002) argues persuasively for us to see it as an ongoing interaction between economists and mathematicians over a period in which both the image and content of both fields are changing. From this complex and contingent historical process, economists came to think about the economic world in mathematical ways and so to represent it to themselves in new languages and new forms of representation. Both were needed, so that over time, the elements of these new mathematical economic worlds, their meanings, how they are symbolised, and what relations are assumed, all came to be taken for granted. Economists arguing for mathematization were proposing, in effect, a new way of world-making,

and philosophy of science, but that do not fully extend the notion to mathematical representations are Lynch and Woolgar (1990) and Baigrie (1996). The classic work on visualization that includes mathematics within its profile is Arnheim (1969). My focus here both contrasts with, and goes along with, that of Bruno Latour in his clever 1986 article on visualization (reprinted in Lynch and Woolgar, 1990, under a different title). One can see the mathematical models of economics as having many of the properties of immutable mobiles that he discusses in that paper. But contra Latour, my aim here is not to think about mobility, but to problematize both visualization and cognition, on which see, from different standpoints and generations, Toulmin (1953) and Nersessian (2008).

one that required *not only new languages but also new representations*. It is from this requirement for new representations that modelling became naturalized in economics.

Two contrasting examples of model-making, one taken from the early nineteenth century by Ricardo, and the other – the Edgeworth Box – from the first real generation of modellers later that century, may help to illuminate the role of models in this process of mathematical world-making. For Ricardo (in the previous chapter), it was natural to turn to the arithmetic of accounting for expressing the relations in the agricultural economy and for his reasoning about it. It was also natural for him as a landlord and financier to use technical or conceptual terms that were close in meaning to those of everyday use and that could match the observable equivalents given in numbers, such as wages, prices, profits, and so forth. Even when, as for rent, his economic concept was not quite the same as that of the people in his economy, it was close enough in definition to be represented in the same accounting terms. It is not just the language of the terms in his model farm that fitted well enough to the common sense of economic arithmetic, but that, as I showed, the format for Ricardo's representations matched the kind of experimental farming reports we found in his early-nineteenth-century economy. So Ricardo took his terms and numbers largely ready made and chose accounting rules for his arithmetic reasoning chains. But his model farm is difficult to pin down as a separate manipulable image, for it emerged only when he worked the bits and pieces of elementary relations – his ingredients – together in his reasoning with them.

In later nineteenth-century modelling, the process of imagining and image-making involved more conceptual work along with the analytical work. In this chapter, we see how Edgeworth fashioned a model to portray abstract concepts: ones that had not previously been displayed in representations, rather than, as Ricardo did, observable things with everyday labels. The visual elements of the Box that carries Edgeworth's name are not illustrations of something seen, but conceptual elements that have to be imagined before they can be imaged. Some of the elements are mathematical, and so have to be expressed in mathematical forms. But mathematics by itself does not dictate the model, for how these conceptual bits fit together is done by making an image of their economic relations, that is, by making a model. The economists who successively contributed to creating the Edgeworth Box had to figure out both the language of representation and the nature of that new representation, both mathematical and economic, in its format. Making a mathematical economic world with models was a tall order. And, despite the best efforts of Edgeworth and others of his generation, it could not, and was not, done all at once.

What then can say of the historical relation between modelling and mathematization? Model-making, I suggest, flowered during the late nineteenth century and throughout the twentieth-century process of mathematization for two reasons. One is that exactly the kinds of qualities needed in making a new mathematical version of the world are those found in model-making, namely, the abilities to be imaginative about the world and to make images of it in new, nonverbal forms. The other is that model-making provided a way of generating the vocabulary and forms of the new way of thinking, and so of providing the new "working objects" on which mathematical economic descriptions could be refined and tested.[6] Model-making became a critical element of this process of mathematical world-making in economics precisely because, by its nature, it involved making the new representations that were a necessary part of that process of world-making. This is my *visualization* thesis in its most broadly construed form, but it encompasses the second thesis developed in this chapter, namely that concerned with *newness*. These two theses – visualization and newness – cannot be argued for separately nor supported independently. The arguments go along together. These new representations that came with modelling and mathematics involved conceptual elements that could not be expressed in the old forms. So, both the nature and content of the new representations, and the grammar they entailed, changed the way economists picture the economy. In learning to create and use these new representations, economists came to understand and see a different version, a newly made version, of the economic world.

4. The Artist's Space versus the Economist's Space

The Edgeworth Box is a small world in a model, fathered by the economists in the late nineteenth century who wanted economics to become a mathematical discipline. It has since had a long and active life that continues into the present time. But I am concerned here not with its life but with its creation story. I present versions of that model's origin and development from three disparate sources: pictures of the Box's development made by an artist of today, the original diagrams from economists' historical development of the Box, and some modern representations of that history. The comparative analysis of these three sets of diagrams provides the materials for me to explore the roles of imagination and image-making in creating economic models and the new conceptual elements that they entail.[7]

I begin this account of model-making with an artist's visualization of the Edgeworth Box made to illustrate a retirement lecture by Prof. Arnold Merkies from the Free University in Amsterdam in 1997. Here is a section of his printed text; the charming illustrations are by Koen Engelen (Figures 3.2a–d).

6 The tag "working objects" comes from Daston and Galison (1992) and its import will be discussed in Chapter 10.
7 It might be argued that I am weighting the scales in favour of my argument about visualization because the model case I use is a diagram, and so its visual components are innate, yet C. S. Peirce treats all mathematical reasoning as 'diagrammatic' (on which see Hoffman, 2004).

Extract from *Zo* by Arnold H. Q. M. Merkies (1997, pp. 8–9), pictures by Koen Engelen (Figure 3.2 reproduced with thanks to, and by permission of, ©A. H. Q. M. Merkies), text translated by Ada Kromhout.

The market economy

What then about the Western method: the much-praised neoclassical system, or, in today's slogan, the market economy. In order to be able to analyse this, mathematical economists tend to simplify the world. We will put the magnifying glass on Koen Engelen's pictures once more:

A closer look at the world

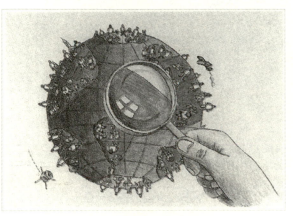

(Figure 3.2a)

First, we isolate two people from the five billion people inhabiting the world:

Two selected individuals with their possessions

(Figure 3.2b)

Next, we concentrate on the possessions of only two of their goods, for example, cheese and wine:

The two individuals with cheese and wine only

(Figure 3.2c)

And, finally, we substitute shadowy figures, who behave according to our wishes, for the real individuals. We now are left with a rectangle, the so-called Box of Edgeworth:

Only cheese and wine

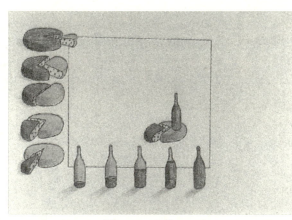

(Figure 3.2d)

In the bottom left corner we have Albert, and Beatrice is in the top right corner. His colour is yellow, and her colour is green. The actual division of their possessions of cheese and wine is indicated in the box. Such a reduction of the rich world into merely some cheese and a bottle of wine is typical of the behaviour of the mathematical economists: reduce the problem to a size on which we can pronounce.

A closer look at the world

Two selected individuals with their possessions

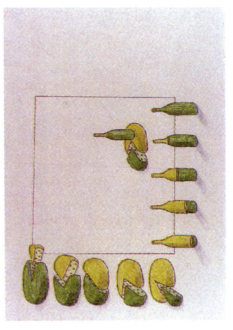

Only cheese and wine

The two individuals with cheese and wine only

Figure 3.2a–d. The Artist's Edgeworth Box by Koen Engelen.
Source: *Zo* by Arnold H. Q. M. Merkies, 1997, pp. 8–9. Reproduced with thanks to, and by permission of, ©A. H. Q. M. Merkies.

As we can see from the text extract and the pictures involved, Merkies' explanation of how we reach the Edgeworth Box model is to start with a picture of the whole world, then "simplify" by taking a magnifying glass to look closely at some detail of the world, then "isolate" two "selected" individuals with all their possessions, then "concentrate" on only two of their possessions, and then, finally, the people are made abstract and their behaviour becomes ideal when we "substitute for the real individuals shadowy figures who behave according to our wishes" (Merkies, 1997, pp. 8–9).

I have picked out certain terms from Merkies' account and repeated them here precisely because they resonate so effectively with the way that philosophers of science sometimes describe the process of creating mathematical models as one entailing simplification, isolation, abstraction, and idealization (a process to be discussed in Chapter 4).[8] According to this account, economists take the world and convert it into something else: something simpler than the complexity that is there; something that isolates a few relevant important parts from the whole; something that is abstract rather than concrete; and something that is ideal and perfect rather than real and messy. What is this something that has these characteristics? Is it even necessarily a model? And does not such a description implicitly assume that economists know the real world that they simplify and idealize, from which they abstract and isolate?

Merkies' description of defining the Edgeworth Box echoes exactly these ideas: take the world, simplify, isolate, abstract, and idealize. Those philosophers seem to have it right after all! But we should not give in to their simplification account so easily here because it omits something crucial, namely that the process also involves making a representation of the economy, making a model of the economy. As the real world is shorn away, first the goods become shadows, the people lose their detailed character and then disappear altogether, but at the same time we see an image gradually emerging, depicting rounds of cheese and bottles of wine lined up along two sides of a box, and a colour coding in the goods that indicates ownership by the absent people (see the colour plate of Figure 3.2). The illustrations by the artist, Engelen, make us realise the important role of developing the image as he makes a new representation at each stage of the model-making.

Modern economists too would create this Box by simplifying the complex world. But they would start with the simplest case of one individual and one good, and then add a second person with another good, gradually building up the elements of the diagram. And, since most economists are familiar with this Box, they will habitually fill in all sorts of other details – details not shown in these pictures, but to be seen in the later figures – without any further thought.

For economists reading this book, I ask please suspend your familiarity with the usual elements, properties, and powers of this well-known little box model and ponder a little these particular pictures. Bring back the imagination to ask: Why do

8 Good examples of this kind of account of how models are made, from philosophers of economics from several different traditions, can be found amongst the papers in Hamminga and De Marchi (1994) and are discussed in Morgan (1996).

the two individuals line up in this antagonistic stance opposite each other? Why did two colours (yellow and green) initially used for cheese and wine suddenly switch to be colour coding for the two individuals so that in the final picture the cheeses and wines become dual coloured? How did the box ever get into the picture in the first place? Indeed, until the last picture, there is nothing in the narrative description about any box, and yet it appears as an element from the first simplification move. And why is it that, with this narrative of Albert and Beatrice and the wonderful pictures, we do not yet have enough elements to make an Edgeworth Box? Indeed, why did the artist stop there and not draw the other elements that economists habitually place in the Box?

Let me begin with the last question and provide some of the following parts of Merkies' narrative, which move beyond that supported by Engelen's pictures:[9]

> The neo-classicists assume that Albert and Beatrice will start negotiating together until they decide upon a division they both consider to be better than their initial situation: barter is taking place. The characteristics ascribed to the two individuals guarantee they jointly find a solution. These characteristics are, among other things, that they both prefer having a bit of both goods to having much of only one good. They have what is called 'convex preferences'. So there is no teetotaller present....
>
> If we expand our small world, we meet with considerably more difficulties. This expansion goes as follows. Suppose we had Albert's possession of money taken as a starting point, instead of his possession of cheese. And suppose that, after some bargaining, Beatrice is willing to give up two of her bottles of wine in exchange for one hundred of Albert's guilders. If Albert agrees, the barter has resulted in a price of 50 guilders per bottle. That is the so-called equilibrium price. Other individuals, with the same convex characteristics as those of Albert and Beatrice, can now enter our small world and also bid for Beatrice's wine. We can also continue this process by exchanging money against all other goods. Thus, ultimately, it appears that it can be mathematically proven that, where there is free barter, equilibrium prices can be established for all goods. This is the so-called Nash equilibrium, named after Nash, who, in 1994, received the Nobel Price for his work published in the early Fifties.
>
> Now, if there are only people of the convex kind living in our world, and if there is freedom of trade under fair rules of play, then the Nash equilibrium is a very attractive situation. Economists then speak of a Pareto-optimal division. It is this division which the neoclassicists envisage as the ideal picture: in a Pareto-optimal division, no one will feel the need

---

9 Merkies' lecture compared various aspects of neoclassical versus socialist economics. The section of his text omitted between my two quotations here, and between the paragraphs in the second quotation, uses the case of Albert and Beatrice and the Box to point out that such a form of analysis in neoclassical economics ignores questions of the *initial* distribution of goods and is concerned only with the benefits of trading what is already owned; see Section 6.i here for further discussion.

to change the situation within the rules of play. Adherents of this theory have an even stronger result: it can be proven that this same Pareto-optimal division can be achieved also through freely varying prices, so through the market mechanism, the invisible[10] hand of Adam Smith. For economists, this is familiar territory. It is the basis of the belief in the working of the market mechanism. (Merkies, 1997, translated Kromhout, pp. 9–10)

It is extraordinary that the use of this little box model takes us so far so quickly. In three paragraphs, Merkies moves the argument from Albert and Beatrice in one act of bartering cheese for wine to equilibrium prices, Nash equilibrium, Pareto optimality, and Smith's invisible hand account of the market mechanism. Of course, these results depend not only on many more assumptions than are evident in the simplifying and isolating ones mentioned in the painter's series of Figure 3.2, but they also require the full Edgeworth Box as developed in historical series of Figures 3.4 and 3.5 rather than the pictorial versions here. The full Box supports such results because it entails additional elements, of which only one is made explicit in this commentary, namely that these are "people of the convex kind". That is, the econo-mist's Box incorporates not only the elements of the perceptual world but also adds in conceptual elements from economic theory that are required for reasoning to such conceptual results as Pareto optimality, Nash equilibrium, and so forth.

The artist has taken the Box picture as far as possible in the realm of percep-tion and illustration, the realm of what can be simplified and isolated from the world. The artist can go no further in representing the world via such a process of isolating and simplifying without becoming an economist. The economist adds in the apparatus of the invisible individuals' indifference curves to represent the preference map of each individual. On these can be built the apparatus of offer curves, contract curves, bargaining ranges, and so forth, all representations of the economic world but expressed in the conceptual terms of Merkies' second piece of text (and whose historical development is discussed below). The contrast is made vivid in Figure 3.3, which sets a modern version of the Box (our Figure 3.1, from Tom Humphrey, 1996) alongside one of the artist's diagrams (our Figure 3.2c, from Merkies, 1997). The conceptual machinery is expressed in this modern Box dia-gram, and it enables economists to argue in conceptual spaces, spaces beyond or behind the perceptual space. The world of people and goods may be illustrated in miniature in the Box by the artist, but the economic concepts have to be visualized: imagined and imaged into that same space by the economist.

The difference between the perceptual space of illustration and conceptual space of visualization is discussed by Michael Mahoney (1985) in relation to per-spective drawing and the new mechanics of the Scientific Revolution. He sets out to

---

10 In the Dutch text here it says 'inwissel hand', which would translate into something like 'exchange hand'. However, the translator suggests that in the Dutch text a typing error was made and assumed that Merkies meant the 'invisible hand' (which would be expected for the text). This typographi-cal error has been confirmed by Merkies in correspondence; however, the notion of an 'exchange hand' is equally inviting in the context here!

(a)

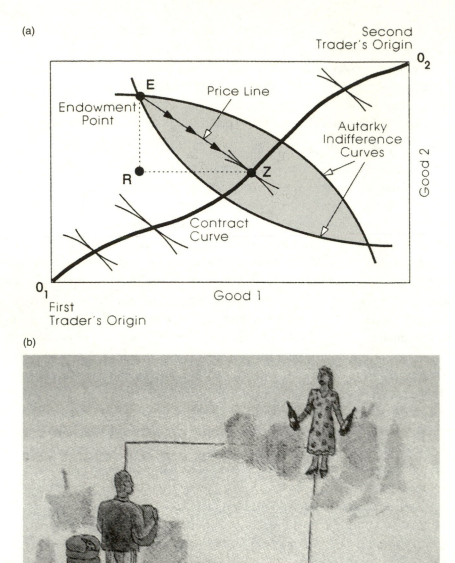

(b)

Figure 3.3. The Artist's vs the Modern Economist's Version of the Box.

Figure 3.3a. Source: Tom Humphrey "The Early History of the Box Diagram" (1996) *Economic Quarterly*, 82:1, 37–75, figure 1. Reproduced with permission from the author, Tom Humphrey, and The Federal Reserve Bank of Richmond.

Figure 3.3b. Source: *Zo* by Arnold H.Q.M. Merkies, 1997, pp. 8–9. Reproduced with thanks to, and by permission of, ©A.H.Q.M. Merkies.

destroy the Edgerton Thesis, namely that there was a direct causal link between the Renaissance improvements in the drawing of machines and the development of the science of mechanics. Mahoney argues that although the engineer-artists of those days drew in new ways (they learned to provide accurate representations of physical objects in three-dimensional space), they did not draw new things; that is, these new ways of drawing did not reveal the inner scientific principles of the machines.[11] Rather, the science of mechanics at that time already treated the machine as

> ... an abstract, general system of quantitative parameters linked by mathematical relations [so]...it is difficult to see how more accurate depiction of the basic phenomena as physical objects could have conduced to their abstraction into general systems. For the defining terms of the systems lay in conceptual realms ever farther removed from the physical space the artists had become so adept at depicting. Those terms could not be drawn; at best, they could be diagramed. (Mahoney, 1985, p. 200)

Reasoning about mechanics was already conducted in the language of mathematics. Mathematical diagrams remained the main form of representing mechanical relations and were used for reasoning through the Renaissance. But, as Mahoney remarks, "It is the mind's eye that is looking here, and it is peering into the structural relations among quantities belonging to many different conceptual (rather than perceptual) spaces" (p. 209). Mathematics here marks out the difference in the source of imagination, from the mind's eye that both imagines and comprehends compared to the body's eye that sees.[12]

For the economist, exploring the economy by model-making involved representing the economy in new ways *and* involved drawing new things. The economic elements inside the Edgeworth Box: the indifference curves, the contract curve, the points of tangency and equilibrium, that is, the mathematically expressed elements, are new, mind's eye, conceptual elements – not body's eye, perceptual elements. Merkies' description of *the Box* (his first quote) accompanies the artist's perception, the body's eye; his description of *the findings with the Box* (his second quote) depends on reasoning in conceptual space, reasoning which cannot be done with the Artist's Box (Figure 3.3b), but needs the full mind's eye version of the Economist's Box (Figure 3.3a).

This distinction between conceptual space and perceptual space tells us how to distinguish when a diagram is doing any work in the argument. If the diagram is about perceptual space but the argument about conceptual space, the reasoning will take place, as Mahoney describes it, "off the diagram". The diagram – in this case, the artist's version – will be, at best, an illustration, rather than a tool for experimentation and demonstration. In contrast, Merkies' second quotation

---

11 And the older drawings of machines were of such inaccuracy that an observer could not see how the machine parts fitted together, nor therefore surmise how the machine might work (in a non-scientific sense) .

12 On the "mind's eye", see Ferguson (1977, 1992).

reports the results of economists' reasoning *with* the Edgeworth Box as the diagram's conceptual apparatus developed over the period from Edgeworth's first diagram in 1881 until the 1950s and beyond. During that period the conceptual resources of the diagram provided a highly creative reasoning tool. Humphrey (1996) reconstructed this history of *using* the Box diagram, especially its important role in deriving economic propositions and proving theorems, and its tremendous versatility to deal with theoretical questions in various domains of economics. Anyone who ever thought the Box diagram was 'merely for illustration' need only read his account to see how using the model was critical in developing the theoretical results of mathematical economics.[13] We turn now to the history of how the diagram itself was made.

5. The History of the Edgeworth Box Diagram – as Told by Itself

The contrast between the artist's illustrations and the scientist's conceptual elements of the Box teaches us something of the content of the economists' model worlds and shows that such models cannot be gained only by a process of taking the world as it seems and subtracting things, for the conceptual content would be lacking. But that contrast does not show us how the model was created. Nor does the artist's sequence of figures – for the artist, Engelen, in showing Albert and Beatrice, cheese and wine, was representing an image *already known* to economists, an image that had long ago established their convention of placing people at corners and lining up their goods along two sides of a box as if along two sides of a graph.

The historical image sequences of Figures 3.4 and 3.5 show the history of how the Box was actually developed. They show how Edgeworth, Pareto, Bowley, and others created the model that culminated in the modern Box diagram. These historical sequences suggest that successive economists created the Box diagram by first portraying how one individual behaves with respect to one commodity, then to consider two individuals exchanging two commodities, and then into more complex diagrams. This process of developing the world in the model by starting with the most simple case and adding details (as a modern treatment would also do) forms the opposite to the process of beginning with a description of the whole world and simplifying downwards into a model world (as in Merkies' account). These are well-accepted alternatives in model-making.[14]

13 Once every economist became familiar with the Box and its results, the diagram's status in the profession changed. It became an illustration for earlier results derived using the Box, and so used as a teaching tool. At the same time, any search of the journals shows that it continues to be used as a referent, as well as in new forms and ways in some of the most highly ranked journals in the academic discipline, for it connects to important results derived from other forms of representation (game theory) and is used in human and computer experiments.

14 On these alternative accounts sometimes known as 'concretization' and 'idealization', see the discussions in Hamminga and De Marchi (1984) and in Morgan and Knuuttila (2012); see Chapter 4 on starting complex and making simple.

These actual historical sequences involve a number of surprising moves and can be usefully compared with a reconstruction of that history using equivalent modernized versions of the Box provided by Humphrey (1996). In reconstructing his history of using the Box diagram, Humphrey modernized along one dimension (the diagrams) to tell the history along another dimension (the theoretical results). This was an effective device, but Humphrey's set of images, also, could have been made only by someone who already knew the Box, was familiar with what it could represent, and with how it could be used.

My question is rather different: How did economists actually *make* this model?[15] When we ask this question, it is clear that both the two generic accounts of model-making (simplifying down or building up) and Humphrey's reconstruction miss an important point, namely, that the materials used in the model have to be imagined before they can be imaged by the economist. Where Merkies' artist could make an *image*, and Humphrey *redraw* the images, the economists who created the Box first had to *imagine* the small world of the model. This is not just the difference between making a model to describe something known and one that has to describe something opaque. Rather the comparison points to the requirement to develop conceptual clarity about those things that are only dimly perceived. This is where the economist's imagination comes in.

In this section, I seek to recreate the unfamiliarity erased by time and usage to understand how this mathematical model – the Box diagram – came into being, how economists used their imagination and built images to create that small world in a model. Recreating this journey takes us from Jevons' utility curve and Marshall's trade diagram (at the start of Figure 3.4), to the extraordinarily complicated and conceptually rich version of the small world created by Leontief (at the end of Figure 3.5). These mark the start and end of the historical sequences of images. This reconstruction of the Box's development requires cognitive attention to see just what is in the history (and – especially for economists – not to overprint into the Box what comes later).

5.i Edgeworth's Imagination and Image

The Edgeworth Box is named after Francis Ysidro Edgeworth (1845–1926), an Irish economist of great originality, whose work in both mathematical economics and statistics continued to be mined throughout the twentieth century. Like Ricardo, Edgeworth came to economics from other fields: originally a student of literature and classics, he trained as a commercial lawyer and taught himself mathematics before becoming a political economist. Edgeworth's version of the Box

---

15 We might both be interpreted as following Lakatos' (1976) example in *Proofs and Refutations*, with actual history below the line, and reconstructed history above. We chose to reconstruct along different lines. And, while he does not show the original diagrams, Humphrey's fine analysis reports many of the historical changes made in the diagrams.

diagram that bears his name – its first appearance – was introduced in his now famous *Mathematical Psychics* (1881), his first main work of economics, a dense and difficult book that develops economics into mathematical abstract forms and applies them to all sorts of questions including those of unionism and cooperatives.[16] Edgeworth begins his book by arguing for the application of mathematics to economics and is gently scathing of those who suppose that one can solve arguments by a form of reasoning which is mathematical but without the symbols that make it mathematical and thus miss the "characteristic advantages of deductive reasoning." (Edgeworth, 1881, p. 3).

For Edgeworth, mathematics is both a *language*, and, because of its special qualities, a *tool* or instrument for the expression of economic ideas and for reasoning about them. But in Edgeworth's mind, it is also an instrument of *imagination* to capture the evidence and behaviour of "things not seen in the world" (Edgeworth, 1881, p. 13). His imaginative speculations and descriptions about economic behaviour were funded by many analogies, ranging from electricity and magnetism to the Fairy Queen as a charioteer, reflecting his erudition in many fields of learning.[17] This is an extraordinary book, perhaps mainly because it does not fit our prejudices of how a mathematical account of the economic world might be written. Brian Rotman (2000) writes, most refreshingly, about mathematicians as follows

> Let us ignore the usual job description given of mathematics (exercise of pure reason, pursuit of objective truth, free play of the mind, and the like) and operate ethnomethodologically. We observe that mathematicians spend their time scribbling and thinking: writing or manipulating ... a prodigious range of symbols, as well as thinking about all manner of imagined worlds and the objects/processes within them. (Rotman, 2000, p. 121)

This well describes Edgeworth's ways of thinking and reasoning about the imagined world of economics in mathematical terms in which – following Jevons – he conceived an account of man as a pleasure machine.[18]

Much more might be said about Edgeworth and his many accomplishments, but the hero of this story is his diagram. So let us dip straight into Edgeworth's account of exchange between two individuals as follows:

---

16 See Keynes' essay (1926) for an early appreciation of Edgeworth's work. For an account of Edgeworth's economic work on this particular topic, see Creedy (1986). For a new edited and annotated version of this important 1881 book, see Edgeworth, ed Newman (2003).

17 For an example: "The invisible world of electricity is grasped by the marvellous methods of Lagrange; the invisible energy of pleasure may admit of similar handling." (Edgeworth, 1881/2003, p. 13). For an account of the metaphors and analogies used in Edgeworth, see Newman's version of 2003, and Mirowski (1994, Part III).

18 See Edgeworth, 1881, p. 15. Jevons' original development of utility graphs depended on analogical thinking (see Maas, 2005, amongst others), and though Edgeworth used physical and psychophysical analogies to present the 'contract curve', when it came to the Box diagram, the discussion (as in Pareto's treatment, see later) became firmly economic, yet expressed in mathematical forms.

> To illustrate the economical problem of exchange, the maze of many dealers contracting and competing with each other, it is possible to imagine a mechanism of many parts where the law of motion, which particular part moves off with which, is not precisely given – with symbols, arbitrary functions, representing not merely *not numerical knowledge* but *ignorance* – where, though the mode of motion towards equilibrium is indeterminate, the position of equilibrium is mathematically determined. (Edgeworth, 1881, p. 4, his italics)

The point at which they *should* settle to make an exchange is "mathematically determined", but the process by which they get there is not known. This is an economic rather than a mechanical problem, and so the analogical content fades away as he begins with his simplest case of two individuals with two goods to exchange where parties are free to contract only by *mutual* consent and without competition from other traders. He defines the locus of points at which exchange might be contracted as that where, whichever direction a move is made away from that set of points, one trader gets more and the other less utility. This set of points he terms the "contract-curve". He then sets about (pp. 20–8) demonstrating the qualities of his defined contract curve by a series of mixed mathematical (calculus rather than geometrical proofs) and verbal reasoning describing these spatial arrangements, to assure himself that the characteristics of the contract curve are sensibly proved by different approaches. These mathematical reasonings are analytic or general in character, and are conducted in the language of mathematics: "let two individuals.... Consider $P - F(xy) = 0$ as a surface" and so forth, but these do not quite settle the questions that interest him about the range of indeterminancy and how that might be overcome.

At a certain point in his mathematical discourse, Edgeworth moves into one of his imagined worlds, and the original version of the Box appears as his figure 1 (see Figure 3.4c) encased in the following text: (my underlinings, his italics):

> It is not necessary for the purpose of the present study to carry the analysis further. To gather up and fix our thoughts, let us <u>imagine a simple case</u> – Robinson Crusoe contracting with Friday. The *articles* of contract: wages to be given by the white, labour to be given by the black. Let Robinson Crusoe = X. <u>Represent</u> *y*, the labour given by Friday, by a horizontal [sic] line measured *northward* from an assumed point, and measure *x*, the remuneration given by Crusoe, from the same point along an *eastward* line (See accompanying figure 1 [Figure 3.4c here]). Then any point between these lines <u>represents</u> a contract. It will very generally be in the interest of both parties to vary the articles of any contract taken as random. But there is a class of contracts to the variation of which the consent of *both* parties cannot be obtained, of *settlements*. These settlements are <u>represented</u> by an *indefinite number* of points, a locus, the *contract-curve*

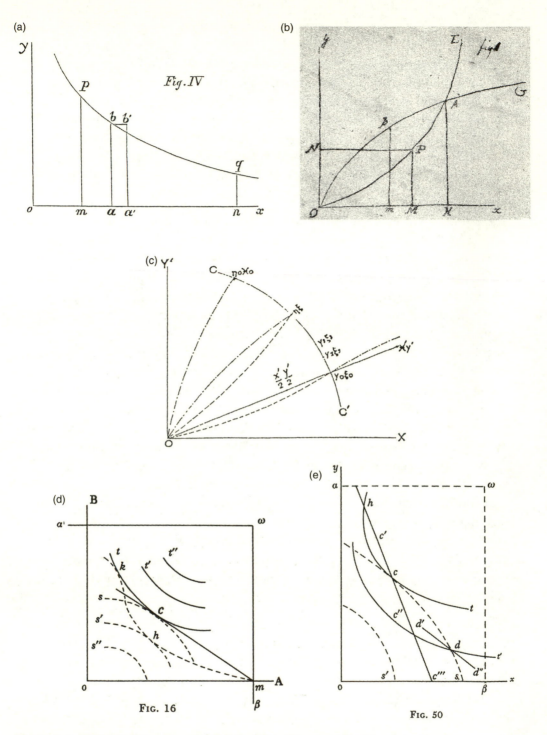

Figure 3.4. Historical Sequence of Original Box Diagrams Part I.

(a) Jevons' Utility Curve (1871).

Source: William Stanley Jevons, *The Theory of Political Economy*, 1871, London: Macmillan & Co., fig. 4 p. 49.

(b) Marshall's First Trade Diagram (1879).

Source: Alfred Marshall, "Pure Theory of Foreign Trade", 1879, figure 1. Marshall Library, Cambridge. (Reprinted, London: London School of Economics and Political Science Reprints of

CC′, or rather, a certain portion of it which may be supposed to be wholly in the space between our perpendicular lines in a direction trending from south-east to north-west. This available portion of the contract-curve lies between two points, say $\eta_0 x_0$ north-west, and $y_0 \xi_0$ south-east; which are respectively the intersections with the contract-curve of the *curves of indifference* for each party drawn through the origin. Thus the utility of the contract <u>represented</u> by $\eta_0 x_0$ is for Friday zero, or rather, the same as if there was no contract. As that point he would as soon be off with the bargain – work by himself perhaps. (Edgeworth, 1881, pp. 28–9, his italics, underlining added)

Thus Edgeworth imagines his Robinson Crusoe and Friday at right angles to each other in the same plane, shoulder to shoulder, as befits those who must mutually agree before exchange can take place. Edgeworth's (x, y) space is a plane, and the indifference curves are projections from three-dimensional utility surfaces; thus he imagines and makes his image accordingly (and so he correctly wrote that for his figure 1 we draw the Y-axis horizontally northwards). The individuals, Crusoe and Friday (X and Y), are not fully and separately distinguished on the diagram from those things that they have to exchange (x and y).

It seems so natural to economists nowadays to represent the two goods for exchange along these two axes, but it was not so in the late nineteenth century when economic diagrams were still in their infancy. Edgeworth's reference two pages earlier to Marshall's 1879 trade diagrams, which use this convention, provides the likeliest clue to their provenance. In Marshall's diagrams, such as in the second of our historical series, Figure 3.4b (another one was shown in Chapter 1), the offer curves depict the amounts offered for exchange at different prices by sellers of English cloth in exchange for German linen and vice versa, one offer curve for each of the two countries. The two goods are represented on the two axes and the whole of the space between is open for trade between two countries. Edgeworth depicts two individual traders alongside their goods in a similar

---

Figure 3.4. (*Cont.*)

Scarce Tracts in Economics, No. 1, 1930). Reproduced with thanks to Marshall Library of Economics, Cambridge.

(c) Edgeworth's Exchange Diagram (1881).

Source: F. Y. Edgeworth, *Mathematical Psychics*. London: C. Kegan Paul & Co., 1881, fig. 1, p. 28.

(d) Pareto's "Optimum" Box Diagram (1906).

Source: Vilfredo Pareto, *Manuale di Economia Politica*. Milano: Societa Editrice Libraria, 1909 Edition, fig. 16, p. 138.

(e) Pareto's "Improvement" Box Diagram (1906).

Source: Vilfredo Pareto, *Manuale di Economia Politica*. Milano: Societa Editrice Libraria, 1906, fig. 50, p. 262.

arrangement, and includes Marshall's offer curves, seen as the two internal dotted curves on Edgeworth's diagram (Figure 3.4c).[19].

Edgeworth's first invention is to draw an indifference curve – the outer dotted lines – for each individual in this trading space: the individual is indifferent between points along their curve, for they represent ones of equal utility to him. This is usually regarded as a critical step forward in the history of neoclassical economics, in which Edgeworth takes Jevons' 1871 "pleasure machine" graph in Figure 3.4a (also discussed in Chapter 4) showing sensations of utility experienced by an individual from consuming *one* good and develops it into a utility map representing the utility of combinations of *two* goods to the individual (Figure 3.4c). And while it seems initially that the whole space is open for trade as in Marshall's Figure (3.4b), Edgeworth's Figure (3.4c) draws the indifference curves through the origin, that is, points at which utility is equivalent to that obtained from zero exchange. This rules out some areas of the 90-degree total space. As he drew in these curves it became clearer that this representation of the problem of exchange restricts the space in which contracts might be made compared to Marshall: the range of indeterminancy of exchange is not the whole plane, but only the area within the indifference curves and the contract curve.

The contract curve: CC′, the second of Edgeworth's innovations – represents the line of most desirable contracts for exchange that Crusoe and Friday might make with each other. As they bargain from the origin point, they can move northeastwards to points where either or both are better off up to the points on the contract curve. Once settled there, no variation is possible without making one of them worse off. Edgeworth's analysis showed the range of bargaining, but exactly where they settle depends on the bargaining strength of each of the two individuals: "This simplest case brings clearly into view the characteristic evil of indeterminate contract, *deadlock*, undecidable opposition of interests" (Edgeworth, 1881, p. 29). And so Edgeworth indicates the role for industrial arbitration "for instance, Robinson Crusoe to give Friday in the way of Industrial Partnership a *fraction* of the produce as well as wages, or again, arrangements about the mode of work" (Edgeworth, 1881, p. 29).

So far, Edgeworth uses the diagram to demonstrate – neatly and effectively – his abstract concepts and spatial reasoning. Then he begins to develop the diagram as

---

19 It is not immediately clear from Edgeworth's 1881 diagram what his two middle curves are. They cannot be indifference curves, because the contract curve is a locus of points at which the indifference curves are at tangency with each other. Edgeworth's footnote, p. 27, noted the close but not identical concepts of Marshall's treatment of instability in trade compared to his own treatment of instability of contract (and he referred to Marshall's figures 8 and 9 – which is consistent as a reference to Marshall, 1879 [1930]). In Edgeworth's 1891 similar diagram, these are Marshallian offer curves, and the consensus of the literature (see Creedy, 1992) is that they are indeed offer curves. I am indebted to Chiara Baroni for her research assistance and translation of various Italian articles of the 1890s which show Edgeworth (1891) repeating the basic elements of his 1881 diagram, and making some comparison with other diagrams of the period, in the context of a commentary on Marshall's trade diagrams. A history of these offer curve diagrams is given by Humphrey (1995), who also discusses other diagrams by Edgeworth from the 1880s. See also Cook (2005) and De Marchi (2003).

an instrument of enquiry to consider what happens with more than two traders: this is the case of 'imperfect competition' (which had previously failed to yield to mathematical analysis). He works with the figure to reason through the process by which agreements might be made and then broken as more traders enter the market.[20] The uncapped axes that he inherited from Marshall's trading diagrams put no limit on the amount of resource that can be exchanged. This enables him to represent agreements at greater (and lesser) exchange amounts as the process of imperfect competition goes ahead. Just as Ricardo had found unexpected insights from developing and using his model farm, Edgeworth gained new understanding from developing his model of exchange contracting and then from his reasoning with it.

Edgeworth was so impressed by the way his own diagram enabled him to generate insights about the *process* (rather than the outcome) of what happened when additional traders joined the market, that he wrote (1881, pp. 36–7, underlining added) that "the figure 1, page 28, is proved to be a <u>correct representation</u>," and that reasoning with it provides "an <u>abstract typical representation</u>" of the process that "will go on as long as it is possible to find a point $x'y'$ with the requisite properties...". In continuing this argument, he notes that this process arrives at the point $\eta\xi$ on his figure 1 (our Figure 3.4c), where the price ray from the origin will be at a tangent to both indifference curves (not shown on his diagram, but shown on the equivalent modern diagram, Figure 3.6b), which is also where the offer curves meet at the contract curve (shown on both). This point, Edgeworth notes, is the limit point to the case of increasing numbers of traders, namely the point obtained when full competition is in place.

It is not the primary aim of this chapter to go into the way that models such as the Edgeworth Box are used (see rather Humphrey's 1996 account) or how economists reason with them in general (see my later chapters). But because of my world-making claims, I need to delve a little further into how Edgeworth viewed this episode. From the beginning of his book, we see Edgeworth arguing for mathematics in economics, imagining how the economy could be described in mathematics and representing the economic world in mathematical terms and models. He arrived at his diagrammatic mathematical model – his figure 1 – by imagining a particular case he took to embody the typical exchange problem and making an image to represent it.

Having made his model to represent two parties in an economic situation, he then used it to demonstrate his previous claims, and to explore and explain other aspects of exchange behaviour that could be represented in his diagram. In this, he was following a pattern of representing trading situations: not only Marshall's diagrams of exchange between England and Germany, but recall also from Chapter 2, Ricardo's earlier arithmetic example of trade between Portugal and England. As we

---

20 At this stage, Edgeworth does not even bother to deal with the case of perfect or market competition since he claims that the results and nature of the equilibrium outcome are well understood from the work of Jevons, Walras, and Marshall.

shall see in Chapter 9, models made to represent situations form a continuing and important tradition in economic modelling. And while such diagrams represent specific situations, by providing convincing demonstrations of a logical kind that might well fit typical cases they seem to acquire broader relevance.

Edgeworth understands the powerfulness of such reasoning with cases, as we can see in his discussion of non-numerical forms of mathematical argument. Although he applauds mathematics because its "very genius is generalisation, [which,] without dipping into particulars, soars from generality to generality" (p. 86), he also claims that mathematics can get general results from arguing single particular cases:[21]

> Indeed, the nature of the subject is such that a *single* instance – by a sort of 'mathematical induction', as it has been called – a single 'representative-particular' authenticated instance of mathematical reasoning without numerical data is sufficient to establish the general principle. (Edgeworth, 1881, Appendix I, "On Unnumerical Mathematics," p. 83, his italics)

This claim about " a sort of mathematical induction" using a "single 'representative-particular' instance" is an apt description of his reasoning about Robinson Crusoe and Friday and what happens to their exchanges when you add traders into their isolated island market, that is, to their economic world in the model. If we take his description "*an abstract typical representation*" as a good one for something we would now denote 'a model', along with his equally interesting description of his mode of reasoning with it as: "*a single 'representative-particular' instance of mathematical reasoning*", then we have an appealing combination of definitions of models and model reasoning.

But there is also an appeal to generality in Edgeworth's reasoning: he claimed mathematics could establish a "general principle" by working with a single instance, a particular representative case, a diagram created from his imagination.[22] This sounds rather grand, and perhaps untenable. Yet the same thing occurred with our parallel example from the last chapter. Ricardo's enquiry into his little arithmetic model of the exchange of cloth and wine between Portugal and England – a very simple and particular case – also produced an outcome that has been taken

---

21 It appears to be in the nature of geometric reasoning that particular cases are taken to provide general proofs; see Arnheim, 1969, chapter 10, for an interesting discussion of this, and Netz (1999) for an account of the origins of such reasoning in Greek mathematics. For much of the nineteenth century, geometry was the exemplar of the mathematical method and *the* way to establish truths via mathematical argument (see Richards, 1988, and Weintraub, 2002 for its relevance for economists in that period). Edgeworth's views might be contrasted with those of Marshall, whose claims for the inductive role of diagrams rested on the possibility of drawing out all the possible cases (see De Marchi, 2003). I suggest however, in Chapter 10, that their two positions can be seen as consistent once one understands how the scope of model findings is extended across cases via mathematics.

22 This seems close to C. S. Peirce's views: "Mathematical truth is derived from observation of creations of our own visual imagination, which we may set down on paper in the form of diagrams" (C. S. Peirce, *Collected Papers*, 1932, Vol. 2, Para 77).

as demonstrative not just for the world in his model, but for a general principle, namely, for the law of comparative advantage.[23] The question of how economists reason with such abstract typical representations and representative-particulars will reappear later in Chapter 10, when I explore how such arguments with cases support claims that might best be described as generic rather than general.

5.ii Pareto's Imagination and Images

Vilfredo Pareto (1848–1923), an Italian contemporary of Edgeworth, was an equally important character in the development of mathematical economics, but his creation of a small economic world in a mathematical model proceeds very differently. Pareto's *Manual of Political Economy* (1906 [1971]) uses two types of mathematical reasoning; the primary one in the text develops through a series of arguments in which diagrams are the main mathematical form, and another, relegated to a long appendix, offers a more general treatment using algebra and calculus (like Marshall, he places some of his mathematical treatment in the background). Like Edgeworth, he relies on general arguments to introduce the specific diagrams, but unlike Edgeworth, these arguments are not analogical in character and he relies on the diagrammatic form much more extensively to work out his arguments and explanations of the economic behaviour of individuals. He portrays individuals as having particular tastes and seeking to do the best for themselves, but they are faced with and constrained by 'obstacles'. Individuals must take various paths to get around the obstacles, a trial-and-error, wandering, process reflected in the various diagrams he uses. Indifference curves between two goods are interpreted as contour lines on a map, for, as with Edgeworth, they are projections from an imagined (but not imaged) three-dimensional utility surface, with equal levels of utility along each contour. So an individual reaches an equilibrium when they have succeeded in getting around the obstacles and they have reached the highest point on their contour map. His description is extremely graphic.

Amongst a plethora of diagrams, the two that move Edgeworth's diagram forward are the first appearance of it as a box: his figure 16 (our Figure 3.4d), and his figure 50 (our Figure 3.4e) in which the diagram is used to develop the notion of what is known as a 'Pareto improvement'. The former figure 16 creates a box from Edgeworth's open axes, and reorientates it (by ninety degrees), with the two individuals at opposite corners, each with a whole set of indifference curves (rather than the single one for each individual drawn in by Edgeworth). The latter, figure 50, is similar but shows only two indifference curves for each individual. One of

---

23 While this law remains as a general foundational tenant of economic science, its ability to account for our observations of the world is more doubtful. Indeed, its failure to explain trade patterns has lead to the development of other trade 'principles', or general claims, some of which were developed through reasoning with the Edgeworth Box.

these individuals is represented as located with axes $0x$ and $0y$ and indifference curves labelled with t, so that as that person moves further away from their origin at 0, they are at successively higher levels of utility or pleasure (Pareto's "ophelimity"), they are moving uphill in Pareto's terminology. The other has axes $\omega\alpha$ and $\omega\beta$ and indifference curves labelled with s, moving uphill as they go away from ω towards 0. They appear with the following theorem and commentary on it:

> We have the following theorem:
> *For phenomena of Type 1, when equilibrium takes place at a point where the indifference curves of the contracting parties are tangent, the members of the collectivity under consideration enjoy maximum ophelimity [utility].* (Pareto (1906[1971] Chapter 6, Para 34, p. 261, his italics)
>
> For phenomena of Type I, we know that the equilibrium point must be at a tangency of the indifference curves of the two individuals. Let c be one of these points. If we move away from it following the route cc', we ascend the first individual's hill of pleasure and descend that of the second; and conversely, if we follow the route cc''. Hence, it is not possible to move away from c helping, or harming, both individuals at one and the same time; but necessarily, if it is agreeable to one, it is disagreeable to the other.
>
> It is not the same for points, such as d, where two indifference curves intersect. If we follow the route dd', we increase the satisfaction of both individuals; if we follow the line dd'' we decrease it for both. (Pareto, 1906[1971], Chapter 6, Para 35, pp. 262–3)

Type I phenomena are those in which neither individual tries to alter the market terms of exchange, that is, where the two individuals' indifference curves meet at a tangency with the price ray (the ratio of exchange between the goods, represented by a straight line) so the equilibrium is at point c as in his figure 16, a point that comes to be called 'a Pareto optimum'.[24] Type II phenomena appear when individuals do have some power to alter the price ratio, and as Pareto argues, at their likely equilibrium point d, there are possibilities for both parties to gain utility by moving in direction d', and for the collective utility therefore to rise: that enquiry, with his new setup in the diagram, lead to the fundamental notion now known as a 'Pareto improvement'. But still the final point of exchange is indeterminate, and here Pareto muses regretfully about the impossibilities for economists – if only they were as lucky as chemists – to conduct experiments with individuals in exchange situations to further these investigations. Several decades later, his wish came true, and an example of such experiments with individuals in the situation depicted in the Box is reported in Chapter 8.

---

24 Point c will be a point on Edgeworth's contract curve: the set of points where the indifference curves are tangencies to each other (which is not shown in Pareto's diagram). When two indifference curves meet back to back at the price ray (that is, where the price ray is a tangent to both indifference curves as at point c) that point comes to be called a 'Pareto optimum' – a notion mentioned by Merkies.

For Pareto, as for Edgeworth, the essential and important reasoning is done with the diagram, not off the diagram, though in the case of Pareto, the diagram is taken as offering neither a typical case nor grounds for a mathematical induction. For Pareto, *the reasoning just is diagrammatic*. His series of specific cases – each one shown in a diagrammatic model – represents his mathematical economic world within which he builds up his arguments. While his 'sketch' account (using his figure 50 diagram) is strong enough to carry the detail required to convince, Pareto, like Edgeworth, argues that rigorous proofs of his theorems can be given only by mathematics (in his Appendix). For both it seems, general analytical treatments are not necessarily of greater importance than the economic reasoning with diagrams in the text. For both, the diagrammatic models provide the arguments for the two-good, two-traders world, and they are sufficient for demonstrating results and gaining conviction about that small economic world in the model.[25]

The Box diagram is, however, an extremely deceptive object. It looks like a very constrained world in the model: What can it possibly have to say more broadly? First, as we saw in Merkies' arguments, despite its small scale and apparently limited scope, Edgeworth's and Pareto's demonstrations with the Box reach towards some fundamental and general results in mathematical economics such as Pareto optimality and so to the "First Fundamental Welfare Theorem" in modern economics (see Blaug 2007). Second, as we know from its later history (see Humphrey, 1996), although this small-scale world was built to represent specific exchange situations, it turned out to have great flexibility over a range of similar trading situations as well as in other domains of economics such as in production and welfare economics. Third, although the Box is a two-dimensional object on paper, the number of things it can represent does not seem to be unduly constrained by that dimensionality. Edgeworth manages to enlarge his small world to argue the case with more traders and, even as early as Pareto's time, the Box represents two individuals, each with two goods in exchange, along with equilibrium points and price rays: that is, it already shows relations among six economic elements.[26]

Given these kinds of flexibility, it is perhaps not so surprising that for both Edgeworth and Pareto, diagrammatic models played an important role in their making a new version of the world for economic science, one that could be reasoned with mathematically. In creating their mathematical diagrams, they followed a process of imagination and image-making. These visualizations embedded new conceptual materials for economic analysis (indifference curves, contract curves, and Pareto improvements). A further historical sequence of diagrams also supports

25 Of course, when economists find models too small and limited in dimensionality, and seek to generalize to bigger worlds (e.g., to cases of more goods and more traders), they may look to other kinds of mathematical demonstrations, perhaps to the general equilibrium account of Walras (and the method of mathematical postulation and proof; see Chapter 1).

26 Lancaster (1957) claimed that later boxes show relations among twelve economic variables, possibly he was including the production elements as well.

deeper and broader claims about newness. For this I return to questions about representation.

6. The World Newly Made in the Model: Questions of Representation?

6.i Visualization

As we observed in discussing the picture sequence within Merkies' text, model-making is a creative process; but the actual historical sequence of visualization observed in Figures 3.4 and 3.5 is very different from that of his artist illustrating an already well-accepted model diagram. When economists *first* make an image of the economy, it is not that they already know how the world works and subtract elements from it to isolate certain parts. Rather it is that they use their imaginations about the hidden workings of the economic world to make representations of those workings in equations or diagrams. Gradually over time, other economists add further elements to the representation. The historical development of the Edgeworth Box model enables us to explore some detailed questions about this process of model-making and to answer certain earlier questions about the representation: Why is it a box? Why are the individuals in an antagonistic stance? And so forth.

Here the relevant comparisons are not between the historical sequence and the artist's pictures, but between the historical sequence and an economist's modernised versions of the Box. If we start with the modern Box representation (as seen already in Figure 3.1), we find two adjacent sides of the Box denoting a fixed amount of the two goods or services or resources available so that the Box represents a world with given and fixed resources. The two antagonistically placed origin points mark the direction of stance of two traders, each with their own two axes (the adjacent ones), and on which their own shares of resources by endowment and by exchange can be marked.

But this was not how Edgeworth imagined the economic world. Our comparison reveals that the most striking thing in this historical sequence of diagrams, evidenced in our second series Figure 3.5a–f, is that Edgeworth's 1881 diagram *is not a box at all, but an open plane*, in which the quantities of goods at issue are not fixed but expandable (in Figure 3.5a).[27] It is equally striking that Edgeworth's *individuals line up side by side*: each trader measures off his resources for exchange

---

27 Economists are now so habituated to the modern diagram that some have difficulty in seeing what imaginative leap was required and what was new about Edgeworth's diagram. My experience in giving this chapter as a seminar paper was that some economists found it difficult to believe that Edgeworth did not conceive of a box – despite his diagram; others argued that he must have fully conceived all the conceptual contents and outcomes before he drew it, that is, that the diagram was "merely illustration" to his argument – despite the textual evidence (quoted above) which suggests otherwise.

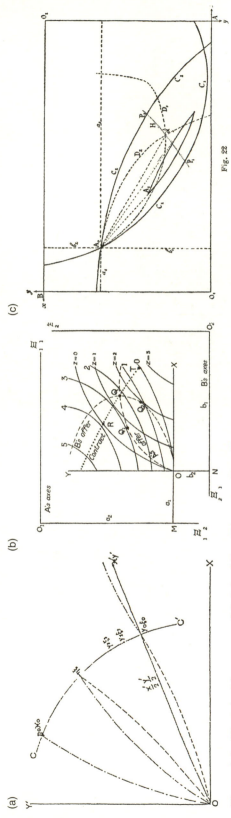

Figure 3.5. Historical Sequence of Original Box Diagrams Part II.

(a) Edgeworth's Exchange Diagram (1881).

Source: F.Y. Edgeworth, *Mathematical Psychics*. London C. Kegan Paul & Co, 1881, fig 1 p. 28.

(b) Bowley's Box (1924).

Source: Arthur Lyon Bowley, *The Mathematical Groundwork of Economics, An Introductory Treatise*. Oxford: Clarendon Press, 1924, fig. 1, p. 5. Reproduced with permission from Oxford University Press.

(c) Lenoir's Box (1913).

Source: Marcel Lenoir, *Études sur la Formation et le Mouvement des Prix*. Paris: M. Giard & É. Brière, 1913, fig. 22, p. 21.

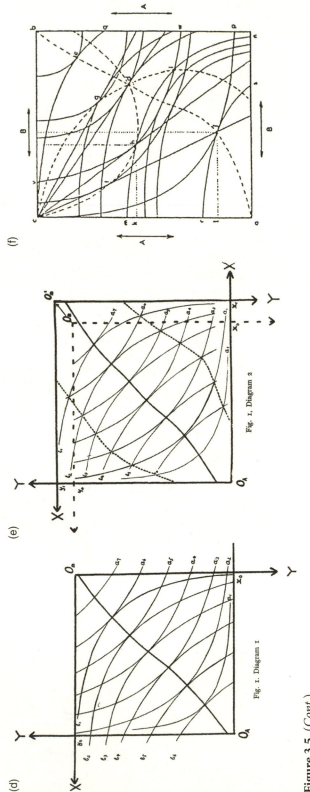

Figure 3.5. (*Cont.*)

(d, e) Scitovsky's Extending Box 1941.

Source: T. De Scitovszky (1941), "A Note on Welfare Propositions in Economics", *The Review of Economic Studies*, 9:1, 77–88, fig. 1 diagram 1 on p. 80 and fig. 1 diagram 2 on p. 81. Reproduced with permission from Wiley-Blackwell.

(f) Leontief's Box 1946.

Source: Wassily Leontief (1946), "The Pure Theory of the Guaranteed Annual Wage Contract", *Journal of Political Economy*, 54:1, 76–79, fig. 1 on p. 77. Reproduced with permission from University of Chicago Press.

along one axis only – one trader X is trying to make a contract by trading his own x for some y offered by Y. What might now be taken as the irreducible shape of the Box – namely a closed set of two amounts of exchangeable items represented by the sides of the Box, and two traders at opposite corners, each with two axes of potential commodities to trade with – are not there from the beginning. In Edgeworth's imagination and diagram, the world is represented very differently from that found in the modern version.

It was Pareto in 1906 (in French in 1909), who without comment, imagines and places the individuals at the SW and NE corners (this new orientation becomes the standard one). By *placing them opposite each other and making the diagram into a Box* as we saw in his figure 16 (Figure 3.4d), he represents a fixed quantity of both goods, but, by extending the axes beyond the rectangle, invites the possibility of extension. Marcel Lenoir (1913), who was familiar with Edgeworth and Pareto's work, picked up the latter's formulation of the Box, and seems to have anticipated Bowley's innovation of moving the starting point for trade inside the Box (Figure 3.5c). Apparently Pareto's contribution was not immediately known in the English-language literature, and this perhaps explains why Bowley's 1924 image (Figure 3.5b) follows Edgeworth in orientation (i.e., potentially NW–SE), while he too presents the two traders at opposite corners. And though he presents almost *a box, it remains open*, or rather, unclosed, and his axes appear flexible in length. Bowley puts numbers on his sequence of indifference curves: he thinks of them as representing nonmeasurable, but ordered, sensations of satisfaction, where the numbers are like readings of heat on a thermometer, except that "The thermometer is calibrated; the imaginary vessel of sensation is not" (Bowley, 1924, p. 2).[28]

Lenoir's and Bowley's most important image change then is *moving the starting point for trade* – the point from which trading commences according to the indifference curves, and that we now call *'the endowment point'* (the point representing how much each trader is endowed with) – *into the middle of the Box*.[29] By contrast, Edgeworth had pictured Crusoe and Friday starting exchange from a position where each owned only the full amount of his own resources. This imaginative move has consequences, for while the indifference curves can be drawn fully inside the Box (as Humphrey shows in our Figure 3.1), the offer curves for the traders must be drawn from their initial endowment point: every change in endowments alters the bargains they are likely to agree to, and thus the range of the solutions.

---

28 This habit relates to a debate over the cardinality or ordinality of utility measures (and so of indifference curves) and the broader relation between psychology and economics – see Coats (1976) for an historical account of these issues.

29 Historians of economics have argued over whether Edgeworth's original diagram can properly be called a box and over the relative contributions of Edgeworth, Bowley, and Pareto to its genesis and development (see particularly Creedy, 1980; Tarascio, 1980; and Wetherby, 1976). Lenoir's contribution was unknown until recovered by Chaigneau and Le Gall (1998). In the British literature, the Box is sometimes known as the Edgeworth-Bowley Box, possibly because, in his continuation of Edgeworth's work, Bowley added these two specific innovations of double axes and endowment points.

Much of neoclassical economics' use of the Box follows this lead of starting from an initial point inside the Box and using that point to address questions of efficiency and optimum outcomes, but these will be optimum only given that initial endowment of goods. So, by *assuming the endowment point is already given*, questions about welfare and equity in the initial distribution of wealth are closed off. Merkies' lecture was concerned with such equity issues, which, as we can now see, became masked by the historical development of moving the endowment point into the Box. Lenoir's and Bowley's version of the diagram thus proved a highly significant move in the history of welfare economics.

As we have seen, the diagram was originally developed to analyse *the exchange outcomes* of two individuals. The question that Edgeworth inherited from Jevons' utility map of pleasure and pain for one individual was to picture what happened with just two individuals – not market exchange with many traders on both sides. He portrays an isolated island economy – of Crusoe and Friday – to provide an imaginative focus for considering how two such individuals would bargain and where they will end up making an exchange. He argues that the exchange point between these two will rest on the contract curve, but exactly where will depend on their relative bargaining power. Pareto develops the Box to define which moves towards an exchange point within the area of possible points are improvements for both. Bowley uses his Box diagram (Figure 3.5b) to argue that the area of bargaining is not on the contract curve, but defined by the range of exchange points bounded by Marshall's offer curves and the contract curve: Bowley's Q_1QQ_2 (if B sets the price ratio, the solution will lie at Q_1 and if A controls the prices, at Q_2). For both Pareto and Bowley then, the exchange outcomes are dependent upon the original endowment point, as well as upon the relative bargaining power of the traders in negotiation as Edgeworth had argued. Leontief (Figure 3.5f) uses the diagram to label another two points – his points *e* and *f*, equivalent to Edgeworth's boundary points on the contract curve (points C and C′ on the modern image Figure 3.6a) – as the solution points for 'perfectly discriminating' monopolists in contrast to Edgeworth's earlier location of the point of perfect competition.

The *Box edges* might seem unimportant, but this aspect of the image too is an element to be carefully considered. While Bowley's two axes continue but do not meet, Scitovsky (1941) (our Figure 3.5d), like Pareto, extends his axes beyond the Box, as indeed does Lerner (1933/52), who, by simply substituting factors of production for goods to exchange, and production maps for utility maps, made *his Box represent production*, not exchange. We see the importance of whether *the Box is joined up, and so resources fixed*, or not in the work of Scitovsky. He uses his diagrams to establish what would happen if the Box grew in size. The critical point of his article is the difference in judging allocative efficiency between situations in which the total resources in the economy are fixed – denoted by a fixed size Box, and those in which the resources change – denoted by a change in Box size. The representation of the effect of this change proves to be quite difficult to understand for the modern user of boxes: it is an imaginative and cognitive difficulty.

It is tempting for the viewer of the model to suppose that by expanding the Box, there are just longer axes, more cheese and wine to be exchanged for a given indifference maps (representing tastes, which have no reason to alter). But of course, these indifference contours are in conceptual space inside the box, and increasing the total resources effectively expands the box from the middle. As the axes are lengthened, perceptual space expands, but so does the conceptual space, so that the contract curve on his first diagram becomes the two dotted lines on the second (see Scitovsky's 1941, Figure 1, Diagrams 1 and 2, our Figure 3.5d and 3.5e). Changing the resources by increasing one axis and reducing the other creates even more dissonance for the modern economist.

Each of these moves, each new addition, each change in shape or content, or reconstruction of the Edgeworth Box diagram – each new image – was prompted by a process of economists' imagining how individuals come to make economic exchanges. We see the results of this process of imagination and image-making by following the original historical sequence of diagrams (Figures 3.4 and 3.5). This gives an impression of a model that begins quite modestly and evolves to stabilize in form around the early 1950s. We see the addition of elements and growing complexity of the diagrams as economists get more confident in visualizing exchange questions and demonstrating answers within this model. At the beginning of the history, as can be seen when comparing some of these original figures with Humphrey's modernized version in Figure 3.1, there is a substantial difference between the originals and the modern version. After Leontief (1946) (Figure 3.5f), the original diagrams are virtually the same as Humphrey's. At that point, we might say the representation became 'modern' and Leontief indeed describes the diagram as "conventional".

If we were to make the reverse comparison, and look at the full sequence of modernized diagrams given by Humphrey to represent these changes compared to the real historical sequence, we would find that sometimes he subtracted elements to focus on what is new, sometimes added elements, and sometimes made extra versions of the Box, to make his modernist form provide the required representative power, arguments, and explanations of the earlier diagrams. His additions and changes are not necessarily because the earlier diagrams lack the resources to show the elements; on the contrary in some ways they are more effective. In part these changes are because the balance between words and diagrams in explanation and argument alters over the period. Earlier users are more economical with their diagrams (perhaps they had to be for printing reasons). For example, compare Leontief's diagram with Humphrey's version of his diagram in Figure 3.6a. They are drawn to represent the same concept set: the indifference maps, the contract curve, the offer curves, and the discriminating monopolist exchange points. The same main points are labelled on both, but notice the incredible complexity of Leontief's diagram compared to Humphrey's. This is because Leontief uses only one diagram to explain all the elements and theoretical results to date, whereas Humphrey, by this stage in his text, is using his ninth diagram. For another part, it is because once the Box has become stabilized into its current closed form, it is not

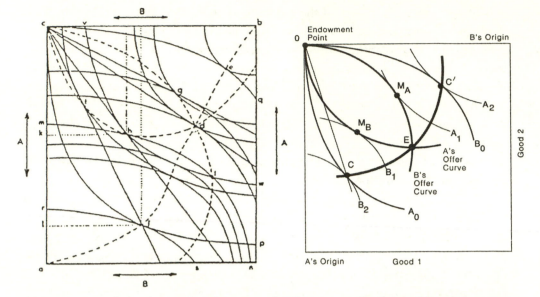

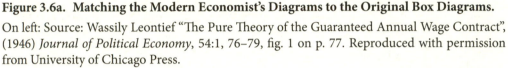

Figure 3.6a. Matching the Modern Economist's Diagrams to the Original Box Diagrams.

On left: Source: Wassily Leontief "The Pure Theory of the Guaranteed Annual Wage Contract", (1946) *Journal of Political Economy*, 54:1, 76–79, fig. 1 on p. 77. Reproduced with permission from University of Chicago Press.

On right: Source: Tom Humphrey "The Early History of the Box Diagram" (1996) *Economic Quarterly*, 82:1, 37–75, figure 9. Reproduced with permission from the author, Tom Humphrey, and The Federal Reserve Bank of Richmond.

so easy to make it represent things in the same way as in the older boxes. As can be seen in Figure 3.6b, Edgeworth, with his open (unboxed) plane of competition, can represent the process of imperfect competition in his one diagram, possibilities that cannot be shown on Humphrey's modernized format in which the Box is already closed and so the total resources of the economy fixed and predetermined. Humphrey needed an additional four diagrams to show what he takes to be the equivalent process.[30] For another example, see the (above) discussion of the Box by Scitovsky (1941), which Humphrey cannot easily represent because the fixed size of the modern Box does not allow it. His modern reconstruction required Humphrey to rethink the images, but not to re-experience the imaginative leaps of the original modellers.

It is the combination of this economy of representation and the flexibility in representational space found in earlier diagrams that makes some of them difficult to understand for modern users. Once the diagram had stabilized in form and content, some of this flexibility disappeared, though at the same time, the range of spaces the Box was taken to represent expanded to include production

---

30 To be fair to Humphrey's account, Edgeworth does then use a second figure (his figure 2, p. 40) – to give a 'close-up' view of how increasing traders moves toward the market solution point.

and international trade domains alongside the original exchange and welfare ones. Economists continued to find new uses for the diagram and turned it into a means of enquiry into other economic realms. The imaginative use of the diagram does not seem to have stopped even though the main image stabilized in form.

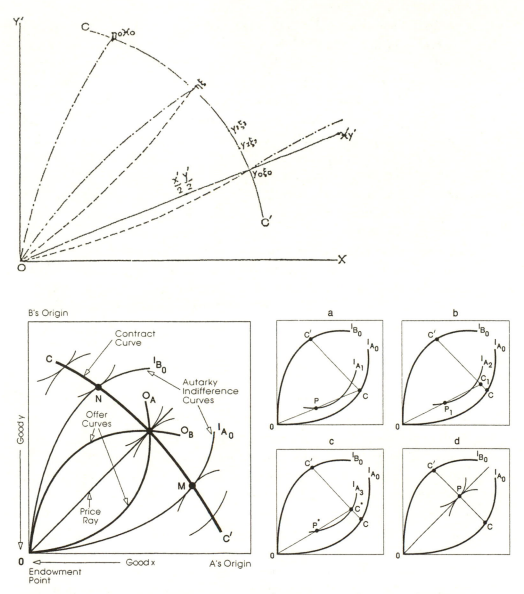

Figure 3.6b. Matching the Modern Economist's Diagrams to the Original Box Diagrams.

On top: Source: F. Y. Edgeworth, *Mathematical Psychics*. London: C. Kegan Paul & Co., 1881, fig 1, p. 28.

On bottom: Source: Tom Humphrey "The Early History of the Box Diagram" (1996) *Economic Quarterly*, 82:1, 37–75, figures 2 and 4. Reproduced with permission from the author, Tom Humphrey, and The Federal Reserve Bank of Richmond.

Perhaps for the non-economist, the strangest element about the history of the Box is the *ciphering of the individuals* and the *conflation* that occurs between *their identity* and that of the *goods* that they own and come to exchange. Remember in Merkies' lecture how the colour coding for the goods – cheese and wine – suddenly morphed to represent the individuals. These conflated elements appear as a set of preference lines in the indifference maps; that is, people are represented both by their origin or endowment points and in their preferences in terms of the two goods. But they have little personality: their indifference maps are drawn to behave according to the 'wishes' of the economist (as Merkies expressed himself). Albert and Beatrice appear as letters on the axes or at the origins: in Bowley's diagram, people A and B trade goods 1 and 2, while in Leontief's paper, people a and b trade goods A and B. In Scitovsky's diagram, we have people A and B, with indifference lines labelled a and b and trading goods x and y! This is pretty confusing, and the lack of any consistency here indicates how unimportant their identities are. These are symbols without any symbolism, without any special meaning, for neither people nor goods in the Box have any particular character worth mentioning. It might have seemed from Merkies' pictures that the individuals and their goods shown around the edge are the most important things in the model. In Edgeworth's Box, they still have characters: Robinson Crusoe and Friday; but by Pareto's time, they really are the shadows they become in the Artist's pictures. I discuss how individuals turn into these shadowy people in economics in Chapter 4; but here it is the conceptual apparatus depicting their exchange behaviour inside the Box that matters and is being imagined, imaged, and so modelled, without much attention to their personalities.

6.ii Newness

Although economists fail to express visually the full particulars of Albert and Beatrice, or their cheese and wine, the diagrams are critical for Edgeworth, Pareto, and the other users of the Box because the Box enables them to place their symbolised individuals into a different form of relationship, and to say different things about that relationship, than in the verbal economics they supplant. The act of representation here involves the direct visualization of the economic world into mathematical symbols and other forms of nonverbal denotation to create a substantial new world in the model. Along with the new forms came substantial new conceptual content.[31]

The contents of the Box traced through the historical model sequence. Figures 3.4 and 3.5 show how the new conceptual elements associated with the model were developed into an analytical apparatus. Edgeworth (1881) made a substantial development of both Jevons' (1871) individual utility graph and Marshall's (1879) trade diagrams

---

31 This relation between new forms of expression and new content echoes Weintraub's (1991) account of how the construction of economic theories about dynamics into mathematical form changed the substance of those theories. For other examples of imagistic reasoning in scientific discovery in relation to innovations in concepts, see Nersessian (1990), Griesemer and Wimsatt (1989), and Toulmin (1953, chapter 2), who also uses Crusoe and Friday to focus his discussion.

in commodity space for two traders (countries) by mapping utility concepts into the commodity space: namely by adding an indifference curve for each trader and their contract curve (see Creedy, 1986). These indifference curves and the contract curve are the critical conceptual innovations that Edgeworth developed, and they are represented for the first time in his diagram. Pareto provides indifference maps, and shows the trading range in which welfare improvements can be negotiated in relation to price rays. Bowley introduces the possibility of initial endowments inside the Box and shows the offer curves from this new 'origin' point clearly on the same map to indicate an alternative bargaining range. Scitovsky develops an analysis of what happens to the utility maps when the size of the commodity space changes. Leontief puts together all the conceptual elements of the indifference map, offer curves, the contract curve, and price rays onto the same diagram. Although some of the ideas associated with these elements have a longer history, the conceptual apparatus is not something that existed before and outside of the model; rather, the conceptual elements are new with the representation and developed inside and alongside the model.

As a test of this proposition of newness, imagine giving a translation of Leontief's diagram in words with a sufficiently exact description so that all the parts, and their relations to each other, are made clear. Such a description could be given, but only by using economists' now habitual mathematical and spatial terms expressing these economic concepts. But these same concepts and terms depended for their definition and their development on the creation of the diagram and on economic reasoning with it. Thus, economists can translate (with some difficulty) their mathematical model world back into verbal terms, but it is a new world being expressed, one that they could not have expressed before they made that diagrammatic world. A similar trial of imagination and cognition is made when an economist of today tries to explain the *Tableau Économique* of Chapter 1. There is an incommensurability in these cases that comes from both the newly conceptualized materials and from their mode of expression.

I should be careful here to point out that when the Edgeworth Box is described as a mathematical model, it is not made of only mathematics. Recall also from Chapter 1 that model-making, in giving more exact form to intuitions about the economic world, at the same time provides rules for reasoning with that model. This is best illustrated (and speaks indirectly to the newness claim) by considering the allowable movements or manipulations that can be made in the Box model. The notion that the two traders will be at some kind of optimum when their indifference curves meet at a tangency makes use of mathematical concepts and logic. But the apparatus of offer curves, indifference curves, and so, for example, the spaces in which trade is ruled out, depend on understanding the new economic conceptual content of the elements in the model. Bowley's movement of the origin into the Box has implications for welfare arguments, which depend on the economic content of the Box. Scitovsky's diagram showing the implications of increasing the resources requires manipulations of the diagram that are determined by the economic meaning of these new curves, which were derived from three-dimensional maps and so do not follow the rules or logic of two-dimensional diagrams. Both mathematical and subject matter conceptual knowledge go into forming the details of the representation, and so reasoning with the model depends not only on the mathematics but also on economic subject information to define the allowable rules of manipulation.[32] From this point of view, there would be as much difficulty in 'translating' the Edgeworth Box into 'just mathematics' with no subject content as into 'just words' with no mathematical content.

A more general sense of what it means to say that we have a new model version of the world is suggested by Michael Lynch (1990) in his discussion of diagrams in social theory. There he remarks, of one example, that it "is a diagram that does not obviously perform an independent representational function. If it were removed from the text, it would not be missed because it adds very little to what the surrounding text says" (Lynch, 1990, p. 5). This is a stronger version, if you like, of Mahoney's observation about "reasoning off the diagram", because of the additional focus on independence, and echoes James Griesemer's parallel argument (of 1991) that diagrams may be ineliminable with respect to other forms of representation in the text. These suggestions about the independence of diagrammatic reasoning support claims about the autonomy of models, namely that it is their independence in functioning that gives models such a potentially powerful epistemic role in science (see Morrison and Morgan, 1999). Here with the Edgeworth Box, that potential rests on its independent representational *content*. And, as we have seen in the preceding discussion, that content is *conceptual*. The Edgeworth Box diagram carries new conceptual apparatus that could not be represented, or manipulated, in verbal form and indeed cannot be entirely expressed in purely (ie subject-matter free) mathematical terms. This is how it comes to carry an independent representational function, and why the Edgeworth Box has had such a long lifespan as an autonomous model able to represent not only individuals in exchange, but also many other elements and relations.

As we saw in Merkies' account, reasoning with the conceptual elements developed with the Box has had such a general reach in economics that we may even see the Edgeworth Box as a shorthand version of modern neoclassical economics: demonstrating – with two consumers, two producers, two factors of production, and two goods – efficient production, maximum utility (consumption), Nash equilibrium outcomes, and Pareto optimality. These are the essential building blocks and main results of neoclassical economics contained in a nutshell. The Edgeworth Box acts as both *a scale model or miniature version of* neoclassical economics and as *a perfect 'logo' or role model for* such economics.[33]

---

32 See Weintraub's (2002) chapter 5 (with Ted Gayer) on Patinkin and Phipps for a good example of how mathematicians and economists can talk past each other because they fail to see this point.

33 I am indebted to Tim Hatton, who suggested this 'logo' aspect (see Chapter 10). See Baden-Fuller and Morgan (2010) on the distinction between scale and role models in a discussion of how certain real firms act as 'business models'.

7. Seeing the World in the Model

I return now to the importance of the particular language of representation in the history of economics. The pioneering mathematical economists wanted to express their economics in new ways, and in this respect, the move from sentences to diagrams may be associated with a somewhat more radical change than that from sentences to algebra. The basis for this claim can be found in the analysis by Larkin and Simon (1987, p. 66), who point to the differences in the way arguments work when a problem is expressed in a "sentential" representation (sentences or algebra) compared to a diagrammatic representation. The diagrammatic form expresses location and spatial relational aspects of a problem; the sentential forms express the temporal and/or logical relations.[34] The relatively greater change required to move from the representational forms of sentences to diagrams (as opposed to from sentences to equations), and their different possibilities, might be one reason why diagrammatic models played such an important creative role in making a new version of economics through mathematization for the first generation of model-makers in the late nineteenth century.

But as I argued in Chapter 1, form also dictates certain aspects of the reasoning rules used with models, or, as Larkin and Simon express the point: "the distinctions between representations is not rooted in the notations used to write them, but in the operations used on them" (Larkin and Simon, 1987, p. 68). From the point of view of how we use a model, it matters little if we denote a person as A or Albert, but the discussion of his relationships and exchange equilibrium works very differently with the Edgeworth Box diagram than when working with a set of sentences, or even a set of equations. Edgeworth found it both very inefficient and extremely difficult to analyse the imperfect competition exchange problem (of an increasing number of traders) verbally or by seeking a general analytical mathematical formulation of the process, yet it yielded to his diagrammatic "abstract-typical" case approach. This returns us to my argument at the beginning of this chapter about the importance of choices of form or language in making new versions of the world in models.

Diagrammatic reasoning may also benefit from a certain cognitive advantage compared to sentential or algebraic representation. It is notable that Larkin and Simon discuss an economics example, the supply and demand Marshallian cross: "the great utility of the diagram arises from *perceptual enhancement*, the fact that it makes explicit the relative positions of the equilibrium points, so that the conclusions can be read off with the help of simple, direct perceptual operations" (Larkin and Simon, 1987, p. 95).[35] The general point to take here is that this

---

34 I am grateful to Marcel Boumans who points out that of course, these sentential forms are not reducible or easily translatable to each other, a stronger version of my point about the 'formal equivalence' of representations in Section 1.

35 The primacy of the visual sense in communication and intelligibility has often been asserted. See Arnheim (1969) for the stronger thesis that thinking is perceptual and Tufte (particularly 1983 and 1997) for a series of books celebrating both views.

perceptual element helps solve the cognitive problem of understanding and using the conceptual spaces of the diagram *only once that diagram is already conceived*. Once the model has been created, perceptual elements may be helpful in reasoning with the Box model, and constructing argument chains with the diagram, as we shall see with the Marshallian cross diagram (in Chapter 7). But it is the creation and development of the Box diagram that allowed the economists involved to open up those new conceptual spaces and resources in economics.

Let me put these bits of argument together in a more general way: the ability to take cognitive advantage of the different perceptual possibilities of different forms of model is determined by the choices the scientist makes in portraying the economic world in the model, both the choice of representational form and within that, the choices of how elements and their relations are represented. I can communicate the importance of this aspect of models by relating it explicitly to an analogous change in visual representation. Ivins (1953), in writing about the introduction of printmaking techniques, gives us an analogy for how economists make models in the first place. He asks: How do etcher-engravers make their visual representations? Much like economic model-makers it seems, for, as Ivins wrote of the former,

> The competent and honest observer and recorder, however, had his very distinct limitations. In the first place, he could only draw a selected and very small part of the things he did observe. More than that, courageous and sharp-sighted as he might be, he had learned to see in a particular way and to lay his lines in accordance with the requirements of some particular convention or system of linear structure, and anything that way of seeing and that convention of drawing were not calculated to catch and bring out failed to be brought out in his statement. For shortness' sake I shall frequently refer to such conventions as syntaxes. (Ivins, 1953, pp. 60–1)

Ivins thus takes us straight back to language and conventions. For the earliest engravers, different visualizing conventions developed in different locations. Apparently, the Italian etchers aimed for three-dimensionality and concentrated on representing the outlines of objects in relation to space, while the Germans paid relatively more attention to representing the textures of the objects. Ivins suggests the effect of this – namely that "even the greatest of them [the Germans] saw objects located in a space that was independent of them and unrelated to their forms, whereas the greater Italians saw that space was merely the relation between objects" (Ivins, 1953, p. 64).

The analogical material here echoes my claims for mathematical economics. A new kind of representation – mathematical models – leads economic scientists to see in a particular way; and each different form of visualization, such as arithmetic, algebra or geometry, diagrams or even machines, leads to a focus on different aspects of the economic elements represented in their models. Portrayal and cognition are intimately linked and both these, in turn, to conception and perception.

Economists do not start out by perceiving the world clearly and describing it in their model but by visualizing how the economic world might be and portraying that intuition in their model – imagining and imaging. In the process of such modelling, economists develop new concepts and so they – and we – come to perceive new things in the economic world (a point I return to in Chapter 10). A new way of looking at the familiar problems of exchange led to a new sense of what the phenomena entailed.

8. Conclusion

I argued earlier that models play an important role in the *process* of the mathematization of economics, first because economists could not make their mathematical version of the economic world all at once and second, because they needed to generate both the new vocabulary and new forms for thinking about the world, just as etchers had to learn the means and develop a language to make new forms of pictures. The history of the Edgeworth Box diagram provides an exemplar for these claims in economics. It suggests how the process of making a new world, a world of mathematical economics, was accomplished gradually by a process of developing mathematical models or representations which stabilized over time. A mathematical economic version of exchange relations in the world was not there to be read off: the situations and processes of exchange had to be imagined and imaged; they had to be visualized into a new representation: the Edgeworth Box.

At the same time, the independent representational content and function of this particular model helped to create the elements for a broader mathematically made version of economics. Creating this Edgeworth Box model and using it as a means of enquiry generated some of the important concepts of mathematical economics, concepts that turned out to be more generally relevant for the further mathematization of economics and so helped delineate the representations and reasoning claims that were allowable in the disciplinary field. These conceptual elements – indifference curves, contract curves, and so forth – have lived a longer life than their initial enclosure within the Edgeworth Box might suggest. Far from being prisoners of a particular model, they proved remarkably free to travel into other models and even to completely different modes of doing economics. Indifference curves, for example, became standard representative devices in microeconomics in general. The range of the contract curve in which settlements would be made within the Box was reconstituted in 1959 as "the core" an important concept in game theory by Martin Shubik (who will turn up as one of the heroes of Chapter 8). 'Lab' experiments have investigated people's exchange behaviour by designing experiments to match the Box situation (as we also find in Chapter 8). Such conceptual content that travels free from its initial model formulation is particularly important for it forms a generic vocabulary, far more useful than technical terms tied to a specific time and purpose. When we find such abstract conceptual elements that are first developed in models and then become more deeply rooted in economics, we begin to understand how and why modelling grew so luxuriantly in modern mathematical economics and why mathematical economics became so dependent on modelling.[36]

Thus, to go back to my original claims for the importance of modelling in relation to both the history of economics and the nature of the science it became, it is not just that (as economists have long argued) mathematics is more exact in expression, or a more efficient workhorse, or more rigorous in argument. The point is that economics did not start with a mathematical version of the economic world; rather, economists imagined how the economic world worked, and made images, or models, of it: a joint process of figuring it out and filling it in. These mathematical models represent something *different* from verbal accounts, they involve *different* concepts, and use *different* kinds of arguments. They represent something independently of the text; that something has conceptual content not (easily) expressible in words, and it is this quality that made models such good building blocks for a mathematically made version of the economic world. Thus models became constitutive – rather than illustrative – of modern economics.

Acknowledgement

This chapter was written for the ECHE conference on "Economic Science and Visual Representation", Montreal, March 2002. It was given a preliminary airing at the Measurement Group in Physics and Economics at CPNSS, LSE in October 2001, and was later presented at seminars at Cambridge, Queen Mary College London, UC Davis, and Pittsburgh; and to the History of Economics Society Annual Conference and at the ANU-Toyota Public Lecture Series 2005 at the National Museum of Australia. My thanks go particularly to Roy Weintraub, Neil De Marchi, Charles Baden-Fuller, Harro Maas, Marcel Boumans, Paul Teller, Tom Humphrey, Tony Lawson, John Davis, Margaret Schabas, Mike Mahoney, Chris Ritter, Robert Leonard, Yves Gingras, Bert Mosselmans, Bob Breunig, Tim Hatton, Paul Frijters, and Thu Nguyen and many others for their helpful comments. I thank my history of science hosts at UC Berkeley and University of Pennsylvania during 2000–01 when I was reading and thinking about visualization; and to the British Academy for originally funding this research. Part of the paper was given at the PSA in November 2002 (and published as Morgan, 2004), and I thank the symposium participants: Mauricio Suaréz, Bas van Fraassen, Andrea Woody, and Ronald Giere (and the anonymous member of Wisconsin's judiciary who came from the courthouse across the road!) for their useful comments. Very special thanks go to Arnold Merkies and Koen Engelen for permission to use their text and

---

36 This is not to imply, of course, that such conceptual content comes *only* with modelling. Ingrao and Israel's account of the invisible hand notions of equilibrium and the development of general equilibrium theory provides a parallel account for conceptual and mathematical developments that are primarily non-model based. As an aside to their main story, they note the development of small-scale modelling in this field in the work in the mid-twentieth century, which they interpret as economists copying physics' use of the modelling method. My account in Chapter 1 suggests a different chronology, and a more important role for models much earlier in the mathematization process.

pictures and to Ada Kromhout for text translation; to Tom Humphrey for permission to use his diagrams; and to Till Gruene and Chiara Baroni for research assistance.

References

Arnheim, R. (1969) *Visual Thinking.* Berkeley: University of California Press.

Baden-Fuller, Charles and Mary S. Morgan (2010) "Business Models as Models". *Long Range Planning*, 43:2–3, 156–71.

Baigrie, B. S. (1996) [ed] *Picturing Knowledge: Historical and Philosophical Problems Concerning the Use of Art in Science.* Toronto: University of Toronto Press.

Blaug, Mark (2007) "The Fundamental Theorems of Modern Welfare Economics, Historically Contemplated". *History of Political Economy*, 39:2, 184–207.

Boumans, M. (1993) "Paul Ehrenfest and Jan Tinbergen: A Case of Limited Physics Transfer". In N. De Marchi (ed), *Non-Natural Social Science: Reflecting on the Enterprise of More Heat Than Light* (pp. 131–56). Annual Supplement to *History of Political Economy*, Vol. 25. Durham, NC: Duke University Press.

Bowley, A. L. (1924) *The Mathematical Groundwork of Economics.* Oxford: Clarendon Press.

Chaigneau Nicolas and Philippe Le Gall (1998) "The French Connection: The Pioneering Econometrics of Marcel Lenoir". In Warren J. Samuels (ed), *European Economists of the Early 20th Century*, Vol. 1 (pp. 163–89). Cheltenham: Edward Elgar.

Coats, A. W. (1976) "Economics and Psychology: The Death and Resurrection of a Research Programme". In S. Latsis (ed), *Method and Appraisal in Economics* (pp. 43–64). Cambridge: Cambridge University Press.

Cook, Simon (2005) "Late Victorian Visual Reasoning and Alfred Marshall's Economic Science". *British Journal for History of Science*, 38:2, 179–95.

Creedy, J. (1980) "Some Recent Interpretations of *Mathematical Psychics*". *History of Political Economy*, 12:2, 267–76.

(1986) *Edgeworth and the Development of Neoclassical Economics.* Oxford: Blackwell.

(1992) *Demand and Exchange in Economic Analysis: A History from Cournot to Marshall.* Aldershot: Edward Elgar.

Daston, Lorraine and Peter Galison (1992) "The Image of Objectivity". *Representations*, 40, 81–128.

De Marchi, Neil (2003) "Visualizing the Gains from Trade, Mid 1870s to 1962". *European Journal of the History of Economic Thought*, 10:4, 551–72.

Edgeworth, F. Y. (1881) *Mathematical Psychics.* London: Kegan Paul, London. (New annotated edition. In Peter Newman (ed), *F. Y. Edgeworth's Mathematical Psychics and Further Papers on Political Economy* (pp. 1–174). Oxford: Oxford University Press for the Royal Economic Society, 2003.

(1891) "Observations on the Mathematical Theory of Political Economy, with a Special Reference to the *Principles of Economics* by Alfred Marshall". *Giornale degli Economisti*, March, 233–45.

Ferguson, Eugene S. (1977) "The Mind's Eye: Nonverbal Thought in Technology". *Science*, 197:4306, 827–36.

(1992) *Engineering and the Mind's Eye.* Cambridge, MA: MIT Press.

Fisher, I. (1892/1925) *Mathematical Investigations in the Theory of Value and Prices.* New Haven, CT: Yale University Press.

Goodman, N. (1978) *Ways of Worldmaking.* Indianapolis: Hackett.

Griesemer, James R. (1991) "Must Scientific Diagrams Be Eliminable? The Case of Path Analysis". *Biology and Philosophy*, 6, 155–80.

Griesemer, James R. and William C. Wimsatt, (1989) "Picturing Weismannism: A Case Study of Conceptual Evolution". In M. Ruse (ed), *What the Philosophy of Biology Is* (pp. 75–137). Dordrecht: Kluwer.

Hamminga, B. and N. De Marchi (1994) *Idealization in Economics*. Amsterdam: Rodopi.

Hoffman, M. (2004) "How to Get It: Diagrammatic Reasoning as a Tool of Knowledge Development and its Pragmatic Dimension". *Foundation of Science*, 9, 285–305.

Hughes, R. I. G. (1997) "Models and Representation". *Philosophy of Science*, 64, S325–36.

Humphrey, T. (1995) When Geometry Emerged: Some Neglected Early Contributions to Offer-Curve Analysis". Federal Research Bank of Richmond. *Economic Quarterly*, 81:2, 39–73.

(1996) "The Early History of the Box Diagram". Federal Reserve Bank of Richmond. *Economic Quarterly*, 82:1, 37–75.

Ingrao, B. and G. Israel (1990) *The Invisible Hand*. Cambridge, MA: MIT Press.

Ivins, W. M. (1953) *Prints and Visual Communication*. Cambridge, MA: Harvard University Press.

Jevons, W. S. (1871) *The Theory of Political Economy*. London: Macmillan.

Keynes, John M. (1926) "F. Y. Edgeworth". *Economic Journal*, 36, 140–53.

Lakatos, I. (1976) *Proofs and Refutations*. Cambridge: Cambridge University Press.

Lancaster, Kelvin (1957) "The Hecksher-Ohlin Trade Model: A Geometric Treatment". *Economica*, 24, 19–35.

Larkin J. H. and H. A. Simon (1987) "Why a Diagram Is (Sometimes) Worth Ten Thousand Words". *Cognitive Science*, 11, 65–99.

Latour, B. (1986) "Visualization and Cognition: Thinking with Eyes and Hands". *Knowledge and Society*, 6, 1–40.

Le Gall, Philippe (2007) *A History of Econometrics in France*. London: Routledge.

Lenoir, Marcel (1913) *Études sur la Formation et le Mouvement des Prix*. Paris: M. Giard & É. Brière.

Leonard, Robert (2003) "Mini-Symposium on Economics and Visual Representation". *European Journal of the History of Economic Thought*, 10:4, 525–686.

Leontief, W. W. (1946) The Pure Theory of the Guaranteed Annual Wage Contract". *Journal of Political Economy*, 54, 76–9.

Lerner, A. P. (1933/1952) "Factor Prices and International Trade". *Economica*, 19, 1–16.

Lynch, M. (1990) "Pictures of Nothing? Visual Construals in Social Theory". *Sociological Theory*, 9:1, 1–21.

Lynch, M. and S. Woolgar (1990) [eds] *Representation in Scientific Practice*. Cambridge, MA: MIT Press.

Maas, Harro (2005) *William Stanley Jevons and the Making of Modern Economics*. Cambridge: Cambridge University Press.

Mahoney, M. S. (1985) "Diagrams and Dynamics: Mathematical Perspectives on Edgerton's Thesis". In J. W. Shirley and F. D. Hoeniger (eds), *Science and the Arts in the Renaissance* (pp. 198–220). Washington: Folger Books.

Marshall, A. (1879/1930) *The Pure Theory of Foreign Trade; The Pure Theory of Domestic Values*. Reprints of Scarce Tracts in Economics, No. 1 (London: London School of Economics and Political Science) and in J. K. Whitaker (ed), *The Early Economic Writings of Alfred Marshall 1867–1890*, Vol. 2 (1975) (pp. 111–236). New York: Free Press

Merkies, A. H. Q. M. (1997) "Zo" Afscheidscollege, September, 1997, Vrije Universiteit, Amsterdam.

Mirowski, P. (1989) *More Heat Than Light*. Cambridge: Cambridge University Press.

(1994) *Edgeworth on Chance, Economic Hazard, and Statistics*. Lanham, MD: Rowan & Littlefield.

Morgan, Mary S. (1996) "Idealization and Modelling". *Journal of Economic Methodology*, 3, 131–48.

(2004) "Imagination and Imaging in Model-Building". *Philosophy of Science*, 71:5, 753–66.

Mary S. Morgan and Tarja Knuuttila (2012) "Models and Modelling in Economics". In U. Mäki (ed), *Handbook of the Philosophy of Economics* (one volume in *Handbook of the Philosophy of Science*. General Editors: Dov Gabbay, Paul Thagard, and John Woods). Amsterdam: Elsevier/North-Holland. Available at: http://papers.ssrn.com/sol3/papers.cfm?abstract_id=1499975

Morrison, M. and M. S. Morgan (1999) "Models as Mediating Instruments". In Mary S. Morgan and Margaret Morrison (eds), *Models as Mediators: Perspectives on Natural and Social Science* (pp. 10–37). Cambridge: Cambridge University Press.

Nersessian, Nancy (1990) "Methods of Conceptual Change in Science: Imagistic and Analogical Reasoning". *Philosophica*, 45:1, 33–52.

(2008) *Creating Scientific Concepts*. Cambridge, MA: MIT Press.

Netz, Reviel (1999) *The Shaping of Deduction in Greek Mathematics*. Cambridge: Cambridge University Press.

Pareto, V. (1906/1971) *Manual of Political Economy*. Translated by A. S. Schwier. London: Kelley/Macmillan.

Peirce, C. S. (1932) *Collected Papers*, Vol. 2: *Elements of Logic*. Cambridge, MA: Harvard University Press.

Richards, Joan (1988) *Mathematical Visions: The Pursuit of Geometry in Victorian England*. Boston: Academic Press.

Rotman, B. (2000) *Mathematics as Sign: Writing, Imagining, Counting*. Stanford, CA: Stanford University Press.

Scitovsky, T. (1941) "A Note on Welfare Propositions in Economics". *Review of Economic Studies*, 9, 89–110.

Tarascio, V. J. (1980) "Some Recent Interpretations of *Mathematical Psychics*: A Reply". *History of Political Economy*, 12:2, 278–81.

Toulmin, Stephen (1953) *The Philosophy of Science*. London: Hutchinson.

Tufte, E. R. (1983) *The Visual Display of Quantitative Information*. Cheshire, CN: Graphics Press.

(1997) *Visual Explanations*. Cheshire, CN: Graphics Press.

Weintraub, E. R. (1991) *Stabilizing Dynamics: Constructing Economic Knowledge*. Cambridge: Cambridge University Press.

(2002) *How Economics Became a Mathematical Science*. Durham, NC: Duke University Press.

Wetherby, J. L. (1976) "Why Was It Called an Edgeworth-Bowley Box? A Possible Explanation". *Economic Inquiry*, 14:2, 294–6.

4

Character Making: Ideal Types, Idealization, and the Art of Caricature

1. Introduction

Economics is about people and their actions. But economists have found that it is as difficult to figure out the economic motivations and behaviour of individuals as to make an analysis of the whole economy. And, though each person is only one small unit in the overall economy, the individual cannot be neglected for his or her behaviour creates exchange, markets, and the aggregate economy. When we search for accounts of the individual's economy, we quickly find that over the past two centuries economists have created a series of economic man portraits, a veritable gallery of economic heroes, each fashioned to fit the style and content of the economics of their day. Whereas early characters appear as descriptions with recognisable human passions, later characters became more shadowy for their design was more clearly driven by the needs of economists' theories. These successive models of economic man were represented initially in verbally drawn sketches, and later in terms that were informed by and fitted to mathematical notions. During the process, economists began to refer to these model people with symbols, and, as we have learnt from the last chapter, labelled them anonymously and interchangeably as X and Y, or A and B. We can treat these as models inasmuch as each one offers a well defined portrait of individual motivations or behaviour strictly limited to the economic sphere. We are dealing here, not with the development of a small world, but with a model person, someone who in some respects appears thinly described but in others appears a caricature: an economic man, not a full man.

These model men may not be workable or manipulable in quite the same way or to the same degree as other models in economics, but they can be reasoned with. These economic men are objects that economists *both enquire into and enquire with*. They *enquire into* them to explore the content and full implications of their ideas about man's economic behaviour. They *explore with* these models of economic man in the sense that each one provides a comparator or benchmark for taking to the real economic behaviour found out in the world, or more recently, in the class-room-laboratory of economic experiment. But economists also *explore with* these models in another rather interesting sense. Economists learnt, during the twentieth century, to refer to their economic man as an "agent" – a term to take seriously when we think about his role in economic reasoning. Economic model man may be thinly characterized, but he has agency: he motivates. He is the actor who shapes the possibilities and outcomes in other economic models such as the exchange situation represented in the Edgeworth Box (Chapter 3) or the Prisoner's Dilemma game (Chapter 9). In other words, enquiries with such economic models depend on the characteristics – particularly his knowledge, ambitions, and preferences – of a model economic man who inhabits those small worlds. Different characterizations of economic man (whether he is selfish or cooperative), or different formulations (whether he is mathematically described or verbally), will provide different rules for his behaviour and so create different outcomes when using those models for reasoning. So, while economic man may be the smallest unit in economists' toolbox of models, he is a very powerful one: his behaviour has all sorts of consequences in other economic models and thus for the rest of economics.

The making of a portrait of economic man is one in which economists have a special entree – for all of us are economic actors, able to observe ourselves and those we interact with in the economy. So, as a starting point, it seems reasonable to think that by observing themselves and others, economists can come to a view of what is important in economic behaviour. And having done so, they can *subtract* everything else, leaving behind just those elements that make a portrait of economic man. While this process of 'idealization', as philosophers like to call it, may provide a good description of the early-nineteenth-century processes of making economic man portraits, it simply does not cover what happened later. If we follow the history of economists' accounts of model man, we find a combination of processes going on, not just subtracting, but abstracting, concept formation, and even adding and exaggerating certain of his features. Nevertheless, in making models of man, economists are making models of people who might be themselves, and so the process has often been the subject of significant and interrogative commentary on the content and nature of economic models. Those reflections have provided two appealing, and especially social science, notions about the making of such models – the creation of ideal types and of caricatures – that I explore in the course of this chapter.

2. Characterizing Economic Man: Classical Economists' *Homo Economicus*

The classical economists from Adam Smith to Karl Marx were very particular in giving accounts of economic behaviour, but few of them created models of economic man. This is certainly so for Smith, the Scottish moral philosopher and founder of classical economics, whose description of economic behaviour in his *Wealth of Nations* (1776) is much too well-rounded a portrait to work as a model. Smith characterized economic behaviour as coming from a complex mixture of instincts (the propensity to exchange as much as self-interest), talents, motivations, and preferences. All of these traits are vital to Smith's account of how wealth is created and spread through the nations. Economic man is "thickly" described, to use a phrase that has haunted both recent historiography and anthropology. Yet this was not considered a realistic portrait by his contemporary scholars, such as Thomas Reid, who regarded it as a fictional device to motivate a virtuous story about commercial society.[1]

Fictional character or not, Smith's characterization of economic behaviour does not constitute a model man. Why not? The character is simply too complicated to reason with. Smith linked man's individual motivations with particular outcomes (e.g., his prudence with investment) but it is not so easy to trace the full outcome of all of his character traits together at the same time because they interact with each other and link up with so many other characteristics and are dependent upon so many circumstances. Nor is it easy to use his account of man to enquire into the economy as a whole, for though Smith's description suggests that causal power lies at the level of the individual, it is the effects of actions in aggregate that create the laws of nineteenth-century political economy such as the subsistence wage thesis or Marx's thesis of capitalist cycles. These laws emerge as the unintended consequences of individuals' actions at the level of groups, and the individuals themselves are powerless in the face of them.[2] We saw just this difficulty in Ricardo's attempts to work out the laws of distribution by starting with individual farmers, and how he managed to wriggle through to a solution by having his model farm represent both the individual farm and the aggregate farm at the same time (see Chapter 2).

1   As such, Smith's account began by persuading us that the fundamental propensity to truck, barter, and exchange was a natural given as a way to draw us into his commercial world picture. I thank Harro Maas for his helpful discussion of this point. (For a history of the actual emergence of a "commercial man", see Bhimani, 1994.)

2   That is, even if Smith's description of the individual economic actor had formed a model, he would have had great difficulty in using it to enquire into the workings of the economy.

Classical political economy was not a science in which a model man could easily function, yet there are examples where he did. Thomas Malthus, a parish priest and great friend of Ricardo, worried about the fast growing population of his day. In his account of 1803, he supposed that this problem arose because of the interaction between man's two primary motives: his self-interest being more than often overwhelmed by his natural proclivity to create children. He also proposed two simple laws of natural reproduction to be always at work (namely that human populations grow geometrically but food supplies only arithmetically). These two motivations, in conjunction with the two laws, would create cycles in the lives of the working poor swinging from poverty with vice to satisfaction at subsistence level. And in accordance with classical ideas about the laws of economics, Malthus supposed that these hypothesized cycles might not be observed because of interference from the other disturbing features in the world.

Malthus' character does form a model man in the sense that he was thin enough in characterization to reason with. He has simple economic and demographic motivations, from which a sequence of population and economic outcomes were derived. In addition, Malthus enquired into the outcomes of his behaviour by a counterfactual thought experiment, that is, by conceiving that the characteristics of his model man might be otherwise and seeing what difference this would mean. So Malthus tells us that if man used his foresight and reasoning power to restrict his family, the law of human population growth would be different (and so Malthus lauds the benefits of education). The arguments that Malthus constructed were important for the development of Darwin's theory of evolution in the later nineteenth century, and continue to resurface periodically whenever the problem of population growth becomes a significant political issue.

In Malthus' work, we find the portrait of a man who functions as a model in economics, that is (as I argued in Chapter 1) whose formulation gives us resources to reason with – both about economic laws and to enquire into the real economy. His model man has direct descendants in modern economics. They reappear with more sophisticated statistical clothing, and amongst many thousands of similar, virtual, people, in Orcutt's computer-based microsimulation model of population dynamics (discussed in Chapter 8). More immediately, Malthus' model man provided an exemplar for John Stuart Mill's only slightly later claims about the requirement for a thinly modelled man to make economics a viable science. Mill, though best known as one of the great philosophers of the nineteenth century, was also a political economist. He defined the science of economics as dealing with an explicitly restricted range of man's motivations and propensities, namely his economic ones, for he argued that only by both delimiting the scope of the subject domain of economics, and defining more narrowly the characteristics of individual economic behaviour, could economists construct a scientific account.

Significantly, Mill's model man character sketch therefore comes intertwined with his definition of economics as:

... the science which treats of the production and distribution of wealth, so far
as they depend upon the laws of human nature. (Mill, 1836, pp. 318, 321–2)[3]

And, despite the fact that both Mill and Malthus were members of the same broad
school of classical economics, the content of Mill's portrait is markedly different
from Malthus' one. The motivations of Mill's economic man consist of one constant positive motivation, namely, a desire for wealth, accompanied by only two
"perpetual" negatives: the dislike of work and the love of luxuries (he downgrades
the Malthusian sexual drive to an important, but nonperpetual, motivation):

> It does not treat of the whole of man's nature as modified by the social state,
> nor of the whole conduct of man in society. It is concerned with him solely
> as a being who desires to possess wealth and who is capable of judging of
> the comparative efficacy of means for obtaining that end. ... It makes entire
> *abstraction* of every other human passion or motive; except those which
> may be regarded as perpetually antagonizing principles to the desire of
> wealth, namely, aversion to labour, and desire of the present enjoyment of
> costly indulgences. These it takes, to a certain extent, into its calculations,
> because these do not merely, like [our] other desires, occasionally conflict
> with the pursuit of wealth, but accompany it always as a drag, or imped-
> iment, and are therefore inseparably mixed up in the consideration of it.
> (Mill, 1836, pp. 321–2, italics added)

In Mill's *homo economicus* (as his character is known), we have the portrait of a
lazy, miserly, but entirely effective, Scrooge. Mill made his thinly characterized economic man very powerful within his account of the economic system, not in the
sense of Malthus' model in giving us specific outcomes (about population), but by
arguing for the breadth of his impact. For example, the laws on property – according to Mill – also flow from this primary desire to possess wealth, for such institutions are designed by man to further his success in accumulating wealth.

Both Malthus and Mill followed processes that enabled them to limn the con-
stitution of economic man according to their own chosen hierarchy of economic
motives. Their strategies might be described as first focus then simplify: first pick
out the economic aspects believed to represent economic motivations and actions
and then subtract away all the non-economic aspects. Yet Mill portrayed his definition as being the result of a process not of subtraction or simplification but of
"abstraction" (as we see above). For him, political economy was an "abstract science"
(1836, p. 325), like geometry, a science of definition, assumption, and deduction.
Hamminga and De Marchi (1994) discuss this notion of abstract science in the more
general context of laws rather than of *homo economicus*. They suggest that the classical
authors' understanding of "abstract" was that it offered a more generalized account.

---

3   There are two edition of this essay: *On the Definition of Political Economy*: in 1836 and 1844 with
    some minor differences between them. The 1844 edition is reprinted in Mill's *Collected Works*,
    Vol. IV (1967), with the changes since 1836 indicated in square brackets.

But, as they point out, this in turn is open to at least two further interpretations, which are equally relevant in thinking about *homo economicus*. For some classical authors, it meant that such a character has general descriptive or explanatory reach so that he is applicable almost *everywhere* (with minor exceptions) – and perhaps this would be so for Malthus, for while neither his population laws, nor the cycles he proposed, could be directly observed in the world, his economic man's behaviour could be found there. For other authors, Mill included, it meant that the character is *not* applicable *directly* anywhere in the real world – because *nowhere* is such a person to be found. As Mill claimed of his economic character, no "political economist was ever so absurd as to suppose that mankind are really thus constituted" (1836, p. 322). However, this does not mean that his *homo economicus* was not relevant for explaining economic behaviour. Quite the opposite. In Mill's view, economics was not only an abstract science, but at the same time a science of tendency laws, wherein general laws might be applied to the concrete cases of the world provided they are always modified by an account of the many specific and disturbing causes that occur there.[4] Mill tendency laws hold for all of us. So, despite this difficulty of application, his abstraction, *homo economicus*, was relevant for explaining *everyone's* behaviour (not just that of some types of people) with allowances for other causes.

3. Concept Forming: Weber's Ideal Types and Menger's Human Economy

"Abstract" has many connotations, and the process of abstracting in the history of economics became associated not just with generalizing, but also with conceptualising, with creating a kind of concentrated notion, encapsulating or reducing (in the cookery sense) some aspects of well-considered phenomena.[5] This kind of concept-forming abstraction creates "ideal types" in the social sciences, a label – indeed a concept in itself – most closely associated with the work of the great German social scientist of the early twentieth century, Max Weber.

---

4 "That which is true in the abstract, is always true in the concrete with proper *allowances*. When a certain cause really exists, and if left to itself would infallibly produce a certain effect, that same effect, *modified* by all the other concurrent causes, will correctly correspond to the result really produced" (Mill, 1836, pp. 326–7). This became the standard defence of why the laws of classical analysis are difficult to validate. On tendency laws in Mill and their modern counterparts in economics, see Cartwright (1989) and Hausman (1992). On Mill's economic man, see Persky (1995).
5 We see this occasionally in the classical school. A good example of what I mean is given by Smith when he attributes an abstract character to labour, the labour that features so strongly in classical economists' labour theory of value, in order to finesse an explanation of how different kinds of labour that cannot easily be compared can nevertheless be understood to determine exchange values:"The greater part of people, too, understand better what is meant by a quantity of a particular commodity than by a quantity of labour. The one is a plain palpable object; the other an abstract notion, which, though it can be made sufficiently intelligible, is not altogether so natural and obvious." (Smith, 1776, Book I, Chapter V, para 5)

Weber's ideal types are generalizations constructed from the "facts of experience", yet in the process, creating abstract concepts that he described as "pure fictions".[6] One of the economists whose work Weber respected and found congenial to his way of thinking was Carl Menger, the late-nineteenth-century founder of the Austrian school of economics.[7] Menger's economic man portrait is located in his concept of the individual or 'human economy' (in contrast to the "national economy" of his contemporaries in the German historical school of economics). In his 1883 work, Menger starts from what he takes to be the most vital elements of human economy, namely,

> ... premeditative activity aimed at satisfying our material needs. ... The direct needs of each economic subject are given in each case by his individual nature ... The goods available to him are strictly given by the economic situation of the moment.... Thus, *the starting point and the goal of every concrete human economy are ultimately determined strictly by the economic situation of the moment.* (Menger, 1883/1985, p. 217, his italics)

Menger's economic man was one who aimed and acted to satisfy his or her needs by choosing between alternative goods, given the constraints of his or her situation of the moment. (We return to the importance of 'situation' in this definition later in this chapter, and more seriously in Chapter 9.) For Menger, all humans had many different needs: for example, man needs water – to drink, to wash, to give to his horse or dog, and so forth, which he wants to satisfy, as well as needs for different goods – food, clothing, heat, and so forth, all of which he also wants to satisfy. Menger represented this in a schedule in his 1871 *Principles* (our Figure 4.1) showing an individual's personal rating of the different goods (Roman numbers, horizontally) and different degrees of satisfaction from each of these goods (Arabic numbers, vertically) and suggested that humans choose quantities of each good, and of different goods, in such a way as to satisfy those needs in a particular order, with necessities first, then less important needs, up to a point where the satisfactions gained from consuming each element of the various goods are equal.

In reflecting on how he arrives at such a conceptual account of human economy, Menger writes about his aim as follows:

> ... to ascertain the *simplest elements* of everything real, elements which must be thought of as strictly typical just because they are the simplest. It strives for the establishment of these elements by way of an only partially empirical-realistic analysis, i.e., without considering whether these in reality are present as *independent* phenomena; indeed, even without

6 See Weber (1904); and for the two quoted phrases, his 1913, p. 98 and 1917, p. 44. See Zouboulakis (2001) on a comparison of Menger's versus Weber's notions of abstraction.
7 See Weber (1908 [1975]). The historical relationship between Weber and Menger is nicely drawn in Bruce Caldwell's recent book (2004) on Hayek.

THE THEORY OF VALUE

I	II	III	IV	V	VI	VII	VIII	IX	X
10	9	8	7	6	5	4	3	2	1
9	8	7	6	5	4	3	2	1	0
8	7	6	5	4	3	2	1	0	
7	6	5	4	3	2	1	0		
6	5	4	3	2	1	0			
5	4	3	2	1	0				
4	3	2	1	0					
3	2	1	0						
2	1	0							
1	0								
0									

Figure 4.1. Menger's Consumption Schedule.

Source: Carl Menger, *Grundsätze der Volkswirtschaftslehre*, Wilhelm Braumüller, Vienna,1871, p. 93 (Reprinted facsimile, London: London School of Economics and Political Science Reprints of Scarce Tracts in Economics, No. 17, 1934.)

> considering whether they can at all be presented independently in their full purity. In this manner theoretical research arrives at empirical forms which *qualitatively* are strictly typical. It arrives at results of theoretical research which, to be sure, must not be tested by full empirical reality (for the empirical forms under discussion, e.g., absolutely pure oxygen, pure alcohol, pure gold, a person pursuing only economic aims, etc., exist in part only in our ideas). (Menger, 1883/1985, pp. 60–1, his italics)

In his political economy work of 1871, Menger successively composed these "real simplest" elements into an account and explanations of economic man's reasoning and behaviour contingent upon his situation. Where Mill had *picked out* – had abstracted – from the full description of man's motivations what he took to be man's main economic motivations, Menger composed his concept of human economy by sequencing together the definitions of the simplest elements to *build up* his abstract notion of typical economic behaviour.[8]

We can gain further insight into Menger's economic man as an ideal type if we recognise that he is neither ideal nor a type in the common meanings of those terms. Machlup (1978, p. 213) suggests that, consistent with the community notions of his time and place, 'ideal' refers not to some elements of perfection, but as the adjectival form of 'idea'; and 'type' refers not to a classificatory kind we meet in the world, but to a 'mental construct'.[9] These are helpful observations for understanding Austrian school economists like Menger. For example, he believed that it is another important part of the character of being human to have limited knowledge,

---

8 This composing notion does not refer to the "compositive definitional mode" that Bruce Caldwell (2004) suggests is the way Austrians economists arrive at aggregate accounts.

9 Fritz Machlup (1978) follows the notion of ideal types from the German-speaking communities' discussions of the later nineteenth century into more recent times.

and so that feature is found in his portrait of economic man. Menger's ideal type economic man is an abstract portrait, but its critical feature is that it offers a *conceptual* model of economic behaviour, neither an idealized character nor a specific natural kind in the world.

Menger thought that by a process of introspective observation and thoughtful, logical method, he could obtain the general or exact laws of the "phenomena of *abstract economic reality*" but not of the "*real*, in part extremely uneconomic, phenomena of human economy" (Menger, 1883/1985, p. 218, italics his).[10] That is, since his economic man was painted in abstract conceptual terms, the account could not be applied to the world, even with difficulty, which speaks to the different notion of 'abstract' we find compared with Mill's portrait earlier. What then is the function of such abstract conceptual – or ideal type – models? Weber's answer goes as follows:

> The ideal type concept will help to develop our skill in imputation in *research*: it is no "hypothesis" but it offers guidance to the construction of hypotheses. It is not a *description* of reality but it aims to give unambiguous means of expression to such a description.... It is a conceptual construct (*Gedankenbild*) which is neither historical reality nor even the "true" reality. It is even less fitted to serve as a schema under which a real situation or action is to be subsumed as one *instance*. It has the significance of a purely ideal *limiting* concept with which the real situation or action is *compared* and surveyed for the explication of certain of its significant components. (Weber, 1904 [1949], pp. 90 and 93, his italics)

So Weber suggests that an ideal type fosters understanding of the social scientist's world, not because it can be directly applied, but as a benchmark device against we can enquire into the world; not because it is a hypothesis, but because it enables us to formulate such hypotheses. Ideal types function neither as theories nor empirical descriptions, but as independent instruments or tools that enable the social scientist to support enquiries into both domains.[11] In other words, they carry the same function we attributed to models as instruments of enquiry in economics in the discussion of Chapter 1. And, like these ideal types, economists' abstract conceptual models form instruments of a subtle and sophisticated kind.

---

10 Machlup interprets Menger as distinguishing between "strict" (ideal) types and "real" types, suggesting a further distinction between economic man as a strict type with no counterpart real types, and other ideal types like "free market price", which have corresponding real types in observable, regular phenomena (1978, pp. 255–6; see also his commentary on pp. 230–32 and Menger (1883/1985, Appendix VI). (See also Mäki, 1997.) Machlup reports the vehemence of contemporary arguments over whether the ideal type may also be, or is in contrast to, a real type and whether it is possible to regain the concrete from the ideal type. See also Hempel's (1965, chapter 7) discussion of the purpose of ideal types.

11 Ideal types don't necessarily form usable scientific models, just as not all analogies do. Once again – as in the Malthus case earlier – it comes down to whether the ideal type is exactly and simply enough formed to be useful in economic reasoning.

We have already found two notions of abstraction in our history of economic man. For Mill's way of making his portrait, the term suggests something like the process of making a reader's abstract: not so much shortening and simplifying, but distilling out the main economic characteristics so that they stand out from the detail of the whole. This contrasts with the notion of abstracting we found in Menger's work: a concept-forming activity, which is not so easy to describe but that clearly involved a more constructive process than subtracting one. Marx Wartofsky suggests we may think of concept forming in science as a process in which the scientist turns perceptions into more abstract mental images.[12] Such perceptions are presumably not literally observations, but rather intuitions and understandings, and the scientists use their cognitive and imaginative talents to turn these into concepts or abstract ideas. Menger's analysis of typical economic behaviour and his creation of an ideal type portrait, work he described (above) as theoretical work to get at the typical empirical form, does indeed seem to fall under this notion of abstracting as concept forming.

But when, as Wartofsky suggests, these abstractions create concepts that can be represented in symbolic form, this opens up all sorts of new possibilities, for concepts transformed into symbols can be manipulated, reasoned with, and extended into different contexts than the original source. In this sense, the most significant difference in the abstracting process behind Menger's human economy compared with Jevons' calculating man is in their language of representation. Though the portraits were contemporaries of each other, and both involved concept-forming work, it was Jevons who, as we see next, moved the portrait from the symbolic languages of verbal expression firmly into those of mathematics, opening up ideas about individual economic behaviour to a different, and more powerful, mode of manipulation. More important perhaps, Jevons' mathematical prortrait could travel easily into many new contexts.

4. Symbolic Abstraction: Jevons' Calculating Man

William Stanley Jevons' (1871) economic man is a calculating consumer, his motivations and actions are defined in psychological terms that are fundamentally unobservable.[13] Like Mill, Jevons explicitly deals only with the economic motivations of man; but whereas Mill's portrait rests upon the classical laws of production and distribution, for Jevons, the main base was the economic laws of consumption. Jevons' portrait is inspired by the economistic moral principle of utilitarianism:

> Economics must be founded upon a full and accurate investigation of the conditions of utility; and, to understand this element, we must necessarily

---

12 See Wartofsky (1968, chapter 2).
13 There is a wonderfully rich literature on Jevons, see particularly Maas (2005a), Schabas (1990), and Peart (1996). On Mill versus Jevons, see Maas (2005b).

examine the wants and desires of man. . . . it is surely obvious that economics
does rest upon the laws of human enjoyment. (Jevons, 1871, p. 102)

This is a move away from Mill's man's desire to accumulate wealth in the form of
goods or money, towards man gaining enjoyment or utility from consumption of
goods, thus replacing the constant positive motive found in Mill's *homo economicus*
with one of his negative motives.

Jevons' portrait was painted in the formal language of mathematics. Calculation
and psychology go along together here, for Jevons' economic man is a pleasure seeker –
he 'maximizes utility' from consumption, where utility is conceived of in a uniform
way.[14] Jevons begins with Jeremy Bentham's psychologically based account of utility, with its seven dimensions: intensity, duration, certainty/uncertainty, propinquity/
remoteness, fecundity, purity, and extent.[15] Jevons regards the last three as being relevant for moral theory, but not relevant for the "simple and restricted problem which
we attempt to solve in economics" (p. 95). He transforms two of the remaining four
"circumstances" – intensity and duration – into quantities, so that each experienced
value of pleasure (or its negative value, pain) could be plotted as Cartesian coordi-
nates in a two-dimensional space. This diagrammatic representation enables him to
depict how man gains pleasure from consuming a good and how that pleasure – or
utility – declines with successive units of the good consumed based on the physiological principle of satiation. While the basic idea has much in common with Menger's,
Jevons interpreted the intensity of pleasure (or utility) as varying continuously with
its duration (or amount of the good), an abstraction consistent with the mathematical
conception of economic man and his behaviour. This can all be seen in Jevons' figure
4 (our Figure 4.2), which charts the amount of good consumed along the horizontal
axis and intensity of pleasure from such consumption on the vertical.

Where Malthus and Mill had earlier reduced the broad classical portrait given
by Smith to a simple set of economic motivations in order that they could reason
about man's behaviour more easily, Jevons reduces the dimensions of Bentham's
utility analysis not just to make it tractable, but to mathematize his treatment of the
consumption feelings and decisions of economic man. By transforming Bentham's
verbal ideas into mathematical conceptions and symbols to represent economic
man's behaviour, Jevons characterizes that man's behaviour with a new level of
exactitude. It also enabled him to take his newly created portrait into the laboratory of mathematics and to investigate his economic model man's motivations
and feelings with mathematical forms of reasoning. As argued in Chapter 1, such
rules of enquiry come with the form of the model: because his economic man is

14 In this respect, Jevons' conception of utility is narrower than that of his contemporary, J. B. Clark
(1899), who had utilities associated with forms, places, time, etc.
15 Bentham's (1789/1970) scientific claims involved a reductionist theory of mind that sensations
(pleasures/pains) lead to mental associations and that pleasure is homogeneous and quantifiable.
Although he used mathematical metaphors: "felicific calculus", "axioms of mental pathology" etc.,
he did not formulate these ideas mathematically.

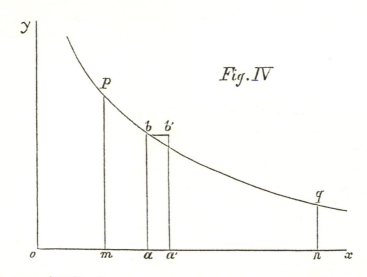

Figure 4.2. Jevons' Utility Curve.

Source: William Stanley Jevons, *The Theory of Political Economy*, 1871, London: Macmillan & Co., fig. 4 on p. 49.

mathematically defined, so are the rules governing his behaviour in the model. Thus Jevons used mathematical rules to dissect his economic man's feelings, using calculus to measure his total amount of utility from consumption (represented by an area on the diagram), and the 'final degree' of utility from consuming successive "marginal units" of the good as marked out along the line of the curve.

The mathematical rules of reasoning used by Jevons to describe the behaviour of the model man are then imputed as the rules of reasoning followed by the man in the model for he implies that real man makes such calculations for himself using the same kind of reasoning and mathematics (as Jevons presents). That is, man makes his economic decisions by weighing up, comparing, and deciding how to maximize his utility from consuming:

> Now the mind of an individual is the balance which makes its own compar-
> isons, and is the final judge of quantities of feelings. (Jevons, 1871 p. 84)

For example, when faced with choice between two goods, Jevons represents his consumer as mentally weighing the utility from successive degrees of consumption of the different goods until they are equal, where they can be exchanged at the margin (and this gives exchange ratios or relative 'prices' for that individual). By portraying his economic man as thinking in terms of these mathematical notions, he revealed his deep sense that this is how economic behaviour is determined.

Jevons defined utility not as a quality within goods, but as "a *circumstance of things* arising from their relation to man's requirements" (Jevons, 1871, p. 105), that is, as a relation between goods and man, so that the utility valuations of his calculating man, – preferences and weighings – are neither observable nor measurable. So, despite the exactitude depicted in the graphs and mathematics of man's behaviour, the terms these symbols represent are fundamentally internal and known only to the subject. Whereas Mill's picture of *homo economicus* still seems to refer to observable behaviour that might be accessed objectively by a commentator, Jevons' calculating man is an introspective character, whose subjectively registered feelings such a commentator could not access.[16] It was only literary licence that allowed Dickens to give us access to Scrooge's wealth seeking (Mill's economic man) from his external behaviour *and* to see him weighing past and future pleasures against pains (Jevons' economic man) in his Christmas dreams!

From Jevons' point of view, in contrast to that of Mill, the *material* of economics is mathematical, so, naturally, economists' portrait of economic man should also be written in the language of mathematics and its methods of analysis must also be mathematical. This move into mathematics turned out to be highly significant and was subject to much debate at the time. McMullin (1985) writes about similar kinds of arguments over Galileo's earlier use of mathematics in the natural sciences, arguments that go back in various forms to differences of opinion between Aristotle and Plato. This difference depends upon whether we understand the Book of Nature for economic science to be written in mathematics or not. If the Book of Nature for economics is *not* written in mathematics, Jevons' mathematization of the portrait imposes a particular kind of abstraction, or idealization for purposes of convenience:

> Mathematical idealization is a matter of imposing a mathematical formalism on a physical [for us, economic] situation, in the hope that the essentials of that situation (from the point of view of the science one is pursuing) will lend themselves to mathematical representation. (McMullin, 1985, p. 254)

That is, we might interpret Jevons' reduction and transformation of Bentham's ideas on utility into two-dimensional geometry and differential calculus as mathematical forms imposed for convenience of the representation and its subsequent usage, rather than because mathematics is the form in which economic man's behaviour is best and most accurately represented. Yet both Jevons here, and Edgeworth as we saw in Chapter 3, took it for granted that economists' Book of Nature was written in mathematics (see Schabas, 1990), just as:

> Galileo took for granted that his geometry provided the *proper* language of space and time measurement, and that arithmetic would suffice for *gravità*. (McMullin, 1985, p. 253, his italics)

Regardless of whether economic man lent himself naturally to a mathematical portrait, or whether his nature was constrained into the mathematical form, this move to mathematical abstractions and concepts was highly significant for the subsequent career of economic model man. The combination of attributes in Jevons'

---

16 Until, that is, recent developments in neuroeconomics (see Section 8 later).

portrait: the psychophysical treatment of motivations, economic man's calculating mentality, and the mathematical nature of Jevons' depiction – all had longer-term implications for the way economists go about the task of abstracting. This is why Jevons is often lauded as one of the founders of modern economics (see Maas 2005a). By his kind of work, methods of creating models of economic man became inextricably linked with 'formalizing'. This entailed changing the language of economics, from the informal and hugely nuanced possibilities of expression found in our verbal languages (but with their limited reasoning possibilities) to the more constrained but more exact and rule-bound symbolic forms of mathematics (with their greater reasoning powers, as discussed in Chapter 1). After Jevons, economic man was generally characterized in ways consistent with a mathematical treatment of his qualities.

Where does this mathematically drawn calculating model man sit in relation to the rest of economics? In Jevons' newly formalized conception of man in marginal economics, and in the neoclassical economic theory that grew out of it, the individual seems to have gained causal power for the laws of economics operate at the level of the individual, not the aggregate as in classical economics. As Chapter 3 records, Edgeworth took Jevons' calculating man into a small-world model – that became the Edgeworth Box – to enquire how his utility maximizing behaviour would enable him to reach exchange decisions with a limited number of other calculating individuals. And, as that chapter also records, Pareto taking advantage of his symbolic abstract form, investigated how such an economic man – an X or a Y, an A or a B – found his or her way around the obstacles on the path to the top of his hill of pleasure. Once formed – as with other models before and since – Jevons' model man was used by other economists to think with and to reason about human economic behaviour in other situations. It was Edgeworth who named Jevons' calculating man an economic 'agent', a motivating agent for plugging into other models and setting the reasoning going. As we shall see (in Chapter 9), his offspring live up to that agency role particularly in modern game theory.

Jevons' model man was not so effective as a model for enquiries into the world, not at least until the advent of experimental economics 100 years later (see Chapter 7) and perhaps neuroeconomics even more recently. It is not just that calculating man's calculations are unobservable, but that, as Jevons carefully explains when he laid out his mathematical theory of marginal utility:

> The laws [of individual economic man's behaviour] which we are about to trace out are to be conceived as theoretically true of the individual; they can only be practically verified as regards the aggregate transactions, productions, and consumptions of a large body of people. But the laws of the aggregate depend of course upon the laws applying to individual cases. (Jevons, 1871, pp. 108–9)

This is not the same aggregation problem of classical economics, as perceived by Malthus or Mill: of disturbing causes covering up, in the aggregate, the behaviour that might be found by the addition of lots of individuals following similar courses of action. The problem here follows from the combination of the actions of individuals following the *same laws* of behaviour but with *different preferences* for goods, subjectively judged. For the 'marginalists', Menger as much as Jevons, each and every valuation decision freely made by the individual economic man can make a difference to the aggregate outcome.

We saw this directly in Chapter 3, when Edgeworth (1881) stressed the ability of each individual, each with different tastes and desires, like Robinson Crusoe and Man Friday, to contract freely in the market place. Equally, we can see the power of each individual calculating model man in the formal mathematical account of general equilibrium by the French marginalist Leon Walras. Defining economic behaviour in terms of individual maximizing of utility turns out to mean that if the preferences for just one good by just one of all the calculating consumers in the economy changes, the demand for that product changes, and the prices of all the other products may also change because of the way these calculating individuals are linked together into the overall market account. This makes it well nigh impossible to think of going back from any individually isolated behaviour to the real world as Mill had proposed. This makes the model man an important feature of neoclassical economics, powerful as a motivating device for other models, and in theorizing. But it creates considerable difficulty, for, to make economic man tractable en masse, later economists must decide whether they really are all the same and might be represented by one particular 'representative agent', or need to have their variability characterized explicitly.[17]

5. Exaggerating Qualities: Knight's Slot-Machine Man

It was the main American exponent of neoclassical economics, Frank Knight (in his thesis of 1915, published in 1921) who worked out the details that allowed calculating man to play his full role in the formal neoclassical theory of the economy. Menger had argued that, unlike his account of 'human economy', it must be assumed that the economic subjects used in price theory do not act in error nor without information about the situation (1921, p. 71). Knight's move was a much more positive one. He argued that only by endowing calculating man with *full* information about everything in the economy (rather than the limited information Menger assumed for his human economy), and with *perfect* foresight about the future (rather than the uncertainty that Jevons had left aside from his calculating man portrait), could the individual person make the necessary calculations that would allow him to judge accurately what actions to take in buying and selling and consuming. These exaggerations are necessary not for understanding man in actual economic life but in order that economic man could play the part required

17 See Hartley (1997) and Kirman (1992).

of him in the overall mathematical theory of the economy being constructed by the neoclassical economists.[18]

Knight was the first to admit that a world peopled by such individuals was no longer a simplification, but an "heroic" abstraction.

> The above list of assumptions and artificial abstractions is indeed rather a formidable array. The intention has been to make the list no longer than really necessary or useful, but in no way to minimize its degree of artificiality, the amount of divergence of the hypothetical conditions from those of actual economic life about us. (Knight, 1921, p. 81)

While the classical economists had pared down to *homo economicus*, neoclassical economists such as Knight exaggerate certain of his characteristics (his calculating ability and his 'perfect knowledge'). Like Mill, he argues that scientific economics places severe limitations on the treatment of man. But in order to arrive at definite analytical results about the workings of markets and the economy as a whole, Knight argues that economic science requires a fully idealized economic man, not just a simplified or abstracted man. Knight's portrait is very different from Mill's. The model man Knight creates was specially designed to live in the highly idealized mathematical world of neoclassical economic theories: a creature of artifice. Only by assuming that there were infinitely many of him, and that each acted independently of the others, could neoclassical analysis depict the perfectly competitive economy and equilibrium outcome that maximized aggregate utility. This model man was an idealized mathematical character designed to behave perfectly in an idealized mathematical world of neoclassical economic science.[19]

The issue of knowledge is a critical one for Knight. Despite, or rather because of, all that information and foresight that he was endowed with, Knight argues that his model economic man has no intelligence:

> With uncertainty absent, ... it is doubtful whether intelligence itself would exist in such a situation; in a world so built that perfect knowledge was theoretically possible, it seems likely that all organic readjustments would become mechanical, all organisms automata. (Knight, 1921, p. 268)

Weber had pinpointed this same question of information as a requirement of acting in a "logically 'perfect' way" in the context of a discussion of what it meant to

---

18 See Giocoli (2003) on the way in which Weber foresaw this requirement. Knight's definitions are verbal despite the mathematical role that the character played.

19 This portrait of economic man was strongly embedded as the central character of formal mathematical theorizing of neoclassical economics. As Knight pointed out in his thesis way back in 1921, and as Arrow has argued more recently (1986), this economic man is one leg of a three-legged stool. He has to be combined with two other basic tenets – perfect competition and general equilibrium theorizing – to get the strong formal results that characterized the middle part of twentieth-century economics, but even there, he was pretty helpless on his own, for each element also depended on the others.

act rationally, but he did so to establish what real people would do by comparison, rather than as a requirement of a broader theoretical aim (1917, p. 42). For Knight, the point is not to establish what real people would do, but what this model man would do inside an economic theory. Knight (later) portrays this idealized economic man as a slot machine:

> The Economic Man neither competes nor higgles ... he treats other human beings as if they were slot machines (Knight, 1947, p. 80),

not even a one-dimensional man, but a purely impersonal utility maximising agent (as economists now say), a pleasure machine that experiences none of Jevons' man's pain or pleasure, nor satisfies his needs as Menger's man does; he has no Malthusian vices, virtues, desires, or children, nor Smithian propensities, talents, or preferences.

Knight insisted that this ideal figure of economic science – his slot-machine model man – does not help to describe actual economic behaviour, and so cannot be used for socially useful economic analysis or policy interventions. Unlike Mill's economic man portrait that he thought held true of everyone at some level, Knight's model man was not to be used in analysing behaviour in the real economy. Indeed, as part of his commitment to liberal democracy, Knight wrote moral commentaries describing man's actual economic behaviour as being driven by competition but acting according to the rules of the social game. He explicitly denied that the rational economic man of his analytical work had any realistic import.[20]

The kind of economic man that Knight created for neoclassical economists' theorizing, slot-machine man as I have labelled it (for it would seem odd to refer to a machine by a personal pronoun), was heaped with important extra information and foresight, qualities accentuated by Knight to enable him to play the central role in the neoclassical system. Weber had already recognised this kind of exaggeration in thinking about the market economy:[21]

> Substantively, this construct [an exchange economy] in itself is like a *utopia* which has been arrived at by the analytical accentuation of certain elements of reality... An ideal type is formed by the one-sided *accentuation* of one of more points of view and by the synthesis of a great many diffuse, discrete, more or less present and occasionally absent *concrete*

20 Although these two domains of his economics were largely separate, Knight created a second economic man character in his portrait of the American economic way of life (see Emmett, 1994). There, we find Knight portrays competition as a human urge or instinct to motivate his description of human behaviour (see Knight, 1923). This characterization of real economic man motivated by some very powerful basic instinct is similar in kind to Smith's propensity to truck, barter, and exchange or Malthus' evolutionary imperative. Knight was following in the same path as the American marginalist J. B. Clark, whose economic man might be called 'social man' (in contrast to the isolated individual usually assumed) and who also had two kinds of economics, one for theorizing and one for describing for the world (see Morgan, 1994).

21 Machlup (1978) suggests that Comte also noted the use of exaggerations in this way; see his p. 228.

individual phenomena, which are arranged according to those one-sidedly emphasized viewpoints into a unified *analytical* construct (*Gedankenbild*). In its conceptual purity, this mental construct (*Gedankenbild*) can not be found anywhere in reality. It is a *utopia*. (Weber, 1904, p. 90, his italics)

Weber's account of this process of exaggeration, or one-sided emphasis in the development of an ideal type is unlike Menger's ideal type human economy, which depended on locating what is typical of real behaviour at its simplest level. The exaggeration we find here is also of a qualitatively different kind than the miserliness left after Mill's *abstraction from* other motivations. Recall that earlier versions of economic man were arrived at by processes of focussing on economic motivations and subtracting or abstracting in the sense of 'to abstract' (of Malthus and Mill) or by the rather different concept-forming abstraction (of Menger and Jevons), all of which suggest, in some way, the filing away of extraneous elements.

If Knight had only taken away uncertainty, as Jevons did when he omitted the uncertainty that Bentham had thought relevant to decisions about utility, this would fit the usual analogical example of the frictionless plane, used as a standard example to illustrate the notion of model-making by idealization in physics. But Knight's slot-machine man is a model arrived at through the *addition* of fictions or falsehoods. He did not just ignore uncertainty or set it at zero, but chose to define its absence as the presence of perfect knowledge.[22] And perhaps it came as a surprise to find that the addition of perfect knowledge – in Knight's terms – means his character has no need of intelligence, and thus we get to the slot-machine model of man, for an automaton does not think. It is this kind of addition that makes the economic man we see in Knight's characterization into the pure concept that Weber remarks upon, for Knight had created the economic model man of neoclassical economists' utopia. Knight's slot-machine man could be used by economists to learn about the idealized (theoretical) economy, and it could do so because it enabled them to explore, within their theories, the economic behaviour of man and its consequences in its most exaggerated form.

6. Making a Cartoon into a Role Model: Rational Economic Man

Just as nineteenth-century classical economics supported different models of economic man's character, so too did twentieth-century neoclassical economics.

---

22 Philosophers of economics, such as Cartwright (1989) and Mäki (1992), usually reserve the term "idealization" for these false statements – and have in mind the kind of under- or overstatements defined by limit cases (such as setting some factor at zero or infinity) in contrast to leaving a factor out (termed 'abstractions' by Cartwright and 'isolations' by Mäki). But there is a difference between setting something (ignorance) to zero and filling in what its opposite – for example, knowledge – might mean. See also the parallel discussion of various kinds of *ceteris paribus* conditions by Boumans in Boumans and Morgan (2001).

We have just seen how Knight's model of economic man was well clothed with artificial assumptions about his knowledge and foresight, even while his underlying character had become decidedly less human, for Knight had black-boxed Jevons' enquiries into what happened inside real man's head and replaced economic man by a wonderfully endowed automaton. A different kind of black-boxing went on in an alternative refashioning of economic man in which he gained the adjective 'rational'. Rational economic man seems to have somewhat more the qualities of a cartoon: he is decidedly two-dimensional in character, and while regarded with affection by economists, he is regarded as a figure of fun by other social scientists.[23] But despite these cartoon qualities, rational economic man came to function as a role model for rational behaviour

The process by which economic man gained the label 'rational' is complex indeed, but my aim here is not to unravel this process, only to sketch in enough to indicate another historically important version of economic man in my gallery of portraits.[24] To this end, I offer just one path through the historical maze, beginning with the distinction between the economic man portraits of Jevons and Menger. Jevons' mathematical analysis of calculating man was concerned with how he made such decisions to maximize utility from consumption assuming that utility was all one kind of stuff, so the nature of man's choices between different kinds of things received little attention. More of a good is better than less up to the point where the extra (marginal) unit no longer gives him pleasure but pain, but beyond that, Jevons' account was limited: his calculating man has no way of choosing between two equal utility-valued goods – he is simply indifferent between them. Edgeworth followed this strand when he expressed the series of points of equal utility valuations for combinations of the two goods as indifference curves in his discussion of Crusoe and Friday (see Chapter 3). In Menger's account, man is an economizer rather than a maximizer. His subjective valuations (based on introspection) are concerned with choices at the margin between satisfying different needs *given his circumstances*, rather than with assessing standardized units of pleasure from consuming different goods as Jevons' calculating man does. It is in this Austrian marginalist tradition in the late nineteenth century that we find an economic man who considers how to choose between things.[25] On the other hand, it was Jevons' and Edgeworth's mathematical formulation of economic man that provided the means of description for rational economic man.

23 Exaggerations of certain features (as noted here in this chapter) have led other social scientists (and critical economists) to make fun of these economic man portraits in ways that reflect these cartoon qualities. For example, J. M. Clark observed that the marginal man of Jevons' variety was "absorbed in his irrationally rational passion for impassionate calculation" (1918, p. 24).

24 I thank the referee who offered me eight different alternative readings of the main elements of rational choice theory! Each no doubt has a history that is mutually entwined with that of the others. See note 26 for further references.

25 His was not the only account that focussed on individual economic choosing. J. B. Clark (1899), the American marginalist, relied on an account of choice influenced by the social group.

This history of what happened to economic accounts of behaviour after Menger and Jevons has been told in various ways, but they mostly agree that this refocusing of the portrait involved two separate moves. On the one hand was a process of stripping away the underlying psychology from both Menger's picture of satisfying needs and from Jevons' picture of maximizing utility that led to the psychological thinness of the new characterization.[26] On the other hand, it involved filling in the notion of what it meant for economic man to be "rational". Historically, economists have used two main notions: one relates to reasoning behaviour, the other to choosing behaviour as Herbert Simon (1976) pointed out. In the early neoclassical economics of Knight, rational meant 'reasoned', goal-directed, activity, a notion that hardly differs from the efficacious pursuit (of wealth) that we found in Mill's *homo economicus*. It was rational in the second 'choosing' sense more associated with Menger that became closely linked to mid-twentieth-century neoclassical economics, and the birth of this man was, as with Mill, closely associated with a change in the definition of economics.

Once again, Weber makes an interesting pointer, taking Menger's concern with satisfying needs given his circumstances into a more general idea:

> Specifically economic motives . . . operate wherever the satisfaction of even the most immaterial need or desire is bound up with the application of *scarce* material means. (Weber, 1904, p. 65, his italics)

This comes close to the standard twentieth-century neoclassical definition of economics as: "the science of the efficient use of scarce resources", for as Lionel Robbins announced in 1932, economists were no longer concerned with "the causes of material welfare", or the creation and distribution of wealth as were the eighteenth- and nineteenth-century classical economists, but with "human behaviour conceived as a relationship between ends and means" (p. 21).[27] The situation of scarcity, noted by Weber and announced by Robbins as defining economics, was one in which choices *have* to be made.

This change in the base definition of economics had great consequences for the portrait of economic man for it places his ability to make choices central to his conception. In the marginalists' conception, whether of Jevons or Menger, model man's desires or his needs (respectively) are the primary components of the portrait.

---

26 A. W. (Bob) Coats (1976) recounts how the late-nineteenth-century attempts to provide psychological underpinnings to economic behaviour gave way in the twentieth century following attacks by pragmatic philosophers in the U.S. and the failure of measurement programmes in the U.K. Using a similar cast of economists that includes Fisher, Pareto, and more, Nicola Giocoli (2003) writes of an "escape from psychology". For a recent dissenting voice, at least as far as some of the story about psychology goes, see Hands (2010). The rise of behaviourism and positivism are also thought to be important factors (on the latter, see Hands, 2007), as are discussions about altruism (see Fontaine, 2007).

27 Robbins references the Austrian tradition, and Caldwell (2004) discusses that relationship though Howson (2004) suggests local roots to his ideas. See Backhouse and Medema (2009) on the acceptance of the new definition and Maas (2009) on the Weber-Robbins comparison.

These were pared away in twentieth-century rational economic man, for whom it is assumed that his desires can be maximized or satisfied only by 'rational' decisions and choices. Characterizing this rationality then became the main object of the portrait. This commitment to a new definition of economic man, and throwing out of the old, was expressed by Lionel Robbins:

> The fundamental concept of economic analysis is the idea of relative valuations; and, as we have seen, while we assume that different goods have different values at different margins, we do not regard it as part of our problem to explain why these particular valuations exist. We take them as data. So far as we are concerned, our economic subjects can be pure egoists, pure altruists, pure ascetics, pure sensualists or – what is much more likely – mixed bundles of all these impulses. The scales of relative valuations are merely a convenient formal way of exhibiting certain permanent characteristics of man as he actually is. (Robbins, 1932, p. 95)

As Robbins took pains to point out, this did not exclude individuals making relative valuations on the basis of their feelings of all kinds, including "virtue or shame", or even an interest in "the happiness of my baker" (Robbins, p. 95, a reference to Smith's self-interest in exchange argument); it is just that these motivations were no longer of interest to the economist.[28] It is this loss of personality as well as of psychology that create the sense of two-dimensionality, and so the cartoon-like character, that this new 'rational economic man' exhibits.

By making choices dominant over desires, mid-twentieth-century economics effectively allowed economic man to have any type of character he liked provided he behaved 'rationally'. Rational economic man was named so because he chose rationally: he wished to maximize his utility (as in Jevons' account) but did so by making choices that were *logically consistent* over a set of goods (rather than by introspectively following by his pleasure or his needs).[29] Here rationality is instrumental – economists working in this neoclassical tradition claimed nothing about the underlying feelings of people, as in marginal economics of Jevons and Menger, nor about their motives as in the classical economics of Malthus and Mill; and, as Robbins implies, economists did not even care. The person in the model ceased to have any explanatory power over the causes of economic behaviour.

Economic man had already became a shadowy figure in the early-twentieth-century Edgeworth Box, labelled with an X or a Y; or as J. M. Clark remarked, "He has become a symbol, rather than a means of description or explanation" (1936, p. 9). When he then acquired propensities to behave rationally, economists used

28 "It is not from the benevolence of the butcher, the brewer, or the baker that we expect our dinner, but from their regard to their own interest. We address ourselves, not to their humanity but to their self-love, and never talk to them of our own necessities but of their advantages" (Smith, 1776, Book I, Chapter II, Para 2).

29 Choices must be 'consistent' and 'transitive' over a number of goods (i.e., if A is preferred to B and B to C, then A must also be preferred to C).

him to enquire into the nature of rational behaviour and to reason with him by asking what constitutes rational behaviour in any given circumstance or situation such as in the situations of game theory (see Chapter 9). Because of his character he came, on the one hand to be seen as offering an account of the rationality of outcomes of economic behaviour in the economy: rational economic man was "designed for interpreting observed *consequences* of men's actions", not for interpreting the actions themselves (Machlup, 1978, p. 281). On the other hand, he was also seen as offering a model for how real man *should* behave:

> The rational man of pure theory is an ideal type in the sense not only of being an idealization where the theory holds without qualification but also of being a model to copy, a guide to action. In pointing out the way to satisfy a given set of ordered preferences, the theorist gives reasons for action. (Hahn and Hollis, 1979, p. 14)

Here, the "reasons for action" are not in the initial feelings of the subjects, but are rationalised (or reasoned backwards) by the economist from looking at the consequences. Model man in this sense is no longer a perfectly distilled, that is, abstracted, version of real man's economic behaviour, or even of the observed consequences of his actions, but for some economists at least, a normative model of behaviour for real economic actors to follow. Economic man became a role model that defined rational behaviour.

7. The Art of Caricature and Processes of Idealization

Let me return here to my larger agenda – the problem of understanding how models are made, for this was the question for the first part of this book. By peering into the history of economic man we have seen how successive generations of economists created their accounts of individual economic behaviour. We have also seen why economists created these model men, for, as they stated quite clearly, they needed a distilled notion of human economic behaviour in order to make economics viable as a science. Making a model of the individual was to create a more carefully limited account of economic man's character, and of the way he behaves, into a form that could be used for reasoning with, either in theorizing or in enquiries into the world.

Various terms have been used here to describe the model-making processes used by these economists: focussing, simplifying, subtracting, reducing, abstracting, isolating, conceptualizing, symbolizing, idealizing, composing, exaggerating, and so forth. Other terms have been used to describe the outcomes: model man as abstractions, utopias, conceptual devices, symbolic abstractions, ideal types, automata, and cartoons. Some of these terms were used by the economists themselves, and others came from my attempts to capture the process they were using or to characterize the outcomes they obtained. We have seen, for example, that Malthus and Mill made their economic man portraits in a relatively straightforward way: they focussed on, or abstracted, only the elements they considered most important. At first sight, such a description seems to be equally relevant for Menger and Jevons. But in these latter cases, it is by no means a sufficient account. Their kinds of abstraction meant that other processes were involved too. Menger's man was made by a process of composing from simplest typical elements and involved abstractions and concept forming in making his ideal type. Jevons used processes of reduction and transforming into symbolic form as well as picking out the salient characteristics for attention and setting others aside. In other words, we quickly find that it is quite difficult to select exactly the right set of terms to capture – with the required nuances – the way that any one economist created his particular model man, and that it is even more difficult to generalize about these processes.

It is tempting at this point to turn to philosophy of science for a way to organise these materials. But when we do so, we face a similar problem. The generic label used by philosophers of science for all these processes is 'idealization', but they do not all share the same understanding of exactly what this term entails, and to add to the confusion, they use the term idealization to refer to both the process and to the end product.[30] This lack of agreement may be partly based on differences in philosophical standpoint, but it is also because it really is difficult to generalize across the differences in the processes that scientists use in model-making. The history of science is usually messier than philosophers would like it to be, and while we can fashion an account that fits well for one process of making an economic model man, it is difficult to pick one process of idealization that generalizes for all the economists, and for their model men who have peopled this chapter. It is not that ideas from philosophy of science are not relevant – for after all, I have been using them during this chapter. The point is rather that clean-limbed philosophical analysis does not so much organise our sprawling historical experience as stumble over it.

Missing from these accounts of idealization is that model-making is a creative activity, as I suggested in my Chapter 3 account of model-making as world–making. A comparison between scientists' processes of making a model and the artists' of making a character portrait invites us to consider where that creative element lies in these complicated and mixed processes of idealization.

To start with, let us go back to the striking example of Knight's slot machine man, whose portrait relied on a particular choice of exaggeration. While the notion of exaggeration had been discussed by Weber (above), it was just such exaggerations

---

30 In addition, their debates juggle a set of additional terms: causal versus construct idealization (see note 40), mathematical idealization, concretization, and isolation (of horizontal and vertical kinds). For discussions of this idealization literature with many references (including the Poznań approach to idealization) in the philosophy of economics, see the essays and references in Hamminga and De Marchi (1994, discussed in Morgan, 1996); and Morgan and Knuuttila (2012). See footnote 38 on the process/outcome conflation.

that gave rise to the terminology of models as "caricatures" used by Gibbard and Varian, (1978) to describe the modelling practices of neoclassical economics.[31]

A caricature relies on the artist taking a *subjective* view in the sense that it relies on distorting or exaggerating certain characteristics beyond the point of objective description. So the kind of representation that just extends a nose or eyebrows so that we can put a name to the character is not what is meant here. The *Spitting Image* puppet of the past British Prime Minister, John Major, is more the kind of thing I have in mind.[32] Major could be recognised in cartoons by his grey suit (as Margaret Thatcher was by her handbag), but when the puppeteers presented Major as grey, not only in his habitual clothing, but in skin and body colour right through, the exaggeration captured an immediately recognisable double set of qualities in the politician: he was boring, and utterly reliably so, even – given his occupation – to the point of trustworthiness! It is exactly this exaggeration of a particular characteristic that enable us to recognise an additional 'something' inherent in the person's character. Thus the insight we gain from caricature comes from comparing that representation with our knowledge of the original in which we must first recognise the similarity in features before we can go on to recognise the additional new understanding these exaggerations or distortions bring.[33]

This art of caricature is reputed to have begun with Annibale Caracci, the Italian artist of the late sixteenth century, who is also credited with introducing the word:

> Is not the caricaturist's task exactly the same as the classical artist's? Both see the lasting truth beneath the surface of mere outward appearance. Both try to help nature accomplish its plan. The one may strive to visualize the perfect form and to realise it in his work, the other to grasp the perfect deformity, and thus reveal the very essence of a personality. A good caricature, like every work of art, is more true to life than reality itself. (Quoted in Gombrich & Kris, 1940, pp. 11–12)

Caracci's notion of caricature can help us understand economic portraiture too. Mill's Scrooge portrait of a man driven overwhelmingly by the motive to gain wealth, as he pointed out, was not intended as a realistic description, but rather to suggest that inside every person there was something of this economic man. By contrast, Knight's slot-machine man is a creature of economic science not of the real world, it was by exaggerating the most extreme characteristics assumed of importance in neoclassical economics that Knight gave the professional economist as the audience (not the general reader) insight into the implications for their theories of adopting a character of full information and foresight – for example, that

---

31 It is significant that this term emerged from one of the earliest philosophical studies of models in economics, rather than in another scientific field.

32 I refer here to the political satire TV show that appeared in Britain in which political figures appeared as rubber puppets during the Thatcher and Major eras, 1984 and 1996.

33 This argument, about similarity supporting new insights, parallels the way new insights are gained from analogical models to be found in Chapter 5.

such a man is one of no intelligence. As Weber noted of his ideal types, caricatures are not descriptions of reality, but allow the economist-scientist to express such descriptions and to explicate the significant elements of their materials. These are sophisticated portraits fashioned in sophisticated ways.

Simple or more daring as these different model outcomes were, like caricatures, they have, as Caracci argued, the potential to be sources of truthful insight into the motivations of economic man or into economists' theoretical accounts of his behaviour. Again, we must first recognise the accurate portrayal of similar qualities in model man and actual man to recognise the additional insight offered in these economists' portraits. Mill's Scrooge character, Malthus' man driven by his passions, Menger's careful chooser, and Jevons' calculating man can all be understood as caricatures – character sketches in which certain inherent characteristics have been featured and emphasized over others in such a way that the viewers – of each time period – were able to recognise the significance of those characteristics. We can view Malthus' and Mill's portraits as caricatures for classical economics just as Knight's character plays the same role for neoclassical economics.[34]

How does this caricature notion speak to our problem of understanding the *process* of making economic portraits? In other words, what processes are involved in the art of creating a caricature? One of the most famous political caricatures in history was the mid-nineteenth century depiction of Louis Philippe of France as a pear. In defending himself in court, the artist, Charles Philipon, drew a series of sketches showing four stages in his caricaturization process (shown here as Figure 4.3).[35] He claimed that he was not representing the King as a pear: his defence hinged on the argument that although the first drawing was indeed Loius Philippe, it gave no sign that he was the King, and the fourth drawing was a only a pear (also, in French, meaning a fathead or dupe). In creating the caricature, the artist must use her or his creativity to overcome the cognitive hurdle for the observer who must recognise Loius Philippe both as King and as pear to gain the insights about the King that came from the meanings of a pear. And once we have gained the insight of the King as a pear, it is not possible to go back and lose that recognition, as was proved by the actions of the French populace who drew pears to refer to their king.[36] Though the artist lost his case, Petrey (1991) recounts the history of how this caricature of the King as a pear rapidly spread through France, and details the ever more ineffective actions of the French state to ban all references to pears!

34 Even Adam Smith's portrait discussed at the beginning of this chapter, though not a model, appears to have been viewed as something of a caricature to his contemporaries (see note 1).

35 The set shown here come from Gombrich and Kris (1940, p. 20, reproduced in Gombrich, 1960). This 1834 set differs slightly from the original set of 1831 reproduced by Petrey (1991) in his semiotic analysis and history of this caricature. Charles Philipon was editor of the journal *La Caricature*, later *Le Charivari*, and the employer of the great nineteenth-century French caricaturist Honoré Daumier.

36 Chapter 9 describes a similar situation, namely that economists see Prisoner's Dilemma models at work in the world, while Chapter 10 discusses the more general claim that economists see their models, including rational economic man, everywhere around them.

Figure 4.3. Philipon's Art of Caricature (1834).

Source: E. H. Gombrich & E. Kris, *Caricature*, Harmondsworth : Penguin, 1940, figure 11, p. 20. Reproduced with permission from Leonie Gombrich, Anton O. Kris and Anna K. Wolff.

It is a wonderful story, but let us not be distracted from how this relates to model-making. Philipon's sequence of drawings shows a process of losing the features of the real person (Loius Philippe) at the same time as gaining features of the caricature of him (the pear). But we can see that it is not just a process of selecting some features in and others out, or even of adding or extending features, but of creatively *transforming* a description of a person into an insightful representation of that person in another form. Descriptions of this process of caricaturization in terms of generalization, subtraction, abstraction, addition and, of course, exaggeration – are all relevant, but no single one of these notions of idealization (taking that as the generic term) fully captures the creative *process of transformation* going on in these sketches, though in combination they come close to it. It is this same complex combination of processes that Philipon uses in making his caricature that we have seen going on in scientific model-making in economics.

Model-making understood as the art of caricaturing – a process of selecting, synthesizing, and transforming elements for an already existing person or account – can be understood as a series of idealizations (used in its generic sense).[37] This comparison with the art of caricaturing suggests an important point about scientific model-making by idealization. It is an obvious point, easy to overlook, that scientists can apply such processes of idealization *only* to some quite well-formed materials they already have in hand.[38] Scientists, like caricaturists, can simplify only from a more complicated description and exaggerate from a representation already available; they can only pick out, reject, and transform elements from the versions of the world that they already have. These are *not newly made* versions of the world (as the Edgeworth Box of Chapter 3); they are *re-made versions* of a world we know much about and have already described.

Where do these initial versions come from in the sciences? This is where the fact that economists are modelling economic man becomes important, for by observing themselves and others, economic scientists have a considerable observational base of knowledge of economic man.[39] And they have other versions in hand as well – in previous theories about economic behaviour and motivations. Economists can use the model men made by earlier economists as the descriptions from which, by further processes of idealization, they come to new models. Thus, the moves from Jevons' calculating man to Knight's slot-machine man or to rational economic man can be interpreted as cases in which economists have been applying their idealizations to already existing models of man rather than to earlier verbal descriptions, or even to their own observations of man's motives and behaviour.[40]

37 This begins to sound a little like Boumans' (1999) recipe account of model-making applied to Ricard's model farm (see Chapter 2). The difference is that idealization processes are carried out on an already existing object or account (e.g., in physics, the pendulum is an object that lends itself to description and then idealization of the description; see Giere, 1988 and Morrison, 1999) rather than being a newly created or imagined account.

38 It is one of the oddities of the idealization literature that this point is overlooked. It may happen because there is an easy slippage, and sometimes conflation, between an idealization as an *outcome* and the *process* of idealization. To idealize (verb), we must already have some kind of description of the world, and then set some bits at zero or ignore them in order to make a tractable model, that is, to arrive at an idealization (noun).

39 Evidence from experimental economics suggests that economists are made by part nature and part nurture. That is, economics students already think and behave more like economic model men than other students, but they come to resemble those models more closely from their economics training. This casts an interesting light on the reflexivity of economists in relation to the models of economic man.

40 McMullin (1985) makes a distinction between "construct" versus "causal" idealizations depending "on whether the simplification is worked on the conceptual representation of the object, or on the problem-situation itself" (p. 255, and see Suárez, 1999). Usually, causal idealizations are designed to simplify the problem situation by taking away causes, as Mill did when he assumed only three constant causes at work in order to make his model man more tractable. Another example of causal idealization is Malthus' suggestion that we might rethink his portrait of economic man to include education and reasoning power – this proposal takes us back to the world level and asks us to rethink the main causes at work in a new idealization producing a slightly different portrait. A move from Mill's *homo economicus* either to Jevons' calculating man, or to Menger's

Although this caricature-making account nicely conveys how model-making involves a complex combination of processes of idealization, it does not tell the economist exactly which items to pick out and which to jettison from amongst the many characteristics that are available, nor how to transform them to make a model portrait. The scientist must play the role of the artist here – responsible for choosing some elements and leaving behind others, working with some of these and leaving others untouched, and for fashioning them all together into the caricature. Whereas two eyes, a nose, and a mouth in particular places within a circle might be sufficient to provide a representation of a face to a growing child, the artist has to do more than this to present the King-as-a-pear to the French population of the 1830s: both the King and his representation as a pear must be recognisable at the same time. Similarly, any particular economist's portrait of economic man depends on that scientist selecting, transforming, and synthesizing his materials in creating a model of economic man and his behaviour that are recognisable within his economic tradition and that still maintains some sense of the real economic man.

But while the art of caricaturing provides an account of the process of creating models of economic man, it does not give much insight into how and why his portrait has changed in such radical ways over time. The economic tradition within which an economist works shapes, in a strong way, the choice of elements and kinds of idealizations made. And, since these models of man provide the objects that economists use to represent man's behaviour in their theories, the elements chosen and their mode of transformation into a new portrait will be different between economic traditions. So, for example, an Austrian school economist of the early twentieth century would not have created, by mathematical idealization, Knight's portrait of perfect knowledge – this is a spurious possibility since Austrian school economists both eschewed mathematics and believed that being human entailed having limited knowledge. Each model man representation, and his process of creation, have to be consistent with and coherent within his broader scientific tradition not only of content, but of form and style as well as scientific practice.

This is just as would expect from our comparison of the way models and caricatures are developed. Earlier caricatures were represented in fine detail in eighteenth-century engravings and nineteenth-century newspapers and their insights into political character are often lost to us now. Twentieth- and twenty-first-century

choosing man, was also a causal idealization. It meant, as we have seen, a return to the real-world object – man – and taking a new direction of simplification and abstraction, to a different account of economic man with different attributes and so causal capacities. In a construct idealization, the scientist alters one or some aspects of an already modelled man rather than going back to the original object. Thus the move from Jevons' calculating man to Knight's slot-machine man could be understood as idealizing on the already conceived mathematical model of man as a pleasure machine to turn it into slot machine. This distinction between causal and construct idealization clarifies the historical moves made between models.

caricatures come to us as cartoon sketches and speak to us by caricaturing matters of our own day.[41] The same dynamics are at work in prompting the successive caricatures of economic man. We find a parallel change in style in economics: whereas Malthus' economic man was drawn with quite a detailed verbal account and it is difficult to understand the milieu in which he made sense, economic man of our own day is created in the abstract formal style of modern economics and is designed to speak to economists' changed scientific concerns about the modern economy.

These changes in model man go along with changes in contents, methods, and modes of doing economic science. As schools of economics rise and fall, they create new portraits, new caricatures that pick out the features that economists of that time and place find most interesting and salient to the analysis of that school. These radical changes in economic man portraits were not so much driven by paradigm change – as exemplifications of them. And if the portrait of economic man is an indicator of more general changes, we seem now to be the midst of another paradigm change.

8. Model Man's CV: De-Idealization and the Changing Roles of Economic Man

Looking beyond the details, we can discern two major shifts in the three-phased career of economic man. In the first phase, economists treated model man as an observational sketch. The second took model man into the centre of economic theory. These two phases of idealizations of various kinds provided the materials for this chapter. The third phase, indicated only briefly here, takes him back to something of an observed character sketch, via processes which might best be described as ones of de-idealization.

In the first phase, we began with the relatively straightforward characters of the classical economics of Malthus and Mill and thence described the more abstract conceptual versions in Menger's ideal type and in Jevons mathematical form. During this historical process, the basic character of model economic man went through several mutations. Malthus portrayed him as driven by physical appetites, Mill as a wealth seeker. Jevons changed him into a man seeking to maximize pleasure or utility from consumption, while Menger presented him as satisfying needs though sensible choices. But these were all model men compared to the rich descriptive portrait we find in other works of social science. Each

---

41 According to Gombrich and Kris (1940), it was only around the turn of the eighteenth to nineteenth centuries that caricatures became associated with the comparative simplicity of cartoon representations, though there were certainly masters of the art before that time. (See Levy and Peart [2010] on nineteenth-century cartoons and caricatures with economic content.) As we have seen, economic man portraits involve a drastic level of simplifying on the grounds of scientific functionality, that is, they have the qualities of cartoons, which is another reason why the notion of caricature models is particularly apt for economics.

model man was made to reduce the complexity of dealing with all human feelings and emotions and actions that flow from them and, at the same time to focus the attention on the explicitly economic aspects of man's behaviour. This sequence of model men was the nineteenth-century economists' answer to the problem of dealing with human behaviour in a scientific way. In each case, model man was taken to represent real man, but pared down to focus on the picture of economic behaviour in its simplest, purest, or most abstract form, unaffected by other considerations and so offered the possibilities of analysis within this narrowed framework. Taken literally he was regarded as a fictional character, but one whom it still seemed possible, by processes of self or other observation (and perhaps by processes of imagination), to compare back with real man. Each of these different models seemed to their economist-creators a sensible scientific strategy compared to the alternative social science approaches in the nineteenth century of studying the real behaviour of man directly with all his feelings and amongst his family, community, or nation.

Jevons' economic man marks a significant turning point into the second phase in this history of such portraits, for his character can be understood both by looking forward from the early-nineteenth century standpoint of classical economics and by looking back at him from the later twentieth-century neoclassical economics. When we trace from Jevons' calculating man, through Knight's depersonalised slot-machine man, to the rational agent of the mid-twentieth century, we can see how certain different economic qualities became exaggerated. He was endowed with calculating power by Jevons, given extraordinary amounts of economic knowledge and certainty to analyse the fullest effect of economizing behaviour by Knight, and he became extremely rational in the neoclassical economics of the mid-twentieth century. These economic men were 'idealized' in the sense that they were endowed with more perfect economic qualities according to the theory of the day. In these traditions, economic man was no longer taken to represent real man, but to be an artificial character created by economists for their mathematical laboratories in which the model man is investigated using model reasoning.

The third phase in the career of economic man may be understood as a series of de-idealizations – processes of adding back elements and bringing the portraits of economic man closer to descriptions of real behaviour. The reputation of neoclassical economic men was at a height in the 1970s. Since then, economists have moved from the all-knowing portrait of Knight's slot-machine and his thinner cartoon partner, rational economic man, to portraits that have more scope for application to the behaviour of people in the real economy. Following attacks in the 1970s – on rational economic man's consistency by Amartya Sen, and on his maximizing ability by Herbert Simon – economists have found good reasons to think about the various ways in which these two central features of economic man's rationality might be limited or "bounded".[42] Behavioural economics, a re-splicing of economics and

---

42 See Sen (1976), Simon (1976), and Klaes and Sent (2005).

psychology, analyses man's abilities to make economic decisions.[43] Economists have replaced Knight's assumption of a man with perfect foresight to investigate "strategic man", one who thinks strategically as in game theory; others have challenged his selfishness by considering his possibilities for altruistic behaviour.[44] Still others have become concerned with the information that economic man knows, chipping away at another of the character traits of Knight's model to rethink model man's ability to act with only limited information; "contractual man" – the ability to make and keep contracts – being one outcome of this rethink.[45] These widespread recent developments in the portrait of economic man began by taking neoclassical economic man as the benchmark ideal and then asking what might happen to modelling outcomes if he were not so perfectly knowledgeable or so rational or so selfish as he was painted. Old models, like old habits, die hard.

While these new portraits of economic man typically start with the models of economic man inherited from neoclassical economics, their refashioning comes in large part from the new ways that they investigate him, that is, the new portraits emerge once again because of changes in the scientific practices of economics. Experimental work investigates individual's economic behaviour in different kinds of situations such as markets or games (see Chapters 7 and 9); simulations use role playing and other kinds of experiment (see Chapter 8); survey work has been investigating how people feel about things economic, and whether they are 'happy'; and neurological investigations (neuroeconomics) seek to trace the physiological aspects of economic behaviour. In conducting experiments *with* him and observing whether he behaves the same or differently from the benchmark or idealized model man of earlier theories, economists have come to treat economic man more like a laboratory rat than a mathematical construct. But by conducting experiments *upon* man to map his model portrait via his brain waves, they seem to be in the process of creating a new biological model organism, one more like the laboratory mouse than the laboratory rat. All these new forms of scientific investigation effectively entail processes of de-idealization, not only to make the portrait more complex, but to make him more descriptively accurate and less driven by theoretical requirements. These modes of investigation and processes of refashioning are fast creating a very different portrait – indeed, a set of portraits – of economic man, ones very different from the verbally and mathematically described models that economists are used to.

These new economic models of man are fast taking economists away from their highly idealized characters of the last two centuries. He is becoming a more rounded and more interesting 'fatter' character – a man who can learn, bargain, act strategically, has memory, and may even be happy. This would be a far cry from the dismal science portrait given us by Malthus, whose economic man suffered

---

43 See Sent (2004).
44 See Giocoli (2003) on strategic man, Fontaine (2007, and 2012 forthcoming) on altruism.
45 See Pessali (2006).

from cycles of starvation and the ill effects of vice. Yet, like Malthus' conception, these modern approaches suggest a return to a biological or physiological analysis of man's behaviour, spliced perhaps with a new cognitive science or psychological account that might be compared to Jevons' conception. His portrait is being radically reconstructed in many different ways.

These three broad phases in the characterization of economic man can be associated then with the long run changes in the ideas, theories, questions, and practices of economic science – in themselves contingent upon many other currents in scientific, political, economic, and intellectual histories. As the focus of enquiry and explanation for economic man's behaviour has changed, these three phases of portraiture have been associated with different functions for economic man within economic sciences. The causal capacities associated with earlier manifestations of model economic men, pictured by Malthus, Mill, and even by Jevons, were the capacities that they thought to be at work in the world. The motivations of Malthus' working man, the character of Mill's wealth-seeker, and even Menger's human economy were understood by economists to be the motives that create changes in the real economy, which is why these portraits were often more useful in reasoning about the world than in theory building. Jevons' man is once again a crossover point. His feelings (eventually) registered in prices in the market place, but his character proved more valuable as a subject for investigation in the mathematics laboratory of the economist (exactly as we saw in Chapter 3 in the Edgeworth Box). From Knight's slot machine, through the twentieth-century history of rational economic man, economic man has lived primarily inside economic theories, representing a set of causal capacities inside a mathematical model account of the world. He plays the role of the individual in whatever problem, situation, or events are portrayed in economists' models of the world: he is the thin person inhabiting those small worlds. Indeed, we meet this character again in Chapter 9, playing his due role in another model. Only in the last few decades, when new, less idealized and more recognisably human versions of economists' model man have grown up, have the causal capacities associated with economic man's character come to be seen once again as representing primarily something active in the world as well as a model for theorizing with. These new model men are manipulated not just in mathematical models but also in experimental situations, and as a consequence are once again becoming usable to enquire into the world, though in radically new ways.

Acknowledgement

This chapter draws on one of the earliest papers on models that I wrote as part of the outcome of the Wissenschaftskolleg in Berlin group on modelling in 1995–6. I am grateful to Margaret Morrison for prompting me to explore the question and for the support of the Kolleg during that year. That paper's 1997 publication under the title "The Character of 'Rational Economic Man' " in *DIALEKTIK*. The topic turned out to be critical for my project on modelling – for what was the small world without a thin man in it? So I resurrected the story here first for a talk at Nancy Cartwright's sixtieth birthday celebrations in June 2005 at LSE, and then added to it for my Presidential Address to the History of Economics Society also in June 2005 (see Morgan, 2006) at the University of Puget Sound and finally into chapter form – which has the benefit of a much extended section on caricatures. I thank Sheldon Steed for his ever-patient research assistance. My thanks go particularly to Harro Maas, Roger Backhouse, Mauricio Suaréz, Bruce Caldwell, Margaret Schabas, Emma Rothschild, and others for their helpful comments. I also thank participants at various seminars in Australia: at University of Sydney (History and Philosophy of Science Department) and University of New South Wales (Economics Department) in October 2005, and at Australian National University (Research School in Social Sciences, Philosophy Group) in November 2005.

References

Arrow, K. (1986) "Economic Theory and the Hypothesis of Rationality". *Journal of Business* 59(4). Reprinted in J. Eatwell, M. Milgate and P. Newman (eds),*The New Palgrave*, Vol. 2 (pp. 69–75). London: Macmillan.

Backhouse, Roger E. and Steven Medema (2009) "Defining Economics: The Long Road to the Acceptance of the Robbins Definition". *Economica*, 76, 805–20.

Bentham, J. (1789/1970) *An Introduction to the Principles of Morals and Legislation*. In J. H. Burns and H. L. A. Hart (eds), *The Collected Works of Jeremy Bentham, 2, 1, Principles of Legislation*. London: Athlone Press, 1970.

Bhimani, Alnoor (1994) "Accounting and the Emergence of 'Economic Man'". *Accounting, Organization and Society*, 19, 637–74.

Boumans, Marcel (1999) "Built-In Justification". In Mary S. Morgan and Margaret Morrison (eds), *Models as Mediators: Perspectives on Natural and Social Science* (pp. 66–96). Cambridge: Cambridge University Press.

Boumans, Marcel and Mary S. Morgan (2001) "Ceteris Paribus Conditions: Materiality and the Application of Economic Theories". *Journal of Economic Methodology*, 8, 11–26.

Caldwell, Bruce (2004) *Hayek's Challenge*. Chicago: University of Chicago Press.

Cartwright, Nancy (1989) *Nature's Capacities and Their Measurement*. Oxford: Clarendon Press.

Clark, J. B. (1899) *The Distribution of Wealth*. New York: Macmillan.

Clark, J. M. (1918) "Economics and Modern Psychology". *Journal of Political Economy*, 26, 1–30; 136–66.

(1936) *A Preface to Social Economics*. New York: Farrar and Rinehart.

Coats, A. W. (1976) "Economics and Psychology: The Death and Resurrection of a Research Programme". In S. Latsis (ed), *Method and Appraisal in Economics* (pp. 43–64). Cambridge: Cambridge University Press.

Edgeworth, F. Y. (1881) *Mathematical Psychics*. London: Kegan Paul.

Emmett, R. B. (1994) "Maximisers versus Good Sports: Frank Knight's Curious Understanding of Exchange Behaviour". In N. De Marchi and M. S. Morgan (eds), *Transactors and Their Markets in the History of Economics* (pp. 276–92). Annual Supplement to *History of Political Economy*, Vol. 26. Durham, NC: Duke University Press.

Fontaine, Philippe (2007) "From Philanthopy to Altruism: Incorporating Unselfish Behavior into Economics, 1861–1975". *History of Political Economy*, 39:1, 1–46.

(2012) "Beyond Altruism? Economics and the Minimization of Unselfish Behavior, 1976–1993". *History of Political Economy*, forthcoming.

Gibbard, A. and H. R. Varian (1978) "Economic Models". *The Journal of Philosophy*, 75, 664–77.

Giere, Ronald (1988) *Explaining Science: A Cognitive Approach*. Chicago: University of Chicago Press.

Giocoli, Nicola (2003) *Modeling Rational Agents: From Interwar Economics to Early Modern Game Theory*. Cheltenham: Edward Elgar.

Gombrich, E. H. (1960) *Art and Illusion: A Study in the Psychology of Pictorial Representation*. Princeton, NJ: Princeton University Press for The Bollingen Foundation, NY.

Gombrich, E. H. and E. Kris (1940) *Caricature*. Harmonsworth: King Penguin.

Hahn, F. and M. Hollis (1979) *Philosophy and Economic Theory*. Oxford: Oxford University Press.

Hamminga, Bert and Neil De Marchi (1994) "Idealization and the Defence of Economics: Notes Toward a History". In Bert Hamminga and Neil De Marchi (eds), *Idealization VI: Idealization in Economics* (pp. 11–40). Amsterdam: Rodopi.

Hands, D. Wade (2007) "A Tale of Two Mainstreams: Economics and Philosophy of Natural Science in the mid-Twentieth Century". *Journal of the History of Economic Thought*, 29, 1–13.

(2010) "Economics, Psychology and the History of Consumer Choice Theory". *Cambridge Journal of Economics*, 34, 633–48.

Hartley, James E. (1997) *The Representative Agent in Macroeconomics*. London: Routledge.

Hausman, Daniel M. (1992) *The Inexact and Separate Science of Economics*. Cambridge: Cambridge University Press.

Hempel, Carl G. (1965) "Typological Methods in the Natural and the Social Sciences". In *Aspects of Scientific Explanation* (pp. 155–171). New York: Free Press.

Howson, Susan (2004) "The Origins of Lionel Robbins's *Essay on the Nature and Significance of Economic Science, History of Political Economy*". 36:3, 413–43.

Jevons, W. S. (1871) *The Theory of Political Economy*. London: Penguin, 1970.

Kirman, A. P. (1992) "Whom or What Does the Representative Individual Represent?" *Journal of Economic Perspectives*, 6:2, 117–36.

Klaes, Matthias and Esther-Mirjam Sent (2005) "A Conceptual History of the Emergence of Bounded Rationality". *History of Political Economy*, 37:1, 27–59.

Knight, F. H. (1921) *Risk, Uncertainty and Profit*. Boston: Houghton Mifflin.

(1923) "The Ethics of Competition". In *The Ethics of Competition and Other Essays* (pp. 41–75). New York: Harper, 1936.

(1947) *Freedom and Reform: Essays in Economics and Social Philosophy*. New York: Harper.

Levy, David M. and Peart, Sandra J. (2010) "Economists, Crises and Cartoons". Working paper, available at SSRN: http://ssrn.com/abstract=1547886

Maas, Harro (2005a) *William Stanley Jevons and the Making of Modern Economics*. Cambridge: Cambridge University Press.

(2005b) "Jevons, Mill and the Private Laboratory of the Mind". *The Manchester School*, 73, 62–9.

(2009) "Disciplining Boundaries: Lionel Robbins, Max Weber, and the Borderlands of Economics, History, and Psychology". *Journal of the History of Economic Thought*, 31, 500–17.

Machlup, F. (1978) "Ideal Types, Reality and Construction"; "The Universal Bogey: Economic Man"; and "Homo Oeconomicus and His Classmates"; all in *Methodology of Economics and Other Social Sciences* (pp. 223–301). New York: Academic Press.

Mäki, Uskali (1992) "On the Method of Isolation in Economics". In Craig Dilworth (ed), *Idealization IV: Intelligibility in Science* (pp. 317–51). Amsterdam: Rodopi.

(1997) "Universals and the *Methodenstreit*: A Re-examination of Carl Menger's Conception of Economics as an Exact Science". *Studies in the History and Philosophy of Science*, 28:3, 475–95.

Malthus, T. R. (1803) *An Essay on the Principle of Population.* P. James (ed), for the Royal Economic Society (1989). Cambridge: Cambridge University Press.

McMullin, Ernan (1985) "Galilean Idealization". *Studies in the History and Philosophy of Science*, 16:3, 247–73.

Menger, Carl (1871) *Grundsätze der Volkswirtschaftslehre* (English Edition: *Principles of Economics*, J. Dingwall and B. Hoselitz [eds]). New York: New York University Press, 1976.

(1883/1985) *Investigations into the Method of the Social Sciences with Special Reference to Economics.* Translation (1985) of *Untersuchungen über die Methode der Socialwissenschaften und der Politischen Oekonomie insbesondere* (edited by Francis J. Nock, translated by Louis Schneider). New York: New York University Press.

Mill, J. S. (1836) *On the Definition of Political Economy.* In J. M. Robson (ed), *Collected Works of John Stuart Mill: Essays on Economics and Society*, Vols. 4–5 (1967). Toronto: University of Toronto Press.

Morgan, Mary S. (1994) "Marketplace Morals and the American Economists: The Case of John Bates Clark". In N. De Marchi and M. S. Morgan (eds), *Transactors and Their Markets in the History of Economics* (pp. 229–52). Annual Supplement to *History of Political Economy*, Vol. 26. Durham, NC: Duke University Press.

(1996) "Idealization and Modelling" (A Review Essay). *Journal of Economic Methodology*, 3:1, 131–8.

(1997) "The Character of Rational Economic Man". *Dialektik* (special issue *Modelldenken in den Wissenschaften* edited by B. Falkenburg and S. Hauser), 1, 77–94.

(2006) "Economic Man as Model Man: Ideal Types, Idealization and Caricatures". *Journal of the History of Economic Thought*, 28:1, 1–27.

Morgan, Mary S. and Margaret Morrison (1999) *Models as Mediators: Perspectives on Natural and Social Science.* Cambridge: Cambridge University Press.

Morgan, Mary S. and Tarja Knuuttila (2012) "Models and Modelling in Economics". In U. Mäki (ed), *Handbook of the Philosophy of Economics* (one volume in *Handbook of the Philosophy of Science*. General Editors: Dov Gabbay, Paul Thagard, and John Woods). Amsterdam: Elsevier/North Holland. Available at: http://papers.ssrn.com/sol3/papers.cfm?abstract_id=1499975.

Morrison, Margaret (1999) "Models as Autonomous Agents". In Mary S. Morgan and Margaret Morrison (eds), *Models as Mediators: Perspectives on Natural and Social Science* (pp. 38–65). Cambridge: Cambridge University Press.

Peart, Sandra (1996) *The Economics of W. S. Jevons.* New York: Routledge.

Persky, Joseph (1995) "Retrospectives: The Ethology of Homo Economicus". *Journal of Economic Perspectives*, 9:2, 221–31.

Pessali, Huáscar (2006) "The Rhetoric of Oliver Williamson's Transaction Cost Economics". *Journal of Institutional Economics*, 2:1, 45–65.

Petrey, Sandy (1991) "Pears in History". *Representations*, 35, 52–71.

Robbins, L. (1932) *An Essay on the Nature and Significance of Economic Science.* London: Macmillan.

Schabas, M. (1990) *A World Ruled by Number.* Princeton, NJ: Princeton University Press.

Sen, A. (1976–7) "Rational Fools". *Philosophy and Public Affairs*, 6, 317–44.

Sent, Esther-Mirjam (2004) "Behavioral Economics: How Psychology Made Its (Limited) Way Back Into Economics". *History of Political Economy*, 36:4, 735–60.

Simon, Herbert (1976) "From Substantive to Procedural Rationality". In S. Latsis (ed), *Method and Appraisal in Economics* (pp. 129–48). Cambridge: Cambridge University Press.

Smith, A. (1776) *An Inquiry into the Nature and Causes of The Wealth of Nations.* Edited by R. H. Campbell and A. S. Skinner (1976). Oxford: Oxford University Press.

Suárez, Mauricio (1999) "The Role of Models: The Application of Scientific Theories: Epistemological Implications." In Mary S. Morgan and Margaret Morrison (eds), *Models as Mediators: Perspectives on Natural and Social Science* (pp. 168–96). Cambridge: Cambridge University Press.

Wartofsky, Marx (1968) *Conceptual Foundations of Scientific Thought.* New York: Macmillan.

Weber, Max (1904) "'Objectivity' in Social Science and Social Policy". In *The Methodology of the Social Sciences.* Translated and edited by Edward A. Shils and Henry A. Finch (1949), pp. 49–112. New York: Free Press.

(1908) "Marginal Utility Theory and 'The Fundamental Law of Psychophysics'". Translated by Louis Schneider in *Social Science Quarterly* (1975), 56:1, 21–36.

(1913) *The Theory of Social and Economic Organisations.* Translated by A. M. Henderson and Talcott Parsons, Part I of *Wirtshaft und Gesellschaft* (1947). New York: Free Press.

(1917) "The Meaning of 'Ethical Neutrality' in Sociology and Economics". In *The Methodology of the Social Sciences* (pp. 1–49). Translated and edited by Edward A. Shils and Henry A. Finch (1949). New York: Free Press.

Zouboulakis, Michael (2001) "From Mill to Weber: The Meaning of the Concept of Economic Rationality". *European Journal of the History of Economic Thought*, 8, 1–30.

5

Metaphors and Analogies: Choosing the World of the Model

1. From Metaphors to Analogical Models

Money is often thought of as liquid: it runs through our fingers, it leaks out of our pockets and we are liable to drown in our debts. The metaphorical use is as extensive and as invasive in the technical language of economics as in our everyday talk. From David Hume's eighteenth-century observation that, like connected bodies of water, the value of money will always come to a common level between places, to the modern-day "liquid assets" (cash and assets that can easily be turned into cash) and the "liquidity preference ratio" (our preferences for a certain proportion of assets held in ready, or easily accessible, money), economists have delighted in the use of metaphorical language.[1] It is not just money that prompts economists' flights of rhetorical fancy. Leon Walras in 1900 described the tendency of the market towards an equilibrium to be "like a lake agitated by the wind, where the water is incessantly seeking its level without ever reaching it."[2] Mechanical metaphors are

1 I thank Margaret Schabas for discussions about the many metaphorical statements about money; see David Hume's "Of the Balance of Trade" in Rotwein (1955).
2 See Walras (1874) Lesson 35, sec 322 in Jaffé (1954), p. 380, for the English language translation quoted here.

equally invasive: Edgeworth held "the conception of Man as a pleasure machine" and Knight, as we have seen, described him as a "slot machine", while Thorstein Veblen portrayed the whole business economy of his day as a vast machine in which firms were as closely connected as cogwheels.[3]

When metaphors are suggestive about the nature of economic objects and economic life, they provide the raw material from which to make substantive analogies, and analogies may be formed into models. By adopting a metaphor, economists can portray the workings of the economy in terms of some other already-formed and known world with which they are familiar, maybe a machine such as a mechanical balance or a physiological system such as the human body. In doing so, economists can be said to have 'chosen' the world of the model. And from imagining some aspect of the economy in terms of something else, economists are able to think anew about the economy from their analogical model.

Turning a metaphor, which begins as a figure of speech and idle likeness, into an analogical model involves both cognitive and imaginative work. And, as with so many aspects of making models, cognition and imagination are intimately linked, both in creatively developing the metaphor into a model, and in making the economic terms fit the analogical world, *and* the analogical terms fit back onto the economic world.

The cognitive issue is one we have already met. Economists don't know well how the economic world works. One option, explored in the history of the Edgeworth Box in Chapter 3, is to imagine how some aspects might be and make an image of them. Another is to start with the bits that are known, and bring them to fit together, as Ricardo did in his model farming in Chapter 2. Yet another is to simplify and abstract an account from the complications of the real world – as in the history of economic model man in Chapter 4. The fourth alternative here begins with metaphors and develops them into analogies with which to explore how the world might be and how it might work if it were like those analogical worlds.[4] In choosing another object/system on the basis of some aspects of similarity between that system and beliefs about how the economy works, economists place significant constraints on the form and content of the model. They develop the analogical model using these constraints as a way to explore the implications of that analogy and whether the model can be used to interpret the economy in those terms (see Morgan and Boumans, 2004). This is a cognitive project in that it is

---

3 For Edgeworth, see his 1881, p. 15; on Knight, see Chapter 4; for Veblen, see his 1904 account. Though McCloskey (1990) characterizes metaphors as models in economics, metaphors are really only a starting point (see Morgan [2001] for discussion of her position).

4 Klamer and Leonard (1994) argue for the importance of the cognitive aspects of metaphors at three different levels. Apart from those that are "pedagogical" (ones that serve to clarify but that do not affect the argument), they label as "heuristic" those that "serve to catalyze our thinking, helping us to approach a phenomenon in a novel way.... metaphor is cognitive here because its respective subjects interact to create new meanings" (p. 33); and as "constitutive" those that offer a "conceptual scheme" to characterize our unknown world (p. 39). In the case of models, I suggest that the two latter levels collapse: If a metaphor becomes embedded into a model, then it is likely to have become constitutive too.

one of comparison and translation between the metaphor's subject matter and the economics' subject matter. The activity of filling in the chosen world of the model presents many questions to answer, and it is in solving these that economists find the potential for gaining a new understanding of the economic system.

In discussing how a metaphor becomes a model, Marcel Boumans suggested that we think of a metaphor as something one-dimensional: to suggest that money is liquid offers an intriguing possibility; it suggests much, but tells us little. To gain the benefit of invoking the metaphor, a scientist needs to develop its various possibilities or dimensions into a model.[5] To fill in a picture of some economic world in which money has the property of being a liquid requires the use of imagination. But first the economist has to choose that world. Is it like blood circulating around a body, as Francis Bacon and some of the early Mercantilist economists thought it?[6] Or is it like water in a natural ecology (as Hume suggested), or like a tidal flow between the oceans and lagoons (as Irving Fisher later suggested)?[7] Such a choice of world is the starting point for a model, and because each of those worlds is more constrained in its possibilities than the original metaphor (that money is a liquid), it provides more explicit guidance about the analogical features and suggests how to depict the properties of the modelled world more exactly. We see this happening, for example, in Irving Fisher's move from his lagoon-ocean metaphor to his analogical model that presented bimetallism as a flow of gold and silver liquids between laboratory flasks (see Morgan, 1999). Only when an economist has used his or her imagination to fill in the full dimensionality of the model, that is, to design and create such a model world, do the properties of the analogical model world become evident and usable to the economist.

Suggesting that the development of a metaphor into a model is a process akin to a change in dimensionality is itself to use a metaphor. Edwin Abbott's (1884/1952) novella *Flatland* captures the cognitive depth and demonstrates the imaginative aspects of changing dimensions in a wonderfully direct way. *Flatland* tells the story of a mathematically defined 'person' (a square) who has lived life in a two-dimensional space yet suddenly finds himself confronting a three-dimensional person and world – at first a thoroughly disorientating and even frightening experience. Making sense of the new dimension, learning to live within it effectively and to act within it safely, requires a cognitive shift in recognising how things are in a three-dimensional world rather than a two-dimensional one. The reader shares this experience most effectively in learning what can*not* be seen in a two-dimensional world, and so comes to understand the potential dangers of living in such an environment. Such recognition is not just an intellectual exercise, for the difference between living in worlds of different dimensions is not experienced as a logical difference, nor one that can be

---

5   This insight prompted some of our joint work on the Phillips Machine and the idea is developed in that paper (see Morgan and Boumans, 2004).

6   "If they [the merchants] flourish not, a kingdom may have good limbs, but will have empty veins and nourish little". (Bacon 1625 in Pitcher, 1985)

7   Hume reference as previously; and see Fisher (1911), chapter VI.

bridged by small incremental steps. Rather it depends upon an imaginative leap into the new world, a transition between dimensions that the reader must also make.

Cognition may be held back by a lack of imagination, just as it was for the inhabitant of *Flatland*, whose imagination was – understandably, given that he had only known a two-dimensional world – unable to stretch easily into the third dimension without guidance and interpretation from a three-dimensional inhabitant. Homer Simpson, a two-dimensional television cartoon character from our modern day, lacked such guidance when he suddenly found himself alone in a three-dimensional computer graphics landscape and promptly fell into a three-dimensional hole, but not before he had discovered his own three-dimensional shape, and its shadow, and the audience had heard his voice echo around his newly three-dimensional world.[8] Imagination and cognition are intertwined in any move from living in one world to another, just at they are in moving from a metaphor to an analogical model world in scientific work.

When a model becomes fully naturalised in a field, the creativity and imaginative leap that were required to overcome the cognitive difficulties in its construction are usually lost. This is so even for everyday models in economics such as the Edgeworth Box but it is particularly so with analogical models.[9] When an analogical model becomes well accepted and well used in its new home in economics, then the economic scientists no longer notice its analogical status, nor what new insights it brought to the field.[10] When a later economist comes to study it, those problems of cognition and imagination arise again in particularly severe form. This has proved exactly the situation in recent attempts to understand and restore the Newlyn-Phillips Machine, a working hydraulic model of the economy built in 1949–50.[11] This Machine – an analogical model for the aggregate economy – forms the main object for discussion in this chapter for it enables us to see what happens when scientists 'choose' the world of the model by working with a metaphor to turn it into a fully dimensional economic model. And it demonstrates how the two main design aspects of developing an analogical model – the cognitive and imaginative – are intertwined.

Later in the chapter, I discuss how economists learn from analogical models. According to literary scholars, metaphors lead us to see the two objects joined

---

8 *The Simpsons, Treehouse of Horror VII* Series 7, Episode 6. In a discussion of how they had done this, the animators suggest that they drew their two-dimensional characters into the story and then made them three-dimensional ones (http://show-links.tv/tv_shows/81760/The_Simpsons_2/7/6/ on January 4, 2008).

9 For example, from my seminar presentations on the history of the Edgeworth Box, it became evident that some modern economists found it very difficult to see how the Box could ever have been first drawn without being a box, even though I showed them the pictures of the original non-box diagram (see Chapter 3).

10 See Mirowski (1989) for a strong metaphor-led view of the history of neoclassical economics and how twentieth-century economists lost sight of the physics metaphor that they introduced in the late nineteenth century. An unnoticed analogy is not quite the same as a dead metaphor because the model may still provide a good working object and provoke new findings and uses.

11 For example, see Moghadam and Carter's account of their 1989 attempts to restore the LSE Machine.

in the metaphor in new ways, and similar claims have been made for analogical modelling in the sciences, namely that scientists have the potential to find new insights about their subject field, find new properties in the objects they study, and develop new theories about their behaviour. This will bring in some comparisons with Fisher's earlier use of a mechanical balance model in 1911. These analogical models were formed by three of the more unusually inventive figures in the history of economics: Irving Fisher, Bill Phillips, and Walter Newlyn.

2. The Newlyn-Phillips Machine

The Newlyn-Phillips Machine is a hydraulic machine that represents the macro-economy. The prototype, built in 1949 by two economists, Walter Newlyn and Bill Phillips, was first demonstrated to the faculty seminar in economics at the London School of Economics (LSE) in November 1949; it was taken to a conference meeting of the AUTE (Association of University Teachers of Economics) in Liverpool, and arrived at the University of Leeds (which had commissioned it) in early 1950. It is pictured here (Figure 5.1) with Newlyn in his local newspaper (the *Yorkshire Evening Post*, January 20, 1950). A report that appeared soon after in the national press described the Machine under the heading "Water keeps running through his hands just like money":

> Tap-water dyed red runs through the veins of the newest member of the staff at Leeds University Economics Department – a mechanical professor with a transparent body and two hearts (ex-RAF electric pumps). He is a bit fat – five feet wide as well as five feet high, but students can learn more from him in one lesson than from a week of text-books…. After talking about economic theory, the lecturer presses a button and Mr. Five-by-Five goes into action. While the students watch, they see the theory come to life. (*Daily Mirror*, January 26, 1950)

This "mechanical professor" is a working hydraulic machine: it is powered by a motor (around the back) that pumps red water up the vertical channel, gravity brings it back down the system, and sensors and valves control the flows. Yet the Machine is at the same time a model of the economic system, for it is designed so that in use it represents the stock and flow relations of the life of the whole economy – the macro-economy. It is an analogical model: the economy modelled as an hydraulic machine.

The photograph (Figure 5.1) shows the prototype model, the Mark I (Newlyn-Phillips) Machine in its actuality, but to see the analogical features clearly, we have to look at a diagram of the model both for a clearer representation and for easier recognition of salient features.[12] This drawing (Figure 5.2) of the Mark

---

12 This is a standard point about scientific illustrations, but still worth making: a salient reference is provided by Law and Lynch (1990), using the topic of field guides in bird-watching.

Figure 5.1. Walter Newlyn Demonstrating the Prototype Machine.

Yorkshire Evening Post, Friday, January 20, 1950. Reproduced with permission from Yorkshire Post Newspapers Ltd.

II (Phillips-Newlyn) Machine exhibits the circular flow of national income in monetary terms around the Machine's economy as flows of water around a series of Perspex tanks, tubes, and channels.[13] Each of these tanks and channels represents different elements of the macroeconomy set up in relation to each other according to the economic ideas and facts of the day. On the diagram, they are labelled with the economic elements that each part of the Machine represents. The red water, representing the flows of money, divides and recombines according to its passage from national income into expenditure, consumption, savings, investment, and so forth. In certain places, it gathers into various tanks, each of which represents a different pool of money for different uses/users. At various points, these flows are governed by valves, activated by sensors, and controlled by "slides" that incorporate the theorized behaviour of economic groups such as investors, savers, consumers, the government, and so forth. These economic behavioural relations can be seen on the diagram as slots cut into rectangular boxes (the slides), labelled with their relations. A number of the engineering solutions for the sensors and the valves are shown in enlarged drawings at the foot of the page. In effect, the economic relationships are to be found represented in the form of the physical arrangements, in the form of the mechanisms that control the flow of water (money) around the system, and in the flows themselves. Taken all together they stand for the national economy.

This drawing of the Mark II model – probably from the American marketing literature – wonderfully manages to conjure up the rushing and splashing involved so that we can almost hear the noise of the water as it moves around the system.[14] A number of these machines were manufactured by a U.K. engineering firm and sold around the world to universities (accounts are scanty, but amongst others named are Cambridge, Harvard, Melbourne, Rotterdam, and Istanbul). Others went to, for example, the central Bank of Guatamala and one of the main motor manufacturers in the USA.[15] At least one other institution, the Free University in Amsterdam, built its own Machine after a visit to London by local instrument makers, a task

13 I call the prototype Mark I the Newlyn-Phillips Machine, since Newlyn played an important role in its invention as we shall see; the Mark II is referred to as the Phillips-Newlyn Machine since it was primarily Phillips who developed the improvements in the later version.

14 The American labels on this diagram show, for example, the central bank that supplies money as the Federal Reserve, whereas on the UK diagrams of the Machine, one of the tanks is labelled "sterling balances" (the overseas-held balances). The exact provenance of this diagram (from the James Meade Archive, LSE) is not known, but labelling the diagram with both Newlyn and Phillips names tells us it must be an early one since Newlyn's name is habitually dropped in later years. It shows the more well known Mark II Machine, which had a few additional features and is also a bit larger, standing 7 ft. by 5 ft. by 3 ft. and so must be post-1950. It was probably drawn to sell the Machine in the USA following its demonstration by Abba Lerner to American economists in the early 1950s.

15 One note in the Suntory and Toyota International Centre for Economics and Related Disciplines (STICERD) archive mentions Ford, but there is correspondence from someone at General Motors (Andrew Court, who wrote articles on hedonic pricing) that indicates that they acquired a Machine. The total number produced is not known. Estimates vary from about 15 (in LSE-STICERD records, when an effort was made to trace those sold) to more like 60 (Newlyn's estimate). (This latter may be an overestimate, but a recent Internet query about the Machine brought out at least one response from an economist in Istanbul who had one in his office cupboard and had not known what it was!)

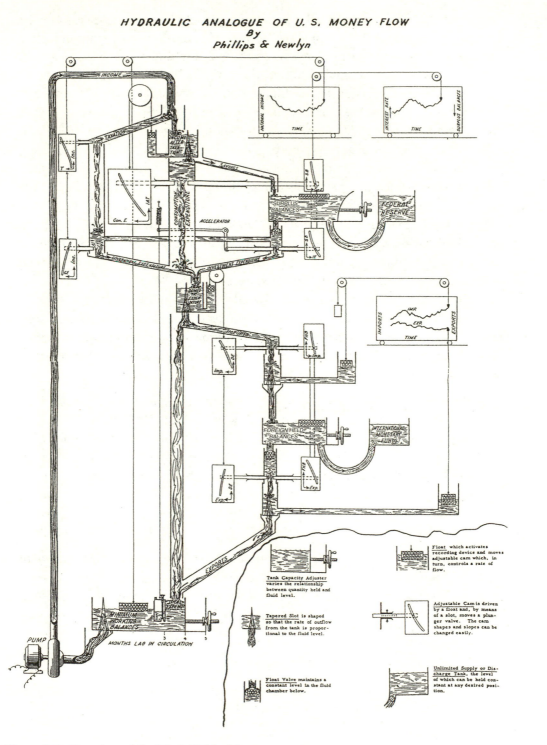

Figure 5.2. Drawing of the Mark II Machine.

Source: James Meade Archive, LSE. Reproduced with permission from estate of James Meade.

requiring ingenuity, and one to be proud of achieving.[16] Such worldwide interest points to the fact that the Machine was designed to be flexible to a range of factual situations (such as institutional arrangements found in different countries) as well as to different theories about how the economy works.[17]

In use, certain parts of the Machine's controls can be set such that some elements can be disconnected, or so that different initial states of the world can be represented, while the functional relations that govern the valves can be chosen to represent different behaviours in specific parts of the system. For this reason, the Machine has also been understood to be a programmable analogue computer, able to solve directly the system of (potentially) nonlinear relations posed in the governing slides and thus show the outcomes for certain variables of this dynamic economic system from each "run" of the Machine as the settings are varied.[18] At the top of both the diagram and the photograph, we can also see some charts where the state of national income (and some other key variables) are automatically drawn out on a scaled graph each time the Machine is used.

The effect of the Machine in action is quite extraordinary. It manages to be, all at the same time: an object whose basic workings everyone can appreciate, a serious scientific model demonstrating obscure arguments in macroeconomics, and a wonderful conceit that amuses both expert and layperson alike when they see it. As a press report in the U.K. said at its launch in Leeds,

> The general logic of the thing is simple enough to be understood by anybody, but the machine has scope to illustrate complicated points of economic theory. You can set the basic adjustments such as national income, rate of exchange and rate of interest in accordance with the facts and see what should happen. Or, if you want to be wildly theoretical, you can set them in accordance with the ideas of Dr. Hugh Dalton [ex-Chancellor of the Exchequer, and sometime lecturer at LSE] and see what shouldn't be allowed to happen. (Gordon, *Yorkshire Evening Post*, January 20, 1950, p. 7)

One of the favourite teaching uses, outlined in the training manual that came with a purchase of the Machine, was to put different students in charge of different elements of the Machine and ask them to coordinate their policies to achieve a certain outcome.[19] At the LSE, where two Machines could be linked together to represent

---

16 I thank Marcel Boumans for this information; see Langman, 1985, which contains a picture of the instrument makers.

17 It provides a good example of how an analogical model too can be built to represent both empirical and theoretical arrangements at the same time, just like Ricardo's model farm in Chapter 2. See also Morrison and Morgan (1999) and the discussion in Chapter 1.

18 See Swade (1995), who, as curator of the computation gallery at the London Science Museum, was responsible for the move of the LSE Machine to the Museum. On the Machine as a computer, see also Swade (2000) and Bissell (2007).

19 Air Trainers Ltd. of Aylesbury, U.K. (who, according to Newlyn's notes, produced the Machine commercially), produced a training manual entitled "National Income Monetary Flow Demonstrator", explaining how to set up the Machine, maintain it, and gave exercises

two national economies, such policy coordination was even more difficult and such lessons usually resulted in water all over the floor!

Over the years since the first prototype was built, it has periodically reappeared in press articles, invariably accompanied either by the kind of joking we see in the reports above, or by a cartoon of the Machine, and often by both. The most famous of these cartoons is that drawn for the satirical magazine *Punch* by Rowland Emett on April 15, 1953, the day after the Budget speech by the Chancellor of the Exchequer.[20] Emett, who had seen the Machine in action, gives a wonderful feeling for the Heath-Robinson aspect of the Machine (its home-made qualities and its quirkiness), which is indeed part of the Machine's charm, whilst simultaneously for us now, depicting the tribulations of economic life and policy in the threadbare postwar days of early 1950s Britain (Figure 5.3). Emett's cartoon itself created a genre of depictions of the economic system as the ad hoc machine of an eccentric scientist, the most recent being a similar one of the global financial system for the front cover of *The Economist* (of November 15, 2008).

The Machine is an exceedingly difficult object to describe and to convey in words. The accompanying article in *Punch* in 1953 referred to the Machine as a "creature", a "financephalograph", "an automechonomist, an economechanical brain, an engine of startling ingenuity", "a creature capable of clarifying the whole situation before the man in the street could say John Maynard Keynes" (Boothroyd, *Punch*, p. 456). The *Daily Mail* of March 8, 1965 headlined it as "the monster money machine that gurgles". The *Financial Times* of April 1/2, 1995 (an apt date indeed) depicted it as half sci-fi creature and half industrial-chemical plant alongside a serious article on the Machine by economist Robert Chote: "The miracle of the liquid

---

for its use in teaching. For example, it suggested ". . . . detail one student to try to maintain internal balance by continuous adjustment of credit and annual adjustments of the budget, and another to try to maintain external balance by, say, annual adjustments of the rate of exchange. A change made by either will upset the attempts of the other unless their efforts are co-ordinated, and the dynamic lags of the multiplier and the accelerator will further increase their difficulties." (p. 16) (Note the multiplier and accelerator elements of the mechanism, paralleling Samuelson's equations model in Chapter 6.) The manual was probably written by, or with the help of, Phillips (neither Phillips nor Newlyn's name are mentioned in it). I thank Robert Dixon of the University of Melbourne for supplying me with a copy of this manual, probably shipped with their Machine in 1953. Vines (2000) reproduces the "operational notes" of this manual (not the set up, nor maintenance notes) in an Appendix to his paper.

20 There a number of unclear dates in this history in the sense that the dates from memoirs do not always agree, nor with those of Newlyn's diary. This is a case in point, though nothing much hangs upon the exact record. The story is that the cartoonist Emett and the Chancellor of the Exchequer both came to see the Machine in action. Newlyn's later notes say it was in late 1949 in those early days of the prototype's demonstrations at LSE (before it moved to Leeds in early 1950), and that the Chancellor was Hugh Dalton (although by then he was ex-Chancellor). Elsewhere he remembers it as Rab Butler, who was indeed Chancellor in 1953, and this fits with the cartoon date but not with a demonstration in 1949: a mystery! Whatever the date, accounts agree that Emett did see a demonstration and the cartoon was the result.

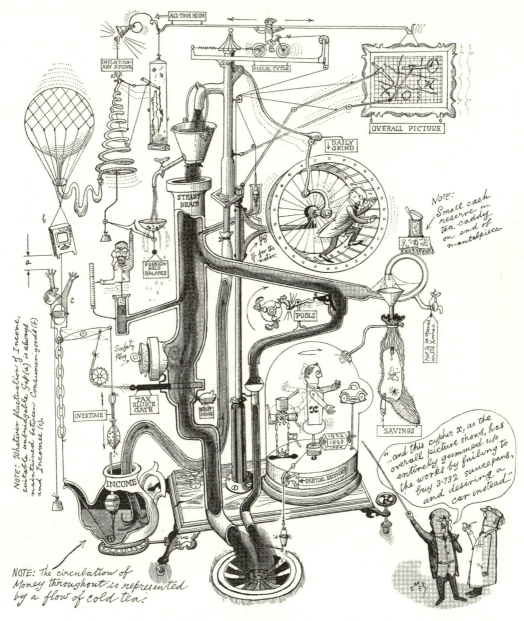

MACHINE DESIGNED TO SHOW THE WORKING OF THE ECONOMIC SYSTEM

Figure 5.3. Cartoon of the Machine from *Punch*.

By Rowland Emett (April 15, 1953, p. 457). Reproduced under licence from Punch Ltd.

economy".[21] In its early years, the Machine even had nicknames. Press reports of the Leeds Machine refer to it as the "Weasel" – possibly named by Newlyn after the nursery rhyme about money that has one verse domiciled in the City of London.[22] In America, by contrast, it was named the "Moniac" by the economist Abba Lerner "to suggest money, the contemporary first generation computer known as ENIAC, and something maniacal" (*Fortune*, March 1952, p. 101).[23] These nicknames, labels, cartoons, and joking descriptions capture some essential dualities of the Newlyn-Phillips Machine, an invention that appears to those who see it in action to be both a machine and a living thing at the same time. They succeed – far better than the serious descriptions, static photos, or analytical diagrams – in capturing the truly analogical nature of the model in use as both a busy, alive, economy and a working hydraulic machine.

The startling character of the Machine has always brought a smile to economists' faces, yet during the 1970s, it came to be seen as a faintly embarrassing reminder of a pre-mathematical age, an historical artefact fit only to languish in dark corners waiting to be scrapped. With the further passage of time, it has gained the status of an icon, a symbol both of economists' attempts to graduate from their predominantly verbal and political culture of the nineteenth century into the more scientific and technocratic practices of their current expertise and of a more "heroic age" when it seemed that a national economy – with great care and attention – could be made not just to run like a machine but be set up to run better.[24] Now, more than half a century after its commissioning, this iconic Machine is treated with more affection. The institutions that own one have, over the last years, sought to restore them and to display them proudly in prominent positions. Four are worth special mention because of their connections with the Machine's inventors. The first prototype is on display at Leeds University (Newlyn's home university), and the Reserve Bank of New Zealand (the home country of Phillips) displays the first production model of the Machine (which has also featured in the 50th Venice Bienniale of

21 See Chote (1995), in which the Machine was described as "may be the only truly tangible achievement in the history of economics"; following an earlier Machine cartoon that accompanied his article for *The Independent on Sunday,* June 5, 1994. For the *Daily Mail* article, see MacArthur, 1965. The *Times Higher Education Supplement* of May 5, 1978 depicted it as a large gaming machine labelled "Economics Without Tears" (see McKie's "Old Economic Pipe-Dream Flows Again", 1965). Another recent discussion came in an article on large-scale economic models (*The Economist*, July 13, 2006, pp. 75–7).

22 "Up and down the City Road, In and out of the Eagle, That's the way the money goes, Pop goes the weasel." The Eagle is the name of a pub on City Road, a road that comes down into the City of London from the north. On the next two lines, there is no agreed interpretation. On one account, to 'pop' means to pawn, and 'weasel' might come from the Cockney rhyming slang for coat – weasel and stoat, so that the whole verse could refer to the weekly circulation of money.

23 ENIAC was the first large-scale digital computer: the Electronic Numerical Integrator and Calculator, then recently built at the University of Pennsylvania.

24 See Morgan (2003) on this engineering view of economics in the twentieth century. The term "heroic age" was used in a letter from Arthur Brown the chair of the Leeds department (who funded the construction of the prototype Machine) in a letter to Nicholas Barr on the occasion of LSE's restoration of its Machine (STICERD archive, Box 2, File 7).

Contemporary Art).[25] The most publicly accessible of these restorations is the LSE Mark II Machine, which was built with certain additional features by Phillips with James Meade at LSE. Since 1995, it has been displayed in the computation gallery of the London Science Museum, directly opposite their specially built Babbage Machine (see Swade, 1995). It is perhaps the only artefact of economic science in the Museum, yet is displayed there as an analogue computer rather than an object of economic science. Meade moved from LSE to Cambridge, which has recently restored its Machine to working order and where it can occasionally be seen in action.

3. The Machine's Inventors: Walter Newlyn and Bill Phillips

The Machine's inventors, Walter Newlyn and Bill Phillips, came from very different backgrounds but experienced the mid-twentieth century in parallel ways and shared more talents in common than at first appears.

Walter Tessier Newlyn was born in Wimbledon in 1915. He left school at sixteen without qualifications.[26] He joined the London office of Darlings, a firm of Australian grain merchants, as junior clerk, and got his first promotion to senior clerk when the latter failed to keep the stamp book in balance. He grew into a young "city gent", enjoying London's social life and enrolling in evening classes in various aspects of shipping and in economics in 1936 (in University of London Extension courses). He continued his studies in economics as an 'external' student during the following two years (and even into the war years, winning the University's Gilchrist Medal in 1943).[27] At the same time, he also rose to become Darlings' chartering clerk and representative on the Baltic Exchange, not only a major grain exchange, but also the main shipping and freighting exchange in the world in the 1930s. Newlyn's experience there is important to the story, for while money was not literally going through his fingers, as the representative of a grain firm on the Baltic Exchange, he worked at the heart of a large wholesale market, trading and chartering space for millions of pounds worth of cargoes on a daily basis. This was the central point of the market economy: such activities as his kept the flow of money and trade going around the world. Just listen to him explaining later on how a firm finances large

---

25 Other restoration projects have been apparent in universities at Cambridge (where Meade, Phillips' second collaborator, was based), Melbourne, and Erasmus (Rotterdam). Currently, the Cambridge Machine restored by Allan McRobie is the only one in working order.

26 I thank Doreen Newlyn for the information provided about Walter Newlyn's early life history in this section, some of which comes from his personal notes "Growing Up" (in which he suggests that he was good at mental arithmetic and not much else), and his CVs of various dates.

27 Newlyn's studies gained him a scholarship to study full time when war intervened, but he continued his "external" studies during the war. He had won the Cobden Prize in his first year of study and the Gilchrist was awarded every three years for the best performance for economics in a Diploma course. This success no doubt eased his way into LSE in January 1946, particularly as he had arrived a semester late.

commodity trades while maintaining zero bank balances, an account that surely draws on his working life in the 1930s:

> Take, for example, the case of a large-scale merchanting firm disposing of a bulk cargo of grain purchased abroad. Having received the cheque at 2.45 p.m. a messenger will have deposited it at the merchant's bank at 2.50. The messenger then proceeds round the corner and at 2.55 deposits a cheque for the same amount drawn on his firm's bank account to one of the London discount houses. Moreover, he probably passes in his walk a messenger of the buying firm who has collected a cheque of similar amount from another discount house and deposited it in the buyer's bank at 2.45 p.m. (Newlyn, 1971, p. 60)[28]

Walter Newlyn's work as a charter clerk on the Exchange set these large cheques in motion (to be cleared within the City of London), and simultaneously sent cargoes of grain around the world.

Alban William (Bill) Housego Phillips was born in Te Rehunga, on New Zealand's North Island, in 1914. As his sister's account of their early life tells, their parents, both mother and father, were ingenious in developing the stream that ran through their dairy farm, both to generate electricity via a water wheel for milking their Jersey cows, and to create a flush toilet: unusual luxuries in their rural neighbourhood of New Zealand in the interwar years.[29] Such systems of electric power dependent upon the stream were then brought inside the house, and governed their daily life:

> Of course, it was wasteful to run a generator when not required. Consequently, Dad built a neat winch into the ceiling in their bedroom and when they decided it was "lights-out" time, the sound of the winch being wound alerted us to the imminent "blackout". … As the winch wound in the cable, the trap-door was raised the water was then diverted to the side of the water-wheel to rejoin the stream…. the wheel stopped turning, generation stopped and LIGHTS-OUT. (Carol Ibbotson-Somervell, p. 5)[30]

Bill Phillips, along with his brother, developed additional ingenious strings and pulleys to make life easier still – bringing light switches within reach of their beds. So Phillips knew about hydraulic systems from the inside, for his family home was run as just such a machine. At fifteen, he left school, becoming an apprentice electrician and, after various wandering employments (including, apparently, crocodile hunting in Australia) made his way via China and Russia (and the Trans-Siberian

---

28 Newlyn may well have accompanied the firm's messenger on some occasions. This description did not appear in the first edition of his *Theory of Money* of 1962, but came into the 2nd edition (1971), along with the Emett cartoon (as a frontispiece) and two diagrams of the Machine to explore monetary circulation. On the Baltic Exchange during this period, see Barty-King (1994).

29 These details come from a memoire written by Phillips' sister, Carol Ibbotson-Somervell, about their early life (from the LSE STICERD archive).

30 I thank Carol Ibbotson-Somervell for permission to quote from her memoire held at the LSE STICERD archive.

Railway) to London, where he joined the London Electric Supply Company.[31] He enrolled in evening classes in social sciences at LSE and completed the Part I exams of a BSc in 1940.[32]

Both our inventors were active in World War II service. In 1938, Newlyn joined the Territorial Army, which was drafted into active service a few weeks before the outbreak of war in 1939. His technical training in the Royal Corp of Signals ensured he could run and mend communication systems, so he became proficient in certain areas of electrical engineering. He served as a signalman in Europe, being evacuated with his brother on "a fishing smack" from the beaches of Dunkirk. Of this dramatic and harrowing event, his diary entry merely records: "31 May: Closed Signals Office Bray Dune 2000 hours and embarked at 2200 hours. 1 June: Landed in England 0800 hours."[33] He was subsequently commissioned and served in the Far East. Phillips' war service was equally active. He received an MBE, both for technical contributions (making Buffalo aircraft function more effectively) and for bravery, and was taken prisoner of war by the Japanese in Java.[34] Amongst the severe deprivations of the camp, he learnt Chinese, and improved his Russian, while using his electrical engineering skills to help make life a little easier for his fellow prisoners (of which more later).

As returning ex-servicemen with some previous university studies in social sciences, which no doubt made up for their lack of school years, both Newlyn and Phillips found their way into LSE: Newlyn became a student in 1945 and Phillips in 1946. This was a fortuitous moment and a shared experience, and they got to know each other well. Newlyn helped Phillips with his economics, and they became great friends, socialising together, both in weekend country walking and having fun on evenings out at London shows (see Newlyn, 2000). Immediately on graduating in 1948 with honours, Newlyn became an Assistant Lecturer in Economics at Leeds University. He was promoted to Lecturer in 1949, the year that Phillips graduated with a bare pass degree in Sociology and Economics. Their idea of creating a machine began even before Phillips had graduated. The two built the first prototype Machine together and demonstrated it in 1949. A Mark II model, improved by Phillips with the help of the already well established economist James Meade, was built by specialist machine makers in 1950 (and this was the one that was subsequently marketed around the world). Thereafter, the prototype was used by Newlyn at Leeds and the improved Mark II version by Phillips in London.

On the strength of this Machine, and his academic papers and thesis on the Machine, Phillips gained an academic position at LSE. The Machine experience led to his subsequent work on dynamics and the use of control theory in economic analysis and policy, for which he gained the Tooke Chair in 1958. He became best

---

31 See also Blyth (1975) on Phillips' early life.

32 This is according to a STICERD Archive CV for Phillips of 1958; at that stage, the BSc (Econ) had a general social science first year of study.

33 I thank Doreen Newlyn for permission to quote from her husband's diary (p. 100 in her personal memoire).

34 See Leeson (2000a) and Blyth (1975).

known for the consequent work that launched the "Phillips curve" into macroeconomics (an empirical relation between unemployment and inflation). In the 1960s, his interests in these kinds of economics problems waned in favour of his longer-standing interest in things Chinese, and in 1967 he went to the Australian National University to work jointly on economics and Chinese studies. He retired due to ill health in 1970 and returned to his native New Zealand, where he died in 1975.

Newlyn had meanwhile achieved a Personal Chair in Development Economics at Leeds University by 1967. His interests, originally in monetary and macroeconomics, turned to development issues, following his visits to Africa that began in the early 1950s. His first visit to that continent on a Houblon-Norman award from the Bank of England enabled him to write about colonial banking, while a later visit to Nigeria in 1953–4 found him measuring inputs and outputs of peasant agriculture. During the next two decades, he worked for periods first as a government advisor, and then a research institute director, in Uganda where he helped found Uganda's first multiracial theatre group. Back at Leeds University, he established the African Studies Unit, co-founded the national Development Studies Association, and was active in the campaign to create a repertory theatre in Leeds. On retirement from Leeds in 1978, he continued to work in development studies with the Sussex Development Studies Institute and died in 2002.

Newlyn and Phillips were both early school leavers, with war experiences to tell, yet enabled by those same circumstances to study at LSE in the late 1940s. Their meeting there resulted in the creation of the most famous physical model in economics. They brought different but complementary resources to that project. Bill Phillips was a highly competent electrical engineer, and had vast experiences in making things work in many different situations, both during his 1930s wanderings around the world and later inside the prisoner of war camp. In addition, he had the kind of deep tacit understanding that comes from his earlier, daily, experience living, literally, inside a domestic hydraulic system. Walter Newlyn had a similarly deep kind of tacit knowledge from his daily work in the City of London before the war, sending money circulating through the international economy. So Newlyn did not just know the theory of money as an economist, but he knew about how money behaved in the economy in ways that very few academic economists could have matched. Newlyn too had a considerable competence in electrical engineering matters, and, as we shall see later, they shared a love of fashioning bits and pieces of equipment into new things.

4. Inventing the Newlyn-Phillips Machine

Newlyn and Phillips chose to model the economy as a hydraulic machine, but there is a long way from using the metaphor that 'money is liquid' to conceiving and constructing such a machine. This returns us to the cognitive problem – how did these two young economists come to this choice, and how did they move from thinking about the economy as a hydraulic system to making a model of the economy as a hydraulic machine? The history of this Machine is usually told placing Phillips at its centre, and concentrates on the LSE end of the story, and on the Machine's later development with Meade (see Barr, 1988 and 2000). Here I am concerned with its invention and the creation of the original prototype Mark I Machine. This means taking Newlyn's participation seriously, for the evidence indicates he was not only a genuine partner in that inventive process, but even the catalyst whose imagination set the Machine project going.[35] And, to understand how two young economists came to model the economy as an hydraulic system, we need to pay attention to the resources they brought to the project: not only their cognitive and imaginative resources that enabled them to see how such a system might be (as I suggested in the introduction), but also their creativity in designing the analogical features to fit together, and work together, in a model.

Let me outline the bare bones of the three steps in this inventive collaboration before a more serious analysis. According to Newlyn's spare historical notes, it began properly with a paper that Bill Phillips wrote during his final year studies and showed to his good friend Newlyn in early 1949.[36] The essay constituted Phillips' attempts to understand stock and flow relationships of economics by re-presenting them in terms of hydraulic systems. Newlyn recognised something significant here, and he suggested to Phillips that a real machine version of the system might be made. During the Easter vacation of 1949, in the second step of their collaboration, Newlyn brought his economic knowledge to the design of such a machine. And he approached his head of department, Arthur Brown, who provided £100 "to cover the cost of materials" of building the Machine for Leeds.[37] In the third step, Newlyn and Phillips built the prototype hydraulic Machine together in the summer of 1949. It was demonstrated at the LSE in late 1949 and arrived at its Leeds home in early 1950.

We gain here an initial picture of collaborative work in which Newlyn's understanding of economics was combined with Phillips' understanding of hydraulic engineering. The impression in the existing literature is that each had something of a cognitive deficit that was made up by the other and this is certainly consistent with the academic papers that each wrote on the launch of the Machine: Phillips' 1950 "Mechanical Models in Economic Dynamics" paper is strong on the engineering, and Newlyn's 1950 paper "The Phillips/Newlyn Hydraulic Model" concentrates on the economics, and particularly the Machine's monetary circulation aspects. It sounds as if turning the metaphor into the model was just a question of getting two smart people with complementary sets of knowledge together. But if we think of the Machine as an invention, this suggests something new. And invention requires imagination.

---

35 Newlyn was a modest man, and at some stage his name became detached from the Machine's authorship, but Phillips always acknowledged the genuine collaboration.

36 Newlyn, in one of his memoirs (see note 46), also notes an earlier conversation on July 28, 1948 as the point when they first discussed the possibilities.

37 Only after the prototype had been demonstrated at LSE under Meade's patronage did the LSE economics faculty under Robbins take the Machine seriously. They then funded the manufacture of the Mark II Machine and supported Phillips to a lectureship in the department.

Where then did the imagination come in? And just what was new about the model of the economy? Filling in the history of their collaboration in turning a metaphor into a machine recovers the creative, imaginative, and new elements in this episode of analogical model-making and reveals more specifically how their complementary – and similar – skills and knowledge came together in the inventive process.

Step 1: Phillips chooses the analogy for his supply/demand model (early 1949)

Let me return to the beginning of the story of the Machine-building collaboration, which began in early 1949 when, meeting by appointment in the LSE refectory, Phillips (still an undergraduate student) showed a paper he had just written to his great friend, and one-year-ahead economics mentor, Newlyn. The paper, entitled "Savings and Investment. Rate of Interest and Level of Income," caught Newlyn's attention so strongly that he saved the original (that Phillips gave to him), for more than five decades.[38] He could recall its importance in his notes on the history, and could lend it to the LSE in 1991 for the occasion of their launch of their restored Mark II Machine in 1992. It was the diagrams in the paper that caught Newlyn's eye, for "they differed significantly from previous stock/flow diagrams in texts".[39]

In this student paper, Phillips turned some conventional economics diagrammatic models into diagrams of hydraulic systems. He began with the supply/demand diagrams usually drawn by economists, showing prices graphed against quantities. These diagrams represent an abstract conceptualization of the marketplace relations for such demand and supply curves cannot be seen in the market; rather these curves are understood by economists as representing the intentions that consumers and suppliers hold about their demand and their supply at different prices. Phillips wanted to get at the process relations between stock and flows of quantities of goods in a market, rather than – as such diagrams were habitually used – to interpret the change in 'equilibrium position' (the points of intersection of the curves) before and after a change in the market relations (as I shall discuss in Chapter 7). The main problem he saw was that such market analysis treats these hypothesized demand and supply quantities without being clear whether these quantities are *stocks at a given point in time* or *rates of flow during a given period of time*. He began by showing how such diagrams could easily support *either* a stock interpretation of quantity at a point in time (his figure 1, our Figure 5.4a) *or* a flow

---

38 Newlyn was shown this paper by his friend when he was visiting LSE in early 1949 (while on a trip to visit R.S. Sayers, the Professor of Money and Banking, for whom he was writing an article, see Newlyn, 2000, p. 31). The original manuscript was given by Phillips to Newlyn, and is now owned by the Oxford economist Martin Slater (Newlyn's son-in-law) and has been lodged with Newlyn's papers in the Brotherton Library, University of Leeds. A copy is in STICERD's collection of papers on the Machine at LSE. Philips' paper is a six-page typed paper – the diagrams are drawn and labelled by hand (the handwriting on the graphs is not like Phillips' normal (terrible) hand, but does match that of the handwritten labels on his thesis diagrams).

39 Newlyn, *RES Newsletter* no. 77, April 1992, p. 12.

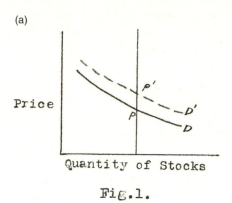

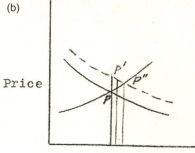

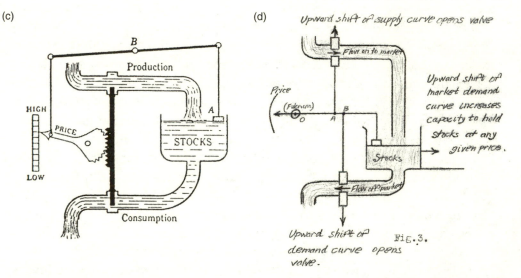

Figure 5.4. Bill Phillips' Undergraduate Essay Diagrams and the Inspiration from Boulding.

(a), (b), and (d) Bill Phillips' 1948/9 undergraduate essay figures 1, 2, and 3. Source: Original essay now in University of Leeds, Brotherton Library Archive.

(c) Kenneth Boulding's plumbing diagram. Source: figure 9, p. 117, from *Economic Analysis* (New York, 1948). Reproduced with permission from The Archives, University of Colorado at Boulder Libraries.

interpretation of quantities over a period of time (his figure 2, our Figure 5.4b) on the horizontal axis. He pointed to the different implications of these two interpretations once the model is used as can be seen from the comparison of the two figures.[40] And, if the quantities of stocks do not remain constant, then "The process

40 One shows the effect of an upward shift in the demand curve when quantity is stocks held and the adjustment is an increase in price only (to p'). The other shows the effects of change in demand when quantity is a rate of flow, where we see (with stocks assumed constant) an immediate response in price to p' but then adjusted to a new position at p". Different interpretations – stocks and flows – provide different processes of change and outcomes.

of change cannot then be shown on a graph, since stocks and rates of flow are as incommensurable as, for example, distance and speed." (Phillips, unpublished, p. 1.) The resources of the conventional diagrammatic model proved too restrictive for his purposes for he wanted to embed an analysis of both stocks and flows at once onto the same diagram.

Prompted by a contemporary analogical drawing of the price system in terms of a piece of domestic plumbing by Kenneth Boulding (1948, shown here too as Figure 5.4c), Phillips offered instead "a hydraulic analogy" of how stocks and flows and their inter-relationship might be integrated together into one model. Phillips' diagram (his figure 3, our Figure 5.4d) turns the conventional economic demand and supply curves (or equations) into a piece of plumbing in which quantities supplied flow into, and those demanded flow out of, a tank containing a stock of the good.[41] In Phillips' version of the diagram, these flows were controlled by a fulcrum attached to a sensor in the tank whose reaction to changes in the stocks was depicted as price changes. His analogical model considerably extends and fills out the economic content of Boulding's analogy, adding in the shifting demand and supply curves from the conventional analysis (via the valves impacting the flow), and representing and interpreting the fulcrum lengths and sides of the tank (see the slight curve at the top of the tank) in terms of price 'elasticities' or responsiveness.

This critical first step consisted in finding the analogy and making good the first analogical representations and interpretations. That is, Phillips takes the metaphor that quantities of economic goods could be conceived in terms of liquids, and, following Boulding's lead, he makes the starting point for the analogical account that the economic system is like a domestic plumbing system (rather than, say, a natural ecology or a bodily physiology). He then fills in that analogy: all the elements of the economic diagram were transformed into the analogous hydraulic diagram in such a way that it is a fully reconceptualized description how the market works, and how adjustments to changes occur, in terms of the three interconnected elements: prices, flows, and stocks of the good. The economists' original conceptual apparatus of supply and demand curves are no longer depicted, but the usually hypothesized movements in them are written onto these new diagrams as causes for valves to open and close. The distinctions between stocks and flow of goods in an economic market that remained opaque in the economics diagrams (and often in the equivalent equations) are made completely clear in the new hydraulics analogy and their relationships laid out to see.

Already we can see something new happening here. As Phillips rethinks economics into his own engineering domain to make sense of it, he depicts the relations in a new way. That new-world model focuses attention onto the stocks and flows and relations between them, rather than onto the shape and position of the hypothetical demand and supply curves. The drawing shows, in a new form, how

---

41 This is clearly a forerunner of his figure 2 in his 1950 paper on the Machine, but this initial analogical diagram is more communicative.

the flows of goods on and off the market and the stocks held in a market are affected by the demand and supply curve positions, their elasticities, and the price changes, interacting altogether, and consequently what it really means to say that there is an equilibrium in the market.

We can also see here how the cognitive problems and the creative process of model-making interact. Phillips, in trying to understand the stocks and flows of an economics market, developed an alternative model by thinking analogically, starting from the imaginative stimulus provided by Boulding. We can almost hear his cognitive struggle in the text that accompanies his attempts to graft stocks and flows onto the traditional models, and we can see the creative work to overcome this impasse in his series of three little diagrams. This sequence of diagrams captures the process by which Phillips took the conventional economics model world and transformed it into another one based on hydraulics.

Phillips' own imaginative leap in his paper becomes evident in the next step into the macroeconomic system. Unlike the well-known supply and demand diagrams of microeconomics, most conventional macroeconomic theories of the time were expressed verbally, and Phillips seems to have been unaware of those that were expressed in diagrams and mathematics (see Chapter 6). So, he drew on his own resources and understanding of hydraulics to move that successful first analogy to another domain. Here the analogy is not that goods can be thought of as liquids, but that money is like water in a hydraulic system, and he presents a diagram of monetary circulation in an aggregate economy (his figure 4, our Figure 5.5). This represents a circular flow of income/expenditure, and flow of savings into, and investment out of, a tank representing money and securities. It is not simply a water flow system, but already a partly engineered system, where the floats and levers offer the elements of control in the system, for example, on savings and investment behaviour.[42] But while some of the economic sectors are represented into hydraulics, two important elements are hardly sketched in at all, namely trade and the government sector. And while there is little economic content in some of the engineering elements, others seem to have captured the economics in creative ways.

The new diagram shows at least one element that would appear in the built Machine: the interesting shape needed to make the hydraulic elements fit to the economic presumptions about liquidity preference in the left-hand side of the money tank. As stocks of money build up in the tank of money balances (M), the interest rate falls and successive increases in the level have less and less impact on investment, indicated by the curved side of the tank. Phillips continued his undergraduate paper (p. 4) by using this segment of his diagram in a discussion of the theory of loanable funds, a theory that he attempts to represent back into a two-dimensional diagram that graphs such investment funds against interest. That graph (not shown) provides a mess of lines (though not quite as bad as Leontief's

---

42 Although Phillips' undergraduate paper has not been published, Newlyn (2000) reproduces Phillips' diagram and gives a fuller description of it there.

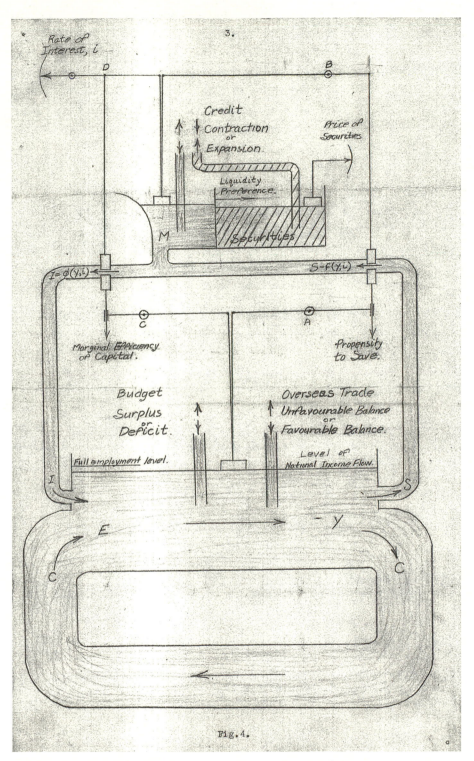

Figure 5.5. Bill Phillips' Undergraduate Monetary-Circulation Diagram.

Source: Bill Philips' 1948/9 undergraduate essay, figure 4. Original essay now in University of Leeds, Brotherton Library Archive.

Box diagram that we saw in Chapter 3), and Phillips complains that "the use of the graph makes considerable demand on the imagination"![43]

While Phillips' discussion relates to the contemporary controversy that, later on, the working Machine most obviously 'solved': namely whether the interest rate is determined by stocks or flows of funds, he had considerable difficulties in making his arguments work in the two-dimensional diagrams of his paper. Vines (2000) argues from his later analysis of this monetary circulation diagram that Phillips must have understood very little of the monetary macroeconomics of his time.[44] Indeed, as Meade noted at the time, Phillips was pretty confused about economics, but

> He was lucky enough to rub shoulders with a fellow student, Mr. W. T. Newlyn, now lecturing on money at the University of Leeds, who was less of an engineer but more of a monetary theorist than himself. Together they discussed how monetary theory could be represented by an hydraulic model. (Meade, 1951, p. 10)

Newlyn had indeed a considerable knowledge of monetary economics, not just from his stint working in the City of London, but from his LSE degree, as is evident in his undergraduate essays of 1946–7. These show familiarity with the professional literature and considerable facility in its analysis, most notably – compared to Phillips' essay – in his comparison and 'reconciliation' of the different contemporary theories of interest rate determination.[45] More surprising perhaps is his sketch of a physical arrangement of pipes to understand the relationships between financial and physical controls over the flow of funds. This analogy was less successful than Phillips' initial hydraulic designs, but does show a certain congruence in their way of thinking about these matters.

Step 2: Newlyn designs the blueprint for a monetary circulation machine (Easter 1949)

Problematic though it now seems, it was the diagram of the whole monetary circulation around an economy (Phillips' figure 4, our Figure 5.5) that especially grabbed

---

43 His paper goes on to a comparison of various theories of the day: the classical system the Keynesian system, Robertson's theory of loanable funds, and the possibilities for fiscal and monetary policy. His two-dimensional graph has some similarities to the famous Hicks IS/LM diagrammatic model of 1937 (see Chapter 6) which Phillips seems not to have known, another sign of his need for Newlyn's superior expertise (see Newlyn's remarks on this section of Phillips' paper, 2000, p. 35).

44 See Vines (2000), p. 66, fn 12.

45 Some of his essays and class presentations in courses on "Banking and Currency" and Professor Sayers's "Advanced Banking Seminar" survive. The one mentioned here was called "A reconciliation between the "loanable funds" and the "Keynsian (sic) theories of the rate of interest" (July, 1947) and covered some of the professional literature of the day, including Hicks' and Keynes' analyses. Others covered sterling balances, the American financial system, the exit from the gold standard, and cheap money policy of 1931–2. Again, I thank Doreen Newlyn for access to these essays.

Newlyn's attention when Phillips showed him the paper in early 1949, and he later claimed that he never read beyond this diagram to the rest of the paper, he was so taken by it (see Newlyn, 2000, p. 34). Newlyn saw Phillips' drawing as full of new possibilities to rethink monetary macroeconomics by the "introduction of a third dimension", namely time, through creating a mechanical version to simulate the economic system:[46]

> ... the innovation in the paper was that it included drawings which showed in detail the mechanical means of effecting the inter-related changes in the levels of stocks and flows of water representing money, thus simulating the economic behaviour of the economy in this sector. (Newlyn, "Historical Summary", dated 8.7.92)

and so "I said to Bill that it should be possible to construct a machine to reflect the articulation of the diagram as a teaching aid" (Newlyn, 2000, p. 34). In particular, Newlyn was struck by the importance that such a machine would have for understanding the timing of monetary relations. From his point of view, the diagram contained a very important insight:

> Implicit in Bill's illustration of an income flow through a tank is a time lag from which it follows that changes in the inflow impart changes in the rate of outflow over time. (Newlyn, "Historical Summary", dated 2003)[47]

Making explicit the importance of time lags between inflows and outflows intrigued Newlyn because he saw that these lags were critical to the circulation of money and thus to the process of how all the monetary macroeconomic elements interacted and evolved through time. These issues informed the way he came to the design of the Machine, and in turn continued into his treatment of money in his subsequent *Theory of Money*. Of course, these issues must also have also resonated with his earlier experiences that we found in his description of a trading community that circulates large flows of money within five or ten minutes while holding no stocks.[48]

The suggestion that such a diagram could be turned into a real machine took root. So, during the Easter vacation of 1949, these two friends, Bill Phillips (who was in his last year of study and should have been working on his sociology) and Walter Newlyn (in a junior academic position at Leeds, but staying at the family home in Wimbledon for the vacation), worked on the specifications for the

---

46 There are various historical summaries of the Machine's history written by Newlyn at different dates. It is in a handwritten version held by Doreen Newlyn that Newlyn referred to "the introduction of a third dimension", the quote below comes from a typed 1992 version that has a copy in LSE STICERD Archive.

47 From Newlyn's memoire account of the model (2003, p. 1), provided by Doreen Newlyn (some of which appears in Newlyn, 2000, or in his 1992). Other details and quotes from the same sources appear in this section.

48 As Arthur Brown wrote at Newlyn's retirement: "His initial career – on the Baltic Exchange – was not altogether irrelevant to his later activities; he has always shown a clearer sense than most economists of how a market really works" (Brown, 1978 pp. 206–7).

Machine. Newlyn tells us that "I drew the full economy version", while Phillips worked on the problem of "converting a diagram into a physical form" (Newlyn, 2000, p. 34). Newlyn's contribution was surely critical here as the full design involved all the major monetary flows in a complete economy with foreign trade, a public sector, a central bank and different kinds of stocks of money.[49] A few elements of the saving-investment sector design were taken over from Phillips' original diagram, but the basic shape is very noticeably different from that. We can see all this in the May 5, 1949 large scale "blueprint" (reproduced here as Figure 5.6) drawn by Newlyn, probably to show Arthur Brown, his head of department at Leeds, to secure funding for the Machine building to come.[50] Though there are some differences between this blueprint and the first published schematic diagrams of the Machine (in his 1950 paper for example, or Phillips' diagram in 1950), it is substantially how the Machine came to be. We can see that the basic components and structure of the Machine are fixed at this stage in Newlyn's diagram, though some rearrangement of the parts occurs, and some elements of the Machine are flipped over right to left relative to the blueprint.[51]

Newlyn's "blueprint" design of May 1949 is a full one in the sense that the economics has been thoroughly represented. Compared to Phillips' first attempt (his figure 4, our Figure 5.5), we see that Newlyn's collaboration has produced a design for a real analogical economic model by instantiating the following economic features into the Machine:

(a) The circular flow of income/expenditure has been divided into savings, investments, consumption, taxes, imports, exports, etc., all in monetary form.

(b) The other main economic sectors (the overseas and government sectors) have been drawn and integrated into the circular flow model.

(c) The flows have been separated from the stocks of money, and those in turn separated into stocks held in four tanks: by the government, in the asset market, in the foreign exchange market, and as working balances for current activity.

49 And, as we shall see during the Machine building period later that year, Newlyn continued to be responsible for explaining much of the detail of macro-economics to Phillips.

50 Newlyn refers to it as a "blueprint" in his letter of January 24, 1991, to Nicholas Stern, then head of STICERD at LSE STICERD Archive (where it exists only as a photocopy in two pieces indicating an original A2 size). Possibly, the existence of this May 5 diagram is the source of the confusion over dates about when Brown was approached. Newlyn (2000, p. 34) tells us that he drew the full economy version (but refers to his later 1950 diagram 1 (equivalent to his 2000, figure 8.2) before approaching Brown for funds to build the Machine and that this was before the Easter vacation in which they worked on the specifications. Yet from his diaries, it seems that they began work on the designs on April 14, 1949. A few days later, Newlyn went back to Leeds, perhaps with Phillips, and less than a month later, his blueprint of May 5 was finished.

51 In their separate 1950 publications, Phillips' more descriptive diagram shows the right–left orientation as in the blueprint, and as in the Mark II Machine which he was then developing, whereas Newlyn's diagram (which is more schematic than descriptive) has the same orientation as the built Mark I.

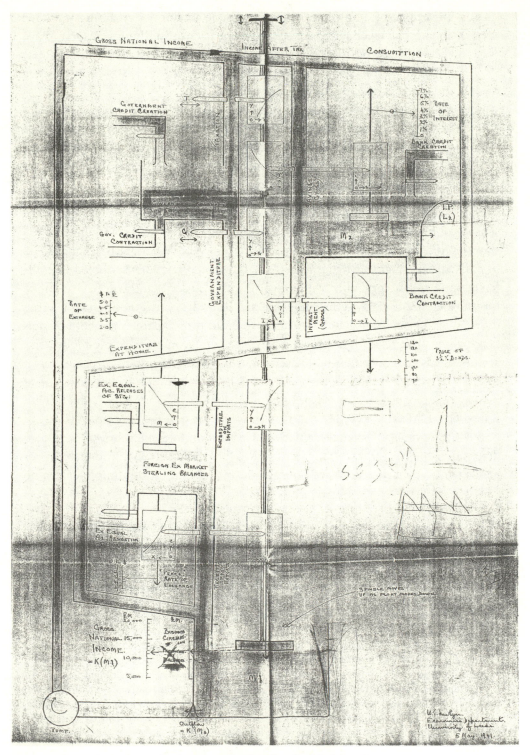

Figure 5.6. Walter Newlyn's Blueprint Design for the Machine, May 1949.

Source: STICERD Phillips Machine Archive. Reproduced by permission from Doreen Newlyn.

(d) The inflows and outflows are given sensible economics meanings.

(e) The functional equations of economic behaviour in Phillips' diagram have been replaced by "slides" which incorporate (as linear or nonlinear functions) those macroeconomic relationships (e.g., the propensity to save slide: Y′ related to S) to control the valves.

(f) The monetary tanks are directly linked to calibrated scales to report changes in national income (£m), the exchange rate ($/£), the price of bonds, and the rate of interest. (In this particular respect, the reporting charts in the design are more ambitious than those developed in the Machine, where, for example, exchange rates are not registered.) [52]

The main hydraulics and controls have also been indicated on this diagram, the sensors for registering changes are in place, and the motive power of the Machine is shown in the pump, so that we can see where Phillips must have also been involved in the hydraulic engineering elements. The functional relations scribbled in a different hand are also probably by Phillips. We can also see that the design might be transformed into a working machine, but still it hardly constitutes an engineering drawing giving sufficient detail for others to build the Machine: it is not an engineering blueprint.[53] Newlyn's drawing privileges the economics of the model, and around the sides of his blueprint, we see some doodled 'mountains', perhaps drawn in Phillips' hand, but that appear in Newlyn's 1950 publication on the Machine as his way of depicting the "time shape of money balances held by an individual" (with time on the horizontal axis; 1950, p. 117) and thus the passage of money in and out of the "active money" balances tank, M1. He goes on to explain how this pattern determines the level in the "idle money" M2 tank, within which money changes hands (finance house to finance house as in his commodity trading) yet has no

---

52 Possibly this was because this aspect of the Machine did not work very well. The Training Manual notes (p. 10) that "The readings on the various scales may be found not consistent with one another, and this is due in part, to basic errors in the Machine. No attempt has been made a achieve a high degree of accuracy" and gave some hints about how to keep inconsistencies to a minimum. It is not clear what accuracy might mean here, though see Morgan and Boumans (2004) for some further discussion. Allan McRobie has restored the Cambridge Machine to be accurate when measured against the solutions to the equations that are taken to represent the Machine.

53 Newlyn reports that during the vacation Phillips "solved some hydraulic problems such as having constant base outflows from the tanks. The final drawings were made" (both quotes: Newlyn, in *RES Newsletter*, no. 77, April 1992). This might suggest that there were separate engineering drawings, but Newlyn's 2000 reference to Phillips' technical specifications refers us only to his 1950 account (p. 284 to top of p. 287), which is a technical verbal description of the Machine's setup. In addition, there is nothing in the STICERD Archive like the full set of engineering diagrams that Phillips produced *after* the building of the Mark II Machine in his LSE PhD thesis of 1954 to cement his LSE career. This evidence suggests that the prototype Machine was built from a version of Newlyn's blueprint diagram and from piecemeal sketches made on the job. (This is compatible with the sketches that were used in Phillips' later work with Meade redesigning parts of the Machine; see Meade's papers at LSE, files 16/2 and 3.)

effect on the level of monetary circulation or income and expenditure through the M1 tank at the foot of the drawing.

Though their new design was set up using the terms, elements, and relations of contemporary macroeconomics, we learn from the discussion of the prototype model in Newlyn's 1950 paper that the way the Machine's elements were defined was not entirely the same as other definitions of the day.[54] For example, as seen above, money is divided in the model according to its activity in the economy, not according to the motivations of individuals who hold it as in Keynes' analysis. There was, at this point, no general agreement amongst economists about these definitions, and, in any case, certain things were defined differently in the Machine just because the medium of expression was different from the verbal or mathematical accounts. And, because of its hydraulic form, the Machine's design particularly required stocks and flows to be accurately and carefully differentiated, as they had not been in verbal versions of macroeconomics at the time.

Newlyn also discusses how a variety of theoretical positions can be understood and demonstrated: the "Keynesian special case", "the Wicksellian process", "Kalecki's accelerator", and so forth (ideal for the teaching purposes that he had in mind for the Machine). Similarly, Phillips, in his 1950 paper, discusses different kinds of "lags" and "multipliers", and so forth, for he understood each theory of the day as being a particular physical setup of the Machine. Newlyn was adamant that the system was designed not only to express a range of different macroeconomics ideas available at that time, but also to describe different institutional arrangements or policy questions in different kinds of economy. For example, the diagram Newlyn drew showed a tank labelled "sterling balances", a category of U.K.-based, but overseas owned, sterling money that provided a worrying problem for the British post-war economy (see on the left in Figure 5.6).

In this second step, it was Newlyn, whose knowledge of macroeconomics was far more advanced than Phillips', and whose special knowledge and interest was in monetary economics, who was important in this basic change of shape and the additions and extensions of the Machine's economy compared to Phillips' original diagram. Whereas in the first step, Phillips had transformed the microeconomics of markets into hydraulics to make sense of it, Newlyn's contribution in the second step was apparently to recognise the macroeconomic possibilities in Phillips' hydraulics and then to show how and where the monetary and macroeconomics could be transposed into hydraulics and thus where the hydraulics could be made to speak to the problems of understanding the aggregate economy. This was a process of comparison and mutual translation between the two worlds that involved both scientists.

54 For example, he explains how the definitions used in the Machine differ from those of the Central Statistical Office's accounts as well as from those of Keynes and of Robertson; see Newlyn (1950), pp. 115–9.

Step 3: Phillips and Newlyn build the prototype
Machine (Summer 1949)

When he found out how badly Phillips had done in his exams, Newlyn felt guilty about the amount of time they had spent working together filling in the specifications that were needed in designing the analogical model during the Easter break (see Newlyn, 2000, p. 34). Nevertheless, after Phillips' final exams, and in the summer break between university terms of 1949 while Newlyn was again in London, the pair set out to make the prototype Machine. Here is Newlyn's description:

> The actual construction was carried out in the garage of Bill's friends in Croydon [South London] during the summer vacation of 1949. My intermittent role was that of craftsman's mate – sanding and glueing pieces of perspex. But one rather long pause in the work was devoted to elucidating the complexities of the reciprocal effects of the external sector, with which Bill was not familiar, but he wanted to understand how the simplified relationships of the model fitted into the theory. (Newlyn, 1992, p. 12)[55]

It was a genuinely collaborative effort, in which Newlyn's expertise in economics complemented Phillips' in engineering. In his 2000 historical account, Newlyn records their working together on the public sector:

> One case in which an economic input from me was needed was the introduction of the Public Sector Borrowing Requirement; it was incorporated by linking the government's working balances to the money market. A hinged barrier in the centre opened and closed to reflect changes in the government deficit/surplus. The other case was that of the external balance. This was a closed book to Bill and, as one would expect, he wanted a full briefing on what lay behind the functions we proposed using to reflect the response of imports and exports to changes in the exchange rate which is determined by differences in the rates of change of imports and exports. I checked my file and found that I drew fifteen graphs to illustrate the multiplicity of the elasticities of domestic and foreign supply and demand which our values should have reflected. (Newlyn, 2000, p. 35)

They each had their own cognitive comparative advantage – and surely each had to be creative and patient in explaining their knowledge to the other. But the resourcefulness of these two inventors was in fact much more balanced than these quotes from Newlyn suggest, for they shared a love of making machines that worked, and to make this Machine work required a labour of love.

Bill Phillips had grown up inventing things to make his life easier, playing around with crystal radio sets and so forth. His habits of mending all things mechanical and electrical – when he visited friends, or in his colleagues' offices – became the

---

55 Perspex is actually a trade name for acrylic glass that came into use during World War II for safety reasons.

subject of fond anecdote. His exploits in the prisoner of war camps are legendary, especially his ability to make and maintain radios out of the smallest and least prepossessing bits of equipment, as Laurens van der Post was to recount later. His invention that allowed prisoners to brew their own tea last thing at night caused the Japanese guards to wonder why the lights dimmed.[56] As Brown remarked of him "Primarily, he was a problem solver.... He wanted to know how systems worked and how they could be made to work better" (Brown, 2000, p. xiv), a remark that serves equally well to characterize Phillips' work in economics.

In many respects, Walter Newlyn had a similar character. His wartime training in communications equipment built upon an earlier aptitude and even necessity for his father, who had been a civil engineer (building bridges and roads in South America) had died in the Battle of the Somme before his young son's first birthday and Newlyn and his brother had grown into his role, using his tools and workshop to keep their mother's home going. Newlyn's wife (Doreen Newlyn) recalls his skills in such diverse but technical tasks as stage management and lighting as they supported travelling theatre expeditions around Africa, and keeping a "great tank of a car alive over 12,000 miles of corrugated murram roads in Nigeria" by nightly maintenance shifts.[57]

Both Walter Newlyn and Bill Phillips were creative in fashioning bits and pieces of equipment into something else, and this is just what they did in building their prototype hydraulic Machine of the economy. They used pieces of Perspex (then a very expensive material) from the windows of bombers, while the engine that pumped the water through the system came from the wind-screen wipers on a Lancaster bomber – perhaps from the airfield near Croydon where they built the Machine. The electric motor for the graphs came from an old clock, while certain of the smaller parts were made by "a friend who owned a factory for making dolls' eyes – known to the small group of friends involved as Mr. Dolls-Eyes".[58] Each and every hydraulic element had to be carefully designed to fit the purposes of the economic meanings, and the Machine built in such a way that each of these bits fitted together in both engineering and economic senses[59]. Their Machine-building is a perfect example of Boumans' (1999) idea of how model-making involves putting together disparate bits and pieces, in this case literally! They celebrated the completion of "the first item, the large tank" by being photographed together holding

---

56 See Leeson (1994, 2000b) for his detective work that pieced Phillips' war experiences together, in which he manages to identify Phillips as the New Zealand magician who kept the radio alive in van der Post's 1985 autobiographical account.

57 I am indebted once again to Doreen Newlyn for filling in these important details, this in a personal communication of August 19, 2006.

58 Newlyn, 2001/3, p. 3 "The Phillips/Newlyn Hydraulic Model: The Leeds Prototype". Unpublished memoire, see notes 46 and 47.

59 In Morgan and Boumans (2004, p. 283) we list the elements that all have to be engineered to make the Machine work effectively. Vines (2000) pays very particular attention to these analogical points and is most admiring of how these two senses of fit – the economics to the hydraulics and the hydraulics to the economics – are achieved.

Figure 5.7. Bill Phillips (left) and Walter Newlyn (right) celebrate completing the first tank during the Machine building in Croydon, Summer 1949.

Reproduced with permission from Doreen Newlyn.

it (Figure 5.7); as Newlyn wrote remembering this event: "It was rather like laying a foundation stone".[60]

Once the Machine was finished, their engineering skills were still required. It was not always easy to get it to work – it often had to be coaxed and sometimes bullied – and it was certainly not easy to maintain.[61] It is a significant sign of Newlyn's engineering abilities that he kept the Leeds prototype Machine going until his retirement in 1978, with only occasional help from his colleagues in mechanical engineering and odd visits from Phillips. Phillips himself regularly had to attend to keep the LSE Machine in working order, and it languished after his departure in the mid-1960s.

Bill Phillips was surely the senior engineer, but Walter Newlyn was certainly qualified as a junior engineer. Senior and junior, these two engineers attempted to calibrate the time for the Machine to get to a position of stable levels of water in the main tank (and thus stable levels of national income on the chart) after a 'policy intervention' experiment using the Machine. Such calibration was not surprisingly quite difficult to achieve and then to interpret in economics terms, and it was a worry that Newlyn expressed in the last part of his article on the Machine in

60 I thank Doreen Newlyn, owner of the photograph, for giving permission to reproduce it; the quote comes from Newlyn's handwritten notes for his history of the Machine that she also holds.

61 Even at the point when Nobel Prize Laureate James Meade arrived at LSE in the early 1990s to make a video record of how to use the Machine, it refused to work without considerable attention from its restorers!

1950. Fifty years after these events, in his short article about Phillips, Newlyn wrote about this as a problem, of getting the analogy between economic time lags and machine time lags correct, as if it were fresh in his mind.

> In the model, perforce, the time-lag is a function of the capacity of the 'active money balances' tank ... which is adjustable within the structural limits .... in the case of the time-lag, the model is not correct, being imposed by the hydraulic analogy as the frequency of the circulation of active balances. But, as in FM radio, it is the *modulation* of the frequency of carrier wavelengths, not the frequency of it, which generates the signal. It is the decisions to change the determinations of the rate of flow of money, with the capacity of the active balances tank [M1] fixed, which should determine the time-lag which will apply to any impulse. (Newlyn, 2000, p. 38, his italics)

No doubt his wartime experiences as signalman made these kinds of analogical comparisons and explanations of second nature.

This three-step sequence of analogical model-making for the Machine really began with verbal economics. Using the stepping stone of the market hydraulics, Phillips first sketched an analogical hydraulic diagram of monetary circulation, then Newlyn developed a full macro-model design and together they built the subsequent prototype Machine. In his 1950 paper explaining the Machine, Phillips then proceeded to expound the mathematics of the economic model that the hydraulic model represented. That is, he used the Machine to get the stocks and flows of money rightly understood, and then undertook to make a mathematical description of the macroeconomic system that the hydraulics represented. Though Newlyn was proficient in electrical engineering, he was not so in mathematics (in his 1950 paper, he footnoted the help of the econometrician Sargan), and as we see from his subsequent use of the Machine in his work on money, he too understood the Machine in hydraulic rather than mathematical terms. Thus, in inventing their Machine, both Phillips and Newlyn reasoned analogically, translating directly back and forth between ideas and knowledge about monetary circulation in the monetary economy and water in hydraulic systems. This was a real substantive analogy between economics and hydraulics and they reaped the real benefits of the analogy in subject matter, as we shall see later.[62]

---

62 Nagel (1961, p. 110) makes the distinction between substantive analogies and formal ones (i.e., mathematical descriptions of substantive systems), It is clear that this was a substantive analogy: the analogical translation did not come via mathematics. And when I have talked about the Machine to engineers, they have usually responded that they would find it very difficult, and probably impossible, to translate back, that is, to write down the mathematics to capture entirely the full workings of the hydraulic flows in the Machine. An additional distinction here is between real analogical systems and paper designs for analogical systems. For example, others during the early 1950s were working with substantive electric analogies, but not with realised systems: see Morehouse et al., 1950; Enke, 1951; and Copeland, 1952 for other paper designs or mathematical descriptions of engineering systems; and for an earlier design, see Barker (1906). For an insightful review and comparison of different electrical circuit designs, see Allen (1955).

Their Machine was invented in a process of analogical modelling – of refashioning economics into another kind of substantive system. This required cognitive, imaginative, and technical creativity of particular kinds. In retrospect, we can see how dependent it was upon a remarkably fortuitous combination of people: Newlyn and Phillips and of their respective experiences, skills, and knowledge.[63]

5. Analogical Models and New Things

The Newlyn-Phillips Machine has often been understood as a merely heuristic device, something to teach with: a wonderful object, an inspired piece of economic model building, but ultimately not really the place to develop new ideas. In contrast the standard account amongst philosophers of science of how analogical models are chosen and used suggest that they are particularly associated with the development of new insights into the nature of the world being modelled.[64] Analogical models have thus been associated with strong claims to act as agents of 'discovery', particularly in Mary Hesse's 1966 classic account. The analogical world is chosen by a scientist because of perceived "positive features": the qualities shared in common between the home field and the analogical case, for example, the way economists perceive money as having the quality of behaving as a liquid. But, as Hesse argues, it is then by systematically investigating the characteristics of the "neutral features", those that are neither recognisably the same (positive features) nor obviously different (the "negative features"), that scientists find potential for new insights. Such neutral features provide likely growing points for theorizing or experimental work, and these may reveal new aspects of the world of interest. Of course, this kind of analysis of positive and neutral features is not one that the scientist self-consciously carries out, but is rather one for the historian or philosopher who wants to understand how, and pinpoint where, analogical models have been fruitful in the scientific work of the past.

63 It was lucky for Phillips to find not just Newlyn to work with, but later Meade, who also loved to make artefacts. Brown remarks on the similar complementary and shared fit by noting that Meade "had started his textbook twenty years before with an exposition of the circular flow of money.... to which the Phillips Machine provided a perfect concrete illustration. Meade had himself dealt in a famous article with the stability conditions of a Keynesian system [see Chapter 6 this volume], and was himself no mean amateur producer of precision artefacts – from kites to cabinets" (Brown, 2000, p. xv). In Meade's archive at LSE, files 16/3 and 16/4, there is an example of this in his design for a rope and pulley machine for teaching macroeconomics, and a correspondence about it with Guy Orcutt (see Chapter 8), who had made his own regression analyser around this same time.

64 These kinds of claims come from an important older tradition in the philosophy of models, particularly the work of Mary Hesse (1966). Her treatment, discussed here, combines a sense of the imaginative and cognitive issues in her philosophy, as does Max Black (1962) (see particularly his pp. 242–3) and, in a broader sense, Steven Toulmin (1953). (See also Achinstein (1964) on models and Ortony (ed, 1994) on metaphors). For more recent work that extends the treatment of analogies in creative ways, see Gentner and Gentner (1983) on cognitive aspects and Schlimm (2008) on analogies in mathematical domains.

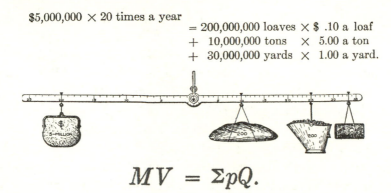

$5,000,000 \times 20$ times a year

$= 200,000,000$ loaves $\times$ \$ .10 a loaf
$+ \quad 10,000,000$ tons $\quad \times \quad 5.00$ a ton
$+ \quad 30,000,000$ yards $\times \quad 1.00$ a yard.

$$MV = \Sigma pQ.$$

Figure 5.8. Irving Fisher's Arithmetical, Mechanical, and Accounting Versions of His Monetary Balance.

Source: Irving Fisher, *The Purchasing Power of Money*. New York: Macmillan, 1911, arithmetic balance, p. 18; mechanical balance, p. 21; accounting equation, p. 26. Reproduced with permission from George Fisher.

Irving Fisher's mechanical balance model of 1911 forms an ideal case where we can see the relevance of Hesse's analysis, and it will provide a good comparative basis for going back to the Newlyn-Phillips Machine to think about this question. It is also a particularly apt comparison, for Fisher, not unlike Newlyn and Phillips, had a passion for making devices. Indeed, he had turned inventor as a teenager when his Father died and he needed income to support his remaining family, and himself through college. Like many professional inventors, most of his inventions were unsuccessful in the marketplace, but his visible card file index system that he invented in 1913 radically cut the time for telephone operators to look up telephone numbers and was sold out to Remington Rand for several million dollars in 1925. Well before this success, he had entered Yale to study physics and ended up with a thesis in economics, his work supervised by the most famous American physicist of the day, Willard Gibbs, and the most famous American economist of the day, William Sumner.

Fisher became a professor of economics at Yale University and a monetary economist of great note, and this is the field of his mechanical analogical model.[65] In his 1911 book on money, he produced these three "illustrations" of his equation of exchange, in arithmetic, diagrammatic, and accounting form (see Figure 5.8). The second diagrammatic form – the picture of the mechanical balance – is an analogical model for the first arithmetic model, a simplified economy with only three goods (where the prices and amounts of coal in the scuttle and cloth in the bale have been changed to fit the balance's scale). The aggregate accounting relation is

---

65 As part of his 1892 thesis he built an operating hydraulic system to demonstrate general equilibrium theory in a three-good, three-consumer economy (shown in Chapter 1). He also designed (on paper) a hydraulic model to demonstrate the various arrangements of the money system – gold standard, silver standard or bimetallic standard. I shall be concerned here only with another paper-based analogical model, however, that of the mechanical balance. See Morgan (1999) and (1997) for more materials on both these episodes of Fisher's model building.

the third model: $MV = \Sigma pQ$ (or later $MV = PT$), and relates aggregate exchanges of goods (all the Qs, or T, times their prices) for money (the stock of M times its velocity of circulation V) in the exchange process.[66] An analysis along the lines suggested by Hesse points us to the positive features that justified Fisher's choice of analogical model, namely that the mechanical balance balances money (M, in the purse) with the goods exchanged (the Qs or transactions T) on each side of the balance in the same way that the arithmetic equation of exchange does.

On the basis of these positive shared analogical features, we can also see how Fisher mapped the velocity of circulation of money (V) as the distance to hang the money purse along one arm, and the prices of the goods (p) along the other arm of the balance in such a way that the arms stay in balance just as the equation does provided, of course, that when any one of its terms are altered, one of the other elements alters to maintain the balance. We might judge these as the neutral features, and since this is a paper model, not a real machine like the Newlyn-Phillips Machine, this analogical work does not have to be accurately calibrated: it only has to work conceptually.[67] Yet even to get the analogical model to work conceptually needs the economic materials to fit well onto the mechanical analogy, requiring creativity and imagination to overcome any initial cognitive dissonance about the relevance of the analogy.

Fisher gained a particularly important new insight from using the neutral features to fit the economics onto the balance. The problem in adopting the analogy came with the move from this arithmetical three-good world to the aggregate level needed to investigate certain theoretical claims, and for this, the aggregate prices and quantities must somehow be mapped along the right arm of the balance. This led Fisher to develop the concept of the "weighted average" for the aggregate version of his equation of exchange (see how the goods formed the "weights" that had to be averaged along the balance arm).[68] From this inspired prompt, Fisher made seminal contributions to the development of index number theory – a fundamental theory of aggregate measurement in economics – in a project that ultimately grew into a massive book of 1922 that still forms the classic text on the subject.

This successful mapping of the economics onto the mechanical diagram also led to Fisher's subsequent *use* of the analogical model for other measuring purposes

---

66 For many, $MV = PT$ might seem either an obvious relation or a tautology, whereas in fact it is an accounting identity. It was by no means uncontentious: other economists favoured other equations; and it was by no means useless: such equations of exchange form the building blocks of macroeconomic reasoning (see Bordo, 1987).

67 In contrast, the Newlyn-Phillips Machine has to work properly otherwise it demonstrates nothing. Further discussion on the difficulties to be overcome to make the Machine work is contained in Morgan and Boumans (2004).

68 See Boumans (2001) for a discussion of how Fisher's index number theory also grew out of his invention of a measuring instrument to arrive at a balanced nutritional diet (a problem with a somewhat similar structure) that he developed during his recovery from TB in the early years of the twentieth century. This device combined Fisher's fad for healthy eating with his inventive capacities.

and for reasoning about various debates in monetary economics, particularly about the nature of the quantity theory of money, and about directions of causality between changes in the elements depicted on the balance.[69] These points could have been made using the general algebraic version of the equation of exchange, but they were demonstrated much more effectively on the mechanical balance diagram.

Analogies grow out of metaphors and, rather like the two-way street of metaphors, they enable the user *to reflect both ways* across the comparison.[70] Analogies prompt scientists to rethink their understanding in two ways: first in translating the economy into the analogous system and then in seeing what new insights that analogous system might suggest to them about their own field.

So, in the first move: making the economics fit onto the mechanical balance, the neutral features of the analogy were extremely fruitful for Fisher, and proved particularly creative in his measurement theory (see Morgan, 1999). But considering the second aspect of his analogical modelling, we should not ignore the negative features – those features which at first sight seemed dissimilar between the economics world and the mechanical one (see Morgan, 1997). Negative features can often be turned to advantage and provide further points of insight because they stem from this second aspect of reflection: the point when scientists reflect back those negative features from the analogous world, to see how they too might fit, onto their own world.[71]

Fisher's work with his mechanical balance illustrates how this second part of two-way comparison works in scientific modelling. In reflecting back from the analogy, he noticed two apparently negative features in the different concepts of balance. Fisher understood his economic equation of exchange to be an accounting identity. And it is the nature of an accounting identity that whenever anything happens in the economy represented in that accounting relation, a balancing change necessarily takes place elsewhere to keep the identity in balance. Of course this is not so with a mechanical balance: the money purse could be increased without any necessary

---

69 He used the analogical model as a means to check his measurements of the velocity of money, the element of the equation that was most difficult to measure (see Morgan, 2007). He used the historical series of statistical data mapped onto the mechanical balance over a period of more than fifteen years to show the impossibility of reading off any empirical or logical proof of the quantity theory of money: the theory, much in dispute at the time, that any increase in money supply automatically increased the price level (see his 1911, figure 12.2, reproduced in Morgan, 1999, and the discussion therein).

70 The claim about metaphor is that we gain insight into both ends of the metaphor: in saying "man is a wolf", we gain potential insight into the wolf-like elements of man's nature and into the man-like elements of the wolf's nature. Here the claim with analogical models is somewhat different – the comparison involves a two-way process of comparison and so potential insight, but both are concerned with learning about only one system of interest, in this case, the economic system, not the machine system.

71 In my earlier account of these negative features, I suggested that Fisher was just unusually creative in turning these negative features to his advantage; here I suggest that the potential of working both ways across the analogy is a more general feature of the double reflective aspect of working with analogical models.

change elsewhere that would maintain the balance at a point of equality – one arm can fall if extra weight is added to it. The two concepts of balance: the economic accounting and the mechanical are apparently incompatible. Another negative feature of the balance comparison lay in the fact that when a mechanical balance is disturbed, it comes to a point of rest with an oscillation, rather than directly to that point, once again, unlike his accounting relation. Fisher, from reflecting on both these physical features of the mechanical balance, changed his economics. His experience of working with the balance model (and the economic statistics he mapped on to it) led him to a reinterpretation of his balance equation: while he still thought that the accounting identity held as an overall constraint on the economic system, he came to see it as only a tendency to equilibrium, rather than a continuous equilibrium outcome at every moment in the economy. And he was inspired by the oscillation problem to see how the theory of cycles in economic life might be integrated with monetary theory as parts of the same system, the cycles being an adjustment to the changes in the monetary elements as depicted on the balance.[72] So he used the behavioural features of a real mechanical balance – the initial non-matching features – to throw light onto and rethink his economic theories about the relationship of money and the economic system in some quite fundamental respects.

Fisher's success with his analogical balance model arose from his working, in quite a systematic way, through both sides of the analogical comparison, as a metaphor invites us to do. First he gained new insights from fitting his economics ideas onto the balance, and second he took features of how a real balance works and fitted those ideas back into his economics to refurnish his economic theories in some fundamental ways.[73] Perhaps, by the time he had finished working with it, Fisher no longer regarded the world in his model as an analogical model for by then he had made his economics into a mechanical model *and* some mechanical features had been incorporated into his economics.

How does this account of the way that analogical models give scientists new insight enable us to appreciate the Newlyn-Phillips Machine as a research machine? We have seen already how Phillips first translated some economics into hydraulics, how Newlyn was instrumental in making the monetary system and hydraulics fit together in a Machine design, and how they then together built the Machine. What insight did this process of making the economics fit the hydraulics provoke? Let me go back to the first demonstration of the prototype Mark I Machine – to the

---

72 See Morgan (1999) for further details of this example. One of the differences between the Mark I Newlyn-Phillips and the Mark II Phillips-Newlyn Machines is that the latter has an 'accelerator' relationship built into it (as may be seen labelled in Figure 5.2); this is the same relation that features in Samuelson's equations model (see Chapter 6). Newlyn suggested that this be left out of the Mark I Machine for ease of use and explanation. Vines (2000) suggests that it is this additional connection that creates cycles and thus integrates cycles into the Machine economy in parallel to Fisher's use of his analogical balance to integrate cycles into his monetary economics.

73 This is a very concise account of the matter: a fuller discussion of how the negative features play an important role is provided in Morgan (1997), and a fuller analysis of the analogical modelling in Fisher is given in Morgan (1999).

LSE faculty assembled under the eye of the sceptical Lionel Robbins in November 1949. When the red water flowed around the Newlyn-Phillips Machine on that day, it resolved for that audience a strongly fought controversy in macroeconomics. In simplified form, Keynesians argued that the interest rate is determined by liquidity preference: people's preferences for holding *stocks* of money versus bonds. Robertson argued that the interest rate is determined by the supply and demand for loanable funds: primarily the *flow* of savings versus that of investment. When stocks and flows *really* work together – as they did that day in the Machine demonstration – it became clear that the theories of Robertson and Keynes were neither inconsistent nor alternative theories but rather were complementary, but more important – they had been integrated in the Machine's economic world.[74]

> They all sat around gazing in some wonder at this thing [the Machine] in the middle of the room …. Then he [Phillips] switched it on. And it worked! "There was income dividing itself into saving and consumption …." He really had created a machine which simplified the problems and arguments economists had been having for years. "Keynes and Robertson need never have quarrelled if they had the Phillips Machine before them". (Robbins in 1972[75])

This controversy over the determination of the interest rate that Robbins suggested the Machine settled is usually portrayed as one arising from the confusion that resulted from relying on purely verbal treatments of the interaction of stocks and flows. This insistence on the problems of verbal economics is somewhat misplaced. There were already a few small diagrammatic and mathematical models (even numerical simulations) and these had been used to explore the workings of the Keynesian system in the late 1930s (as we shall see in Chapter 6). Yet, as we have also seen from Phillips' undergraduate paper, economists' diagrammatic models failed to elucidate certain problems because they could not *show* both stocks and

74 In a short correspondence prompted by Robertson's reading of Phillips' 1950 paper about the Machine, Robertson wrote: "I have just been reading the account of the God (with frontispiece – he is certainly handsomer than most human economics)…." (Letter, 27.8.50 Robertson to Meade), it seems that Robertson, who had not seen the demonstration, could not see this point. In reply, Phillips suggested of the Machine "that by distinguishing between stock and flow schedules (which, incidentally, can only be done in a continuous analysis), and by putting income effects into the model instead of having to allow for them by making shifts in the curves, the process is at any rate shown more clearly, and the different parts of the theories integrated into a wider formal system." (Reply from Phillips to Robertson, September 19, 1950. Both letters, Meade Papers, File 4/1, LSE Library Archives.)

75 Notes by Chapman from a 1972 conversation with Lionel Robbins, at whose seminar at LSE the prototype Machine was first demonstrated in 1949 (LSE STICERD Archive). Being an LSE account, Newlyn had already been written out, but by all accounts, Phillips always insisted on the important role played by Newlyn in developing the first Mark I Machine, and Meade, in his early remarks made the same points. Thus when Meade wrote to Arthur Brown at Leeds (on December 12, 1949) asking to keep the Mark I prototype for a few more months he was most hesitant: "When I mentioned the matter to Phillips he was shocked by it and stressed very heavily the moral obligation which he was under to you [Brown had funded the Mark I] and to Newlyn who is, of course, co-inventor…." see Meade Papers. file 16/2, LSE Library Archives.

flows at once. In the analogical Machine, both stocks and flows work separately and combine together to determine the interest rate, and they do so in a way that makes use of the necessary time gap, or lag, in the interactions between investment and income. In Newlyn and Phillips' model world, such time lags played an important role in the circulation of liquid around the Machine and the levels of national income.

So, Phillips and Newlyn did not just create a machine to solve the stock-flow problem. Rather they invented an economic model world in which the dynamics and time relations of these circular flows and stocks of money in the economic system could be more fully represented and integrated than in other media. Their new way of representing the economy as a hydraulic one in which money is red water enabled them to combine the many macroeconomic elements and allow for their interaction, and gave users a new way of exploring the complex system experimentally by different runs of the model. This was the first part of the two-way analogical comparison: namely to see and gain understanding from making an economic system behave as a hydraulic system. The Machine enabled a new understanding about these matters because in this new model world, the elements were liquid stocks and flows and fully obeyed the laws of stocks and flows; and the system was genuinely dynamic – the liquid did take time to circulate. It was this newfound compatibility between the materials and the theories that economists had been struggling to express in words and diagrams that not only provoked satisfaction and enjoyment at the sight of it happening in the circulation of water in the Machine, but also deepened their understanding of the economic system that had been represented in the analogical model.

These claims about the Newlyn-Phillips Machine are difficult to make convincingly just because they depend on the real Machine in action, and so commentators have struggled to see what was so special about the Machine for professional economists. More recently, as part of a volume of essays in honour of Phillips, the economist David Vines studied a Mark II Machine in Cambridge to find out what it really could tell him (see his 2000). Vines, with a background in maths and physics, carried out, through visual study of the passive Machine, the set of actions suggested by the original training manual that told the user how to set up and run particular experiments: conjunctions of initial settings and interventions on the Machine.[76] And, at the end of each suggested 'experiment', he reflected on what he had learnt from the Machine as opposed to what was known (then and now) from conventional theoretical mathematical modelling and verbal discussions. He found that there is always some additional insight that comes from the four aspects of the analogical model that we have already noted: the fact that stocks and flows are really working together; that time matters; that the continuous and sequential

76 Vines (2000) reads as if he actually carried out the experiments on a working Machine, but it turns
    out that these were close study of a passive Machine during the 1990s (in a personal communi-
    cation August 28, 2006). At that stage, the Cambridge Machine had not been restored to working
    order. See note 19 for information on the training manual.

pattern of changes gives a real dynamics (as apposed to a sequence of statics); and that the interactions of the various elements are really working, as opposed to us thinking about them working (although of course, in this case Vines was visualizing them working).[77]

Vines came to have an appreciation not just for the engineering, but for the fitness between the economic and the hydraulics in the Machine, which in effect, gives credit to the imaginative, cognitive, and creative work undertaken by both the original inventors, Newlyn and Phillips. He came to see the Machine as "truly progressive" *as well as* being an incredible heuristic device:

> It is not true that 'everything is in the machine' .... But there is in fact much more in the machine on these subjects than is allowed in macroeconomic conventional wisdom. And it is immensely visible. It easily stimulates further thoughts and conjectures .... (Vines, 2000, p. 49)

Such further thoughts and conjectures are evident in the work of our two inventors: we can find insights from their interaction with the Machine's hydraulics reflected in their subsequent economics. Just as Fisher had used insights from his analogical balance model to question and rethink his account of the monetary economy, so too did Newlyn and Phillips. Vines (2000) makes a strong case that the ways in which the Machine problematizes issues of time lags, dynamics, and control provided the prompts for Phillips widely recognised and influential later contributions in econometrics, control theory, and stabilization theory. In Newlyn's case, the pattern of reflection from the Machine is more difficult to trace because he soon turned to development economics. But we can see how he develops his ideas about monetary circulation from his work with the Machine, first in the charts and diagrams in his 1950 paper on the Machine, and then through his book on monetary theory (1962 and several editions). We can see these machine insights in his questions about, and the attention he gives, to the circulation patterns of the "active money" (depicted in the Machine), which in turn depended on the behaviour and speed of reaction times of different individuals in the economy: "It is not the frequency of payments in which we are interested but the speed of reaction to amplitude" (Newlyn, 1962, p. 85).[78]

Just as Fisher took his insights from the behaviour of his mechanical balance into his ideas about economic balance, so too did Newlyn and Fisher use their experiences of how their hydraulics model worked to rethink some of their economics.

---

77 The sequence of moves, or 'comparative statics', on a diagrammatic model was the usual way economists investigated dynamics, at that time, as we shall see later in Samuelson's simulated model of the macroeconomy in Chapter 6.

78 In these, he interpreted the multiplier time not as the time lag between income reappearing as expenditure (or v.v.) but the response time for individuals to react to a change in volume of payments. While this relates to earlier ideas about the velocity of circulation that indeed go back to Irving Fisher's work on velocity with his equation of exchange (see Morgan, 2007), the details of the trails left by Newlyn's writings suggest that they are the development of his own studies with the Machine.

So creativity, imagination, and cognition came not just in the process of developing an analogical model, but in bringing insights back from that analogy into their economics. As with *Flatland*, the three-dimensional reader who succeeds in using his imagination to understand a two-dimensional worldview not only gains insight into the nature of the two-dimensional world, but learns something new about his own three-dimensional world too.

Reflecting both ways across the analogy – first in fitting the economics onto the hydraulics in building the Machine, and then in later work, developing insights from the hydraulics and engineering in their economics – appears to have been a source of fruitful ideas in the work of both these economists. But, just as no economists nowadays will think of Fisher's mechanical balance when they use the term "weighted average", the faint traces of the Newlyn-Phillips hydraulic Machine have become lost over time as the insights they drew from their engineering became taken for granted in those parts of economics where they have been used.

Despite this memory loss, the Newlyn-Phillips Machine might be regarded as one of the most inventive models in economics. Indeed, it was so inventive – almost a piece of science fiction – that people did not know how to take it. At the first public outings of the prototype, the reactions of the economists were ones of amazement that it worked, of enjoyment at the spectacle, and of enlightenment about the dynamics of the macroeconomic system. Such a mixture of delight and insight were remarked whenever the Machine's workings were displayed. The newspaper reports after the Leeds demonstration argued that it was a purveyor of both facts and a machine to sort theories, a knowledge maker with a personality, yet a technocratic object. Cartoons ever since have fixed on similar features: as a personality: a somewhat makeshift character; as an economy: a vibrantly alive and eccentric system; yet as a purveyor of ideas: something of an economics 'fruit-machine' spewing out new sets of results with each experiment conducted by its scientist-attendants. Economists loved the Machine for its sheer boldness and eccentricity, but it proved a difficult thing to work with, dependant upon the care of its inventors Newlyn, Phillips, and later Meade, to keep it alive. And despite the fact that few people have seen the Machine at work, it remains perhaps the only economic model to have seeped into the public imagination. From the original Emett cartoon, to a recent cover of *The Economist*, the Newlyn-Phillips Machine exists as a folk object for people who have never seen or even heard of the original economic model.

Acknowledgement

The main case study for this chapter grew out of a paper written jointly with Marcel Boumans (2004) on three-dimensional models and the Phillips Machine, but the question here is a different one, and offers an analysis based on some new historical materials: drawn both from the LSE Archives (Meade's papers) and the STICERD Phillips Machine Archive (thanks to Sue Donnelly and Angela Swain respectively) and from information from correspondence and conversations with Mrs. Doreen Newlyn, in turn based on her husband's diaries, records and notes. My very sincere thanks go to Mrs. Newlyn for digging out the answers to my questions and her willingness to share her records and photographs and give me permission to use them in this chapter. Thanks also to Lesley Chadwick, Martin Slater, Martin Carter, Greg Radick, Mike Flinn, in connection with Newlyn's history and the Leeds Machine; Robert Dixon in connection with the Melbourne Machine; Brian Silverstone and Robert Leeson for their help with the New Zealand end of the story; David Vines for email discussions of his "experiments"; and participants at seminars at LSE, Leeds, Amsterdam and the History of Economics Society (especially Roy Weintraub). The chapter also uses in very concise form and for comparative purposes, materials from my study of Fisher's mechanical balance model (the full stories are given in Morgan, 1997, 1999). Finally, I thank Marcel Boumans for permission to draw on our earlier joint work on the Machine and for his many helpful comments on this chapter.

References

Abbott, Edwin A. (1884/1952) *Flatland. A Romance of Many Dimensions*. New York: Dover.

Achinstein, Peter (1964) "Models, Analogies, and Theories". *Philosophy of Science*, 31:4, 328–50.

Allen, Roy G. D. (1955) "The Engineer's Approach to Economic Models". *Economica*, 22, 158–68.

Bacon, Francis (1625/1985) In John Pitcher (ed), *The Essays*. London: Penguin Classics.

Barker, D. A. (1906) "An Hydraulic Model to Illustrate Currency Phenomena". *Economic Journal*, 16, 461–6.

Barr, Nicolas (1988) "The Phillips Machine". *LSE Quarterly*, 2, 305–37.

(2000) "The History of the Phillips Machine". In Robert Leeson (ed), *A.W.H. Phillips: Collected Works in Contemporary Perspective* (pp. 89–114). Cambridge: Cambridge University Press.

Barty-King, Hugh (1994) *The Baltic Story: Baltic Coffee House to Baltic Exchange*. London: Quiller Press.

Bissell, Chris (2007) "The Moniac: A Hydromechanical Analog Computer of the 1950s". *IEEE Control Systems Magazine*, 27(1), 59–64.

Black, Max (1962) *Models and Metaphors. Studies in Language and Philosophy*. Ithaca, NY: Cornell University Press.

Blyth, C. A. (1975) "A.W. H. Phillips, M.B.E.: 1914–1975". *The Economic Record*, 51, 135, 303–7.

Boothroyd (1953) "The Financephalograph Position: Serious Lag in Production." *Punch*, April 15, p. 456.

Bordo, Michael D. (1987) "Equations of Exchange". In J. Eatwell, M. Milgate, and P. Newman (eds), *The New Palgrave: A Dictionary of Economics*, Vol. 2 (pp. 175–77). London: Macmillan.

Boulding, Kenneth J. (1948), *Economic Analysis* (revised edition). New York: Harper.

Boumans, Marcel (1999) "Built-In Justification". In Mary S. Morgan and Margaret Morrison (eds), *Models as Mediators: Perspectives on Natural and Social Science* (pp. 66–96). Cambridge: Cambridge University Press.

(2001) "Fisher's Instrumental Approach to Index Numbers". In Judy L. Klein and Mary S. Morgan (eds), *The Age of Economic Measurement* (pp. 313–44). Annual Supplement to *History of Political Economy*, Vol. 33. Durham, NC: Duke University Press.

Brown, Arthur J. (1978) "Appreciation at Retirement". *University of Leeds Review*, 21.

(2000) In Robert Leeson (ed), *A. W. H. Phillips: Collected Works in Contemporary Perspective* (pp. xii–xv). Cambridge: Cambridge University Press.

Chapman, Shirley (1972) Some notes on Bill Phillips and his machine … from a conversation with Lord Robbins. 1 Dec. 72 (Box 3, LSE STICERD Archive).

Chote, Robert (1994) "The Dangers of Stirring up Chaos". *The Independent on Sunday*, June 5.

(1995) "Miracle of the Liquid Economy". *Financial Times*, Weekend Section, April 1/2, p. I–II.

Copeland, Morris A. (1952) *A Study of Money Flows*. New York: National Bureau of Economic Research.

Daily Mail (1965) See MacArthur.

Daily Mirror (1950) "Water Keeps Running through His Hands Just Like Money". January 26, 1950.

The Economist (2006) "Big Questions and Big Numbers". July 15, pp. 75–7.

The Economist (2008) November 15–21, front cover.

Edgeworth, F. Y. (1881) *Mathematical Psychics*. London: Kegan Paul, London. (New annotated edition. In Peter Newman (ed), *F. Y. Edgeworth's Mathematical Psychics and Further Papers on Political Economy* (pp. 1–174). Oxford: Oxford University Press for the Royal Economic Society, 2003.

Emett, Rowland (1953) "Machine Designed to Show the Working of the Economic System. Cartoon, *Punch*, April 15, p. 457.

Enke, Stephen (1951) "Equilibrium among Spatially Separated Markets: Solution by Electronic Analogue". *Econometrica*, 19, 40–7.

Financial Times (1995) See Chote.

Fisher, Irving (1911) *The Purchasing Power of Money*. New York: Macmillan.

(1922) *The Making of Index Numbers*. New York: Pollak Foundation for Economic Research.

Fortune (1952) "The Moniac: Economics in Thirty Fascinating Minutes". March, p. 101.

Gentner, D. and D. R. Gentner (1983) "Flowing Waters or Teeming Crowds: Mental Models of Electricity". In D. Gentner and A. L. Stevens (eds), *Mental Models* (pp. 99–129). Hillsdale, NJ: Lawrence Erlbaum.

Gordon, Con (1950) "New Machine Shows How the Money Goes". *Yorkshire Evening Post*, January 20, p. 7.

Hesse, Mary (1966) *Models and Analogies in Science*. Notre Dame, IN: University of Notre Dame Press.

Hume, David (1955) "Of the Balance of Trade". In E. Rotwein (ed), *David Hume: Writings on Economics* (pp. 60–78). Madison: University of Wisconsin Press.

Ibbotson-Somervell, Carol (1994) "A.W.H. Phillips, MBE: 1914–1975, A.M.I.E.E., A.I.L., Ph.D.Econ., Professor Emeritus; Sibling Memories, Press Cuttings, Selected Biographical Notes". Unpublished memoire, LSE STICERD archive, Box 7, File 6.

The Independent on Sunday (1994) See Chote.

Klamer, Arjo and Thomas C. Leonard (1994) "So What's an Economic Metaphor?" In Philip Mirowski (ed), *Natural Images in Economic Thought* (pp. 20–51). New York: Cambridge University Press.

Langman, Michiel (1985) "Geld als Water; De Droom van Elke Econoom. *Economisch Bulletin*, Oktober: 8–11, p. 9.

Law, J. and Michael Lynch (1990) "Lists, Field Guides, and the Descriptive Organisation of Seeing: Birdwatching as an Exemplary Observational Activity". In M. Lynch and

S. Woolgar (eds), *Representation in Scientific Practice* (pp. 269–99). Cambridge, MA: MIT Press.

Leeson, Robert (1994) "A.W. H. Phillips M.B.E. (Military Division)". *The Economic Journal*, 104, 605–18.

(2000a) [ed] *A.W.H. Phillips: Collected Works in Contemporary Perspective*. Cambridge: Cambridge University Press.

(2000b) "A.W. H. Phillips: An Extraordinary Life". In Robert Leeson (ed), *A. W. H. Phillips: Collected Works in Contemporary Perspective* (pp. 3–17). Cambridge: Cambridge University Press.

MacArthur, Brian (1965) "All Done by Water …". *Daily Mail*, March 8, p. 10.

McCloskey, D. N. (1990) "Storytelling in Economics". In Don Lavoie (ed), *Economics and Hermeneutics* (pp. 61–75). London: Routledge.

McKie, Robin (1978) "Old Economic Pipe-Dream Flows Again". *Times Higher Education Supplement*, May 5, 1978.

Meade, James (1951) "That's the Way the Money Goes". *LSE Society Magazine*, January, 10–11.

Mirowski, Philip (1989) *More Heat than Light: Economics as Social Physics, Physics as Nature's Economics*. Cambridge: Cambridge University Press.

Moghadam, Reza and Carter, Colin (1989) "The Restoration of the Phillips Machine: Pumping up the Economy". *Economic Affairs*, October/November, 21–27.

Morehouse, N. F., R. H. Strotz, and S. J. Horwitz (1950) "An Electro-Analog Method for Investigating Problems in Economic Dynamics: Inventory Oscillations". *Econometrica*, 18, 313–28.

Morgan, Mary S. (1997) "The Technology of Analogical Models: Irving Fisher's Monetary Worlds". *Philosophy of Science*, 64, S304–14.

(1999) "Learning from Models". In Morgan and Morrison (eds), *Models as Mediators*, pp. 347–88.

(2001) "Models, Stories and the Economic World". *Journal of Economic Methodology*, 8:3, 361–84. Reprinted in U. Maki (ed), *Fact and Fiction in Economics* (pp. 178–201). Cambridge: Cambridge University Press.

(2003) "Economics". In T. Porter and D. Ross (eds), *The Cambridge History of Science*, Vol. 7: *The Modern Social Sciences* (pp. 275–305). Cambridge: Cambridge University Press.

(2007) "An Analytical History of Measuring Practices: The Case of Velocities of Money". In M. Boumans (ed), *Measurement in Economics: A Handbook* (pp. 105–32). Philadelphia: Elsevier.

Morgan Mary S. and Marcel Boumans (2004) "Secrets Hidden by Two-Dimensionality: The Economy as an Hydraulic Machine". In Soraya de Chadarevian and Nick Hopwood (eds), *Models: The Third Dimension of Science* (pp. 369–401). Stanford, CA: Stanford University Press.

Morgan, Mary S. and M. Morrison (1999) [eds] *Models as Mediators*. Cambridge: Cambridge University Press.

Morrison, M. and M. S. Morgan (1999) "Models as Mediating Instruments". In Mary S. Morgan and Margaret Morrison (eds), *Models as Mediators: Perspectives on Natural and Social Science* (pp. 10–37). Cambridge: Cambridge University Press.

Nagel, Ernest (1961) *The Structure of Science*. London: Routledge & Kegan Paul.

Newlyn, Walter T. (1950) "The Phillips/Newlyn Hydraulic Model". *Yorkshire Bulletin of Economic and Social Research*, 2, 111–27.

(1962/1971) *Theory of Money*. Oxford: Clarendon Press.

(1992) "A Back of the Garage Job". *RES Newsletter*, no. 77, April, 12–13.

(2000) "The Origins of the Machine in a Personal Context". In Leeson, 2000 (ed), pp. 31–8.

Ortony, Andrew (1994) *Metaphor and Thought*, 2nd ed. Cambridge: Cambridge University Press.

Phillips, A. W. (Bill) H. (1950), "Mechanical Models in Economic Dynamics". *Economica*, 17, 282–305.

Schlimm, Dirk (2008) "Two Ways of Analogy: Extending the Study of Analogies to Mathematical Domains". *Philosophy of Science*, 75, 178–200.

Swade, Doron (1995) "The Phillips Economics Computer". *Resurrection* no. 12, 11–18.

(2000) "The Phillips Machine and the History of Computing". In Robert Leeson (ed), *A. W. H. Phillips: Collected Works in Contemporary Perspective* (pp. 120–6). Cambridge: Cambridge University Press.

Times Higher Education Supplement (1978). See McKie.

Toulmin, Stephen (1953) *The Philosophy of Science*. London, Hutchinson University Library.

van der Post, Laurens (1985) *The Night of the New Moon*. London: Hogarth Press.

Veblen, Thorstein (1904) *Theory of Business Enterprise*. New York: Scribner.

Vines, David (2000) "The Phillips Machine as a 'Progressive' Model". In Robert Leeson (ed), *A. W. H. Phillips: Collected Works in Contemporary Perspective* (pp. 39–67). Cambridge: Cambridge University Press.

Walras, Leon (1874) *Elements d'Economie Pure*. English translation by William Jaffé (1954). London: Allen and Unwin.

Yorkshire Evening Post (1950) See Gordon.

6

Questions and Stories: Capturing the Heart of Matters

1. Introduction

Scientific models are not passive objects but form sophisticated instruments of enquiry.[1] Models are objects to enquire into and to enquire with: economists enquire into the world of the economic model, and use them to enquire with into the economic world that the model represents. What kind of reasoning turns these pieces of mathematics or little diagrams into a means of enquiry? And how is it that these enquiries lead economists to feel that they have captured something of the heart of the matter, either of their theories or of the economic world, in their models?

The question: 'How do economists use models?' is, in one sense, easy to answer: they ask questions with them and tell stories! Or more exactly: they ask questions,

---

1 See Morrison and Morgan (1999) and Morgan (1999).

use the resources of the model to demonstrate something, and tell stories in the process. At first sight, it is difficult to see exactly why questions are needed, or what the stories do.[2] How does asking questions of models and telling stories with them enable them to function as epistemic instruments that economists might learn from using and that might capture the heart of anything? Let me begin with an example that shows how stories can shape the reasoning resources of models before going on to show how and why economists working with models typically ask questions and tell similar kinds of stories when they reason with them.

2. Stories to Shape Model Resources: Frisch's Macro-Dynamic Scheme

One of the greatest challenges for economists in the 1920s and early 1930s was to get to the heart of the matter of business cycles. This was a theoretically complex puzzle, namely to work out what particular combinations of economic elements, and their relationships, might be responsible for creating business cycles. It was also a real economy problem, evidenced in the deep depression of 1921–2 and the Great Depression of 1929 onwards.

Against these backgrounds, the Norwegian economist Ragnar Frisch (1933) set himself to solve one important aspect of this puzzle: to figure out what kind of mathematical model of the economy could produce a cyclical pattern in general economic activity in the world of the model.[3] He began his modelling of the economic system from his visual sketch of the economic system, a *Tableau Économique*, depicting the elements and circulating flows of the economy from which he fashioned a simpler, mathematical, model, both shown in Chapter 1 (Figure 1.6).[4] This latter

2 Several commentators have discussed stories: McCloskey (1990a, 1990b and 1994) and Mäki (1992), or questions and stories: Gibbard and Varian (1978), in the context of economic models. My own account, of 2001 and here, begins with the last named work for they raise and note some important aspects of modelling – including that both questions and stories are involved; but they do not really explain how, and so why, stories are critical to the identity of a model. (More recent work has discussed models as fictions; see, e.g., Suárez [2009] and Frigg [2009]; or Le Gall [2008] for economic models, but my focus here is on the role of narratives in model usage, not on the status of models; of course not all stories are fictional.)

3 Frisch (1895–1973), the Norwegian equivalent to Keynes in terms of his position and professional stature, was, along with Tinbergen, one of the leaders of the econometric movement and together, they were responsible for developing the ideas and practices of modelling in the interwar period. Mathematical modelling was pretty unusual at this time, and the term 'model' was not yet introduced, so Frisch talked of his "macro-dynamic system". See Chapter 1 here for the history of modelling in general, and Boumans (2005) for the early history of business cycle mathematical modelling.

4 The story of Frisch's model has been told several times in the history of economics. Boumans (1999) tells how and why he picked out elements to make a model at "the extreme limit of simplification" (1933, p. 174), and how he moulded them together with a mathematical formalism to make a "new recipe" for business cycles; Morgan (1990) concentrates on its place in the history of econometrics; and Louçã (2007) on its analogical aspects.

"macro-dynamic system" had the resources – of both mathematical and economic content – for Frisch to think of it as a kind of machine. It was a machine that could produce cycles in economic activity in the world of the model in a seamless process of change, and these cycles gradually died down over time of their own accord. These two qualities of the world created in his model were vitally important in fulfilling Frisch's requirements for the model, for while cycles were a feature of the real economy, it was a widely held theory amongst economists of the time that, if the economic system were left to itself and without disturbances, the cycles would die out and the economy would tend towards a position of rest or 'equilibrium'.[5] Frisch went on to show, by adding some reasonable guesses about the numbers in his simple model system, that it could produce cycles that matched the lengths of economic cycles in the real economic system. So, his little model was consistent with theoretical assumptions, and he took comfort from its ability to mimic the length of real economic cycles.

But this neat cyclical activity produced in the world of the model was just too neat to fit the more unruly pattern of activity found in the real world, *and*, as he said, "in reality the cycles we have occasion to observe are generally not damped" (Frisch, 1933, p. 197). These observations led Frisch to ask:

> ... in what respect do the dynamic laws need to be completed in order to explain the real happenings? .... what would become of the solution of a determinate dynamic system [such as his little model] if it were exposed to a stream of erratic shocks that constantly upsets the continuous evolution, and by so doing introduces into the system the energy necessary to maintain the swings. (Frisch, 1933, p. 197)

This is where the final, third, step of his model-making occurred, and where stories with extended analogies began to play a serious role in shaping his model.[6]

In this third step of his model-making, Frisch followed the lead of the preeminent Swedish economist Knut Wicksell, who had distinguished between the *propagation* problem (the economic machine that created the cycles) and the *impulse* problem (what kept the cycles going) with a memorable story-cum-analogy: "If you hit a wooden rocking-horse with a club, the movement of the horse will be very different to that of the club" (Frisch quoting Wicksell, p. 198). The motion of the horse is a rocking one (the propagating element), but the horse will gradually come

---

5 On the history of this assumption, see Ingrao and Israel (1990); and for discussion of its importance in mathematical economics and the econometric models of the mid-twentieth century, see Weintraub (1991) and Morgan (1991).

6 Stories were critical to his model design here but not all analogies involve good stories. Thus Frisch rejected an alternative analogy, which conceived of the long, several-year, period of the business cycles as waves on a stream's surface with the yearly seasonal variations in economic activity as ripples caused by stones on a river bed. There was no narrative to connect the elements. A contrasting example of where an analogy worked well without narratives is found in creating the Newlyn-Phillips hydraulic Machine of Chapter 5. For a case of stories figuring in model construction in physics, see Hartmann (1999).

to a position of rest unless there is some reason for it to continue to rock by the boy hitting it with a club (the impulse). For Frisch, the propagating part of his model and the impulse part were different motions and there was no reason for them to be concurrent or for the impulses to be regular: imagine a small, angry boy hitting his toy horse with a stick at random intervals and with random amounts of force, and you have the right idea.

How then did Frisch turn this story about impulses into an element that could be joined to his economic mathematical (propagation) model? He found inspiration in the statistical experiments reported in 1927 by G. Udny Yule and Eugen Slutsky.[7] Yule in England had used a story of small boys shooting peas at a moving pendulum to explain his statistical experiments in which an harmonic process was disturbed by random elements, a story rather similar to Wicksell's. Slutsky, across the other side of Europe in Russia, had picked out and summed a series of successive lottery numbers to create a second series of numbers that showed a maintained cyclical pattern but with jagged shapes that were very similar to those of business cycle data (see Chapter 8, Figure 8.5). These stories were attached to demonstrations: graphs that showed Frisch how random shocks or erratic elements could provide data patterns that looked much more like business cycle data than the smooth waves created by his economic mechanism model.

Using these stories and their statistical demonstrations to motivate his own model design, Frisch added a set of random shocks into his economic mechanism, introducing them in such a way that the mathematical model of economic activity carried along the random shocks (or propagated them) through following time periods. Using these stories of small, mischievous boys to shape his model so that it contained both mathematical and statistical resources, Frisch was able to produce simulations that demonstrated not only how his world in the model could produce the kinds of damped cycles required of contemporary business cycles theorizing, but could at the same time imitate the kind of jagged and maintained cycles of data produced by the real world (that we see in the financial reports of newspapers and television).

Emulating the data pattern was a useful attribute of the model, but the small boy story of impulses had no obvious equivalent back in the economic world. Frisch sought an economic interpretation in another story using an analogy, a pendulum mechanism fed by a stream of water through a valve, that he designed and drew to understand Joseph Schumpeter's theory of cycles (see Louça, 2007). According to this account, cycles were maintained in the economy because of the role of innovations in the economic system: innovations in technology, in the organisation of work, in finding new supplies and markets, and in new products. Frisch argued that such innovations "accumulate in a more or less continuous fashion, but are put into practical application on a larger scale only during certain phases of the cycle"

---

7 See Yule (1927) and Slutsky (1927); Slutsky's work was published in Russian but immediately abstracted and known by European and American economics (see Morgan, 1990; Judy Klein, 1997; and Barnett, 2006).

(Frisch 1933, p. 203), so that, as he put it, it is not the innovations themselves, but their pattern of utilization in the economy that "constitutes the new energy which maintains the oscillations" (Frisch, 1933, p. 204). Frisch adopted Schumpeter's account to provide an economic explanation for the maintenance of cycles that occurred in *using* his model. So here we see a story being used in a different way, not to shape the creation of the model as the rocking horse story did, but now as a means of relating the modelling result back to the world to offer an economic explanation of why the economic world behaves as it does.

In this now classic paper of 1933, written in the depths of the Great Depression, Frisch had set about modelling why the economy experienced business cycles. He began with a visual schema of economic activity, developed a smaller mathematical model of the economy as a mechanism that would produce damped cycles, and combined it with a random shock element so that it would produce patterns that matched business cycle data. In other words, he succeeded in capturing some important elements of the theory and of the world behaviour in his model world. Stories, or story analogies, were critical in building up or creating the model and joining the elements together. But his last story analogy was also critical for pointing to the way the model could be used to provide explanations. It is this latter role of stories that features regularly in the way that economists *use* their models.

3. Questions and Stories Capturing Keynes' *General Theory*

The appearance of Frisch's model in 1933 was a rare event, for this was a period when the majority of the economics profession did not indulge in mathematical modelling about the economic system as a whole. But the extended length and depth of the Great Depression into the 1930s meant that many economists became obsessed by the question of why the cycle had got stuck in a depression and why the economy did not right itself and recovery begin. The most important theoretical contribution to this problem was the publication of John Maynard Keynes' *General Theory* in 1936 – a book generally taken to epitomise the development of macroeconomic theory, a theory that replaced business cycle theories (at least, for half a century). Those who approach this famous book now will find its argument mode opaque, for it is a curious mixture of mathematics and words.[8] Its opacity was equally true then, for the immediate reaction of a number of young economists of the day was to create various algebraic and geometric models in their attempts to understand and capture the heart of Keynes' theory. In some cases, they tried to provide a representation of his ideas that would allow comparison with other systems, particularly the classical system.[9] The most influential of these attempts was

---

8 See Andvig (1991), Solow (1997), and Lucas (2004, p. 13), who noted that "you had to have an intermediary to get close to the *General Theory*. Somebody had to help you get at it."

9 Though not all these attempts were self-described as 'models', Darity and Young (1995) have rightly referred to these attempts in the two or three years following publication of Keynes' book as

the one by John Hicks, which morphed into one of the most ubiquitous models of macroeconomics, namely the IS/LM diagram. I concentrate initially on two others, one by the young British economist James Meade, and one by the young American economist Paul Samuelson, to introduce my discussion of the typical questions and storytelling characteristics of model usage in economics.[10]

3.i Modelling Keynes' *General Theory*: Meade

James Meade's paper began:

> The object of this article is to construct a simple model of the economic system discussed in Mr. Keynes' *The General Theory of Employment, Interest and Money*, in order to illustrate:
>
> (i)   the conditions necessary for equilibrium;
> (ii) the conditions necessary for stability of equilibrium; and
> (iii) the effect on employment of changes in certain variables. (Meade, 1937, p. 98)

Meade began with seven assumptions about specific elements in the economy (e.g., that the prime cost in every industry is wages); these were followed by a list of the eight conditions (e.g., that prices of goods are equal to marginal costs; and that total income equals wages plus profits) under which an economy based on the seven initial assumptions will be in short-period equilibrium. From these, Meade constructed eight relationships, mirrored in a mathematical model. (Just as Alfred Marshall [1890] kept his diagrams in the footnote, Meade kept his mathematical model in his Appendix, clear evidence that such models were still not the accepted and acceptable way of doing economics.) It is these eight relationships – the model – that Meade reasoned with in the rest of the paper, telling us that:

> By means of these eight relationships we can show that the volume of employment is determined for every given supply of money, for every given money wage-rate, and for every given proportion of income saved. (Meade, 1937, p. 99)

We might ask where this requirement to determine the volume of employment came from? It did not come from the model itself, which is Meade's interpretation of the main contribution of Keynes' book: namely the development of a

---

"models purporting to represent Keynes's message" (p. 1). Their survey of these models (translated into common format, and with modern modelling terminology) discusses eight papers, reviews, or responses that appeared in print in the period 1936–8.

10 This is the same Meade who helped Phillips design the second, or Mark II hydraulic machine at LSE (see Chapter 5). Meade's (1907–95) training and career were associated with Oxford, London School of Economics (LSE), and Cambridge; Samuelson (1915–2009) was associated with University of Chicago, Harvard, and MIT; and Hicks (1904–1989) was associated with Oxford, LSE, and Manchester. All three economists became Nobel Prize winners.

macroeconomic aggregate account that integrated the real and monetary side of the economic system. It came rather from an understanding of the main economic problem and policy question of the day that Keynes' book addressed: solving the unemployment problem of the Great Depression.

But before he could get to grips with that question about employment, Meade had to satisfy himself about the nature of the world in his model. Just as Frisch had checked that his model world could generate cycles in economic activity and that these would dampen down to make sure it fulfilled the necessary requirements to be a business cycle model, Meade first checked that his mathematical model world would return to an equilibrium situation following a change in one element of the system, and that this equilibrium point would be a stable one (his points (i) and (ii) in his introduction). This habit of checking if certain general mathematical qualities that fit broader economic assumptions hold in the world of the model is a general feature of modelling in economics, and so often features as the first usage of a model. And, as we have seen with Frisch, it was the general assumption of his generation of economists that the economic system is one that tends to return to positions of rest following a disturbance.[11] Somewhat disarmingly, Meade concludes his model checking with: "It is of course possible that in the real world the system is unstable" (p. 102) but he continues with his model on the basis that it would be difficult to carry out his analysis of employment unless the system were stable (a point illuminated by Samuelson's work; see below). And while this comment might have struck a reader living in the earlier 1930s as ironic (given that so many economies did seem to be stuck at the bottom of the cycle), by 1937, the economy was beginning to recover, which seemed to support economists' beliefs about the nature of the economic system.

We have already noticed that, in this domain of model questions, the demand for labour – the most pressing problem of the Great Depression in the U.K. context – is the critical criterion for Meade. He works through four cases to answer the questions: What is

> ... the effect on employment of (1) a reduction in interest rates, (2) an increase in the total supply of money, (3) a reduction in money rate-wages [sic], and (4) a reduction in the proportion of income saved? (Meade, 1937, p. 102)

In addressing these questions, he works through the model, tracing the effects of changing one thing in the model (while holding certain others constant) to see the outcomes of such changes on all the intervening elements (whether it raises or lowers other things in the model) as well as on the "short-period demand for labour".

---

11 These checks – to see what happened to the short-period equilibrium of the model when some element in it was changed – were discussed verbally in the text and demonstrated formally in the appendix with the mathematical model. On the history of mathematical analysis of dynamics and stability analysis, see Weintraub (1991), who gives considerable attention to Hicks and to Samuelson (he does not discuss Meade's work).

For each question put to the model, the answer involves an implicit set of causal links, signalled by the order in which the tracing process is followed. This tracing allows consideration of whether each of the linked changes that occur are plausible ones in the context of the economic world portrayed in the model, but perhaps also in the context of the economic world that Meade lived in. These are *the narratives of model usage*: each answering argument to each question offers a narrative sequence of connected events as each change alters the value of some other element in the model; this requires tracing all these changes through the various relationships in the model.

At one point Meade traces through the effect of *two* of these critical factors changing at once, and unusually the changes are specified in size. This provides an effective illustration of model narratives, so I report the narrative reasoning verbatim here:

> Suppose that there were a 10 per cent reduction in all money wage-rates combined with a 10 per cent reduction in the supply of money. Then *if* output and employment remained unchanged, the marginal prime cost and so the price of all commodities would fall by 10 per cent in view of the 10 per cent fall in the money wage-rate; and in consequence all money incomes would fall by 10 per cent. Ten per cent less money would be required to finance current transactions, and, as the total supply of money is also reduced by 10 per cent, the supply of "idle" money would also have fallen by 10 per cent because of the 10 per cent fall in money incomes. Money investment would also have fallen by 10 per cent if expected profits had fallen by 10 per cent; for the rate of interest being unchanged, and supply price of capital goods and the expected money yield on them having fallen by 10 per cent, there would be no incentive to change the value of *real* investment, so that ... (Meade, 1937, p. 103, his italics)

Meade's text shows how this tracing process produces the narrative that accompanies his use of the resources of the model: each narrative begins with a starting point given by the question asked, and follows the order that the model is solved to reach outcomes.[12]

We can see the general features of model usage here: in using his model to answer economically interesting problems, Meade began with questions (about employment in relation to other things in the economy). He used his model resources (the eight equations) to answer them, and in doing so told a series of stories with the model – for these questions required attention not only to final outcomes but also to the multiple intervening elements, processes, and side effects, on the path to them. The stories were shaped by the mathematics of the content and constrained by it, but not fully determined by it. The decision what to change depended on

---

12 Readers may recognise that this is fundamentally the same method used by Ricardo in arguing with his accounting model farm, discussed in Chapter 2.

the economic question, and the description of what happened depended on the economic content of the model, so that the narratives were economic stories about the world depicted in the model. In the process, the effect of whatever happened on the demand for labour (*the* 1930s problem) was assessed in its own terms but also for various other impacts on other elements in the model. So, the way the question was asked, the objects of interest, what else was held constant and what allowed to vary, and the order of solution: all these affected the way any particular story was told. As Barthes wrote in a very different context: "meaning is not 'at the end' of the narrative, it runs across it" (1982, p. 259).

3.ii Reasoning with Models: The External and Internal Dynamics

Reasoning with models involves four closely related elements. Scientists create a model to answer a set of questions they find of interest. They manipulate the model to demonstrate the answers to those questions. In the process they tell narratives about the world in the model, narratives that might also be useful for understanding the world that the model is made to represent. We can write these down as four steps, but of course as we have already seen with Meade, they are not completely separate, or indeed separable, activities:

> Step 1: *Create or Construct* a model relevant for a topic or problem of interest.
> Step 2: *Question* that model world: the 'external dynamic'.
> Step 3: *Demonstrate* the answer to the questions using the model's resources: the 'internal dynamic'.
> Step 4: *Narrative* accompanies the demonstration to link the answers back to the questions and to their domains: both to the world in the model and the world that the model represents.

Model-making: the activity of representing or denoting some aspect of the world into a model was discussed in the earlier chapters of this book.[13] The features that are unusual in the account here are my insistence on questions as a separate element in the way models are used and the claim that demonstrations with models are inextricably bound up with *narratives* or *stories* (at least in the way that economists use models). These narratives not only provide the form in which questions are answered but also help economists to learn and understand things about *the world in the model*, and/or provide interpretations and insight into *the world that the model represents*. So these narratives provide the correspondence

---

13 Steps 1, 3, and 4 here are parallelled in R. I. G. Hughes' (1997) DDI account of the way models are used in physics: *Denote, Demonstrate* and *Interpret. Denotation*, is his word for the model-making practices analysed in my previous chapters. His terminology follows Nelson Goodman (1968, p. 5), who points out that denotation entails representation, but is independent of resemblance and I am happy to follow Goodman's sense of the matter (see Chapter 1 for a further discussion). I add in as Step 2: *Questions*, for they are essential to the way that a model is used. For his final Step 3: *Interpretation*, I use the term *Narrative*.

links between the demonstration made with the model and the events, situations and processes of change in the real world. I discuss *questions* and the model resources that enable *demonstrations* next; *stories* or *narratives* are discussed later in the chapter.

Models have to be '*questioned*' to make use of their resources. I call such questions the '*external dynamic*' because they are the prompt for the economist to begin manipulating their model. Economists typically begin their model usage with a question about something in the model or in the world. For example, a query may be raised by a casual observation about something in the world that needs accounting for. Or the prompting question might occur by considering a change to some term in the model implied by a policy option. Equally it may be a question about the world in the model, for example, about the modification of an assumption that seems interesting from a theoretical point of view such as whether the model has a tendency to equilibrium. Such questions as "How does it happen that . . . . . ?", "What happens if . . . ?" or a "Let us assume that . . ." prompt some term or element in the model to be set at a new value or a modification is made to the model to represent the question or arrangement, just as in Meade's account, which we can take as fairly typical. So, the external dynamic is not 'external' in the sense that it is motivated by the events of the world rather than the contents of the model but in the simple sense that it comes from the scientist-user.

Then, it is in using models to answer questions that we find *demonstrations* going on; and these depend on the '*internal dynamic*'. This term comes from Hughes work on physics:

> Its [the model's] function is epistemological. To be predictive, a science must provide representations that have a dynamic of this kind [provided by mathematics] built into them. That is one reason why mathematical models are the norm in physics. Their internal dynamic is supplied – at least in part – by the deductive resources of the mathematics they employ. (Hughes, 1997, p. 332)

It is indeed tempting to think that the deductive work of models is determined only by their mathematics. But deductive resources of models in economics are not restricted to any particular form: the model could be mathematical (geometric, or algebraic, or arithmetic) but need not be, for there are deductive resources in many diagrammatic or material object models (think of the hydraulic machine of Chapter 5). But it is an essential characteristic of models that they have resources that can be manipulated to produce outcomes; otherwise no demonstrations are possible.[14]

---

14 It is a good place to note here if it is not already obvious that the 'internal dynamic' of a model does not require a model to have dynamic properties, nor to have conventionally understood deductive resources, in the mathematical sense. Similarly, not all models appear as mechanisms that have to be 'cranked' to make demonstrations. The claim is merely that to be useful in economics, models must have some manipulable resources that can be put to work to answer questions, whether this is by arithmetical simulation, algebraic solving, or setting a machine to work, or whatever.

And, as I have already suggested in Chapter 1, the workable content of a model hangs not just on its manipulable resources, but on a broader combination of those resources as well as their rules for manipulation. In my account, these together form the *internal dynamic* used in model demonstrations. We can see both illustrated in Meade's case.

The *rules of reasoning* that are applied to any model can be understood as language rules, and content-based rules (as also discussed in Chapter 1). If a model is created as a set of equations as Meade's model, the rules for manipulating it or for reasoning with it come from algebra, so he could use the deductive reasoning mode of that particular mathematical language to demonstrate certain outcomes of the model. But the particular economic content of a model also determines some of the rules for manipulation or reasoning. For Meade, the assumptions in Keynesian macroeconomics determine the allowable starting points and forbid other starting points, and they dictate the causal ordering of the variables in the order of model manipulation. But these two sources of rules may not be easily separable into language and subject matter for, of course, the economics has been expressed into that language in making the model. Nevertheless, economic content does supply some of the rules of model manipulation and thus the possibilities for reasoning with the model. We saw how Ricardo's model farm (Chapter 2) used an accounting logic, and the rules for manipulating his farm accounts were set by that language; but the economic content in his model – his classical laws and assumptions – also dictated some of the rules, and constrained the ways in which he manipulated his model farm accounts.

It is evident, of course, from the examples in this chapter, that these rules of reasoning must have content to work upon, namely the *model resources*. Meade's model of eight equations contained many such resources. In contrast, Frisch's *Tableau Économique*, a visual sketch, provided some resources to reason with, but little that could be used deductively until he turned it into a mathematical model, which contained fewer subject matter resources, but more manipulable qualities. So, the resources of any model provide the materials on which the rules of reasoning appropriate to it can be used and it is this 'internal dynamic' that scientists use to demonstrate answers to their questions.

One of our earlier cases in which the rules and resources are very clearly demarcated is the material object model of the Newlyn-Phillips Machine discussed in Chapter 5. There the language of the model is not a mathematical one, but the language of real hydraulics, and the economic content has been denoted into flows, stocks, and tanks of water too. The circulation and manipulation of the flows of water representing the flows of money are governed by the hydraulics. But the flows are, in turn, controlled by valves and "slides" in which the economic relations are expressed. Evidently the reasoning rules – the subject matter rules and the language rules – come from different sources, but they work simultaneously together on a machine with many resources for demonstration. Together, they create the internal dynamic of that model in making demonstrations.

3.iii Modelling Keynes' *General Theory*: Samuelson

We can see how the questions or external dynamic and the internal dynamic together create and enable demonstrations in another of the contemporary attempts to make sense of Keynes' ideas by the use of modelling. Alvin Hansen is generally regarded as the American interpreter of Keynes, and the young Paul Samuelson, in one of his earliest papers in 1939, adopted Hansen's model of Keynes' ideas to explore the joint roles of the "multiplier" and "accelerator", the two relations that came to be understood as important for total effective demand in the Keynesian system. Samuelson's model was:

$$(1) \qquad Y_t = g_t + C_t + I_t$$
$$(2) \qquad C_t = \alpha Y_{t-1}$$
$$(3) \qquad I_t = \beta(C_t - C_{t-1})$$

where Y is aggregate national income, g is government expenditure, C is consumption expenditure, I is induced private investment, and t is the time indicator. In this model, equation (1) is the normal Keynesian aggregate (national) income identity; relation (2), the Keynesian aggregate consumption function is interpreted as the multiplier relation, and (3) is interpreted as the accelerator relation. In this model, when government spending increases, income rises, but in successive time periods the initial increase in national income that this creates is 'multiplied' by an increase in consumption and 'accelerated' as the increase in consumption induces increases in private investment. These interpretations rely on the time dependencies in the relations (noted in the subscripts) and the format of the model, which links decisions by different groups of people in the economy through time, based on the modelling practices of the Dutch economist Jan Tinbergen and the younger economists of Wicksell's Stockholm school. As Samuelson argued, this combination of the multiplier and accelerator relations was responsible for the novelty of his results, but also their complexity. Rather than checking that his model exhibited "well-behaved" stable equilibria in advance of his more specific questions, as had Frisch and Meade, Samuelson chose first to use simulations to examine how this model world worked and to show that it was not always well behaved.

Samuelson's question, the external dynamic, was: "What happens if government expenditure increases?" and was primarily an enquiry into the world of the model, the world of Keynesian economic theory. He first carried out some arithmetical simulations of the model to show how the two relations (2 and 3) in the model interact. Each simulation is based on injecting into the model world a continuous stream of single units of government spending in each period, setting off, via the model equations, a sequence of changes in aggregate income over succeeding time periods. He traces out several such sequences for aggregate income in tabular form (his table 2, our Figure 6.1), according to the values chosen for the parameters in the two relations (seen in the top row of the table). These different starting points and settings are what Samuelson calls his "hypotheses" about the world in

TABLE 2.—MODEL SEQUENCES OF NATIONAL INCOME FOR
SELECTED VALUES OF MARGINAL PROPENSITY TO CON-
SUME AND RELATION

(*Unit: one dollar*)

Period	$\alpha = .5$ $\beta = 0$	$\alpha = .5$ $\beta = 2$	$\alpha = .6$ $\beta = 2$	$\alpha = .8$ $\beta = 4$
1	1.00	1.00	1.00	1.00
2	1.50	2.50	2.80	5.00
3	1.75	3.75	4.84	17.80
4	1.875	4.125	6.352	56.20
5	1.9375	3.4375	6.6256	169.84
6	1.9688 *	2.0313	5.3037	500.52
7	1.9844	.9141	2.5959	1,459.592
8	1.9922	− .1172	− .6918	4,227.704
9	1.9961	.2148	−3.3603	12,241.1216
.. ..	.....	....	....	....

* Table is correct to four decimal places.

Figure 6.1. Samuelson's Arithmetic Simulation.

Source: Paul Samuelson (May, 1939) "Interactions between the Multiplier Analysis and the Principle of Acceleration", *The Review of Economics and Statistics*, 21:2, 75–78; table 2 on p. 77. Reproduced with permission from MIT Press Journals.

the model. The first of these columns represents the model with only the multiplier relation at work (β is set at zero), and shows an increase in aggregate income up to a certain point, but no cycles. Of these other three simulated sequences where both relations are active, one produces cycles that are regular but undamped, one explosive cycles in aggregate output, and the last one exponential increases in output. That is, the question and model do not alter, but with different parameter values for the same model, the internal dynamic of the model – its resources and reasoning rules – enable Samuelson to demonstrate different sequences in the arithmetical simulations and so tell a set of different narratives. And these different narratives suggest that, for many values of the parameters, unlike Meade's model, the system is not stable nor does it have a well-behaved tendency towards equilibrium.

As Samuelson noted of these demonstrations with the model:

> By this time the investigator is inclined to feel somewhat disorganized. A variety of qualitatively different results emerge in a seemingly capricious manner from minor changes in hypotheses [settings of the model]. Worse than this, how can we be sure that for still different selected values of our coefficients new and stronger types of behaviour will not emerge? Is it not even possible that if Table 2 [the arithmetic simulation results in our Figure 6.1] were extended to cover more periods, new types of behaviour might result for these selected coefficients?
>
> Fortunately, these questions can be given a definite negative answer. Arithmetical methods cannot do so since we cannot try all possible values of the coefficients nor compute the endless terms in each sequence. Nevertheless, comparatively simple algebraic analysis can be applied which

will yield all possible qualitative types of behaviour and enable us to unify our results. (Samuelson, 1939, p. 76)

Using his model (above), Samuelson then solves for the different roots of the equation system as a whole.[15] He maps these solutions onto a graph (Figure 6.2) where the axes denotes the values of the parameters (α and β) in the multiplier and accelerator relations, so that

It can be easily shown that the whole field of possible values of α and β can be divided into four regions, each of which gives qualitatively different types of behaviour. ..... Each point in this diagram represents a selection of values of the marginal propensity to consume and the *relation* [the accelerator relation]. Corresponding to each point there will be a model sequence of national income through time. The qualitative properties of this sequence depend upon whether the point is in region A, B, C, or D. (Samuelson, 1939, p. 77, his italics)

Each region (on Figure 6.2) marks out an area with a different *qualitative* story as to what happens to the behaviour of aggregate income as the *quantitative* values of the two parameters in the model vary together. The government action is also allowed to vary: that is, the external dynamic changes to ask what happens if government spending is a single impulse, or a continuous impulse (as in his first arithmetic simulations), or follows a cyclical pattern. So, for example, a single period of government spending creates a gradual return back to the original level of aggregate income in region A, damped oscillations around that level in region B, explosive oscillations in C, and explosive growth in D. The effects of alternative government actions within the world of the model are also explained in the qualitative stories for each region of the map. The behaviour of aggregate income is thus characterized in terms of periodicity, damping factors, and effectiveness of government expenditures used to pump-prime national income.

So, by the use of analytical solution methods, Samuelson is able to take account of joint variation in both multiplier and accelerator parameters and to demonstrate how these varied together over the full range of values, rather than just for those values chosen in his earlier arithmetic simulations. He is also able to demonstrate, using the model's resources of the multiplier and accelerator relations, how some rather bizarre narrative results come from what seemed to be simple assumptions about parameter values in those behavioural relations and about policy actions. For example, as he explains, in region D, with large values of the two parameters (as in his fourth column of his table 2), either single or constant increases in government expenditure will send national income increasing dramatically; but there is a downside too, for a small disinvestment by the government will "send the system ever downward at an increasing rate. This is a highly unstable situation, but corresponds most closely to the pure case of pump-priming" (Samuelson, 1939, p. 78).

---

15 For example, where g_t (government expenditure in time t) equals 1 unit, the system to be solved becomes: $Y_t = 1 + \alpha[1 + \beta]Y_{t-1} - \alpha\beta Y_{t-2}$

CHART 2.—DIAGRAM SHOWING BOUNDARIES OF REGIONS YIELDING DIFFERENT
QUALITATIVE BEHAVIOR OF NATIONAL INCOME

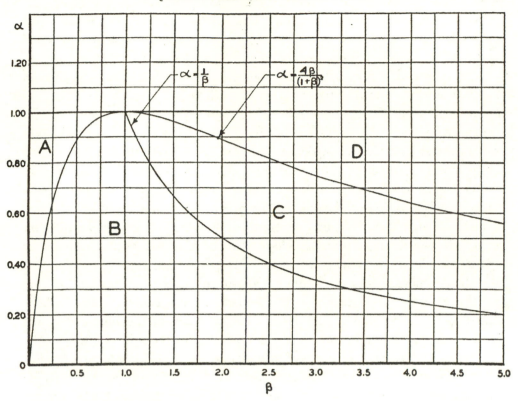

Figure 6.2. Samuelson's Model Solution Graph.

Source: Paul A. Samuelson (May, 1939) "Interactions between the Multiplier Analysis and the Principle of Acceleration", *The Review of Economics and Statistics*, 21:2, 75–78; chart 2 from p. 78. Reproduced with permission from MIT Press Journals.

The chart and its regions enable Samuelson to demarcate, and type, the full range of possible stories about what will happen to aggregate income in the world of his Keynesian model from using the model resources (the internal dynamic) to answer questions about changes in government spending (the external dynamic). Samuelson claims that the generality – meaning both the full range and their classification – of these new stories compared to previous analyses is useful. But note that it is not the equation solutions themselves that are interesting here. Rather it is the range of government actions assumed in the questions (the external dynamic), the range of parameter values in his hypotheses, and the patterns of economic behaviour reported in the narrative answers attached to the map. These narratives succinctly summarise the relations between questions, hypotheses, and outcomes: it is these that are demonstrated by using the internal dynamic of the model.

With Meade and Samuelson we have a range of examples of questions (the external dynamic) and answers in which we see how the internal dynamic of their models are used to demonstrate different outcomes, or even kinds of outcomes, as each question changes the set-up or details in the model. They both used small algebraic Keynesian models, Samuelson's a much simpler model than Meade's. Meade kept the same model throughout and asked different questions, telling different stories as he manipulated the model resources to trace through answers to those questions. Samuelson asked variations on the same general question of his one model, but with different parameter values creating different stories in conjunction first with arithmetic simulation methods and then with analytical solution methods. While Meade had checked the 'good behaviour' of his model (that it fulfilled certain requirements of stability) before using it to investigate the possibilities of government policy, Samuelson showed how certain government actions could destabilize the behaviour of the economic world in the model. As we see from this brief comparison with Meade, there are different ways to manipulate the same kinds of model resources, even while these manipulations are still determined by the same language of the model and its similar economic content. Different questions and different modes of demonstration create different stories, showing the importance of understanding the nature of the internal dynamic to the possibilities of demonstrations made with the model.

These examples also point to the important role of the scientist both in asking the questions and in carrying out the manipulations necessary for the demonstrations. The model itself does not pose the question and the internal dynamic does not work without an external dynamic. Scientists pose the question or the 'external dynamic', and put the model to work to make use of its 'internal dynamic' to demonstrate some answer with the model. The model cannot demonstrate these answers by sheer deductive logic or unadulterated mathematics without the prompt given by the subject matter question, which both determines and constrains, how those deductive resources are used. Then, using the appropriate rules of reasoning, elements in the model have to be mentally or physically shifted around on the diagram, or the algebra has to be manipulated and solved through, for the economist to demonstrate answers. Even with models in which the system can be programmed to solve itself (so to speak), as in computer simulations with certain kinds of mathematical models or the hydraulic Newlyn-Phillips machine (see Morgan and Boumans, 2004), each time the scientist asks a question, the model has to be calibrated properly and set going to answer the relevant question. Models may require more or less human manipulation to provide demonstrations, but they do not manipulate (or solve) themselves, nor will they do so in the absence of an external dynamic provided by the scientists' questions.

4. Finding New Dimensions and Telling New Stories

4.i Modelling Keynes' *General Theory*: Hicks

In 1937, John Hicks, another British economist, introduced a 'little apparatus', a model in two diagrams (derived from three equations) that grew into the celebrated IS/LM model of the Keynesian system. Hicks first gave his account at a meeting of the Econometric Society in Oxford in 1936, a meeting where those interested in developing statistical and mathematical modes of reasoning into economics had gathered. These included the two economists most closely associated with the development of macro-modelling, the Norwegian economist, Ragnar Frisch (whose 1933 model was discussed above) and Jan Tinbergen, the young Dutch economist who introduced the term "model" into economics, and had by this time produced the first macroeconometric model and fitted it to data for the Dutch economy.[16] Though these two later (in 1969) won the first Nobel Prize in economics for these developments, it was Hicks' diagram that gained longevity as a working object in economics. His model, first developed to represent Keynes' ideas, "became the organizing theoretical apparatus of the emerging discipline of macroeconomics" in the postwar years, and remained a generic tool for macroeconomic analysis.[17]

Hicks' agenda was to find a way to compare Keynes' account of the macroeconomy with the older classical account to pinpoint what was truly innovatory in Keynes' work. To do this he created a model within which he could represent both accounts. He began by denoting with symbols the elements in the Keynesian theory and, with these, constructed a small system of three functional relationships. He produced four sets of these three relations, of which two sets are given here (from his pp. 152 and 153).[18]

$$\text{Classical theory:} \qquad M = kI, \qquad I_x = C(i), \quad I_x = S(i,I)$$
$$\text{Keynes' } General\ Theory: \quad M = L(I, i) \quad I_x = C(i), \quad I_x = S(I)$$

where M is the given quantity of money, I total income and I_x investment, and i the interest rate. Hicks' use of such symbols hardly went further than labelling the terms in the equations and using them to outline verbally his understanding of the existing theories. From this kind of analysis, he claimed that there was nothing particularly new in this second set of these equations – those he took to represent Keynes' *General Theory* – compared to the theory around in Cambridge of the time.

In this kind of Keynesian macroeconomics, it is very difficult to follow the verbal arguments and see what is determining what in any given discussion.[19] It was just such kinds of convoluted verbal reasoning that, continuing in macroeconomics

---

16 This model too had been questioned for historical explanations and simulated for policy options (see chapter 4, Morgan, 1990).

17 For more general accounts of the history of the IS/LM model, see De Vroey and Hoover (2004), particularly their introduction (p. 3 quoted here); and on what was lost as IS/LM became the dominant model, see Backhouse and Laidler (2004) in that volume.

18 The other two sets denote Hicks' version of "Mr Keynes' *special theory*" and the "Treasury View" (Hicks, 1937, p. 152).

19 Indeed, students nowadays find Hicks' original paper as impenetrable as Keynes' book, for the model, and what it might show, are both opaque to them. In contrast, Samuelson's paper holds no horrors for them. This demonstrates rather nicely how both Samuelson (and Meade's) papers can be considered 'modern' in modelling terms, while Hicks' IS-LL diagram became clarified and understood only through much usage and further development by others.

into the 1950s, prompted Newlyn and Phillips to turn macroeconomics into an hydraulic machine (as we saw in Chapter 5). Hicks' reasoning possibilities also proved limited by the deductive resources of his equations and he, like Frisch, Meade, and Samuelson, found the need for a more workable model to make progress in representing the complicated project of Keynes' work and to understand the difference between the two sets of equations – of Keynes and of the classicals. As he said, "Is there really any difference between them, or is the whole thing a sham fight? Let us have recourse to a diagram" (Hicks, 1937, p. 153).

Hicks' diagrammatic model, his figure 1 (left side on Figure 6.3) was not simply a transposition from one form (equations) to another (diagrams), but involved a second move of abstraction in which he moved from the labels and terms (as in the equations) to derive relations from these that revealed more clearly the implications of their connections. The *LL* curve represents, for a given quantity of money, the relation between aggregate income (on the horizontal axis) and the rate of interest (on the vertical axis), drawn from the first equation in the Keynesian system. The *IS* curve came from the two other equations and was drawn to show the relations between income and interest "which must be maintained in order to make saving equal to investment" (p. 153). This derivation of the curves for his diagrammatic model appears an effective conceptual innovation, one that prompted Hicks towards a new analysis.[20] Though he had found nothing new in the equations, this diagrammatic modelling changed the dimension of the representation in a way that enabled him to recognise and define what he took to be the real novelty in Keynes' account:

> Income and the rate of interest are now determined together at *P*, the point of intersection of the curves *LL* and *IS*. They are determined together; just as price and output are determined together in the modern theory of demand and supply. Indeed, Mr. Keynes' innovation is closely parallel, in this respect, to the innovation of the marginalists. The quantity theory tries to determine income without interest, just as the labour theory of value tried to determine price without output; each has to give place to a theory recognising a higher degree of interdependence. (Hicks, 1937, pp. 153–4)

The point here is not whether Hicks had 'the correct interpretation' of Keynes' theory, but that in making the conceptual leap into this new model diagram and answering questions with it, he created a form of Keynesian economics not just for himself but for a generation of economists.

Hicks' attempts to figure out further aspects of Keynes' work prompted him to think about the shape of the *LL* curve and to create his figure 2 (right-hand side of Figure 6.3), where he argued that there was some minimum level of interest rate in practice (a topical issue for the 1930s), and some maximum level of income

---

20 This situation is similar to the way Edgeworth's development of indifference curves in the Box diagram created new conceptual resources (see Chapter 3).

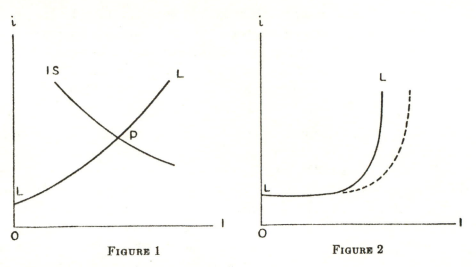

FIGURE 1   FIGURE 2

Figure 6.3. Hicks' IS-LL "Little Apparatus".

Source: J. R. Hicks (April, 1937) "Mr. Keynes and the 'Classics'; A Suggested Interpretation" *Econometrica*, 5:2, 147–159; figures. 1 and 2, p. 153. Reproduced with permission from The Econometric Society.

that could be financed with the given quantity of money. Using this second figure enabled him to compare theories in a way that illuminated their differences. He characterized the classical theory (in its recent Cambridge version) as the situation when the *IS* curve cut the *LL* curve on the rising section to the right: where

> An increase in the inducement to invest will raise the rate of interest, as in the classical theory, but will also have the subsidiary effect in raising income, and therefore employment as well (Mr. Keynes in 1936 is not the first Cambridge economist to have a temperate faith in Public Works). But if the point *P* lies to the left of the *LL* curve, then the *special* form of Mr. Keynes' theory becomes valid. A rise in the schedule of the marginal efficiency of capital only increases employment, and does not raise the rate of interest at all. We are completely out of touch with the classical world. (Hicks, 1937, p. 154, his italics)

The shape of the *LL* curve represented different states of the economic world; the difference in theories came down to where the *IS* curve cut this *LL* curve. If the money supply increases, the *LL* curve moves to the right (see the dotted line on Figure 6.3). But if *P* remains on the left-hand section, then such a monetary policy will fail to change the rate of interest and so fail to restart the economy.

Demonstrations with these curves enabled him to explain why the classical policy response of increasing money in the system would not get the economy out of the Great Depression. But they also showed him why his diagrammatic model and reasoning mode was helpful, for they revealed that the problem was more complex than his initial version of the Keynesian equations suggested. Hicks regarded his diagram almost as a physical piece of apparatus:

> In order to elucidate the relation between Mr. Keynes and the "Classics," we have invented a little apparatus. It does not appear that we have exhausted the uses of that apparatus, so let us conclude by giving it a little run of its own.
>
> With that apparatus at our disposal, we are no longer obliged to make certain simplifications which Mr. Keynes makes in his exposition. (Hicks, 1937, p. 156)

The diagram encouraged him to rethink some of the equations, so he made his investment equation dependent not only on the interest rate but also on income. This version of the equations had the effect of creating a more gradual rising *LL* curve on a new version of the diagram so that the slopes of both curves became critical in determining the effects of changes in any elements in the diagrammatic model.

Hicks had made himself a model that he could work with: one that he could ask questions of and demonstrate answers with, and that enabled him to go beyond the "simplifications" be found in Keynes' book. It enabled him to explain and "elucidate" the differences between the two systems of theory, the classicals versus the Keynesian one. And, it enabled him to tell a story about what happened in Keynes' special case when there was no response of investment to lowering of interest rates. In addition, he used it to work out and tell stories about other outcomes, associating these, wherever possible, with the names of other economists whose positions they represented. For example, he considered the interesting possibility that the *IS* curve might be horizontal, another special case version of the model that he labelled as Wicksell's account. He was able to represent and discuss different theories from different economists quite easily in the world of his little diagram. Finally, he was also able to represent different states of the world using his model, ones that might arguably be relevant for discussing and telling narratives about the real world of the Great Depression.

Despite the many states of the economy he managed to represent, and the multiple economists whose ideas he managed to express as special cases within the model, and the demonstrations that enabled him to show and explain things with his model, Hicks ended by describing his invention as a "skeleton apparatus" for there were all sorts of things that "you cannot get into a curve" (p. 158). Nevertheless, it is because of its flexibility to express lots of different theoretical identities and so be used for different demonstrations that this new IS/LM diagram (it was renamed by Hansen) had such a long life as a model. In some senses it never really died but continued hidden inside policy models even though it fell out of fashion for theorists. And, despite its multiple identities, and multiple users, it has remained firmly attached to Hicks' own name as inventor.

4.ii Demonstrations, Variety, and Fruitfulness

We have seen, with these three different reactions to Keynes' work, how modelling works as a method of enquiry, into both the nature and details of Keynesian theory and into its portrait of the real economy. The answers to the questions that economists raise depend on their model demonstrations, and this is where economists learn new things from using their model that they did not know before, new things about the world in the model that perhaps reflect insight into the world that the model represents for, as Hughes (1997) suggested, "From the behavior of the model we can draw hypothetical conclusions about the world over and above the data that we started with" (p. 331). Of course, these "hypothetical conclusions" are conclusions only about the world of the model and whether they transfer to the world that the model denotes is a very tricky topic to which I return (later and in Chapter 7). It is evident from these three cases that for models to be useful for enquiry, that is, for economists to learn new things from their demonstrations, their models need certain qualities.

First, we have seen in these examples the importance of my argument that models need sufficient resources that can be manipulated to demonstrate or show certain things with the model if they are to be useful as a means of enquiry. They must have sufficient internal dynamic to answer some questions, that is, to make some relevant demonstrations; models that have few resources have very limited potential to produce demonstrations. As we saw, Hicks' little sets of equations did not provide him with the resources or rules of manipulations to do more than characterize the differences between the theories he was investigating. It was only when he moved to a new form of representation, his "little apparatus", that he had a model with sufficient internal dynamic to develop some new insight into questions about Keynes' theory. Samuelson's model, a minimalist model, nevertheless provided the resources, via two different ways of reasoning (simulation and analytical solutions), to explore certain aspects of the Keynesian claims, with results that proved quite surprising. Meade's model – a causal model of the macroeconomy – had the resources for him to develop quite complex accounts of how the macroeconomy he portrayed might behave under a wide range of possible actions. In other words, all these modellers produced different models of Keynes' *General Theory* that we might call 'workable' – they could be put to work to demonstrate certain characteristics, processes, independencies, outcomes, and so forth, often ones that were unexpected or new to the investigator.

Second, size in relation to content matters. Models must be sufficiently small or simple to be manipulable, and yet sufficiently complex or sizeable to embody the kind of resources that allow for fruitful investigation, and so demonstrations that develop new or unexpected findings. Yet models must not be too open-ended; rather they must constrain in some degree, otherwise their demonstrations may not be productive. Samuelson's models produced almost too many outcomes: any pattern in aggregate behaviour seemed consistent with his model.

Third, to generate interesting answers to questions in these demonstrations, there must be some economic subject matter content in the workable resources. We saw first in Frisch's case how the physical (non-economic) stories shaped the bits of his model, but that he required an economic understanding of his model before he could interpret the resulting demonstrations in a meaningful economic way. For Meade, Samuelson, and Hicks, the internal dynamic already had economic content so that it could be immediately reflected in the narratives told with the model demonstrations. These economics resources were based on time relations (Samuelson), on causal orderings (Meade), or on possibilities of alternative inter-pretations (Hicks). And critically perhaps, these resources might be at a different conceptual level than those portrayed in the verbal language theorizing as we saw in Hicks' IS/LM diagram.

Fourth, models give rewarding demonstrations when they embody the kinds of resources that create a certain amount of variety. Hicks' model had the resources for showing, and allowing him to compare, the different theories of many economists. Samuelson's model had the resources to demonstrate an extraordinary different range of behavioural outcomes from the same stimulus of government expendi-ture, with very different implications. The variety in Meade's model was developed in the range of behavioural or causal accounts and policy analyses he could make with the same model. The possibility of variation allows explorations of different theoretical positions, of the relative importance of different assumptions, and of different world situations and behaviours.

Making demonstrations is the modelling activity that enables economists to find things in the world of the model that are new to them, that are not previously recognised, or not fully understood. Clearly it is useful if a model demonstrates things that accord what the economist already knows, but the payoff from model-ling lies in the unexpected outcomes, the demonstrations that surprise the econo-mist (a topic to which I return in Chapter 7). And while these cases of Keynesian modelling enable us to recognise the characteristics that made these particular models useful for enquiry in terms of fruitfulness and variety of the demonstra-tion possibilities, there is no metric that allows us to recognise or guarantee these possibilities in advance. While it is probably self-evident that the possibilities of the Newlyn-Phillips machine (of Chapter 5) are of an almost endless variety because of the nature and mixture of the resources in both hydraulics and econom-ics, it would probably not have been easy to predict that the Edgeworth Box (of Chapter 3) would have been a fruitful model. In its initial version, it does not look to have much workability or variety of applications as an instrument of enquiry, yet it developed into a kind of nutshell model that has somehow come to represent the neoclassical system of theory as a whole (see Chapter 10). Similarly, no one could possibly have predicted the manifold usefulness, fruitfulness, and long working life of Hicks' IS-LL diagram at its birth, despite Hicks' ability to use it to demonstrate aspects of many different versions of macroeconomics.

While it is difficult to predict that a model will create new outcomes, or show fruitfulness and variety – it is rather easier to recognise these qualities *post hoc* from the narratives that go along with their usage. Narrative is the place where these demonstrations are interpreted within the world of the model and in terms of the things in the world that the model describes. The interpretations are not where novelty lies; novelty and learning come in the things demonstrated with the models, and narratives are the way to understand their importance and relevance in answering the questions asked.

5. Capturing the Heart of the Matter with Narratives

Storytelling is not just a curious feature of Meade's and Samuelson's work, for it is a matter of observation that economists commonly tell stories or narratives when they carry out investigations with models. And though this practice is now mostly evident in their spoken rather than written arguments, it remains an essential element of seminars and explanations using models. Commentators especially interested in the practices of economists have discussed the prevalence of stories; for example, McCloskey made the following observation on the rhetoric of economists:

> Economists, especially theorists, are for ever spinning 'parables' or telling 'stories'. The word 'story' has in fact come to have a technical meaning in economics, though usually spoken in seminars rather than written in papers. It means an extended example of the reasoning underlying the mathematics, often a simplified version of the situation in the real world that the mathematics is meant to characterize. (McCloskey, 1983, p. 505)

The account of such model stories in this chapter suggests that they are not primarily a rhetorical practice but an epistemic one, and perhaps this is why economists remain uneasy about recognising the role of stories in their modelling work. Perhaps they think that economic models, particularly mathematical models – that is, 'scientific' models, ought to be governed solely by deductive or mathematical modes of arguing. Yet when economists use models, they typically also make use of this other logic – the logic of narrative. The source of the tension may lie in a confusion over the role of models in economics. Recognising – as I pointed out in Chapter 1 – that economic modelling is not primarily a method of proof, but rather a method of enquiry, in large part dissolves that tension.

To make these inquiries with models valuable, economists seek to capture the heart of the matter in two senses, in two domains: the world of the model and the world that the model represents or denotes. Model questions are designed to prompt explorations of the relationships represented in the model. And since economic models are not only pieces of mathematics, but also pieces of economics, so their demonstrations need to be interpreted, understood, and explained in economic terms. These model narratives provide not only the means to understand the economic world of the model, but also to link the model with the economics of the world.

5.i Narratives and Identity in the World of the Model

How do narratives relate to enquiries into the world of the model? What do narratives teach economists? Nancy Cartwright has suggested that models are "fables" in their relationship to scientific laws and "parables" in relation to the world that they purport to represent.[21] Following the first of these claims, she describes models as

---

21 See Cartwright (2010). A fable is usually defined as "a short story with a moral", and a parable as "a story used to illustrate a moral lesson" (OED definitions).

fitting out laws, just as a fable fits out an abstractly stated moral as a way for us to explain or fully appreciate that moral.[22] This seems an apt description of the way that Frisch's modelling went on, with two general theses that might together be taken as the scientific equivalent of a moral: an abstract law that economists thought governed the economic cycle (a damped harmonic process) and an empirical law that described their data (maintained, but disturbed harmonic movements). With the help of story-analogies both these elements were fitted out in the model's construction – in the economic hypothesis about the rocking horse (the propagating mechanism) and in the description of stochastic processes inherent in the small boy with the club (the impulses). Frisch's fitting out, and fitting together, of these elements in his model, and demonstrations with his model, showed why an adequate business cycle model needs both kinds of 'laws': the ones from theory, and the ones that describe empirical characteristics and how they could be made to work together. In fitting out these two laws in the shape of the model, he produced a "new recipe" (see Boumans, 1999) with tremendous demonstrative power and so value for other economists who came to understand and appreciate both the difficulties of modelling business cycles – and so the neatness of his solution. Or, to put the same point in another way, other scientists learnt from the "mere existence" of Frisch's model (as Schlimm, 2009, suggests). He *showed* 1930s' economists how to put these abstract elements together and fit them out to make their own meaningful models that could be used to tell business cycle narratives, and enabled Tinbergen to fashion the first macroeconometric model.

We could equally well describe the way that Meade, Samuelson, and Hicks developed their models as a process of 'fitting out' Keynes' *General Theory*. His theory (or laws), like the moral of a fable, were not hidden in one of their models to be revealed by it, but were already given by him and written into their models by these younger economists. But in these cases, we should ask not just what was learnt from the fitting out process of making their models, but what was understood from *using* their models. And we might answer, recalling Samuelson's demonstrations, that "anything can happen"! But this judgement ignores the role and power of the narratives that come from using such Keynesian models, which is where economists really came to understand and appreciate Keynes' ideas. The problem was well described by Solow, who learnt Keynesian economics from such "explanatory articles" that turned Keynes book into models:

> *The General Theory* was and is a very difficult book to read. It contains several distinct lines of thought that are never quite made mutually consistent. ..... These articles reduced one or two of those trains of thought to an intelligible *model*, which for us became "Keynesian economics" .... [an]

22 See Cartwright's 1991 paper, where she argues that "Fables transform the abstract into the concrete .... they function like models in physics" (p. 57). This is consistent with her simulacrum account (1983) in which models make the link between a prepared description of the phenomena and the laws that are thought to govern the phenomena.

illustration of the clarifying power of the model-building method. (Solow, 1997, p. 48, his italics)

These models clarified Keynes' theory, and they did so by fitting out the same general theory in different ways (just as different fables can be created to fit out the same moral). But crucially those different models also produced different kinds and pieces of information from the narratives associated with *their usage*. By working through the full range of more particular Keynesian stories that could be told by *using* their models, each with specific details, they learnt things about the Keynesian system that they did not know in advance. For example, even though Samuelson knew the equations of his simple little Keynesian model, he still learnt lots of unexpected and complicated things about that Keynesian model world, including that it was compatible with some implausible and bizarre stories as well as some meaningful and plausible ones. The same kind of comments might be made with respect to Meade and Hicks and their Keynesian models. No doubt, these economists made their models in order to understand the Keynesian system, but they came to that understanding not primarily from creating those models, but by using them to tell a variety of stories.

This focus on particulars is just what we might expect from Cartwright's account of fables and their morals, for she agrees with Gotthold Lessing's claim that "the general only becomes graphic, or visualizable, in the particular" (Cartwright, 1991, p. 59).[23] This is an epistemic claim: just as the fable provides the particulars to understand the moral, so here, the scientists comes to grasp the general or abstract in the model by working through the particular narratives that can be associated with it.[24] That these particulars are given and found in narrative form is flagged in the parallel field of law, where Neil MacCormick argues that it is stories that enable one to understand what more abstract legal statutes mean:

> Undoubtedly, when one reads and tries to make sense of a complex statutory text, or a legislative proposal, it can be difficult to see what it means, unless you try to figure out how it might work in practice. You come to understand it by figuring hypothetical situations it would cover, that is by figuring stories that match the text. (MacCormick, 2005 p. 208)

Placing stories – not just particulars – as the vehicle for understanding a piece of law resonates with the role of narratives in the practical usage of economic modelling. Think of Meade's task of taking the reader through all the different effects of

---

23 In contrast, Hayden White claimed, for the narratives of history that "We understand the specific story being told about the facts when we identify the generic story-type of which the particular story is an instantiation" (1975, p. 58); see Morgan (2001) for further discussions of narratives in science.

24 As Cartwright (1991, p. 61) points out, these particulars might still be abstract in relation to other more concrete levels, just as Frisch's model-based insight into business cycle data in general was more abstract than Tinbergen's statistical model of the Great Depression. See also Grüne-Yanoff (2009) and my Chapters 7.2.iii, 9.4.iii and 10.3 on the importance of the levels at which models operate.

a couple of small changes prompted by his question about the hypothetical world in the model: communicating and understanding the outcomes from a complicated eight-equation set of relationships works rather easily with a narrative mode. Think of Samuelson, who was able to summarise the variety of output patterns from a couple of relationships in a few succinct narratives. These narratives report the model demonstrations and their outcomes. These model narratives were neither 'merely heuristic' nor 'just rhetoric' – important though heuristics and rhetoric are – but the way economists came to understand what lies at the heart of the Keynesian system.

At the start of the chapter, I showed how economists sometimes use stories in creating their models as Frisch with his rocking horse model. More usually, narratives appear with model usage and enable economists to figure out the characteristics and nature of the economic world in their model, as we saw with Meade, Samuelson, and Hicks. In carrying out model explorations and providing stories in answers to their questions, these economist-scientists explored the behavioural characteristics of the models they had made. From these they learnt the possible processes and outcomes compatible with the mathematical and economic content of their models. By identifying the specific stories that could be told with their models (and the ones that they could not tell), these economists came to understand the identity of the world that had been captured in their models.[25]

5.ii Model Narratives and Making Sense of the Economic World

What can models tell us about the world we live in? In *creating* the model, economists represent or denote the situation in the world in such a way as to incorporate their theoretical claims or hypotheses about the world (e.g., Frisch's beliefs about cycles or the Keynesian account of the macroeconomy). But these denotations are not very informative, for a diagram or an equation on its own can explain nothing, or at least very little, about how the world works.[26] If the activity of denoting or model-making is the step of making connections *from* the world *to* the model, it is the activity of using models to tell narratives that not only enables economists

---

25 The example of the Edgeworth Box diagram (Chapter 3) suggests that some models may carry many different identities. This box has been used for the last 100 years to tell stories about consumers in exchange situations, about firms and production decisions, about countries and trade policy, about welfare questions, and so forth (see Humphrey, 1996). The basic form of the model remains the same but the interpretation of the elements differs according to the domain, and the stories that are told alter. Knowing that a piece of economics uses an Edgeworth Box diagram does not even enable you to predict the domain of the economics, let alone the story it will be used to tell.

26 For example, economists can denote aggregate consumption in the world with a C, and then interpret C to refer back to aggregate consumption in the world; similarly with the consumption function. This is basically the way that Gibbard and Varian (1978) understand stories: as an interpretation of the assumptions, terms, and structure of the model, rather than of the demonstrations made with the model, so there is no reason in their account why these interpretations need a narrative form.

to understand their theories (e.g., the Keynesian system) *but at the same time may* form the connections from the model *back* to the world. While the validity of such *back inference* from models will feature in the discussions of later chapters, here in this chapter, I want to focus on the way that these correspondence links are made. In model usage, *narratives provide the possible correspondence links between the demonstrations made with the model and the events, processes and behaviour of the world that the model represents.* Narratives may show how to apply the model to the world, and to offer potential insights, understandings, or even explanations of how the world (that the model represents) works.[27]

At first sight, the modelling efforts by Hicks, Samuelson, and Meade were solely enquiries into the world of the model. But for any economist of the day, who had just lived through the Great Depression, their model explorations spoke also to the real economic problems of the period. Hicks' enquiry can be understood to be asking not only how different theories expressed in the model compared but also whether the real economy behaves like the classical system or was better characterized by the newer theory. Meade's enquiry could be understood as an exploration of policy options for the Great Depression. The patterns found by Samuelson's arithmetic simulations indicated, for example, that Keynesian policies based on the two factors determining growth in the Keynesian model world might produce not only growth in economic activity, but also cycles, or other more unexpected kinds of economic behaviour. For economists, these model stories were not just stories about the Keynesian theory, but models designed to tell Keynesian stories about the real world.

These model narratives function at a certain level: they construct a version of events that is relatively simplified but yet also detailed in some respects. Elsewhere in this book (Chapter 7) I have described this level as generic – for example, Hicks' diagrams showed differently sloped curves to describe the kinds of relationships that might occur in the world. But the point I want to make here is somewhat different. Yes, the models discussed in this chapter were each one created to be more specific and limited in certain respects than Keynes' *General Theory*, and Meade, Samuelson, and Hicks consciously picked out different sections of that work to form the central elements of their model as the most relevant for study. But in *usage*, we saw that the stories that were told with these different models about the world in those models were even more particular, more detailed, and more differentiated. For example, Meade could tell stories about complex combinations of events that could arise in his model usage, and describe those particular events in numerical form. Samuelson too could tell a range of very different, but highly particular, stories about the world in his model, qualitative stories that depended on subtly different patterns of reaction as he varied the numbers to see what the impact of government policies might be. With this range of patterns, he could tell

---

27 A parallel example is the way that chemical formulae were first used with short narrative devices to explain the details of how chemical reactions actually took place: see Ursula Klein (1999).

stories about specific events that seemed likely, such as what happened when the government withdrew its spending, as well as ones that seemed very unlikely, such as the economy either collapsing to nothing or growing exponentially!

But the events of the world we live in are not only particular, they are also concrete, so that narratives must function not only to link the more general to the more particular, but also to link the particular and the concrete. By linking the general to the particular and the particular to the concrete, narratives provide explanatory services for an economic science based on models.[28]

There are two different ways to understand how narratives work in a scientific context. On the first account, we can characterize the role of model narratives as stories about the world that the model represents by seeing them as a linking device, a device that links demonstrations from the abstract, generic level, of the model to the concrete particulars of the world. We can see *how* and *why* this is might be so by looking at a parallel, once again in the case of law, where interpretations of events made by lawyers have to bridge between abstract legal and everyday discourses. They typically depend on narratives or stories to make their interpretations comprehensible: stories operate or function as that bridge:

> Stories thus function not as some kind of optional, aesthetically-pleasing form, but as a response to the cognitive problems of abstraction and information overload. (Jackson, 1988, p. 64)

Notice that there are two cognitive problems here that have to be overcome together in making the narrative function effectively – the abstraction (of the law) and the information overload of the concrete and specific details of the facts and events in question.[29] The modelling activity of the economist might be seen as like that of the detective who first puts together a case using various hypotheses and an array of disjointed facts, or the lawyer who later must construct that same case so that it will pass muster with a jury. Such stories necessarily have degrees of flexibility and of constraint in their construction. The economist, like the detective, has ideas, theories, or hypotheses about how some set of events occurred, and an array of bits of knowledge about the world, but is not sure which bits fit together and how they do so. Modelling might be seen as a way for economists to try out their hypotheses and solve the fitting together problem. So, in this account, narratives operate as a cognitive bridge between the abstract and still relatively general economic model with its demonstrations and the much more detailed accounts of the concrete events of the real economic world. In making these correspondence links, narratives offer potential explanations for those real-world events.[30]

---

28 The standard account of how explanation works in science is by figuring out which scientific law 'covers' any particular phenomenon or event, and then arguing that the general law 'explains' that event. For a flavour of more recent discussions, see, for example, the essays in de Regt et al. (2009).

29 Jackson (1988) reports experiments that suggest that both overly simple stories and highly detailed and complicated ones are equally problematic in making a case persuasive.

30 A fuller discussion of the explanations offered by models in economics is found in Chapter 9.

Alternatively, the explanatory function of narratives, and the level of account of the world that narratives offer, can be understood as an epistemic claim, rather than as a cognitive one. Louis Mink argues that narrative helps us to understand the world *not* because it *links* the general and particular but rather because it offers a distinctive form and level of understanding that *sits in-between* the general theory and the fully detailed account of the world and does so by configuring the events of world so that they can be understood.

> On the one hand, there are all the occurrences of the world – at least all that we may directly experience or inferentially know about – in their concrete particularity. On the other is an ideally theoretical understanding of those occurrences that would treat each as nothing other than a replicable instance of a systematically interconnected set of generalizations. But between these extremes, narrative is the form in which we make comprehensible the many successful interrelationships that are comprised by a career. (Mink, 1978, p. 132)

In this second account of narrative, there is no appeal to the abstract or general theoretical account in seeing how models might function to make sense of, or explain, the events of the world (as in the standard account of scientific explanation).[31] Nor do narratives pretend to be a complete and exhaustive description of events in the world. The focus here is on the understanding narratives offer, and the kind of comprehension that they provide. On this account, model narratives are not a special kind of story, nor do they play a special role, nor are they a ground-level version of something more general. Rather narratives, wherever they are found, are accounts that configure – they make sense of or explain materials – at an intervening level between complete and exhaustive detail and full systematic generalization.

Whether we think of narrative as a playing a cognitive bridging role or providing a configuring account, it is the qualities and the criteria that the narrative form brings to explanations of the world that are used to judge them. MacCormick (2005) suggests that good narratives need to show both 'consistency' and 'coherence', qualities that are as important in the sciences as in the field of law. Consistency refers to the characteristic that the facts do not contradict each other just as, for economists, the assumptions of a model must not contradict each other. Coherence refers to a positive feature, namely that narrative makes a series of events hang together. We expect coherence in a narrative whether in fictional stories or in the factual accounts of law and history.[32] Coherent stories both suppose a certain amount of complexity and impose causal connections onto a set of disjointed elements: a coherent narrative is one that fits apparently unconnected things together, puts

31 See footnote 28.
32 I thank Jon Adams here for several helpful discussions and his insights into the functions of narrative. In addition, there are interesting questions about the nature of the causality involved with narratives, and their inherent ambiguity over whether relations in them are ones of time, causal necessity, or contingency (ambiguities that are consistent with the ways that economists think about economic relations; see Morgan, 2001).

things in order, fills in gaps, and makes sense of the relations of people and events. This might be termed the logic of narrative explanation, not in terms of a literary or linguistic analysis, but in terms of its epistemic role in science: narratives put together materials in ways designed to make sense of events in the world. A coherent model narrative *about the world* offers possible explanations of the world, not explanations of possible worlds.[33]

Models in economics offer the same kind of explanatory services that planetary motion models offered to early astronomers in showing them how the elements of the universe that they observed fit together into a systematic account. Models show economists, for example, how all the elements of the Keynesian system work together, or how both the multiplier and accelerator might together create economic growth for the world. But, in using small abstract economic models to get a grip on their concrete economic world, it is the coherence of these narrative-based explanations that serve to pull disparate elements together, and to provide accounts of the world. Economists don't expect these narratives to be exactly true to every last detail of any particular concrete events of the world. If they were, they would probably not be good stories. But they trust that their models will capture some of the heart of the matter, and that by telling such stories, they try to reconnect their simple models with the facts of the messy economic world we all live in.

5.iii Narrative as a Testing Bed for Models

Economists use narratives as an informal test of the validity of the model, with criteria that suggest in various ways why and how they find their models useful. As we have seen from the examples of Keynesian models and their usage in this chapter, model narratives function *both to take apart and explore the world in the model, and to put together and make coherent accounts of the world that the model represents*. This double function may account for their endemic quality in economics, but it does make it more difficult to figure out what economists' own criteria for their model narratives might be. It seems that some models are considered better than others because they can be used to tell better stories, so that the judgement of models relies on judging the narratives. Hints about this are found in the kind of reflective, but nonanalytical, accounts that economists occasionally give of their own practice that recognise the importance of storytelling. For example, Krugman, in autobiographical mode, noted

> The models I wrote down that winter and spring were incomplete, if one demanded of them that they specify exactly who produced what. And yet they told meaningful stories. (Krugman, 1993, p. 26)

33 This is an important distinction: other commentators prefer to think of models offering explanations of possible worlds (e.g., Rappoport, 1989) as a way to get around the problem of "unrealistic assumptions", an issue that goes back to Milton Friedman (1953).

Or Franklin Fisher, commenting on the literature of industrial economics:

> At present, oligopoly theory consists of a large number of stories, each one an anecdote describing what might happen in some particular situation. Such stories can be very interesting indeed. (Fisher, 1989, p. 118)

The notion that the quality of model narratives provide an informal test of a model lurks in such comments. They suggest that narratives attached to models have qualities beyond those of consistency and coherence explored in the last section. Two terms – 'meaningful' and 'plausible' – capture the sense of how economists think about this matter.

'Meaningful' is a quality that refers to narratives told about *the world of the model*. This has two aspects for economists. On the one hand, model stories need to be theoretically meaningful. It is not just that a model has to have consistent assumptions (the consistency check we saw paralleled in legal narratives), but that a model must also have characteristics that are meaningful in terms of economists' theories, which, of course, has implications for the narratives that can be told. For example, business cycle models are meaningful only if they can generate cycles and, in Frisch's period, this meant damped cycles, just as later Meade needed to check that his model had equilibrium tendencies.

On the other hand, the narratives need to be economically interesting in the behaviour they reveal in the world in their model. Economists would even prefer that these narrated behaviours and explanations are a little surprising, for economists want to get more out of their modelling than they know to start with. (Narratives that just repeat back what they already know are not very interesting.) Those that reveal some strange elements, or surprising behaviour, or unusual connections and effects, are more interesting to the economist, and so may be more meaningful for them. Narratives of bizarre events might be problematic, but are often equally useful in revealing things about the model and thus re-enforce the ways in which narratives provide a test-bed for the model.

'Plausible', in contrast, captures the idea that the stories map adequately to certain characteristics of the phenomena in *the real world* that the models aim to describe and that economists seek to explain. To get a useful narrative test of the plausibility of a model, the model users first have to make sensible choices about what specific phenomena of the world their model might explain and then consider how to connect their model with those specifics. That is, they need to decide where to start their tale and the order of solving the model and to carry through the demonstrations that provide the narratives with care and attention – as we saw with Meade, Samuelson, and Hicks. In other words, they first need to ask plausible questions of their small mathematical models before they can tell stories that are plausible about the events of world. But the term 'plausible' suggests not only that the world of the economic model has been made to fit (in some loose way) the world the model represents, but also that it offers some insight into the economics of why it is as it is. For example, Frisch's model was not only meaningful in economic terms (with its damped cycles and equilibrium tendency), but also plausible in terms that fit the world (it could produce cycles that fit the data pattern of the world), and that could be explained by the way innovations came into the economy (rather than by its mechanical pendulum analogy).

Economists do not take the plausibility of narratives as a proof, or even a sign, of the truthfulness of a model. Yet, naturalistic accounts of economic modelling (as mine here and others discussed in this section) have noticed how storytelling about the world often invokes shades of inference, as well as explanation, in the way economists think about these stories. This is reflected in Gibbard and Varian's (1978) account of "casual application": the way economists apply mathematical models to events in the world in contrast to the serious application of econometric models. In that latter domain, the models are applied to data from the world, and are validated with statistical testing. But in the domain of mathematical and diagrammatic models, as we have seen, the narrative forms the place where a looser 'casual' mode of connection of the model to the world goes on and the criteria of validity are similarly loose.[34] But they are not absent. So, economists such as Hicks, Samuelson, and Meade did not claim to learn from using a model whether Keynes' *General Theory* is generally true for the world. They did learn – from enquiry into the world of the model – how to use the elements of his theory to tell meaningful Keynesian narratives of kinds of events (depressions), and to give plausible narrative explanations of particular concrete events that happened in their real world, such as the Great Depression. Using such models narrative, they could also suggest how Keynesian policies might work in the world that the model represents, though the looseness of the criteria of plausibility always make it doubtful, difficult, and potentially dangerous, to use these little mathematical models to intervene directly in the economic world.[35]

When storytelling with a model succeeds in offering accounts that are both meaningful in their theoretical terms and plausible, and perhaps striking, in terms of the explanations these narratives offer for real-world events, economists are rather pleased with their efforts. Such a model may be understood by economists as one that has already offered suggestions about the way that the economic world might work, and might be used to generate additional insights. But what counts as meaningful and plausible both change over time.

Consider first what might counts as meaningful for economists. Whereas the primary theoretical criteria for the macro-models that we saw economists using in the interwar period was their equilibrium behaviour, by the second half of the twentieth century, such an aggregate model also needed adequate 'micro-foundations' before it could count as meaningful. Thus, Gibbard and Varian in 1978 noted that economists liked models that were meaningful in theory terms *and* that offered an explanation of some easily noticed phenomena by some simple, but plausible, behaviour of individuals:

---

34 Exactly how these narratives about the world are matched to the events of the world will become much clearer in the discussion of game theory in Chapter 9.
35 See Cartwright (2009).

In some cases, an aspect of the world (such as price dispersal, housing segregation, and the like) is noticed, and certain aspects of the micro-situation are thought perhaps to explain it; a model is then constructed to provide the explanation. If the model turns out to have striking features, a casual search for economic situations with those features may then be conducted. In either kind of case, no measurement that goes beyond casual observation is involved. (Gibbard and Varian, 1978, p. 672)

MacCormick labels a narrative that offers such a kind of explanation "credible", meaning that it is not only coherent, but also provides a satisfactory "causal or motivational account of the whole complex of events" (2005, pp. 226–7). Robert Sugden, a microeconomist and reflexive commentator of modelling practises in modern economics, has the same sense, calling such model worlds that succeed in capturing something of an observed pattern of a phenomenon by a simple behavioural rule followed by individuals: "credible worlds".[36] Sugden's paradigmatic example to exemplify this notion is Thomas Schelling's (1978) model of segregated housing: an analogical model, wherein the 'individuals' are treated as pieces on a checkerboard, each piece's behaviour follows certain simple rules, and the outcome is a pattern of pieces in which the colours are segregated. Sugden judges such a model world as a "credible but counterfactual world(s), *paralleling* the real world" (Sugden, 2009, p. 4), where the judgement of credibility hinges on the "sense that it [the model world] is compatible with what we know, or think we know, about the general laws governing events in the real world" (p.18). He offers, as an analogy for this sense of credibility, the feeling we experience from reading "realistic novels" (2009, p. 18) – which brings us back to both plausibility and narrative.[37]

But the licence for inferring that a model narrative parallels the real world, that is that the model is credible, as with Gibbard and Varian, hangs on a pretty loose sense of resemblance, or similarity, in the outcomes. In the Schelling case, the similarity lies in the outcome checkerboard pattern that mimics, or 'looks like' the ones we observe in the world of segregated neighbourhoods. But for Sugden, the economically striking thing that he notices about this parallel world is that the checkerboard segregated outcome is *not* the result of an rule based on *strong* colour preferences but only on *mild* preferences in individual behaviour of the pieces.

---

36 See Sugden (2000, 2009). Sugden's "credible worlds" account of modelling is in some ways quite close to Gibbard and Varian's account (1978) and in many ways compatible with my own here: all three are practice-based accounts, and discuss the informal way that models are judged. But it is not quite clear that "credible worlds" are a different kind of model, or that Sugden offers a different philosophical account of how models are made and used. For example, Schelling's model-making may be understood in the tradition of analogical modelling (where the mimicking is both at the level of the simple rules of games and of the phenomenal outcome), a characterization that offers a strong contrast with the idealization accounts of modelling (associated with Cartwright and Mäki); see my Chapter 1. However, the possibility to explain phenomena with a credible world model still needs an account of how models are used, and still relies on similarity claims to sustain inference however loosely these claims are made.

37 See also Grüne-Yanoff (2009).

This in turn reveals why the model is especially interesting for the economist: it is not just that the model narrative satisfies economists' current preferences for good, theory-based, explanations in that it has micro-behaviour creating an aggregate level phenomenon, but that the particular assumption about individual behaviour needed to get the result (mild colour/racial preferences of the pieces) is appealingly unexpected, but yet credible.

We have seen that the elements in a narrative that make a model count as *meaningful* are contingent on local scientific knowledge: they depend on what economists of a certain time take to be a good explanation of human behaviour or of the behaviour of the whole economy; they depend on the theories and assumptions of the time and place and group of economists involved. But this is equally so of the *plausibility* of models in relation to the world, for what counts as plausible depends in part on the particular events to be explained. Where Depression-era model narratives were plausible stories for the 1930s, and Keynesian stories told with models were seen as plausible to many economists and policy makers and the public during the 1950s and 1960s, they came to be seen as implausible during the stagflation of the 1970s, only to be resurrected, in certain respects, in the economic crisis at the end of the first decade of the twenty-first century. So what constitutes plausibility, like meaningfulness, is by no means a stable or universal criterion.[38] In part, this is of course because, as we know from the history of economic science: economic theories, ideas, evidence, and methods change – just as for any other science. But we also find from historians of what happens in the economy (economic historians) that their subject matter is not necessarily stable – economies develop; there are crises, new phenomena to be explained, and old ones to be reevaluated. Plausibility, like meaningfulness, depends on both content and context.[39]

These changing judgements of plausibility in modelling reflect the in-between level at which model narratives offer explanations, between general laws and everyday particulars, between the abstract and concrete levels. Model accounts are designed to be more specific in content than laws, so they are regularly adapted to fit new problems or new phenomena. At the same time, new theories and new abstract concepts prompt changes in the character and content of models.

In addition, the notion of what even counts as plausible is moulded in a much more general way by the epistemic genre – of modelling – within which economists operate. In Chapter 1 (Section 3), I explained how individual branches of the sciences adopt particular modes of reasoning (modelling, laboratory experiment, statistical reasoning, etc.) that form the context within which certain kinds of arguments seem reasonable and right, and so plausible. As I also pointed out there, this means that the knowledge obtained in each branch is relative to the mode of doing science, but that each of these modes of doing science is considered

---

38 Thanks again to Jon Adams for helping me think this issue through.
39 See Hawthorn (1991) on the notion of "plausible worlds" for the social scientist.

valid. Modelling forms this broader context within which economic models are judged plausible.

In other words, the effectiveness of model narratives in 'explaining' the world, depends upon a lot of implicit and explicit, time and place dependent, science-based knowledge that is both conceptual and empirical, both historical and theoretical as well as methodological. Models are 'tested' *against* this knowledge *within* the accepted community norms of scientific argument with models, and found meaningful, plausible, and credible, or found wanting. This situation seems to be not incompatible with Cartwright's (2010) idea that while models are "fables" in relation to laws, they are "parables" in relation to the world. Unlike fables, the moral of a parable is not written into the story but has to be drawn out of it. Conceived as a parable, the meaning of a model for the 'target system' – the real world the scientist is trying to understand – is a matter for interpretation and has to be drawn out of it, with the help of other information, theory, concepts, and things economists already know about the world: the contingent scientific knowledge. But with parables, as with fables earlier, *the narrative form really matters*. Narratives are not just the vehicle for drawing out those interpretations, for narratives bring qualities and criteria of their own. For economists, good model narratives have to be consistent and meaningful with respect to the world in the model and they have to be coherent, plausible, and even credible with respect to the world that the model represents. These criteria for narratives are the means by which economists test out the quality of their models: what counts as a good model depends on the good qualities of the narratives that can be told with it.

6. Where Next?

It is a nice paradox of the way models are used that a humanistic notion – narrative or storytelling – is critical to the way that models are used as a mode of enquiry in economic science whether the model narrative is a story about the world portrayed in the model or a correspondence story about the real world, past, present, or future. Narratives are evident both in enquiries into the somewhat abstract world of the model as much as in enquiries with the model into the more particular and concrete world we live in. The discussion of narratives here has identified two elements that need further investigation in the following chapters.

Following the first track, I follow up my observation that narratives are used to explore the world in the model by telling stories about more particular kinds of cases and situations than are provided for in more general theories or laws. As we have seen, with slightly different questions or slightly different arrangements or slightly different values in the model – narratives provide different outcomes for that world in the model. An unintended side effect of such model usage turns out to be the provision of classificatory services alongside the explanatory services. These two outcomes of model usage – of particularity in terms of the levels of explanation that models offer, and the way that leads to classification – are first taken up in Chapter 7 and, then, more strongly but in a different kind of way, in Chapter 9. In that latter chapter, I also follow up my investigations into narratives in the context of game theory, where narratives are found to play an even more critical role in model reasoning.

On a different track, I have suggested here that model narratives offer some kind of inferential possibilities. This interpretation rests not only on the way that economists place reliance on the credibility and plausibility of their model stories, but even more so on the demonstrations that occur in model usage and that are paralleled in model naratives. As we saw in this chapter, a model demonstration is the result of a manipulation by the scientist, a manipulation that may equally be redescribed as a mode of experiment but one with more limited possibilities of inference. This interpretation of model reasoning is explored in Chapter 7 in the context of supply and demand models. The mode of demonstration is even more obviously an experimental mode when we come to the model simulations of Chapter 8. This leads me to consider several ways in which judging the validity of model results might be understood as questions of inference.

Acknowledgement

This chapter was originally written at Nuffield College, Oxford, during my period in residence as the Norman Chester Senior Research Fellow, Autumn 1997, for presentation at a conference at Erasmus University, Rotterdam, November, 1997. It circulated in revised form as a University of Amsterdam Working Paper in 1999 and was published, more or less in that form as Morgan (2001). Since then, this chapter has lost some of the literary materials on narrative, but gained those on law, along with the discussion of the steps of model usage (from Morgan, 2002) – and so it gained Sections 2, 3iii, 4, and 5.iii. I thank the Warden, Fellows, and Students at Nuffield for their hospitality and many discussions of the role of models and my NAKE students (classes of 1997 and 1999) for pertinent questions when I taught the topic. I thank participants at the Rotterdam conference, as well as at subsequent seminars at Nuffield College, Oxford, at Groningen, at the WRR (Dutch Scientific Council for Government Policy) in the Hague, and at the HES meeting in Montreal; and Ben Gales, Roger Backhouse, Deirdre McCloskey, Margaret Morrison, Harro Maas, and Nancy Cartwright for their comments. I thank Till Grüne for research assistance for the revised version of the chapter and Jon Adams for helpful discussions on the nature of narrative.

References

Andvig, Jens Christopher (1991) "Verbalism and Definitions in Interwar Theoretical Macroeconomics". *History of Political Economy*, 23, 431–55.

Backhouse, Roger E. And David Laidler (2004) "What Was Lost with IS-LM". In Michel De Vroey and Kevin D. Hoover (eds), *The IS-LM Model: Its Rise, Fall and Strange Persistence* (pp. 25–56). Annual Supplement to *History of Political Economy*, Vol. 36. Durham, NC: Duke University Press.

Barnett, Vincent (2006) "Chancing an Interpretation: Slutsky's Random Cycles Revisited". *European Journal for the History of Economic Thought*, 13:3, 411–32.

Barthes, Roland (1982) "Introduction to the Structural Analysis of Narratives". In S. Sontag (ed), *A Roland Barthes Reader* (pp. 251–95). London: Vintage.

Boumans, Marcel (1999) "Built-in Justification". In Mary S. Morgan and Margaret Morrison (eds), *Models as Mediators: Perspectives on Natural and Social Science* (pp. 66–96). Cambridge: Cambridge University Press.

(2005) *How Economists Model the World to Numbers*. London: Routledge.

Cartwright, Nancy (1983) *How the Laws of Physics Lie*. Oxford: Clarendon.

(1991) "Fables and Morals". *The Aristotelian Society*, Supplementary Volume 65, 55–68.

(2009) "If No Capacities Then No Credible Worlds. But Can Models Reveal Capacities?" *Erkenntnis*, 70:1, 45–58.

(2010) "Models: Parables v Fables". In R. Frigg and M. Hunter (eds), *Beyond Mimesis and Convention: Representation in Art and Science* (pp. 19–31). New York: Springer.

Darity, William and Warrren Young (1995) "IS-LM: An Inquest". *History of Political Economy*, 27, 1–41.

de Regt, H., Leonelli, S., and Eigner, K. (2009) [eds] *Scientific Understanding: A Philosophical Perspective*. Pittsburgh: Pittsburgh University Press.

De Vroey, Michel, and Kevin D. Hoover (2004) [eds] *The IS-LM Model: Its Rise, Fall and Strange Persistence*. Annual Supplement to *History of Political Economy*, Vol. 36. Durham, NC: Duke University Press.

Fisher, Franklin M. (1989) "Games Economists Play: A Noncooperative View". *RAND Journal of Economics*, 20:1, 113–24.

Friedman, Milton (1953) "The Methodology of Positive Economics". In *Essays in Positive Economics* (pp. 3–46). Chicago: University of Chicago Press.

Frigg, Roman (2009) "Models and Fiction". *Synthese*, 172:2, 251–68.

Frisch, Ragnar (1933) "Propagation Problems and Impulse Problems in Dynamic Economics". In *Economic Essays in Honour of Gustav Cassel* (pp. 171–205). London: Allen & Unwin.

Gibbard, Allan and Hal R. Varian (1978) "Economic Models". *The Journal of Philosophy*, 75:11, 664–77.

Goodman, Nelson (1968) *Languages of Art*, 2nd ed, 1976. Cambridge: Hackett.

Grüne-Yanoff, Till (2009) "Learning from Minimal Economic Models". *Erkenntnis*, 70:1, 81–99.

Hartmann, Stephan (1999) "Models and Stories in Hadron Physics". In Mary S. Morgan and Margaret Morrison (eds), *Models as Mediators: Perspectives on Natural and Social Science* (pp. 326–46). Cambridge: Cambridge University Press.

Hawthorn Geoffrey (1991) *Plausible Worlds: Possibility and Understanding in History and the Social Sciences*. Cambridge: Cambridge University Press.

Hicks, John R. (1937) "Mr. Keynes and the "Classics": a Suggested Interpretation". *Econometrica*, 5, 147–59.

Hughes, R. I. G. (1997) "Models and Representation". *Philosophy of Science*, 64, S325–36.

Humphrey, Thomas M. (1996) "The Early History of the Box Diagram". Federal Reserve Board of Richmond. *Economic Review*, 82:1, 37–75.

Ingrao, Bruna and Giorgio Israel (1990) *The Invisible Hand*. Cambridge, MA: MIT Press.

Jackson, Bernard S. (1988) *Law, Fact and Narrative Coherence*. Liverpool: Deborah Charles Publications.

Keynes, John M. (1936) *The General Theory of Employment, Interest and Money*. London: Macmillan.

Klein, Judy L. (1997) *Statistical Visions in Time: A History of Time Series Analysis, 1662–1938*. Cambridge: Cambridge University Press.

Klein, Ursula (1999) "Paper Tools and Techniques of Modelling in Classical Chemistry". In Mary S. Morgan and Margaret Morrison (eds), *Models as Mediators: Perspectives on Natural and Social Science* (pp. 146–67). Cambridge: Cambridge University Press.

Krugman, Paul (1993) "How I Work". *The American Economist*, 37:2, 25–31.

Le Gall, Philippe (2008) "L'Économie est elle une Science *Fiction*? Récit et Fiction en Modélisation Economique et en Art". Unpublished paper, University of Angers.

Louçã, Francisco (2007) *The Years of High Econometrics*. London: Routledge.

Lucas, Robert E. Jr. (2004) "Keynote Address to the 2003 *HOPE* Conference: My Keynesian Education". In Michel De Vroey and Kevin D. Hoover (eds), *The IS-LM Model: Its Rise, Fall and Strange Persistence* (pp. 12–24). Annual Supplement to *History of Political Economy*, Vol. 36. Durham, NC: Duke University Press.

MacCormick, Neil (2005) *Rhetoric and the Rule of Law: A Theory of Legal Reasoning*. Oxford: Oxford University Press.

Mäki, Uskali (1992) "On the Method of Isolation in Economics". In G. Dilworth (ed), *Intelligibility in Science* (pp. 319–54). Studies in the Philosophy of the Sciences and Humanities, Vol. 26. Amsterdam: Rodopi.

Marshall, Alfred (1890) *Principles of Economics*, 8th ed, 1930. London: Macmillan.

McCloskey, Deirdre N. (1983) "The Rhetoric of Economics". *Journal of Economic Literature*, 21, 481–517.

(1990a) "Storytelling in Economics". In D. Lavoie (ed), *Economics and Hermeneutics* (pp. 61–75). London: Routledge.

(1990b) *If You're So Smart*. Chicago: University of Chicago Press.

(1994) *Knowledge and Persuasion in Economics*. New York: Cambridge University Press.

Meade, James E. (1937) "A Simplified Model of Mr. Keynes' System". *Review of Economic Studies*, 4:2, 98–107.

Mink, Louis O. (1978) "Narrative Form as a Cognitive Instrument". In R. H. Canary and H. Kozicki (eds), *The Writing of History* (pp. 129–49). Madison: University of Wisconsin Press.

Morgan, Mary S. (1990) *The History of Econometric Ideas*. Cambridge: Cambridge University Press.

(1991) "The Stamping Out of Process Analysis in Econometrics". In Neil De Marchi and Mark Blaug (eds), *Appraising Economic Theories* (pp. 237–63 and 270–2). Cheltenham: Edward Elgar.

(1999) "Learning from Models". In Mary S. Morgan and Margaret Morrison (eds), pp. 347–88.

(2001) "Models, Stories, and the Economic World". *Journal of Economic Methodology*, 8:3, 361–84; reprinted in U. Mäki (ed), *Fact and Fiction in Economics: Models, Realism and Social Construction* (pp. 178–201). Cambridge: Cambridge University Press.

(2002) "Model Experiments and Models in Experiments". In Lorenzo Magnani and Nancy J. Nersessian (eds), *Model-Based Reasoning: Science, Technology, Values* (pp. 41–58). New York: Kluwer Academic/Plenum Press.

Morgan Mary S. and Marcel Boumans (2004) "Secrets Hidden by Two-Dimensionality: The Economy as a Hydraulic Machine". In S. de Chadarevian and N. Hopwood (eds), *Models: The Third Dimension of Science* (pp. 369–401). Stanford: Stanford University Press.

Morgan, Mary S. and Margaret Morrison (1999) [eds] *Models as Mediators: Perspectives on Natural and Social Science*. Cambridge: Cambridge University Press.

Morrison Margaret and Mary S. Morgan (1999) "Models as Mediating Instruments". In Mary S. Morgan and Margaret Morrison (eds), *Models as Mediators: Perspectives on Natural and Social Science* (pp. 10–37). Cambridge: Cambridge University Press.

Rappaport, Steven (1989) "Abstraction and Unrealistic Assumptions in Economics". *Journal of Economic Methodology*, 3:2, 215–36.

Samuelson, Paul A. (1939) "Interactions Between the Multiplier Analysis and the Principle of Acceleration". *Review of Economics and Statistics*, 21, 75–8.

Schelling, Thomas C. (1978) *Micromotives and Macrobehaviour*. New York: Norton.

Schlimm, Dirk (2009) "Learning from the Existence of Models. On Psychic Machines, Tortoises, and Computer Simulations". *Synthese*, 169(3), 521–38.

Slutsky, E. E. (1927) "The Summation of Random Causes as the Source of Cyclic Processes". *The Problems of Economics Conditions*. The Conjuncture Institute, Moscow, 3:1, 34–64 (English Summary, 156–61).

Solow, Robert M. (1997) "How Did Economics Get That Way and What Way Did It Get?" *Daedalus*, Winter, 39–58.

Suárez, Mauricio (2009) [ed] *Fictions in Science*. London: Routledge.

Sugden, Robert (2000) "Credible Worlds: The Status of Theoretical Models in Economics". *Journal of Economic Methodology*, 7, 1–31. Reprinted in U. Mäki (ed), *Fact and Fiction in Economics: Models, Realism and Social Construction* (pp. 107–36) [2001]. Cambridge: Cambridge University Press.

(2009) "Credible Worlds, Capacities and Mechanisms". *Erkenntnis*, 70:1, 3–27.

Weintraub, E. Roy (1991) *Stabilizing Dynamics: Constructing Economic Knowledge*. New York: Cambridge University Press.

White, Hayden (1975) "Historicism, History and the Figurative Imagination". *History and Theory*, 14:4, 48–67.

Yule, George Udny (1927) "On a Method of Investigating Periodicities in Disturbed Series with Special Reference to Wolfer's Sunspot Numbers". *Philosophical Transactions of the Royal Society of London*, Series A, 226, 267–98.

Model Experiments?

1. Introduction

How can we characterize the way scientific modelling works? In Chapter 1, I suggested economists use models as a means of investigation or enquiry: they both enquire into the small worlds in their models, and use those enquiries as a way to interrogate the nature of the world. In this chapter I explore how these kinds of enquiries work by treating model-based reasoning as akin to experimental investigations.

Treating model reasoning as a form of experiment inevitably raises questions about the nature of such experiments. In Chapter 6, I portrayed model usage as a process of asking questions about the circumscribed and limited world in the model and using the model to derive answers about that small world. This is a process in which scientist and model are jointly active participants: neither is passive – the scientist experiments by manipulating the model, that is, he or she uses the model's resources (both its subject specific and deductive resources) to demonstrate answers to questions of interest to the scientist. In this chapter I show how the heart of the experimental action lies first in the ways a model's resources are used to demonstrate answers to questions about that model world, and second in using these experimental demonstrations to make inferences from that model world to the real one.

First then, in making demonstrations, we will see that models feature in a variety of different experimental modes of enquiry. On the one hand, economists create mathematical models and experiment on them, that is, they experiment within the small model world. On the other hand, economists undertake laboratory or classroom experiments, in which, as we shall see, models generally play a rather more passive but still essential role. But in between, there is a whole range of hybrid forms of experiments in which models feature in the experimental design, undergo controlled variation in the experiment, and so forth. In other words, models feature either as the object of manipulation or set the constraints within which experimentation takes place: there are both experiments in or on models and models in experiments.

Second, the notion of model reasoning as offering a kind of experiment enables me to take up the challenging problem, flagged in Chapter 6, of how economists make inferences from their model work, and what range of inferences such model demonstrations support. In this context, I end with a discussion of the contrast in epistemic power of model and laboratory experiments. On the way, however, I explore how these model-based experiments prompt the development of more generic categories for analysis, conceptual work that is an important but unexpected side effect of the historical shift to model-based reasoning in economics. These generic categories both define and limit the relevant domains for model-based inferences.

I take as my exemplar model for this chapter one of the most common and well-used models in economics, namely the supply and demand model, which appears in textbooks now either as a diagram with supply and demand curves (each relating prices and quantities in the marketplace) or as a set of three equations (the two functions and an equilibrium condition). Economists became so used to working with this model that it seems always to have been there. But while arguments about the laws of demand and supply may long have been at the centre of discussions about markets, that does not mean the model itself did not have to be developed. As I pointed out in Chapter 1, the transition from a verbal to a model-based science took place between the late-nineteenth and the mid-twentieth centuries and the earliest examples of supply and demand models shown in this chapter come from the beginning of that period. Not surprisingly, this change in what counted as scientific ways of doing economics required a shift in both cognition and perception: economists had to learn to think in models and to perceive the world in terms of models, and each depended upon the other. So the manner in which these earliest experiments on models were conducted and explained was all rather clunky. As such model-based reasoning became more commonplace, economists became more adept at it, and the model-experimental process became smoother.

The benefit of choosing this supply and demand model as the exemplar for this new mode of doing science is that it enables me to show how the means of modelling became standardized and even 'black boxed'; it provides a site for study that is more revealing than later examples. But it was also one of the first models to feature in classroom experiments with real subjects, enabling me to compare model and laboratory experiments as well as to show how models also feature in this latter kind of experiment. As new forms of using models and doing experiments flooded into economics in the later twentieth century, we find a variety of hybrid forms of supply and demand experiments to fill in our comparison. Models lie at the heart of these hybrids too, so that the historical trajectory of this model provides rich materials for analysis.

2. Experiments in the World of the Model

We can start out by thinking of model experiments as a kind of glorified thinking or mental experiment.[1] I call them 'glorified' only because such pen-and-paper experiments are too complicated to be done in the head. Writing down a model and manipulating it allows economists to think through in a consistent and logical way how a number of variables might interrelate, and to find the solutions to questions about such systems. This habit of making and using models extends the powers of the mind to ask questions and explore the answers in complicated cases. Sometimes such questions are about theories, sometimes about possible interventions (policies), sometimes about phenomena in the world. In this way, model experiments have come to function both in the domain of theory development and for understanding the world. But to treat this extension of the powers of the mind as a kind of experiment requires not only some credible evidence of such model usage in economics but also a convincing analysis of how such work goes on.

The development of an effective supply and demand model, and of its usage, is usually associated with Alfred Marshall, who was an English economist of the late nineteenth and early twentieth centuries, famous for his writings about the nature and workings of industry. But, as historians of economics have shown, there are several important predecessors for this work, dating from the mid-nineteenth century.[2] Their histories tell us that in 1838, the French economist Antoine-Augustin Cournot was the first to make a supply and demand diagram, and to experiment

---

1 I want to avoid the label "thought experiments" since commentators tend to treat these as a rather distinct category; see particularly Margaret Schabas (2008) and Julian Reiss (2002) for discussions of thought experiments in economics.

2 This chapter does not provide a history of exchange theory (on which see Creedy [1992 or 1998], the latter having extracts from original texts) or of the use of supply/demand diagrams (on which see Humphrey [1992], who retains the original diagrams in his commentary). Both of these authors cover French, German, and English literature. For a neat account of the French tradition in geometric analogies beginning with the pyramid analogy to demand, and considering Dupuit's work,

with it in a discussion of tax incidence. He was closely followed in 1841 by the German contributor, Karl Heinrich Rau, who built and used the diagram to discuss how market adjustments occur. Though the use of the diagram remained uncommon until the later nineteenth century, two other contributors, Hans von Mangoldt and Fleeming Jenkin, are particularly important for my discussion of the development of model experiments as the way to construct arguments with models. Mangoldt worked in the classical tradition in Germany (and cited Rau's work), but found his analytical approach overlooked by the historical economists dominant in his country in that later part of the century. Jenkin's work was also overlooked, possibly because he beat his more mainstream British compatriots to the new ways of arguing with diagrams! Yet the work of both show us how the supply and demand model and the method of reasoning with it co-evolved.

2.i Mangoldt and Jenkin

Hans von Mangoldt's 1863 discussion of demand and supply uses the same concepts as Adam Smith in his 1776 *The Wealth of Nations*. So the "natural" price (or "centre of gravity" price) is one that supply and demand adjustments will tend to restore following some change in the market. (And only rarely is this price called an "equilibrium" price.) But Mangoldt, like Ricardo earlier in the nineteenth century, found that attempting to give more general and logical answers than Smith to questions about the principles of economics produces verbal arguments that are just too complicated to be viable. Therein his turn to diagrams, equations, numerical examples – and to experiments with them – to answer the same questions as Smith, using Smith's concepts and terms, but with a different mode of reasoning using models.

Mangoldt's discussion of the exchange ratio of goods used a large number of demand and supply diagrams and they played an important role in demonstrating his arguments. I use the term 'demonstrate' here, and take it seriously, to differentiate it from 'illustrate'. The importance of this distinction came up explicitly in the Edgeworth Box discussion (of Chapter 3, Section 6ii), where we saw how the independent representational function of models goes beyond illustration in the sense that more information is found in the diagram than in the text, and often the text is dependent on the mathematics or the diagram (as in Figure 7.1, showing Mangoldt's figures 3 and 4, 7, and 8). For example, by laying out the various different shapes that the demand and supply curves might take, Mangoldt was able to explain the reasoning that lay behind those shapes. His diagrams and texts are mutually dependent, even though his initial use of the diagrams did not involve experiments:

> The more general and more urgent is the need satisfied by a particular type
> of goods, and the less capable of being satisfied by other means, the more

see Ekelund and Thornton (1991). For a more detailed and wider treatment of the French tradition that includes supply and demand, see Ekelund and Hébert (1999). For a useful introduction to the diagrammatic work of Marshall, see Whitaker (1975).

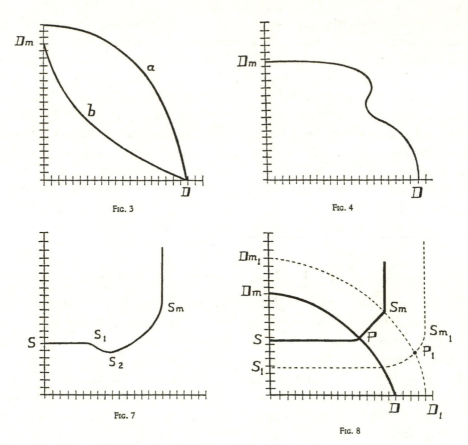

Figure 7.1. Mangoldt's Supply and Demand Model Experiments.
Source: Hans K. E. von Mangoldt, *Grundriss der Volkswirtschaftslehre*, 1863, figures 3 and 4, p. 49; figures 7 and 8, p. 50.

slowly will demand diminish at low prices and the more quickly at high prices. The demand curve will have a strong bulge. If, on the other hand, a type of goods has a limited demand and is easy to dispense with or to substitute, then a rising price causes demand to contract more sharply even at relatively low price levels and the demand curve will quickly approach the price scale. Similar effects follow from the distribution of wealth. If wealth is evenly distributed, demand will fall very gradually; if wealth is concentrated in a few hands, demand will contract sharply at first and slowly afterwards. In the one case the demand curve will be concave, in the other convex (to the origin) as shown in Figure 3.

The rule of diminishing demand at rising prices is occasionally subject to exceptions. Vanity or fear may cause demand not to fall, but to grow when prices rise (Figure 4). (von Mangoldt, 1863/1962, p. 35)

Read carefully, these passages show how Mangoldt's accounts of the shapes of the curves in his diagrams enabled him to characterize, classify, and compare typical cases, an important modelling activity in itself, as we shall see later (and as I argue further in Chapter 9). But though there were questions and answering stories attendant on these different slopes in the demand curves, and it was these that enabled him to define and categorize the different cases, there was nothing that we would yet want to call an experimental intervention in the model. Similarly with his figure 7, which showed how a supply curve might fall over some range due to economies of scale, but rise over others.

Other examples, such as his figure 8, do show how he conducted experiments on his diagrams.

> Economic progress and the advance of civilization tend to cheapen the supply of goods through better production methods and to extend it through increased knowledge and mastery over nature. As a result the supply curve tends to shift downwards and the point at which it goes off vertically to infinity is moved further outwards. This tendency contrasts with that other tendency of progress which we have mentioned, namely to extend and raise demand (see figure 8). The latter tendency is apt to push up the natural price, the former works in the opposite direction. Whether the natural price of any particular type of goods will shift upwards or downwards, therefore depends on the prevalence of one over the other tendency of progress. (von Mangoldt, 1863/1962, pp. 36–7)

This example is beautifully clear: an implicit question about the effect of progress answered by an experiment with the diagram. In this context, we can see how models offer the kind of power to demonstrate associated with experimental demonstration, just as we found Ricardo (in Chapter 2) used his arithmetical reasoning chains to demonstrate outcomes rather than to illustrate his text discussions. This demonstration also clarifies the benefits of reasoning with the diagram: by separating out the two kinds of tendency and their opposing relative strengths, he provides an explanation as to why there is no general and simple answer to what happens to prices during a period of "progress".

Mangoldt is particularly recognised by historians of economics for his treatment of far more complex cases, particularly that of interdependent demand and supply for two goods. Here, his textual discussion became exceedingly convoluted and intertwined with equations, numerical examples, and diagrams. For example, a verbally conducted experiment convinces him that if demand rises for one good, it will also rise or fall for the connected ('dependent') good, depending on the nature of the connection and which kinds of goods are involved. But then the more difficult question arises: What happens to the price of the dependent good? This begins a more specific discussion starting with the case of complementary goods where an increase in demand for one good (A) led to an increase in demand for the other related good (B). I quote the passage extensively on its own just to show how difficult it is to follow such verbal reasoning without the help of diagrams; patience is required:

> Assume that in a given state of the economy two goods whose consumption is directly related are consumed in a certain proportion and that the price

of both is their natural price. This means that for both goods the price has settled at a level at which demand and supply are equal at which the given proportionality obtains. Suppose now that nothing alters except for a change in a price factor of the principal good *A* – for instance, new productive capacity raises the volume of supply possible at each price. The centre of gravity of the *A*-price would then shift, and equilibrium between demand and supply would come about only at higher consumption than hitherto. Given the assumed proportionality in the consumption of both goods, demand for the dependent good, *B*, would also tend to rise. By assumption, the means of payment available for the purchase of good *B* remain constant; proportionality in the consumption of both goods can, therefore, be reestablished only if the consumption of *A* contracts sufficiently to liberate enough funds to raise demand for *B* to the appropriate level. (von Mangoldt, 1863/1962, p. 42)

And so the text continues on, for a further twenty odd lines, densely describing the assumptions and conditions under which the price of the dependent good will rise in various cases of possible changes in prices and quantities, and movements in output and consumption. This reasoning covered so many elements that it is really difficult to follow. Nevertheless, Mangoldt manages to finish his text argument with a general claim that the demand for the dependent good will rise so as to use up all the funds available for the purchase of both goods and the price of B will be its "new natural price" (p. 43).

It then turns out that all this text is merely preliminary discussion, for he then changes his mode of reasoning: "Let us again clarify the argument by a graphical exposition" (p. 56 in original, my translation[3]). As before, Mangoldt's diagrams serve both to demonstrate the outcomes of different assumptions or questions about particular cases and to characterize different kinds of cases. But here the diagrams work in conjunction with an algebraic treatment of the basic supply and demand relations and with a mixture of analytical and numerical methods of solution.[4] In these experiments, a set of supply quantity and price values for *A* and the supply curve for *B* are assumed, but the construction of the demand curve for *B* is based upon the algebraic relations and certain numerical assumptions (about

---

3 This is my alternative translation of the original German (the page reference is to the 1962 translation).

4 Commentators focus on different aspects of these methods. Schneider (1960) discusses Mangoldt's algebraic treatment, and quotes at length one of his numerical experiments, but in explaining Mangoldt, he transposes his experimental numerical solution method into a four-quadrant diagram, a favourite device of Schneider's day and a sure indication of the dimension of difficulty! Creedy (1992) pays attention to the numerical method and offers an alternative interpretation of what he did in algebraic form. Creedy also points out that the English translation alters the way the numerical experiment is reported from the original German, making the historical interpretation even more difficult.

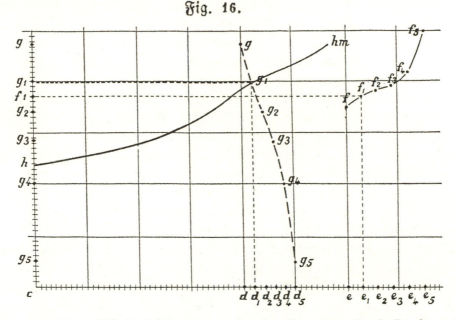

Figure 7.2. Mangoldt's Model Experiment for Complementary Goods (his figure 16, where *hm* is the assumed supply curve for good B; the supply curve from the numerical experiment for good A is labelled with successive f_n; and the demand curve for good B derived from the numerical experiment is labelled with successive g_n, where the *n* represent successive numbers.)

Source: Hans K. E. von Mangoldt, *Grundriss der Volkswirtschaftslehre*, 1863, figure 16, p. 56.

the demand ratio of the goods and total funds available) which enable him to use numerical methods of solution. These experimental results are reported on the diagrams, so, for example, we can see the calibrated values from one of his numerical experiments mapped onto his figure 16 (our Figure 7.2), even though the calibrated numbers are not written onto the figure. The accompanying discussion gives a series of little numerical examples or experiments to motivate the claim that the price of *B* goes up as the supply quantities of *A* move rightwards. Further experiments consider different cases so that in all, he provides diagrams, equations, and numerics, for changes in demand and in supply of both substitute and complementary goods.

Mangoldt's analysis as a whole has been described as brilliant and innovative in content (see Schneider 1960 and Humphrey, 1992), and so it is. It is equally innovative in its reasoning mode: it bears the hallmarks of a scientist understanding the value of models, indeed arguing and reasoning with models and making experiments with them, but still, holding no strong grip on the concept of a model. Unfortunately for the history of economics, Mangoldt's diagrams and equations and his experiments with them were cut out of the 1871 reprint of his book by the editor who thought that "it is utterly inconceivable to me that graphs or mathematical formulae could facilitate the understanding of economic laws".[5] This surely made his text even more difficult to follow – at least it does for modern economists! Mangoldt's innovatory use of models seems to have been lost until Edgeworth found it in the later part of the nineteenth century and then historians rediscovered his work in the following century.

Fleeming Jenkin's arguments with diagrammatic models of the laws of supply and demand of 1870 are equally brilliant, but much more confidently model-oriented and the text is rather an addendum to the diagrammatic work, for all of Jenkin's model work is demonstrative. Like Mangoldt's, many of Jenkin's diagrams laid out various cases and categorized them. For example, he created representations of Henry Thornton's discussion of the behaviour of buyers and sellers of single goods such as horses, and spoiling goods such as fish. Other diagrams demonstrated the differences between Dutch and English auctions. Elsewhere (1871–2, in his 1887) he used the diagram to demonstrate tax incidence. Like Mangoldt, Jenkin used his diagrams in explicitly experimental mode, making use of the internal resources of the diagram to answer questions. In the initial design of his diagram, Jenkin had defined the "whole supply" as the amount for sale "then and there", while the supply and demand curves were functional relations in which the supply or demand depended on a given price. We see his "laws of supply and demand" demonstrated in his figures 3 to 6 (our Figure 7.3 and 7.4) where the diagrams were designed and used to distinguish the "first law", namely that the market price will be where the "curves cut", from the "second law", namely the effect of a change in the whole supply or demand. The experiments with the first law diagrams (his figures 3 and 4) demonstrated the effects of alterations in the slope of the functions in the graphic relations, while the experiments on the second law diagrams (his figures 5 and 6) demonstrated a whole set of "probable effects": changes that followed from "an increase in the whole supply" or "in the purchase fund" (i.e., amounts available for demand). As we can see, each diagram showed the analysis of the experiment by labelling the lines and giving a written list underneath of the elements in the experiment and how they change, almost like a laboratory notebook reporting what happened in the experiment.

The marketplaces envisaged in Jenkin's model world were still dominated by competition amongst buyers and amongst sellers but the language of discussion was no longer entirely Smithian, for example, the intersection point in the first law is referred to in his text as the "theoretical price" (p. 79 of 1887/1996) and the diagrams were presented as showing "a pair of imaginary demand and supply curves for corn" (p. 77) useful for his demonstration of aspects of the "laws of supply and demand". Yet these curves are also quite empirical, for they, like Ricardo's arithmetic chains, showed that the corn was to be bought and sold in "quarters" and priced in plausible amounts of shillings per quarter. The corn law battles over the

5 Quoted in Creedy (1992, p. 46); this section was the first part of his text to be translated into English in 1962.

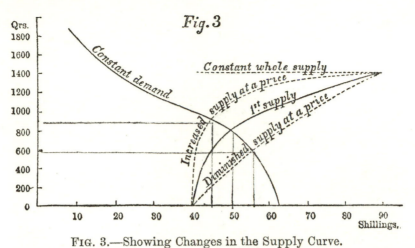

FIG. 3.—Showing Changes in the Supply Curve.

If the supply curve rise to the upper dotted line the market price will fall to 45s., and
900 quarters of wheat will change hands, instead of 800 as in Fig. 1.

If the supply curve fall as shown by the lower dotted line the market price will rise to
55s., but only 600 quarters will be sold.

The whole supply, the price at which all would be sold or none sold, all bought or none
bought, may all remain unaltered, as well as the demand curve. In practice some
or all of these elements would generally vary when the supply curve varies.

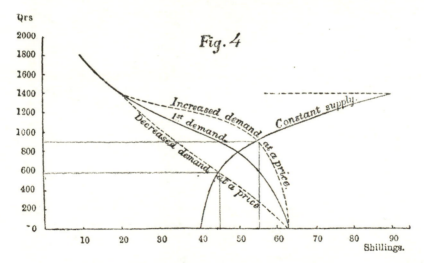

FIG. 4.—Showing Changes in the Demand Curve.

If the demand curve rise, as in the upper dotted line, the market price will be 55s., and
the quantity sold be 900 quarters.

If the demand curve fall, as in the lower dotted line, the price will fall to 45s., and the
quantity sold to 600 quarters.

As in Fig. 3, the whole supply, the price at which all would be sold or none sold, all
bought or none bought, is left unaltered, as well as the supply curve.

In practice some or all of these elements would generally vary when the demand curve
varies.

Figures 7.3 and 7.4. Fleeming Jenkin's Supply and Demand Curve Experiments.

Source: Fleeming Jenkin, "The Graphic Representation of the Laws of Supply and Demand,
and Their Application to Labour" in his *Papers Literary, Scientific, etc*, Vol. II, edited by
S. Colvin and H. A. Ewing, 1887, London: Longman and Green. Figures 3, p. 80; 4, p. 81;
5, p. 82; 6, p. 82 (Reprinted facsimile, 1996, London: London School of Economics and
Political Science Reprints of Scarce Tracts in Economics, No. 3.)

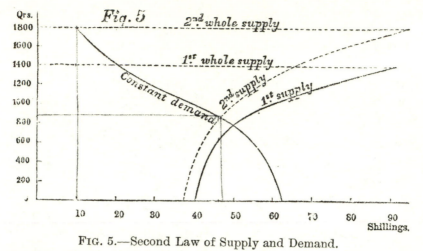

FIG. 5.—Second Law of Supply and Demand.

Fig. 5 shows probable effect of increase in the whole supply.
The dotted line on right shows probable effect of increasing the whole supply to 1,800
    quarters.
The price at which whole supply would be sold rises to 95*s*.
The price at which the whole supply would be bought falls to 10*s*.
The market price falls to 47*s*.
The price below which no sale could take place falls to 38*s*.
The price above which no sale could take place may remain unaltered.
The quantity which will be sold rises to 870 quarters.

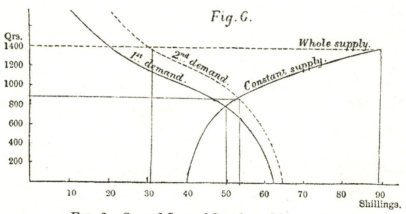

FIG. 6.—Second Law of Supply and Demand.

Fig. 6 shows probable effect of an increase in the purchase fund.
The dotted demand line shows the probable effect of increasing the purchase fund.
The price at which the whole supply would be sold may be unaltered.
The price at which the whole supply would be bought rises to 30*s*.
The market price rises to 53*s*.
The price below which no sale would be effected may remain unaltered.
The price above which no sale would take place rises to 65*s*.
The quantity which will be sold rises to 850.

Figures 7.3 and 7.4. (*see previous page for details*)

tariff on wheat, which had kept the price high in Ricardo's day, were over, for the tariff had been abolished by 1846. However, wheat remained the main staple for the British consumer at this time, and its price an important political fact. In parallel to Ricardo's hypothetical farm accounts, Jenkin's imaginary set of curves, demonstrating how the laws of political economy worked in the market for wheat, offered not an abstract argument, but one with immediate relevance.

Note that contrary to the earlier work by Mangoldt and to modern convention, but consistent with the mathematical conventions of the day about the placing of dependent and determining variables, prices were shown on the horizontal axes. Jenkin was a classic Victorian polymath – a well-recognised engineer who wrote literary criticism, plays, medical tracts, political economy, and so forth. By his mathematical economic analysis with his diagrams, he scooped Marshall, as the latter recognised.[6] Yet Jenkin's work was to be snubbed by Marshall and Jevons, who both claimed priority with the "scissors diagram" or "Marshallian cross" as it later came to be known.[7] Marshall developed the use of the diagram and obtained a particular facility in experimenting with it compared with Mangoldt and Jenkin. Indeed, it is his smoothness of experimental method with the model, rather than any particular original finding with the model, that I wish to stress in the discussion that follows.

2.ii Marshall

In the chapter of Marshall's *Principles of Economics* (1890 and many later editions) that I analyse here (book 5, chapter 13), Marshall used the now standard version of a supply and demand diagram in which, by convention, prices are given on the vertical axis, and quantities on the horizontal. Six of these diagrams are shown in Figure 7.5, where the DD' curve represents the potential demand by consumers for a good at various prices and the SS' curve the potential supply by producers over the same price range. In an analysis that was typical for him (the argument went on in the text, and the model manipulations were shown in footnotes), Marshall asked four questions, conducted ten model experiments and six associated mental experiments (all in less than ten pages), and then used the answers to provide a commentary on both the policy and theoretical implications of the answers. I have taken any case where the diagram was used to demonstrate a point as a 'model experiment', and any case in which Marshall did not bother to work through the diagram, but pointed directly to the answer, as a 'thinking' or 'mental' experiment. These mental experiments are cases where the question asks the reader to think of the reverse of the just conducted model experiment. So he does not actually diagram them, but the reader's ability to do these mental experiments depends on the original ones in the small world model being already understood. This means that

6 According to the later account by Foxwell, see Whitaker (1975).
7 See Humphrey (1992).

the difference between his mental experiments and his model experiments is not as clear-cut as it sounds. Overall, however, the number of experiments is indicative of the classificatory work going on – it takes sixteen cases to answer four questions.

The first question Marshall asked is: What would happen in an industry when there was some "great or lasting" change in normal demand? To answer this, the model is manipulated: an increase in demand at all prices means that the demand DD' curve shifts upwards to the right to the position dd' (see his figures 24–6, the top row of Figure 7.5). This experiment shows the curves' new intersection point (the point at which all exchanges are believed to take place, or the "equilibrium point"): a, compared to the old intersection point: A. In the first case, where the commodity supply "obeys the law of constant return", the price is determined on the production side and the new point shows a rise in quantity (H to h), but no change in price (A is the same height as a). However, according to Marshall's text and diagrams, there are two other alternative shapes that the supply schedule can take: either upward sloping, or downward sloping like the demand curve (respectively his figures 25 and 26). In the former case, the experiment shows that equilibrium quantity and price both rise, while in the latter case that quantity rises but price falls. Thus, one question and three similar experiments with diagrammatic models reveal that equilibrium quantity always rises, but that price changes depend on the shape of the supply function. He is also able to rank the size of the quantity changes in the three cases. The first two of these three experiments could have been done mentally, but only once the *model diagram* was already sufficiently well known to the economists to be seen in their minds' eyes, and *its rules for manipulation* understood. When Marshall first produced his *Principles* text, this would not of course have been so. But the third case is difficult to treat, and to produce the answer to his question, without the actual diagram and its manipulation, even when the model is well known. Marshall then asks his second question: What happens if there is a decrease in normal demand? He does no model experiments here; knowing the answers to the first question provides immediate answers for each case: the simple mental experiment is sufficient.

Marshall's third question is: What happens if there is an increase in the facilities of supply? This question prompts a further three model experiments in which there is a shift to the right or downwards of the supply curve from SS' to ss' (as shown in his figures 27–29, the bottom row of Figure 7.5). These model experiments allow him to answer that regardless of the shape of the supply curve, equilibrium price falls and quantity rises, though there is a range of price changes in the three cases. They also enabled him to classify the relatives sizes of the changes in the three cases, and this turned into a discussion of elasticity of demand and (in his figure 29) of whether the new equilibrium point would be stable or not:

> The three figures 27, 28, 29 represent the three cases of constant and diminishing and increasing returns, respectively. In each case DD' is the demand curve, SS' is the old position, and ss' the new position of the supply curve.

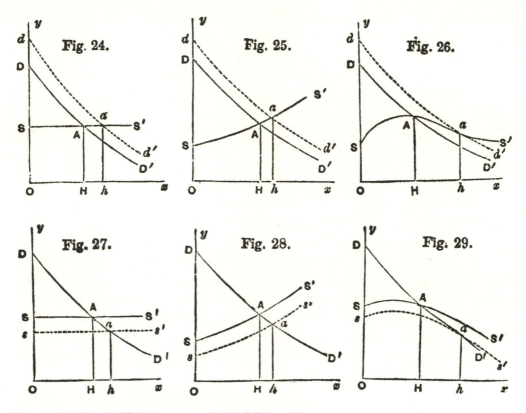

Figure 7.5. Marshall's Diagrammatic Model Experiments.

Source: Alfred Marshall, *Principles of Economics*, 1st edition, 1890. London: Macmillan & Co. Book V, chapter XIII, figures 24–26, note 1, p. 464 and figures 27–29, note 1, p. 466. Reproduced with acknowledgement to Marshall Library of Economics.

> *A* is the old, and *a* the new position of stable equilibrium. *Oh* is greater than *OH*, and *ah* is less than *AH* in every case: but the changes are small in fig. 28 and great in fig. 29. Of course the demand curve must lie below the old supply curve to the right of *A*, otherwise *A* would be a point not of stable, but of unstable equilibrium. But subject to this condition, the more elastic the demand is, that is the more nearly horizontal the demand curve is at *A* the further off with *a* be from *A*, and the greater will be the increase of production and the fall of price. (Marshall, 1890, p. 466, fn1)

Marshall's fourth question is: What happens if a tax or bounty is placed on the price of the good? Here the reasoning necessary to follow through the answers to the question requires quite complicated model experiments, but using exactly the same set of diagrams. The answers hinges on what happens to the "consumers' surplus" which is the triangle defined by, for example, the points *DAS* on his figure 24. If a tax is placed on a good, the price paid by consumers will rise, and their share of this "surplus" (the difference consumers would have been willing to pay and the amount they will actually pay at the market equilibrium price, *A* or *a*) will consequently fall. The answers given by the model experiments lead to two further sets of observations in which Marshall relates the findings to wider issues. On the one hand, the experiments prompt a discussion of the principles of taxation in relation to both the model's final outcomes and the indirect changes in elements in the model revealed by the experimental manipulations. On the other hand, the model work leads to theoretical discussions on the validity of general claims about the nature of the equilibria involved and to certain general issues of ethics and distributive justice.

In introducing his first set of diagrams, Marshall suggests that diagrams are of "special aid in enabling us to comprehend clearly the problems" (Fn 1, p. 464) of his chapter. But as things get more difficult, Marshall's dependency on the diagrams and their manipulation get stronger so that on the next set of diagrams, he argues that his explanations "can be most clearly seen by the aid of diagrams, and indeed there are some parts of the problem which cannot be satisfactorily treated without their aid" (Fn1, p. 466). Marshall was famous for railing against the unnecessary use of mathematics – he only wanted mathematics that helped in understanding economic problems; otherwise he had no use for it. Here we find him advocating the use of diagrammatic models as such helpful mathematics, first in understanding economic problems and then in using the models to demonstrate answers to his questions.

2.iii Conceptual Work: Defining Generic Categories

While all these three authors, Mangoldt, Jenkin, and Marshall, developed and used the same basic diagram, their conceptual apparatus and understanding of demand and supply and their notion of the intersections were not entirely the same. What is shared is that they took very little for granted in their style of reasoning. The practice of asking questions and manipulating diagrams to demonstrate the answers to questions was foreign to the majority of economists of the day, and no doubt that is why their texts make such a point of laying out the method of reasoning. Some of Mangoldt's and Jenkin's quoted examples are rather clear, though others (as we can see from the second example of Mangoldt) were much more laboured. With Marshall, the method of reasoning begins to seem natural to the material. My interpretation of these activities as 'model experiments' seems to fit easily onto all three economists' usage of the supply and demand diagram, even though the term 'model' was not yet in use and the style of reasoning had not yet been labelled 'modelling'.

For both Mangoldt and Jenkin, the use of specific numbers on the graphs remains important; as for Ricardo and his model farm numbers, their model experiments function as examples in which the claims are partly general and partly designed to fit likely problems, causes, and plausible numbers of their day. Though the examples have this dual quality, their reasoning with the models is consistently demonstrative, not illustrative: they could not have made these arguments without their diagrams, that is, without their models.[8] For Marshall, the diagrams and their demonstrations have become just a little more abstracted from the immediate world, but he too, like Mangoldt and Jenkin before him, uses them to compare, categorize, characterize, and classify during his analysis of the different cases. And for each different kind of case, he produces 'generic' claims, by which I mean claims that are not completely general (about the law of demand) nor entirely specific (about the demand for fish or horses), but about markets in which demand curves have certain kinds of shapes and certain characteristics.

The ability to define kinds of cases is an important outcome of the way models are used. Marshall's ability to answer his "What happens when or if ...?" questions require that he commits himself to the shapes of the curves in his diagrams. Once these different possible shapes have been given form in the model, the experiments on the model immediately take him not to one answer, but to a set of answers matching the set of cases he had laid out: remember he had four questions and it took sixteen experiments to answer them for the different cases. Even when empirical examples prompt the question, such as in Jenkin's consideration of a market for a single horse, or for fish at the end of the day, the economist must conceptualise the form of the law of demand for such a case in the diagrammatic model. Thus model questions and experiments take economists not so much to general answers or very particular cases, but more often to relevant categories of cases, or generic cases, which prompt them to develop the conceptual details of the laws of demand and supply relevant for those categories in their model experiments.

This analytical and categorizing work of model experiments fits in neatly with the late-nineteenth-century notion of what it meant to do "formal work" in economics. For example, W. E. Johnson's taxonomy of methods from the encyclopaedia of the day (Old Palgrave, 1894–6), refers to formal methods as those that "analyse and classify" concepts and involve the "logical processes of definition and division". (These formal methods were contrasted with "constructive" methods that "establish laws and uniformities".) This is not so very different from modern commentaries on models. As Hausman (1992) and others have argued, mathematical model work is conceptual theorizing work, concerned with classifying and characterizing. In earlier chapters, we saw how economic concepts were formed in the *creation of models* – as for example, the indifference curve and the contract curve in the Edgeworth Box case. Here, we have found another aspect of how this concept developmental work gets done consistent with Johnson's and Hausman's ideas; namely *in using models*, the process of analysis prompts definition and division to produce more specialised versions of the general laws of demand and supply and so more closely specified models. So their model experiments enabled these economists to explore the laws of demand and supply by defining and dividing into different generic kinds the materials *to which* those laws applied, and by classifying and categorizing the generic ways *in which* they applied. In so doing their model

---

8 See Chapter 3 for a discussion of the independent representational function played by models.

experiments, Mangoldt, Jenkin, and Marshall created new kinds or categories of relations by differentiating them, and generally characterizing the shape and behaviour of supply and demand curves in ways that developed the conceptual content of economic theories about markets.

Perhaps then we can regard modelling experiments in economics as a kind of testing ground, not for seeking to prove or disprove the general law of demand, for a model experiment could hardly do this, but one more like that of a creative design workshop. Such model experimental work allows the economist to test out intuitions and ideas and so come to understand what their laws of demand and supply mean in different circumstances much as architects use experiments with their models in the process of designing buildings, either to see how different designs might look or how their buildings might be constructed.[9] Another useful comparison may be found in material sciences and pharmaceuticals, where the aim of much experimentation is to make new substances; indeed hundreds of thousands of new things are made each year in laboratories: they are 'synthesized' and then 'analysed'. This creative, exploratory, character of experiments in such fields seems to be paralleled in the model experiments of economics[10]. Economists create, in their small model worlds, new categories and new manifestations of the basic demand or supply relations, which can then be analysed in further model experiments. This is how and why model experiments were instrumental in generating new elements that developed the much older 'laws' of supply and demand.

3. Models in 'Laboratory' Experiments

These historical cases of the late nineteenth century show how model reasoning involves experimental work on the model or in the world of the model. The economic relations of interest – the supply and demand curves – are represented in the model, questions are asked, and the manipulation of the resources of the model is used to provide answers. But if this way of using models is a form of experiment, we need to ask how experimental controls are instantiated, and what type of demonstration is involved in such experiments. To answer these questions, it helps to have the comparison case of economists' classroom experiments ready to hand. This brings our history to the years just after the mid-twentieth century, when such experiments on the supply and demand model began in economics. The classroom was the initial site of the economist's laboratory, its students the people in the modelled economy. Here we will see how models typically came into the experimental design, and we might even conceive of them as part of the experimental apparatus. But at the same

---

9　See Yaneva (2005) and Valeriani (forthcoming) for two examples from the literature on the use of architectural models in the creative and construction process.

10　The hybrid experimental work of Hommes and Sonnemans (to be discussed in part 5 of this chapter) contains the same combination of exploratory and classificatory work as they vary combinations of inputs and models to see what happens to the outputs from their experiments.

time, the models are still the object of experimental interest: Do people really behave as had been assumed in those Marshallian diagrammatic model experiments?

Economists have long assumed that market outcomes will have certain characteristics, in particular that a group of buyers and sellers in a market will arrive at an equilibrium price, that is, at the intersection of the demand and supply curves in Marshall's diagram. This assumption has now driven almost a century of research into the conditions under which this assumption will hold, relying on mathematical work and modelling experiments to investigate the features of this theory. However, many questions remain about how markets work and how the independent individual buyers and sellers arrive at a price in the real world as opposed to in the idealized markets portrayed in economists' theory and in their models. These questions were the first ones to be investigated in a classroom experiment in economics and there is now a record of more than fifty years of such experiments on this topic. Let us pass the argument to Edward Chamberlin, who conducted the first such experiments in economics at a time when modelling had just become well established. He opened his experimental report in 1948 thus:

> It is a commonplace that, in its choice of method, economics is limited by the fact that resort cannot be had to the laboratory techniques of the natural sciences. On the one hand, the data of real life are necessarily the product of many influences other than those which it is desired to isolate – a difficulty which the most refined statistical methods can overcome only in small part. On the other hand, the unwanted variables cannot be held constant or eliminated in an economic "laboratory" because the real world of human beings, firms, markets and governments cannot be reproduced artificially and controlled. The social scientist who would like to study in isolation and under known conditions the effect of particular forces is, for the most part, obliged to conduct his "experiment" by the application of general reasoning to *abstract* "models." He cannot observe the actual operation of a *real* model under controlled conditions
>
> The purpose of this article to make a very tiny breach in this position: to describe an actual experiment with a "market" under laboratory conditions and to set forth some of the conclusions indicated by it. (Chamberlin 1948, p. 95, his italics)

The last part of the first paragraph is particularly significant in our context: for Chamberlin, experimenting with "a market" is a way to observe "a real model" in place of the "abstract models" of mathematics and diagrams.

Chamberlin described a set of forty-six classroom experiments in which class students were divided into groups of 'buyers' and 'sellers'. They were each given a different card showing either the maximum price they, if buyers, would be willing to pay (their 'reservation' prices) for a unit of a good or the minimum price, if sellers, they would be willing to accept for a unit. (These reservation prices for buying:B and selling:S are listed in the column titled "Market Schedules" in his table 1 on our Figure 7.6.) Each participant could trade one unit during a short period when "the market" was in operation by circulating through the marketplace (the classroom) and trying to strike a bargain to buy or sell privately with another participant. Once a contract was concluded, the transaction price (third column of the left side of his table 1) was written on the class board, but not their reservation prices. This is Chamberlin's "real model" operating under controlled conditions.

In these experiments, the reservation prices (for buying and selling) written on the cards were even numbers drawn from a supply and demand model with conventional shaped curves, that is, downward sloping demand and upward sloping supply, that were neither particularly steep nor flat. If drawn out, however, as Chamberlin did in his report (see his figure 1, in our Figure 7.6), we see

TABLE 1

TRANSACTIONS			MARKET SCHEDULES	
B	S	P	B	S
56	18	55	104	18
54	26	40	102	20
72	30	50	94	26
84	34	45	90	28
44	44	44	86	30
102	42	42	84	32
80	20	40	82	34
60	28	55	80	36
48	40	45	76	40
76	36	45	74	42
94	52	55	72	44
68	58	62	68	46
66	46	55	66	50
82	32	58	60	52
90	72	72	58	54
104	54	54	---	---
52	50	50	56	58
86	64	64	54	62
74	62	69	52	64
			50	66
LEFT OVER			48	68
			44	70
38	68		38	72
50	66		34	74
28	82		32	78
32	88		30	80
18	90		28	82
26	84		26	84
22	104		24	88
24	78		22	90
30	80		20	98
20	98		18	104
34	74			
58	70			

FIG. 1

Equilibrium sales. 15
Actual sales. 19

Equilibrium price. 57 (56–58)
Average of actual prices. . . 52.63

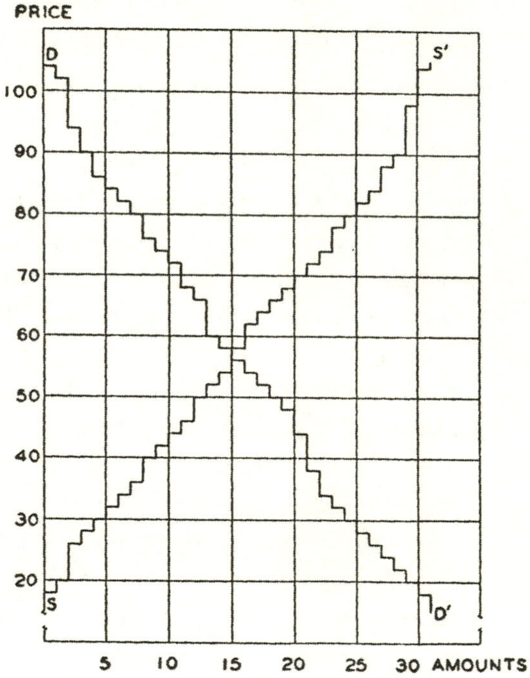

Figure 7.6. Chamberlin's "Real-Model" Experimental Results.

Source: Edward H. Chamberlin (April 1948), "An Experimental Imperfect Market", *Journal of Political Economy*, 56:2, 95–108; table 1 and figure 1 on p. 97. Reproduced with permission from University of Chicago Press.

immediately that unlike the smooth continuous curves drawn by Marshall in his diagrams and assumed in most models, these schedules have steps, for these prices were set at even numbers and for trades at quantities in whole units, so a schedule does not provide a smooth line. Since Chamberlin's experiment often went on with a less than full set of price cards handed out (because of a limited number of class participants), the schedules sometimes also had considerable gaps (or larger steps) in them.

In most of his experimental outcomes, Chamberlin found that the average price of transactions in this laboratory market was lower than the equilibrium price predicted by the Marshallian model (i.e., at the intersection of the demand and supply curves used in his experiment) and sales were higher than the amount predicted, as can be seen from the exhibit showing the actual transactions in the experiment and the numbers given out to students forming the demand and supply "market schedules" (see foot of his table 1, in Figure 7.6).

Much of the rest of Chamberlin's paper was given over to further experiments with different instructions or rules for trading in the classroom 'market' to explore why these findings might have arisen. He particularly sought to explain the difference between average prices found in the experiments and the equilibrium price expected from theory as the intersection of the two schedules of the model used in his experimental design. From his experiments, Chamberlin came to doubt that there was even a tendency towards this equilibrium:

> It would appear that in asserting such a tendency, economists may have been led unconsciously to share their unique knowledge of the equilibrium point with their theoretical creatures, the buyers and sellers, who, of course, in real life have no knowledge of it whatsoever. (Chamberlin, 1948, p. 102)

In 1955, Vernon Smith started his first series of classroom experiments, or, as they were known then: "experimental games", meaning role-playing experiments (see Chapter 8) in which the

> ... experimental conditions of supply and demand in force in these markets are *modeled closely* upon the supply and demand curves generated by limit price orders in the hands of stock and commodity market brokers at the opening of a trading day. (Smith, 1962, p. 111, italics added)

Smith followed an experimental design very similar to Chamberlin's[11]. Each class participant was given a card labelled as buyer or seller and each had a reservation price drawn from the schedules of a supply and demand model. But every

---

11 Vernon Smith's contributions in developing the field of experimental economics have been recognised by a Nobel Prize in economics. At the time he started such work, few other economists were undertaking experiments, though by the late 1950s and early 1960s, experimental work had begun to flourish in a small way in economics, partly in cooperation with experimental work by psychologists, a point briefly discussed again in Chapter 8 in the context of Shubik's work. See Guala (2008) for a short history of experimental economics.

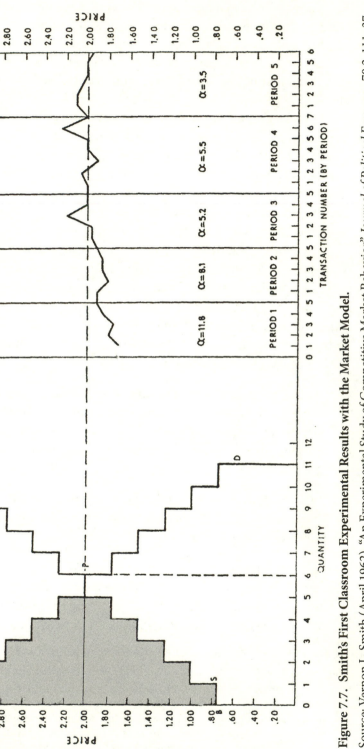

Figure 7.7. Smith's First Classroom Experimental Results with the Market Model.

Source: Vernon L. Smith (April 1962), "An Experimental Study of Competitive Market Behavior", *Journal of Political Economy*, 70:2, 111–37; chart 1 on p. 113. Reproduced with permission from University of Chicago Press.

experiment had several periods during which "the market" operated, and in each time period, each person could make one new trade. In addition, contracting was conducted openly by students raising their bids and offers in public so that everyone knew what all the bids and offers were. These two features meant that students had more chance to learn about the demand and supply reservation prices held by others in 'the market'. Smith carried out ten sets of experiments, varying the shapes of the demand and supply schedules, sometimes changing their levels in mid-experiment, and sometimes letting participants trade two units. With these design features, Smith found overall a much greater evidence of convergence of exchange prices, than had Chamberlin, towards the 'equilibrium' prices indicated in the various supply and demand models that he used to generate the reservation prices in each of the experiments he conducted. We can see in the report of Smith's first experiments, shown in his chart 1 (in Figure 7.7), both the stepped model schedules that generated the prices on the cards that he gave to participants and the convergence to that model market equilibrium over time in the sequence of runs of his first experimental market.

These early experiments from Chamberlin and Smith are regarded as classics in the field, and their charts of the model curves and numerical outcomes have become totems within the experimental community used both to motivate the rationale for experiments and to convey succinctly the kinds of experimental results that opened up investigation of long held assumptions within economics. I will come back to this sequence of classic classroom experiments later in the chapter.

4. Comparison: Model Experiments and Laboratory Experiments

4.i Controls and Demonstration

To compare these two kinds of experiments: economists' model experiments and their classroom experiments, we need some grip on the notion of experiment in its ideal form namely, in the laboratory. These ideals might be most easily communicated by thinking about the example of chemistry, which provides the typical idea of the layperson's laboratory science with test tubes, Bunsen burners, a range of apparatus, jars of chemicals, and a workbench[12]. In this ideal experimental milieu, the environment is controlled (e.g., all the apparatus is clean), the inputs to the experiment are controlled (e.g., the amounts are of specified quality and carefully weighed quantity) and the experimental intervention itself requires a level of control in order that the effectiveness of the change can be properly assessed. That is, for example, the amount and process of adding chemical A to chemical B

---

12 Chemistry has also provided the basis for one of the most convincing accounts of tacit knowledge in creative laboratory work in the form of Collins' investigation into crystal growing (see Collins, 1990).

(under the controlled conditions) must itself be carefully controlled in order for the effect of the experimental intervention to be properly assessed. In such laboratory experiments, a particular process of interest cannot be isolated, accessed, and assessed without rigorous attention by the experimenter to all kinds of control.

The experimental scientist must work hard to take account of all conditions and factors that are likely to interfere with the process of interest. Here it is useful to draw upon Marcel Boumans' (1999) dissection of *ceteris paribus* conditions, which extends the analysis of such factors by distinguishing between three sorts of control conditions: *ceteris paribus*, *ceteris neglectis*, and *ceteris absentibus*.[13] Some disturbing causes may be declared absent if the experimenter can physically rule them out of the setup (*ceteris absentibus*). Of the causes that are present but *are not the subject of experiment*, some may be thought to be so minor in effect that they can be neglected (*ceteris neglectis*), while others that are present have to be controlled for by procedures that hold them constant during the experiment (*ceteris paribus*). These control conditions make the setup of the laboratory experiment somewhat (more or less) artificial, but it remains of the real world for all that because however ingenious the scientist, the material world can be controlled only to an extent. Of course, the subject of interest is not the controls, but the process and outcomes of the experimental manipulation: the careful adding of A to B and its assessment.

Experimentalists in economics follow the same ambitions as in other laboratory sciences, and indeed, soon came to refer to their classrooms as "laboratories".[14] They sought to remove or control interfering factors in the environment that might invalidate the experimental results and to conduct the experimental intervention in such a way that economic behaviour could be isolated and its experimental variation become known. In economics, as in other fields, these controls are enforced in economics as much through experimental design choices as through direct physical means. Chamberlin and Smith exerted little control over the environment of the open classroom, but exerted control over the behaviour of the participating subjects by limiting what they could know and how they could trade, thus controlling both inputs and allowable variations in behaviour. For example, Chamberlin used his experimental design to set separate limits on the contract price for each person and he controlled the distribution of those limits using the schedules from his demand and supply model. He also set controls on the amount that could be

13 Boumans' work on this problem in the context of the functioning of economic models as measuring instruments connects to Hasok Chang's (2001) discussion of the development of thermometers. Both works are outcomes of the joint "Measurement in Physics and Economics" research project at the London School of Economics (Centre for Philosophy of Natural and Social Science) and University of Amsterdam's History and Philosophy of Economics group. For a much fuller treatment of these issues in the measurement context, see the books by Chang (2004) and Boumans (2005). For a discussion of ceteris paribus assumptions in the supply and demand context, see especially Hausman (1990); and in the general economics context, see Boumans and Morgan (2001) and Mäki and Piimies (1998) and the references in both.

14 Such experiments later moved into computer 'laboratories' (where much greater levels of control over personal interaction and so environments and inputs are possible) when experimental economics really took hold in the 1980s and 1990s.

Table 7.1. Model Experiments and Laboratory Experiments

	Model Experiment (Mangoldt, Jenkin, and Marshall)	Ideal Laboratory and Classroom Experiment (Chamberlin and Smith)
Materials of the Experimentable World	Create an artificial world in a model	Create a controlled real world within an artificial environment
Experimental Control	By model design and assumption of *ceteris paribus* conditions	By experimental design and physical controls/rules
Demonstration Method	Deductive in model	Experimental in laboratory

Note: This and the following Table 7.2 were developed from comparisons first made in Boumans and Morgan (2001), Morgan (2002a, 2003), and finally in Morgan (2005), some of which also bring in the econometrics comparison but not those of field and natural experiments.

contracted in each period by each person and the amount of information made publicly available. We can think of these controls as "rules" (known to economists as "institutions") that participants had to follow. But he left room for variation in action because he left open how bargaining negotiations were conducted.

How such controls are instituted forms one of the dimensions of contrast between model experiments and laboratory experiments. As we see in Table 7.1, in the laboratory experiment, the experiment is in the real world and elements are controlled physically and by rules of behaviour. In contrast, in the model experiment, the experiment is in the world of the model, where controls are made by assumption in the process of creating and using the model. The model experimentalist has control over the design of the model: he or she decides its elements and their relationships, 'isolates' them by excluding other factors (as Edgeworth did in choosing a desert island economy, as in Chapter 3), and 'idealizes' away awkward features (as in the history of economic man, Chapter 4). The modeller assumes that minor causes can be neglected; that certain things are zero; and that certain things are unchanging. In fact, economists state the phrase *ceteris paribus* to imply that all three of Boumans' conditions hold by assumption without discriminating between them. In contrast, the laboratory economist has to enforce physically these different types of conditions: in the design of the experiment to ensure an adequate experimental procedure and on the environment within the laboratory. Whereas the modeller can impose, by assumption, a total independence between two or more elements in the model (however implausible that might be) in order that the model will be tractable for experimental manipulation, that degree of independence might not be obtainable in the equivalent real material system. Related elements or confounding causes may prevent experimental isolation and demonstration in the laboratory experiment whereas they can so easily be assumed away in the model experiment: everything else *may* not be the same or may not be ruled out when manipulating the real world system whereas it *can* be held the same or set at zero when manipulating the model.

We can see how these model controls work if we go back to our late-nineteenth-century experimentalists. There were certain things in Marshall's model experiments that he did not bother to make any specific assumptions about. For example, he motivated his first experiment by listing five reasons why normal demand might have risen: change in fashions, new use for the good, new market for the good, decline in supply of a substitute good, and increase in wealth or income. But it made no difference to the model experiment which of these were relevant for he assumed that all these causes had the same effect, namely, a rise in normal demand that was the starting point of the experiment. He also assumed away all sorts of potentially disturbing factors, such as events in closely related markets (though he did consider these in other chapters). There were also many hidden assumptions, such as that of automatic adjustment to equilibrium, that the curves were smooth, cut the axes, and so forth, which were required to make his model experiments work neatly.

The importance of these assumptions becomes particularly evident if we compare Chamberlin's laboratory experiment with Marshall's earlier model experiments. We can see that Marshall's outcomes depended on the assumption that before the experiment (as it were) trading was at the intersection point of a supply and demand curve and that there was an automatic adjustment to the new intersection (or equilibrium) point whenever one of the curves was shifted in the experimental manipulation within the model. In Chamberlin's classroom experiments, by contrast, reservation prices were controlled by a design based on a pair of imagined curves of potential supply and demand from Marshall's diagrammatic model. But while those numbers on the stepped curves limited each participant's range of behaviour, there was nothing in the experimental design that enforced buyers and sellers to trade at those prices, or for their behaviour in 'the market' to lead to the intersection point of those curves. As Smith wrote about his chart 1 (Figure 7.7), participants were free to trade within the shaded area of the graph, but,

> We have no guarantee that the equilibrium defined by the intersection of these sets [of reservation prices – the stepped lines] will prevail, even approximately, in the experimental market (or any real counterpart of it). The mere fact that, by any definition, supply and demand schedules exist in the background of a market does not guarantee that any meaningful relationship exists between those schedules and what is observed in the market they are presumed to represent. All the supply and demand schedules can do is set broad limits on the behavior of the market. (Smith, 1962, pp. 114–5)

This difference between the materials of the laboratory and model experiments is summarized in the top row of Table 7.1: the laboratory scientist *creates a controlled real world within an artificial environment* while the modeller *creates an artificial world in a model*.[15] But in the laboratory case, it is not only the experimenter

---

15 Boumans (2002) shows how this latter idea is now the self-conscious aim of many economists. See also the discussion of "credible worlds" in Chapter 6. The terminology of "artificial worlds" has been

who places controls on the experiment, for the agency of nature also creates boundaries and constraints on the experiment. There are constraints in the mathematics or diagrammatics of the model too of course, but the critical point is whether the assumptions that are made there happen to be the same as those of the situation in the world that the model is held to represent, and there is nothing in the materials of the model to ensure that they are. This fundamental difference between the 'experimental world' and the 'model world' has considerable implications, as we shall see in later Sections 5 and 6.

Another fundamental point of difference between model experiments and laboratory experiments lies in the nature of their demonstration (the third line of Table 7.1). It is easier to recognise, and to label, this difference as that between experimental demonstration and deductive demonstration than it is to provide a characterization of the difference. It is tempting to portray model demonstration as superior on the view that it is grounded in some form of abstract diagrammatic or mathematical logic, compared to experimental demonstrations that, as we have learnt from modern science studies, depend on all sorts of technological and human and social attributes that defy philosophical codification.[16] But this apparent superiority of mathematics may be regarded as doubtful since Lakatos's seminal *Proofs and Refutations* (1963) recognised that mathematical argument too has its own informal nature. And, as we have already seen, the kinds of diagrammatic model reasoning that Marshall used depended critically on all sorts of shared disciplinary views from economics (some labelled 'theory') about the economic elements represented in the model, about automatic adjustment processes, and, most critically, on what constitutes a valid manipulation of the elements in the model.

Knowledge of what counts as a valid experimental manipulation of elements in a model can be understood as equivalent to a knowledge of valid experimental protocols in the laboratory. In laboratory experiments, some protocols are about conditions and control, but others are about the order and range of permitted interventions. The situation is similar with model experiments. As discussed in Chapter 1, the deductive resources in model demonstrations depend on both the language of the model and its economic content, so its manipulation is subject not only to the protocols of legitimate mathematical manipulation but also to the legitimate subject-specific rules about what can be done to what, what ranges a parameter might take, and so forth. For example, in Marshall's diagrammatic supply and demand model, the curves can be shifted only in certain ways in response to particular questions raised, and if a sequence of changes is involved, the order of this is not open. The use of the model resources are also shaped, as we have seen in

---

independently applied to understand Marcel Lenoir's work on the supply and demand model; see Le Gall (2007), chapter 6.

16 On the one hand, science studies has debunked experiment for us (e.g., see Gooding et al., 1989; Gooding, 1990; Hacking, 1983; and Franklin, 1986, 1990) while at the same time philosophers have also moved away from defining experiment in any simple way (see Heidelberger and Steinle, 1998; Radder, 2003; and Rheinberger, 1997).

Chapter 6, by the need to provide a plausible or meaningful economic account of the sequences of changes and outcomes demonstrated in the model experiment. So the validity of demonstration depends on following valid subject matter protocols in both model and laboratory experiments.

4.ii Experimental Validity and The Inference Gap

In Chapter 1, I argued that models served as an instrument of enquiry rather than a mode of truthmaking, and that models were both objects to enquire into and to enquire with. In experimenting on models, economists enquire directly into the world of the model, and only indirectly into the world represented in the model. The question of whether an experimental result in any field, and for any kind of experiment, can be taken as valid for the uncontrolled real world is an important and complicated problem. Model experiments are no exception. The worries appear different because couched in different terms, but for communities of both model users and laboratory experimentalists, they are directly related to issues of control and representation. For laboratory scientists, the main problem can be seen as one of 'external validity'.[17] Do the processes and results obtained in the laboratory hold true in the world? Has the world been sufficiently well replicated in the laboratory? Does the artificial, controlled environment created for the laboratory experiment nevertheless allow the experimentable materials to behave sufficiently naturally to justify inference from the laboratory to the world? For economists using models, this same issue can be understood as a question of 'similarity' or 'parallelism'. Has the real world been well enough represented in the created, circumscribed and parallel world in the model for inferences to be made from the model experiment to the world. These two related points of contrast in the materials of the experimentable world – control and representation – have implications for the range of potential inference from the two types of experiment. These differences are displayed in Table 7.2, an extension of Table 7.1.

In experimental economics, the validity of experimental results is defended by referring to the design of the experiment. Experiments are designed to recreate or replicate part of the real world in the classroom 'laboratory'. Control is dependent on the choice of experimental setup, circumstances, and procedures (institutional rules, rewards, and so forth). These choices are guided by the experimenter's need to design the experiment in such a way that *real economic* behaviour is made

---

17 In Morgan (2005), I discuss Harré's (2003) argument that there are two different kinds of experiment, ones that intervene on natural objects, and others that create artefacts that are not paralleled in the natural world. It was this that suggested to me that the inference problem of parallelism (from the latter kind of experiment) might be considered differently from that of external validity (for the former kind), and that this has relevance for how to think about inferences from models. On 'parallelism' in experimental economics, see the work of Francesco Guala (another member of the "Modelling" and "Measurement in Physics and Economics" projects at LSE), particularly his 1999b. He also treats experiments as playing the same kind of mediating function as models (see Guala, 1999a, 2002, 2003 and his 2005 book). Conversations with Francesco Guala have helped me clarifying my thinking about many aspects of laboratory experiments in economics.

Table 7.2. **Model Experiments, Laboratory Experiments, and Inferential Scope**

	Model Experiment (Mangoldt, Jenkin, and Marshall)	Ideal Laboratory and Classroom Experiment (Chamberlin and Smith)
Materials of the Experimentable World	Create an artificial world in a model	Create a controlled real world within an artificial environment
Experimental Control	By model design and assumption of *ceteris paribus* conditions	By experimental design and physical controls/rules
Demonstration Method	Deductive in model	Experimental in laboratory
Inference to World	Different materials: "casual"* but wider range, weaker validity; relies on accurate representation	Same materials: specific but narrower range, stronger validity; relies on accurate replication
Potential of Results**	Surprise	Confoundment

* This term derives from Gibbard and Varian's 1978 description.
** See Section 6 of this chapter.

manifest in the experiment. Although there are arguments as to whether experimental subjects, such as the students in Chamberlin's and Smith's classroom experiments, really do behave 'naturally' in such artificial environments, nevertheless they share the quality of being humans in economic action. This 'natural' claim is obviously more of a problem where the students are asked to role play, for example, managers in industries. Nevertheless, this element in the inference gap is surely less than for model experiments, where the humans are represented by model men, symbols that behave as programmed by the economists (see Chapter 4).

The quality of economists' experimental design and their real human inputs can be adduced as reasons why the results experimentalists find in their controlled situations might carry over and be considered valid in the external, that is, the uncontrolled real world. These qualities may make it possible to infer to very similar situations (in terms of behaviour, objects, rules, and circumstances) in the world, but that very same tightness of controls and the high levels of specificity involved in the laboratory experimental setup make inferences to situations and circumstances in the world that are not exactly the same more problematic. Thus, Chamberlin could make some inferences about the behaviour of people (acting under similar market rules and within a similar kind of demand and supply market as given by his model) in the world, but could not say much about their behaviour in markets with different characteristics or where the rules are very different. Smith found it possible to make somewhat wider inferences about behaviour under his rules because he found stable results over a set of experiments with considerable variation in supply and demand curves. Taking the Chamberlin and Smith cases together, economists might perhaps make comparative inferences about how people behave, and the effects of this, under two different kinds of market rules of interaction. But still, the validity of their results was limited in scope because, their experimental work had shown them that the details of rules or 'institutions' matter to outcomes. Their results have a certain strength in external validity, but that validity is narrowly limited to like situations in the world.

In contrast, for mathematical modellers the problem of inference from model experiments is understood as directly related to the kinds of assumptions involved in creating their small world models. Their model versions of the world are not already given; they have to be created. As we know from the first half of the book, this involves processes of imagination, abstraction and simplification in representing the economic relations and events into a model. In Marshall's cases, these processes created a model world of supply and demand relations in which the economist gains experimental control by making assumptions about the connecting, confounding, and disturbing factors in that model world. It is these assumptions and simplifications that make the model world tractable so that experiments on it will produce results.

While these abstractions, simplifications, and controls by assumption all limit the applicability of the model-experimental results to any particular concrete events in the world, yet paradoxically, it is these same qualities that make it easier for economists to 'apply' the results of their model experiments 'approximately', or even as Gibbard and Varian (1978) suggest, "casually", to a wider number of objects and circumstances in the economic world: namely, to all those that share some common traits with the model world. Thus, for example, Marshall's experiments on models provide potential inferences about the direction of change in quantity in response to a shift in the demand curve due to a whole range of causes. But, unless – to continue with Marshall's example – an economist knows the exact shape and slope of the curves, he would be hard pressed not only to make general inferences from such experiments, but equally to provide narrative explanations or useful inferences about any particular case in the real world. This is where the dividing and categorizing work of modelling comes in. As we saw, Marshall broke down the general case into different sub-cases or classes – of different shaped and sloped curves, suggesting that inference could be valid back to a set of applications in the world where those generic kinds of curves might hold. But at the same time, this inference is relatively weak, because such models still lack the host of details required for vaid inferences in any particular concrete case. The generic level at which models operate – at the level of a class or typical kind – means that their experiments attain a degree of particularity at the same time as a degree of generality.[18] This explains why the range of inferences from model experiments is less than that from general theory, but broader than from laboratory experiment (where inferences are bound by the specifics of experimental design) and than econometric modelling (where inferences apply only to a specific time and place), both of which have narrower domains but stronger claims to validity.

18 This classification element of modelling is nicely reflected in John Sutton's 'class of models' approach that relies on modelling to categorise industries into different kinds that can then be more effectively worked with than by taking the set as a whole (see Sutton, 2000 and Morgan, 2002b).

At this point in the discussion of inference, it is worth returning to the four steps of model reasoning outlined in Chapter 6: create a model for the problem of interest, ask questions, make experimental demonstrations in the world of the model, and tell narratives of inference and explanation. These must necessarily be connected: so the possibility for making inference from a model experiment depends upon the question that prompts the experiment. An entrance to this connection comes from considering May Brodbeck's aphorism: "Model ships appear frequently in bottles; model boys in heaven only" (1968 [1959], p. 579). We can't get much help in understanding how ships can transport goods or explain why boys are naughty from these models. Why not? To understand exactly how a ship can float, *simplifying* into a model that fits into a bottle doesn't help, but simplifying to capture the relations among length, draft, and displacement may do. Similarly, an *idealization* process that provides a model of the behaviour of a boy in heaven may not be very useful to social scientists seeking to answer questions about real boys in the world. Rather, scientists need to represent or denote in their model some of the essential characteristics relevant for understanding boys in the real world if experiments with the model are to help them answer questions about real boys. Scientists have to capture the elements and relations in their model that are relevant to the question asked if they are to provide a model demonstration in answer to that particular question: that is, the question (the external dynamic) and the resources of the model (the internal dynamic) have to be aligned.

The challenge to economists then is to make their model world descriptively and analytically useful at precisely that point where the question is to be answered. If the problem at issue is how different pricing strategies affect a supply and demand market outcome, then the market input strategies have to be considered very carefully. If questions are about what happens when the demand curve shifts, both demand and supply curves need to be effectively represented, but particularly, as Marshall showed in his experiments, the latter, since the experimental manipulation of the demand curve traces out the shape of the supply curve on which the experimental results for that kind of model depend. This is the classic 'identification problem', as it is known in econometrics.[19] And in this respect, model experiments have the same structure as laboratory experiments, for it is the elements of the model or classroom manipulation that are the focus of the economists' questions, and that require careful model or experimental design, in order for the experimental interventions to provide informative output.

Both kinds of experiments depend on controls of some part of the system as well as the environment to make their interventions work, even though these controls make those aspects of the laboratory or the model world artificial. And both kinds of experiments have problems in isolating and capturing the part of the world that they want to interrogate. A comparison emphasises these aspects in common.

---

19 For a history and analysis of that problem, in the same supply/demand domain, see Morgan (1990), and Boumans (2005).

We might say that in the case of laboratory science, successful experiments depend on *accurate replication in the artificial environment of the laboratory* of the elements, changes, and outcomes *in that part of the world relevant to the question*. Or, as Cartwright has suggested, "when features of the situation of the [experiment] are just right to manifest the natural characteristics of the process", then inferences might be made from the results of experiment to teach something about the world.[20] In the case of a modelling science, a parallel claim would be that successful experiments depend on *accurate representation in the artificial world of the model of the parts of the world relevant for the questions of interest*.

But there is of course a serious catch-22 situation here. Economists create models in an effort to find out how the world works and it is because they don't already know how it works that they also don't know whether they have an accurate model representation! The real problem therefore lies in that the sciences do not have *formal procedures and inference criteria* for deciding when a representation is a good one. This might be called 'forward inference' from the world to the model during the process of model-making, in contrast to 'back inference', from the model experiment to the world when using the model. If a model is a good representation, an experiment with it may well be informative. But, this back inference too lacks formal criteria.[21] This is not just a problem for model experiments, for the methods of back inference from laboratory experiments are mostly informal too.[22] And even when economists do have formal back inference procedures based on statistical theory (as in econometrics) these do not mean that it is easy to make valid inferences in practice. This general lack of principles and procedures for making inferences from models are why, as we found in Chapter 6, economists using models to comment on, or act in, the world fall back on the credibility and plausibility of their narratives.

Strangely perhaps, the most obvious element in the inference gap for models (in comparison with that for laboratory experiments) lies in the validity of any inference between two such different media – forward from the real world to the artificial world of the mathematical model and back again from the model experiment to the real material of the economic world. The model world is at most a parallel world.[23] This parallel quality does not seem to bother economists. But materials do

---

20 Cartwright (2000, p. 6), a sentiment that goes back to Bacon.

21 It is generally agreed that this requires some kind of outside evidence or additional information for models as well as for hybrid experiment setups, and simulation procedures (see Oreskes et al., 1994 and Oreskes, 2000). What kind of evidence is not agreed: for example, economists take the accuracy of the representation to depend on the realism of the model assumptions; Cartwright (2000) suggests we need outside knowledge of causes; and Hartmann (1996) argues that we need independent reasons for believing the model to be used.

22 See, however, Deborah Mayo (1996).

23 It is because the model world is a parallel world that the inference problems for model experiments can be labelled as 'parallelism', in comparison to the laboratory experiment where the inference question is one of 'external validity'. This 'parallel world' terminology can be found also in the discussion of "credible worlds", see Chapter 6.

matter: it matters that economic models are only *representations of* things in the economy, not the things themselves.

The inference gap is not just a matter of language, important though that is, but also a matter of the distance this creates in the experimentable materials. In Chapter 1, I characterized the modelling tradition of economics as one concerned with thin men acting in small worlds. Early discussions of the supply and demand diagram were premised on an economic man who still had some content and feelings, so that we found Mangoldt arguing about people behaving from vanity or fear. Jenkin's discussion of buyers at auctions tells us their judgement of the market depends "partly on the quickness of the bids, and partly on their former experience and general knowledge" (Jenkin, 1887/1996, p. 84). But as my Chapter 4 history of this model of economic man recounts, the fatter character of the nineteenth century gave way to a more thinly characterized rational economic man in twentieth-century economics who became the animating device assumed to be acting inside small worlds like these market demand and supply diagrams. This model economic man is predictable, for he behaves, as Merkies (1997) suggested about the people in the Edgeworth Box, "according to the wishes of the economist" (see my Chapter 3). But the implications of his behaviour have to be worked out for each model in which he is placed (as we shall see in Chapter 9). Economic man is not any real economic man, any more than the supply and demand curves are the real marketplace.

We can express this in a more philosophical way by adopting the language that Rom Harré (2003) used when he made this same point about his "domesticated world" experiments, those conducted using colonies of fruit flies that scientists have captured and tamed to live in their laboratories.[24] In contrast to the *representations* provided by mathematical models, these fruit flies can be taken as *representatives of* fruit flies in the world and may even serve as *representatives for* other kinds of flies.[25] There are epistemological consequences of this shared ontology. It is because real experiments are made of the same stuff as the world that their epistemological power is greater: inference back to the world is likely to be easier and more convincing than for the case of model experiments where there is no shared stuff, no shared ontology of things and materials.[26] The inference gap is much harder to bridge – for example – for model economic man than for his domesticated version in the economists' classroom or laboratory. I will return to this point when I up take up the hint of the last row in Table 7.2 on "surprise versus confoundment". Meanwhile,

---

24 See Weber in Creager et al. (2007) and references therein.

25 See Morgan (2003) on these issues of representing; and Baden-Fuller and Morgan (2010) for the representativeness idea with respect to 'business models'.

26 My commentary in this chapter is concerned with the difference between experiments on mathematical models (and, later on, computer models) of natural or social systems and experiments directly in the material of the natural or social worlds. There are other kinds of experiments wherein the materials of experiment differ from those of the focus of interest and I discuss experiments with analogical models in Chapter 5 and in Morgan and Boumans (2004).

I turn to my final case of model experiments in economics. The discussion so far suggested we could make a rather clean cut between experiments in mathematical, small-world, models and those where models featured in experiments in classrooms and laboratories. But as experimentalists became more ambitious, and their techniques of experiment developed further, they wove models more deeply into their experimental designs. Thus the distinctions that I have made between experiments in the world of the model and models that play a role in experiments, or between model experiments and laboratory experiments, have become increasingly difficult to make.

5. Hybrids

The ideal of experiments given above suggests that successful laboratory experiments rely on the object or process of interest having a high degree of detachability (so that the *ceteris paribus*, *absentibus*, and *neglectis* conditions hold) and of manipulability (so that the scientist can vary or manipulate the process of interest in a controlled way in order to make an experimental demonstration and get some results). But many of the things scientists want to learn about cannot be studied in a laboratory experiment because those things do not have these joint qualities of detachability and manipulability: the weather system and the economic system are two obvious examples of systems that are neither isolatable nor controllable in the laboratory.[27] Economists can reproduce reasonably complex situations and induce certain kinds of economic behaviour in the laboratory (see Guala, 1999b), but cannot easily recreate the open environment of market forces and laws in which those actions occur. As we saw in the classroom experimental work of Chamberlin and Smith, models can offer substitute controls for the market, but these are often far from the open market institutions of interest to economists. Yet mathematical models of these systems are equally likely to be insoluble and intractable for analysis. And even where a system has the qualities necessary to enable model investigation, the ways in which the model's elements and capacities can be manipulated may not be at the level the scientist wants to investigate. It is in these situations, where real-world experiments and model experiments are both equally problematic, that various forms of hybrid experiments and simulations – all of which use models in some way or other – have become important in scientific work.

5.i Virtually Experiments

I take as my case here the work of two of my colleagues at the University of Amsterdam: Cars Hommes and Joep Sonnemans, who wanted to learn about market behaviour at a level of complexity beyond that which could be easily investigated

---

27 On climate models, see Dahan Dalmedico in Creager et al. (2007).

in straightforward lab experiments *and* that was also too complex for mathematical model work (which is typically where simulation comes in; see Chapter 8).[28] In a series of three experiments (see Sonnemans et al., 1999 and Hommes et al., 1999), they joined Hommes' mathematical experiments and numerical simulations using a model to Sonnemans' laboratory experiments on learning. Their aim was to allow role-playing participants to behave as if operating in a market, but to fit their behavioural inputs together in ways that model a market. So here the model device that brought these experiment participants together was an active element in the experiment itself.

The individuals in their laboratory experiments are told that they are each advising a hypothetical supplier who operates in a market where he or she must make output decisions based on the expected price (because of production lags) while buyers made decisions on the actual price. So, the experimental subjects are asked to predict the price for the following year (and to design strategies for predicting future prices) for the supply of the good, knowing only the current and previously realized prices (that is, not knowing how anyone else in the market will act). Such experiments are now conducted in 'laboratories' where 'market' participants are linked via computers rather than 'trading' in an open classroom. These one-period-ahead predictions (or the alternative written down strategies) are then used, either individually or in randomly selected groups, by the experimenting scientists as inputs into a market model, for unknown to the experimental participants, the hypothetical market has demand and supply functions that are already specified by the researchers in mathematical form. But while the model gives a structure of relations to the market, it also functions as the calculation instrument in the experiment, taking the experimental subjects' expected prices as inputs and using them to determine the 'realized' market prices for each period.[29] These model outputs are then taken as existing prices relevant for the prediction of the next period's price, as the experiment runs over several periods.

The values of the parameters in the two functional relations in the model are also varied experimentally so that, according to the participants' predictions, a sequence of prices over time may behave nicely (converge towards a stable market equilibrium level), or get stuck in a cycle, or result in chaotic behaviour, but in theory at least, the participants should be able to learn from their experience to reach the stable level. But there are a number of twists in the experimental design that complicate the ability of the experimental subjects to learn about the mathematical model market in which they are participating over the experimental runs. For example, random 'noise' is added to the demand side, and the demand and supply

---

28 Cars Hommes worked at CeNDEF – Centre for Nonlinear Dynamics in Economics and Finance and Joep Sonnemans at CREED – the experimental unit in the Faculty of Economics and Econometrics at the University of Amsterdam.

29 In fact, this part of the experiment is computerized, so that the computer also acts as the interface among participants, the model, and the experimental outputs.

functions change levels (but not shape) during, or even within, the course of the experimental sessions so that realized prices and the market equilibrium level both change.[30] So variations in the model create some of the experimental variation to which the individuals respond.

Like all laboratory experiments in economics, these ones have both an air of artificiality about them (stemming from the combination of strict rules and structured responses) and a real-world quality (stemming from the natural variation that comes from the participants' behaviour and their predicament). The controls in the experimental situation meant, for example, that participants' price predictions had to be within a fixed range determined by the mathematical model, although they could write down any pricing strategy they liked – so long as it could be programmed.[31] The mathematical model of the market used was a 'cobweb model', well understood from decades of empirical work.[32] But here, the parameter values that govern its shape were chosen by Hommes and Sonnemans to allow for a range of outcomes according to the participants' responses, thus enabling the variation in participants' inputs to be reflected in variations in experimental outputs. The experimental participants were students given small monetary incentives to predict prices in the experimental environment rather than industry managers whose jobs might depend on their abilities to predict prices in the market. Yet, just as in the real world, they had to make decisions about pricing, and pricing strategies, without knowing either the demand relation in the market model or about their rival suppliers' pricing strategies.

The presence of such real-world inputs in these kinds of experiments has led me to describe them as 'virtually experiments' (based on a comparable example on the structural strength of bones tested in computer experiments).[33] By this I mean that although certain aspects of the experimentally defined world are artificially constructed, other aspects are of the real world, or so close to it, that the experiment is virtually a laboratory experiment. Here the human subject inputs are real-world material, while the world they operate in is a model world. Because of this real-world input, the experimental setup allows for unexpected variations in the experimental outcomes. For example, in these experiments in which the participants wrote down their strategies for responding to realized prices, those strategies were fed into the model to calculate long period dynamics of the equivalent realized market prices. The 102 strategies proposed by the experimental participants were all different, and though they could be grouped according to certain types, there was no

---

30 Further variability is provided by varying the number of suppliers (in one experiment there are many and in another, only one); and in learning (in one experiment, subjects can learn as they go along, in the other, they can plan out a strategy in advance and learn only between experiments).

31 They were checked by the experimenters to make sure they were clear, complete, provided unique predictions for each situation, and used only the information available at that time.

32 The cobweb model is based on empirical work in the 1930s on agricultural goods markets, see Morgan (1990).

33 See Morgan (2003) for an analysis of this comparable example.

'typical' strategy; there was no one strategy that could be taken as 'the' representative strategy. This variability in turn limited the inferences that could be made from the experiments. Even when the effect of their different predictions and strategies were combined together via the mathematical model of the market, the patterns were sufficiently ordered only to infer a fivefold classification. These results could then be compared with other results obtained by simulations and analytical work with the model, where the inputs were mathematically modelled people that 'behave' according to certain theoretical or hypothesized rules, such as following "rational" or "adaptive expectations".[34] By using real people, not model economic men, in their experiments, Hommes and Sonnemans enabled a legitimate comparison to be drawn between these real-people experiments and the equivalent model-men experiments where 'the market' was characterized only in a model.

These hybrid forms stretch into simulations: experiments with statistical or mathematical models that generally rely on iterative, rather than deductive, modes of demonstration. Simulation has a comparatively long tradition in economics that predates the computer simulations of the type so familiar nowadays, and often such models may not be built as small world models but only aim to mimic something in the world. These models are used as raw materials in experiments to see whether they generate particular kinds of data patterns that look like those produced by the world. (I discuss simulation models at greater length in Chapter 8 and consider their inferential possibilities there.)

Experiments conducted by Cars Hommes, this time in conjunction with William Brock, provide a example of the range of elements involved in simulating models to mimic patterns in stock market prices (see, e.g., Brock and Hommes, 1997). Such studies use, as inputs, mathematical decision rules appropriate for different kinds of behaviour, labelled with classifications that separate "fundamentalists': those who believe that stock prices reflect fundamental values of the companies concerned, from "technical traders" or "chartists": those who trade on observed patterns of price changes, and "trend followers": those who follow trends (and may overreact in doing so). Hommes and Brock (amongst others) use model experiments to explore what happens when various different such kinds of mathematically described 'traders' are put together in simulated 'markets'. And to the extent that traders in the real stock market act on the decision rules as proposed in the models, or that the mathematical rules real traders use are those used in the model experiments, then we might also accord these model experiments the status of 'virtually experiments'. It appears here that, rather than the model offering a representation in a different kind of material of the rational behaviour decisions made by humans, the mathematical model is itself an input of the real world: that is, the mathematics here is not a model of the behaviour, but provides model-based rules on which economic action is taken, including computer-based trading directly on such models

---

34 These mathematical modelling comparisons drew on Hommes' earlier work (see, e.g., Brock and Hommes [1997] and text below).

without intervening human traders. These models have become "performative", for as Mackenzie (2006) argues, these finance models are "an engine not a camera" – they do not represent what is happening the financial markets; they are the active power in those markets. The models themselves have become part of the market.[35]

5.ii The Status of Hybrids

The range of experiments discussed in this chapter – laboratory, model, and hybrid experiments – have used versions of the same basic supply and demand apparatus and framework. In the exploratory, analytical tradition represented by Marshall's model work (see Section 2), experiments consisted of manipulations of the model enabling the economist to explore deductively what happens in the model when specified events, policy interventions or structural changes affect certain variables. This branch of model-experiment activity relies on small abstract models based on assumptions that often have limited correspondence with the real-world economy. Such model-based experiments are designed to explore the range of possibilities in answering questions posed by various theoretical hypotheses about economic behaviour. In using their internal resources to answer their questions, economists come to understand how the elements of the model fit together; they learn the range of forms the model can take and the variations in response to experimental manipulation that they exhibit, and how to classify them in terms that are generic: they are neither completely general, nor particular to individual cases, but specific for a kind of case. In Marshall's experiments, the model world was both the subject and the object of experiment.

In the laboratory experimental work of Chamberlin and Smith, the active resources were provided by the experimental subjects while the model was largely passive, for it was neither the subject nor object of experiment but part of the experimental design. Even there though, it played two roles; namely, it placed rather loose limits on each participant's behaviour and it acted as a benchmark to assess their experimental results against those obtained from Marshall's model experiments. So the experimental work into the nature of real economic activity depended also on the world conceived in the model, both in performing such experiments and in making inferences from them.

The hybrid cases show us how models and experiments come together in ways that mix real-world and abstract elements. In some of these experiments, there are no people and we are close to the model experiment except that the dynamic of demonstration operates in simulation mode not in deductive mode. In others – the virtually experiments of Hommes and Sonnemans – elements of both laboratory

---

35 This thesis, and the term "performativity", are due to Michel Callon (1998); MacKenzie's (2004, 2006) account offers many insights into this in the case of economic market-making, in particular how the use of models may make a market more efficient at one point, but then be blamed for its failure at another – "counterperformativity". See also MacKenzie (2009), MacKenzie et al. (2007), and Callon et al. (2007) and further discussion in Chapter 10.

and model experiments are embodied at both the design and experimental stage, for the 'market' consists of real people (laboratory inputs) operating in conjunction with a mathematical model and each part is subject to its own kinds of 'control'. In a pragmatic mixture, Hommes and Sonnemans instituted laboratory control where real-world material could be isolated and manipulated and substituted model-based controls in those areas that could not be isolated by experimental means. The demonstration method also involved a mixture of experimental and mathematical methods (of calculation). The model was part of the structure of the experimental world, and was itself varied in an experimentally controlled fashion. (It was also part of the experimental apparatus, used as an instrument to calculate the outputs depending on the various real-world inputs.) The model behaviour was of interest, but so was the behaviour of the participants.[36]

When we add the hybrids to the different kinds of experiments using the supply and demand models in this chapter, it becomes much harder to make clear distinctions between the different kinds of experiments and the role of models in them. Rather, as we have seen, models play many different roles in experiments; sometimes they are the object of experiment, sometimes part of the experimental apparatus, sometimes both, and sometimes models may even create the part of the economic world that they represent.

6. Materials Matter: Surprise versus Confoundment

Let me return, however, to the hard and fast distinction in order to make a final point about inference from model experiments. The archetype of experiment assumes that however much the experimental situation is constrained, controlled, and even constructed, it is nevertheless an experiment on a real-world system. However artificial the environment that is created, however artificial the outcome, the experimental intervention itself involves an action upon or the creation of a material object or phenomenon in the same kind of stuff as the world it investigates. In contrast, much of modern economics functions by using extended model experiments in which the material world of the economy remains absent: model experiments are investigations into a world made of bits of mathematics, diagrams, and so forth, not real people in real markets.

It is tempting to see this contrast between model and real experiments as one between a system in which the outcome to the question is already built into the model that is created and another where experiments may give really new

---

36 Finally, it is worth mentioning briefly another hybrid or intermediate case provided by the kind of model-based experiments found in the econometrics in the same domain of demand and supply models; see Morgan (1990, part II) for discussion and examples. The typical econometric model incorporates a mathematical model as its structure and 'real-world' statistical observations from the economy are used for valuing its parameters. It thus incorporates a lesser degree of control but some greater degree of real-world materiality than a mathematical model experiment (see Boumans and Morgan, 2001).

information. On this view, economists should not be surprised by their model experiments because, of course, they *know* the resources that created their results because they built the model that provides the experimental setup.

However, this mistakes the case. Economists do find themselves surprised by the results of their mathematical model experiments. They know the elements that they put into their model so that the outcomes of model experiments are already built into the model. But the answers to their questions found from experiments on their models are not fully known, or not fully understood, in advance. They created the model because they could not figure out how a number of elements behave together, or how a variation in one thing will affect all the other elements and relationships that they are juggling. As we found in the history of the supply and demand model, model experiments extend the possibilities for scientists to figure out those complicated problems. Scientists want their experiments with models to tell them things they know already – because that way they gain confidence in the model's quality. But they really want their experiments with their models to surprise them for this betokens that they have learnt something new from their model experiments. In principle though, having been surprised, economists can go back through the model experiment and understand why such surprising results occurred.

We saw this in the models built to understand the new macroeconomics of the 1930s. Recall (from Chapter 6) Samuelson's expression of surprise in experimental results as he varied the parameter values in a very small macro-model:

> A variety of qualitatively different results emerge in a seemingly capricious manner from minor changes in hypotheses. Worse than this, how can we be sure that for still different values of our coefficients new and stronger types of behaviour will not emerge: Is it not even possible that if Table 2 [his simulation experiment results] were extended to cover more periods, new types of behaviour might result for these selected coefficients? (Samuelson, 1939, p. 76)

Samuelson's reaction to the "capricious" results of experimenting with his model was to solve the model analytically and classify and characterize all the possible kinds of results (according to different values of the parameters). It is more doubtful that such 'surprise' was something that Marshall would admit too, but we see in his classification work, as in Mangoldt's work, the same desire to characterize, to classify, and to develop concepts interpreting the varying different kinds of results that come from their experiments with models. Surprise marks the unexpected things that economists learn from enquiring into the world of their model and that are associated with the kinds of conceptual development work that we noted in this chapter.

In model experiments, surprise comes from ignorance about the model world. In laboratory experiments, ignorance comes in a different place – it is ignorance not about the model behaviour, but about the world behaviour. So economists experimenting in their classrooms and laboratories might have the wrong account or hypothesis about what they expect to happen in the economy, or their knowledge of the economic behaviour of the subjects they are investigating might be seriously incomplete. We can characterize the contrast between these different kinds of experiments – in the model and in the laboratory – by saying that in experiments on mathematical models of physical, biological, or economic systems, scientists may be surprised, but in real-world experiments directly on those systems, they may be confounded. That is, in the laboratory, there is always the possibility not only of being surprised but of being confounded because the scientists' greater level of ignorance may prevent them from explaining why a particular set of results occurs, and the limits on experimental manipulability may prevent them easily reaching an understanding of why such results occur.

In our examples from Hommes and Sonnemans, it is the unexpectedness which results from their real-world inputs, revealed (by the participants) to the experimenters but not designed or known by them beforehand, which creates the possibility of genuinely experimental outcomes, that is, ones that might confound the experimenters' expectations. Recall that they found so much variation in one part of their experiment that though they were able to suggest interpretations for some of the patterns of behaviour that emerged, others were even without pattern.[37] Chamberlin too was confounded by many of his results. For example, some showed that after a movement towards the expected equilibrium level, the path then diverged further from it. There were others in which "the most diverse patterns appear, with no apparently predominant tendencies to be noted" (Chamberlin, 1948, p. 101). Another set of results appeared to contradict an analytical point that "proved at the time exciting at least to the writer and to one particular group of students" (1948, p. 98). The more that the behavioural inputs are of the real world, the more empirically rich they are, the more possibilities there are for confoundment, that is, for turning up unexpected regularities (or even none at all), or for results that don't fit either the standard theory, or the existing knowledge of the economy, or even certain intuitions about the economic world, and so for genuine learning from experiments. This points to the importance of maintaining as much real-world input as possible into economic experiments, and so of allowing participants in the experiments a certain degree of the freedom to behave within the experimental setup. The danger for the economic experimentalists is that they control the behaviour of their participants so closely to their models of how people should behave that those subjects have no freedom to act in ways not dictated by economic science.[38] In such a case those economists might as well have conducted the experiment in the world of the model rather than the laboratory of the real world.

In the contrast between model experiments and laboratory experiments in Section 4, it was suggested that inference from model experiments is weak but

---

37 See Sonnemans et al. (1999, p. 20).

38 See Santos (2007), who has taken up the challenge of discussing the trade-off between control and agency.

wide and from real experiments is strong but narrow. These were comparisons of the scope of inference to apply to more or less detailed cases and circumstances in the world. Here I am pointing to a different aspect of inference: its focus. Real experiments, in the same materials as the world, have a potentially greater epistemological power than model ones with respect to the world – such experiments give the possibility of observing new patterns, of establishing new stable regularities and so uncovering new phenomena unexplainable given the existing body of knowledge and so confounding the scientist (see Morgan, 2005 for further discussion of this). Model experiments offer less inferential power to learn about the world. But the possibility of model experiments to surprise, that is, to produce results that are unexpected against the background of existing knowledge and understanding, remains an important, even powerful, way in which economic theories and concepts are developed and refined. The surprising results of model experiments lead *not to the discovery of new phenomena in the real world, but to the recognition of new things in the small world of the model,* and thence to the development of new categories of things and new concepts and ideas in economics.

Acknowledgement

I thank the British Academy for supporting my research during the initial work on this topic. This chapter has grown out of several papers. The first was prepared for the workshop "Towards a More Developed Philosophy of Scientific Experimentation" (Amsterdam, June 2000) at the invitation of Hans Radder and appeared as Morgan (2003). The paper was prompted by two events: Tony Keaveny's seminar on bone experiments at UC Berkeley in Fall 1999 which formed the example for my commentary on Nancy Cartwright's paper on experiments prepared for the Princeton Workshops on "Model Systems, Cases and Exemplary Narratives" during 1999–2000. I was able to present these ideas to the British Association Festival of Science in 2002. My thanks go to Tony Keaveny and his colleague, Michael Liebschner, and the Princeton workshop organisers, Angela Creager, M. Norton Wise, and Liz Lunbeck. The second was a joint paper with Marcel Boumans written at the invitation of the editors of *Journal of Economic Methodology* entitled "*Ceteris Paribus* Conditions: Materiality and the Application of Economic Theories" (2001). I thank Marcel for an extremely stimulating joint writing experience! The third paper, drawing on the previous two, was prepared for "Model Based Reasoning" (Pavia, May 2001), given also at "Language, Logic and Logistics: Modeling and Cross-Disciplinary Discourse" (State University of New Mexico, January 2001) and published as Morgan (2002a). I thank Cars Hommes for discussions about his experiments. The extension of materials on categorization were developed for a session on models at the ASSA 2005; and those on "confoundment versus surprise" for a meeting on experiments (Nottingham, 2003) that led to Morgan (2005). I particularly thank Marcel Boumans, Francesco Guala, Rom Harré, Arthur Petersen, Hans Radder, Norton Wise, Angela Creager, Rachel Ankeny, Margaret Morrison, Dan Hausman, and participants at the above meetings and subsequent seminars at Nijmegen, INEM (Amsterdam), Melbourne, ANU, and A Coruña for all their useful questions and comments.

References

Baden-Fuller, Charles and Mary S. Morgan (2010) "Business Models as Models". *Long Range Planning*, 43, 156–71.

Boumans, Marcel (1999) "Representation and Stability in Testing and Measuring Rational Expectations". *Journal of Economic Methodology*, 6, 381–401.

(2002) "Calibration of Models in Experiments". In Lorenzo Magnani and Nancy J. Nersessian (eds), *Model-Based Reasoning: Science, Technology, Values* (pp. 75–94). New York: Kluwer Academic/Plenum Press.

(2005) *How Economists Model the World to Numbers*. London: Routledge.

Boumans, M. and M. S. Morgan (2001) "*Ceteris Paribus* Conditions: Materiality and the Application of Economic Theories". *Journal of Economic Methodology*, 8:1, 11–26.

Brock, W. A. and C. Hommes (1997) "Models of Complexity in Economics and Finance". In C. Heij, J. M. Schumacher, B. Hanson, and C. Praagman (eds), *System Dynamics in Economic and Financial Models* (pp. 3–44). New York: Wiley.

Brodbeck, May, 1968 [1959] "Models, Meaning and Theories". In M. Brodbeck (ed), *Readings in the Philosophy of the Social Sciences* (pp. 579–601). New York: Macmillan.

Callon, Michel (1998) *The Laws of Markets*. Oxford: Blackwell.

Callon, Michel, Yuval Millo, and Fabien Muniesa (2007) [eds] *Market Devices*. Oxford: Blackwell.

Cartwright, N. (2000) "Laboratory Mice, Laboratory Electrons, and Fictional Laboratories". Paper for Princeton Workshop on Model Systems, Cases and Exemplary Narratives, January 2000.

Chamberlin, E. H. (1948) "An Experimental Imperfect Market". *Journal of Political Economy*, 56:2, 95–108.

Chang, Hasok (2001) "Spirit, Air and Quicksilver: The Search for the 'Real' Scale of Temperature". *Historical Studies in the Physical and Biological Sciences*, 31, 249–84.

(2004) *Inventing Temperature: Measurement and Scientific Progress*, Oxford: Oxford University Press.

Collins, Harry M. (1990) *Artificial Experts, Social Knowledge and Intelligent Machines*. Cambridge, MA: MIT Press.

Cournot, Augustin (1838/1960) *Researches into the Mathematical Principles of the Theory of Wealth*. Translated by Nathaniel T. Bacon. New York: Kelley reprint.

Creager, Angela, Elizabeth Lunbeck, and M. Norton Wise (2007) [eds], *Science Without Laws: Model Systems, Cases, and Exemplary Narratives*. Durham, NC: Duke University Press.

Creedy, John (1992) *Demand and Exchange in Economic Analysis*. Aldershot: Edward Elgar.

(1998) *Development of the Theory of Exchange*. Cheltenham: Edward Elgar.

Dahan Dalmedico, Amy (2007) "Models and Simulations in Climate Change: Historical, Epistemological, Anthropological and Political Aspects". In Angela Creager, Elizabeth Lunbeck, and M. Norton Wise (eds), *Science Without Laws: Model Systems, Cases, and Exemplary Narratives* (pp. 125–56). Durham, NC: Duke University Press.

Ekelund, Robert B. and Robert F. Hébert (1999) *Secret Origins of Modern Microeconomics; Dupuit and the Engineers*. Chicago: University of Chicago Press.

Ekelund, Robert B. and Mark Thornton (1991) "Geometric Analogies and Market Demand Estimation: Dupuit and the French Contribution". *History of Political Economy*, 23:3, 397–418.

Franklin, Allan (1986) *The Neglect of Experiment*. Cambridge: Cambridge University Press.

(1990) *Experiment, Right or Wrong*. Cambridge: Cambridge University Press.

Gibbard, A. and Varian, H. R. (1978) "Economic Models". *The Journal of Philosophy* 75:11, 664–77.

Gooding, David (1990) *Experiment and the Making of Meaning*. Dordrecht: Kluwer Academic.

Gooding, David, T. Pinch, and S. Schaffer (1989) *The Uses of Experiment*. Cambridge: Cambridge University Press.

Guala, Francesco (1999a) *Economics and the Laboratory*. Ph.D. thesis, University of London.

(1999b) "The Problem of External Validity (or 'Parallelism') in Experimental Economics". *Social Science Information*, 38:4, 555–73.

(2002) "Models, Simulations, and Experiments". In Lorenzo Magnani and Nancy J. Nersessian (eds), Model-Based Reasoning: *Science, Technology, Values* (pp. 59–74). New York: Kluwer Academic/Plenum Press.

(2003) "Experimental Localism and External Validity". *Philosophy of Science*, 70, 1195–1205.

(2005) *The Methodology of Experimental Economics*. New York: Cambridge University Press.

(2008) "History of Experimental Economics". In S. Durlauf and L. Blume (eds), *The New Palgrave Dictionary of Economics*, Vol. 3 (pp. 152–6). London: Palgrave-Macmillan.

Hacking, Ian (1983) *Representing and Intervening*. Cambridge: Cambridge University Press.

Harré, Rom (2003) "The Materiality of Instruments in a Metaphysics for Experiments". In Hans Radder (ed), *The Philosophy of Scientific Experimentation* (pp. 19–38). Pittsburgh: Pittsburgh University Press.

Hartmann, Stephan (1996)"The World as a Process: Simulations in the Natural and Social Sciences". In Rainer Hegselmann, Ulrich Mueller, and Klaus G. Troitzsch (eds), *Modelling and Simulation in the Social Sciences from the Philosophy of Science Point of View* (pp. 77–100). Dordrecht: Kluwer Academic.

Hausman, Daniel M. (1990) "Supply and Demand Explanations and their *Ceteris Paribus* Clauses". *Review of Political Economy*, 2, 168–87.

(1992) *The Inexact and Separate Science of Economics*. Cambridge: Cambridge University Press.

Heidelberger, M. and F. Steinle (1998) *Experimental Essays: Versuche zum Experiment*. Baden-Baden: Nomos Verlagsgesellschaft.

Hommes, Cars, J. Sonnemans, J. Tuinstra, and H. van de Velden (1999) "Expectations Driven Price Volatility in an Experimental Cobweb Economy". University of Amsterdam CeNDEF Working Paper, 99–07.

Humphrey, Thomas M. (1992) "Marshallian Cross Diagrams and Their Uses before Alfred Marshall: The Origins of Supply and Demand Geometry". *Economic Review*, 78:2, 3–23.

Jenkin, Fleeming (1887) "The Graphic Representation of the Laws of Supply and Demand, and Their Application to Labour". In *Papers Literary, Scientific, etc*, Vol. II. Edited by S. Colvin and H. A. Ewing. London: Longan and Green; and as *LSE Scarce Tracts in Economics*, III (1996). Routledge/Thoemmes Press.

Johnson, W. E. (1894–6) "Method of Political Economy". In Robert H. Inglis Palgrave (ed), *Dictionary of Political Economy*, Vol. II (pp. 739–48). Reprinted 1917. London: Macmillan.

Lakatos, Imre (1963) *Proofs and Refutations*. Edinburgh: Nelson.

Le Gall, Philippe (2007) *A History of Econometrics in France: From Nature to Models*. London: Routledge.

MacKenzie, Donald (2004) "The Big, Bad Wolf and the Rational Market: Portfolio Insurance, the 1987 Crash and the Performativity of Economics". *Economy and Society*, 33, 303–34.

(2006) *An Engine, Not a Camera*. Cambridge, MA: MIT Press.

(2009) *Material Markets*. Oxford: Oxford University Press.

MacKenzie, Donald, Fabian Muniesa, and Lucia Siu (2007) *Do Economists Make Markets*. Princeton, NJ: Princeton University Press.

Magnani, Lorenzo and Nancy J. Nersessian (2002) *Model-Based Reasoning: Science, Technology, Values*. New York: Kluwer Academic/Plenum Press.

Mäki, Uskali and Piimies, Jukka-Pekka (1998) 'Ceteris paribus'. In John B. Davis, D. Wade Hands, and Uskali Mäki (eds), *The Handbook of Economic Methodology*. (pp. 55–9). Cheltenham: Edward Elgar.

von Mangoldt, Hans K. E. (1863/1962) *Grundriss der Volkswirtschaftslehre*, Book III, Chapter 3, Part 1 translated as "The Exchange Ratio of Goods" by Elizabeth Henderson, *International Economic Papers*, No. 11, pp. 32–59 (2nd, abridged edition of original German, 1871).

Marshall, Alfred (1890) *Principles of Economics*, 8th edition, 1930. London: Macmillan.

Mayo, Deborah (1996) *Error and the Growth of Experimental Knowledge*. Chicago: University of Chicago Press.

Merkies, A. H. Q. M. (1997) "Zo" Afscheidscollege, September, 1997, Vrije Universiteit, Amsterdam.

Morgan, Mary S. (1990) *The History of Econometric Ideas*. Cambridge: Cambridge University Press.

(2001) "Models, Stories and the Economic World". *Journal of Economic Methodology*, 8:3, 361–84 (also in Mäki, Uskali [2002] *Fact and Fiction in Economics* (pp. 178–201). Cambridge: Cambridge University Press.

(2002a) "Model Experiments and Models in Experiments". In Lorenzo Magnani and Nancy J. Nersessian (eds), *Model-Based Reasoning: Science, Technology, Values* (pp. 41–58). New York: Kluwer Academic/Plenum Press.

(2002b) "How Models Help Economists to Know". [Commentary on John Sutton's *Marshall's Tendencies. What Can Economists Know?* (2000)] *Economics and Philosophy*, 18, 5–16.

(2003) "Experiments Without Material Intervention: Model Experiments, Virtual Experiments and Virtually Experiments". In Hans Radder (ed), *The Philosophy of Scientific Experimentation* (pp. 216–35). Pittsburgh: Pittsburgh University Press.

(2005) "Experiments vs Models: New Phenomena, Inference and Surprise". *Journal of Economic Methodology*, 12:2, 177–84.

Morgan, M. and M. Boumans (2004) "Secrets Hidden by Two-Dimensionality: The Economy as a Hydraulic Machine". In S. de Chadarevian and N. Hopwood (eds), *Models: The Third Dimension of Science* (pp. 369–401). Stanford, CA: Stanford University Press.

Oreskes, N. (2000) 'Why Believe a Computer: Models, Measures and Meaning in the Natural World'. In J. S. Schneiderman (ed), *The Earth Around Us: Maintaining a Livable Planet* (pp. 70–82). San Francisco: W. H. Freeman.

Oreskes, N., K. Shrader-Frechette, and K. Belitz (1994) "Verification, Validation, and Confirmation of Numerical Models in the Earth Sciences". *Science*, February 4, 263, 641–6.

Radder, Hans (2003) [ed] *The Philosophy of Scientific Experimentation*. Pittsburgh: Pittsburgh University Press.

Rau, Karl Heinrich (1841) *Grundsätze der Volkswirtschaftslehre*. Heidelberg: C. F. Winter.

Reiss, Julian (2002) "Causal Inference in the Abstract or Seven Myths about Thought Experiments". *Causality, Metaphysics and Methods Technical Report*, 03/02, CPNSS, London School of Economics.

Rheinberger, Hans-Jörg (1997) *Towards a History of Epistemic Things: Synthesizing Proteins in the Test Tube*. Stanford, CA: Stanford University Press.

Samuelson, Paul A. (1939) "Interactions Between the Multiplier Analysis and the Principle of Acceleration". *Review of Economics and Statistics*, 21, 75–8.

Santos, Ana C. (2007) "The 'Materials' of Experimental Economics: Technological versus Behavioral Experiments". *Journal of Economic Methodology*, 14:3, 311–37.

Schabas, Margaret (2008) "Hume's Monetary Thought Experiments". *Studies in History and Philosophy of Science*, Part A, 39:2, 161–9.

Schneider, Erich (1960) "Hans von Mangoldt on Price Theory: A Contribution to the History of Mathematical Economics". *Econometrica*, 28:2, 380–92.

Smith, Adam (1776) *An Inquiry into the Nature and Causes of The Wealth of Nations*, edited by R. H. Campbell and A. S. Skinner. Oxford: Oxford University Press, 1976.

Smith, Vernon L. (1962) "An Experimental Study of Competitive Market Behaviour". *Journal of Political Economy*, 60:2, 111–37.

Sonnemans, Joep, C. Hommes, J. Tuinstra, and H. van de Velden (1999) "The Instability of a Heterogeneous Cobweb Economy: A Strategy Experiment on Expectation Formation". University of Amsterdam CeNDEF Working Paper 99–06.

Sutton, John (2000) *Marshall's Tendencies*. Cambridge, MA: MIT Press.

Valeriani, Simona (forthcoming 2012) "Models as 'In-Between-Knowledge' in the Construction of St Paul's Cathedral", in *Proceedings of the Conference 'The Model, a Tool in the Architectural Project'*, Ecole de Chaillot, Cité de l'Architecture et du Patrimoine, Editions Lieux Dits.

Weber, Marcel (2007) "Redesigning the Fruit Fly: The Molecularization of *Drosophila*". In Angela Creager, Elizabeth Lunbeck, and M. Norton Wise (eds), *Science Without Laws: Model Systems, Cases, and Exemplary Narratives* (pp. 23–45). Durham, NC: Duke University Press.

Whitaker, J. K. (1975) *The Early Economic Writings of Alfred Marshall, 1867–1890*. London: Macmillan/Royal Economic Society.

Yaneva, A. (2005) "Scaling Up and Down: Extraction Trials in Architectural Design", *Social Studies of Science*, 35:6, 867–94.

8

Simulation: Bringing a Microscope into Economics

1. The Birth of a New Technology

It is evident that one of primary places of use for models in modern sciences lies in various kinds of simulation. Economics is no exception: a distinctive culture of simulation emerged in the social sciences in the years around 1960. This sudden explosion in the use of the term "simulation" covered a very broad range of practises: a variety of types of 'experiments' including people in role-playing experiments (known then as "gaming"), computation machines, probability setups, statistical data, mathematical models, and games of chance.[1] All these elements fitted under the same umbrella, and so apart from the notion of mimicking, or imitation,

---

1 A search of the electronic journals at JSTOR in economics (including some management), statistics, and demography journals shows that "simulation", used in those senses, had 4 mentions between 1951 and 1954; 36 usages in 1955–8; and 180 in the years 1959–61. (The term had other meanings before 1950, when it was used to refer either to workers feigning sickness in insurance schemes, or to the use of policy to create the conditions for perfect competition.)

inherent in the meaning of the term 'simulation', the possibilities of giving a neat definition are small. The extraordinary range of the term is revealed in a bibliography in the house journal of the American Statistical Association, and in a symposium in the house journal of the American Economic Association, both in 1960.[2] These documents allow us to explore the connotations of the new term 'simulation' in economics and to trace back its separate roots into the interwar period. Each of the elements has its own longer tradition, yet, like a family tree where the same first names keep reappearing through the generations, the elements of simulation in economics often tangle together and reappear.

My particular interests in this literature are twofold. The first is to understand the historical dynamic by which the newly emerged method of modelling came to be combined with an older experimental tradition from statistics, a newer experimental mode in social sciences, and the new research tool of the computer, to form the technology of simulation.[3] This is, not by intent but by content, a largely American history, situated within the immediate context of the Cold War and its research technologies. My historical enquiry focusses on two figures, Martin Shubik and Guy Orcutt, who played an important developmental role in creating simulation techniques in economics. Their personal histories help us to understand how the new technology was broadly constituted out of some old and some new techniques and ideas, and yet encompassed a considerable variety of simulation types.

This literature of 1960 also serves my second interest, namely to understand how models fit into in the technology of simulation and to see how this technology, in turn, fits into the history of reasoning modes in economics. In this context, 1960 is an apparently undistinguished moment in the history of social sciences in America. It is not a moment when the world of social science changed because simulation dropped into the tool box of methods. Rather it is a moment when the multiple possibilities of experiments with models and real experiments (that had emerged already in several different forms, as we saw in the last two chapters) coalesced together as a new technology under the all-embracing single term: simulation. This coalition was relatively short-lived, for as experimental economics grew in strength, it developed into its own self-confident field and style of reasoning. But at this point of time, an *American Economic Review* (*AER*) Symposium of 1960, and the 1962 publication of a book of readings entitled *Simulation in the Social Sciences*

---

2   For the bibliography in the *Journal of the American Statistical Association* (*JASA*), see Shubik (1960a). The *American Economic Review* symposium (to be discussed later in the chapter) contained an essay survey of simulation in the economics of firms and industries by Shubik (1960b), Guy Orcutt's (1960) first substantive report of his microsimulation studies, and a paper by Clarkson and Simon (1960) reporting their attempt to programme a computer to mimic bankers' investment decisions. A slightly later view of the field might be found in the entries on "Simulation" in the *International Encylopedia of the Social Sciences* in 1968 (edited by Sills).

3   Simulation is nowadays often taken to refer narrowly to a substitute for analytical techniques in mathematical work, but not in this time nor in the social sciences disciplines.

(Guetzkow, 1962), provide evidence of simulation as a combined methodology. The literature of those years around 1960 is self-conscious in a way that earlier and later literature is not: simulation as a way of doing social science was perceived as new, and because of its newness, it had to be explained, justified, and recommended to readers.[4]

My two questions about models in relation to simulation fit naturally into broader enquiries into simulation undertaken by historians and philosophers of science in recent years, although there seems no generally accepted definition or account of simulation. The notion has been difficult to pin down because it has involved different elements and practices at different times and in different subject communities.[5] For this 1960s group of scholars in the social sciences, simulation was broadly perceived to be a technology of investigation that used experiments to reveal aspects of the models under study, and from which inferences might be made. In certain crucial respects, we can think of the technology of simulation as bringing a microscope to economic models. Like the specimens placed under the slide of a microscope, simulation puts the world in the model under greater scrutiny than other modes of model analysis. Later in this chapter, I explore this analogy of the simulation technology as taking a microscope to the models of economics, to understand what is involved in the preparation of models for such scrutiny and what kind of invasive techniques are used to observe the worlds in those models.

Economic models are also instruments to enquire with into the nature of the world (see Chapter 1). In this respect, the association of the word simulation with that of mimicry suggests that the credibility of models relies – in some way or other – on their ability to mimic. My analysis of simulation as a technology akin to microscopy suggests not only how, and so why, inferences about the real world that rely on this mimicking power of models may be misleading, but also when and why such inferences might be justified.

---

4 Ten years later, an equivalent collection of essays (Guetzkow et al., 1972) betrays a much greater degree of maturity and assumes that the simulation approach is understood and acceptable.

5 Apart from biographical and autobiographical pieces, and brief histories from field participants, there has been little historical evaluation of the development of the technology as a broad movement, but there are a number of specific studies. For example, Peter Galison (1997), working on physics of this period, suggests we see in simulation something that is not quite theory and not quite experiment. Evelyn Fox-Keller (2003), on physics and AI, concentrates on the thing that is being simulated in computer experiments, and points to the change in meaning of the notion from something that is false to something that imitates. In Sergio Sismondo's edited volume (1999) on simulation and modelling, Eric Winsberg looks at the many model layers required in simulation and Deborah Dowling portrays simulation as a method of experimenting on theories. Hartmann (1996) discusses a variety of functions that simulation play while Humphreys (2004) focusses particularly on computer aspects of simulation. More recently, there has been an explosion of interest in the subject with specialist meetings and at least two special issues of journals devoted to simulation in the sciences (for examples, see those edited by Knuuttila et al. [2006] and by Frigg et al. [2009]).

2. Simulation: Content and Context

The 1960 bibliography on "Simulation, Gaming, Artificial Intelligence and Allied Topics" was prepared by the economist Martin Shubik (see his 1960b), then a consultant to the General Electric Company. Looking at this material enables us to take a wide-angled lens to the historical question: What was simulation in 1960? The first major point to notice is its extraordinary range of subject matters, and while statistics is certainly one of the main roots of simulation methods (the bibliography was published in the *Journal of the American Statistical Association*), Shubik was reporting an essentially multidisciplinary activity.[6] The social sciences and engineering sciences were linked into a network via a number of in-between topics and fields (see Figure 8.1). The broad span of issues – from logistical ones to individual rationality and the behaviour of organisations – cover the space from management to political science, from decision making to weapons, and from engineering to psychology. Shared between the fields, we see various kinds of games – war games with sand tables or in logistics labs, business games based on company histories, and role-playing games; different connotations attach to the term 'games' in relation to the subject fields.[7] Economics finds its place both around and within this circle, with a considerable number of articles about firms/markets and industries, in role-playing experiments, and in econometric and computer simulations of models.

Shubik placed the majority of the works he surveyed into the two categories labelled "simulation" and "gaming" (role-playing experiments), from which I have drawn the map in Figure 8.1. But, like many undertaking such bibliographic exercises, Shubik clearly had difficulty in separating out his two categories and in classifying his material.[8] He tried to use the following definition:

> Gaming usually (though not always) makes use of a simulated environment to study the behavior of, or to teach individuals, while simulation is directed towards studying the behavior of a system given the behavior of the individual units or vice versa. Gaming always involves the presence of decision-makers. Simulation does not necessarily entail the involvement of individuals. In most instances a simulation involves only the machine manipulation of a model. (Shubik, 1960a, p. 736)

But Shubik's attempts to make this taxonomy of simulation work were defeated both by the recalcitrance of his material and by the contemporary users of the terminology, who understood simulation as a research approach that defined a set of

---

6　For a more extended discussion of the coverage of this bibliography, see Morgan (2004).

7　There are a number of possibly interesting links (e.g., between war gaming and management games) that have not been much researched, though see two papers by Rowley (1998, 1999).

8　Similar difficulties beset the third section on Monte Carlo studies. Applied examples using Monte Carlo were included within the simulation category in his section I and technical papers on developments in Monte Carlo appeared in his section III.

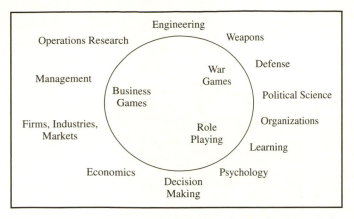

Figure 8.1. Shubik's 1960 Bibliography: Subject Map for the "Simulation" and "Gaming" Categories.

Source: Mary S. Morgan (2004) "Simulation: The Birth of a Technology to Create 'Evidence'" *Revue D'Histoire des Sciences*, 57:2, 341–77, p. 345. Reproduced with permission of *Revue D'Histoire des Sciences*.

research methods.[9] At that moment of time, "simulation" covered both simulated environments and simulated processes and these were not neatly separable.

Shubik's perceptions of the shared spaces of simulation were not idiosyncratic. Guetzkow's 1962 book of readings on simulation in the social sciences contained accounts of dynamic flight simulators; role-playing air-defence experiments from RAND's Systems Research Laboratory; computer simulations of thinking; a management game report; and examples from engineering, transport queuing, and role playing from political science, along with computer simulations of elections.[10] In contrast to the generous nature of the subject fields found within Shubik's categories of "simulation" and "gaming", the majority of the "Monte Carlo" section in the bibliography came from mathematics, statistics, and computation with some papers from natural sciences and engineering (see Figure 8.2). This forms a further set of axes for techniques and ideas which feed into the fields outlined in Figure 8.1: a set of elements that includes the research tools of computers and yet another kind of game, games of chance.

9 Even in Shubik's own division of items between categories, we find people-based experiments (i.e., "gaming") in amongst the "simulations" and machine-based research (i.e., "simulations") in amongst the "gaming"! He also wondered if it might be useful to separate "strategic" from "tactical" simulation, "analogue" from "digital" computer simulations, and both from "man–machine" simulation. Though he did not make use of these classifications, they are all ones that reappear in other discussions of the day.

10 Two similarly named collections of essays provide useful contrasts: the 1972 collection (Geutzkow et al., 1972) contained role-playing and computer-based simulations within a more restricted traditional social sciences range, whereas a 1996 collection (Hegselmann et al., 1996) contained no gaming or experiments with people. After 1960, the pattern of usage of the term 'simulation' waxed and waned, and in settling down, its range of meaning was reduced to that of computer simulation.

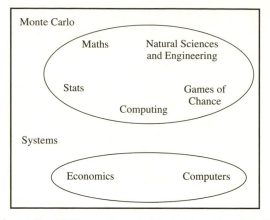

Figure 8.2. Shubik's 1960 Bibliography: Subject Map for the "Monte Carlo" and "Systems" Categories.

Source: Mary S. Morgan (2004) "Simulation: The Birth of a Technology to Create 'Evidence'" *Revue D'Histoire des Sciences*, 57:2, 341–77, p. 347. Reproduced with permission of *Revue D'Histoire des Sciences*.

It is also evident from the publication sources that what we have here is the intersection between the sciences and two kinds of secretive establishments: we are warned by Shubik that there were many other papers that could not be included in his bibliography for either they were classified as part of the defence establishment's Cold War stance or they were company documents and reports considered to constitute commercial secrets.[11] So we must extend the military–big (natural) science complex that grew up in World War II and the Cold War period to the social sciences including management studies, and we must add to that the military–industrial complex familiar to economic historians and going back to World War I (and intermittently to the mid-nineteenth century).[12] Shubik's bibliography shows how entrenched that military–industrial–science complex had become for the social sciences, for U.S. Defense Department research contracts in this field of simulations and gaming employed a mix of social scientists, mathematicians, and defence experts. This mix included not only some already known multidisciplinarians such as John von Neumann and Herbert Simon, but also a host of younger talents who later became leaders in their own fields in American academe. With the work of Mirowski (2002), it is becoming increasingly clear that much of the basic and technical research in economics in the USA during the Cold War period was funded directly or indirectly by various arms of the defence establishment.

11 Not all US Defense Department contract material was classified during the Cold War. The bibliography contained many RAND reports and many other research papers that originated from Defense Department funding of various kinds. The three most populous outlets in Shubik's simulation and gaming (his Categories I and II) came from RAND, from the *Journal of the Operations Research Society of America* and from a collection of management journals.
12 For recent discussions of Cold War big natural science, see Galison (1997); for the social science and industrial side, see Hounshell (1997), Jardini (1996), and Mirowski (2002); for the management studies connections, see Rowley (1999).

From the point of view of this newly established history of Cold War economics, there is one striking omission from Shubik's bibliography, namely, game theory. The omission is striking both because game theory was fostered within some of the same institutions leading the field of simulation within the military–science context (e.g., RAND) and because – as we will see – Shubik himself was known as a game theorist at this time; indeed, he surveyed the use of game theory in industrial economics in a parallel paper in May 1960 (Shubik, 1960c). The absence of game theory in his bibliography makes an important point for my interests. While it may be tempting to think that the connection between *game theory* (the theory of games of strategy) and *gaming* is a very intimate one, the former being the theory for the latter, this quite mistakes the meaning of the term gaming as it was used during this period. 'Gaming' was understood to be a broad-based experimental research and training method involving people playing roles (either simulating the behaviour of others, or possibly playing their own usual roles) in an actual or simulated environment – for example, to investigate how team learning took place. 'Game theory' was a mathematical body of work about decision making in strategic interaction, as we shall see in Chapter 9. In the late 1940s and early 1950s, mathematical game theorists, such as Shubik, invented "playable games" of strategy to illustrate and explore their pathological or paradoxical properties and played such games with each other. But Shubik regarded this as an informal "trying-things-out" activity, a practice he separated from the carefully designed and controlled role-playing experiments falling under the label "gaming".[13] For Shubik, game theory was neither simulation nor experiment, and there was no reason to confuse them, yet he carried out gaming (i.e., role-playing experiments) on game theory as well as contributing to both fields.

3. Shubik and Simulation

3.i Martin Shubik's History

A simulation of a system or an organism is the operation of a model or simulator which is a representation of the system or organism. The model is amenable to manipulations which would be impossible, too expensive or impracticable to perform on the entity it portrays. The operation of the model can be studied and, from it, properties concerning the behavior of the actual system or its subsystems can be inferred. (Shubik, 1960b, p. 908)[14]

13 See next section, and for this part of Shubik's history, see his 1992, p. 159 and pp. 248–52 (in Weintraub, 1992). For an explicit statement of the separation of gaming and games – see Shubik 1966 (p. 10), and more generally, his 1975 book.

14 One way to notice the importance of Shubik's claim about the nature of economic models used in simulations is by contrasting it with those models used in operations research (OR) at that same point in time, where the aim was to be prescriptive for how firms ought to behave, rather than accurately descriptive of how they do behave. For example, contrast our authors' notion of a representing model with Dorfman's 1960 description of OR, where the activity is described as one of

How did Shubik come to know the technology of simulation so intimately that he could assemble an authoritative and wide-ranging bibliography on it within a few years of his Ph.D. thesis? Shubik's career history speaks both to the content and context of simulation evident in his bibliography and its range in economics at that time.

Shubik chose mathematics as his field of study at the University of Toronto, despite a highly variable performance in mathematics at high school.[15] The choice was instrumental: the young Shubik fancied a career in politics, and finding the social science studies available in 1943 unimpressive, decided that at least he would gain some useful tools. At the same time, as a navy reservist, he gained experience in electronics. This start proved effective for his continuing graduate studies in economics, but both these and his extracurricular activities in left-wing political parties and union schools made him disillusioned with his chances of changing the world by using his economics within a political career. The seminal moment in his history, according to his own hindsight, was when he picked up John von Neumann and Oskar Morgenstern's *The Theory of Games and Economic Behavior* (1944) while browsing the library one day. He gained entry to the economics department at Princeton in 1949 and was, as he says, "swept into the excitement" (Shubik, 1997, p. 97), the excitement of being just in the right place at the right time, for Princeton was one of the two main research centres at which the theory of games was being developed in the late 1940s and early 1950s. The location of the excitement was the mathematics department's seminar, in which a number of economics students along with one of its professors, namely Morgenstern himself, were active participants.[16]

Shubik's enthusiasm for game theory is evident in his first professional publications dating from the early 1950s. Only a year after earning his Ph.D. in 1953 and while still at Princeton, he published a book of readings in game theory, which began

"formulating [the] problem by means of formal mathematical models" and a model is defined as "a symbolic description of a phenomenon in which its observable characteristics are deduced from simple explanatory first principles (ie assumptions) by manipulating symbols in accordance with the laws of some formal logic" (p. 577). Shubik's and Orcutt's emphasis on the model's representational role is the usual accompaniment to definitions and descriptions of simulations, where the representing capacity relates to the need for validating the model. If the model does not represent the economic system, the mimicking 'evidence' produced by simulation has little value in telling us anything about that economy (but see Section 7). Where OR might use similar experimental techniques of model solution, *they do not aim to mimic* and the validation issue is not important. The OR aim of simulation is to determine what the economic system ought to be like to ensure best performance, whereas, as discussed here, the aim is to understand the working features of the economic system as it is. See also Thomas and Williams (2009) on the different aims of social science simulations in this period.

15 This section draws on Shubik's autobiographical accounts (1992, 1994, and 1997). He was born in New York, educated in England and Canada, and was a member of the Royal Canadian Navy (Reserve) from 1944 to 1950, starting off as "Stoker" and ending as Lieutenant (Electronics and Radar).

16 From this seminar grew Shubik's long-term collaboration in game theory with Lloyd Shapley, a graduate student in the mathematics department.

by attributing the failure of earlier mathematical thinking in the social sciences to their basis in physical analogies (Shubik, 1954 pp. 2–4). He asserted that there were six new interconnected theories where there was a mathematics appropriate for, and adapted to, the social sciences.[17] He had already used two of these – game theory and information theory – in a short paper of 1952 (based on work funded by the Office of Naval Research) in which he took issue with neoclassical economics and claimed to unify the existing economic theory of competition (in which forms of monopolistic competition were then treated independently from that of perfect competition).[18] In doing so, he redefined the firm as "an organization designed to obtain, process, store, and act on information", in other words, the firm as an organisation was like a computer (Shubik, 1952, p. 146).

His was not a straightforward academic career. From Princeton in 1954, following a year at the Center for Advanced Studies in the Behavioral Sciences at Stanford, Shubik went to work at the General Electric Company (in the Operations Research section) in 1956, which "changed his views about how firms actually worked" (1997, p. 103). It grounded his earlier abstract definition of a firm as an information processor:

> In particular, at General Electric, I felt that the future of long-range planning lay in the development of good detailed computer models of firms and the industries they were in. My vision, which still has not been realized, was to see the simulation integrated into the data-gathering system of the firm and used both for the generation of contingent forecasts and long-range planning and for both training and operational gaming. (Shubik, 1994, p. 252)

He supposed that planning, operations, and training would all be managed using the data that flowed every day into the firm and using simulation models and management games both developed for the computer and built specially for that firm.

Meantime, Shubik's thesis was growing into *Strategy and Market Structure* (1959a), the first full-length serious integration of the ideas of game theory into the field of industrial economics (see also Chapter 9, Section 4.iii). His importance in this initiative may easily be overlooked. Economists take it for granted that game theory is about economics. But in the early years, game theory was both a mathematical topic and a series of social (sometimes intensely antisocial) real games, whose most obvious applications were found in military problems and Cold War strategy, rather than in mainstream economics. Shubik was instrumental in making the mathematical part of game theory into a theory for economics, particularly

---

17 The most well developed of these, he claimed, was game theory, wherein analogies connected human and social activities to other human and social subject matters. With our hindsight, we can see that the six fields he mentioned – game theory, information theory, statistical decision theory, choice theory, learning theory, and organization theory – were all well chosen.

18 This was obviously a big claim for a Ph.D. student to make, particularly in the house journal of the Economics Department at the University of Chicago, one of the foremost departments of the day.

the economics of firm and industry behaviour (the subject of his Ph.D. thesis). His contribution has been lauded as the turning point: ".... in 1959 came Shubik's spectacular rediscovery of the core of a market in the writings of F. Y. Edgeworth (1881). From that time on, economics has remained by far the largest area of application of game theory" (Aumann, 1987 p. 467).[19] To reinterpret the new game theory concepts and results in terms of the classic eighty-year-old work of Edgeworth (discussed in Chapter 3) was to establish game theory's place in the heart of modern neoclassical microeconomics.

Shubik's continuing enthusiasm for game theory was moderated from the mid–later 1950s by his growing appreciation of the usefulness of role-playing experiments or gaming and a growing belief that game theory could be tested by "experimental and empirical techniques of simulation" (1959a, p. 556). Why and how did he make this move from game theory to gaming? As early as his 1952 paper, he was considering how people in an organisation argued and came to agreement, and thought about a little role-playing experiment to imagine how this process occurred. But Shubik tells us that his first attempts at experiments in the economics of industry were undertaken with Siegel and Fouraker only in 1957–9, after a chance meeting with Siegel while camping at Yosemite.[20] By 1960, Shubik was undertaking such experiments on his own account (reported Shubik, 1962a), in which he explored various theoretical solution concepts from game theory in a series of different experiments in which games were played under experimental conditions.[21] Meanwhile, following a year's leave at Yale in 1960, he had gone to a research laboratory at IBM working on experimental and business games and forecasting problems. He collaborated there to develop a business game that had a sufficiently rich environment to make a good training tool, but with enough "clean basic structure that it could be analyzed for many game theory and oligopoly theory results" (Shubik, 1994, p. 253).[22]

By 1960 then, Shubik had successfully covered the grounds of simulation and gaming experiments (including the man–machine simulations of business games) as we see in Figure 8.3, which picks out and assembles these elements of Shubik career. It is no wonder that he could write with such authority in surveying the topic

---

19 This comes from the historical survey piece on game theory in the *New Palgrave* (the modern encyclopaedia of economics) and surely overstates the case both in implying Shubik (1959b) turned the tide singlehandedly and that economics took game theory to its heart immediately after 1959 (see Weintraub [1992]). In fact, it was rather slow at taking a general hold in the community. Nevertheless, Shubik's result remains fundamental in the community history.

20 See Shubik (1994, pp. 252 and 257); these experiments that Shubik participated in were reported in Fouraker and Siegel (1963).

21 This work was undertaken while Shubik was at the Cowles Commission at Yale and was completed by February 1961, with, again, funding from the Office of Naval Research. In 1975, Shubik, that student of both game theory and gaming, made the join in a book: *Gaming for Society, Business and War: Towards a Theory of Gaming*.

22 He seems to have specialised in making business games work as research tools: in the 1970s he succeeded in a double aim of creating an artificial player for a business game in a joint research initiative into competitive behaviour and an exploration of the Turing test (see 1994, p. 255).

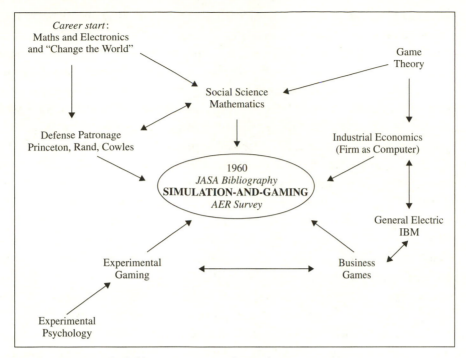

Figure 8.3. Martin Shubik's Experiences of Simulation.

Source: Mary S. Morgan.

of simulation both in his bibliographic treatment of the broad field (1960a) and his survey paper for the *AER* symposium on simulation (1960b). Both were based on a deep, insider's, practitioner's, knowledge of simulation, its research methods, and the economic topics involved.[23]

3.ii Models, Simulated Environments, and Simulated Behaviour

Models are always to be found somewhere in these economic simulations though their location is not always obvious. On the one hand, they are often hidden in the various combinations of factual and fictional resources that economists use

---

23 Shubik's immense knowledge and understanding of the field led him to further survey and critical assessment work in the 1970s, and its range and content speak to the continuing importance of the context I have been painting in here. Thus, in 1970, Shubik and Brewer, under the umbrella of RAND, were commissioned, by the Defense Advanced Research Projects Agency (ARPA, an arm of the U.S. Department of Defense), to inquire into the state of modelling, simulation and gaming in the various parts of the defence establishment in the USA. Their survey covered several hundred models and led to a number of technical reports aimed at their sponsor (e.g., Shubik and Brewer, 1972a, 1972b, and Shubik et al., 1972]). Out of this work, the two men produced a most impressive account for public consumption of their several-year research endeavour, namely *The War Game* (see Brewer and Shubik [1979]). Here Shubik and Brewer provided a measured and detailed but deeply critical study of the use of models, games and simulations (MSGs) by the U.S. military. The book was copyrighted RAND, but was published from the heart of the academic establishment, namely, Harvard University Press.

in simulation, hidden at least compared to econometrics (the statistical branch of economic modelling) where both the model and inputs of real data are clearly flagged.[24] On the other hand, simulations are experiments and, as we already found in our discussion of the varieties of hybrid experiments in Chapter 7, the place and role of models are sometimes quite opaque, particularly – as here – where human subjects and mathematical models are being used in different combinations with computers. Shubik picked out a selection of examples to provide a more detailed account of simulation in his *AER* symposium paper "Simulation of the Industry and the Firm" (1960b); for us, they provide good cases to illustrate the many ways in which models were used in simulations in this period.

Gaming (that is, people in role-playing experiments) in the economics of industry and firms was represented (in Shubik's survey paper) by two different kinds of activities: the environment might be 'rich' as in business games, or more strictly controlled as in (what we would now label) economic experiments. Economic experiments were still rather new, and in this sub-field of economics might be well represented by the work of Shubik's collaborators: Siegel and Fouraker (1960). Following the practices of experimental psychology (Siegel's field), they conducted careful laboratory experiments into the outcome of price bargaining in the situation of isolated exchange between two persons: representing the problem of bilateral monopoly in industrial economics. This was a version of the problem described in the celebrated Edgeworth Box model, which they referred to as an "ancestor model" (discussed in Chapter 3). By tradition dating from Edgeworth (1881), this outcome was thought to be analytically indeterminate, solved in practice by the relative bargaining power of the two individuals. The experimenters used students as their subjects to play the role of firms and placed them in a controlled environment. They constrained their behaviour according to a simple economic model of profits for each of the pair of players, rather as we saw Chamberlin and Smith constrained their experimental subjects with a supply and demand model in Chapter 7. The two students "bargained" in such a way that the experimenters could track the exchange prices and quantities as they were determined in their set of experiments.

Business games, by contrast, embodied very complicated models with many different elements of information. These games emerged in the late 1950s and were just beginning to become popular.[25] The best known one, "The Carnegie Tech Management Game" (see Cohen et al., 1960), used the detergent industry of the day to provide the raw material of economic details for its industry model. This was a "man–machine" simulation: the industrial environment (the model) was programmed on the computer and the people playing the game took the role of managers making the decisions required by the firms participating in the industry and responding to the environment; the computer acted as the calculating device

---

24 Econometric models are not discussed directly in this book, but see Chapter 1 for some comparative points and references, including Morgan (1990) and Boumans (2005).

25 According to Cohen et al. (1960), there were twenty-one business games around at that point.

that solved the individual plans according to the model of industry level activity.[26] In part a teaching tool, the game also provided a research platform for the study of oligopoly industries, and material for a study of team actions, and for a number of other aspects of decision-making behaviour.

Simulations (that is, no role-playing participants) in industrial economics were represented in Shubik's *AER* paper by examples spanning from ones using very detailed descriptions and input data from a real industry or firms to ones where the firm modelled was entirely fictitious and no empirical data were used. Jay Forrester's "Industrial Dynamics" (1958), now considered a classic, set up a complicated model of an individual hypothetical factory's flow of information, orders, inventory, production, and distribution with lags and feedback control mechanisms (see Thomas and Williams, 2009). This "systems analysis" model was then simulated to understand how the information flows and their timing creates certain patterns in other parts of the industrial system. In a similar vein, a mathematical model of an entirely fictitious industry consisting of an initial 100 firms was programmed in Hoggatt (1959) to simulate what will happen in that industry under certain conditions as an exercise in model exploration using a computer.

At the other extreme from these fictional industry models is the famous department store model found in Cyert and March (1963). Together with the researcher C. G. Moore, they carried out a very detailed field study of the decisions that determined the pricing and output decisions of a certain number of departments within a department store. By not only studying carefully the details of the decision processes, but also collecting a quantitative history of pricing (e.g., of "marking up and down", according to circumstances), sales, and so forth, they were able to use all these empirical materials to create a very detailed process model that, using computer help, predicted prices particularly accurately. Another example of empirically based models came in Cohen (1960), who simulated the "shoe, leather, hide sequence" – the sequence of economic activity from raw materials to final output of the shoe industry. In order to model the behaviour of a typical firm in this industry, he required data at a very detailed level and full institutional descriptions of the firms in the sector, both of which were available in the work of Mack (1956). His process model of the whole industry used real input data to estimate a closed dynamic model of the system of relations within the industry. The consequent aggregate industry model was immensely complicated, so he simulated it to produce simulated streams of output data for a long set of future periods.

Somewhere between the fictional firms and industries modelled by Forrester and Hoggatt and real firms and industry models of Cohen and of Cyert and March,

---

26 Business games that used computers as an interface nominally fell into the gaming category, but not all man–machine simulations fulfilled the aims of gaming as Shubik defined them. Sometimes the people participating were taken as given, that is, they and their behaviour are not the subject of investigation; rather, they were the "cheapest effective simulator" of the real life individuals that they were representing (see, e.g., Chapman et al. [1962]).

we have the example of a "paper-machine" simulation exercise. Cyert, Feigenbaum, and March (1959) aimed to develop an accurate model of the behaviour of a generic firm by specifying how firms make decisions in a series of nine steps. This "process model" was built as a "flow diagram", which could be easily translated to computer format and used to simulate the decision processes of two firms in a duopoly industry over hypothetical time. The simulation results were compared to the actual market share and profit ratios from the tin can industry (Continental Can Co. and American Can Co.) over the period 1913–56. The authors claimed a "good fit" (p. 93), that is, between their simulated 'evidence' and the real stream of evidence, though they denied that this demonstration validated their model. I will return to this point later in the chapter.

We can see from these case examples from the 1960 period how simulations and gaming in the economic behaviour of individuals, firms, and industries used models, people, experiments, and computers in a considerable variety of arrangements. Some models involved lots of real firm information, and some relied on hypothetical or fictional firms created by the economist. The computer played perhaps a more important part in the simulations than in the gaming experiments that relied on role-playing, but they were particularly important in the so-called "man–machine" simulations where role playing and complicated models were combined (such as business games).

During his own work with simulation and gaming experiments, including the man–machine business games, Shubik had come to appreciate the advantages of these simulation approaches compared to methods that relied solely on the analysis of simple mathematical economic models, and he gained a very healthy respect for the difficulties involved in these genres of research. His later autobiographical declamations echo, with even more passion than his earlier statements, his discontent with abstract economic models and their idealizing or simplifying assumptions. He explains here how those seeds found in his earliest 1952 examination of game theory grew into the firm belief that the rational economic model man of economics (whose history I gave in Chapter 4) should be replaced with a model of economic man as a sensory computer:

> .... I have tried to escape the early indoctrination, via mathematics, game theory, and economics, in models of the abstract, all-knowing rational decision maker. The rational decision-maker model of the human is at best a poor first-order approximation of a far more complex, intelligent creature who is able to make decisions with highly aggregated information in a limited time and with capacity constraints on calculation. The passions probably are the manifestations of highly complex programs designed to enable us to deal with sensory inputs that would otherwise overwhelm us. (Shubik, 1994, p. 256)

Shubik's vision of man as a computer who manifests passion as outputs from complex programmes working on a bundle of sensory inputs is a far cry from Jevons' late-nineteenth century portrait of a rational economic decision maker whose mind could judge, with the fineness of a mechanical balance, very fine degrees of utility (see Maas, 2001). Shubik's vision reflects how a small number of economists, including those with such divergent ideas as Herbert Simon and Friedrich von Hayek, thought about man's economic behaviour in ways that were very differ-ent from the mainstream views about rational economic agents in the 1950s and 1960s.[27]

4. Guy Orcutt's History and "Microsimulation"

Simulation is a general approach to the study and use of models.... An indi-vidual simulation run may be thought of as an experiment performed upon a model..... A model of something is a representation of it designed to incorpo-rate those features deemed to be significant for one or more specific purposes. (Orcutt 1960, pp. 893 and 897)

A very different trajectory into simulation can be found in the history of Guy Orcutt. His microsimulation method was first introduced to the community of economists in his 1960 *AER* symposium paper and an immediately following book (Orcutt et al., 1961). This microsimulation approach is recognised and referred to by the economics profession as the opening of a new research tradition in economics and demography in which simulation is essential to the research method: that is, the research method is founded on simulation whereas other forms of simulation in economics often form a complementary technology, complementary to real experi-ments, to econometrics, to mathematical modelling and so forth.[28] Orcutt's meth-ods and models, developed through the 1960s, became used routinely in the United States to assess the distributional, economic, and demographic consequences of changes in welfare regimes, tax regimes, and so forth during the 1970s, and later spread to other countries.

Orcutt's first interests lay in electrical engineering, an interest fostered at home, in the field of his first college study, and evident in his later work.[29] He moved from electrical engineering to physics, but switched to economics in graduate school (at the University of Michigan) for the same reasons as Tinbergen earlier – to a more socially useful science, a science that might prevent a second Great Depression (this was after all the late 1930s). During his first job, at MIT, he built an electric

---

27 See Simon's (1991) biography; and on Hayek's work on the brain, see Caldwell (2003). Mirowski's (2002) book explores the considerable scope and depth of economists' engagement with comput-ers and AI in this period. See Chapter 4 here for an account of mainstream views.

28 See, for example, Greenberger et al. (1976), Watts (1991), and the special issue of *Journal of Economic Behavior and Organization* (1990, Vol. 14) reporting papers at a conference in honour of Orcutt for assessments of his role.

29 Biographical details about Orcutt are taken from the assessment sources (see previous footnote) and from autobiographical pieces: Orcutt (1990a, 1990b, 1968). See also Solovey (1993).

regression analyser (i.e., a computer to calculate statistical regressions), and took this with him for his postgraduate work at the Department of Applied Economics in Cambridge between 1946 and 1948. This was, by his own accounts, a most formative experience: there, under Richard Stone's guidance, but using his own purpose-built computer, he initiated a series of analyses of the correlation structures found within aggregate macroeconomic time-series data. His first paper (1948 with Irwin) analysed the data used in the first U.S. macroeconometric model built by Tinbergen (1939). Tinbergen had, in the mid-1930s, built the first ever macroeconometric model, a model of the Dutch economy (Tinbergen, 1937), by relying on the model design proposed by Frisch 1933 (discussed at the beginning of Chapter 6). Empirical data had been used to estimate the parameter values on the equations representing the economy and he had then carried out simulations of that estimated model to explore the effects of six different policy prescriptions to get The Netherlands out of the Great Depression (see Morgan, 1990, chapter 4). Such simulations of policy options became a standard part of econometric model usage in the postwar period.

Though Orcutt greatly admired Tinbergen's macroeconometric work, he came to the conclusion that these aggregate data and their associated empirical business cycle or macro-models were not good material for analysing the economy, nor for undertaking simulation-based examinations of policy changes. It was not that such models necessarily provided bad representations of the macroeconomy, but that the data used for their measurement meant that the possibility of validating the model was extremely doubtful, for the presence of correlation problems in the data rendered the simulations useless. This was the reason Orcutt wanted to move to microeconomic, or individual level, data, taken from across the population, for he believed this would enable him to avoid the problems he had identified in aggregate time-series data. It was individuals who made economic and demographic decisions: if these could be satisfactorily modelled with empirical support, they could be summed to provide a more reliable representation of the aggregate economy.

Orcutt's 1960 *AER* symposium paper opens with a general account of simulation, and then, as an example, lays out his first substantive report on his new micro-analytic simulation method. He describes how he first created a "sample" of 10,000 "individuals" (not real individuals, but virtual individuals) using data from the census with additional information from a small interview-based sample survey to assign relevant characteristics to them so that they constituted a representative sample of the individuals in the whole U.S. population at 1950. He then prepared a description of the demographic behaviour of the representative sample of individuals covering their births, deaths, marriages, and divorces; and he simulated the dynamics of the demographic changes undergone by these individuals, following their behaviour in his sample, month by month, over simulated time. Finally he blew the sample up to aggregate level to assess both the resulting cross-section and the time-series characteristics of that virtual population compared with the actual population figures and patterns of 1960.[30] It sounds straightforward, although incredibly ambitious given the technology of the day. The real difficulty was to figure out how to simulate the individual microdynamics. To do this, as we shall see, Orcutt used knowledge from his own previous experiences and a considerable creativity in solving these new problems to make his microsimulation work.

Steeped as Orcutt was in the problems of statistical business cycle work, he was already familiar with the tradition of statistical experiments using sampling devices and random numbers. From physical devices in the early days (e.g., Galton's quincunx), through thought experiments (the balls in the urn model), and computer-based Monte Carlo methods in latter days, statisticians have used experiments to explore and demonstrate properties of statistical distributions and the outcomes of statistical processes. In the 1920s, such explorations of time-series data problems had led to Yule's statistical experiments to analyse "nonsense correlations" (in 1926) and Slutsky's use of random numbers to generate an artificial data-series that mimicked business cycle data (1927) (that we heard about in Chapter 6 and of which more later).[31] Orcutt's own late 1940s investigations, using his own computer, into aggregate economic time-series data relied on similar investigative techniques.[32] He used statistical experiments and simulations involving "experimental models" and random numbers to generate artificial series, whose properties could then be examined and compared with those of real economic data.

As we noted, Orcutt had come to distrust the results found by Tinbergen, but his own microsimulation approach combined elements of both Tinbergen's economic evidence-based model approach and Slutsky's use of a statistical randomising procedure. Orcutt's (1957, 1960, and 1961 et al.) microsimulations were based on empirical evidence at two points: the "status" variables, which determine the characteristics of all individuals in the sample, were taken from census and sample survey data of the day so that the sample of 10,000 virtual individuals was constructed to be a representative sample of the population at the beginning of the period. The "operating characteristics", which determine the demographic behaviour and so history of the individuals over time, were estimated from the demographic evidence of the day: they provided the probabilities of outcomes for the set of individuals sharing similar characteristics. Only at the last point did the randomizing element come in, for whether a demographic change occurs for any particular virtual individual in the sample depends on the probabilities which govern – in a statistical sense – these events. Here Orcutt made use of the statistical experimental technique of Monte Carlo – the sampling techniques that pick out and so determine which individual events occur, though the probabilities that govern these are determined empirically.

---

30 In Orcutt et al. (1961), they report the full details of this work, and add in preliminary form, a considerable degree of extra economic content by combining the demographics with labour force, spending, and saving behaviour of the individual decision units.

31 See Morgan (1990), Chapter 3 and Hendry and Morgan (1995).

32 See Orcutt and Irwin (1948), and Orcutt and James (1948).

There are two elements in Orcutt's adoption of Monte Carlo techniques worth commenting on here. First, he generated these random selections by the computer, rather than as Slutsky did by sampling from lottery tickets, or by drawings from Holbrook Working's or later Kendall's random numbers table. This was, perhaps, for Orcutt, just another small innovation in this long statistical tradition of statistical experimenting using random numbers, but one he surely found easy to understand because of his own experiences. The second comes in using a computer to pick out and reassemble the individual behaving elements in the sample as a feasible way to carry out the microdynamics.[33]

Several more aspects of Orcutt's personal history can be found embedded in his microsimulation approach. One is that his simulation design incorporated "block recursiveness". This notion came out of arguments over simultaneous equations versus recursive form models between the Cowles Commission econometricians and Herman Wold in the 1940s and 1950s, a debate to which Orcutt had contributed.[34] Wold argued that, in principle, to be behaviourally realistic, economic models should be formulated to allow for individual decisions to be made in a sequential way and be linked in a causal chain, and that this recursiveness property required close attention to the time units in which decisions where made. Simon, in investigations of the structure of econometric models, argued for a slightly less stringent requirement – namely, block recursiveness – on grounds not just of causal ordering but their identification properties. Orcutt chose his time units (one-month slots) and blocks (individual family units) to gain a reasonable degree of verisimilitude in his model but also to maintain a practical design for the model work following Wold's and Simon's ideas.[35] In addition, as he pointed out, block recursiveness was neatly compatible with the sequential operations of the computer technology.

Another aspect of his model design presumably related more closely to his practical experience in electrical engineering. His idea of "plugable components" made it easier for the researcher to test the coherence of the model for each bit could be tested independently. Bits of the model – such as parameters in the operating characteristics or the status characteristics – could be independently revised

---

33 There was a considerable argument at the time between the statisticians and the mathematician/ physicists about who invented Monte Carlo techniques. The argument is more usefully understood not as a priority dispute over the method (for the evidence is clearly on the statisticians' side), but over its domains of application. The statisticians' version of the argument appears in the comment by M. S. Bartlett in 1953 (p. 48): "This 'artificial sampling' or 'Monte Carlo method' is well known to statisticians, so much so that tables of random numbers are a familiar item in their libraries. In recent years, however, it has also been seriously considered by mathematicians as an aid to the solution of differential or other mathematical equations...". Another contemporary discussant (Marshall, 1954) drew a contrast between the historically established usage of Monte Carlo methods in probability cases (as here in Orcutt) and the novelty of the physics' usage in applying the method to solve deterministic cases. (See also McCracken, 1955.) On the relevance of the technique in the history of physics, see Galison (1997).

34 See Morgan (1991), Orcutt (1952), and Hendry and Morgan (1995).

35 For discussion of these ideas of Wold and Simon, see Morgan (1991) and Boumans (2006, 2009, 2010).

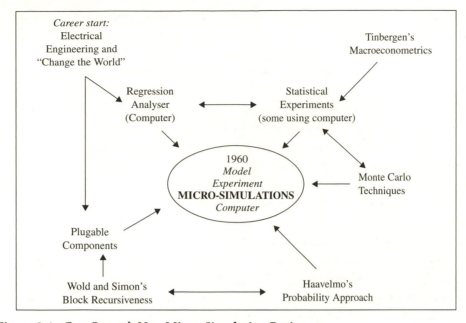

Figure 8.4. Guy Orcutt's New Micro-Simulation Recipe.
Source: Mary S. Morgan.

and reinstated (rather than the whole model having to be redesigned). Related to both this and the block recursive approach was the use of a smaller number of component types within the large number of individual components: that is, there were a limited number of family types within his sample of 10,000 individuals in the simulation model. This also made his simulation design more practicable.

Finally, Orcutt consciously adopted the probability approach developed by Haavelmo (1944) for econometrics.[36] Conceptually, the sample of component individual units had to be understood as "probability samples of the components in more extensive conceptual models of economic systems" (Orcutt, 1960, p. 903). It was this that justified the blowing up of the representative sample to make valid comparisons with the real findings for aggregate population gained from the census.

So Orcutt's work in developing his microsimulation models was an outcome of a personal history steeped in the history of the fields of statistics, computation, and econometrics with the additional element of making the computer the instrument of population aggregation. We have here an excellent example of Boumans' (1999) idea that a model is like a recipe – made up from lots of different elements mixed together, but with the added benefit that we can see rather clearly in this case how these elements were part of Orcutt's own history (see Figure 8.4). And, again following Boumans' ideas and terminology, we can see how, out of his own past work and interactions, Orcutt had developed a new model recipe. But it was much more than this. Orcutt, just as Tinbergen with his "macroeconometric model" earlier,

---

36 See Morgan (1990, chapter 8).

had created a new kind of scientific object for economics, one that required the development of a new technology of model usage. New object and new technology are both implicit in the new title he gave it: "microsimulation".

This book began with the idea, in Chapter 1, that models are technologies: instruments of enquiry – economists enquire into the world of the model and enquire with the model into the world. And, as we saw in Chapters 6 and 7, there are various different ways of experimenting with models that give economists insights into the small worlds in their models, and then different ways of making inferential connections between that small model world and the real economic world. The same has been found in the materials discussed in this chapter, showing a continuum from simulations with small mathematical models of fictional firms to others using real data on firms, to Orcutt's massive microsimulations based on survey and census data. (And, though not discussed here, these simulations coexisted with econometric work in the 1960s in which models were estimated using real data to produce parameter values, and then simulated to produce a further 'evidence' stream in a validation exercise or in policy analysis.[37]) The possibilities of making inferences from model simulations to learn about the nature of the world is an important issue, one that I put off until the final section of this chapter.[38] Before that, I explore this new mode of using models – simulation – to suggest that the common features of this new technology worked primarily to investigate the world in the model.

5. Bringing a Microscope into Economics

Back in 1954, Oscar Morgenstern's account of economic experimentation likened the computer, then a brand-new instrument in science, to both a telescope and microscope – instruments for economists that could bring both large things from far away and things normally too small to be seen into focus for them to study.[39] Martin Shubik, who may well have inherited this metaphor from him, described

37 Though Orcutt felt Tinbergen's macroeconometric model simulations were not worth pursuing, that path was followed, *ca.* 1960, in the work of Adelman and Adelman (1959), and of Duesenberry et al. (1960); see additional details in Morgan (2004). Looking back to the 1930s, it is possible to see a parallel continuum running from the small mathematical model simulations Samuelson used in 1939 to explore the combination of multiplier and accelerator mechanisms in one model (see Chapter 6) to Tinbergen's simulations on his Dutch econometric model based on data from the real economy to simulate the policy possibilities to get the economy out of the Great Depression (see Morgan, 1990, chapter 4).

38 In this context, some gaming might count as simulation (where the role-playing involves people playing not their usual roles – for example, students playing business games as in Cohen et al. [1960]) whereas others might just count as experiments (where people play their own roles – for example service men playing their usual role in a logistics experiment; see Chapman et al., 1962).

39 Morgenstern (1954, pp. 539–41) focussed on the possibility of observing new kinds of data and new patterns by the analysis of greater masses of economic data. He also commented on the use of computers in solving Leontief's input–output model on the Navy's Mark II computer at Harvard in 1947 (which took 48 hours). Morgenstern's work was part of a Princeton economics project, again funded by defence spending. Crombie, writing more broadly about reasoning in

the digital computer in 1960 as fulfilling a double duty as laboratory equipment for economics:

> ... it promises to provide the economist with the means for constructing both the instruments for observation and the equipment for experimentation that have been the earmarks of the traditional sciences. Used in one way, the computer supplies a viewing equipment to the economist in a manner analogous to the microscope for biologists (however, a great amount of work goes into setting up the "specimens" to be observed). (Shubik, 1960b, p. 908)

The digital computer, he went on, allows the economist to study masses of data at various levels of aggregation; it enables the use of more "realistic", that is, complicated, models that do not have to be solved analytically, but can be analysed by numerical methods; and it enables simulation. Shubik also points us to the role of analogue computers, that is, to the use of models that may substitute for the computer in the simulation and particularly mentions the Newlyn-Phillips Machine (of Chapter 5) as providing "an analogue simulation of the macroeconomic system" (1960b, p. 909).[40] But simulation as a technology is neither uniquely nor necessarily dependent upon the computer, and while the presence of the computer, digital or analogue, is helpful, it is the mode of investigation that is really the focus of attention here. It therefore seems more appropriate to understand simulation (rather than the computer itself) as the technology that brings a microscope into economics.

It is the exploratory and investigative power of simulation, the power to make economic things observable, that is the focus for our discussions here. In this context, it is worth remembering that there is no one technology of observation in the sciences, but many different instruments working in different ways.[41] Understanding simulation as an instrument of observation like a microscope provides us with a

---

science (see Chapter 1), suggested implicitly that modelling was a substitute for telescopes and microscopes: "Hypothetical modelling was a means of gaining insight into phenomena inaccessible to direct observation or analysis because they were too remote like the rainbow or the heavenly bodies, or too minute like the microscopic structures and processes of matter postulated to account for the observable effects which alone were available to us, or because they could not be investigated immediately without destroying them like the operations of the human brain" (Crombie, 1994, p. 1241), but he gave no account of how this access was achieved nor did he discuss simulation.

40 While there is no doubt that the digital computer greatly increased the possibilities of simulation in economics, and it has perhaps become one of its major instruments in many fields, its usage is not a necessity for simulation. In economics, mathematical and statistical simulations were carried out by hand (e.g., Slutsky, 1927; Samuelson, 1939), and as we have just learnt, there were a whole range of non–computer-based simulations (i.e., 'gaming') in economics. On the Newlyn-Phillips machine as an analogue computer, see Morgan and Boumans (2004).

41 For example, Hoover (1994) has suggested that econometrics should be regarded as an technology of observation rather than one of measurement while Boumans (2005) argues for measurement as observation with a measuring instrument. Three chapters by Maas, Morgan, and Porter in Daston and Lunbeck (2010) suggest other modes of economics observation, while a broader picture of observation in the history of economics will be found in Maas and Morgan (2012).

neat way into understanding the technology of simulation in economics. It draws our attention to three elements in the Morgenstern/Shubik discussion that provide the basis for using our analogy: the viewing instrument, the specimen, and the matter of scale/degree. The idea is that simulation conceived as a microscope allows economists to see the details of things at a scale far smaller than they can normally see, but that the things economists 'see' with the instrument are not 'natural objects' – rather they are specially prepared and treated specimens of those objects – that is, models. And they are observed with an instrument that is not simply a magnifying glass but a complex scientific instrument. Each of these elements needs to be considered with care if we are to make good use of the analogy.

5.i Introducing the Analogy

Hacking (1983), in the classic modern philosophical treatment of microscopes, discusses particular aspects of the instrument to argue that there is no natural seeing for two fundamental reasons. First, the instrument relies in critical ways on the physical laws of light (utilized in various ways according to the different kinds of microscope) to enable us to access the materials we seek to study. Second, we make up the specimen in various ways to enable us to access its material in different ways. In addition, of course, successfully seeing with the microscope depends on many technical elements that enhance the power and accuracy of the instrument and a fair amount of tacit knowledge and skill in the user. (I shall return to these important aspects later.) On the basis of this instrumental reliance, Hacking stresses that we don't see *through* a microscope, we see *with* a microscope.

What is it that we see with the microscope? As we all know, scientists use microscopes to study phenomena at a level of detail and scale much smaller than they can naturally see. But small scale is not necessarily the only, nor the most critical, quality the instrument investigates. As Hacking's discussion shows, the microscope and the preparation of specimens on the slide extend the scientist's natural powers so that the process observation is active, even invasive of the materials: it *brings into observation particular hidden details and structures*. This is a typical feature of instruments such as modern sophisticated medical MRI scanners, for they manifest this active, invasive observation in an obvious way. It is therefore useful to broaden our understanding of microscope here to focus on its 'scoping' property that enables us to see and investigate *hidden* things. This is a common property of all sorts of modern scoping instruments: for example, while electron microscopes may be mainly instruments to reveal characteristics at a particularly small scale, X-ray crystallography techniques are designed to uncover different aspects of the structures that they investigate.[42] Scoping instruments enable us to reveal different

---

42 See Rheinberger's survey paper (2008), which indirectly speaks to this theme; for more details of X-ray crystallography see de Chadarevian (2002) and for electron microscopy, see Rasmussen (1997).

kinds and aspects of things for they extend observation not only in scale but in *analytical power*, the power to take apart the material studied to access different kinds of information. Older microscopes and modern instruments are devices of 'active' or 'analytical observation'. Modern scopes may even synthesize, as well, that is put back together into an overall picture those things taken apart by the techniques involved.

If our analogy between the technology of such 'scopes' (interpreted broadly) and simulation works well, it should provide resources to help us to understand simulation in economics. I divide this epistemological side of my enquiry into simulation into three sections. In the rest of this section, I discuss the analogical features of scale and slide preparation. In Section 6, I consider how simulation conceived as a microscope functions as a technology of observation. Finally (in Section 7), I explore how this analogical comparison can help us understand certain issues about judging the quality of simulations, namely about the inference problem. That is, I question how the active observational strategy of model simulation can give economists access to information about the things in the world that they are trying to mimic.

5.ii Matters of Scale and Kind

Let us start by returning to the issue of scale, for the microscope analogy first suggests that simulation allows us to observe much tinier things than those we can study or see without such instruments. Indeed, the very word embodies this ides of smallness. Yet in economics, simulations were first associated not with small things, but with statistical studies on big things, the whole aggregate economy, using econometric models in the 1930s. With the advent of machine (computer) based simulation in the 1950s and 1960s, it became feasible to process very much larger amounts of data, and carry out far more calculations, than hitherto.[43] But once aggregated, these wholes are not easy to look into, and then the aggregation itself turned out to be worrying. Orcutt expressed a more general complaint: "There is an inherent difficulty, if not practical impossibility, in aggregating anything but absurdly simple relationships about elemental decision-making units into comprehensible relationships between large aggregative units" (1957, p. 116).

In the 1960s, the power of immense calculation in computer simulation did indeed enable economists to move away from large things, away from the aggregates, to the divisions of those aggregates into smaller units. We can find this scale argument well understood in this simulation literature of 1960, where we find the

---

43 While the calculation requirements of working with aggregates may be considerable, this is and was more due to the model estimation techniques than the scale of the entity in itself. The first time a computer was used to estimate a large macroeconometric model was the Klein-Goldberger model in (see their 1955), before this, econometric model estimation was a laborious method using hand calculators.

claim that simulation, with the benefit of the computer, means economists can work at a much finer grained level of analysis than before. For example, Shubik wrote:

> The methodological tools provided by gaming and by simulation are making it feasible to uncover and examine in an organized manner much of the important fine structure of the firm and markets in which firms operate. (1962b, pp. 41–2)

Simulation with the computer expands the power to cut the economic world up into smaller units of both time and activity. Economists could, for example, with this new approach, examine the economy at the level of the shoe industry, where before they were forced by the constraints of calculation to see only the manufacturing sector. They could, if they wished, see what is happening at the level of individual family demography, month by month, instead of the population as a whole once every ten years in the census data. Having got down to this level of detail, however, the computer simulation also enabled them to aggregate back up to a complex or aggregate level, as several of our simulators, for example, Orcutt, noted. In this sense, computer simulation techniques do have powers less like a microscope and more like those of the more modern magnetic imagers in medical science, for, as economists claim about simulation with the computer – they provide the means both to see at the level of detail and to recompose the detail into the big picture again, where the big picture is an aggregation of the individual units, not one that started from an aggregate-level analysis.

But, as we have already discussed, microscopes are instruments that are not just for observing smaller things, but for revealing hidden aspects of things: details we don't really appreciate, maybe even new characteristics that had not been thought of before. Similarly in economic simulation, where very careful study of models might reveal things that can surprise the economist. Recall, for example, Samuelson's use of a little Keynesian model, where his arithmetic simulations uncovered a variety of behaviours that were implicit in his model, including some quite capricious ones (see Chapter 6). In the context of firms and industries, economists already had the option to study the small units such as individual family histories, or the individual firm in a case study, and did so. But working with individual cases does not reveal aspects of the individual in relation to other units. In both of these two examples, the shoe industry and the family demography, it is not the individual element alone whose behaviour needs to be understood – it is the individual's behaviour in relation to, or in conjunction with, other individuals. It is their inter-relations and inter-actions that are normally hidden in higher levels of aggregation that the method of simulation might reveal from the models. Thus Orcutt sought a "new type of model" consisting of "various sorts of interacting units" (1957, p. 117). Smallness, it seems here, is interesting only because of those units' place in the picture at a higher scale, or in the dynamics of interaction with other small units, rather than as stand-alone small-scale objects. It is in this sense that authors, such as Shubik and Orcutt, involved in the *AER* symposium argued that the new technology marks an improvement in realism and complicatedness of the things studied, compared to both the methods of aggregate level study, such as macroeonometric modelling or the simple mathematical models of microeconomics.

5.iii Specimens = Models

What constitutes the specimen in the microscope slide in these economics simulations? This is a much more difficult problem. The specimens, if they were natural objects, ought to be the small-scale bits or at least small cut up bits of the economy, they should be the individual family unit, the typical shoe firm. They are not. They are, rather, models of those things. Now of course, many sciences use models as simulation devices, and sometimes these are material models – for example, the early earthquake simulations reported by Oreskes (2007) used small-scale, especially built, physical models made out of various materials, substituting, for example, pancake batter or wax for rock. Even so, economists' models made of statistical or mathematical materials don't seem anything like the natural, though highly prepared, objects that biologists place under the microscope and whose behaviour or structure they want the instrument to reveal. The natural objects of economics are the individuals, families, and firms, making decisions and taking actions in relation to their economic affairs. It is descriptions, accounts, and theories about these that economists "prepare" into models – using bits of mathematics and statistical data, random numbers and so forth to make up the model – and that are investigated by the simulation process.

But the difference is neither so great, nor so straightforward as it seems. On the one side, in biology, the specimens are specially chosen, cleaned, and prepared for the instrument – but they may also be stained with chemicals or dyes to bring out certain salient features, flattened, and, for the electron microscope, coated with a metallic covering (see Rheinberger, 2008). So much for 'natural' things!

On the other side, in economics, the simulation slide has as its object a model, and as Shubik warned us, "a great deal of work goes into setting up the 'specimens' to be observed" (1960b, p. 908). In fact, we can find just as long a process to prepare these economic model specimens as their biological counterparts. If we think back to the example of Orcutt's microsimulation discussed earlier, it takes little imagination to understand the careful work required to construct the model: creating the 10,000 virtual-person sample to be representative of the population, and clarifying the characteristics that describe their behaviour, in order that the simulation can take place.[44] In the shoe industry case, we would need to include Mack's extensive work in collecting, checking, and cleaning statistical information, and Cohen's

---

44 In Orcutt's case the individual used as components were ciphers – model people, not real people. But in some of the gaming experiments where real people role-play, we can conceive of these people as model components.

work in preparing the data to the correct format both for the calculations by the computer and to be consistent for the model he had built. In the department store case, we would need to include Moore's extensive field work that went into Cyert and March's modelling of the department store's decision process.[45]

A good example of specimen preparation that shows how difficult it is to draw the line between economics and biology in this respect is given by the third paper in the 1960 *AER* symposium by Clarkson and Herbert Simon: "Simulation of Individual and Group Behavior".[46] Their aim was to programme a computer to select stocks for investment: a typical and traditional economics' decision problem of how people make choices in the face of, at one and the same time, lots of information and considerable uncertainty. Clarkson (1963) explained how his simulation modelling began by observing exactly how investment trust officers in banks chose stocks for a portfolio. He interviewed trust officers and observed their meetings; he made an historical analysis of past decisions; and he made "protocols" or written records of the investment decision processes. This time-consuming and exacting task of building up of an 'expert system' record provided the basis for programming the computer to make the same such decisions, namely to select stocks for a portfolio, on the basis of the same information that the trust officer held. The raw material of information about stocks and their performance, about clients and their requirements, and about the legal requirements for trusts all had to be gathered and entered into the computer's programme in a way compatible with the decision process described in detail in the protocols so that the computer could make the decisions as far as possible in the same order on the same information with the same elements of memory as a trust officer.

In this case, it is not clear how to locate the difference between the natural materials used for decision making and the ones being used in the simulation slide. Trust officers form beliefs and take action on information, information that in part comes to them in the form of accounts, statistics, graphs, and the like. These paper forms are not raw unadulterated economic materials; the information has all been prepared for the trust officer, just as it has all to be prepared for the simulation model and for the computer. No wonder that Shubik thought that, in due course, the firm would channel its normal incoming information through channels that would include simulations as part of the firm's decision processes.

Shubik (1960b, p. 914) had argued that for most of the economics simulations he discussed; the preparation of the model involved a long set of translations:

---

45 When we consider the details involved, it seems that creating and preparing a model for simulation goes well beyond that normally required for mathematical model analysis: both the level of detail that has to be specified and the checking involved for model simulation is much greater than that for model solution. Indeed, as Shubik reminds us several times, "one of the most valuable contributions of simulation has been the discipline imposed by the necessity of precisely defining for the computer the model to be investigated. Fortunately in some ways, the computer is literal-minded and has little imagination" (Shubik, 1962b, pp. 5–6).

46 This was apparently Clarkson's thesis work, so I shall refer also to a chapter of that work reprinted in a 1963 collection.

"to go from a verbal description of an economic process through to a computer simulation .... may entail the use of as many as five languages": starting from the verbal description, passing to a mathematical model, to flow diagrams, to a computer program and finally to machine language. In contrast, for Clarkson and Simon, it was this ability of computers to handle "non numerical computations" that allowed a more immediate match in their simulation model to the individual decision-making process:

> To write a heuristic program of a decision-making process, we do not first have to construct a mathematical model, and then write a program to simulate the behavior of the model. We can directly write a program that manipulates symbols in the same ways that (we hypothesize) the human decision-maker manipulates them. (Clarkson and Simon, 1960, p. 925)

We can see then that the slide (model) preparation for the simulation in the Clarkson and Simon's investment decision case (as in the department store model of Cyert, Feigenbaum, and March) involved fewer translations, that is, less transforming preparatory work, between the raw economic materials and the model specimen than in some of the other simulations discussed in Shubik's survey. And, at the same time, the materials in the slide were more closely attuned to the requirements of the instrument being used in the simulation. As Clarkson and Simon described this quality of the computer – the computer can read and compare symbols and be programmed to process symbols and act on that information just as an expert decision maker reads symbols, compares information, and acts on these comparisons. Although there seems to be a tradeoff between preparing the slide and the role of the computer in this simulation, their relationship is difficult to pin down. It is, perhaps, better just to admit that they – object and apparatus – jointly fulfil the role of "epistemic mediators".[47] Where the biologists prepare slides so that they can 'see' certain things with the microscope, economists prepare models so that the relevant parts of the world they study can be 'read' by the computer.

6. How Do Simulations Work as Microscopes?

If our analogy for simulation as a scoping technology is to be useful, then we need to consider what kind of study of models as specimens a microscope offers, and what power the microscope has to offer the scientist the kind of active or analytical observation that we noted earlier. These questions require some understanding of the instruments involved with two elements being important here.

First, there are various different kinds of microscope, but each design relies on harnessing particular laws of nature into their working principles and technical

---

47 This useful phrase comes from Lorenzo Magnani (at the Model-Based Reasoning Conference, Pavia, May 2001; see Magnani, 2002).

design. Hacking's account of the microscope pays good attention to the way in which the use of different properties of light (e.g., polarizing, UV) are incorporated into different kinds of instruments and how they can pick out different kinds of structures, or the same structures in different kinds of ways, in the material under observation. In other words, scopes reveal characteristics in the materials of interest that are not directly observable by making use of some kind of instrumentally invasive action offered by the scope. In providing a technology of observation to investigate hidden structures of objects, microscopes use the laws of nature from one field to investigate objects obeying their own different laws of nature – namely, life under the slide.[48]

Second, we may think that microscopes, not unlike telescopes, are focussed to observe independent objects. But it would be wrong to conclude from this independence that the materials under the slide – even though specially prepared – are entirely passive. According to popular history, Brownian motion was discovered in 1827 by Robert Brown using a microscope but only because the behaviour of pollen and dust particles made that motion visible in the slides. Modern revealing instruments often rely on an explicit experimental intervention into the object being observed to reveal behaviour in the materials. For example, X-rays are used to map the processes of the live body by an intervention that is designed to reveal those processes, such as tracking a barium meal through the digestive system. Similarly, the imaging techniques used to map the brain activity at the micro level depend on a certain amount and kind of brain activity to prompt the mapping, and these in turn are sometimes prompted by external stimuli. The new field of neuroeconomics makes use of these qualities of invasive observation when they map brain activity of subjects as they perform economic experiments while their subjects are under scanners. There must be an active intervention by the scientist and collusion from the specimen for these kinds of scoping instruments to work. As Hacking says (1983, p. 189): "Don't just peer: interfere".

Both of these characteristics of scopes – the use of other field laws (of nature) within the instrument and the scientist's intervention into the object studied to provoke elements to be observed – prompt further analysis of our analogy between scopes and simulation, for each has the potential to offer insights into the technology of simulation in economics.

Let us once again look more closely at the case provided by Orcutt's microsimulation to explore these points. This model specimen in the slide consists of several layers. First, there is a sample of "individuals" or "components":

> The basic components of the model are individuals and combinations of individuals such as married couples and families. The family units form,

---

48 Hacking's point here is an interesting version of the theory-ladenness of observations, where the theory is the one involved in the instrument's functions. I don't regard this as a problem – on the contrary, it is in the nature of instruments to have some theory embedded in their functions, and if that comes from an independent field, that seems to be an advantage. This point will come back in the final section of the chapter.

grow, diminish, and dissolve as married couples have children and get divorced and individuals age, marry, and die. (Orcutt, 1960, p. 903)

Then, each simulation "month", these "individuals" in the model have the possibility of changing their "status" according to their initial status description, the probabilities and behavioural parameters of the model that describe their behaviour, and whether they are picked out by the random sampling device to "experience" such a change. These changes then have to be made to all the chosen individual components in the sample: "Solution of the model was achieved by simulation on a large electronic computer" (Orcutt 1960, p. 904). In this way, the initial representative sample was updated each simulation month, according to both the behavioural stochastic laws and the random process selecting individuals for changes in status, to reach its final outcome at the end of the simulation period. This final sample outcome was then grossed up to compare with the actual population change.

In such a model under observation then, the field laws used in the simulation instrument are those of mathematics and statistics. These are applied to the component materials at several points in the simulation experiment: in picking out the individuals, in applying the behavioural parameters, in carrying out the simulation, and in grossing up the sample. This is how the field laws of the simulating instrument are used to "interfere" to reveal the characteristic behaviours of the material in the slide: namely, the model of population under investigation.

The economic models used in the cases described here are specially prepared devices, but unless the method of simulation prompts them to manifest their characteristic patterns of behaviour, there is nothing to observe. We saw how the process went on in Samuelson's arithmetic simulation of his little Keynesian model (in Chapter 6): each arithmetical simulation of the model with different parameters revealed different outcomes in national income. Orcutt's microsimulations worked in the same kind of way, except of course that it was much more complicated. By design, he created variability in the individuals and potential variability in their behaviour in order that he could use his innovative technology of simulation to 'observe' that behaviour. The simulation technology also demonstrated the outcomes of that variability and those behavioural intersections in the effects on the 'population' as a whole. By such experiments, Orcutt was able to study and observe the behaviour of the demography of his model sample and of its population.[49]

---

49 We need the slide materials to be responsive to the experimental intervention to reveal their characteristic behaviours but also that those behaviour patterns remain unaltered for sufficient time that those investigating them can observe them. For some scopes, there may be a fine line between revealing and altering – X-ray technology reveals, but also, over the long run, harms some parts of the structures it investigates. The electron microscope, as Rheinberger points out, generally destroys the specimen under observation. If the effect of the observation technology interferes with the relevant characteristics of the specimen under experimental investigation, there is clearly a problem. Here, luckily, the people whose behaviour patterns were revealed by the simulation were only virtual people.

But we can push this point about model experiment and model participation further. It is not just nice if there is life under the slide, it is a necessity. There needs to be potential variability in the behaviour of the elements in the slide for their hidden characteristics to be made visible and identifiable. In econometrics, hidden relations in the data can be identified only if Nature's experimental process has created the necessary variability in the materials that are "passively" observed, just as Brownian motion was visible only because of the motions of the particles of pollen and dust. In contrast, in simulation, the scientist can use each experimental run as an opportunity to stimulate, in an organised way, the variability inherent in the slide's materials. Thus, in model simulations, it is the scientists who create the possibilities for observing the hidden details of the behaviour of their models, while the poor econometricians, though they share some of these powers of model investigation, ultimately have to rely on Nature's cooperation in creating variability in order to reveal the hidden characteristics of their data.[50]

This is the sense in which – although clearly the models used in economic simulation experiments are not live specimens of nature – scientists must nevertheless create their active collusion: they must induce their models to exhibit those models' variability and characteristics in the simulation experiment. So, the concept of the active or analytical observation that I earlier associated with microscopes, and we have now seen for simulations, relies both on an instrumental technology of observation using man-made laws of manipulation (maths and stats) and a collusive or manipulable specimen (the model) in the slide for the experimental runs.

Although our analogy enables us to think separately about the role of the model and the laws that reveal its behaviour, it is often not at all easy to say or to see what exactly is happening inside the simulation. In Orcutt's case, we can point to the separate elements of the model-specimen and to the probability laws used to reveal the behaviour of the model but it is in fact quite difficult to draw a line between them. It occurs somewhere in the behavioural part of the model, which is labelled as part of both the slide and the revealing laws. We found this same fuzzy divide in the investment decision case earlier, where the line between the object of investigation (the investment decision process as the specimen on the slide) and the instrument (the computer) seemed equally difficult to locate. Both cases prompt us to ask: Where does the specimen in the slide finishes and the apparatus begin? Where does the object of experiment end and the experiment begin? This makes the commentator's life difficult, but is not an unusual situation in science. Parallels are found in Hans-Jörg Rheinberger's discussion of such intersections between instrument and experiment in the case of biological investigations. He challenges us to answer:

---

50 Of course, this overstates the case. Econometrics does allow us to take apart the behaviour based on passive observation, but it is still in the final resort dependent on Nature to produce the variability on which its statistical analyses work. For the necessity of variability in the materials for identification to occur see Morgan (1990), Hendry and Morgan (1995), Boumans and Morgan (2001), and Boumans (2005). In case the comparison seems strained, no less an authority than Haavelmo (1944) argued for econometrics as a form of experiment; see Morgan (1998).

"Where does the experiment take place? Is it at the instrument, with, before, within the instrument?" He concludes that

> The investigative value of an instrument depends on the shape of such intersections; they decide about whether a particular instrument and a particular object can be brought together at all and bound into a fruitful analytical constellation. (Rheinberger, 2008, pp. 1–2)

Simulation *can be* a successful instrument of observation of the world in the model, even if we are unable to strictly divide up its parts and relate them to functions.

The other side of this technological problem is that faced by the economist. This suggests another caveat that follows from this analogy of the technology of simulation with microscopes, namely, that such simulation instruments are man-made and mass-produced. Like modern microscopes and imaging instruments, pre-programmed simulation packages on the computer come ready to use. They have all the features of 'black boxes': that is, these simulation packages are complex enough that they require tacit knowledge and associated practical skills to get them to work, yet the economist does not need to understand how the instrument works to use these programmes to carry out simulation experiments. Economists are therefore in a strange, but not unusual, situation: they have instruments that use certain kinds of laws to manipulate their models to reveal certain aspects of those models, but they don't necessarily understand exactly how those instruments work. There are two sets of worries that arise with such a black box technology, both relate to the status of what is observed. First, simulation is a kind of experiment, and as such brings with it the problems of creating experimental artefacts, raising questions about how to distinguish genuine characteristics of behaviour from artefactual ones created by the technology of manipulation.[51] Second, while simulation begins as a technology of enquiry into the world in the model, an economist's purpose may be to seek insight about the real-world economy from that enquiry. This is the problem of *interpreting* the behaviour of the model in the slide, a problem to which I turn in the last section of this chapter.

7. The Observation–Inference Problem

As I have argued earlier, economic models have to be used for economists to learn about the world in the model and about the world the model represents. To learn from models, economists need to ask them questions, manipulate them, demonstrate with them, observe their behaviour, use them to tell narratives and prompt inferences (as discussed in Chapters 6 and 7).[52] From studying the world in the

---

51 See, for example, Gooding et al. (1989) and Guala (2005) on economics experiments.

52 To go back to those points: gaming and simulations share the same epistemological character. Games have to be played just as model experiments have to be run! I discuss this games = models equivalence in the paper related to this chapter (Morgan, 2004), but it was also recognised at the time; see Cushen (1955).

model with various kinds of experimental means and understanding how the model works, they often hope to gain understanding about how the real world works.[53] Just so in these kinds of simulation: in studying models, economists first study life under the slide, and hope that at some point it will tell them something useful about life beyond the slide.[54]

In the laboratory experimental situation, the scientist seeks to infer from the revealed behaviour of the experiment back to the natural (uncontrolled) world. The instruments of experiment are relevant here. Harré (2003) argues that if the laboratory apparatus used is a "registering instrument" (such as thermometers) the causal laws operate directly on the instrument, making inference from the instrument relatively unproblematic. For example, with a thermometer, the laws of heat create changes in the mercury column, from which legitimate inferences about temperature might be made.[55] A microscope is an instrument that allows the scientist to observe things by making use of laws of nature, but it is not primarily an instrument that is acted upon in a causal way by a law of nature in order to register the effects of those laws. Rather, it is an instrument that uses the laws from one field to reveal aspects of material in another field. What kinds of inference does it enable?

Let me explore this question by using one of the simplest – and classic – simulations mentioned briefly earlier in this chapter (and that appeared in Chapter 6).

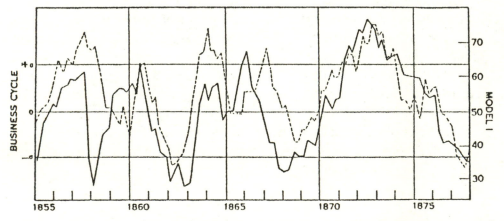

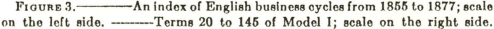

FIGURE 3.————An index of English business cycles from 1855 to 1877; scale on the left side. ---------Terms 20 to 145 of Model I; scale on the right side.

Figure 8.5. Slutsky's Random Shock Simulation.

Source: Eugen Slutsky (1927 April 1937) "The Summation of Random Causes as the Source of Cyclic Processes", *Econometrica*, 5:2, 105–46; figure 3, p. 11. Reproduced with permission from The Econometric Society.

---

53 For additional cases of learning about the world from manipulation of models, see Morgan (1999, 2003).
54 But it is important to note that not all simulations share this aim; see footnotes 3 and 14.
55 This seems a reasonable claim, though see Chang (2004) for a discussion about the history of exactly what can be inferred in such a case.

In the 1920s, Slutsky took a series of numbers drawn randomly from the People's Commissariat of Finance Lottery and summed them into a simple 10-period moving average. He charted this series next to a section of U.K. business-cycle data from the nineteenth century to show how closely his summed random number series mimicked the business cycle series (Figure 8.5).

As we know, microscopes use the laws from one realm to reveal the behaviour of some other system. In Slutsky's case, the simulation used the laws of arithmetic (moving summation) to reveal something of the hidden properties of random numbers in his model specimen that we see in the dashed line on his graph (the data output series labelled A in the schema below). His filled line, on the other hand, is the registration of irregular but roughly cyclical behaviour of the economy that we take to have been the result of operations by another kind of law: the laws of economics, that generate the real world data (labelled B here).

Simulation
Microscope   **Real Materials**

laws of arithmetic   *laws of economics*
operating on   *generate*
model specimen
generate ⟹ **data output A**   ⇓
        mimics ⟹ **real world data B**

Slutsky's simulation, showing the power of summations of random numbers to mimic business cycle data, was widely understood at the time to suggest that the cause of business cycles might lie in series of random events. Frisch interpreted Slutsky's work almost literally in his famous rocking horse model of 1933, in which the economic system was conceived as acting as the adding up device (the "propagation" device) to carry through external shock events that hit the economy (the random "impulses") to create the kind of business cycles we see in the data (see Chapter 6, Boumans [1999] and Morgan [1990]). In other words, Frisch recognised that both the motivating laws of arithmetic and the characteristics of the materials (the random numbers) were involved in the simulation technology.

The Slutsky case emphasizes how inference in simulation is not just about a mimicking of output data, but will tend to run backwards (as Harré's term "back inference" implies) to ask about the mimicking of the model and laws that created those data. Here, the mimicking of the real data by the model data outputs is central to the back inference, for it is this evidence that links the two entirely different realms. That is, the inference is not just from simulation data back to real data, but from the model specimen and the laws that reveal its behaviour back to the real economy and its governing laws. This is just the inference that Frisch took from Slutsky's simulation, and built into his model design for the macroeconomy (though contemporary readers also held other interpretations; see Barnett [2006]). It is all too easy to concentrate on data mimicking, and slide into the further inference about a mimicking relation between the models and their laws of operation, forgetting that these simulations may involve different kinds of operative laws from those of the system being modelled. In this case, the inferential slide had fruitful consequences, for after Frisch had used Slutsky's model to explore the world of his own mathematical macromodel, Tinbergen adapted the idea to develop econometric models to explore the statistical data of the business cycle generated by the real world.

Our survey of economics simulations around 1960 (in Section 3) showed how economists shared Slutsky and Frisch's desire to use artificial means, in various different ways, to create a stream of outputs that look like the real observations they have from the world – that is, to create 'evidence' that would match or mimic the empirical or real evidence, namely, the little data facts of the world (see Morgan, 2004). A comparable example discussed in Chapter 6 was the checkerboard model of Thomas Schelling (1978) that, when simulated, created patterns of segregation that matched those found in urban areas in the world.[56] Such inferences as those made from Slutsky's random numbers or Schelling's checkerboard model essentially rest on a mimicking ability, in contrast to econometric work where mimicking is not so obviously a part of the structure of the back inference relation between model results and the world.[57] It is this mimicking element that seems to me one of the most salient features of the simulation technology, namely, its production of output which can be compared directly to empirical information such as observational data without further transformation or interpretation. But this mimicking leaves open the question of what can be learnt from such comparisons. Boumans (1998) suggests that whether we can interpret or treat such 'evidence' as evidence valid for the real phenomena is a kind of Turing test in economics. Indeed, the kind of simulations undertaken in the process models of the department store (Cyert and March) or the trust officers' decisions (Clarkson and Simon) are very like a Turing test in privileging the role of the computer as a decision making, rather than calculating, machine.

The answer to these problems of legitimate inference, and whether simulation 'evidence' can be usefully compared with empirical evidence, takes us back to the content of the model and to the rules or laws governing its operation. Let us return to Slutsky, and a so far unnoted third element in the laws governing the behaviour of the elements in his graph. Despite the fact that early business cycle indicators were called "barometers", the rise and fall of economic activity revealed in business cycle data are not registered directly by the laws of economics acting on a "registering instrument" like a barometer. In fact, the economic data (B) in the schema may come from an accurate registering or recording instrument, but

---

56 In comparison, the estimation methods of econometrics provide a different kind of "fit", one in which parameters of behavioural relations have to pass tests of both statistical adequacy and economic interpretation. See Morgan (2004) for a further discussion of this creation of matching evidence.

57 Hartmann (1996) makes mimicking part of his definition of simulation, in contrast to Humphreys (see his 1990, 2002, 2004), who focusses more on the computational aspects of simulation. In the '1960 moment' when simulation seemed to suddenly arrive in economics, the aim of understanding the world through model simulation marked out the difference with the contrasting aims of OR simulations that were normative (see footnote 14, and, more generally, footnote 5 references).

one – if we look inside this particular black box – that is governed by a completely different set of laws: bureaucratic or commercial ones in which economic organisations such as firms, or banks, or tax authorities, fill in forms according to legal requirements or habitual conventions. Most data collections in economics are undertaken according to social laws and the data themselves are assembled according to some quantitative design, labelled by Ted Porter (1994) in his historical analysis of social science measurement as a "standardized quantitative rule" (SQR). So these 'real' economic data (B) are not governed by the laws of economics directly, although, indirectly, the individual values recorded are expected to be the results of the behaviour of the economy. This gives us three sets of governing laws: those arithmetic ones used in the simulation to reveal aspects of random number behaviour; those bureaucratic ones that directly govern the collection and aggregation of the economic data, and those economic ones that indirectly govern the values of the data collected, as in the schema below:

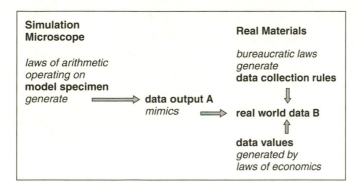

This prospect in turn raises another interesting possibility. While the bureaucratic laws (the SQRs and their conventions) may be dissimilar to those laws that govern the behaviour of the market, yet, curiously, they may be rather similar to those that govern the simulation model. Suppose – as is the case with some economic data series – the relevant statistical authority collects the data on business activity by random sampling of all the returned forms and adding together the amounts from those that they sample to make each separate data point, they are in effect using a similar model and laws of addition as Slutsky used in his simulation device![58] This suggests that when the simulated series mimics the data series, that mimicking power and its back inference might, with more justification, point us not to the economic laws but to the bureaucratic laws.

---

58 This was indeed how the U.K. authorities used to measure and aggregate the trade figures during the period of exchange controls when banks returned forms for all import and export payments; this sometimes created some quite strange outcomes. Such sampling in a standardized form is a regular feature of measurement structures in the social sciences.

8. Conclusion

Using an analogy should give insights on both positive and negative sides, and here they seem to be mirrors of each other. The technology of simulation conceived as microscopy has reminded us exactly why we need to be wary of back inference based on mimicking power, for the analogy tells us that the laws that run the simulation experiment and reveal the behaviour of the material in the slide are not necessarily from the same realm as the laws of behaviour governing the real economic materials. This is in contrast to domesticated (real) world experiments, where the causal laws creating effects or behaviour in the laboratory are believed to be the same ones as in the wild. Once again, as in Chapter 7, we see why model experiments have less inferential power than real experiments (see also Morgan [2003, 2005]). Yet using the analogy also offers positive features. It has focussed attention on how simulation works as an investigative technology dependent upon operative laws to reveal hidden aspects of the model's behaviour. And, even when the model specimen and the governing laws can not easily be disentangled (as in Slutsky's simulating device wherein his model integrated the laws of arithmetic and the random materials), we can see that they maintain an identity separate from the real-world economy under study. In simulation the scientist uses not a specimen from the real-world domain, but a model that only represents or denotes the real-world economy. This separate and different identity of the model from the world, a problem for back inference, nevertheless gave Slutsky, and then Frisch and Tinbergen the creative resources to investigate the behaviour of real economic material using their models. The attentive reader will appreciate the paradox that the strength of the microscope analogy for simulation as an instrument of investigation lay in showing us how using laws from one realm can reveal the behaviour of a specimen from another realm, just as its weakness in back inference follows from that same independence.

Orcutt's example provides an interesting contrasting case. On the one hand, the lines between the model, the governing laws, and the technical apparatus were almost impossible to draw, so that independence was highly compromised. On the other hand, Orcutt's simulations of the socioeconomic had a high degree of credibility that supported back inference because there was mimicking power at both the level of the model and the level of the investigative laws. Let me explain.

First, the model specimen was chosen as a representative sample of the population. This representative sample was constructed according to a statistical analysis of the population and a sample survey of certain households so as to mimic certain statistical features of the population it represents, though of course, it was not a sample of real people. We could say then that when Orcutt created his model sample for simulation he did so in such a way that it embodied a statistical notion of mimicking.

Second, the investigative laws that revealed the behaviour of the model also came from probability and statistics. These were chosen because, as already established by demographers in past times, such statistical or probabilistic laws can be said to *govern* the behaviour of our population. We individual people know better – we know that births, marriages, and deaths are determined by a whole realm of social, economic, medical, physiological, and other laws, which determine whom we fall in love with, whether we have children, why we die, and when any of these happen to us. However, not only do our scientific statistical laws of demography *describe* these behaviours at the population level rather accurately, they also have considerable analytical edge that make them an excellent choice for the experimental intervention in Orcutt's simulation microscope. Because of this, they could be used *to reveal the behaviour of the virtual people in Orcutt's model, even while they did not determine the behaviour of the real people modelled.*

Thus, mimicking was built into this microsimulation at two points: first at the level of the model specimen built to mimic the population in the economy of Orcutt's time and place: 1950s, United States; and second in the probability laws governing his experimental intervention (i.e., to make the simulation run), again calibrated to his time and socioeconomic world. When we analyse the case like this, we see that the model and the investigative laws were both formulated in statistical and probability terms, though, as I have explained, these were descriptively adequate, not causally adequate, for the material being modelled. Perhaps then it is not only the previously well attested power of both model and investigative laws to represent the materials they were asked to study, but also the close attunement of the model preparation with the laws in the scope, which gave Orcutt's technology of simulation the potential to be a "fruitful analytical constellation" (to use Rheinberger's phrase again). It is this mimicking at two levels that enabled Orcutt's simulation to offer both accounts of the world in the model, and a credible basis for inferences to the real world that the model represents.

Acknowledgement

This chapter was created from several papers. Initial ideas were discussed at the LSE CPNSS and the History of Science meeting at in Vancouver 2000. The main historical parts were developed further at the invitations of Amy Dahan and Bernard Walliser at the Centre Alexandre Koyre, Paris, colloquium "Modeles et Modelisations, 1950–2000: Nouvelles Pratiques, Nouveaux Enjeux", and of Ursula Klein and Eric Francoeur at the Max-Planck-Institute for History of Science, Berlin, workshop "The Digital Workbench: Computer Modeling, Data Processing, and Visualization in Science and Technology", both in December 2001. The sections on microscopes were developed at the invitation of Johannes Lenhard for the workshop "Simulation: Pragmatic Constructions of Reality" at Bielefeld in June 2004. I thank Carl Hoefer, Nancy Cartwright, Naomi Oreskes, Marcel Boumans, Rachel Ankeny, Hans-Jörg Rheinberger, and other participants at these meetings for pertinent questions and comments; Till Grüene-Yanoff and Xavier Lopez Del Rincon Troussel for research assistance; Jon Morgan and Lisa Chin for editorial work; and the British Academy for funding the first half of this chapter's research. Sections 1–4 of the chapter draw mainly on my publication in the *Revue d'Histoire des Sciences* (2004); Sections 3.i, 4, and 5 are substantially developed from that version, and Sections 6 and 7 are newly developed from the Bielefeld talk.

References

Adelman, Irma and Frank L. Adelman (1959) "The Dynamic Properties of the Klein-Goldberger Model". *Econometrica*, 27:4, 596–625.

Aumann, R.J. (1987) "Game Theory". In John Eatwell, Murray Milgate, and Peter Newman (eds), *The New Palgrave: A Dictionary of Economics* (pp. 460–82). London: Macmillan.

Barnett, Vincent (2006) "Chancing and Interpretation: Slutsky's Random Cycles Revisited". *European Journal of the History of Economic Thought*, 13:3, 411–32.

Bartlett, Maurice S. (1953) "Stochastic Processes or the Statistics of Change". *Applied Statistics*, 2:1, 44–64.

Boumans, Marcel (1998) "Lucas and Artificial Worlds". In John B. Davis (ed), *New Economics and Its History* (pp. 63–88). Annual Supplement to *History of Political Economy*, Vol. 29 Durham, NC: Duke University Press.

(1999) "Built-In Justification". In M. S. Morgan and M. Morrison (1999), pp. 66–96.

(2005) *How Economists Model the World to Numbers*. London: Routledge.

(2006) "The Difference between Answering a 'Why'-Question and Answering a 'How Much'-Question". In J. Lenhard, G. Küppers, and T. Shinn (eds), *Simulation: Pragmatic Construction of Reality* (pp. 107–24). Sociology of the Sciences Yearbook, Vol. 25. New York: Springer.

(2009) "Understanding in Economics: Gray-Box Models". In H.W. de Regt, S. Leonelli, and K. Eigner (eds), *Scientific Understanding: Philosophical Perspectives* (pp. 210–29). Pittsburgh: University of Pittsburgh Press.

(2010) "Measurement in Economics". In U. Mäki (volume ed), *Handbook of the Philosophy of Science: Philosophy of Economics*, Vol. 13 (pp. 333–60). Philadelphia: Elsevier.

Boumans Marcel and Mary S. Morgan (2001) "*Ceteris Paribus* Conditions: Materiality and the Application of Economic Theories". *Journal of Economic Methodology*, 8:1, 11–26.

Brewer, Garry D. and Martin Shubik (1979) *The War Game: A Critique of Military Problem Solving*. Cambridge, MA: Harvard University Press.

Caldwell, Bruce (2003) *Hayek's Challenge*. Chicago: University of Chicago Press.

de Chadarevian, Soraya (2002) *Designs for Life: Molecular Biology after World War II*. Cambridge: Cambridge University Press.

Chang, Hasok (2004) *Inventing Temperature: Measurement and Scientific Progress*. Oxford: Oxford University Press.

Chapman, Robert L., John L. Kennedy, Allen Newell, and William C. Biel (1962) "The Systems Research Laboratory's Air-Defense Experiments". In Harold Guetzkow (ed), *Simulation in Social Science* (pp. 172–88). Englewood Cliffs, NJ: Prentice-Hall.

Clarkson, Geoffrey P. E. (1963) "A Model of the Trust Investment Process". In Edward A. Feigenbaum and Julian Feldman (eds), *Computers and Thought* (pp. 347–71). Malabar, FL: Kreiger.

Clarkson, Geoffrey P. E. and Herbert A. Simon (1960) "Simulation of Individual and Group Behaviour". *American Economic Review*, 50:5, 920–32.

Cohen, Kalman J. (1960) *Computer Models of the Shoe, Leather, Hide Sequence*. Englewood Cliffs, NJ: Prentice-Hall.

Cohen, K. J., R. M. Cyert, W. R. Dill, A. A. Kuehn, M. H. Miller, T. A. Van Wormer, and P. R. Winters (1960) "The Carnegie Tech Management Game". *Journal of Business*, 33:4, 303–21.

Crombie, Alistair C. (1994) *Styles of Scientific Thinking in the European Traditions*, Vols. I–III. London: Duckworth.

Cushen, Walter E. (1955) "War Games and Operations Research". *Philosophy of Science*, 22:4, 309–20.

Cyert, R. M., E. A. Feigenbaum, and J. G. March (1959) "Models in a Behavioral Theory of the Firm". *Behavioral Science*, 4, 81–95.

Cyert, Richard M. and James G. March (1963) *A Behavioral Theory of the Firm*. Englewood Cliffs, NJ: Prentice-Hall.

Daston, Lorraine J. and Elizabeth Lunbeck (2010) [eds] *Histories of Scientific Observation*. Chicago: University of Chicago Press.

Dorfman, Robert (1960) "Operations Research". *American Economic Review*, 50, 575–623.

Dowling, Deborah (1999) "Experimenting on Theories". In Sergio Sismondo (ed), *Modeling and Simulation*. Special issue of *Science in Context*, 12:2, 261–74. Summer.

Duesenberry, James S., Otto Eckstein, and Gary Fromm (1960) "A Simulation of the United States Economy in Recession". *Econometrica*, 28:4, 749–809.

Edgeworth, Francis Y. (1881) *Mathematical Psychics*. London: Kegan Paul (New Edition, edited by Peter Newman, Oxford: Oxford University Press, 2003).

Forrester, Jay W. (1958) "Industrial Dynamics: A Major Breakthrough for Decision Makers". *Harvard Business Review*, 36:July–August, 37–66.

Fouraker L. E. and S. Siegel (1963) *Bargaining Behavior*. Hightstown, NJ: McGraw-Hill.

Fox-Keller, Evelyn (2003) "Models, Simulation and 'Computer Experiments' ". In Hans Radder (ed), *The Philosophy of Scientific Experimentation* (pp. 198–215). Pittsburgh: Pittsburgh University Press.

Frigg, Roman, Stephan Hartmann, and Cyrille Imbert (2009) [eds] *Models and Simulations 1*. Special Issue, *Synthese*, 169:3, 425–626.

Frisch, Ragnar (1933) "Propagation and Impulse Problems in Dynamic Economics". In *Economic Essays in Honour of Gustav Cassel* (pp. 171–205). London: Allen & Unwin.

Galison, Peter (1997) *Image and Logic: A Material Culture of Microphysics*. Chicago: University of Chicago Press.

Gooding, David, Trevor Pinch, and Simon Schaffer (1989) *The Uses of Experiment*. Cambridge: Cambridge University Press.

Greenberger, Martin, Matthew A. Crenson, and Brian L. Crissey (1976) *Models in the Policy Process: Public Decision Making in the Computer Era*. New York: Russel Sage Foundation.

Guala, Francesco (2005) *The Methodology of Experimental Economics*. New York: Cambridge University Press.

Guetzkow, Harold (1962) [ed] *Simulation in Social Science*. Englewood Cliffs, NJ: Prentice-Hall.

Guetzkow, Harold, Philip Kotler, and Randall L. Schultz (1972) [eds] *Simulation in Social and Administrative Science*. Englewood Cliffs, NJ: Prentice-Hall.

Haavelmo, Tryvge (1944) "The Probability Approach in Econometrics". Supplement to *Econometrica*, 12.

Hacking, Ian (1983) *Representing and Intervening*. Cambridge: Cambridge University Press.

Harré, Rom (2003) The Materiality of Instruments in a Metaphysics for Experiments". In Hans Radder (ed), *The Philosophy of Scientific Experimentation* (pp. 19–38). Pittsburgh: Pittsburgh University Press.

Hartmann, Stephan (1996) "The World as a Process: Simulations in the Natural and Social Sciences". In Rainer Hegselmann, Ulrich Mueller, and Klaus G. Troitzsch (eds), *Modelling and Simulation in the Social Science from the Philosophy of Science Point of View* (pp. 77–100). Dordrecht: Kluwer.

Hegselmann, Rainer, Ulrich Mueller, and Klaus G. Troitzsch (1996) [eds] *Modelling and Simulation in the Social Sciences from the Philosophy of Science Point of View*. Dordrecht: Kluwer.

Hendry, David F. and Mary S. Morgan (1995) *The Foundations of Econometric Analysis*. Cambridge: Cambridge University Press.

Hoggatt, Austin C. (1959) "A Simulation Study of an Economic Model". In *Contributions to Scientific Research in Management – Proceedings of the Scientific Program Following the Dedication of the Western Data Processing Center* (pp. 127–42). Los Angeles: University of California.

Hoover, Kevin D. (1994) "Econometrics as Observation: The Lucas Critique and the Nature of Econometric Inference". *Journal of Economic Methodology*, 1:1, 65–80.

Hounshell, David (1997) "The Cold War, RAND, and the Generation of Knowledge, 1946–62". *Historical Studies in the Physical and Biological Sciences*, 27, 237–67.

Humphreys, Paul W. (1990) "Computer Simulations". *PSA Proceedings of the Biennial Meeting of the Philosophy of Science Association* Vol. 1990, Volume Two: Symposia and Invited Papers, pp, 497–506.

(2002) "Computational Models". *Philosophy of Science*, 69, S1–11.

(2004) *Extending Ourselves: Computations Science, Empiricism and Scientific Method*. Oxford: Oxford University Press.

Jardini, David R. (1996) "Out of the Blue Yonder: The RAND Corporation's Diversification into Social Welfare Research, 1946–1968". Ph.D. dissertation, Carnegie Mellon University.

Klein, Lawrence R. and Arthur S. Goldberger (1955) *An Econometric Model of the United States, 1929–1952*. Amsterdam: North Holland.

Knuuttila, Tarja, Martina Merz, and Erika Mattila (2006) [eds] *Computer Models and Simulations in Scientific Practice*, Special Issue, *Science Studies*, 19:1 at http://www.sciencestudies.fi/v19n1

Maas, Harro (2001) "An Instrument Can Make a Science: Jevons's Balancing Acts in Economics". In Judy L. Klein and Mary S. Morgan (eds), *The Age of Economic Measurement* (pp. 277–302). Annual Supplement to *History of Political Economy*, Vol. 33. Durham, NC: Duke University Press.

(2010) "Sorting Things: The Economist as an Armchair Observer". In L. J. Daston and E. Lunbeck (2010), pp. 206–29.

Maas, Harro and Mary S. Morgan (forthcoming) [eds] *Observing the Economy: Historical Perspectives*. Annual Supplement to *History of Political Economy*, Vol. 44. Durham, NC: Duke University Press.

Mack, Ruth (1956) *Consumption and Business Fluctuations: A Case Study of the Shoe, Leather, Hide Sequence*. New York: National Bureau of Economic Research.

Magnani, L. (2002) "Epistemic Mediators and Model-Based Discovery in Science". In L. Magnani and N. J. Nersessian (eds), *Model-Based Reasoning: Science, Technology, Values* (pp. 305–30). New York: Kluwer Academic/Plenum Press.

Marshall, A. W. (1954) "An Introductory Note". In Herbert A. Meyer (ed), *Symposium on Monte Carlo Methods* (pp. 1–14). New York: Wiley, and London: Chapman & Hall.

McCracken, Daniel D. (1955) "The Monte Carlo Method". *Scientific American*, 192:5, 90–6.

Mirowski, Philip (2002) *Machine Dreams: Economics Becomes a Cyborg Science*. Cambridge: Cambridge University Press.

Morgan, Mary S. (1990) *The History of Econometric Ideas*. Cambridge: Cambridge University Press.

(1991) "The Stamping Out of Process Analysis in Econometrics". In N. De Marchi and M. Blaug (eds), *Appraising Economic Theories* (pp. 237–63 and 270–2). Cheltenham: Edward Elgar.

(1998) "Haavelmo's Methodology". In J. B. Davis, D. Wade Hands, and Uskali Mäki (eds), *Handbook of Economic Methodology* (pp. 217–20). Cheltenham: Edward Elgar.

(1999) "Learning from Models". In Mary S. Morgan and Margaret Morrison (eds), *Models as Mediators: Perspectives on Natural and Social Science* (pp. 347–88). Cambridge: Cambridge University Press.

(2003) "Experiments Without Material Intervention: Model Experiments, Virtual Experiments and Virtually Experiments". In Hans Radder (ed), *The Philosophy of Scientific Experimentation* (pp. 216–35). Pittsburgh: Pittsburgh University Press.

(2004) "Simulation: The Birth of a Technology to Create "Evidence" in Economics". *Revue d'Histoire des Sciences*, 57:2, 341–77.

(2005) "Experiments Versus Models: New Phenomena, Inference and Surprise". *Journal of Economic Methodology,* 12:2, 317–29.

(2010) "Seeking Parts, Looking for Wholes". In Lorraine J. Daston and Elizabeth Lunbeck (eds), *Histories of Scientific Observation* (pp. 303–25). Chicago: University of Chicago Press.

Morgan Mary S. and Marcel Boumans (2004) "The Secrets Hidden by Two-Dimensionality: The Economy as a Hydraulic Machine". In Nick Hopwood and Soraya de Chadarevian (eds), *Models: The Third Dimension in Science* (pp. 369–401). Stanford: Stanford University Press.

Morgan, Mary S. and Margaret Morrison (1999) [eds] *Models as Mediators: Perspectives on Natural and Social Science*. Cambridge: Cambridge University Press.

Morgenstern, Oskar (1954) "Experiment and Large Scale Computation in Economics". In O. Morgenstern (ed), *Economic Activity Analysis* (pp. 483–549). New York: Wiley.

Neumann, John von and Oskar Morgenstern (1944) *The Theory of Games and Economic Behavior*. Princeton, NJ: Princeton University Press.

Orcutt, Guy H. (1952) "Actions, Consequences and Causal Relations". *Review of Economics and Statistics*, 34:4, 305–13.

(1957) "A New Type of Socio-economic System". *Review of Economics and Statistics*, 39:2, 116–23.

(1960) "Simulation of Economic Systems". *American Economic Review*, 50:5, 893–907.

(1968) "Research Strategy in Modeling Economic Systems". In D. G. Watts (ed), *The Future of Statistics* (pp. 71–100). New York: Academic Press

(1990a) "From Engineering to Microsimulation". *Journal of Economic Behavior and Organization*, 14, 5–27.

(1990b) "The Microanalytic Approach for Modeling National Economies". *Journal of Economic Behavior and Organization*, 14, 29–41.

Orcutt, Guy H., Martin Greenberger, John Korbel, and Alice M. Rivlin (1961) *Microanalysis of Socioeconomic Systems: A Simulation Study*. New York: Harper.

Orcutt, Guy H. and J. O. Irwin (1948) "A Study of the Autoregressive Nature of the Time Series Used for Tinbergen's Model of the Economic System of the United States, 1919–32". *Journal of the Royal Statistical Society*, Series B, 10:1, 1–53.

Orcutt, Guy H. and S. F. James (1948) "Testing the Significance of Correlation between Time Series". *Biometrika*, 35:3/4, 397–413.

Oreskes, Naomi (2007) "From Scaling to Simulation: Changing Meanings and Ambitions of Models in the Earth Sciences". In A. Creager, Liz Lunbeck, and M. Norton Wise (eds), *Science Without Laws* (pp. 93–124). Durham, NC: Duke University Press.

Porter, Theodore M. (1994) "Making Things Quantitative". In Michael Power (ed), *Accounting and Science: Natural Inquiry and Commercial Reason* (pp. 36–56). Cambridge: Cambridge University Press.

(2010) "Reforming Vision: The Engineer Le Play Learns to Observe Society Sagely". In Lorraine J. Daston and Elizabeth Lunbeck (eds), *Histories of Scientific Observation* (pp. 281–302). Chicago: University of Chicago Press.

Radder, Hans (2003) [ed] *The Philosophy of Scientific Experimentation*. Pittsburgh: Pittsburgh University Press.

Rasmussen, Nicolas (1997) *Picture Control: The Electron Microscope and the Transformation of Biology in America, 1940–1960*. Stanford: Stanford University Press.

Rheinberger, Hans Jörg (2008) "Intersections: Some Thoughts on Instruments in the Experimental Context of the Life Sciences". In Helmar Schramm, Ludger Schwarte, and Jan Lazardzig (eds), *Instruments in Art and Science: On the Architectonics of Cultural Boundaries in the 17th Century* (pp. 1–19). New York: de Gruyter.

Rowley, Robin (1998) "Assisting Managerial Decisions: The Search for Operating Rules and the Origins of Management Science". Working Paper, McGill University (History of Economics Society, Conference Paper).

(1999) "Normative Microeconomics and the Creation of a Revised North American Tradition: The Emergence of Management Science, 1935–1960". Working Paper, McGill University (European Society for the History of Economic Thought, Conference Paper).

Samuelson Paul A. (1939) "Interactions between the Multiplier Analysis and the Principle of Acceleration". *Review of Economics and Statistics*, 21, 75–8.

Schelling, Thomas C. (1978) *Micromotives and Macrobehaviour*. New York: Norton.

Shubik, Martin (1952) "Information, Theories of Competition, and the Theory of Games". *Journal of Political Economy* 60:2, 145–50.

(1954) *Readings in Game Theory and Political Behavior*. New York: Doubleday.

(1959a) *Strategy and Market Structure*. New York: Wiley.

(1959b) "Edgeworth Market Games". In A. W. Tucker and R. D. Luce (eds), *Contributions to the Theory of Games*, Vol. IV (pp. 267–78). Princeton, NJ: Princeton University Press.

(1960a) "Bibliography on Simulation, Gaming, Artificial Intelligence and Allied Topics". *Journal of the American Statistical Association*, 55 (Dec), 736–51.

(1960b) "Simulation of the Industry and the Firm". *American Economic Review*, 50(5), 908–19.

(1960c) "Game Theory as an Approach to the Firm". *American Economic Review*, 50(Papers), 556–9.

(1962a) "Some Experimental Non-Zero Sum Games with Lack of Information about the Rules". *Management Science*, 8(2), 215–34.

(1962b) "Simulation and Gaming: Their Value to the Study of Pricing and Other Market Variables". IBM Research Report RC-833.

(1966) "Simulation of Socio-Economic Systems. Part I: General Considerations". Cowles Foundation Discussion Paper, No. 203. New Haven, CT: Yale University.

(1975) *Gaming for Society, Business and War: Towards a Theory of Gaming*. New York: Elsevier.

(1992) "Game Theory at Princeton, 1949–1955: A personal Reminiscence". In E. Roy Weintraub (ed), *Toward a History of Game Theory*. Annual Supplement to *History of Political Economy*, Vol. 24. Durham, NC: Duke University Press.

(1994) "Some Musings on Gaming and Simulation". *Simulation and Gaming*, 25(2), 251–8.

(1997) "On the Trail of a White Whale: The Rationalizations of a Mathematical Institutional Economist". In A. Heertje (ed), *The Makers of Modern Economics*, Vol. III (pp. 96–121). Cheltenham: Edward Elgar.

Shubik, Martin and Garry D. Brewer (1972a) "Models, Simulations, and Games – A Survey". Report for Advanced Research Projects Agency, R-1060-ARPA/RC, Santa Monica, CA: RAND.

(1972b) "Review of Selected Books and Articles on Gaming and Simulation". Report for Advanced Research Projects Agency, R-732-ARPA, Santa Monica, CA: RAND.

Shubik, Martin, Garry D. Brewer, and E. Savage (1972) "The Literature of Gaming, Simulation and Model-Building: Index and Critical Abstracts". Report for Advanced Research Projects Agency, R-620-ARPA, Santa Monica, CA: RAND.

Siegel, Sidney and Lawrence E. Fouraker (1960) *Bargaining and Group Decision Making: Experiments in Bilateral Monopoly.* New York: McGraw-Hill.

Sills, David L. (1968) *International Encyclopedia of the Social Sciences*, Vol. 14 (pp. 262–74). New York: Macmillan & Free Press.

Simon, Herbert A. (1991) *Models of My Life.* New York: Basic Books.

Sismondo, Sergio (1999) [ed] *Modeling and Simulation.* Special issue of *Science in Context*, 12:2, Summer.

Slutsky, Eugen E. (1927) Reprinted in translation (1937) "The Summation of Random Causes as the Source of Cyclic Processes". *Econometrica*, 5, 105–46.

Solovey, Mark (1993) "Guy Orcutt and the Social Systems Research Institute". In R. J. Lampman (ed), *Economists at Wisconsin* (pp. 178–84). Board of Regents of the University of Wisconsin System.

Thomas William and Lambert Williams (2009) "The Epistemologies of Non-Forecasting Simulations, Part I. Industrial Dynamics and Management Pedagogy at MIT". *Science in Context*, 22:2, 245–70.

Tinbergen, Jan (1937) *An Econometric Approach to Business Cycle Problems.* Paris: Hermann.

(1939) *Statistical Testing of Business Cycle Theories.* Geneva: League of Nations.

Watts, Harold W. (1991) "Distinguished Fellow: An Appreciation of Guy Orcutt". *Journal of Economic Perspectives*, 5:1, 171–9.

Weintraub, E. Roy (1992) [ed] *Toward a History of Game Theory.* Annual Supplement to *History of Political Economy*, Vol. 24. Durham, NC: Duke University Press.

Winsberg, Eric (1999) "Sanctioning Models: The Epistemology of Simulation". In Sergio Sismondo (ed), *Modeling and Simulation.* Special issue of *Science in Context*, 12:2, 275–92, Summer.

Yule, George Udny (1926) "Why Do We Sometimes Get Nonsense Correlations Between Time-Series?" *Journal of the Royal Statistical Society*, 89, 1–64.

9

Model Situations, Typical Cases, and Exemplary Narratives

1. Introduction

The model that forms the heart of this chapter is the Prisoner's Dilemma game, in which we find two thin model men making a strategic choice within a small model world. The characters are the rational economic men whose history we charted in Chapter 4, while the small world is one of those characteristically small and constrained model worlds like the Edgeworth Box (of Chapter 3) or the supply and demand model (of Chapter 7). In this chapter, the Prisoner's Dilemma game shows how the thin man inhabits the small world in a way that epitomises modelling in modern economics.

The Prisoner's Dilemma game is not just a standard working object in economics, but represents an important general problem in a shorthand way for economists. It is one of a number of simple 'games' studied in the social sciences that represent not just situations of conflict in which choices must be made, but situations in which the players face a dilemma in choosing what actions to take. But, significantly, the Prisoner's Dilemma game also presents a dilemma for social scientists, particularly economists, studying the game, for the outcome of the rightly reasoned or 'rational' action by the individuals taken separately leads to an outcome that seems to be wrong or 'irrational' when the individuals are taken together, that is, for society. This combination of qualities has turned the Prisoner's Dilemma game into an exemplary model not only for such situations in the economic world but also with respect to fundamental beliefs that economists hold about the economy.

The third dilemma consists in working out how these small model worlds can be used as a means of enquiry into the real world. Game thinking does not fit easily with modern economists' picture of their science as a mathematical discipline, producing and applying general theories derived deductively from general principles of rational behaviour. Yet, game theory does seem to provide ways to describe and analyse economic situations and to suggest explanations for economic behaviour of "agents" – the people or firms – in those situations. Compared with the materials examined in the last few chapters, these game theory models offer fewer resources for experimental activity and we will find them more dependent on narratives and more involved in classifying activity. My analysis of model reasoning here hinges on the idea that games, such as the Prisoner's Dilemma, provide models for situations in the world, while the narratives are a flexible device that match the world in the model to the world that the model represents.

2. War Games

Game theory was born and nurtured in the war and Cold War years of the 1940s/50s American military–industrial–scientific establishment, that same environment that saw the development of model simulation methods discussed in Chapter 8. That establishment included social scientists along with mathematicians, engineers, computer scientists, physicists, and chemists. Game theory was a shared domain of research into rational strategic action, played out in games and in theorizing, particularly involving the political scientists, the psychologists, the mathematicians, and the economists. But not all of those concerned with game theory were part of the Cold War establishment: although game theory was associated with Cold War policy analysis and advice on both military and foreign affairs fronts, a number of those involved in developing game theory warned against such use.[1]

Unlike many games in game theory, the Prisoner's Dilemma 'game' actually began life as a game. It was possibly first played at RAND during January 1950 in an experiment designed by Merrill Flood and Melvin Dresher (and reported in Flood, 1952) in work funded by the military. In the game, each of two players (John Williams from RAND and Armen Alchian from UCLA) had to choose,

---

1 On the history of game theory in economics and this context, see particularly Weintraub (1992), Mirowski (2002), Giocoli (2003), and Leonard (2010). I discussed the war contexts at greater length in the original version of this paper (see Morgan, 2007).

simultaneously, and in the absence of knowledge of the other's choice, one of two actions, and for which they received payoffs that both players knew about in advance. Howard Raiffa, working at the University of Michigan on contracts for the Office of Naval Research, was at the same time investigating a similar game, and carrying out experiments with it (reported in 1951; see Raiffa 1992, pp. 171–3). Though there is some debate about who first worked on the game matrix, all agree that the name and story were attached to the game by Albert Tucker (a Princeton mathematician) when he wanted to use the game in a lecture to psychologists.[2]

The basic ideas of the Prisoner's Dilemma game were depicted in a telling cartoon by R. O. Blechman that accompanied Anatol Rapoport's discussion of game theory in the context of the Cold War in *Scientific American* in 1962 (shown in Figure 9.1b).[3] The situation depicted – the denouement of Puccini's opera *Tosca* – is hardly an everyday affair: the heroine Tosca faces up to the Chief of Police, Scarpia, who holds her betrothed, the painter Cavarodossi, under threat of execution. The cartoon was accompanied by tables (matrices) of numbers depicting the benefits of two different choices each of them might make in this situation. (In the matrix shown here as Figure 9.1a, Tosca's choices are the row choices, and her "payoff" numbers are on the left; Scarpia has the column choices and numbers on the right. (Cavarodossi does not appear in the matrix, for he has no choices to make.) Tosca promises to grant sexual favours to Scarpia, who promises in return to order blanks be fired at the execution. But neither side keeps its promise. Tosca decides that she should in fact stab Scarpia when she meets him hoping, by that time, he will have already ordered that blanks be fired, thus gaining her lover's freedom and retaining her virtue (a double benefit from double crossing Scarpia depicted as her sung "+10" in the cartoon). At the same time, Scarpia has decided he can order real bullets for Cavarodossi, believing that this way he can win Tosca and rid himself of her lover. He thus anticipates a similar double benefit of "+10", from double crossing Tosca, but he realises only the penalty of death sweetened by that of revenge, "-5",

	Scarpia: blanks	Scarpia: bullets
Tosca: sex favours	R (5) R (5)	T (10) S (-10)
Tosca: stabs Scarpia	S (-10) T (10)	P (-5) P (-5)

Figure 9.1 Game Theory in Tosca.

(a) Matrix of "payoffs."

2 For this history, see Poundstone (1992 pp. 116–8) and Roth (1995, pp. 9–10 and 26–7). Raiffa (1992, p. 173) gives an account of the disputed provenance (with RAND) of the type of game, suggesting that it was "folk knowledge" of that time.

3 Rapoport used this platform – and a variety of other cartoons – to warn against the usage of game theory to guide Cold War actions.

Game theory in "Tosca": Tosca double-crosses Scarpia

Scarpia derives satisfaction from the thought of what is going to happen

Tosca and Cavaradossi discover the double double cross

Figure 9.1 Game Theory in Tosca.

(b) Cartoon. Source: Anatol Rapoport, "The Use and Misuse of Game Theory", *Scientific American*, Dec 1962, pp. 108–18. Cartoon by R. O. Blechman, p. 111. Reproduced with permission from R. O. Blechman and with acknowledgement to *Scientific American*.

as he dies (rather than the full penalty of "-10" had he let Tosca win her betrothed's freedom). She, finding her lover executed, realizes that she too has been double crossed, so her earlier triumphant "+10" turns into a dejected "-5" (not "-10", for she still has the satisfaction of having double crossed Scarpia). Both Tosca and Scarpia would have been better off if they had kept their bargain, but both fear the worst of each other and want to get the best outcome for themselves. Both end up paying the penalty for their selfishness and lack of trust. Their situation, their actions, and their payoff numbers taken together have all the characteristics of the Prisoner's Dilemma game.

The USA/USSR superpower relationship of the day, particularly their nuclear relationship, was depicted as sharing the same structure and offering the same strategic choices. If they could agree not to use their nuclear arsenals, and could stick to that agreement, both countries would be better off. But given the lack of trust, the strategic analysis of rational action in such a game suggested that they would each be better off if they bombed the other one before they were bombed themselves.

As dramatic as these two examples are, the Prisoner's Dilemma game has been used as a model for many more conventional situations and has become a mainstay in economic discussions about all sorts of things. The Prisoner's Dilemma game has gained exemplary status in representing a certain kind of difficult situation that seems endemic in economic life. And, as we will see, analysis of that game situation cuts into the heart of some well-trusted economic beliefs.

3. The Exemplary Narrative

3.i The Prisoner's Dilemma: Collaborate or Defect?

I start this account of the Prisoner's Dilemma game with its first written appearance in R. Duncan Luce and Howard Raiffa's now classic 1957 text, *Games and Decisions*.[4] (As with the Edgeworth Box, there is something to be gained by going back to see how a well-known model began its life history.) Here is a version of one of their three matrices, showing the strategic choices and utility payoffs for

---

4 This is also the text that the *Oxford English Dictionary* uses to notify first written usage of the term "prisoner's dilemma". (The OED entry also notes Albert Tucker's more general claim to the game's provenance; see footnote 3.) The founding text in game theory is von Neumann and Morgenstern (1944), but the important contribution of Luce and Raiffa's book was immediately recognised: "The theory of games and decision-making theory may well provide the base for a unified conceptual structure for the social sciences (c.f. Shubik, 1959, and Luce and Raiffa, 1957)" (Siegel and Fouraker, 1960, p. 2). We noted the importance of Shubik's book in the last chapter (as one of the first books to integrate game theory thoroughly with industrial economics); it returns in this chapter for its role in building a taxonomy. Luce and Raiffa's book remains a highly respected reference book for the game theory field.

the Prisoner's Dilemma game, the one they suggest is "intuitively" useful for their discussion that follows (p. 95):

	Player B, Strategy 1	Player B, Strategy 2
Player A, Strategy 1	5 \ 5	6 \ -4
Player A, Strategy 2	-4 \ 6	-3 \ -3

where B, the column player, has outcome payoffs on the right, and A the row player, has outcomes payoffs on the left, from whatever joint choices they make.

Here I have presented the game in the form it most usually appears in economics writings, namely as a particular matrix of payoffs. Many variations of the numbers may be used, and while the matrix is usually symmetric, it need not be.[5] But this variation in numbers is potentially misleading, for the numbers used cannot be just any numbers. Even slight changes in the numbers may change the matrix to represent a different game, maybe even another dilemma game.[6] The relations between the numbers in a Prisoner's Dilemma game matrix must conform to a set of inequalities that are very important in defining a Prisoner's Dilemma game, for they provide a more general description of the payoffs, and constrain the numbers although – surprisingly – they are rarely given:[7]

a) $T > R > P > S$, and
b) $2R > (T + S) > 2P$

Of course, these inequalities are defined in terms that make no sense yet, and they make no sense because so far I have not reported the narrative text that goes with the game.

The text plays an important role in defining the structure of the game (as we will discuss in a later section), and whereas the game often appears without these inequalities, it (almost) never appears without the text. In fact, the identity of the Prisoner's Dilemma game consists in the triple: matrix, inequalities, and narrative. Just as we needed the opera's denouement to understand the numbers in *Tosca's* matrix and cartoon, we need the Prisoner's Dilemma story to understand their game, and neither the text nor the matrix (even with the inequalities as constraints) will on its own characterize that game.

5 For example, in one of the first records of the game played experimentally, at RAND (reported in Flood, 1952), the matrix was not symmetric, to make it less clear what the situation was.

6 For example, the "Battle of the Sexes" or "Chicken" are two other classic two-person dilemma games usually discussed alongside the Prisoner's Dilemma game, both also used widely as examples. In terms of the Cold War context, the Cuban missile crisis was discussed as a game of Chicken (two young men driving towards each other down the middle of the road to see who gives way first).

7 See, for example, Rasmussen (1989, p. 30) or Axelrod (1984, pp. 9–10).

The text attached to the matrix is the story of two prisoners and their dilemmas. The narrative of the Prisoner's Dilemma game goes as follows, quoting from Luce and Raiffa's text immediately following their matrix (given above):

> The following interpretation, known as the prisoner's dilemma is popular: Two suspects are taken into custody and separated. The district attorney is certain that they are guilty of a specific crime, but he does not have adequate evidence to convict them at a trial. He points out to each prisoner that each has two alternatives: to confess to the crime the police are sure they have done, or not to confess. If they both do not confess, then the district attorney states he will book them on some very minor trumped-up charge such as petty larceny and illegal possession of a weapon, and they will both receive minor punishment; if they both confess they will be prosecuted, but he will recommend less than the most severe sentence; but if one confesses and the other does not, then the confessor will receive lenient treatment for turning state's evidence whereas the latter will get "the book" slapped at him. (Luce and Raiffa, 1957, p. 95)[8]

Each prisoner faces the same strategic choice, but this choice poses a dilemma for him: Should he choose to collaborate with his fellow prisoner and not confess to the police, he may end up with the rewards of a small prison term, but if his fellow prisoner does the opposite it makes his own situation the worst it could be. If he follows his own self-interest and confesses, hoping his fellow will not, and thus enforce the best outcome for himself and the worst outcome for his fellow, there is the danger that his fellow will also confess, thus leaving them both worse off. The dilemma lies between whether to trust a fellow prisoner and so chance the outcome of being a "Sucker" (not confessing when his fellow does) or giving into the "Temptation" to tell tales on the fellow. Of course, he may hope that they can both reap the "Reward" of collaborating with each other, but there is always the possibility that both will pay the "Penalty" of defection. The dilemma of whether to "Collaborate" and reap the joint rewards or "Defect" to your own advantage and to the loss of your opponent was experienced by the two players involved in that first recorded playing of the game, as we can learn from the transcripts of their ongoing personal commentary as the game was played over and over again for 100 times (the full transcript is given in Poundstone, 1992, chapter 6). It is the dilemma faced by Tosca and Scarpia each time their opera plays itself out.

This analysis of the narrative text reveals the meaning of the constraints on the matrix numbers and we can now see where the inequalities terminology comes from: T is the payoff from giving into Temptation and Defecting; R is the reward to both from Collaboration (with each other); P is the Penalty to each when both Defect; and S is the loss from being a Sucker, the player who Collaborates when his fellow player Defects. So the previous matrix can be reinterpreted to link the payoff numbers with the inequality symbols:

---

8   At this point, Luce and Raiffa also give a matrix of utility payoffs in terms of months and years in jail!

	Player B, Collaborate	Player B, Defect
Player A, Collaborate	R(5) / R(5)	T(6) / S(-4)
Player A, Defect	S(-4) / T(6)	P(-3) / P(-3)

In the analysis of this dilemma, the economist assumes that each prisoner is a rational economic actor (the character whose history I traced in Chapter 4) and will seek to maximise his individual utility (his payoff). That is: for A (row player), it is better to play row D regardless of what B (column player) does [6 > 5 and –3 > –4]; and for B (column player) it is better to play column D [6 > 5 and –3 > –4]. Both prisoners will act rationally by defecting (confess to the police) and both end up with penalties of (–3). Although both prisoners could do better than this if they could agree to collaborate (neither confess), the payoff structure shown in the inequalities is such that the individual temptation to defect is overriding. As Luce and Raiffa wrote:

> Since the players each want to maximise utility, α_2 and β_2 [D and D in my symbols] are their "rational" choices. Of course, it is slightly uncomfortable that two so-called irrational players will both fare much better than two so-called rational ones. Nonetheless, it remains true that a rational player (an α_2 or β_2 [D] conformist) is always better off than an irrational player. In further support of these strategy choices, we may point out that .. [D, D] .. is the unique equilibrium pair of the game ... (Luce and Raiffa, 1957, p. 96)

In this Prisoner's Dilemma case, the economists' game solution is, at one level, straightforward: rational economic man, the model man who inhabits economic theories and makes them what they are, follows an individual utility maximising aim that translates into a choice that ends up with both players paying a penalty rather than reaping rewards. The joint collaboration outcome (CC) cannot be an "equilibrium solution" because, according to economists' assumptions of how a rational model man will play the game, both have an individual incentive to defect; only the DD outcome that follows from both prisoners fully following their own self-interest creates a valid equilibrium solution.

The Prisoner's Dilemma game carries the hallmarks of 'good' economic theory within the neoclassical programme: the individual rational actions of these model economic men create an equilibrium outcome. These two hallmarks form the basic rules of reasoning in game theory. Unfortunately, in the Prisoner's Dilemma game, that outcome is not a good one.

3.ii The Economists' Dilemma: Individual Rationality or Invisible Hand?

Economic theory has long assumed a model 'economic man' to lie at the heart of economic reasoning. The traditional *homo economicus* was established for economists by John Stuart Mill in 1836, who argued that only by adopting a thinly characterized account of economic motivations and behaviour could economics make any progress as a science, and he pictured man as governed overwhelmingly by wealth-seeking self-interest. From Mill onwards then, such abstractions and idealizations of economic man were thought to capture the essential elements of economic behaviour, but known to be inadequate as a description of actual behaviour, which was subject to many other impulses, economic and otherwise. In the late nineteenth century self-interested economic man became a subjective valuer and calculating consumer. By the mid-twentieth century (according to the history I related in Chapter 4), neoclassical economists' model of economic man had turned into a rational economic agent who seeks to maximise his utility by choosing the best actions in any given situation. This model man who inhabits game theory must play his part, but as in many such games, he lacks knowledge of what the other player will do.[9] So, when faced with the strategic choice in the Prisoner's Dilemma game, the best he can do is to act rationally in his own *individual* interest.[10]

Neoclassical economists' emphasis on such narrowly defined, hard-edged individual economic rationality created a particular problem in the Prisoner's Dilemma game, wherein the theoretical analysis of individually rational and strategic behaviour leads to an outcome that is jointly irrational. That is, by following the economists' injunction to maximise their individual gain, the two individuals in the game both end up with a worse outcome than if they had both collaborated with each other. This combination of individual self interest and self-defeating joint outcome makes economists uncomfortable, as we can see from the way that Luce and Raiffa (1957) used their narrative to argue that this solution to the Prisoner's Dilemma game still remains rational in their terms:

> One might try to argue that the differences between [6 and 5] and between [–3 and –4] are so small that even a criminal's ethics would make him select the first strategy so that they would not both be caught in the "stupid" [–3, –3] trap. Such an argument is inadmissible since the numerical utility values are supposed to reflect all such "ethical" considerations. No, there appears to be no way around this dilemma. We do not believe that there is anything irrational or perverse about the choice of α_2 and β_2 [D and D], and we must admit that if we were actually in this position we would make these choices. (Luce and Raiffa, 1957 p. 96, replacing the numbers in their matrix above into their text)

---

9 In other words, he is not endowed with the perfect knowledge and foresight of Knight's slot machine man; see Chapter 4.

10 Game theory has in turn developed an idea of economic man as strategic man; see Giocoli (2003) for a recent history of the development of the modelling of strategic behaviour within the economic man portrait.

The belief that there was nothing wrong with the individual choices here but that the outcome is 'wrong' in some sense created a dilemma for economists, expressed with feeling by Luce and Raiffa:

> The hopelessness that one feels in such a game as this cannot be overcome by a play on the words "rational" and "irrational"; it is inherent in the situation. "There should be a law against such games!" (Luce and Raiffa, 1957, pp. 96–7)

But perhaps, economists argued, the result might not hold if the two people play a succession of such games. It is tempting, after all, to suppose that a succession of games would ensure the cooperative outcome. Even here, the *theoretical* analysis led to the same result. The usual method of analysing what would happen in a Prisoner's Dilemma game repeated a finite number of times was one of "backward induction".[11] First work out what will happen in the last game: because it is the last game, there is no reason for the individual to cooperate and every reason to defect, hoping that the opponent will not and thus reap the best outcome, as in the single-game case. Since both individuals follow the same rationality, the last game is a DD result. Then move back one game to the penultimate game, where the same analysis goes through. Rational economic man has no learning power, no power to trust, only to choose strategically the best option in any given situation. The analytical sequence continues back to the beginning, so the theoretical result is a series of bad outcomes.[12]

These theoretical results left the economist extremely uneasy – either the rationality assumption is wrong, or the outcome equilibrium is wrong. But neither could easily be given up in the 1950s and 1960s: too much was at stake.

On the one hand, the model of rational economic man was deeply embedded in the 'high theory' of that day. Because of the position of this rational character as a central building block of modern neoclassical theory, softening or broadening the rational man portrait would undermine more than just the Prisoner's Dilemma result or even game theory.

On the other hand, economists relied equally on another important result in economic theory, namely the 'invisible hand' thesis that individuals following their own self-interest will end up doing naturally what is best for each other. According to the invisible hand argument, the outcome for a game where the players follow their own self-interest should be a good one. Economists and philosophers seem to have a deeply ingrained belief that the invisible hand is a benevolent one. This is most often dated back to Adam Smith's use of the term, and his argument is often taken to be epitomised in the following quote:

---

11 "Inductive modelling", as Rapoport termed the process, in which he imagined how hypothetical reasoning on the part of the individuals might result in different behaviour, led him to the same conclusions (see Rapoport, 1966, Chapter 10).

12 This result does not necessarily hold for the game repeated an infinite (or perhaps unknown) number of times.

It is not from the benevolence of the butcher, the brewer, or the baker, that we expect our dinner, but from their regard to their own interest. We address ourselves, not to their humanity but to their self-love, and never talk to them of our own necessities but of their advantages. (Smith, 1776, I.ii.2)

This invisible hand argument is the basis of the idea that free individuals operating in a free market will provide a more efficient outcome than that arising from government planning. The invisible hand concept and argument is the basis for economists' claims that a free market is good for everyone.[13]

Thus, the *theory* of what happens in the Prisoner's Dilemma game puts economists in a particularly nasty double dilemma: If the individual play is constrained according to economists' cherished notion of rationality, they must accept the irrational outcome that both players are worse off than if they collaborated. But accepting that irrational outcome creates a problem for economists' equally cherished belief in the benevolence of the invisible hand, and thus the efficiency of the market in such contexts. But if they weaken or widen the rationality of individual self-interest, economists potentially undermine their results in mathematical work on general equilibrium analysis and perfect competition that give technical substance and formalization to their informal invisible hand arguments.

Economists have made various attempts to get around these dilemmas. We can classify these ways as attempts to broaden individual rationality to get both prisoners to the good outcome, or as ways to broaden the invisible hand argument to accept bad outcomes. This way of posing economists' solutions to their dilemmas with the Prisoner's Dilemma game is signified by seeing where economists place the apostrophe. If it is the individual prisone*r's* dilemma, the question focuses on individual rationality. If it is the joint prisone*rs'* dilemma, the focus is on coordination or 'social' outcomes. Most economists use the term Prisone*r's* Dilemma, and focus on the individual problem (a rare exception being David Kreps in both his microeconomics text, 1990a, and his book on modelling and game theory, 1990b). But when economists write about the dilemma as a problem of invisible hand outcomes and issues of coordination, they more often use the form Prisone*rs'* Dilemma (e.g., Tullock, 1985).

Theoretical ways around the prisone*r's* dilemma seem to depend on arguments that each individual without any opportunity to collaborate will nevertheless rationally play the cooperative move in the first place. Perhaps people have a "disposition" to trust each other? Perhaps people follow a moral code that makes them trust each other? Perhaps people begin by trusting until that is proved wrong? On the whole, economists have not found these attempts to broaden their rationality principle in terms of trust issues very convincing (see, e.g., Shubik, 1970), and have left these

---

13 And thus, of course, it is intimately bound up with the economic ideology of the Cold War; see Morgan (2003).

kinds of speculations to those more philosophically inclined (see Campbell and Sowden, 1985, and Hargreaves Heap and Varoufakis, 1995).

However, *experimental* work on how the Prisoner's Dilemma game is played by real people for money reveals differences from economists' theoretical account of how rational economic man plays the game.[14] For example, the original experiments at RAND showed that, in repeated rounds of the game, some collaboration would occur. Since then, there have been many experiments with the game, in both economics and psychology.[15] The most famous of these is probably the extensive set of experiments conducted by Rapoport and Chammah (1965) showing how players tended to converge to either CC or DD outcomes over a series of experiments, but they also reported considerable variations in outcomes, and that outcomes vary with the numbers in the matrix. Axelrod's series of tournaments reported in his 1984 book investigated various "strategies" or sequences of moves in playing a repeated Prisoner's Dilemma game in a simulation. These strategies were played out against each other in a computer tournament, and those that did best turned out to be those that were rather collaborative and rather forgiving – 'nice' strategies if you like. (Once again, as with Samuelson's simulations of Chapter 6, some surprises turned up for the investigators.) The results of such *experimental* studies of the game hit at the heart of the *theoretical* results obtained from analysing the Prisoner's Dilemma game.

The continued experimental investigation of trust and collaboration in this context have occupied the psychologists more keenly than the economists. Economists have been more interested in what it means to be rational. And, since the 1970s, they have broadly opened up the question of what it means to be economically rational, with experimental and theoretical studies of bounded rationality, learning theory, contracting theory, and how people value different choices in different kinds of situations. These explorations of economic behaviour increasingly maintain the rational economic model man only as a benchmark, a function he continues to play in the Prisoner's Dilemma case.

If the question is concerned with the prison*ers'* dilemma, the solution lies not in the game itself, but in the nature of the invisible hand argument. There is no necessity for the aggregate outcome of many individual self-interests to be benevolent, as the Prisoner's Dilemma case demonstrates so easily.[16] While economists' commitment

---

14 In the experimental tradition, it is usually assumed that monetary payoffs can be related to individual utility and preferences in comparable ways, though for some commentators, this is a controversial assumption. See Roth (1995, pp. 26–8) for a very brief overview of the findings of experiments with this game.

15 The two disciplines do not necessarily make the same inferences from the same experiments, as Leonard (1994) shows in the context of experiments with bargaining games.

16 Ullman-Margalit's (1978) insightful discussion of invisible hand explanations points out that, on hearing them, we should find them both plausible and surprising. The Prisoner's Dilemma game, I think, fits this description, and is often associated with invisible hand explanations as we see hereafter (even though it does not strictly fit her other requirement that they are aggregate outcomes, unless we interpret two people as an aggregate as this literature seems to do). The

to the benevolence of the invisible hand has *appeared* to remain just as strong and deep-seated as ever – as with the notion of rationality, and over the same time period since the 1970s (see Chapter 4) – there have been subtle changes in thinking. It would be a challenging task to trace the winding and possibly many paths by which neoclassical economists came to modify their belief in the all-pervasiveness and complete benevolence of Smith's invisible hand argument linking individual behaviour and social outcomes. Nevertheless, I believe I am on safe ground in arguing that game theory was an important element in that change. For example, in 1975, Martin Shubik, one of the developers of game theory in economics, stated:

> ... one of the most important lessons that game theory has to teach is that a concept of individual rationality does not generalize in any unique or natural way to group or social responsibility. Social rationality could easily be a concept defined independently from individual rationality and may not even be consistent with it. (Shubik, 1975, p. 24)

The classic example of the Prisoner's Dilemma game functioned, and continues to function, as an exemplary narrative in making and marking this turn. As game theory first gained professional dominance during and after the 1970s, the Prisoner's Dilemma game turned up in many different contexts. As we will see later, it has been used to interpret all sorts of unfriendly outcomes from the free market, such as free riding problems, differential wages, and environmental externalities. When game theory trickled down into the classroom, it proved equally powerful, and as evidence of the general change in belief, I can do no better than quote from one of my London School of Economics colleagues, Margaret Bray, in teaching students the lesson drawn from using the Prisoner's Dilemma game during an intermediate level, undergraduate course in economic theory:

> The first law of economics is that individuals left to follow their own self-interest will reach a mutually beneficial outcome; the second law of economics is that this won't necessarily happen! (Bray, 2000)[17]

This power of the Prisoner's Dilemma game to function as an exemplary model with wide relevance, stretching to the laws of economics themselves, marks it out as a special case within game theory.

I will now turn to the Prisoner's Dilemma game as a model in another sense: for showing us how game theory is applied by matching typical cases to economic situations.

---

issue of benevolence has been a more formidable obstacle than might be supposed. The pre-Smith manifestation of the invisible hand argument available within the tradition of political economy, namely Bernard Mandeville's *Private Vices, Publick Benefits* of 1705/14, pictured the invisible hand as a partly malevolent one. In his fable, private vices lead via an invisible hand process to public benefits, but the participants in the economy interpret the process as a bad one.

17 Quoted from game theory lectures in "Microeconomic Principles" (or intermediate microeconomics), Autumn 2000, by permission, from Margaret Bray.

4. The Commentator's Dilemma: Fitting Together Situations, Narratives, and Cases

When we look into the way game theory, including the Prisoner's Dilemma game, is applied to understand the world, as opposed to the theoretical and experimental study of the games themselves, we find a problem of how to characterize its usage and role. On the one hand, we find that game theory spawns models that have a specified range, not general applicability (as with Marshall's versions of the supply and demand models in Chapter 7). On the other hand, the use of mathematical notation and model arguments is inextricably bound up with narratives (as with the Keynesian macroeconomic models of the 1930s in Chapter 6). The analysis here rests on an additional key element: the way situations are modelled. In this genre of model reasoning, the narratives provide explanatory depth, while general theory is replaced by typical cases, from which classifications and taxonomies are developed to gain explanatory breadth. Together with the situational analysis, these characterize the way that game theory enables economists to reason about the economic world using models.

4.i Reasoning about Situations

The application of game theory to the world involves reasoning about situations. We might start by reminding ourselves of another moment in the history of model man in economics (from Chapter 4). Recall that for Menger, the founder of Austrian economics, "*the starting point and the goal of every concrete human economy are ultimately determined strictly by the economic situation of the moment.*" (Menger, 1883/1985 p. 217) [italics his.]. During the 1930s and 1940s, economics had been more generally redefined to focus on economic man as making choices given the constraints of his situation. Friedrich von Hayek's seminal paper "Economics and Knowledge" (of 1937) develops this Austrian tradition into an account of how man's knowledge constrains and determines his choices of economic behaviour in any given situation; his account prompted his fellow Austrian emigré, the philosopher Karl Popper, towards an analysis of the logic of economic situations. Popper's "Models, Instruments, and Truth" of 1963 grew up in the context of two other, related, debates in contemporary philosophy (of the late 1950s and early 1960s).[18] First, could the scientific mode of explanation developed for natural sciences be considered relevant *not only* for social sciences *but also* for history? And, what

---

18 Originally a 1963 lecture (given to the Department of Economics at Harvard University), Popper explicitly recognised the Hayek connection (1963/94, pp. 154 and 181). Revisions were undertaken in 1964 and the lecture was finally published in full only in 1994. Many of the relevant elements discussed here can also be found in Popper (1967) and there are earlier hints of the "logic of the situation" in his 1945 essay.

does it mean to explain historical events in terms of the rational actions of the individuals involved?[19]

Popper characterized "situational analysis" as *the* method for economic analysis, arguing that explaining or predicting a "*kind or type* of event" is "most easily solved *by means of constructing a model*" where "the '*models*' of the theoretical social sciences are essentially descriptions or reconstructions of *typical social situations*" (Popper, 1963/1994, pp. 163 and 166, his italics).[20] This reconstruction includes not only the typical personal knowledge of the individual in such a situation, but also the environment, institutions and structural relations within which the individual operates. The universal laws found in the natural sciences are replaced by an "animating" or "rationality principle" consisting of acting "appropriately to the situation". Here is where Popper's work intersects with William Dray's contemporaneous development of the argument that historical explanation should be based on the analysis of a "rationale" of action by the historical actors given their situations.[21]

Dray's account of historical explanation was first formalized into a schema by Carl Hempel (1961–2), and then by Noretta Koertge (1975, p. 440) in discussing Popper's recipe for explanation in the social sciences as shown here (as Box 9.1).[22]

Box 9.1 Koertge's Schema.

1. Description of the situation	Agent A was in a situation of type C
2. Analysis of the situation:	In a situation of type C, the appropriate thing to do is X
3. Rationality principle:	Agents always act appropriately to their situations
4. Explanandum:	(Therefore) A did X

Source: Noretta Koertge "Popper's Metaphysical Research Program for the Human Sciences." *Inquiry*, (1975) 18, 437–62, p. 440. Reproduced (reset) with permission from Taylor and Francis Ltd. (http://www.informaworld.com).

---

19 See Dray (1957); and for entry into the concurrent arguments about historical and scientific explanation, see Gardiner's 1974 collection.

20 In principle according to his analysis, both natural and social science events may be explained either under a covering law (with initial conditions) or by constructing models. But, in practice, according to Popper, the covering law kinds of explanations can rarely be applied using the kinds of theories of the social sciences; instead, such sciences work by constructing models. For a more recent discussion of the covering law mode of explanation in economics, and the relevant literature, see Hands (2001).

21 See particularly Dray's "The Rationale of Actions" in his *Laws and Explanation in History* (1957) and his "The Historical Explanation of Actions Reconsidered", 1963, in Gardiner (1974).

22 Hempel first outlined such a schema in his 1961–2 paper (p. 12) on rational action, where he referred to Luce and Raiffa as well as Dray, both of 1957. He discussed the schema further in his 1965 (p. 471) essay on explanation in the natural and social sciences and in history, which Koertge references. I follow her later formulation because, like Popper, she emphasises the importance of "the situation", which is critical here for the discussion of models.

The idea is that an analysis of the situation combined with a principle of rational action will define what it is logical (i.e., rational) for agents to do in a particular type of situation, and thus enable the social scientist to "explain" such actions. Since the description of the situation includes the relevant aims and knowledge of the agent, the rationality principle is "almost empty", a "zero-principle" (Popper 1963/1994, p. 169). It is not supposed to have empirical content, nor is it a psychological assertion. The consequence of Popper's recipe for social science explanation is that we "pack or cram our whole theoretical effort, our whole explanatory theory, into an analysis of the *situation* – into the *model*" (Popper, 1963/1994, p. 169).

One important element of this formulation has been neglected in both these earlier and subsequent discussions.[23] Wade Hands (1992, pp. 27–31) has argued that situational logic is indeed exactly how economists do argue in standard microeconomics. But both Hands' and Bruce Caldwell's (1991) commentaries omit the important word "type" when they reproduce Koertge's formulation. This little omission has serious implications that are not easy to appreciate either from Popper's original account of social science explanation nor Hempel's account of Dray's historical explanation. My point is this: If there are no *typical* situations, the explanatory power of models – to describe and analyse these typical situations – breaks down. Either all situations are the same, in which case general scientific laws provide the "cover" (or give the basis) for explanations, or every situation is different and we are in a world of singular cases and explanations where Dray's "rationale" for each and every action must be fully explored as in history.[24] We can see then how situational analysis, if it refers to *typical situations*, offers a middle level of explanatory reach in which scientific explanation covers a subset of instances with the same well-reasoned account, provided the instances are all one of class of events or "type" of situation. When we take this notion of a *typical situation* fully into account, we have a form of reasoning that depends on models, in which economists offer analyses and seek explanations at some intervening level between those for the single events of history and those for the recurring phenomena of the natural sciences, that is, at level of the typical situation described in the model.

This intervening level, the level of types, has come up before in my account of models. We saw in the analysis of supply and demand models in Chapter 7 that experimental work with these diagrammatic models generated an analysis

23 Most of the literature on situational analysis (in the philosophy of economics) concentrates on the problems of Popper's rationality principle, as does Koertge (1979). Latsis' 1972 analysis adapts Popper's views into his own "situational determinism" account of the history of industrial economics in terms of a Lakatosian research programme. He compares his notion of "situational determinism" to "economic behaviouralism", and so his emphasis too turns out to be the status of the rationality principle rather than the model or situation description.

24 See Van Fraassen (1988) for a neat example of the contrast in these forms of explanation. The problem he discusses is to explain the length of a shadow formed from a particular tower. Initial conditions (the height of the tower, etc.) and the general laws of physics explain the length of the shadow, but the height of the tower itself is explained by an historical narrative about why the castle owner built the tower just so high as to cast a shadow over a terrace at evening time.

of different typical cases: those where supply or demand curves had particular kinds of shapes; those in which market participants or the goods were of particular kinds; and so forth. A contrasting example might be given by the notion of "business model" in which a real firm acts as a role model and provides the means for description of what constitutes "the type" (see Baden-Fuller and Morgan, 2010). Popper himself uses the example of market structure in industrial organisation to reinterpret a standard area of economic theorizing in terms of his situational analysis. He describes the cases of perfect competition and the pure theory of monopoly and duopoly, as "idealized and over-simplified social situations" (1963/94, p. 170), three different 'typical' situations (models) within which economists explain how firms act in terms of the logic of the situation. These economic situations are usually defined by different specific technologies, institutions, goods, or markets. But in deciding what is appropriate in such typical model situations, microeconomists rely on a general behavioural postulate – firms act rationally to maximise profits – to animate the analysis of the situation described in the model and so provide standard outcomes for each type of situation. Thus, for example, economists theorize that any firm operating within a perfectly competitive industry will operate differently than any one that is a monopolist, though both will be following a rational profit-maximising rule. The animating principle of profit maximising is needed to kick start the analysis, but does little explanatory work for the economist. Rather the explanation of the different outcomes hinges upon the differences in the way those types of industry situation are described and analysed in their models.

Game thinking seems an even better example of these ideas. In game theory applications, the game type acts as a model for a type of situation in the economic world, that is, the game type acts as a model situation. Classifying an economic situation as a particular type of game, in which the appropriate logical action in that type of situation has already been defined in game theory, enables the economist to explain or predict what will happen using the game type as the model for the economic situation. The agents in the model situations are motivated by a simple rationality principle of utility maximising, but their actions that follow from this animating principle vary according to the specifics of the model – namely, to the type of game: to the precise situation defined there, including its rules, the level of knowledge, and the sequence of choices and payoffs. The almost empty rationality principle makes little difference, but small differences between model situations and so types of games may really bite, so that the outcomes of games are not easily predictable. As economists explore the effect of changes in the game type, they also explore the impact of such changes in the model for the economic situation.

Characterizing game theory in this way suggests that its applications will depend on being able to match a description of an economic situation, real or hypothesized, to the description of a type of game so that the "appropriate" economic behaviour can be defined. As we have seen already in this context, 'appropriate', for economists usually means not just an animating rationality principle, but some kind of an equilibrium outcome. And, while much of economic game *theorizing* has been concerned with defining the natures of different equilibrium outcomes in different types of game situations, in *applying* game theory, using it to explain things in the economic world, economists put all their effort into describing, analysing, and reconstructing the elements of the situation as typical of a kind of game. The thin but definite rationality principle associated with their model characterization of man as a rational agent who acts to further his self-interest is very close to the zero principle that Popper describes. If model man were fatter, he could be problematic in this form of model reasoning: imagine Malthus's model man parachuted into game theory, with his sexual drive only under the limited control of his reason; he might fit in the Battle of the Sexes game, but what would he do in the Prisoner's Dilemma game? The rational economic man of mid-twentieth-century economics acts according to a rationality principle that constrains, but has little substantive content of its own (as economists themselves have long recognised), so its animating power to provide explanations that connect to the world depends entirely on the work that has gone into describing and analysing the model situation within which economists' model man or model firm acts.

We see now how the model man of modern economics I described earlier fits into reasoning about the economic world using game theory. His thin profile needs little attention; instead, economists can concentrate their activity into modelling his economic situation. How does that modelling go on, how do economists describe, analyse, shape, and reconstruct the situations they find in the economy into a model or typical situation? How is the matching between game type and economic situation achieved, since the ability of economists to use model situations as explanatory devices depends on the empirical adequacy of that match?[25] Here is where narratives are particularly important, for in game theory they are the device that helps both to define the model situation, and to obtain the match between the type of situation portrayed in the world of the model and the one described from the real world.

4.ii Explanatory Depth: The Roles of Narratives

When I first started attending to the role of narratives in economics, I took the trouble to listen carefully to how, and where exactly, narratives were involved. In most economics seminars, narratives were mainly employed in the way economic models were used to answer questions. As I outlined in Chapter 6 (see also Morgan, 2001, 2002a) questions prompted economists to experiment with their mathematical or diagrammatic models and narratives made sense of their deductive demonstrations in terms of hypothetical events that might be theoretically interesting or that might occur in the world. Narratives occurred primarily in economists' explorations into the world of the model and so – as I suggested in that chapter – they

---

25 As Popper observed, "the empirical explanatory theories or hypotheses are our various models, our various situational analyses. It is these which may be empirically more or less adequate" (Popper, 1963/94, p. 166).

come *to form part of the identity of the model.* Of only secondary importance was that they provided the format for making informal or casual inferences from the model experiments to the events of the economic world.[26]

But in attending seminars that employed game theory, the role of narrative seemed truncated – narratives seemed merely to fill in the middle space between a set of individually rational actors, a matrix of numbers and an equilibrium solution. Although there are stories that are all middle, it seemed odd to label these as stories.[27] And while the narratives gave accounts of the situations, as stories they were curiously unsatisfactory, for the situation was already well specified, the actors had little or no economic character, and an equilibrium outcome was already presupposed: the whole problem was how to get from the situation to an outcome that had the right characteristics (or how to "solve" the model). There seemed little work for the narratives to do. However, my sense that only thin middles were involved was misleading, for when I studied them more seriously I saw that narratives assumed a more important role in game theory than in other kinds of economics; indeed narratives played three different roles.

In the first place, narratives, in game theory, are closely connected with the description, analysis, and reconstruction of the situation, namely with the creation of the model.[28] *Narratives here are built into the identity of the model from the start*, and, as we saw with the Prisoner's Dilemma text, they are an essential element, for without it, the matrix and inequalities of the game make no sense. You cannot describe the Prisoner's Dilemma game without the text, any more than the matrix alone tells the story of *Tosca's* final drama.

But the role of narrative does not stop once the model or game has been created. Rather, as I explore in this section of the chapter, narrative work continues as a flexible way of matching a game situation to an economic situation in applying game theory to the world. This process gives more serious consideration to model application compared to the informal inferences we found in Chapter 6. Here, narratives provide the means to reason about the model situation, and they give depth to such explanations because the narratives are grounded in thick situation descriptions.[29] But this back and forth matching between the narrative of the game and that

---

26 In one example in Chapter 6, I showed how narratives made correspondence links between theoretically based Keynesian macro models and the world of the 1930s. In another example there, I pointed to the role of stories in mimicking models, where model outcomes were seen as "credible" if they mimicked some phenomenon of the world.

27 Ursula Le Guin (1980, p. 194) gives an example of a minimalist middle that she is prepared to label "a whole story", carved in runes in Carlisle Cathedral: "Tolfink carved these runes in the stone". This is clearly sufficient of a story to narrate a situation and outcomes, as we will see in my argument's continuation (though it is not sufficient to be a game situation unless the runes have been misread and two people were there: Tol and Fink!).

28 See Chapter 6.2 for the way stories were used to develop Fisher's economic model, and Hartmann (1999) for a case of stories used in model construction in physics.

29 In contrast to these thick descriptions, the narratives that accompanied the model experiments detailed in Chapter 6 relied heavily on manipulable resources and informal inference.

of the world has the effect of collapsing the gap between the model situation and the world situation. Thus, this second function of *narratives as a matching device* does not solve, but rather to some extent dissolves the inference gap between model experiments and the events of the world by smoothing out the differences between them.[30]

There is also a third function of narratives in game theory. Remember, from the last section, that models represent *typical* situations, not one-off cases. Narratives play a role in constructing and shaping an account of the economic world that *locates the typical features of such situations*, and so, by characterizing what is particular about different situations, *contributes to the categorizing and classifying activity of modelling* (as we shall see in the next section). Narratives, in defining and giving structure to these typical situations, sometimes point to problems – as indeed the Prisoner's Dilemma narrative did.[31]

How and where does narrative do all this work? When we look carefully at the account of the Prisoner's Dilemma game given by Luce and Raiffa and the several parts of their text given earlier, we can see that it is the matrix and the text that, taken together, characterize the game situation, but it is the interpretative text, not the matrix, that contains the *explicit* rules of the game (i.e., non-collaboration, simultaneous moves, etc.) as well as the economists' *implicit* traditional assumptions about the individual rationality that characterizes the players (and that must in turn entail the necessary equilibrium character of the outcome or 'solution' as a requirement of 'good' economic accounts). The narratives bound up with the text motivate the assumptions about individual rationality in discussing the reasoning of the prisoners and the equilibrium outcome. As we found already, these are the general requirements that tell economists how to reason with game theory models (in the sense of rules of reasoning, introduced in Chapter 1). The narratives also constrain the outcomes, since although both prisoners might do better if they could agree not to confess, later parts of their text embody the rules of the game that forbid any discussion between them. These are the rules for the specific game, not only for the individuals imagined in the game, but for the economists reasoning with the model. We might say that the narrative texts serve to 'fill in' the middle of the story by embedding the economic assumptions into a description of the situation (including the knowledge and aims of the individuals). Narratives contain the economists' resources to explain why the outcome is as it is, and sometimes how the situation might even be resolved.

We have seen how narrative elements were part of the creation of the Prisoner's Dilemma game. But we can also see how they helped Luce and Raiffa in thinking how to resolve their dilemma with the Prisoner's Dilemma game. Their narrative, for

---

30 From an epistemological point of view, we can describe this process as "built-in justification", as Boumans (1999) did for different reasons in his study of some of the earlier macro-models.

31 See also Grüne-Yanoff and Schweinzer (2008) for a development of my discussion of narrative in the theorizing activity of finding game *solutions* or deriving valid outcomes.

example, emphasises the economists' interpretation of the rationality assumption, namely that "neither suspect has moral qualms about or fear of squealing" (Luce and Raiffa, 1957, p. 95). And they go on to explore the possibility that if cooperation were allowed, the prisoners would reach the cooperative outcome with some kind of binding agreement, though they immediately reject this by pointing out that this goes against both the rationality assumption of each player maximising individual returns and the equilibrium outcome that follows from that assumption taken with the payoff matrix.[32] Nevertheless, this formal issue seems less strong for Luce and Raiffa than their narrative musings about whether a binding agreement to cooperate would be broken by double-crossing, and these are generated by the situation and considerations of whether the game can adequately represent that situation:

> Within the criminal context, such a "double cross" may engender serious reprisals and so it might be argued that it would not be worth while. This seems, however, to deny the utility interpretation of the given numbers [in the matrix]. If we have ignored such considerations in abstracting a game from reality, we had better include the breaking of a binding agreement as an integral aspect of an enlarged game purporting to summarize the conflict of interest. Alternatively, we may suppose that the effect of breaking a binding agreement is so disastrous that it is not considered. (Luce and Raiffa, 1957, p. 96)

In other words, these ways around the outcome of the Prisoner's Dilemma game would lead to the respecification of the rules or the game and/or the revision of the matrix of payoffs to reflect the changes in utility.

Luce and Raiffa felt that neither of these re-descriptions of the game situation suggested by their narratives really solved the problem or got around their dilemma with the game. There seemed no way to redefine rationality to fit the case and generate the collaborative outcome: as they said (and I quoted earlier):

> The hopelessness that one feels in such a game as this cannot be overcome by a play on the words "rational" and "irrational"; it is inherent in the situation. "There should be a law against such games!"

They went on at this point:

> Indeed, some hold the view that one essential role of government is to declare that the rules of certain social "games" must be changed whenever it is inherent in the game situation that the players, in pursuing their own ends, will be forced into a socially undesirable position. That such social and economic games exist is illustrated in the next paragraph. (Luce and Raiffa, 1957, pp. 96–7)

---

32 A more modern text would argue that even if the prisoners could agree to collaborate, the agreement is not "credible" or "enforceable" and so the individual temptation to defect remains overriding.

And they then tell us why the government should step in and "pass a law against such games". Can the government legislate against the Prisoner's Dilemma game? Clearly not. But, in expressing such sentiments, economists are no longer arguing about the Prisoner's Dilemma game, but about the analogous situations to which it is applied, to those "social and economic games" that exist in the world, where governments habitually do legislate against the *outcomes* that arise in those kind of Prisoner's Dilemma situations.

That economists recognise this slide between the world in the Prisoner's Dilemma model and the situations in the world that it represents serves almost as a litmus test of my argument about the way that the Prisoner's Dilemma game is used, namely that economists reason about economic situations by using games as model situations for them. And here the interpretative text remains as necessary as the matrix of payoffs in enabling economists to use the game to reason in economic terms about situations and cases in the economic world. For example, the Prisoner's Dilemma game has been used as a model for a very common form of economic situation: "It [the prisoners' dilemma] arises as a problem of **trust** in every elemental economic exchange because it is rare for the delivery of a good to be perfectly synchronised with the payment for it…" (Hargreaves Heap and Varoufakis, 1995, p. 149; bold in original). That is, the Prisoner's Dilemma game may be relevant whenever we have trade at a distance over time or space (by mail, Internet, or for future delivery). In these cases, both buyer and seller have to trust each other to deliver and not to cheat on the deal to their own advantage and the disadvantage of the other exchange party. We can characterize this situation by saying we often (perhaps even daily) face such a Prisoner's Dilemma situation. But institutions or habits of exchange and trust, those very habits that economists since Hume have thought essential to the mechanism of the market, mean that we (generally) end up with the mutually beneficial outcome rather than the mutually bad outcome. Here we take it for granted that our market institutions and exchange habits are backed by a law of contract that legislates against the outcome of the kind of situations modelled by the Prisoner's Dilemma game, namely, to curtail double crossing (see Hargreaves Heap and Varoufakis, 1995).

The identification of a model-world case with a real-world case in game theory is not so much a matter of formal analogy but of narrative elements that allow the economist to slip easily between the two cases. The narratives translate the prisoners' situation into the economic situation – real or hypothetical – and vice versa. Narratives link the particulars of the economic situation to the typical situation depicted in the game and so 'explain' how it is, for example, that two large firms can end up doing damage to each other just as the prisoners end up with the double-defect outcome. The Prisoner's Dilemma game has often been used to characterize situations of competition between firms, and it has become commonplace to use the Prisoner's Dilemma game to reinterpret the findings of famous past economists. For example, Kreps (1990a) is one of many who use it to reestablish

Cournot's mid-nineteenth century arguments about the behaviour of rival mineral water companies:

> While the story [the Prisoner's Dilemma story] is fanciful, the basic structure of options and payoffs that characterize this game occur over and over in economics. In this basic structure players can cooperate to greater or to lesser extent. If one player unilaterally decreases the level of her cooperation, she benefits and her rival is made worse off. Consider, for example, the case of Cournot duopolists [imagine Evian and Perrier] each (independently) choosing a quantity level to bring to the market. Typically, if one firm increases its production (which is a less cooperative strategy), its profits increase, as least for a while, and the profits of its rival decrease. But (past the monopoly level of output) if both firms increase their levels of output, both do worse. (Kreps, 1990a, p. 504)

Notice how Kreps moves seamlessly from the Prisoner's Dilemma game between two players into the Cournot competition between two firms, and how, some pages later, the game rules moved from a Prisoner's Dilemma game (where no collusion is allowed) to one of possible cooperation, when Kreps continues:

> With collusion, identical firms could each supply half the monopoly quantity, and together they would obtain the monopoly profits. But this isn't an equilibrium; if one side provides half the monopoly quantity, the other side has the incentive to supply more .... This isn't identical to the prisoners' dilemma game, since there we had a strictly dominant strategy for each side. But here, as there, we have (in equilibrium) each side taking actions that leave both worse off than if they could collude. (Kreps, 1990a, p. 524)

Now we see it isn't quite a Prisoner's Dilemma game, but the characteristic outcome of the Prisoner's Dilemma equilibrium remains. This, once again, is the exemplary point of the game type: that the self-interest outcome is not the best one for the two individuals taken together. Once again the narrative matches the situation of the Prisoner's Dilemma game with the economic case and enables a smooth transition in reasoning between the two while allowing a subtle change in the game specification.

Another example brings Marx into the Prisoner's Dilemma, game-theory, fold with his characterization of capitalists as paying their own workers low wages to maximise their own profits while hoping that all other capitalists will pay their workers high wages, thus increasing consumption demand (Hargreaves Heap and Varoufakis, 1995, p.154, quoting from Marx). This of course is a version of the 'free-rider' problem that is endemic in economic situations ranging from environmental pollution to labour supply of work effort. But here, the commentators have used the narrative to move the situation surreptitiously from a two-person game to an n-person Prisoner's Dilemma game. This is also exactly the move made by Luce and Raiffa. Having discussed the Prisoner's Dilemma matrix and text (see above), they give the following "alternative interpretation" for the Prisoner's Dilemma game in a familiar narrative about farmers:

> As an *n*-person analogy to the prisoner's dilemma, consider the case of many wheat farmers where each farmer has, as an idealization, two strategies: "restricted production" and "full production." If all farmers use restricted production the price is high and individually they fare rather well; if all use full production the price is low and individually they fare rather poorly. The strategy of a given farmer, however, does not significantly affect the price level – this is the assumption of a competitive market – so that regardless of the strategies of the other farmers, he is better off in all circumstances with full production. Thus full production dominates restricted production; yet if each acts rationally they all fare poorly. (Luce and Raiffa, 1957, p. 97)

As we have noted earlier, economists seek to solve the dilemma in situations that they perceive as a version of the Prisoner's Dilemma game by altering the rules of the game, or some other aspect of the game played, or by widening the notion of rationality. And, once again, these ways around the problem are driven by the situation narrative that provides the interplay between game type and economic case.

> In practice the equilibrium [of full production – see above] may not occur since the farmers can, and sometimes do, enter into some form of weak collusion. In addition, a farmer does not play this game just once. Rather it is repeated each year and this introduces..... an element of collusion. Finally, sometimes the government feels as we do, steps in, and passes a law against such games. Of course, in this analysis we have neglected the consumer. When he is included collusion may not be socially desirable even if it is desirable for the farmer. (Luce and Raiffa, 1957, p. 97)

In this further narrative, the commentary has moved us from a single game to a repeated Prisoner's Dilemma game, and this, as Luce and Raiffa already knew in 1957 from the experiments of the 1950s, moves us into a different game, where collusion is more than likely, particularly as in the farmers' situation where the number of rounds is unknown.[33]

In applying the models of game theory to the world, either to real or hypothetical situations, the plausibility of the match – the game type with the economic case – is explored in the narrative sequences that surround the application and which integrate together the general economic assumption of individual rationality, the matrix of payoffs, the institutions and rules of the game, and the description of the situation. The narratives also provide the means for probing the description of the case and so the nature of the game and its type, changing the latter if necessary to fit the former. If the match seems ill-fitting, if the game is not an appropriately specified model for the economic situation, then the game specification is altered.

33 But it is also, as economists only learnt later, a game in which the "folk theorem" holds: that is, if the future is not too heavily discounted, collaboration is highly likely but many equilibria occur, and so almost any outcome is possible (see Fudenberg and Tirole, 1991/ 1998, section 4.3).

Narratives function as the means by which the economists re-describe the world situation into a game theory model, that is, into a type of situation, while the rationality of the actors involved remains constant. In binding the game type to the economic case, narratives also provide a means of reasoning about that case. Game thinking thus enables economists to maintain their thin rationality, but gain *explanatory depth* by using narratives to explore exactly what will happen, and why, in each particular type of situation, each model situation.[34] But in using narratives as the device both to create the model and to ensure its empirical adequacy – to ensure the match between game model and real-world situation – the difference between the model account and the description of the world has all but disappeared. In effect, this process elides the distinction I made in Chapter 1 between two kinds of enquiries: those *into* the world of the model seem to overwrite those *with* the model into the world with implications for the way that economists see the world that I explore in Chapter 10. But of course, as pointed out at the end of Chapter 7, there is still a world of difference between economists' models of the world and the world itself: between the Prisoner's Dilemma matrix, its set of inequalities and its text, and the set of farmers and their actions in their fields and in the market.

4.iii Explanatory Breadth: Taxonomies, Kinds, and Cases

Game theory gains *explanatory breadth* across different economic situations by developing many different variations in the model situations or types considered. By multiplying the games they study, economists generate more types of situations and by rethinking economics into game theory terms, they find more real-world situations that can be matched to game types. Marshall and his forerunners generated a set of different cases, forming a taxonomy, of the more obvious types of supply and demand models by asking different questions and experimenting with different diagrammatic models. Here I suggest two other mechanisms by which game theory explanations come to cover more and more types of cases, that is, to cover more and more model situations.

On the one hand, game theory has traditionally grown by a theorizing activity that fills in the empty cells in a taxonomy. Luce and Raiffa (1957) introduce the Prisoner's Dilemma game in a chapter on "Two-person non-zero-sum non-

---

34 My characterization of the way game theory works in economics is unlikely to transfer to other social sciences. For example, Anatol Rapoport (1962), a psychologist, defines the failure of the thin rationality to provide plausible explanatory devices in game situations as one of the most important aspects, even important achievements, of game theory – game theory reveals all too clearly what social scientists don't know about how humans behave. It may be helpful to contrast the differences in interest between psychologists and economists in this context. We can think of economists holding a thin but unchanging rationality principle and varying the situation or game while psychologists vary their characterization of rationality while keeping the game situation constant. This might be pictured on a two-dimensional graph of 'rationality' versus 'situation', in which economists explore along one dimension and psychologists along the other.

co-operative games", thus placing the game as of a particular type in a taxonomy with six categories (two- versus n-people, zero-sum versus non-zero-sum, and cooperative versus non-cooperative games). Of course, faced with such a taxonomy, the natural theorist will find ways to fill the empty boxes by investigating extensions of particular games within a certain class: extending a two-person game to an n-person game; extending a game without cooperation to one with cooperation; games with one period to finite periods to infinite periods; games with zero-sums to non-zero sums; and so forth. An explicit example of this taxonomising work comes in Rapoport and Guyer's "A Taxonomy of 2×2 Games" (1966).

The taxonomies themselves also change radically over time: new categories emerge out of old types; new questions generate new types. Thus cells within the taxonomies have not just grown in number over the last fifty years, they have also altered in categories. The categories recognised in Luce and Raiffa in 1957 have changed entirely by the time of Fudenberg and Tirole (1991), the text through the 1990s. In the 1990s, "static" versus "dynamic" games with "complete" versus "incomplete information" provide the basic four-cell taxonomy with subcategories of "multistage" and "repeated" games, games in "normal or strategic" versus "extensive" form (the form in which games are represented), and so on. And as would be expected from my Chapter 1 discussion about the relation of forms to rules, these forms exhibit different aspects of a game and are associated with different reasoning rules.[35]

The labelling of a particular game also changes as cell boundaries are revised and these too change as the economists come to focus on different aspects of game playing and so analyse different features of the games. The Prisoner's Dilemma game is classified in the 1991 text as a static game of complete information, and its repeated version as a dynamic game of complete information, whereas in the 1957 text, it was classified under two-person, non-zero-sum, non-cooperative games and its n-person version in an equivalent n-person cell.

On the other hand, game theory also extends by attempts to characterize particular economic situations, empirical or hypothetical ones, as game situations, and thus to type them or place them within a particular category of game. Shubik in 1953 (p 27) produced a taxonomy in which he had sorted and matched categories of industrial market situations into game types in a table with a grand title – "A General Theory of Games" – indicating that general theory in this field was itself a set of typical games. His categories of games were "Cooperative Games" "Semi-Cooperative Games", "Non-Cooperative Games", and his types of industrial structure included not just "pure" competition and monopoly but various kinds of duopolies (such as Cournot and Bertrand), oligopolies, and cartels.

---

35 The "normal or strategic form" is the matrix of choices and payoffs as in this chapter, but a game may also be represented and described in its "extensive form" (a branching tree diagram showing the choices and payoffs); or even in early days in terms of its "characteristic function" (the individual and combined maximum rewards possible).

New categories in a taxonomy also grow from the narratives, which, as we have found, go through a process of matching the economic situation with the game situation and then exploring how and why it does not fit. When it does not fit, a new version of the game may be developed with a slight change in the rules, or payoffs, or information arrangements, and so forth. We can see this, for example, in Luce and Raiffa's narrative attempts (discussed earlier) to resolve the prisoner's dilemma first by altering the game to a cooperative one, then to a game with many people, and then to one with many time periods. Sometimes such a revision turns out to be a different type of game, sometimes it is like the original type. This kind of reasoning has perhaps been most clearly evident in the industrial economics literature, where a serious tradition of using game reasoning to extend the scope of the economic theory of firm competition, and to understand the exact details of empirical cases, goes back to Shubik's seminal 1950s work.

This integration of game theory into industrial economics begun by Shubik (1959) enabled him to re-explore a number of classic works in the field of the theory of the firm (from the nineteenth century through the 1930s), and to extend results for those cases and compare their 'solutions'. Game reasoning appeared to provide a new and constructive tool of analysis here: it offered the possibility for the analysis of firms' strategic decisions based on the model situations offered by game theory in conjunction with more traditional microeconomic analysis of the theory of the firm and its profit-maximising possibilities (ie its pay-off regimes). The approach seemed to combine the benefits of situation-based thinking along with older, more general, theories and generic models of microeconomic behaviour.

But by the early 1990s, the outcome of this extension of game theory into industrial economics proved less rewarding than had been hoped. First of all, as became clearer, the possible ways of characterizing models situations as games grew enormously as each game depended on many detailed specifications. For example, Peltzman (1991) wrote down a "non–exhaustive list" of twenty "questions that arise in formulating and solving game-theoretic models – questions whose answers can crucially affect results" (1991, p. 207). These ranged from the simple ones of how many players there are and who moves first to more difficult ones of the nature of the equilibria in the model. The answers characterize the rules and institutions of either a hypothetical situation imagined in the model, or an empirical situation under study. Peltzman was pessimistic that "the interminable series of special cases" (1991, p. 206) generated by theorists had been of any help in analysing empirical cases or in producing any powerful generalizations.

Franklin Fisher was equally sharp about the way in which theoretical cases multiplied and how little they were able to provide reliable help for an analysis of oligopoly in his comment on the 'folk theorem', the theorem, known by experience, that

> ... any outcome that is individually rational can turn out to be a Nash equilibrium ..... anything that one might imagine as sensible can turn out to

be the answer ... This is a case in which theory is poverty-stricken by an embarrassment of riches. (Fisher, 1989, p. 116)

For game theory, framed both historically and philosophically as we have seen by the two guiding assumptions of individual rationality and equilibrium solutions, the multiplicity of equilibria that proved possible in so many game situations seemed surprisingly threatening. Nevertheless, Fisher did not accept that the series of special cases that resulted was pointless. He interpreted the outcome not as one of a failed general theory, but a good example of "exemplifying theory", particularly useful in thinking about cartels and oligopolies, where general theories had been least effective:

> When well handled, exemplifying theory can be very illuminating indeed, suggestively revealing the possibility of certain phenomena. What such theory lacks, of course, is generality.... the theory of oligopoly is that of exemplifying theory. We know that a lot of different things *can* happen. We do not have a full, coherent, formal theory of what *must* happen or a theory that tells us how what happens depends on well-defined, measurable variables.... At present, oligopoly theory consists of a large number of stories, each one an anecdote describing what might happen in some particular situation. Such stories can be very interesting indeed. Elie Wiesel .... has said that "God made man because He loves stories", and economists (not merely game theorists) are plainly made in the divine image in this respect. (Fisher, 1989, p. 118, his italics)

Game-theoretic models exemplify typical situations or typical cases and such cases are used to characterize empirical situations. In this sense, both theoretical work and empirical work proceed in the same way in this field, as examples of case-based reasoning. But, whereas at the end of the 1930s, industrial economists had four typical or model situations, in their box of exemplars (perfect competition, monopoly, and two types of imperfect competition), and Shubik had added a few more in the 1950s, by the 1990s game theorists had filled their box of exemplifying theories, or models situations, to overflowing. For Fisher and Peltzman, typical situations had degenerated into a series of special cases or particular stories. Where Fisher had found this liberating, John Sutton (1990) was more critical, and portrayed the flexibility of game theory to "capture various situations" as embarrassing because "given any form of behaviour observed in the market, we are now quite likely to have on hand at least one model which "explains" it – in the sense of deriving that form of behaviour as the outcome of individually rational decisions" (Sutton, 1990, p. 506). The question for game theorists, as Sutton so bluntly stated it, was "In 'explaining' everything, have we explained nothing? What do these models exclude?" (1990, p. 507). With every economic situation potentially matched by more than one candidate model from game theory, and with individual rationality being compatible with many different equilibrium outcomes, the possibilities of using game theory for explanations in terms of types of situations – the middle-level explanatory power of situational analysis – is lost.[36] Explanatory breadth, obtained by the development of further typical cases, and so to cells in a taxonomy, appears to have drowned in a sea of one-off individual cases and anecdotes.

All three of these critiques by Peltzman, Fisher, and Sutton support my analysis of the way game theory provides explanations in reasoning about model situations. They recognise that cases form the basis of such reasoning, for game theory provides models for typical economic world situations and so empirical study; that stories are an important element in matching the theory of what may happen in a typical model situation to a particular world situation; and that the heart of the endeavour is explanation. However, the three also give a clear sense of the way in which such explanatory power became limited by the proliferation of individual cases. This points back to my stress on the importance of the typicality of model situations – once typical cases have been lost, explanatory power goes with them.

5. Conclusion

There were two distinct parts to this chapter. The first part of the chapter discussed the way in which a particular game, the Prisoner's Dilemma game, had grown into an exemplary model. The Prisoner's Dilemma game provides an exemplary case that epitomises the dilemmas and antisocial outcomes that follow from economists' joint assumptions of individual rationality and equilibrium outcomes in certain kinds of situations. The game works at the meta-level in discussions of the invisible hand, and this same exemplary quality applies at the case-based level where the Prisoner's Dilemma game functions as a model of specific economic situations. Just as political scientists may use the case of Athenian democracy if they wish to discuss the institutions of any particular democratic government (see Ober, 2007), economists use the case of the prisoner's dilemma if they wish to discuss particular situations in which individual 'rationality' leads to an 'irrational' answer.

The second part of the chapter fitted together the analysis of three elements to build up a picture of how game theory is applied to provide explanations of economic world events. Situational analysis focusses the explanatory power into accurate descriptions and so analyses of typical model situations, so that even with a thin notion of rational behaviour – a thin model man – specific outcomes can be deduced from the game-theoretic model for an economic situation of that type. Narrative plays the important role of enabling the economist to check that the economic situation is accurately described in the model, that the chosen model type matches the economic situation, and by exploring the features of that

---

36 In Sutton's case, this outcome has lead to the development of his "class of models" approach which, in my view, re-establishes the middle level of explanatory power at a level based on industry characteristics (see Sutton, 2000 and my commentary, Morgan, 2002b).

match provides a sense of explanatory depth for the specific cases being discussed. Explanatory breadth is derived from the development of a full taxonomy of typical cases, so that different model situations span the various empirical situations in such a way that all the individual real-world cases can be classified in terms of a type of case or model. This combination gives local explanatory power at the level of types of cases. But, since each type of case is different, and since explanatory power resides in the accurate description of the model situation not in the general but thin rationality that animates the models, game theory claims both explanatory depth from its model narratives, and explanatory breadth from its taxonomies of models, yet does not achieve generalized explanations.

Despite this, or perhaps because of it, game theory came to be found everywhere in economics. In his 1984 book on the evolution of co-operation, Axelrod remarked on the infectious quality of the Prisoner's Dilemma game in social psychology: "The iterated Prisoner's Dilemma has become the *E. coli* of social psychology" (p. 28).[37] The Prisoner's Dilemma infection seems to have been equally invasive in economics. Once economists started thinking about the nasty outcomes in economics that might be described in terms of a Prisoner's Dilemma game, they began to see such Prisoner's Dilemma game situations everywhere in the economy, not just in the habitual problem of trust in individual exchange. For example, "Inflation: The Invisible Foot of Macroeconomics" uses the two-person game to model the inflationary outcome from the interaction between government and unions.[38] It has been used to model Gresham's Law that bad money drives out good (Selgin, 1996), international fishing wars, productivity problems (Leibenstein, 1982), and so forth and so on. In the long history of applying the Prisoner's Dilemma game model to Prisoner's Dilemma game situations in the world, the distinction between the world in the model and the world that the model represents grew less clear. Where the Prisoner's Dilemma game was once the model lens through which economists studied certain less than happy outcomes in the economy, it became the things economists saw in the economy.

Acknowledgement

This chapter comes from a paper written for the Princeton Workshop in the History of Science: "Model Systems, Cases and Exemplary Narratives", 10th February, 2001 under the title "The Curious Case of the Prisoner's Dilemma: Model Situation? Exemplary Narrative?" I thank the workshop organisers: Angela Creager, Elizabeth Lunbeck, and Norton Wise for their invitation and responses, and Suman Seth for his commentary. The paper came out as Research Memoranda in History and Methodology of Economics, 01–7, University of

37 During the first drafting of this chapter, there was a TV quiz show that advertised itself as a Prisoner's Dilemma game show – the infection had spread beyond academe.
38 See Carter and Maddock (1987). Hargreaves Heap (1994) surveys the ways in which the Prisoner's Dilemma game (and others such as the Chicken game) can be used as a model for understanding the institutional backgrounds for macroeconomic performance.

Amsterdam, and was published in *Science Without Laws: Model Systems, Cases, Exemplary Narratives* (ed Creager, Lunbeck, and Wise; Duke University Press, 2007). The current version has removed the Cold War discussion, clarified a number of matters, and included a cartoon! I am grateful to my LSE research assistants, Till Grüene and Gabriel Molteni, who showed incredible patience with my library requests and the British Academy who funded this research. Amongst many colleagues who read and discussed these materials with me, I thank particularly Bruce Caldwell, Robert Leonard, John Sutton, Margaret Bray, Nancy Cartwright, Ned McClennen, and my colleagues at the University of Amsterdam and at the LSE (in both the Centre for Philosophy of Natural and Social Science and in the Department of Economic History). Section 4.i of the chapter was drafted for the INEM conference at Stirling in September 2002 under the title "Game Theory Explanations in Economics: Reasoning about Model Situations", and subsequent versions were given at the History of Science Society Meeting in Austin, Texas, and the 2nd Siena Workshop on the History of Economics (both November 2004). I thank the discussants and participants at all these meetings for their comments.

References

Axelrod, R. (1984) *The Evolution of Cooperation*. New York: Basic Books.

Baden-Fuller, Charles and Mary S. Morgan (2010) "Business Models as Models". *Long Range Planning*, 43, 156–71.

Boumans, Marcel (1999) "Built-In Justification". In Mary S. Morgan and Margaret Morrison (eds), *Models as Mediators: Perspectives on Natural and Social Science* (pp. (66–96). Cambridge: Cambridge University Press.

Caldwell, Bruce J. (1991) Clarifying Popper". *Journal of Economic Literature*, 29:1, 1–33.

Campbell R. and L. Sowden (1985) *Paradoxes of Rationality and Cooperation*. Vancouver: University of British Columbia Press.

Carter, M. and R. Maddock (1987) "Inflation: The Invisible Foot of Macroeconomics". *Economic Record*, 63(181), 120–8.

Dray, William (1957) *Laws and Explanation in History*. Oxford: Oxford University Press.
   (1963) "The Historical Explanation of Actions Reconsidered". In Patrick Gardiner (ed), *The Philosophy of History* (pp. 66–89). Oxford: Oxford University Press.

Fisher, F. M. (1989) "Games Economists Play: A Noncooperative View". *RAND Journal of Economics*, 20:1, 113–24.

Flood, M. (1952) "Some Experimental Games". *Research Memorandum* RM-789. Santa Monica, CA: The RAND Corporation.

Van Fraassen, B. (1988) "The Pragmatic Theory of Explanation". In J. C. Pitt (ed), *Theories of Explanation* (pp. 136–55). Oxford: Oxford University Press.

Fudenberg, D. and J. Tirole (1991/98) *Game Theory*. Cambridge, MA: MIT Press.

Gardiner, Patrick (1974) *The Philosophy of History*. Oxford: Oxford University Press.

Giocoli, Nicola (2003) *Modeling Rational Agents: From Interwar Economics to Early Modern Game Theory*. Cheltenham: Edward Elgar.

Grüne-Yanoff, Till and Paul Sweinzer (2008) "The Role of Stories in Applying Game Theory". *Journal of Economic Methodology*, 15:2, 131–46.

Hands, D. Wade (1992) "Falsification, Situational Analysis and Scientific Research Programs". In Neil De Marchi (ed), *Post-Popperian Methodology of Economics: Recovering Practice* (pp. 19–53). Dordrecht: Kluwer
   (2001) *Reflection Without Rules*. Cambridge: Cambridge University Press.

Hargreaves Heap, S. P. (1994) "Institutions and (Short-Run) Macroeconomic Performance". *Journal of Economic Surveys*, 8:1, 35–56.

Hargreaves Heap S. P. and Y. Varoufakis (1995) *Game Theory: A Critical Introduction*. London: Routledge.

Hartmann, Stephan (1999) "Models and Stories in Hadron Physics". In Mary S. Morgan and Margaret Morrison (eds), *Models as Mediators: Perspectives on Natural and Social Science* (pp. 326–46). Cambridge: Cambridge University Press.

Hayek, F. A. von (1937) "Economics and Knowledge". *Economica*, 4:13, 33–54.

Hempel, Carl G. (1961–2) "Rational Action". *Proceedings and Addresses of the American Philosophical Association*, 35, 5–23.

(1965) *Aspects of Scientific Explanation*. New York: Free Press.

Koertge, Noretta (1975) "Popper's Metaphysical Research Program for the Human Sciences". *Inquiry*, 18, 437–62.

(1979) "The Methodological Status of Popper's Rationality Principle". *Theory and Decision*, 10, 83–95.

Kreps, David M. (1990a) *A Course in Microeconomic Theory*. New York: Harvester.

(1990b) *Game Theory and Economic Modelling*. Oxford: Clarendon Press.

Latsis, Spiro J. (1972) "Situational Determinism in Economics". *British Journal for the Philosophy of Science*, 23, 207–45.

Le Guin, Ursula (1980) "It was a Dark and Stormy Night; or, Why Are We Huddling about the Campfire?". In W. J. T. Mitchell (ed), *On Narrative* (pp. 187–96).Chicago: University of Chicago Press.

Leibenstein, H. (1982) "The Prisoners' Dilemma in the Invisible Hand: An Analysis of Intrafirm Productivity". *American Economic Review*, Papers and Proceedings, 72: May, 92–7.

Leonard, R. J. (1994) "Laboratory Strife: Higgling as Experimental Science in Economics and Social Psychology". In N. De Marchi and M. S. Morgan (eds), *Higgling: Transactors and Their Markets in the History of Economics* (pp. 343–69). Annual Supplement to *History of Political Economy*, Vol. 26. Durham, NC: Duke University Press.

(2010) *From Red Vienna to Santa Monica*. New York: Cambridge University Press.

Luce, R. D. and H. Raiffa (1957) *Games and Decisions*. New York: Wiley.

Mandeville, B. (1705/14) *The Fable of the Bees, Or, Private Vices, Publick Benefits*, edited by F. B. Kaye (1924), Oxford: Clarendon.

Menger, Carl (1883/1985) *Investigations into the Method of the Social Sciences with Special Reference to Economics*. Translation (1985) of *Untersuchungen über die Methode der Socialwissenschaften und der Politischen Oekonomie insbesondere*. Edited by Francis J. Nock, transl. Louis Schneider. New York: New York University Press.

Mirowski, P. (2002) *Machine Dreams: Economics Becomes a Cyborg Science*. Cambridge: Cambridge University Press.

Morgan, Mary S. (2002) "Models, Stories and the Economic World". *Journal of Economic Methodology*, 8:3, 361–84.

(2002a) "Model Experiments and Models in Experiments". In L. Magnani and N.J. Nersessian (eds), *Model-Based Reasoning: Science, Technology, Values* (pp. 41–58). New York: Kluwer Academic/Plenum.

(2002b) "How models help economists to know" [Commentary on John Sutton's *Marshall's Tendencies. What Can Economists Know?*] *Economics and Philosophy*, 18, 5–16.

(2003) "Economics". In T. Porter and D. Ross (eds), *The Cambridge History of Science*, Vol. 7: *The Modern Social Sciences* (pp. 275–305). Cambridge: Cambridge University Press.

(2007) "The Curious Case of the Prisoner's Dilemma: Model Situation? Exemplary Narrative?" In Angela Creager, Elizabeth Lunbeck, and M. Norton Wise (eds), *Science*

Without Laws: Model Systems, Cases, and Exemplary Narratives (pp. 157–85). Durham, NC: Duke University Press.

Morgan, Mary S. and Margaret Morrison (1999) [eds] *Models as Mediators: Perspectives on Natural and Social Science.* Cambridge: Cambridge University Press.

Neumann, John von and Oskar Morgenstern (1944) *The Theory of Games and Economic Behavior.* Princeton, NJ: Princeton University Press.

Ober, J. (2007) "Democratic Athens as an Experimental System". In Angela Creager, Elizabeth Lunbeck, and M. Norton Wise (eds), *Science Without Laws: Model Systems, Cases, and Exemplary Narratives* (pp. 225–43). Durham, NC: Duke University Press.

Oxford English Dictionary, online version at http://dictionary.oed.com/

Peltzman, S. (1991) "The Handbook of Industrial Organization: A Review Article". *Journal of Political Economy*, 99:1, 201–17.

Popper, Karl R. (1945) "The Autonomy of Sociology". In D. Miller (1985) [ed], *Popper Selections* (pp. 345–56). Princeton, NJ: Princeton University Press.

    (1963/1994) "Models, Instruments, and Truth". In M. A. Notturno (ed), *The Myth of the Framework. In Defence of Science and Rationality"* (pp. 154–84). London: Routledge.

    (1967) "The Rationality Principle". In D. Miller (1985) [ed], *Popper Selections* (pp. 357–65). Princeton, NJ: Princeton University Press.

Poundstone, W. (1992) *Prisoner's Dilemma.* New York: Doubleday/Anchor.

Raiffa, H. (1992) "Game Theory at the University of Michigan, 1948–52". In E. Roy Weintraub (ed), *Toward a History of Game Theory* (pp. 165–76). Annual Supplement to *History of Political Economy*, Vol. 24. Durham, NC: Duke University Press.

Rapoport, A. (1962) "The Use and Misuse of Game Theory". *Scientific American*, Dec, 108–18.

    (1966) *Two-Person Game Theory.* Ann Arbor: The University of Michigan Press.

Rapoport, A. and A. M. Chammah (1965) *Prisoner's Dilemma.* Ann Arbor: The University of Michigan Press.

Rapoport, Anatol and Melvin Guyer (1966) "A Taxonomy of 2 × 2 Games". *General Systems*, XI, 203–14.

Rasmussen, E. (1989) 2nd ed, 1994 *Games and Information.* Oxford: Blackwell.

Roth, Alvin E. (1995) "Introduction to Experimental Economics". In John H. Kagel and Alvin E. Roth (eds), *The Handbook of Experimental Economics* (pp. 3–109). Princeton, NJ: Princeton University Press.

Selgin, G. (1996) "Salvaging Gresham's Law: The Good, the Bad, and the Illegal". *Journal of Money, Credit and Banking*, 28:4, 637–49.

Shubik, M. (1953) "The Role of Game Theory in Economics". *Kyklos*, 6:21, 21–34.

    (1959) *Strategy and Market Structure.* New York: Wiley.

    (1970) "Game Theory, Behavior, and the Paradox of the Prisoner's Dilemma: Three Solutions". *Conflict Resolution*, 14:2 181–93.

    (1975) *The Uses and Methods of Gaming.* Amsterdam: Elsevier.

Siegel, S. and L. E. Fouraker (1960) *Bargaining and Group Decision Making. Experiments in Bilateral Monopoly.* New York: McGraw-Hill.

Smith, A. (1776) *An Inquiry into the Nature and Causes of the Wealth of Nations.* Edited by R. H. Campbell and A. S. Skinner (1976). Oxford: Oxford University Press.

Sutton, J. (1990) "Explaining Everything, Explaining Nothing?" *European Economic Review*, 34, 505–12.

    (2000) *Marshall's Tendencies. What Can Economists Know?* Gaston Eyskens Lecture, University of Leuven. Cambridge, MA: MIT Press.

Tullock, G. (1985) "Adam Smith and the Prisoners' Dilemma". *Quarterly Journal of Economics*, 100, 1073–81.

Ullman-Margalit, E. (1978) "Invisible-Hand Explanations". *Synthese*, 39, 263–91.

Weintraub, E. Roy (1992) *Toward a History of Game Theory*. Annual Supplement to *History of Political Economy*, Vol. 24. Durham, NC: Duke University Press.

10

From the World in the Model to the Model in the World

1. Introduction

Models and modelling have changed the science of economics, the way that economic knowledge is used in the world, and the way that economists see and understand the world.

If we look back two centuries again, as we did at the start of Chapter 1, we now have a much better view of the way in which economics has changed. Adam Smith's *Wealth of Nations* of 1776 covered the whole territory of what then constituted the art and science of political economy in an expansive verbal treatment. His text provided a closely sequenced set of arguments linking the laws of political economy together, and simultaneously illustrating and supporting those laws by the evidence of common experience and of history. Modern economics is qualitatively very different. It has became a social science largely dependent on small mathematical or diagrammatic models, each separately representing different bits of the economy and each treated largely independently of the others, while its evidence base rests largely on statistical, and now experimental, methods. So the changes in economics might be found both in these new objects: models, as a way of expressing economic ideas and content, and in the new way of reasoning with them: modelling.

Over the last hundred years, models and modelling became the primary way of doing economic science. The chapters of this book have explored how some of these individual models were created and came to maturity and how they were investigated and used in economics. I have described how reasoning with models involves demonstrations that embed both mathematical and experimental notions and analysed the ways in which models work as theorizing instruments. I have shown how narratives both help to describe the phenomena to be modelled and then link formal deductions made within the world of the model to the world that the model represents. In this final chapter, I take a step back from these individual studies of how models are created and reasoned with to discuss the nature of models in a more general and integrated way, and to discuss the wider implications of modelling for the way economics goes on in the world.

The first half of this chapter (Sections 10.2 and 10.3) takes models for what they have become: the 'working objects' of modern economics. I consider what qualities make things into good working objects for the sciences, and discuss how mathematical and diagrammatic models fulfil those requirements for the purposes of economics. I suggest that even though economic models form small and artefactual working objects, for economists these creations may nevertheless express sophisticated accounts of the things they want to describe and understand. At the same time, the characteristic of individual economic models to represent typical kinds of things in the economy suggests how working with models may offer more general results.

The second half of this chapter looks at the consequences of modelling, both for economic knowledge and for the way such knowledge is used in the wider world. I argue in Section 10.4 that though individual models appear to occupy separate niches, they are in fact held together by ties of practice: of community, of common constraining assumptions, and of the flexibility inherent in modelling as a shared epistemology. The broader consequences of the modelling revolution for the way that economic knowledge is used in the world are considered in the final section (10.5) of this chapter – and so of the book. Economics has long been a social science with considerable power not just to give us a particular understanding of the economy but also to intervene in that economy. Models have helped create a different mode of interacting with the economy, an engineering mode that shapes our economic world in ways somewhat differently from the impact of the general laws of prior generations of economists. But at the same time, the cumulative effect of the modelling revolution has been more than the sum of the models, or their individual uses, in shaping the world. It has created a perspectival change in the way economists view their field: they began by looking at the economic world through the lens of their models and ended by seeing their models in the world.

2. Models: The New Working Objects of Economics

During the last century, as outlined in Chapter 1, economists came to rely on models as a way of doing economics: they learnt to create models to represent economic life at many levels, to reason and theorize with them, and to apply that new knowledge to understand their world. In the process, models became *the* 'working objects' for modern economics. An understanding of what this entails, that is, of just what makes something a useful working object for a scientific field, begins by comparing economic models with the working objects for other sciences. There is an important proviso: throughout this book, I have argued that these models of economics provide 'small-world' accounts. So there is a double aspect here: the characteristics of models that enables them to function as working objects must be shared to a considerable degree with those characteristics of being small worlds, and here useful comparisons can be made with small worlds from the arts.

2.i Model Worlds and Working Objects

No doubt all scientists develop or adopt some objects, specific to their particular science, that form the materials for their scientific investigations – labelled "working objects" by Lorraine Daston and Peter Galison (1992). For the natural and human sciences that they were discussing, these were often naturally found objects, such as the snails and finches that Darwin worked with and that prompted his understanding of evolution. Their focus was not so much on the work that these objects did as individuals, but on the way in which they denoted something broader than their individual objectivity might suggest:

> Working objects can be atlas images, type specimens, or laboratory processes – any manageable, communal representatives of the sector of nature under investigation. No science can do without such standardized working objects, for unrefined natural objects are too quirkily particular to cooperate in generalizations and comparisons. (Daston and Galison, 1992, p. 85)

In drawing out the concluding threads of this book, I focus attention on working objects that are artefactual rather than natural ones, and slant my gaze towards the work that such objects are made to do in relation to the qualities they have.

The working objects for any science are not predetermined – rather scientists choose their working objects for their own science with two main criteria in mind. One quality is their typicality, or perhaps their possibilities for being representative of, or for, certain kinds of natural object (a problem I take up in Section 10.3). The other quality is the object's possibilities to reveal some of the secrets of the nature that they embody or represent. Both of these qualities are needed to make an object a useful working object.

This quality of being a revealing object is neither easy to define nor to recognise in advance, and so whether it is likely to be present depends on the skills of the scientists, and on their imagination and good fortune, in choosing their objects and fashioning them for use. This criterion has its prosaic side: a working object must be, as Daston and Galison put it: "manageable" and "communal" (see above). "Communal" implies a resource that can be shared with others so that knowledge gained can be validated by the community. The notion of being "manageable" has several dimensions. It encompasses the notion of scale in relation to the cognitive abilities of the investigating community of scientists *and* to their purposes. I prefer the term 'workable', however, for it focusses on the possibilities for the object to play a revealing role in their science. It suggests something like tractability of content, or, as in the earlier discussions in this book, the object's resources for productive manipulation. Examples of such working objects that carry these qualities of being communal and workable are found in the 'model organisms' of the life sciences: a limited set of particular life forms (standardized ones, such as the lab mouse), used for intensive experimental investigation, with each object studied by its own community of specialists. And, as we know from their histories, each one of those working objects has been chosen for its especially useful qualities in researching a particular subject or question: it must be "the right tool for the job".[1] For example, fruit flies proved good for genetic studies because – amongst other qualities of manipulability – they reproduce quickly enough to exhibit genetic change during a reasonably short period of scientific investigation. Here, scale applies not just to size, but equally to time: life-cycles must be of an order that can fit the processes of investigation.[2]

For many other sciences, working objects are not naturally found or even specially prepared natural objects (such as the laboratory communities of fruit flies), but are established through the creation of *artefacts* that represent a particular sector of nature. In this respect, consider maps. Maps are not natural objects, but represent natural and social objects in standardized ways by following conventions in their representations (rather than through picking out a typical form of snail found in the field, or by standardizing the natural object itself, as in the strain of fruit fly used in the laboratory). By choosing convenient ways of representing things, map-makers might denote the contours of the land and the minerals beneath, they may show forests of different kinds as a uniform green, and waters may be shown blue regardless whether they are salt or fresh.[3] They can denote roads of various sizes,

---

1 See, for example, essays in Clarke and Fujimura (1992), Lederman and Burian (1993), Leonelli (2007), and especially Kohler (1994). For a broader comparison, see Rheinberger, 1997, chapter 7, for an account of models in the life sciences and biochemistry which parallels in some respects this account here; and see Meli, 2006, for an account of working objects in mechanics that offers points of contrast.

2 On time scales, see Griesemer and Yamashita (2005, translation of a 1999 Princeton colloquium talk). For a comparative economics case: the Newlyn-Phillips Machine of Chapter 5 had to be calibrated to make the machine circulation time fit the usual circulation of money around the macro-economy.

3 These conveniences turn into conventions, but may take many generations to do so. For example, in the fifteenth century, oceans were variously coloured sandy brown, dark brown, green, or white as well as blue. Maps of the sixteenth century onwards more often had seas coloured blue, but this was by no means a universal convention, and perhaps depended upon the intended use of the map, as well as on changes in what was represented (e.g., the point at which skies, that were more regularly coloured blue, no longer appeared on maps). See Whitfield (1994/2010) for evidence.

railway stations, youth hostels, windmills, and so forth with standard markers. If we habitually use maps, we understand the conventions of representation, and can read the symbols and understand the relationships of the parts to the extent that we think of a good map as one that describes the terrain sufficiently for us to measure distances between places and to use it to get around. For those who use maps and understand the conventions, it is easy to forget how little the map *looks like* the thing it depicts, and to be surprised when others who know just where something is in their town, and could get there with no problem, at the same time cannot read a map or use it to tell a stranger how to get there. This may seem a trivial purpose – but it is no accident that the centuries of sea-based exploration were those when cartographers mapped the globe: map-making and exploration were co-dependent. Maps describe the natural object only for those who know how to read the representation and know how to use that object.

If the notion of working objects stretches from carefully chosen natural objects to the representations of natural objects such as maps, then we can also surely include economic models. Such models – the working objects of modern economics – are in many ways like maps. Both are representations of natural or social objects that are not easy for outsiders to understand. Like maps, economic models are pen-and-paper objects, not objects of, or in, the world but artefacts made to represent – to depict, denote, or describe – things in the world such as economic markets, consumption behaviour, and so forth. The models of economists are diagrams, sets of equations, or accounts, in which economists adopt standardized and formalized conventions to denote their phenomena of interest just as map-makers do. The early chapters of this book showed how economists struggled to describe and depict market and exchange relations into mathematics and diagrams, as in the Edgeworth Box (Chapter 3) and their supply and demand diagrams (Chapter 7). Over their first decades of existence, these models not only came to have standardized forms, but also developed convenient symbols of representation for the phenomena they were to depict, so that prices, quantities, consumers, and their preferences, could all be denoted with letters, lines, and curves.[4] Things that begin as conveniences in making descriptions of the economy turn into conventions for later users, but like maps in relation to the physical environment, only those who know the conventions and are taught to read and use the representations will see economic models as accounts of the elements and phenomena of the economy.

Like maps, the models of economics are also manageably small worlds. Maps, like models, rely in part on *omission* to become small worlds: they do not represent every detail of the terrain and have more or less specific content depending upon the scale that is chosen for the representation. The scale in turn depends upon the purpose: a map good for hiking requires a large scale and lots of detail,

---

4 For example, we saw the convention established of putting prices on the vertical axes in the sequence of original supply and demand diagrams in Chapter 7.

a map designed to show the relationships of countries and continents needs a very small scale as we find in world globes. And while there is a direct relation in maps between scale and content – the larger the scale, the more detail that can be shown, and the smaller the scale, the less detail can be fitted into it – map-makers have been ingenious in the extraordinary degree to which content can be expressed even at very small scale. Thus walking maps may include sketches of peculiar or recognisable features of the landscape to draw attention to important nodes of the route.[5] Like map-makers, those creating economic models must pick out what they take to be the salient points of the economy so that their representations not only remain manageable but also focus on the elements and their relationships that are of particular interest to them. Ricardo's model farm picked out the classes of labourers, farmers, and landlords, and their wages, profits, and rent to characterize the economic life of his day (Chapter 2). In contrast, 150 years later, Newlyn and Phillips (Chapter 5) picked out the monetary flows of income and expenditure through a Keynesian system to characterize the economic life of their day. In both cases, much of the detail of these system-wide accounts was necessarily omitted from the models to make them manageably small enough to manipulate and experiment upon.

Relations between content and scale are equally important to the way other sciences form objects small enough to work with, where this involves not omissions but *transposition* or substitution of materials. For example, geologists used sand, plaster of paris, and wax to represent the qualities of rock in scale models of earthquakes before computer simulations took over (see Oreskes, 2007). Models created by engineers in the laboratory to understand the performance of deep sea cables may transform not just the cable materials (by the use of PVC to get the required elasticity and lead particles to get the required density) but also the environment (substituting glycerine for salt water to get the required viscosity).[6] For economists, habituated as they are to their mathematical accounts of their world, it is easy for them to forget that they too are transposing or substituting materials. Whereas Ricardo used the language of accounting to describe his economy, a language used in the economic life of his day, later economists turned away from the vernacular to specialised scientific languages – diagrams, and mathematics of various kinds, and even, in the case of Newlyn and Phillips, to the language of real hydraulics in their economic model accounts. Working objects make content manageable and manipulable in many ways. And while it is these shorthand conventions of representation found in pieces of mathematics and diagrams that economists found particularly useful for their small-world accounts, it is these same languages and conventions that are the sources of potential disquiet.

---

5 Other kinds of maps may need to be enlarged in scale for the scientist to interpret and work with – for example, genetic traces.

6 I thank Susan Sterrett for this example, and her reference to Herbich (1999, p 330–1); on scale models, see Sterrett (2006).

2.ii Small Worlds, Miniature Worlds, Compressed Worlds?

To an outsider coming to the field of economics, one of the most striking things is the way that economists feel that they can express so much of what happens in the economy within their small worlds, within these little chunks of mathematics or puzzling diagrams. Don't they seem much too small? Surely those economists must have ignored too much, and the model descriptions be much too different from economic life as it is lived, to be the way to do science? Even some inside the field question whether models are a valid way of doing economic science because of this combination of scale reduction, simplification (to omit things), and transposition into mathematical and diagrammatical forms. Economic models have occasionally been referred to as 'toy models' (by both critics and users), conjuring up images of the scale models of farm animals and fire engines – objects of the playroom rather than the serious work of social science. And, of course, to some extent this label and these criticisms are right: economic models are – in certain respects – like those toy assembly kits that enable a child to construct and manipulate a model plane or a crane. Such constructions omit many features, even though they may capture sufficient salient details of real things to be recognisable as models of them. And as toys, they are made out of plastic perhaps, rather than the serious scale models of engineering (where, as we have seen above, the materials have to be right for the scale of the model). But economic models don't even have the virtues of those toys in as much as their equations and diagrams do not even *look* like anything recognisable in the economy such as consumer goods, factories, or tax bills. Of course the economists who are committed to economic models, and know how to read them, do recognise these pieces of mathematics as accounts of economic life – though perhaps they are too conjectural, abstract, and idealized, to be labelled as 'descriptions'.

These oft-repeated complaints about their size, and the lack of realistic qualities in models, focus on what a model is not, rather than what it is or might be. In an earlier discussion of the model of economic man: rational economic man (and his ancestor, *homo economicus*), I suggested that while other social scientists might regard him as a cartoon character, such a model could be understood as the outcome of a sophisticated process of caricaturization. I return again here to the arts for comparisons since they have proved especially adept at modes of depicting life in small, manageable forms without creating toys.

Smallness of size in the arts sometimes betokens *miniaturization*, wherein certain important details are kept in play even in very small objects. The small-scale portraits known as 'miniatures' involve a very considerable scale reduction, but they do not achieve this primarily by simplifying the portrait of the person painted, and it is perhaps the source of their charm that their creators aim to capture the special qualities of their subject in just as much detail as other portraits, ones that are as large as life, or larger. Other kinds of minute representations, full of tiny details, yet more or less idealized according to the artistic sensibilities and genres of the day, are found inscribed into the capital letters of illuminated mediaeval manuscripts; displayed in carvings of jade, gold, or wood; and embossed onto seals. Small-scale representations are to be found in the fine and decorative arts of civilizations ancient, medieval, and modern. As modern viewers, we are not always aware how often such representations follow specified forms, formulae, and rules. The ubiquitous presence of dates and sovereigns' portraits to be found on coins (in certain societies and over long periods) are obvious examples of such conventions. A less obvious example is found in the religious icons of early modern times: these were designed to be small enough to be transportable, but they were also painted according to rules, of what could be represented and how, that were legislated by church authorities to ensure the correctness of religious interpretation and observance.[7]

Consider another art form, that of poetry, in which smallness equates neither with simplification, nor with miniaturization, but rather with something like *compression* in the way accounts of life are created in verbal language. Here, smallness certainly does not stand in the way of an expressive, even expansive, account of the world and our experience of it. Take, as an example, the sonnet – a succinct form of poetry that goes back to the thirteenth century. Sonnets, like economic models, are constructed to observe formal rules in representing content: in their case, ones of length, structure, metre, and rhyme. The exact combinations of these formal rules depends upon the kind of sonnet (although historically they have all consisted of only 14 lines). There are more compressed kinds of poems, with equally strict requirements, the most well-recognised probably being the Japanese haiku. And even the less high-brow forms of poetry, such as the limerick, obey formal rules of length, metre, and rhyme. The point to see is that their smallness of size, and the strict requirements of their form, nevertheless go along with an expansive space within the poem.[8] Think only of the depth of expression, the subtlety of ideas, and the complexity of feelings that can be found in the greatest of sonnets, all within the confines of that narrow formula.

There is no equation in the arts between smallness and simplification, nor between small size and thin or mean content. But equally, there is no claim that small is automatically effective: there are beautiful sonnets and inexpressive ones, witty limericks and terrible ones, exquisite icons and slapdash, crudely painted, ones, just as there are good models and bad models. So, yes of course, economic models don't capture all the detail of the world in their mathematical languages. They are simplified, but that does not mean that what is expressed is necessarily

7 I am indebted to Annabel Wharton for this consideration and for discussions of the control of religious paintings during the counter-reformation as documented by the canons of the Council of Trent in the sixteenth century (which codified actions that had probably been quite widely implemented earlier).

8 This reflective comparison of models with poems was prompted by a TV interview with the new British poet laureate, Carol Ann Duffy (in early 2010), who talked about the space for expression within a poem not being constrained by its small size.

simplistic or silly, or even simple to understand – though individual models might well be all those. The point is rather that, for the sciences that rely on artefactual working objects such as maps and models, those artefacts may render the world, and denote the things in it, at a small scale fitting to the scientist's work, but yet articulate the contents with a considerable degree of intensity just as sonnets and miniature art works do.

And if we understand the small worlds expressed in economic models as cousins to the small worlds of the sonnet, we can see how both offer combinations of carefully chosen and arranged ideas, succinctly expressed within a formal structure. Models for the economist, like sonnets for the poet, are means to express accounts of life in an exact, short form, using languages that may easily abstract or analogise, and involve imaginative choices and even a certain degree of playfulness in expression, all within a structure that follows certain rules – of mathematics or of length and metre. We saw just this process of capturing and articulating the nature of economic activity in the neatest possible way, when Edgeworth (1881) created his diagram to imagine and express the exchange problem faced by Robinson Crusoe and Man Friday (in Chapter 3). Similar creative ways of compressing and expressing can be found in mapping: many people know Charles Minard's 1861 map tracing Napoleon's Russian campaign showing, in its thick sand-coloured strands, a confident band of outward marchers who dwindled into a pathetically vulnerable, thin black line on their retreat from Moscow to Paris. But when Minard's map is analysed by Edward Tufte (1983), he shows us how it not only denotes the size of the army, but also captures five other elements of the advance and retreat (latitude, longitude, direction of travel, dates, and temperature). And just as with maps for the geographer or geologist and models for the economist, understanding sonnets takes not just knowledge of the form but also considerable cognitive attention on the part of the reader to unravel the content and meanings so carefully compressed into those standardized and constraining structures.[9]

There are two points to take from these comparisons about the nature of models and how their qualities might be regarded. First, economic models may be small, simplified, and not recognisably like the things that they depict in the world, but this does not invalidate them as working objects, for the sciences – like the humanities – rely on such objects in their search to comprehend the world. Second, economic models may be constructed and played with like toys, but for the economist-scientist who works with such objects, models can be understood as articulate artefacts – compressed accounts of things in the world expressed in an appropriately specialised form and language.

---

9 It is perhaps easy to underestimate the importance of both knowledge and cognitive attention needed to unravel poetry: a brief acquaintance with Empson's work on ambiguity (1st edition, 1930) reveals the wondrous difficulties. I am indebted to David Russell for this reference.

3. The Work of Working Objects

3.i Materials for Describing and Theorizing

Working objects not only come in different forms, from natural objects to artefacts, but they also fulfil different functions in the various sciences. Daston and Galison (1992) presented their set of such things – natural objects and their images – as an empirical resource: "If working objects are not raw nature, they are not yet concepts, much less conjectures or theories; they are the materials from which concepts are formed and to which they are applied" (1992, p. 85). In contrast, the studies of this book suggest that the working objects of economics are already abstracted and conceptualized images, used primarily for conjecture and theorizing. This theorizing/describing border does not map easily – or not in any general way – onto the line between artefactual and factual working objects nor onto that between manipulable and non-manipulable objects. The artefactual maps of geographers can be used to find things out about the world described while the more passive rocks and fossils may prove to be objects for conjecture, theorizing, and concept formation.[10] Moreover, the distinction between theoretical and empirical objects may even be very hard to draw, and rather than a continuum between these theorizing and describing functions, working objects may fulfil both to different degrees in different sciences. As Weber (1904) claimed for his own working objects, his 'ideal types' were neither hypotheses nor descriptions, but enabled the scientist to develop and express both (see Chapter 4). So, rather than worrying about the distinction, it makes more sense to ask and see why the mathematical economic models of economics became more closely connected to theorizing than to describing.

In describing the creation of economic models in the first half of this book, I showed how economists built models to depict some particular phenomenon or to figure out some puzzle or problem about a set of relations in the economic world. Creating these artefactual accounts involved economists in a certain amount of conjecture and even concept formation in how to represent the sector under study, just as ancient and early modern map-makers had to make conjectures in representing some elements of the world that they could not bring into perspective, or the outlines of which were not fully known to them. So, Edgeworth conjectured in mathematical terms the shapes of the exchange relationship between Crusoe and Friday, and conceptualised the curve of points of exchange (the "contract curve") to make a map or image of that relationship that grew into the Edgeworth Box (Chapter 3). And once conjectured, and accepted as an account of economic exchange, the Box diagram came to be used for analysis and theorizing the behaviour of those involved, to investigate at what points exchange would be made under different circumstances, and so forth. Model accounts of phenomena turned – through

10 For example, on reasoning with maps, see Frigg (2010) and on the role of fossils, Rudwick (1988).

usage – into objects for various kinds of theorizing: hypothesis formation, solving theoretical puzzles, and further concept development.

But it was not just through the process of making and using models that such development occurred. History is important here – which returns us briefly, once again, to the account given in Chapter 1. No doubt, there were both descriptive and analytical aims for the early economists who created models, but there came a marked divergence after the interwar period so that statistical (econometric) modellers concentrated on theoretically informed descriptions that could be used for measurement and hypothesis testing, while mathematical modellers concentrated on providing accounts that established concepts and sparked hypothesis formation and theory development.[11] We saw this latter focus clearly in the attempts of economists in the later 1930s to make sense of Keynes's general theory by developing mathematical models of it (Chapter 6). These models set the way that Keynesian ideas were developed and analysed and even in some respects, conceptualised. This (often fuzzy) division of labour in economic modelling meant that increasingly through the twentieth century, concepts and theories came to be developed, and came to be accepted within the profession largely through the vehicle of mathematical models: they became the communally accepted working objects for expressing, developing, and regenerating theories.

Yet there remained a tension at the heart of all this, a tension that derives in part from the practical problems of doing any science. To generalise, and investigate broad similarities and differences, as Daston and Galison pointed out above, scientists need working objects that are not too "quirkily particular", but what this may entail differs between sciences and between kinds of working objects. In economics, the intimate connection that mathematical and diagrammatic modelling came to have with economic analysis and theorizing asked for a rather generalized account in the model, but at the same time, as we have seen in several chapters of this book, models were also designed to account for the particularities of the world. The process of modelling in economics pressed for any more general economic account, such as that for the law of demand, to be broken out to show how it applied to – was relevant for – different kinds of cases in the world (as we found in Chapter 7). The tension between general account and more specific cases had to be resolved *in each model* in the context of the practical problem at issue.

This tension between general and specific, between analysis and description, was most famously played out during the early years of modelling in the "empty economic boxes" debate of 1922. Here the empiricist economic historian John Clapham lambasted the analytical economist Arthur Pigou for the empty economic boxes lying on "the shelves of his mind" (Clapham, 1922, p. 305), boxes that were labelled with reference to an analytical feature of the production process: 'decreasing, increasing and constant returns to scale'. Pigou (1922) agreed that his boxes

---

11 Statistical or econometric models provide something more like empirical working objects, but they are not the subject of this book – see rather Morgan (1990) and Boumans (2005).

were not full of hats or hose – that is, of firms or industries that exist in fine degree in the world – due to the immense difficulties of allocating firms or industries correctly into his analytically labelled boxes (as Clapham himself pointed out). But, Pigou claimed, nor were his boxes empty: each box bearing one of those analytical labels was full of smaller boxes, each one a subdivision of the bigger box for, as he argued, the interesting *analytical* distinctions, lay at a more specific level that cut across those of the individual firms or industries existing in the world. His boxes held the working objects of economics: accounts of *conceptualized types* or *kinds* of things in the economic world. Like Weber's 'ideal types', economists could theorize with these accounts and use them to explore relevant similarities and differences found in the phenomena of the economy. These boxes held the models of economics.

3.ii "Abstract Typical Representations" and Model Inductions

It was as an historical project, then, that economic models were developed to lie between general accounts and particular descriptions, and thus were created both to describe or depict phenomena and to theorize about them. And, while we have seen how this dual aspect enables models to mediate between these two levels, we have also seen how slippery and difficult that duality has been for giving an account of their roles as scientific instruments with epistemic functions that enable economists to find out about their world. This brings us to the second major quality required if working objects are to do work for the scientist.

If working objects are to be epistemically useful to a science, they need not only to be small scale enough to be manageable and to have sufficient content that their investigation will be revealing for the scientists, but at the same time they also need to be justifiable as typical or representative (in certain respects) of things in the natural or social world. It is this last quality that enables the scientist working with such objects to gain knowledge that has a wider inferential scope beyond the particular specimen to the class of which it is typical. An object that, on being investigated, tells us only about itself may have rather limited value. Economic *historians* have been extremely fond of researching the Great Depression, but its importance as a working object for *economists* became evident only with the financial crises of 2008 and its aftermath, for it was seen to offer perhaps the only valid comparison. And while the contrast invoked by extreme events may help the scientist to understand normal events, such contrast is only possible because working objects representing those normal events have already been developed (e.g., the features of a normal economic depression). An object that is representative, in some respect, of a class of things can be used not only for investigating that class of things, but also for making comparisons with other classes of objects as well as with one-off or extreme events.

The claim to typicality that is needed to make good working objects for a science can be cashed out in various ways, even when those objects are various different sorts of model. For example, the model organisms of biology are particular organisms that come to represent not only the narrow kind of which they are a member, but also their wider class: the laboratory mouse may be considered representative *of* mice, and representative *for* mammals in general. The mouse is not exactly like other mammals in all respects, but as a mammal, it has the typical features of that wider class of organism, just as the fruit fly does for the class of all insects. These working objects of life sciences enable biologists to learn not just about the particular species, but, *possibly*, to infer their experimental findings from the individual model organism to the larger group that it represents.[12]

Models act as working objects in other fields by invoking different notions of typicality and play out this representative role in other ways. For example, 'business models', which have recently become working objects for the management field, are generally understood by making reference to certain individual firms, such as McDonald's or Google, that serve as the exemplar case *for* a particular way of organising a firm and doing business.[13] The workings of such an exemplar firm are taken to be typical – in the sense of being representative for – a way of doing business, rather in the way that characteristics of a particular model organism are taken to be typical for their kind or class. And because these exemplar businesses are taken as typical for a certain way of doing business, they also function in a normative way as a role model, providing a recipe to be copied by other firms.

Unlike these laboratory mice or business models, economic models are themselves only depictions or representations *of* things in the economic world and so an economic model's claim to *typicality* must lie not in the model itself, but in the level of those things that it is taken to represent. Economic models are abstract but not thereby general – rather each is created to represent a typical situation, action, event, behaviour, relation, or system in the economic world.[14] Edgeworth used the felicitous phrases – "abstract typical cases" and "abstract typical representations" (Edgeworth, 1881, pp. 34 and 37) to describe his diagram and the results he obtained from reasoning with it. We may recall (from Chapter 3) that Edgeworth designed his abstract model diagram to capture the features found in the exchange relation between Crusoe and Friday. His diagram was understood by him and his community not only to be a *representation of* the situation of those two fictional characters on their island, but also to capture, in abstract form, what was typical in exchange relations between any two factual people, firms, or countries in a relatively isolated situation who needed to come to an exchange agreement. Thus, his economic model, in representing that one particular case, could also be considered

---

12 See Ankeny (2007) for a discussion of this inductive move and see Ankeny and Leonelli (2011) for a useful distinction between representational scope and target in the context of biologists' use of model organisms; see also Morgan (2003a, 2007).

13 See Baden-Fuller and Morgan (2010) on business models.

14 This is so even when the cases are odd cases – for example, 'corner solutions' in the Edgeworth Box; these are not the unique working objects of history, but analytically constructed, extreme cases, which can yet be treated as a category.

representative of and *for* a class of such cases. Similarly the supply and demand model for fish could be considered relevant for any kind of consumer good that spoils quickly; and if the good was understood to be a long-lasting one, the model would be configured in a slightly different way.

Edgeworth went on to describe his *reasoning* with such diagrammatic and mathematical objects (that economists later came to label models) as a "sort of 'mathematical induction'" in which "a single 'representative-particular' authenticated instance of mathematical reasoning without numerical data is sufficient to establish the general principle" (Edgeworth, 1881 p. 83).[15] Once such a general principle had been established by reasoning with the "representative-particular" case, that general result could be carried over to other cases. This carry-over has two dimensions. First, the puzzles unravelled in earlier work with the Edgeworth Box model did not have to be reestablished by later economists from manipulating the model each time but could be taken as already proved; they formed the baseline to extend the possibilities for answering further questions with the model as we saw in the history of the Box diagram in Chapter 3. Second, that same general principle also provided the means to transfer results from the representative-particular model (of Crusoe and Friday) to any similar model case (of two countries, or two abstract agents: A and B or X and Y) represented mathematically in the same way.

Edgeworth's "mathematical induction" might be labelled then a 'model induction' – inferring results obtained on one model that depicts a typical case to further examples of that class of models. So, once economists have developed 'the right model for the job' (echoing the point about model organism choice): once they have decided what type of case is involved, *and* have got a model for that typical case that allows them to answer the questions they want to address – then they can apply the earlier findings again through such model inductions. To illustrate the point another way: economists have used two different versions of a model to capture the differences between two typical kinds of industry: one model of competitive firms treats an industry with lots of firms and another model of monopoly where there is only one firm. Model inductions can be made within each strand of

---

15 The precise meaning of mathematical induction in Edgeworth's time and place seems a little obscure. Whereas mathematical induction is now considered a form of proof that generalizes by repeatability in number theory or by "recurrence" (as Poincaré, 1902/1905, chapter 1 has it), it is used here by Edgeworth to apply to his diagrammatic figures and other forms of "unnumerical mathematics" as he calls them. It might be that he is calling on an analogy with scientific induction. It might be that he is thinking of the way proofs are constructed in Greek geometry, where Netz (1999) suggests that such induction is based on implicit or intuitive repeatability for generalizing results over a set of points that are agreed to lie within a valid class (see Netz's 1999, and particularly his p. 269 comments). (I thank Roy Weintraub and Ivor Grattan-Guinness for discussions of this issue.) In the context of this history of modelling, however, an interesting parallel is offered by Simon Patten, a contemporary of Edgworth, who suggested that Ricardo's method of reasoning (see Chapter 2) was a "concrete deductive" method that depended on generalizing from a concrete example that he took to be typical (Patten, 1893, p. 30). See also footnote 21, Chapter 3, for further discussion.

modelling, but not necessarily across the strands as the parent models for each kind of case are somewhat different. This is why, for Alfred Marshall, one of the pioneers of modelling, the possibility of describing the industrial world as a whole, and for getting results for all empirical cases of firms and industries, depended on being able to draw out – make diagrammatic models of – all the possible analytical kinds or types of cases that he thought existed in the world (see De Marchi, 2003). Once all analytical kinds of industries and firms were depicted in his diagrams, then each of the individual cases (of any kind) requiring investigation and analysis could be dealt with by induction from the model for that typical case.

While such model inductions are the means by which mathematically proved points about the world in the model provide the basis for further work within the world of the model, they do not, of course, validate inductions from the model to the world. As discussed in various places in this book (in Chapter 1 and in 6 to 9), this is a particularly thorny problem and there are many aspects to consider. What we have added to that discussion here is that such model-based inferences will also depend on making valid claims about the class in which the case falls, so that the model chosen is indeed, 'the right model' for the kind of case at issue and for the question to be addressed.

Economic models function as working objects in economics by representing, in abstract form, *typical* things in the economic world. That is, they offer accounts in between full generality (capturing something limited but possibly true of *all* cases in the world) and complete particularity (aiming at a full description of every element but only for *one* case). I called this the 'generic level' in Chapter 7 (Section 2.iii), not just because it lies in between those other levels, but because it refers to a genera or class of things.[16] The generic level that models operate at enables them to be more succinct (than the full description) and so makes them more manageable as objects to investigate. But at the same time, this generic quality relies on economists picking out the details that are similar to a number of individual cases in order to represent not the full and varied nature of all things in their world, but to make that world comprehensible by locating what is typical across a number of individual cases. In Chapter 9 (Section 4.i), I discussed the role of defining typical situations for the possibilities of explanation using models. When models generalize too much, they cease to have sufficient granularity to be useful as working objects, just as they do when they particularise too far. As we saw in that account of game theory, when the rationality description became too thin, it became too general to do much work in the model beyond initial motivation; and when the game situations became so finely described that idiosyncratic differences became paramount, those models ceased to be useful

---

16 This generic quality of economic models is enhanced by the processes of idealizing and abstracting that go on in model-making that we have seen in earlier chapters. For example, the idealizing of exchange relations in the Edgeworth Box case abstracts from the particularities of the goods exchanged and the people making those exchanges.

in offering explanations to the industrial economist. In operating at this generic in-between level, models not only smooth over the minor variations found in the real natural objects whose class they represent, but they also clarify the major differences between types of things in the economy. It is essential for their manageability and tractability as working objects in economics that an in-between or intermediate level of representing is maintained, but at the same time, this generic level is the source of their representative quality so that as small worlds they can offer accounts of typical things in the economic world and support the generalization of results, although only *within the scope* of those modelled small worlds.

4. Modelling: The New Way of Practising Economics[17]

While their function for both describing and theorizing, and their epistemic qualities for model inductions about generic kinds of things, may well explain *why* models became so central as working objects within economics, puzzles remain. If models offer only generic accounts of typical things, then what kinds of coverage did models obtain over the field of economics? And if each model grows separately, as they seem to do from the cases studied in this book – how do they fit together, if they do? And if models don't cover the field, or quite join up, then why did they become so invasive? The answers lie in several different levels of the practical way that modelling goes on. Modelling is a general way of doing science, and it forms one of the several 'epistemic genres' discussed in Chapter 1. But each science that adopts modelling (or any other way of doing science) develops its own version – its own form of models, its own practices of model investigation, and its own form of reasoning with and making inferences from such models. So modelling in economics developed its own set of practices that may be unusual, if not unique, to that field.[18] One of these special features in economics is the practical role of two assumptions that act as key mathematical rules for the way modelling is done. The second feature lies in the many different ways that models get stitched together, or come to play central roles, in different parts of economics – so that even while they seem isolated islands, they are joined in practice by many causeways. And, of course, that version of modelling that became specific to economics created its own community aspect, a factor that should not be underestimated in creating its own historical dynamic.

17 The phrase "new practice" comes from Marcel Boumans (2005).

18 Not only do different sciences call different kinds of things models, but modelling works in very different ways in different sciences. For example, Godfrey-Smith (2006) writes of "The strategy of model-based science" as a way of theorizing in evolutionary science, though that "strategy" he describes does not seem to me to fit economics so comfortably – even though economics also relies on model-based theorizing. I suspect that there is *no one strategy* of model-based science.

4.i Assumptions in Practices

If we look to the most salient difference between economics of 200 years ago and economics of today it is that the notion of 'laws' has almost disappeared from economics. Historians have argued that there were few laws left over from the classical system of political economy by the mid nineteenth century, the laws of supply and demand being the most obvious remainders when models started to arrive in the late part of that century. There are also only a few *general theories* left over from the nineteenth and early twentieth centuries, for example, the quantity theory of money. This loss of general law-like claims and theories about how the elements of the economy behave and are related together is exemplified by the fact that, in practical terms, economists have collapsed the distinction between 'theories' and 'models'. When pressed, economists might suggest that theories are more general than models, or that they are less conjectural, but they don't usually find the need to distinguish between them.

Modelling, as we have seen, provides economic science with lots of 'middle level stuff': in-between, generic-level accounts of what economists take to be typical in economic life rather than descriptions of particulars or very general accounts. Models result both from dividing general accounts and gathering particular empirical cases together. So what then holds economic ideas together? One could argue that it is those two general assumptions that modern economists came to share and use: the *individual utility maximization* of economic man (of Chapter 4), and the *equilibrium tendency* in the aggregate system models (evident in Chapter 6), and their combination which proved so important to the argument about the Prisoner's Dilemma model (in Chapter 9). During the twentieth century, these two general assumptions seem to have replaced the interlocking jigsaw of laws of the classical system that we saw at work in Ricardo's model farm and model farming (of Chapter 2).

It is helpful here to identify just what role these two assumptions play in models and modelling, for to those observers coming to the field, they are both powerful and somewhat mysterious. Observing that these two assumptions function as requirements in the development and on the use, of models takes us back to the discussion of rules and formalism in Chapter 1. The argument there was that models gave *form* to ideas about the economic world but at the same time made those ideas *formal* or rule bound, which dictated how the model could be reasoned with. I suggested that there were two sources of such rules. One source came with the mathematics chosen for the model, that is, with the language. The other source of rules came from the economics content that determined what manipulations were allowable and which ones were not, depending upon, for example, the causal or time relations pictured between elements in the model. What emerges from the cases treated in the book is that both of these two assumptions of neoclassical economics – maximization and equilibrium – are integrated rules: they are each rules of both language and content at the same time. That neither of these two assumptions can be understood or expressed as mathematical *or* economic, but only as conjoint rules for modelling, is surely why they appear so powerful in the creation and usage of models. They are more powerful than the many other separate mathematical and subject rules that govern any particular model, but that are not shared necessarily with other models.

But these two assumptions are not all-powerful. There are two points here. One is that these two rules do not both appear in all models. There may be only one of them, as we saw in the utility maximizing portrait of economic man in Chapter 3 or in the equilibrium qualities of macroeconomic models of Chapter 6. Sometimes both appear, as in the Prisoner's Dilemma case of Chapter 9. So while one or other or both of these rules are to be found in models, they do not in themselves bind the models themselves very closely together. This has not gone unnoticed by economists, for whom the most obviously worrying lack of connection has been that which exists between the models of individual units of the economy and models of the system as a whole. This lack of consistency has driven attempts to ensure that the equilibria of macro-models have foundations in individual maximization.[19]

The second point is that these two rules are necessary but not sufficient to build a model. While these two economic assumptions provide motivations, strategies, and constraints for modellers, and indeed as mathematical rules sometimes grip very strongly, they are not independently or solely generative of models. In some they are dominant and drive the way the analysis is carried on, as we saw in the Prisoner's Dilemma case (of Chapter 9); in the macro-models we looked at they stay more in the background as prior criteria to be fulfilled (in Chapter 6). Models must exhibit at least one of these two assumptions, just as, in parallel again, sonnets have to fulfil requirements of length, structure, metre, and rhyme. In sonnets, those rules too are formal ones: they give form to the poem and make it rule bound; they do not determine the content, but they do shape the content because they have very strong control over how it is articulated, In economic models, the two assumptions are rules of content too, so they do somewhat more than dictate the way that the content works. Rather, as Axel Gelfert succinctly expressed the power of such shared mathematical formalisms in modelling, they come "to embody theoretical, ontological, and methodological commitments" (2011, 'Abstract').

In effect then, we have a picture of modelling in which individual small-world models are tethered at one end to one or both of these two assumptions and, at the other end, to economists' desire to develop accounts of phenomena in the world that will enable them to analyse and answer questions about those phenomena. In between lie the many practical requirements of developing idealized, simplified, and tractable accounts of the world. In this most flexible practice, modellers are free to express any small-world description as long as they fulfil the relevant formal

---

19 This is a call for foundational links between the models of microeconomic accounts of individually optimizing people, firms, organisations, and so forth and the equilibrium tendency required for aggregate level accounts of the economy as a whole: that is, for 'micro-foundations' of macro-models.

assumptions in the articulation of their models. This means that modellers can share these same assumptions, yet offer different accounts of the same things on the ground, whereas in contrast, the details of the early nineteenth century arguments between Ricardo and Malthus about matters of fact rested on their disagreements at the levels of laws and definitions. It also means that though economists' detailed accounts of economic phenomena – of causal relations, of processes, and so forth – have become understood primarily through modelling, and models are to be found everywhere in neoclassical economics, nevertheless they neither fully interlock with each other, nor entirely cover the ground.[20]

4.ii Network of Models

That models appear as largely independent and separate objects, isolated islands rather than joined-up continents, is, in one part, an historical outcome: the modelling project was never a unifying one, but rather its practical aspect was from the start to customize and typify. We have seen this in several examples of the modelling process. The laws of supply and demand came to be found and expressed in a huge sequence of offspring models depending on the goods or markets or questions under analysis (Chapter 7)[21]. But that very sequence focussed not on what was law-like about them all, but what was *typically* different between their *kinds* in an analytical sense, just as in Pigou's riposte to Clapham about the contents of the labelled boxes. We saw how taxonomic processes spawned many new *kinds* of game in the industrial economics of game theory (in Chapter 9). And we saw how economists provided interpretations of Keynes' theories into a series of different, but still 'Keynesian', models (in Chapter 6). These various historical processes by which models came to gradually colonise areas of economics established some links between models, but of a variety of different sorts.

Economists have themselves commented on this disconnected outcome. Kelvin Lancaster (one of the later developers of the Edgeworth Box) wrote:

> Model-makers often like to think of ourselves as creating the bricks out of which a magnificent structure representing the whole economy will one day be built, using all our contributions. The better analogue, however, seems to be that we are trying to construct some giant computer program, with each of us writing code for our own particular piece, but unfortunately we are not all using the same computer language or interfacing with each other or with the same databanks. (Lancaster, 1997, p. 70)

20 The world sketched out by economists seems a "patchwork of models" in contrast to the "dappled world" that Nancy Cartwright (1999) envisages for science, that is a world operating *under* a "patchwork of laws" where the law-like behaviour suggested by science might be recovered only in situations that are well represented by the models in those sciences.

21 On kinship in models, see Hoover (1991) for an analysis of the models of new classical economics.

George Akerlof (discussing the paper he wrote while an assistant professor that won him the Nobel Prize in economics) suggested this disconnectedness might be due to a change in style that occurred in the last third of the twentieth century, when modelling was no longer an exploration of deviations from a standard model (as in the supply and demand case above), but rather:

> ... economic models are tailored to specific markets and specific situations. In this new style, economic theory is not just the exploration of deviations from the single model of perfect competition. Instead in this new style, the economic model is customized to describe the salient features of reality that describe the special problem under consideration. Perfect competition is only one model among many, although itself an interesting special case. (Akerlof, 2003)[22]

While the practices of modelling did not create a united empire across the subject domain of economics, they did create a network of connections between models beyond those of kinship, interpretations, or cells in a taxonomy.

As Pigou foretold back in 1929, certain models became *keystone* models, that is, they act as the stone at the head of the arch that holds all the lower stones around the arch in place.[23] One of the best examples of a keystone model might be found in the later history of Hicks' IS/LM diagram, where the other major elements and sectors of macroeconomics were modelled in such a way that they could be hung around its edges, literally joining on to it, via shared axes, to create multi-quadrant models (evident in textbooks as well as academic papers).

In other cases, models *stitch* certain elements of economics together. For example, the models of returns to scale in production (the boxes that Clapham and Pigou argued about) directly inter-relate with the modelled shapes of supply curves, while the utility maps of Edgeworth and Pareto can be pieced together to create demand curves; so these two curves that form the supply and demand cross in Marshall's market model rely on independent causes – one side of the cross is about the behaviour of consumers and the other of producers.[24]

More often, models link subfields together by being transferred across subfields because of their considerable *flexibility* to fit into different theoretical domains. The model of rational economic man is obviously the most well travelled and well used model endemic to microeconomics. In fact it lurks inside every micro-model for it embodies one of the principled constraints of individuals' utility maximization. Economists also find the model of supply and demand flexible enough to fit onto anything that can be classified as a 'good' in economic terms, that is, to any object that is not freely available, or can be made not free: from consumer goods, to children, to wage labour, to money, to clean air and water as much as to waste products.

---

22 The notion that models are tailored to very specific questions and situations is the language also used by Mansnerus (2011) to account for the way models are constructed in epidemiology.

23 Reported in his 1931, discussed in Chapter 1.2.

24 See Chapter 7 examples.

Such models are movable from site to site, subfield to subfield, rather as partial differential equations in physics or the Lotka-Volterra model in biology.[25] These models may look like Latour's fast travelling – because formalised – immutable mobiles, and in a sense they are.[26] But while the forms travel, the point about economic models is that they are not just *working* objects but *workable* objects: they are *mutable* mobiles. And so with each new user and for each new use, the model acquires idiosyncratic elements relevant for the new phenomenon that it aims to describe, or for the new questions it is used to address, or the new theoretical development it prompts.

Some models have become critical in holding economics together by providing a *resource for concept development* and associated theorizing. The Edgeworth Box has been a central working object in the development of modern economics in the sense that new concepts critical to the development of neoclassical mathematical economics were developed within the Box. Humphrey (1996) showed how the model was used subsequently in many different domains (exchange, production, and their relationships, and welfare economics) for developing many different theoretical results. It became a workhorse model, flexible, hardworking, well understood and developed to its capacity. In the process it turned into a nutshell model or *logo* for the field of neoclassical economics for it demonstrated and gathered together into one space the main conceptual elements and theoretical results of the approach: optimum exchange points between consumers, efficient production points for producers, the Pareto optimum, welfare judgements, and so forth (see Chapter 3).[27] It may even be taken as a logo for *the modelling approach*, that is, for this way of doing economic science.

Other models form *the exemplar case* most widely used to refer to particular results that have important implications. We saw, for example, in Chapter 9 how the Prisoner's Dilemma case gained its exemplary status because of the way in which it shows how the usually unspoken but deeply held belief of neoclassical economics (inherited from Adam Smith) that self-interest will lead to the best outcome for all is subverted into the claim that this does not necessarily hold. The model embeds both the neoclassical assumptions of rationality and equilibrium, but in ways that show how those rules may be curiously at odds with each other.

It is not easy to generalize why certain models come to function as *keystones, stitches, conceptual resources, logos, exemplars*, or *flexible travellers*. As

---

25 See Wise (2009) and Kingsland (1985).

26 Readers familiar with Latour's 1986 work on immutable mobiles may have been wondering why his language has not been used in this chapter, given our shared my interests. The answer is that my agendas are different from his. I am less interested at this point in visualization (which I discussed in Chapter 3), and I get to cognition later (see Section 10.5); I am more interested in the way working with hands changes things, and so have focussed on models as mutable, changeable, analytical tools – whereas his agenda is their immutability and associated mobilization (see Morgan, 2011).

27 See Chapter 3 and previous thanks to Tim Hatton for introducing this logo idea to me after hearing my account of the Edgeworth Box.

working objects, they must contain those two general qualities defined earlier: the possibility to reveal and to be justifiable as typical. But these general qualities do not tell us why certain models become more central than others, that is, why they become the right model for the job. There are good contingent reasons: historical and epistemic, in each case, as in the choice of model organisms. And, as with model organisms, there is a tendency for one model to become 'the model' for a domain of phenomena, or as the site for solving certain kinds of theoretical puzzles, so that there is a snowball effect – one model becomes more and more central to the practice of the scientific domain or problem for which it offers a working object.[28]

4.iii Community Matters

We know that during the twentieth century, modelling became *the way* to do economics. The term 'model' changed from being a noun to being a verb as economists adopted a new way of reasoning and of finding out about the world.[29] 'To model' and 'modelling' became understood, used, and accepted as the way to reason properly in the field (as I outlined in Chapter 1). This has two main aspects, one technological and the other professional, though they can hardly be pulled apart in any meaningful way.

The epistemic genre of creating and reasoning with models requires a craft skill working with highly formal instruments. This shared practice of craft work – as for any other mode of doing science and in any other scientific community – operates as a flexible methodological glue for doing that science in a particular way. If it comes to be thought to be 'the right way' to do that science, it becomes a community commitment. So when economists became linked by their shared commitment to modelling as an epistemic genre, they were first and foremost linked by the practices and techniques of that shared technology, one that – as suggested above – is a rather flexible practice.

And of course, once modelling became the way to reason rightly in economics, any new question or topic that was taken up had to be developed into a modelling project not just as a matter of professional habit but as a signal of professional quality. Since the acceptance of a new way of doing science is a community matter, it depended on disciplinary training, norms, and purposes that reinforced, but also constrained or even policed, professional practices (see, for a comparative example, Tala, 2010).

So once modelling became the way to do economics, the way to reason rightly, that approach itself created a professional commitment that became very hard to

28 And once the method of modelling became autonomous in the discipline, and accepted by the community, then it not only gave safer passage to any individual new model but it also made it possible for particular models to gain a life of their own, just as, of course, certain experiments gain a life of their own (see Hacking, 1983) or certain facts do (see Howlett and Morgan, 2011).

29 See Warsh (2006, Chapter 13).

break out of, or indeed for a new way of doing economics to break into.[30] Once modelling was so accepted, newer developments and methods, such as experimental economics, and simulations, then grew up equally dependent upon models. We saw in Chapter 7 how the models of demand and supply went into experimental economics in formulating the hypotheses that were to be tested and in the design and construction of experiments. In Chapter 8 we saw how models were spliced with survey data, probability schemes, and statistical instruments to create sophisticated simulation instruments. Modelling interacted easily, and become hybridized with, other modes of doing economics. It is difficult now to find a part of economics in which the practices of modelling, in one way or another, are not present.

5. Models in the World

5.i Models: New Instruments for Acting in the World

Economics as a discipline has always been considered both a science and an art: an investigation into how the economic world works and an associated set of recipes for shaping it to work better in some way or other, so carrying a moral or normative element. The question here is how much difference the technocratic development of models and modelling made to this traditional interventionist aspect of economics?

This joint tradition of science and art in economics has changed in content over time. The scholastics – religious commentators – of the mediaeval period laid out the moral duties required of economic behaviour consistent with the divine responsibilities of the sovereign, and with the everyday responsibilities of man, both dictated by their understanding of God's laws.[31] The mercantilists and the physiocrats both argued for the importance of the sovereign acting in accordance with (rather than against) the natural laws of the economy – they simply disagreed what these natural laws were. The merchant-economists of the fifteenth to the eighteenth century supposed that trade was a zero-sum game: the more that a nation could export and gather treasure in payment, and monopolise the carrying trade, the better. So the king could best secure wealth to his nation by navigation acts, granting trading companies a regional or commodity monopoly, and so forth. In contrast, the physiocrats of eighteenth century France, at least as represented by Quesnay's *Tableau Économique* (in Chapter 1), were convinced that 'nature alone affords a surplus' upon which a nation could grow wealthy, and argued that the king – who ruled by

---

30 This is evident in the difficulties experienced by economists in the new field of experimental economics to break into publishing in mainstream journals.

31 For example, they held that it was a moral duty of the sovereign to keep the currency honest (by not clipping or shaving it) and of man to behave morally, so, for example, they advocated usury laws that forbade exploitative rates of interest.

divine right – nevertheless needed to fashion his policy in accordance with those natural laws of the economy and so support – inter alia – large-scale farming.

The classical economists of the late eighteenth and nineteenth centuries, more clearly than those before, distinguished between the two different notions of 'principles': those revealed by the scientific investigation as the natural laws of the economy, and those policies by which an economy should be governed. The match between the science and the art determined the proper domain of governmental action to create good outcomes in the economy. So for Adam Smith, the primary source of wealth, and the process by which it was spread through the nations, was the division of labour and exchange of the resulting surplus production, a position that drove the argument and desire for free trade throughout the classical period.[32] Even when, later in the nineteenth century, economists turned towards historical and social laws, we find these same ambitions and connections at work between science and art. So, for example, the Soviet attempts to rid their economy of money in the post-revolutionary years of the early twentieth century, followed a Marxian definition of money as a damaging feature of the capitalist exchange economy to be discarded in a socialist one.

While both economic ideas and the relationships between economic science and governance have changed, and those relationships have in turn shaped economic phenomena over the centuries, the relationship between the history of economic science and the history of economies is a difficult one. It would be rare indeed for any historian to claim that economists of any period or place had succeeded in remaking the economic world in the image of their laws or theories of the economy – for things economic have proved malleable only up to a point. The various attempts by governments following socialist economics to make fully socialist economies have been no more fully successful than the attempts by capitalist states following free market economics to fashion markets that work free of all regulation, though both groups have succeeded in shaping their economies and the ways that they work.[33]

And the process of interaction between the economy and economists has never been one-way. Just as economists as policy advisers have tried and sometimes succeeded in shaping things economic, so sudden and unexpected changes in economic behaviour and events have equally shaped and prompted changes in economics. Feedback loops go in both directions. It is well understood, for example, that the

32 Similarly, we can find Malthus's account of the laws of population attended by policy advice about ways to discourage population growth, and Ricardo's analysis of the laws of rent dictated a tax regime that fell on the landlords. See, for example, Winch (1996) as a good example of historical studies on the art of political economy in the early nineteenth century.

33 Historians have shown how these changes in economic theories and ideas overturned older laws and characteristics of the economy and helped to create new economic phenomena. For examples: on the changes wrought with mercantilism (the monopoly trading companies such as the East India Company or the Hudson's Bay Company), see Appleby (1978); for the Soviet attempt to create an economy without money, see Dobb (1928); and for essays on economics and the Cold War, see Coats (1997).

policy failures of the Great Depression and success of managing demand in World War II were the main factors creating the economic consensus around Keynesian theories of demand management in the immediate post-war period. But then, governments acting under the guidance of that same Keynesian economics – this time embodied in models – were blamed for the 'stagflation' that beset economies in the 1970s. Historians of economics see an ongoing mutual shaping and reshaping of economics and the economy: neither are static, nor fully responsive. Yet the joint theses that economics shapes the economy and is mutually shaped by it has often been a hard problem to evidence in any detail because there are so many paths of transfer and many mediators on the way between economic ideas, theories, laws, and accounts and the associated actors, actions, and interventions in the economy.

This example of Keynesian economics is nevertheless symptomatic for the twentieth century, which had seen economics turn into a tool-based, technical discipline. These tools were ones of description, depiction, and analysis but equally ones that helped to fashion interventions so that, in this public realm, economics had taken on more of an engineering aspect (see Morgan, 2003b). Mathematical models played an important part in this transposition towards economics as an engineering, tool-based science, but were not coextensive with it. Statistical measurement and analysis, survey information, national income accounting, econometric models, time-series forecasting models, input–output analysis, all formed sophisticated instruments that economists and governments used to understand and engineer the economy (or at least to try to do so), at aggregate or local level, in various different ways.

Yet diagrammatic and mathematical models did offer quite a distinctive instrument in this tool box. The difference between the model-based discipline that economics has become and the earlier manifestations of the art of political economy relies on the fact that models are designed to offer accounts at a lower level, a generic or typical level, whereas the more general 'laws' of demand were neither so easily evidenced nor manipulated. Models – particularly of microeconomics such as of the behaviour of people, firms, markets and so forth – offer materials in a format that can be more easily operationalized at a relatively closely focussed level. So while models can be used to help design legislation as in the older law-based traditions of economics, they also offer recipes for acting directly in the world.[34] Wartofsky argued early on that this was an essential element of models:

> I cannot mean by a model anything quite as narrow as either an imitative version of something already existing, as in scale models, or simply

---

34 It is helpful to distinguish here between using models explicitly to intervene 'with' to change things in the world, as opposed to the way that economists do things 'to' models as part of their investigations of them. See Guala (2007), for parallels in the use of economic experiments, and on using models for interventions in biology, see Fox-Keller (2000). (Her, 2003, also distinguishes between models *of* things and models *for* things, where *for* denotes that modelling always has some purpose – and thus differs from the of/for distinction of representativeness made earlier in this chapter.) On the general point about representing and intervening, see Hacking (1983).

a prototype or plan for some future embodiment. At best, these are what models may look like but not what they function as. To stretch the term 'model' even further, let me suggest that what I mean by model is not simply the *entity* we take as a model but rather the *mode of action* that such an entity itself represents. In this sense, models are embodiments of purpose and, at the same time, instruments for carrying out such purposes. (Wartofsky, 1968, in 1979, pp. 141–2)

Recent studies in the history of economics and in economic sociology have provided case-work evidence of this mode of action that models possess – showing how economists' models (and/or experiments) have been used to make or remake certain aspects of economic markets. Sociologists studying these phenomena like to talk about such intervention and shaping as 'performativity' though, as I suggest above, it may be seen as a more general practice of economics, one longer understood by historians of economics.[35] Just as the merchants offered trading companies as a recipe to make themselves and the commonwealth richer in the early modern period, and the physiocrats provided 'maxims' by which a healthy economy could be developed on the basis of agriculture, so – in more recent times – the Black-Scholes-Merton model has provided a formula for financial trading, auction models provided designs for telecom auctions, natural resource models provided designs to prevent overexploitation, and emissions trading schemes to reduce greenhouse gases were designed on economic models. These models are used as a 'mode of action', directly in the economy by traders and firms or by the government to organise or create markets within the economy.[36]

One might even see the "Freakonomics" phenomenon as another manifestation of the modelling revolution, one that has spilled out from the broad professional realm of economists – in academia, business, and government – into the everyday world. Here, economists have begun a process of translation, from the results of tool usage in modern economics back into the verbal domain of common communication. These works concentrate on the descriptions and explanations given by economic models of everyday phenomena. We can see them particularly in the newspaper columns in the *New York Times* (by Levitt and Dubner) and the London *Financial Times* (by Harford).[37] In the latter, Tim Harford writes two columns. One, "Undercover Economist", muses on some phenomenon of life and

---

35 Recent work in economic sociology, from Callon's 1998 starting point, through MacKenzie (2006, 2007, 2009), and particularly MacKenzie et al (2007), offer the main examples from economic sociology. See footnote 33 for history of economics contributions.

36 And the fact that these mathematical model usages of economics are more successful in intervening to shape economic behaviour to be more like the economists' world in the model and to create new markets and phenomena than the equivalent use of contemporary macroeconometrics models that are used for intervention in the aggregate economy says less about the aim of those latter models to be effective than about the much greater complexity of the task they are being used to tackle. See Greenberger et al. (1976) and den Butter and Morgan (1998).

37 For other examples in this vein of literature, see Tim Harford (2008), Robert Frank (2007), and Steven Landsberg (1995). I thank Tiago Mata for discussions of these popularisations.

uses economics – past wisdom and recent, academic, model work – to analyse them and explain them. In the second, he acts as an agony uncle, answering questions addressed to: "Dear Economist". Here, readers write in to ask "Can a cheap wine be a winner at dinner? How can we stop our child buying sweets? Should I try to make school fees fairer? How can I win back my girlfriend?" and again, he uses some standard models to answer these questions. Levitt and Dubner (2005) have a similar agenda, though the academic material is often less evident in explaining, for example "why drug dealers still live with their moms", or the behaviour of real estate agents. In this genre of popularisation, the professed aim is to show how the hidden logic of economics can be used to explain almost anything, and to announce the explanations as a form of common sense but with a twist of something counterintuitive or surprising that the economic analysis uncovered.[38] By interpreting the problems of everyday life using economic models, the medium of model analysis provides the message, but the message itself is re-conveyed in the everyday medium of communication so that we can all begin to share economists' understanding of how the world works according to their small-world models.[39]

The theories, principles and laws of past economics embodied explanatory accounts at a rather general level, but they also – in their distinction between science and art – carried implicit normative suggestions about how the economy would or should behave, given the right governance. Models have inherited this positive (how the economic world is) and normative (how it should be) mix from earlier economics. But because models operate at a less general level than laws, they tend to embed the normative elements at a level closer to practical matters (however idealized the models themselves might appear to be). Indeed, it is this integration of the normative and positive aspects in models that prompts the way they are taken into the world and used directly as recipes to remake the world, and to change the behaviour of its people, as economists think it and they should function – that is, according to their models. This normative ethos is indeed the basis of the advice column "Dear Economist".

---

38 Harford's column is misleadingly entitled "Resolving readers' dilemmas with the tools of Adam Smith" – models are clearly not the tools of Smith, though Harford does share with Smith the facility of making the ideas of economics seem matters of commonsense. (These examples from his weekend column for the *Financial Times* come randomly from January–April, 2010.) Levitt and Dubner (2005, p. 13) too refer to their economic work as one of tool use: "Since the science of economics is primarily a set of tools, as opposed to a subject matter, then no subject, however offbeat, need be beyond its reach." It is fair to add that this genre of popularization it is not only the results of mathematical models, but also econometric models, that are translated back to the vernacular.

39 Of course the reference here is to Marshall McLuhan, whose famous book was in fact titled *The Medium Is the Massage* (not message). Freakonomics – as economics for the masses – provides a natural link in this context. It is little known that McLuhan held in high esteem his colleague, and preeminent Canadian economic historian, Harold Innis, who wrote on the history of communication in relation to civilizations.

But, just because the application of economic ideas via models *seems* easier, it does not guarantee that the effectiveness of interventions using models has been more successful than earlier attempts to change the world with moral teaching (of the scholastics), or via the actions of states following a set of verbally expressed general laws (of the classicals and mercantilists). This is an important question but one very difficult to answer, for we lack both the kinds of comparative historical studies that might address this, and any kind of metric for making judgements on such comparisons even when we know something about the extent and depth of these re-shapings.[40]

We are left then with the more general outcome. Economics has for many centuries sought to shape and to remake the economic world. That it now does so via the medium of models, and at many different levels, means that since we all live in that world – we live in a world that has been and is being shaped by these small-world economic models. Exactly how, and at what degree is less certain.

5.ii Seeing Small Worlds in the Big World

There is a significant perceptual and cognitive shift involved in this historical shift to modelling. Economists began by expressing small worlds in their models, but by and by, those models came be the things that economists found or saw directly at work in the world. This has heralded a change in economists' view of the world, and that change came not just from the new form of expression, but from working with these objects.

We know historically, that modelling involved a change in language and format of expression to create new working objects that represented the economy in models that held certain qualities of smallness, typicality, manageability, and expressiveness. The modelling revolution meant not just that claims were more closely specified and argument was more rigorous, but rather that economists made new versions of the economic world for themselves, and regardless of how these models were created, it was through working and arguing with these new versions of the world that economists came to their new understanding of the economy and how it worked. So, when economists came to talk about some phenomena or puzzle in the economic world they used the conceptual elements of their models, and the investigative resources of those models, to explain them. Economists came to understand – in the sense of both *perceive* and *recognise* – their economic world in terms of their models, and by working with such objects, they came to see the world differently than before. This cognitive and perceptual shift is a necessary precursor to acting with such models in the economy, and to the extent that these actions change the world for us all, their new ways of world making make new worlds for us all to live in.

This is a more general point of course: new ways of world-making change perceptions of the world – for scientists moving to mathematics just as for

---

40 See Greenberger (1976) for an attempt at survey and assessment.

artists moving to abstract formalism.[41] Here I take up the theme of Chapter 3: the relation of imagination and portrayal to cognition and perception that comes with the shift from words to models in economics. World-making through modelling in economics involved three moves. Economists looking at the world make an account of it in their small-world models. These accounts then function as an instrument: by analysing those models and experimenting with them, that is, by *working with them*, economists come to see new things in the world that were previously hidden to their view. As time goes on, these newfound things become so familiar that the model moves from being the lens that enables economics to interpret the world in this new way, to being the things they find and see in the world. So, economists begin by positing rational economic man, or the Prisoner's Dilemma game, or supply and demand curves as their way of depicting the world and the things in it. Investigating these workable objects then leads them to interpret economic things in the world in terms of these models. Finally, they move to a point where they no longer use those models to interpret the world, but they see those models at work in the world – the point at which model-designed interventions seem natural.

At a more prosaic level, we often see this process happening, or experience it ourselves. The Underground Railway map of London is sometimes held up as an example that prompts such a perceptual and cognitive process. This map is both idealized and abstract, and makes relationships between stations linear in such ways that all the stations can be fitted onto the map and they are attached to their correct transport lines. Visitors come to understand London's geography by studying and using that Underground or Tube map to travel around under the ground. They then experience the places and the neighbourhoods of London on the surface as having the same spatial relationships as those on the map; acting on the map they move around London on the surface, taking the Underground map as a good description of that space above ground. This example tells how a map leads to a re-description of the world in terms of the spaces of that diagram and is one example of the habitual way in which representations of a particular bit of the world changes the way that particular part of the world is recognized and understood. The Tube map, long regarded as a classic piece of graphic design, naturalises the way we see the relationship of places to each other. It offers a prime example of one of Latour's (1986) "immutable mobiles", a visualization that has perceptual and cognitive consequences.

Economists have experienced the same kind of change as those users of the Tube map. Moving to a mathematical or diagrammatic way of describing the world and of reasoning with it is not just a change in the mode of representation for them,

---

41 For the general point in art, the classic reference is Gombrich (1960), although Goodman (1976) remains a more useful resource for the comparison with science because his analysis goes beyond issues of perception towards ones of creation in his concept of 'world-making'. For science, amongst many possible discussions, see particularly Rheinberger (1997, chapter 7) for an account of models in the life sciences and biochemistry, and Toulmin (1953) in relation to how new modes of representations and reasoning (including models) create new understandings in a science.

nor even just an historical change in the way of world-making and shaping, but it naturalizes what they see: what they recognise and understand in the world. Economists came to see the economy *differently* after they had learnt to represent it in models, to express claims about it, and reason about it in terms of those models. So the introduction of modelling has wrought a more powerful change in economics than can be understood from noting the downgrading of general laws and theories. Rather, it is these changes in the representations of many particular bits of the world taken together that – for economists – led to a broader creation of a whole new way of looking and seeing that involved depicting, understanding, and theorizing everything in the economy in terms of their models. This is why models and modelling involve changes in imagination, perception, and cognition for economists of a kind that parallels the effects of radical changes in other fields of representation.

One of the most effective parallels in historical terms is given by the introduction of perspective drawing into art. Historians of art claim that this innovation *changed* our visual perception of the spatial relationships between things in the world. But the situation can be more finely graded, for there were different versions: Northern Dutch perspective is different from Italian perspective. As Svetlana Alpers (1983) explains: the Dutch provided us with wide-angled townscapes, the Italians with the narrow, but long-distance, focus.[42] But for W. M. Ivins (1938), the nature of the change wrought by the development of perspective drawing and painting was not just a question of developing a particular new way of portraying and seeing, or even various ways of seeing. The important thing, he said, is that in the previous system of pictorial symbols

> ... there was no rule or grammatical scheme for securing either logical relations within the system of pictorial symbols or a logical two-way, or reciprocal correspondence between the pictorial representations of the shapes of objects and the location of those objects in space. (Ivins, 1938/73, p. 9)

Perspective drawing – so the claim goes – achieved both, and thus its importance to our scientific as well as our artistic cultures, for the "logical relations" were understood to rest upon, or be consistent with, scientific knowledge of the laws of nature.

Ivins went on to point out that the logic of perspective drawing was a solution to the problem of geometric optics: a mathematical or scientific solution, not a human one of physiological or psychological optics. Thus he claimed, the "solution may be regarded as a convention, but a convention of such great utility and so exceedingly familiar that for practical purposes it has the standing of a 'reality'" (Ivins 1938, p. 14).[43] In other words, the persuasive power of perspective drawing

---

42 And Elkins (1994, p. 87) suggests that there were many more than variants than the two contrasted by Alpers.

43 These new ways of drawing provided conventions, but not *mere* conventions, for Ivins, like Nelson Goodman (1978), takes our 'world-making' as a matter of creating alternative versions (see Chapter 3).

ultimately rests on its utility and familiarity, rather than its status connection with a law of nature, either geometric or physiological. These alternative new perspectival forms of art proved to be in sufficient coherence with human experience to be of considerable utility whether they were based on the wide-angled lens the Dutch used to show their towns or the narrow zoom ones that the Italian used to espy the distant landscape viewed through their buildings.[44]

There is a similar difficulty in making the parallel claim that the advent of economic modelling – as a whole – provided an economic world pictured as a system of internally logically related symbols because, as suggested above, the relationships between models may be absent or insecure. And it remains even more doubtful how far modelling has secured any general two-way or reciprocal correspondence between economists' representations and the economic events and behaviour in the real world.[45] Economists' models offer mathematical accounts of the world, but there is nothing even that guarantees that mathematics in its various forms offers accurate ways to describe the economic world. We could indeed point to the specific examples studied by the sociologists and their accounts of how economic models have remade certain parts of the economic world (mentioned above), but these examples do not provide any general rule for making correspondences between models and the world. We could point to the historians' accounts of co-dependency, but these offer no logical links, only causal and contingent ones. We cannot sensibly appeal to the 'laws of nature' of economics as embedded in models, and suggest that the reciprocal relationship is assured because those laws are true of the world. Such an answer betrays an innocence of scientific method, of modelling as an epistemic genre, and of the immense difficulties of ensuring truthful knowledge from science.[46] Nevertheless, for economists, such a correspondence has been wrought in *perceptual* and *cognitive* terms – if not in *logical* or even *scientifically stable* terms – as we can see from the way that they confidently describe, analyse, and explain all kinds of activities of life in terms of their models.

And so, for economists over the past century, their small worlds acquired utilitarian qualities: they offered accounts of sufficient coherence with their experience

---

44 We could take another form of perspective, and find it equally useful and make it equally familiar because it coheres reasonably well with our experience even though it too relies on something not quite correct. As Ivins points out, photographs were initially thought to suffer from a particular form of 'distortion': the camera is one eyed where we are two. Nowadays, no one notices that there is any difference until indeed, they look through special glasses at a stereoscopic pair of pictures. Similarly, cameras incorporate a sloping back so that vertical elements remain upright – as we think they should look – rather than have the 'true' perspective of moving together as they get farther away from us.

45 Indeed, much philosophical debate has been concerned with just this difficulty of correspondence conditions, and, in the context of models, the possibility of isomorphic, or more reasonably, homomorphic, relations between model and world. This book, in treating model usage as a form of experiment, has treated these as inference problems – see Chapters 6–8.

46 These difficulties were evident both in the problem of making inferences from models (discussed in Chapter 7), and in the use of informal narratives as a substitute for inference links between models and world (in Chapters 6 and 9).

of the economy as to be usable and useful working objects to explore and gain an understanding of the economic world. In the process, those small-world models of their science became so familiar to economists that now, when economists look at their small mathematical models they see the real world, and when they look at that big real world they see it as a sequence of their small models.

Acknowledgement

My thanks go to Rachel Ankeny and Dan Rodgers for helpful comments on this chapter in draft. I also thank my four closest readers throughout the process of writing this book: Marcel Boumans and Harro Maas gave me their usual penetrating comments (although I have resisted their respective invitations to include discussion of Bertholt Brecht's sonnets and homeopathic medicine in this final chapter); Roy Weintraub once again provided an invaluable sounding board for the ideas; while my most faithful reader, Charles Baden-Fuller, after much patient encouragement told me once again where to cut and when to stop.

References

Akerlof, George A. (2003) "Writing the 'The Market for Lemons': A Personal and Interpretive Essay", November 14th 2003. Retrieved September 28, 2010 from: http://nobelprize.org/nobel_prizes/economics/laureates/2001/akerlof-article.html

Alpers, S. (1983) *The Art of Describing*. Chicago: University of Chicago Press.

Ankeny, Rachel (2007) "Wormy Logic: Model Organisms as Case-based Reasoning". In Angela Creager, Elizabeth Lunbeck, and M. Norton Wise (eds), *Science Without Laws: Model Systems, Cases, and Exemplary Narratives* (pp. 46–58). Durham, NC: Duke University Press.

Ankeny, Rachel and Sabina Leonelli (2011) "What's So Special about Model Organisms"? *Studies in the History and Philosophy of Science*, 42:2, 313.23 doi:10.1016/j.shpsa.2010.11.039

Appleby, Joyce Oldham (1978) *Economic Thought and Ideology in Seventeenth Century England*. Princeton, NJ: Princeton University Press.

Baden-Fuller, Charles and Mary Morgan (2010) "Business Models as Models". *Long Range Planning*, 43, 156–71.

Boumans, Marcel (2005). *How Economists Model the World to Numbers*. London: Routledge.

Callon, Michel (1998) "Introduction: The Embeddedness of Economic Markets in Economics". In M. Callon (ed), *The Law of the Markets* (pp. 1–57). Oxford: Blackwell Publications and *Sociological Review*.

Cartwright, Nancy (1999) *The Dappled World: A Study of the Boundaries of Science*. Cambridge: Cambridge University Press.

Clapham, John H. (1922) "Of Empty Economic Boxes". *Economic Journal*, 32:127, 305–14.

Clarke, Adele E. and Joan H. Fujimura, eds (1992) *The Right Tools for the Job*. Princeton, NJ: Princeton University Press.

Coats, A. W. (1997) *The Post-1945 Internationalization of Economics*. Annual Supplement to *History of Political Economy*, Vol. 28. Durham, NC: Duke University Press.

Creager, Angela N. H., Elizabeth Lunbeck, and M. Norton Wise (2007) [eds] *Science Without Laws: Model Systems, Cases, Exemplary Narratives*. Durham, NC: Duke University Press.

Daston, Lorraine and Peter Galison (1992) "The Image of Objectivity". *Representations*, 40, 81–128.

De Marchi, Neil (2003) "Visualizing the Gains from Trade, mid 1870s to 1962". *European Journal of the History of Economic Thought*, 10:4, 551–72.

Den Butter, Frank and Mary S. Morgan (1998) [eds] *Empirical Models and Policy Making Economic Modelling* Special Issue, 15:3.

Dobb, Maurice (1928) *Russian Economic Development since the Revolution*. New York: Dutton.

Edgeworth, Francis Y. (1881) *Mathematical Psychics*. London: Kegan Paul.

Elkins, J. (1994) The *Poetics of Perspective*. Ithaca, NY: Cornell University Press.

Empson, William (1930) *Seven Types of Ambiguity*. London: Chatto and Windus.

Fox-Keller, Evelyn (2000) "Models of and Models for: Theory and Practice in Contemporary Biology". *Philosophy of Science*, 67, S72–86.

(2003) "Models, Simulation and 'Computer Experiments'". In Hans Radder (ed), *The Philosophy of Scientific Experimentation* (pp. 198–215). Pittsburgh: Pittsburgh University Press.

Frank, Robert H. (2007) *The Economic Naturalist: In Search of Explanations for Everyday Enigmas*. New York, Basic Books.

Frigg, Roman (2010) "Fiction and Scientific Representation". In Roman Frigg and Matthew Hunter (eds), *Beyond Mimesis and Nominalism: Representation in Art and Science* (pp. 97–138). Berlin and New York: Springer.

Gelfert, Axel (2011), "Mathmatical Formalisms in Scientific Practice: From Denotation to Model-Based Representation" *Studies in History and Philosophy of Science*, 42:2, 272–86.

Godfrey-Smith, Peter (2006) "The Strategy of Model-Based Science". *Biology and Philosophy*, 21, 725–40.

Gombrich, E. H. (1960) *Art and Illusion: A Study in the Psychology of Pictorial Representation*. Princeton, NJ: Princeton University Press for The Bollingen Foundation, NY.

Goodman, Nelson (1976) *Languages of Art*. Indianapolis: Hackett.

(1978) *Ways of Worldmaking*. Indianapolis: Hackett.

Greenberger, Martin, Matthew A. Crenson, and Brian L. Crissey (1976) *Models in the Policy Process*. New York: Russell Sage Foundation.

Griesemer, J. and G. Yamashita (2005) "Zeitmanagement bei Modellsystemen. Drei Beispiele aus der Evolutionsbiologie". In H. Schmidgen (ed), *Lebendige Zeit. Berlin: Kulturverlag Kadmos* (pp. 213–41). German translation of paper "Managing Time in Model Systems: Illustrations from Evolutionary Biology". Presented at Princeton Colloquium, October 1999.

Guala, Francesco (2007) "How to Do Things with Experimental Economics" In Donald Mackenzie, Fabian Muniesa, and Lucia Siu, *Do Economists Make Markets? On the Performativity of Economics* (pp. 87–127). Princeton, NJ: Princeton University Press.

Hacking, Ian (1983) *Representing and Intervening*. Cambridge: Cambridge University Press.

Harford, Tim (2008) *The Logic of Life*. London: Little, Brown.

Herbich, John B. (1999) *Developments in Offshore Engineering: Wave Phenomena and Offshore Topics*. Houston: Gulf Publishing Co.

Hoover, Kevin D. (1991) "Scientific Research Program or Tribe? A Joint Appraisal of Lakatos and the New Classical Macroeconomics". In Neil de Marchi and Mark Blaug (eds), *Appraising Economic Theories* (pp. 364–94). Aldershot: Edward Elgar.

Howlett, Peter and Mary S. Morgan (2011) [eds] *How Well Do Facts Travel?* Cambridge: Cambridge University Press.

Humphrey, Thomas (1996) "The Early History of the Box Diagram". Federal Reserve Bank of Richmond *Economic Quarterly*, 82:1, 37–75.

Ivins, W. M. (1938). *On the Rationalization of Sight* (1973) New York: Da Capo Press.

Kingsland, Sharon E. (1985) *Modeling Nature : Episodes in the History of Population Ecology.* Chicago: University of Chicago Press.

Kohler, Robert, E. (1994) *Lords of the Fly: Drosophila Genetics and the Experimental Life.* Chicago: University of Chicago Press.

Lancaster, Kelvin (1997) "Welfare, Variety and Economic Modelling". In Arnold Heertje (ed), *The Makers of Modern Economics*, Vol. III (pp. 55–73). Cheltenham: Edward Elgar.

Landsberg, Steven E. (1995) *The Armchair Economist: Economics and Everyday Life.* New York: Free Press.

Latour, Bruno (1986) "Visualization and Cognition: Thinking with Eyes and Hands". *Knowledge and Society: Studies in the Sociology of Culture Past and Present*, 6, 1–40.

Lederman, Muriel and Richard M. Burian (1993) [eds] *The Right Organism for the Job*, part issue, *Journal of the History of Biology*, 26:2, 233–368.

Leonelli, Sabina (2007) "Growing Weed, Producing Knowledge. An Epistemic History of *Arabidopsis thaliana*". *History and Philosophy of the Life Sciences*, 29, 193–224.

Levitt, Steven D. and Stephen J. Dubner (2005) *Freakonomics*. New York: Harper Perennial.

MacKenzie, Donald (2006) *An Engine, Not a Camera*. Cambridge, MA: MIT Press.

(2007) "Is Economics Performative? Option Theory and the Construction of Derivative Markets". In Donald Mackenzie, Fabian Muniesa, and Lucia Siu (eds), *Do Economists Make Markets? On the Performativity of Economics* (pp. 54–86). Princeton, NJ: Princeton University Press.

(2009) *Material Markets*. Oxford: University Press.

MacKenzie, Donald, Fabian Muniesa, and Lucia Siu (2007) *Do Economists Make Markets?: On the Performativity of Economics*. Princeton, NJ: Princeton University Press.

Mansnerus, Erika (2011) "Using Models to Keep Us Healthy". In Peter Howlett and Mary S. Morgan (eds), *How Well Do Facts Travel?* (pp. 376–402). Cambridge: Cambridge University Press.

McLuhan, Marshall (1967) *The Medium Is the Massage*. New York: Random House.

Morgan, Mary S. (1990) *The History of Econometric Ideas*. Cambridge: Cambridge University Press.

(2003a) "Experiments Without Material Intervention: Model Experiments, Virtual Experiments and Virtually Experiments". In H. Radder (ed), *The Philosophy of Scientific Experimentation* (pp. 216–35). Pittsburgh: University of Pittsburgh Press.

(2003b) "Economics". In T. Porter and D. Ross (eds), *The Cambridge History of Science*, Vol. 7: *The Modern Social Sciences* (pp. 275–305). Cambridge: Cambridge University Press.

(2007) "Reflections on Exemplary Narratives, Cases, and Model Organisms". In Angela Creager, Elizabeth Lunbeck, and M. Norton Wise (eds), *Science Without Laws: Model Systems, Cases, and Exemplary Narratives* (pp. 264–74). Durham, NC: Duke University Press.

(2011) "Travelling Facts". In Peter Howlett and Mary S. Morgan (eds), *How Well Do Facts Travel?* (pp. 3–39). Cambridge: Cambridge University Press.

Netz, Reviel (1999) *The Shaping of Deduction in Greek Mathematics*. Cambridge: Cambridge University Press.

Oreskes, Naomi (2007) "From Scaling to Simulation: Changing Meanings and Ambitions of Models in Geology". In Angela Creager, Elizabeth Lunbeck, and M. Norton Wise (eds), *Science Without Laws: Model Systems, Cases, and Exemplary Narratives* (pp. 93–124). Durham, NC: Duke University Press.

Patten, Simon N. (1893) "The Interpretation of Ricardo". *Quarterly Journal of Economics*, 7, 322–52.

Pigou, Arthur C. (1922) "Empty Economic Boxes: A Reply". *Economic Journal* 32:128, 248–65.

(1931) "The Function of Economic Analysis". In Arthur C. Pigou and Dennis H. Robertson (eds), *Economic Essays and Addresses* (pp. 1–19). London: P. S. King & Son.

Poincaré, Henri (1902/1905) *Science and Hypothesis*. In French in 1902; translation 1905. Reprinted, Dover Publications, New York, 1952.

Radder, Hans (2003) [ed] *The Philosophy of Scientific Experimentation*. Pittsburgh: University of Pittsburgh Press.

Rheinberger, Hans-Jörg (1997) *Towards a History of Epistemic Things*. Stanford: Stanford University Press.

Rudwick, Martin (1988) *The Great Devonian Controversy: The Shaping of Scientific Knowledge among Gentlemanly Specialists*. Chicago: University of Chicago Press.

Smith, A. (1776) *An Inquiry into the Nature and Causes of The Wealth of Nations*, edited by R. H. Campbell and A. S. Skinner. Oxford: Oxford University Press, 1976.

Sterrett, Susan (2006) "Models of Machines and Models of Phenomena". *International Studies in Philosophy of Science*, 20:1, 69–80.

Tala, Suvi (2010) "Enculturation into Technoscience: Analysis of the Views of Novices and Experts on Modelling and Learning in Nanophysics" *Science and Education*, 30:7/8, 733–60.

Toulmin, Stephen (1953) *The Philosophy of Science*. London: Hutchinson.

Tufte, Edward (1983) *The Visual Display of Quantitative Information*. Cheshire, CT: Graphics Press.

Warsh, David (2006) *Knowledge and the Wealth of Nations*. New York: W. W. Norton.

Wartofsky Marx W. (1968) "Telos and Technique: Models as Modes of Action". In Marx W. Wartofksy, *Models: Representation and the Scientific Understanding* (1979) *Boston Studies in the Philosophy of Science*, Vol. 48 (pp. 140–53). Dordrecht: Reidel.

Weber, Max (1904) "'Objectivity' in Social Science and Social Policy". In *The Methodology of the Social Sciences* (translated and edited Edward A. Shils and Henry A. Finch , 1949). New York: Free Press.

Whitfield, Peter (1994) *Image of the World: 20 Centuries of World Maps*, 2nd edition, 2010. London: The British Library.

Winch, Donald (1996) *Riches and Poverty : An Intellectual History of Political Economy in Britain, 1750–1834*. Cambridge: Cambridge University Press.

Wise, M. Norton (2009) "On the Historicity of Scientific Explanation: Technology and Narrative." History of Science Society Distinguished Lecture, forthcoming in Uljana Feest and Thomas Sturm (eds), special issue of *Erkenntnis*.

Index